The
Economics
of Banking
Operations

The Economics of Banking Operations

A Canadian Study

by

JOHN ALEXANDER GALBRAITH

MONTREAL
McGill University Press
1963

To Audrey, John, and Jane

Preface

The Economics of Banking Operations is concerned with fundamentals in the economics of banking, over which there is still much debate and controversy. The analysis attempts to show the impact on the banking system and on the stability of the economy of various banking operations and transactions, classified for this purpose into domestic, inter-regional, international, government, and central-bank operations. The treatment is theoretical or abstract, the sub-title, "A Canadian Study," being indicative not so much of the precise scope of the study as of the background against which it was carried out.

Such an austere approach helps, I believe, to clarify the nature of banking. It leads naturally to a theory of the banking firm which contributes, in a modest way, to the integration of banking theory with general economic theory. Through it new light is thrown upon the relationship of banking profits to competition and to monetary policy. The contribution of branch banking to the mobility of funds within an economy is seen to differ from what existing thought would have it. The strictly analytical method also makes possible a fuller discussion of the flow of international and government transactions through the banking system than is usually granted to these important transactions. Applied to central banking, the analytical approach lays bare the basis of monetary control which the existence of various supplementary control devices has obscured.

The discussion is intended for those interested in proceeding beyond the area covered in elementary books on banking. Hence, some acquaintance with the general principles of banking economics is a pre-requisite for the reader; but aside from Chapter Two and parts of Chapter Seven, no advanced knowledge of general economic theory is required for following the argument.

The book is based upon my Ph.D. dissertation presented to the Faculty of Graduate Studies and Research, McGill University, in October 1958. For publication some attempt was made to take at least partial account of the many new contributions in this field in the interval between submission of the dissertation and early summer of 1961, when I carried out the revisions. These revisions were, of necessity, restricted to additions to footnotes and to small textual changes, which I am afraid do less than justice to all the new material that has come forward. In addition, Chapter Three was completely rewritten and some new analysis dealing with non-bank competition, monetary policy, and monetary control, added in the process. A major piece of post-doctorate research is incorporated into Chapter Seven under the head of the *Modus Operandi* of Monetary Control. The Appendix, which deals with the expansion of banking systems, is also new. With these exceptions, the work stands as it was written in 1957–58.

The dissertation itself would not have been written without the generosity of two institutions: The Ford Foundation and The Royal Bank of Canada. I am deeply grateful to the former for a doctoral dissertation fellowship and to the latter for an unconditional eight-month leave of absence from the Economic Research Department of the Bank, both granted during the academic year 1957–58. Neither institution, of course, assumes responsibility for the results of its generosity.

The work as a whole also owes much to my employment with the Bank. In my nine years at the Bank I have had unexcelled opportunities for learning about those aspects of banking of most interest to economists, a learning process that was much accelerated by the many knowledgeable people with whom I have the good fortune to work. I mean no ingratitude to this large group in naming only a few: those who proved particularly helpful in special areas of banking. Among these I must include E. A. Robson and R. M. Mitchell for expert direction and guidance through the tangled and bewildering maze of foreign-exchange transactions. On banking routine I gained much from W. H. Ruel and N. J. M. McLeod. When it came

to questions touching on bank accounting M. G. Clennett was ever
willing to provide the answers. For education in investment activities
I relied heavily on J. E. Morgan and R. S. Sneyd. To add that to
these last two I owe many of my most exciting and productive in-
sights in no way diminishes my debt to the others.

In the special field of documentation and bibliography I count
myself fortunate to have had the expert help of Miss M. H. Tees,
librarian of The Royal Bank of Canada, who settled so many stubborn
problems for me. My task was also eased considerably by having had
at my disposal over the long course of this work two extremely capable
typists: Mrs. Von Scheliha and Miss R. Laframboise.

Other benefits accrued from the comments of Professors Earl Beach
and Murray Kemp on an early version of Chapter Two, and from
the opportunity to present the subject matter of Chapter Four in a
paper read at the Annual Meeting of the Canadian Political Science
Association in June 1958. I am also much in debt to Mr. J. R.
Ferguson and Professor J. C. Weldon for their kind help in the final
stages of preparation for publication.

As is customary, I have left acknowledgement of the greatest debts
to the last. To my teacher, director of research, and immediate super-
visor, Dr. Donald B. Marsh, formerly of McGill University and now
an assistant general manager of The Royal Bank of Canada, my
indebtedness cannot be encompassed within any narrow bounds. His
contribution ranges from suggesting the topic, through facilitating
the difficult passage from initial idea to finished dissertation, to pressing for culmination in publication. No one could do more, and at all
stages his aid and encouragement were indispensable.

To my wife, to whom along with our children this book is dedi-
cated, I also owe a special debt of gratitude. She brought at all times
to the tedious task of editing innumerable drafts such industry and
patience as one would scarcely hope to find even in the most dedi-
cated of fellow workers.

In short, I have had exceptional material to work with, unexcelled
opportunities and facilities for carrying out that work, and the best
of teachers and assistants. In addition, I could not have had a
more competent and conscientious editor than I had in Mrs. J. R.
Mallory, of McGill University Press. I have, therefore, no one to

blame but myself for any imperfections in the final product. I am equally alone in being responsible for all views, opinions, and conclusions expressed.

J. A. G.

Montreal
May 1962

Postscript

After this book was completed and in proof, a note, by another author, appeared in the *Economic Journal*, December, 1962, pages 1002–5 of which unaccountably contain passages strikingly similar to those on pages 391–7 of this book. On checking further I have discovered that the passages in the *Economic Journal* came from the unpublished Ph.D. dissertation of the same author, submitted to Columbia University in 1960. Examination revealed that large parts of that dissertation, including the above mentioned passages in the *Economic Journal*, correspond very closely to passages in my own Ph.D. dissertation, submitted to McGill University in 1958, many of which are now contained in Chapter Seven of this book.

Therefore, since it might appear that several passages in Chapter Seven of this book were taken from the 1960 work of another person, I feel it necessary to declare here that the original source for this chapter is my own 1958 Ph.D. dissertation.

J. A. G.

April 1963

Contents

List of Figures

Introduction

This study attempts to assess the economic consequences of various types of banking operations and transactions. The general problem examined is therefore a broad one, but fortunately it resolves itself easily into a series of smaller ones, which may be put as follows:

1. How do banks carry out domestic banking operations, and do they affect the stability of the economy?
2. What determines and influences the lending behaviour of the banking firm?
3. How do banks influence the geographical distribution of the money supply within a country?
4. How do international payments flow through the banking system?
5. How do government debt and fiscal policies affect the banking system?
6. How do central-bank transactions work their influence through the banking system?

The foregoing questions suggest topics worthy of study—topics which, despite the voluminous literature in the economics of banking, have not by any means been exhaustively explored in previous works. Proof of this is only too evident in the continuing controversy over monetary policy and banking theory that has been a feature of general and academic discussions on monetary matters in recent years.

The first chapter considers preliminary matters; such as, for example, what modern banks do and how they do it. Special attention is given to the question of the role banks play in the saving-lending process. These are questions of fact and analysis one would expect to have been settled long since, but, as the documentation within the chapter itself indicates, the authorities are far from agreement. Because previous attempts to settle the question are far from satisfactory, the question of whether bank credit is inherently unstable is also examined in the chapter.

The second chapter deals with the economics of bank lending in an attempt to provide an analysis of lending behaviour more satisfactory than that given by the "availability doctrine"—the only existing theory of lending behaviour. The pure theory of production is applied to the banking firm in an effort to explain "output" behaviour in banking. Credit rationing naturally enters into the discussion, and accordingly an attempt is made to treat this subject in a more systematic manner than has hitherto been done.

Profit-maximization is a predominant theme running through the analysis of Chapter Two, but nothing is said there about what form banking profits take. This is more a matter of banking mechanics than of economic theory; yet the nature of profit-taking in banking is sufficiently different from that in other fields to provide material for fruitful discussion. Chapter Three is therefore devoted to this topic as well as to various aspects of competition and monetary policy which bear on bank profits.

Chapter Four examines the relationship between banking operations and the geographical distribution of the money supply within an economy: a not unimportant matter for countries the size of the United States and Canada. The question is discussed mainly from the point of view of branch banking, since existing thought about branch banking and the mobility of funds is completely confused and entirely misleading.

In Chapter Five international payments are analyzed in order to determine how they flow through the banking system and affect the money supply and internal balance within an economy. The latter point is discussed with reference to international capital movements: a reference of particular relevance for countries like Canada and Australia. The banking mechanics of international payments have not perhaps received the treatment they merit; at least one gets the impression that there is a gap here between banking literature and the literature of international trade. The former usually does not go far enough in its treatment of the international payments mechanism, while the latter stops short of detailed involvement of the banking system. Chapter Five, then, attempts to bridge this gap.

Budget surpluses and deficits, and the debt policy of the government, work through the banking system in devious ways; the purpose of Chapter Six is to chart some of these. Accordingly, the financial operations of a central government are discussed, mainly in terms of how they alter bank deposits; and some attention is given to the possibilities of manipulating government deposits as a means to monetary-policy ends.

The last chapter, Chapter Seven, deals with central banking. It attempts to differentiate central banking from ordinary banking and treats central-bank transactions in terms of open-market operations and bank-rate manipulations. These are topics often discussed but seldom explained in any satisfactory analytical fashion. The abstract treatment accorded to them in this study helps perhaps to pave the way for a generalized treatment of the basis for monetary control—yet another matter on which the analyses and opinions presented in banking literature are far from clear.

Such is the manner in which this study is organized. The problems considered arise in other banking systems as well as in the Canadian system so that the analysis may be generally applicable. The background, however, is a Canadian one. It is for the reader to judge for himself whether this qualifies the analysis in any significant way; he is at least forewarned of the possibility.

Chapter One: THE NATURE AND
CONSEQUENCES OF DOMESTIC
BANKING OPERATIONS

This chapter considers what modern banks do and
how they do it from the point of view of their activities as borrowers,
lenders, and investors: that is from the point of view of their activities
as suppliers of funds to the community. Specifically, the following
matters are examined: the conditions and restrictions under which
banks provide funds; the stability of the funds they supply in total;
and the part banks have in the saving-lending process. The examination is confined to domestic banking operations that bear on the
private sector of the economy and ignores transactions in foreign
exchange or foreign assets. This excludes a general discussion of international payments and of transactions involving the central government or the central bank. Accordingly only the cash reserves, deposits, loans, and security holdings of the banks are discussed fully;
income transactions in banking, the capital accounts of the banks,
and the other excluded topics are dealt with specifically in later
chapters. What is discussed here is organized under the following
major heads: the banks as borrowers, the banks as lenders, the banks
as investors, and the consequences of domestic banking operations.

THE BANKS AS BORROWERS

The Individual Bank

Banks are usually considered to be borrowing institutions; they do
not to any great extent operate with their own funds. The traditional
view is that a bank borrows its working funds from its depositors who

thereby become the chief creditors of the bank.[1] This view requires greater elaboration than it usually receives because the mechanics of borrowing by a bank can be a source of confusion, especially in comparing the behaviour of banks with other financial institutions.

An individual bank borrows from the private sector when it issues or creates a liability on itself in exchange or payment for some asset or service acquired. The liability the bank creates is a deposit, which is only a special form of "accounts payable." Although the notion of a bank creating deposits suggests much more, it reflects no more than an act of borrowing; it is an act not peculiar to banking: any other organization, such as a trust company, that accepts deposits from the public does the same thing.[2]

A bank may go into debt for non-cash transactions, that is for transactions that do not bring an addition to its cash balances or cash reserves. It makes a direct entry to its deposit accounts in exchange for some income transaction, such as interest payments on savings accounts, and for non-cash assets, such as securities and loans, that it acquires. Conversely, it accepts payment for sums due to it when it is authorized by its debtors to make direct entries to their deposit

1. Thus, F. Cyril James, *The Economics of Money, Credit and Banking*, 3rd ed. (New York, The Ronald Press Company, 1940), p. 89, states that "commercial banks trade on borrowed funds, and the chief creditors of such an institution are the depositors who place in its hands the surplus funds that they do not intend to spend immediately."

Morris A. Copeland, *A Study of Moneyflows in the United States*, Publications of the National Bureau of Economic Research, Inc., Number 34 (New York, National Bureau of Economic Research, Inc., 1952), p. 318, holds that banks "can borrow money" by expanding their deposit liabilities.

This view is most fully expounded by J. G. Gurley and E. S. Shaw, "Financial Aspects of Economic Development," *American Economic Review*, 45 (Sept. 1955), 519; "Financial Intermediaries and the Saving-Investment Process," *Journal of Finance*, 11 (May 1956), 262n5; and *Money in a Theory of Finance* (Washington, D.C., The Brookings Institution, 1960), p. 291.

2. John Maynard Keynes, *A Treatise on Money* (New York, Harcourt, Brace and Company, 1930), 1, 24, argues that a bank creates deposits when it receives cash deposits just as it does when it makes loans. G. W. McKinley, "The Federal Home Loan Bank System and the Control of Credit," *Journal of Finance*, 12 (Sept. 1957), 322-4, generalizes the argument by attempting to show that any institution which accepts deposits creates credit in the same way as does a bank.

accounts with the bank to reduce them by the amount owing. In making direct entries to its deposit accounts for these non-cash transactions, the bank is altering its position as a debtor to the public.

However, the borrowing activities of a bank are more usually discussed in connection with the creation of deposits in exchange for cash brought to the bank by the public for the specific purpose of getting or increasing deposits. When the public brings currency to the bank for deposit, the bank by writing up its deposits in exchange for the currency is viewed as borrowing the currency brought to it.

More commonly, it is cheques and monetary instruments of that nature that are brought to a bank for deposit. When these monetary instruments are drawn on other banks or on the central bank, or when they are issued by other institutions, the receiving bank gains an addition to its cash balance or deposit at the central bank by simply clearing the instruments to the issuing institutions. Therefore, the receiving bank by accepting these monetary instruments from its depositors and giving them in exchange deposits, in effect borrows or acquires for itself cash balances or reserves. That is, the thing borrowed is not the deposit created but the cash reserves represented by the instruments deposited.

When the monetary instruments deposited with a bank are drawn upon it, the bank in accepting them in exchange for deposits merely carries out a transfer of the ownership of the deposits already on its books. Where the monetary instruments have been issued by the bank itself, an increase in its deposits follows. This may be viewed as a passive borrowing of the cash reserves that the bank would have lost had the holders of the instruments exercised their option of depositing the instruments elsewhere.

But all cash borrowing by a bank, in the sense of the last three paragraphs, is of a passive nature; it depends on the depositors coming to the bank.[3] And when the cash position of the bank requires accumulating additional cash, the bank does not actively offer its borrowing instruments on the market, although it may take what steps it can to attract depositors through higher interest rates, lower service charges, or more advertising. (Short-run adjustments in the

3. Keynes, *Treatise*, *1*, 25, who speaks of banks passively creating deposits against the receipt of liquid resources from their customers.

cash position, however, are effected by selling assets or borrowing from the central bank.)

In this respect the borrowing activities of a bank differ slightly from that of non-deposit receiving financial institutions, such as finance companies, which operate with borrowed funds. These institutions, through brokers, may offer more actively their borrowing instruments to the public. Aside from this minor difference, there is no point of principle that differentiates the borrowing activities of a bank from that of any other borrowing financial institution. Both, in borrowing from the public, receive, in exchange for their debt instruments, currency and cheques, which add to their cash balances. The borrowing instruments used may differ, but the instruments employed, whether they be deposits or not, all serve the same general purpose: to provide the holders with a convenient financial asset. From considerations such as these it has been argued that banks are really no different from other financial institutions using borrowed funds;[4] as far as borrowing by an individual bank from the public is concerned, the inference seems warranted.

The Banking System

The inference seems less warranted when the borrowing activity of the banking system as such is considered. Certain differences from other financial institutions come to light in the whole that do not appear for the parts.

While one bank may be considered to be borrowing cash reserves when it receives for deposit cheques drawn on other banks, the banking system itself cannot be viewed as borrowing by accepting bank cheques for deposit. Obviously there can be no change in total deposits or in the cash position of the banking system as a result of the cheque-depositing acts of the public when all cheques are drawn on existing deposits with the banks. Only when the cheques deposited with the banking system are drawn on non-banking institutions that

4. The argument has been advanced most vigorously by Gurley and Shaw, "Financial Aspects of Economic Development," p. 521; "Financial Intermediaries and the Saving-Investment Process," p. 259; "The Growth of Debt and Money in the United States, 1800–1950: A Suggested Interpretation," *Review of Economics and Statistics*, *39* (Aug. 1957), 250; and *Money in a Theory of Finance*, pp. 198–9.

keep their cash balances with the central bank or are drawn on the central bank itself, can the banking system increase the total of its cash balances through accepting cheques for deposit. However, in this instance, whether the banking system really does gain cash reserves depends not on the act of passively accepting cheques for deposits but on the decision of the monetary authorities: it is by now a familiar principle that the final say on the amount of cash reserves in the banking system rests with the authorities, not with the banks.

Given that cheques received by the banks for deposit are drawn either on themselves or other members of the banking system, there can be no net increase in the cash reserves of the banking system: hence no additional borrowing of cash reserves by the banking system from the public. However, the deposits that the banking system already holds might be viewed as having been borrowed from the public since the public does have a choice between holding currency and holding deposits. But considering that the deposits created by the banking system constitute a major part of the money supply and that all the money in existence must be held by someone, lending to the banking system by holding the existing supply of deposits is nearly automatic with scarcely any element of discretion involved. It thus differs from other lending-borrowing relationships where the element of discretion is usually very much in evidence and much less automatic.

There is perhaps more discretion involved in the banking case when the public alters its preference between currency and deposits. This is a preference reflected in the ratio of currency to deposits held by the public, and a change in the ratio does alter the cash balances of the banks. This currency ratio, as it is called, is not particularly stable,[5] but nevertheless it is generally concluded that a change in the

5. James W. Angell, *The Behaviour of Money: Exploratory Studies* (New York, McCraw-Hill Book Company, Inc., 1936), pp. 20, 23, found that in the United States the ratio of currency to deposits had not remained constant over time and that currency in circulation did not fluctuate in a fixed relationship with movements in deposits. Fluctuations in the currency ratio still occur in the United States. Stephen L. McDonald, "The Internal Drain and Bank Credit Expansion," *Journal of Finance*, *8* (Dec. 1953), 408–9. Neither has the currency ratio been constant in England. "Bank Deposits and Currency: Divergent Fluctuations," Midland Bank *Review*, Nov. 1957, p. 2. The Bank of Canada estimates corporate

preference of the public between currency and deposits is not a significant factor in altering total bank deposits.[6] Furthermore, central banks usually act to smooth out the effect of changes in the currency ratio on the cash reserves of the banks.[7]

Assuming that changes in the currency ratio are not permitted to upset the cash reserves of the banking system, banks as a group cannot through their own acts gain from the public an increase in their cash balances; they cannot add to their cash reserves either by

holdings of Canadian currency by assuming a constant ratio of 3 per cent between the chartered-bank deposits and the currency holdings of corporations. Non-corporate holdings of currency are then found by calculating the difference between currency in the hands of the public and currency held by corporations—that is, it is not obtained by applying a constant currency ratio to the non-corporate sector, which suggests, as do the data themselves, that the currency ratio is not constant in Canada either. Bank of Canada, "General Public Holdings of Certain Liquid Assets," Research Memorandum (Ottawa, The Bank, 1953), p. 13 (mimeographed); idem, *Statistical Summary*, Financial Supplement, 1956, p. 32.

6. However, the point is still a controversial matter. Erich Schneider, "The Determinants of the Commercial Banks' Credit Potential in a Mixed Money System," Banca Nazionale del Lavoro (Rome), *Quarterly Review*, Sept. 1955, p. 133, concludes that for Germany, where the currency ratio has been fairly constant, variations in bank deposits must be attributed solely to changes in the amount of cash reserves and in the reserve ratio; further, he concludes that even where the currency ratio is not constant the effect of changes in the ratio can be suitably modified by central-bank action. A similar conclusion is reached by R. S. Sayers, "The Determination of the Volume of Bank Deposits: England, 1955–56," Banca Nazionale del Lavoro, *Quarterly Review*, Dec. 1955, pp. 179–81, who criticizes A. Gambino, "Money Supply and Interest Rate in Recent Macro-Economic Conceptions," Banca Nazionale del Lavoro, *Quarterly Review*, Sept. 1954, for concluding on the basis of experience with the currency ratio in the United States and Italy that changes in the ratio are a significant factor in determining the amount of deposits. Mr. Sayers points out that in England, where the currency ratio has not been constant, changes in it have not disturbed bank deposits because the Bank of England has acted to neutralize movements in the ratio. However, A. Gambino, "Further Considerations on the Determinants of the Volume of Bank Deposits," Banca Nazionale del Lavoro, *Quarterly Review*, Jan.–June 1956, p. 40, rejects the argument.

7. J. J. Polak and W. H. White, "The Effect of Income Expansion on the Quantity of Money," International Monetary Fund, *Staff Papers*, 4 (1954–55), 404n6, say it is usually considered the legitimate function of central banks to offset the effect on banking reserves of a loss of currency to circulation.

issuing or creating more deposit liabilities or by disposing of other assets. For example, when the banks as a group have an excess or deficiency in their cash reserves and they try to spend the excess or make up the deficiency, they cannot affect the total amount of cash reserves in the banking system when these are held constant by the central bank; all they affect is the total of bank deposits. Thus, if the banks as a group are trying to eliminate a cash deficiency of, say, one million dollars by selling securities to that amount, they succeed, under the conditions postulated, only in reducing bank deposits by one million dollars. If the banks are working to a 10 per cent cash-reserve ratio, a cash deficiency of one million dollars requires a reduction of ten million dollars in deposits in order to restore the ratio to 10 per cent. Therefore, in the example given, the banks as a group must keep on selling securities until they have sold ten million dollars worth. At this point their deposits will be ten million dollars lower and their reserve ratio will be restored to the desired level.

This differs from the situation facing non-deposit receiving financial institutions. A group of such institutions by actively offering more of their debt instruments to the public may gain an increase in their cash balances; they induce the public to give up some of their deposits in exchange for the additional debt instruments offered in the market. These non-bank institutions can also as a group add to their cash balances by disposing of some of their assets for cash. In short, non-bank financial institutions may as a group increase their borrowing from the public and so gain additional cash balances: banks as a group, when they expand their deposits, only alter their liabilities relative to their cash balances.[8]

The Nature of Cash Reserves

How much banks may borrow is determined by their cash balances or reserves, because banking practice is to keep liabilities to the public in some given proportion to cash reserves. With cash reserves fixed for the banking system, the limit to deposits is set by the ratio, of cash to deposits, that the banks work to. The system then cannot through the acts of its members expand its liabilities beyond this point.

8. Cf. David A. Alhadeff, "Credit Controls and Financial Intermediaries," *American Economic Review*, 50 (Sept. 1960), 660.

Other financial institutions are usually not limited in their borrowing by the amount of cash that they have; for them the limit is set by the cost at which they can borrow and the demand of the public for their liabilities. Given their willingness to accept a given cost, demand sets the limit to the amount that such institutions borrow from the public. Although these non-bank financial institutions may also operate with some notion of a minimum that their cash should bear to their liabilities, such a ratio is not as crucial for them as it is for banks, because unlike banks they have a greater facility for increasing their cash balances; furthermore their liabilities are likely to be less subject to unpredictable calls.

The reserve ratio is thus crucial in banking. The lower the reserve ratio—the less cash a bank must hold against its liabilities—the more profitable the situation. Law or custom both determine how low the ratio will be in any particular banking system, and the profit motive can usually be counted upon to keep the ratio from rising for any length of time above the minimum deemed necessary.[9]

Given the reserve ratio that banks work to, then, the limit to their borrowings or deposits is set by the amount of cash reserves that the central bank permits the banking system to have; the maximum amount of deposits for the system is simply the arithmetic product of the total for cash reserves and the reciprocal of the reserve ratio.[10] Consequently, any fluctuation in total bank deposits is due to fluctuations in the level of cash reserves; and since determination of the level of cash reserves lies not with the banks but with the central bank, the former are not therefore responsible for variations in the level of bank deposits, so long as they maintain a stable cash-reserve ratio or a stable demand for cash. In short, if the central bank keeps cash reserves constant, the stability of bank deposits is guaranteed by a fixed reserve ratio.

Stability of bank deposits, however, does not of itself guarantee stability of the money supply (deposits plus currency held by the

9. A. F. W. Plumptre, *Central Banking in the British Dominions* (Toronto, The University of Toronto Press, 1940), pp. 17–18, gives a brief account of some of the considerations that set upper and lower limits for the reserve ratio banks maintain and which results in a fairly stable ratio.

10. Cf. Keynes, *Treatise*, 2, 49–50.

public). A constant currency ratio is also required. For if the central bank pursues a policy of fixing cash reserves, it must offset the effects of variations in the currency ratio on the cash reserves; if it does, bank deposits remain constant but the money supply fluctuates according to the changing preference of the public for currency. If the central bank fixes the total of its deposit liabilities and notes outstanding and remains indifferent to shifts between the two categories, changes in the currency ratio produce changes not only in the money supply but also in bank deposits. Thus the items that determine the size of the money supply are the amount of cash reserves in the banking system, the cash-reserve ratio the banks work to, and the currency ratio.[11] To say that these determine the supply of money, however, obscures all the numerous forces operating on the money supply that the central bank has constantly to assess.[12]

The main point here is that any fluctuation in total bank deposits is more easily explained in terms of variations in the cash reserves supplied by the central bank than in terms of deliberate alterations by the banks in the extent to which they borrow from the public. In contrast, fluctuations in the liabilities to the public of other groups of financial institutions are more easily explained in terms of these institutions deliberately accepting more or less funds from the public than in terms of their being supplied with cash reserves.

11. A geometrical presentation of the determination of the money supply, based on the factors noted, is given by Arnold P. Collery, "A Graphic Analysis of the Theory of the Determination of the Money Supply," *Journal of Finance*, *11* (Sept. 1956), 328–31.

12. Thus various writers approach the problem of assessing changes in the supply of money by considering a wide variety of different factors. The statistical approach is to record all the factors that produce increases or decreases in the money supply. Cf. Edward C. Simmons, "A Note on the Causes of Instability in the Money Supply," *Journal of Finance*, *6* (Sept. 1951), 333–7. R. A. Radford, "Canada's Capital Inflows, 1946–53," International Monetary Fund, *Staff Papers*, Feb. 1955, p. 256, presents a calculation of changes in the Canadian money supply, and the causal factors involved, for the years 1946–53. Sayers, "The Determination of the Volume of Bank Deposits," p. 187, lists twelve factors that he considers relevant to the determination of total bank deposits.

THE BANKS AS LENDERS

The Individual Bank

Cash reserves not only set a limit to the liabilities of the banking system but also limit its lending, and the same is true for the individual bank. What an individual bank can lend depends on its cash balances, just as what other lenders can lend depends on their cash balances. The nature of that dependence for a bank, however, is obscured by the fact of deposit creation, and is the cause of controversy over what banks lend in making loans.

One group argues that banks lend the funds of their depositors.[13] This may be called the banking view: that what a bank lends depends on its deposits.[14] Ricardo perhaps inspired this school of thought by his often-quoted sentiment that the distinctive function of the banker begins as soon as he uses the money of others.[15] The opposing group

13. "Commercial banks, the authors believe, individually and as a system . . . receive on deposit and lend out for investment the balances and savings of their clients." R. E. Speagle and L. Silverman, "The Banking Income Dilemma," *Review of Economics and Statistics,* 35 (May 1953), 128. Similar statements implying that banks lend their deposits appear in Rollin G. Thomas, *Our Modern Banking and Monetary System* (New York, Prentice-Hall, Inc., 1946), p. 59, and in Ray B. Westerfield, *Money, Credit and Banking* (New York, The Ronald Press Company, 1938), pp. 174, 178.

14. ". . . the banks are strictly limited in their lending operations by the amount which the depositor thinks fit to leave with them." Walter Leaf, *Banking,* Home University Library of Modern Knowledge, Vol. 124 (London, Williams and Norgate, Ltd., [1926]), p. 102.

15. The original quotation upon which subsequent adaptations by others are apparently based is as follows: "There is this material difference between a Bank and all other trades: A Bank would never be established, if it obtained no other profits but those from the employment of its own capital: *its real advantage commences only when it employs the capital of others.*" David Ricardo, *Proposals for an Economical and Secure Currency, with Observations on the Profits of the Bank of England, as they Regard the Public and the Proprietors of Bank Stock,* in *The Works and Correspondence of David Ricardo,* Piero Sraffa, ed. (Cambridge, at the University Press, 1951), 4, 108.

Walter Bagehot, *Lombard Street: A Description of the Money Market* (New York, Charles Scribner's Sons, 1902), p. 21, apparently misquoted Ricardo (he makes no specific reference) when he wrote "the distinctive function of the banker, says Ricardo, 'begins as soon as he uses the money of *others*;' as long as he uses his own money he is only a capitalist." In another place (pp. 242–3), Bagehot expresses

speaks of a bank actively creating deposits by lending and investing,[16] with no mention of lending what is borrowed. Banks supply funds of their own creation, it is argued, rather than lend the funds of others.[17]

The controversy may perhaps be settled by a few considerations on types of lending. There are two general ways in which a lending institution may carry on its lending activities. One way is to lend assets (usually cash balances) that it owns or has borrowed; the lender thereby alters the composition of his assets without changing their total or altering his liabilities. The other general way of lending is to create in favour of the borrower a liability on the lending institution that the borrower can use for his own purpose. The process is most commonly represented by an exchange of deposits for the debt instruments of borrowers, and the effect on the balance-sheet of the lender is a simultaneous and equal increase in assets and liabilities.

---

himself as follows: "Thus a banker's business—his proper business—does not begin while he is using his own money: it commences when he begins to use the capital of others."

It is Bagehot's contrast between a banker and a capitalist, based on Ricardo's views quoted above, that writers on money and banking are fond of pointing out. Cf. James, *Money, Credit and Banking*, p. 89; Westerfield, *Money, Credit and Banking*, p. 174; "Banker," *Encyclopaedia Britannica* (14th ed.), *3*, 37.

Ludwig von Mises, *The Theory of Money and Credit*, trans. H. E. Batson, new ed. (London, Jonathan Cape, 1953), p. 262, refers to the Bagehot-Ricardo distinction as constituting the definition of banking held by the English "Classical School." Oddly enough, Charles Rist, *History of Monetary and Credit Theory from John Law to the Present Day*, trans. Jane Degras (New York, The Macmillan Company, 1940), p. 172, argues that Ricardo presented the creation view of banking and not the intermediation view. His interpretation is based largely on the *Proposals*, the same piece of writing in which Ricardo states that the advantage of banking lies in using the funds of others. Rist makes no reference at all to this statement.

16. Keynes, *Treatise*, *1*, 25.

17. Herbert Joseph Davenport, *The Economics of Enterprise* (New York, The Macmillan Company, 1918), p. 348, one of the earlier sources to give a clear account of the process of credit creation in banking. Also cf. L. J. Pritchard, "A Note on the Relationships of Bank Capital to the Lending Ability of the Commercial Banks," *American Economic Review*, *43* (June 1953), 365-6, and "Toward a More Meaningful Statistical Concept of the Money Supply," *Journal of Finance*, *9* (Mar. 1954), 45n13.

B

Clearly these are two completely different ways of lending. The first describes the lending mechanics of the financial institution that does not create deposits of any kind; the second, the lending mechanics of banking. The non-bank lends from its cash balances by advancing borrowers currency and cheques drawn on its bank deposit. Borrowers by depositing the cheques of the lender in their own bank accounts cause the cash balances (deposits) of the lender to fall. Banks also may lend currency, in which case they differ in no way from other lenders, but they do not usually lend that part of their cash balances represented by deposits with the central bank by issuing cheques on those deposits to borrowers. Instead, non-currency loans are made by creating additional deposits in favour of the borrowers. In other words, the same type of debt instrument serves to acquire the debt instruments of borrowers as serves to acquire cash balances for the bank. That is, the same financial instrument—the deposit—serves both as a medium for borrowing and as a medium for lending.

This again emphasizes the difference in lending technique between banks and other lenders. In making loans by creating deposits the bank is not lending the same thing as it borrowed; it is not lending its cash balances or reserves.[18] Recognition of this difference by those

---

18. "In fact, also, even when the deposits in the bank are not derived from the lending activity of the bank, but are really funds deposited from outside sources, these funds are commonly used by the bank as a reserve basis on which loans are extended rather than as funds which are themselves loaned out by the bank." Davenport, p. 263.

J. Brooke Willis, *The Functions of the Commercial Banking System* (New York, King's Crown Press, 1943), p. 31, maintains that cash reserves are loaned only in the sense that their availability for withdrawal permits loans to be made; but he goes on to point out (p. 33) that "loans are not made out of reserves. This is obvious since any given aggregate of reserves will be the same before as after the expansion of bank deposits."

The main exception to this are certain types of money-market loans that may be viewed as an advance of cash reserves by the lending bank. One example of such loans is provided by advances of American banks in the "Federal funds" market. Cf. "Money by the Day," Federal Reserve Bank of Chicago, *Business Conditions*, Jan. 1958, pp. 11–16. Another example is represented by the "daylight overdrafts" granted by the Canadian chartered banks in the form of certified cheques to money-market dealers. Cf. J. S. G. Wilson, "The Canadian Money Market Experiment," Banca Nazionale del Lavoro, *Quarterly Review*, Mar. 1958, pp. 29–30.

who argue that banks fall into the same category as other lenders would end much fruitless debate. However, of more importance than the difference in lending technique is the question whether the effect of lending on the position of the lender differs with the technique used.

The effect of lending on the position of the non-bank lender is obvious: he loses cash directly to the borrower or to the institution with which the borrower holds his cash balances. The lending bank may also lose cash as a result of lending; but if it does, it loses cash not to the borrower but to the person or institution to whom the borrower's funds get paid. The lending bank may not, of course, lose cash to the full extent of its loans: it retains some of its loan-created deposits. But the act of retention represents only passive borrowing from the public[19] as a result of some beneficiaries from the spending of borrowers depositing their receipts with the lending bank.[20] The non-bank lender can place itself in exactly the same position as the lending bank by actively borrowing from the public; in this way it can match the performance of the lending bank that retains a portion of its loan-created deposits.

Likewise, the lending bank that loses cash reserves because of its lending activities is placed in the same position as a non-bank lender that does not borrow to replenish its cash. If it did not have excess cash balances before, the lending bank must build up its cash balances by disposing of other assets for cash. The lending ability of a bank, like that of all other lenders, depends on its cash balances; not because it lends its cash balances, as other lenders do, but because it too loses cash balances when it lends. It can, however, like other lenders, preserve its cash balances during the lending act by attracting funds through borrowing from the public. If both types of lender are able to borrow equally successfully from the public, both, given

19. It represents forced borrowing when banks require borrowers (as is sometimes American practice) to keep a portion of their loans on deposit with the lending bank; in effect, the borrower then has to borrow in order to lend to the bank.

20. This is perhaps what Davenport, p. 263, had in mind when he wrote that banks are mainly intermediaries between debtors and creditors because the borrower becomes indebted to the bank and then nominates someone else to be a creditor of the bank by spending his loan proceeds.

similar cash-balance policies, can extend their loans to the same
degree.

Therefore, although the lending technique differs, the effect of
lending on the position of the lender does not differ in principle
between a bank and a non-bank. Lending depends in both cases on
cash balances and the ability to preserve that cash balance by borrowing and by liquidating other assets. Any confusion that exists in
the literature that compares banks with other lenders arises because
some writers emphasize the difference in lending techniques while
others emphasize the similarity of effects.

The Banking System

When the lending activity of the banking system as such is considered, the matter is a little different. The usual way of drawing the
distinction between the lending activities of an individual bank and
that of the banking system is to formulate a paradox the gist of which
is that, while for an individual bank loans depend on deposits, for all
banks deposits depend on loans (interpreting loans widely to mean
all forms in which banks provide deposits to the community).

Phillips in his classic treatment of the subject put it in these words:

> It follows that *for the banking system* deposits are chiefly the
> offspring of loans. For *an individual bank* loans are the offspring of
> deposits.[21]

The metaphor is not altogether illuminating. To say that the loans
of a bank are the offspring of its deposits is correct in the sense that
the deposits on the books of a bank reflect cash reserves gained or
retained,[22] for the loans of a bank depend on its cash reserves. For the

21. Chester Arthur Phillips, *Bank Credit: A Study of the Principles and Factors
Underlying Advances Made by Banks to Borrowers* (New York, The MacMillan Com-
pany, 1921), p. 64 (italics in the original). This was stating more clearly the
relationship between loans and deposits which Keynes had expressed earlier as
follows: "It is natural to think of a Bank's loans as being the children of its deposits.
But it is at least as true to think of the deposits as being the children of its loans."
J. M. Keynes, "The Prospects of Money, November, 1914," *Economic Journal, 24*
(Dec. 1914), 617.

22. Unspent balances in loan deposits are an obvious exception, but all other
credit entries in the deposit accounts of a bank represent either the receipt of cash
or the decisions of the public to keep deposits with that bank. Great Britain,

banking system too loans depend on having cash reserves. Hence, the distinction between the banking system and the individual bank does not lie in the source of loans: the distinction lies in the effects of making loans. An individual bank in making loans is likely to find its cash reserves reduced by more than its deposits are increased; in the banking system an increase in loans is likely to increase deposits by more than it reduces cash reserves.

This way of stating the distinction between lending by one bank and lending by all banks emphasizes the fact that in the deposit-creation process leakages from cash reserves for the banking system are less than for the individual bank. In the course of lending to the private sector the banking system only loses cash reserves through a drain of currency into circulation and through a possible loss of cash to the other depositors of the central bank. Aside from these minor exceptions, there is no loss of cash reserves from the banking system as a result of banks making loans.[23]

Committee on Finance and Industry, *Report*, Cmd. 3897 (London, His Majesty's Stationery Office, 1931), p. 34, recognizes that it is natural to think of the deposits of a bank as being created by the public through the deposit of cash but criticizes this view by arguing that most deposits arise out of the actions of the banks themselves. Strictly speaking, the natural view is correct: it is the action of the public that keeps the deposits at a given bank, not the act of creating them.

The possibility of confusing all deposits in the banking system with cash reserves has been ably put by Willis, *Commercial Banking System*, p. 34, as follows: "At some point in the banking process individual banks, or the banks severally, wrote up by way of credits to borrowers the very deposits which the individual banker says were brought to him in the form of cash by his depositors. But once generated, their identity with the transaction by which they were created is soon lost somewhere along the devious routes and bypasses of the flow of funds, with the result that to the individual banker who later acquires these funds, because his customers transfer them to him in the form of reserves from banks by which they were originally issued, they appear as funds entrusted to him which he can safely lend or invest."

23. During the financial crises of 1914 in the United Kingdom at the outbreak of World War I, there was apparently some apprehension that if the joint-stock banks lent more freely the deposits of the Bank of England would become depleted. Keynes, "The Prospects of Money," pp. 616–17, in commenting on this stated: "How much the Clearing Banks lend to their customers . . . it will not in the least diminish the aggregate of the free balances held by them at the Bank of England. At the most it can only affect the names to whose credit these balances stand."

No aggregation of non-bank lenders produces the same results; individually or collectively non-bank lenders do lose cash balances when they lend, except when borrowers transfer their loans from one lender to another—a minor qualification. Furthermore, non-bank lenders, individually or collectively, can add to their cash balances by expanding their liabilities to the public: banks as a group cannot, as already explained, unless the central bank acquiesces. This distinction between banks as a group and other groups of non-bank lenders has policy implications, but before these are discussed it is necessary to consider the implications for lending policy of this inability of the banking system to alter the amount of cash reserves available to the system.

The Nature of Bank Loans

With a given amount of cash reserves there is a certain maximum of loans that a bank or a banking system can make—a maximum that is set mainly by the reserve ratio. On the one hand it is natural to think that banks would prefer to extend their loans to the maximum possible. There is undoubtedly a profit advantage in lending which is probably not present in other activities in which banks engage.[24] On the other hand, banks play a fairly passive role in the lending process, which makes it difficult for them to be always as fully loaned as they would like to be. That is, the initiative in the bank-loan market lies with the borrower, not with the banks.[25] The point is made very effectively by Schumpeter, as follows:

> The above statement that a bank cannot normally take the initiative in its business with its customers merely meant that it cannot initiate the individual transaction. Its truth becomes ob-

24. Roland I. Robinson, *The Management of Bank Funds* (New York, McGraw-Hill Book Company, Inc., 1951), p. 94.

25. Cf. Canada, Royal Commission on Banking and Currency in Canada, *Report* (Ottawa, King's Printer, 1933), Addendum by Sir Thomas White, p. 83; Robinson, p. 97. Graham Towers, then Governor of the Bank of Canada, stated in 1954 that one of the prerequisites for an increase in bank loans is "the desire and credit worthiness of customers to secure the loans." Canada, Parliament, House, Standing Committee on Banking and Commerce, *Proceedings: Decennial Revision of the Bank Act*, 1st Sess., 22nd Parl., 1954, p. 142.

vious if we consider what that would involve. As far as the financing of enterprise is concerned, it would involve suggesting definite plans to, or urging on, people who have every motive to go ahead and must normally be expected to know the ground on which they are standing better than any banker can. . . . there are occasions— they may be the high points in the career of a great banker—in which a bank can successfully make itself responsible for an enterprise by pledging its support and committing itself to seeing the entrepreneur through. But it is evident how risky this is. As a rule, it augurs ill for a proposition if it has to be forced on the primarily responsible man. But the same applies, in a lesser degree, even to current transactions. A bank often sees reason to restrain, but it is rarely in a position to ask its customer: Won't you borrow in order to do this or that? . . .

It might be urged that initiative need not go as far as this but can be exerted without any particular suggestions by assuming a general attitude of encouragement, which consists mainly, though not wholly, in offering attractive conditions and in conveying to wavering customers the impression that if they go ahead they will not do so alone. Even a small bank may do that if it observes that others do it, but a bank important enough to influence situations by its own action or example seems particularly able to impart such a stimulus. . . . It has been pointed out in the preceding chapter that the end of recession is the only stage to offer possibilities of corporative initiative by banks. The reason why more use is not made of these possibilities is analogous to the reason why initiative action by banks could do but little once a downward cumulative process has set in. Banks control one element only of the situation in which businessmen find themselves, and that situation contains so many hitches and untenable positions that such action, besides becoming extremely difficult, cannot be expected to be effective.[26]

Thus it is difficult for banks as a group actively to increase the

26. Joseph A. Schumpeter, *Business Cycles: A Theoretical, Historical, and Statistical Analysis of the Capitalist Process* (New York, McGraw-Hill Book Company, Inc., 1939), 2, 641–3.

total of bank loans outstanding. It is almost equally difficult for them to refrain from making acceptable loans when the growth in loans outstanding is threatening the cash position of the banks.[27] This is because

> bankers commonly regard their relations with regular customers as extremely valuable. This gives them a strong and persistent motive to accommodate their customers. It is a motive that is reinforced by competitive considerations. A bank that does not take care of the legitimate needs of its customers when money becomes somewhat tight takes the strong risk of losing them permanently, and of having too few good customers when money is not so tight. Hence, commercial banks have a continuing incentive to take care of their regular customers. . . .[28]

Therefore, banks cannot as a rule refrain from making new loans solely out of consideration for their cash balances, nor can they increase their loans at will to utilize excess cash balances. Furthermore, they cannot, for good practical reasons, call in loans simply to restore their cash-reserve ratio;[29] calling loans produces difficulties for borrowers, creates ill-will against the banks, injures bank-customer re-

---

27. "Every banker is conscious of how important it is for the bank not to have to refuse, merely because its cash position is not strong enough, normal accommodation to firms of good standing or seasonal loans within the limits in which they are usually granted. . . ." Pasquale Saraceno, "Liquidity Problems from the Standpoint of the Individual Bank," *Bancaria* (Monthly magazine of the Italian bankers association [Associazione Bancaria Italiana, Rome]), English Supplement to No. 11, 1951, pp. 24–5, which summarizes papers prepared for the International Credit Conference, Rome, 1951.

28. United States Congress, Joint Committee on the Economic Report, *Monetary Policy and the Management of the Public Debt: Their Role in Achieving Price Stability and High-level Employment—Replies to Questions and Other Material for the Use of the Subcommittee on General Credit Control and Debt Management*, 82nd Cong., 2nd Sess., 1952, Pt. 1, p. 108, henceforth cited as U.S. Congress, *Monetary Policy . . . Public Debt: Compendium*.

29. This refers to customer loans and not loans to the money market, which are made with the understanding that they will be called when necessary for adjusting the cash positions of the banks.

lationships, and in general may do long-term damage to the lending business of the banks.[30]

However, the usual situation has been for the banks not to be under pressure to make additional loans but for them to be generally under-loaned. Indeed, a conspicuous feature of twentieth-century banking has been the general decline in the importance of bank loans in developed economies. The facts for Canada are briefly as follows. From 1900 till 1930 the percentage of loans to total bank assets seldom fell below 40 per cent, but after 1930 the percentage dropped to below 20 per cent and in many years since then it has been below 30 per cent. The low point (17 per cent) was reached in 1946. Since then the percentage has risen until at the end of 1956 it stood at just

30. Canadian banks do not have a history of liquidating loans to protect their cash position. Two statements for periods when there might have been grounds for the practice serve to support this view:

"The funds that are employed as current discounts are regarded as more or less fixed. It will quite probably be the case that the bank could force payment on a large part of these advances whenever it chose. But to do so . . . would cause great inconvenience to the customers, loss of valuable accounts, and perhaps excite alarm among depositors. So, as a rule, these discounts have to be allowed more or less to run their natural course. The gross amount will rise and fall with the seasonable . . . changes in the trades and in industries of the country." H. M. P. Eckardt, *Manual of Canadian Banking*, 4th ed. (Toronto, Monetary Times, [1913]), p. 188.

"There is no evidence that, at any time during the period under study [1900–13], they [the Canadian banks] used their power over the volume of loans to adjust their cash reserve ratios. There is abundant evidence, on the other hand, that the first consideration of the banks was the meeting of the credit needs of their customers, and that they neither contracted nor expanded their current loans primarily because of the state of their cash reserves." Jacob Viner, *Canada's Balance of International Indebtedness, 1900–1913: An Inductive Study in the Theory of International Trade*, Harvard Economic Studies, *26* (Cambridge, Mass., Harvard University Press, 1924), p. 176.

The situation was not always so. In earlier days of Canadian banking—around the 1850's—the chartered banks did follow the practice of calling in their out-standing loans in order to protect their position. Adam Shortt, "The History of Canadian Currency, Banking and Exchange: The Crisis of 1857–58," *Journal of The Canadian Bankers' Association, 11* (Apr. 1904), 206.

A striking example of loan liquidations by a large Canadian bank in the 1860's is recorded by G. Hague, "The Late Mr. E. H. King," *Journal of The Canadian Bankers' Association, 4* (Oct. 1896), 24.

over 40 per cent.[31] The same tendency for loans to decline relative to total bank assets, over a long period of time, appears in other banking systems as well.[32] Indeed, the fall in bank loans relative to total bank assets has been so prevalent as to lead some observers to talk of a secular decline in the demand for bank loans and to conclude that bank loans have become less necessary in financing economic activity.[33] Support for this argument as it applies to Canada may be

31. J. D. Gibson, "The Trend of Bank Loans and Investments in Canada," *Readings in Money and Banking*, ed. Elizabeth M. Rosengren (Toronto, University of Toronto Press, 1947), pp. 58, 60, which is reprinted, with editorial comment, from *Canadian Investment and Foreign Exchange Problems*, ed. J. F. Parkinson (Toronto, University of Toronto Press, 1940); "The Postwar Growth in Bank Lending," The Bank of Nova Scotia, *Monthly Review*, Sept.–Oct. 1953, pp. 3–4; Bank of Canada, *Statistical Summary*, Financial Supplement, 1956, p. 19, from which current ratios can be calculated.

After 1956 the Bank of Canada, *Statistical Summary*, does not tabulate total bank assets but instead gives the smaller figure of total Canadian and net foreign assets. Also the loan series has been revised back to September 1956 and is not strictly comparable with the earlier loan figures. Total loans in Canadian currency as a percentage of the foregoing asset aggregate stood at about 44 per cent at the end of 1956 and at about 46 per cent at the end of 1960. Bank of Canada, *Statistical Summary*, Financial Supplement, 1959, p. 19, and Mar. 1961, pp. 139–40.

A chart plotting the percentage of chartered-bank Canadian loans, insured mortgages, and non-government securities to total assets over the years 1954–60 appears in Bank of Canada, *Annual Report*, 1960, p. 65.

32. E. Browaldh and L. E. Thumholm, *Changes in Bank Balance Sheets, 1938–1952* (Paris, Institut International d'Etudes Bancaires, 1954), pp. 16–17, who calculate the ratios of loans to total assets in eleven European banking systems for the years 1938 and 1945–52. In the United States the decline in the importance of bank loans is commented upon in C. R. Whittlesey, "Memorandum on the Stability of Demand Deposits," *American Economic Review*, *39* (Dec. 1949), 1196; and in the article, "Monetary Policy: Our Changing Economic Environment," Federal Reserve Bank of Philadelphia, *Business Review*, Apr. 1957, p. 4.

33. R. S. Sayers, *Modern Banking*, 3rd ed. (Oxford, Clarendon Press, 1951), pp. 240–4; Plumptre, *Central Banking*, p. 214; Gibson, "The Trend of Bank Loans and Investments in Canada," pp. 57–9; A. E. Phipps, "The Banking Situation in Canada," *Journal of The Canadian Bankers' Association*, *36* (Jan. 1929), 125–6, an address delivered at the Annual General Meeting of The Canadian Bankers' Association, Nov. 8, 1928; U.S. Congress, *Monetary Policy . . . Public Debt: Compendium*, Pt. 1, p. 534; H. G. Johnson, "Some Implications of Secular Changes in Bank Assets and Liabilities in Great Britain," *Economic Journal*, *61* (Sept. 1951), 549.

seen in the ratio of bank loans to gross national product—a ratio that fell steadily from the early 1930's till the early 1940's and which has risen only slightly since then.[34] Contrary evidence is suggested by the recent behaviour of bank loans in Canada, which increased from $4.1 billion at the end of 1954 to $5.4 billion at the end of 1956 and to $6.5 billion at the end of 1960—an increase that appears even more impressive when viewed against the slow but steady rise in bank loans since 1946, when they amounted to only $1.6 billion.[35]

Any slack left in the balance-sheets of banks by the failure of loans to attain their maximum values is taken up by increased security holdings, with the result that modern banks may be not only important lenders but also large investors.

THE BANKS AS INVESTORS

Banks have long been holders of securities. In England it has long since been a matter of sound banking practice for banks to hold a large portion of their surplus funds in government securities,[36] and

34. "The Postwar Growth in Bank Lending," p. 3; Bank of Canada, *Statistical Summary*, Financial Supplement, 1956, pp. 19, 105, and Mar. 1961, pp. 139–40, 177, from which more recent ratios of bank loans to gross national product can be calculated. Possibly the greater importance of public activity in generating gross national product, together with the different financial requirements this involves, accounts for the lower ratio of loans to gross national product that now prevails.

35. Ibid., p. 19, and Mar. 1961, pp. 139–40. The conclusion that the decline in the importance of bank loans in the 1930's and 1940's meant a growing independence from the need for bank loans by business in general was not universally accepted. One study concluded that while there had been great structural changes in the business of commercial banking since 1900 there was "no evidence of a persisting tendency for the business lending function of commercial banks to decline." Neil H. Jacoby and Raymond J. Saulnier, *Business Finance and Banking*, Financial Research Program: Studies in Business Financing (New York, National Bureau of Economic Research, 1947), p. 18. This view is restated by Mr. Jacoby in U.S. Congress, *Monetary Policy . . . Public Debt: Compendium*, Pt. 2, p. 1035, and is supported elsewhere in the same source, Pt. 1, p. 534, and United States Congress, Joint Committee on the Economic Report, *Monetary Policy and the Management of the Public Debt: Report of the Subcommittee on General Credit Control and Debt Management*, 82nd Cong., 2nd Sess., 1952, p. 35.

36. James W. Gilbart, *The Principles and Practice of Banking*, new ed., ed. anon. (London, Bell and Daldy, 1871), pp. 201–10 passim, discusses the high regard of

American banks have been significant investors in securities since the 1890's.[37] However, the rise in the importance of securities in the balance-sheets of banks has been most noticeable in this century. In Canada, security holdings of the chartered banks, as a percentage of bank assets, began their upward rise in 1915, although not until 1930 did they really become noticeably large. Thus, from 1900 to 1930 bank holdings of Dominion and provincial government securities seldom exceeded 10 per cent of bank assets, but from 1930 to 1945 the percentage rose steadily until it exceeded 50 per cent in 1945. It then fell to 40 per cent by 1950, and to less than 30 per cent by 1953. And since mid-1955 the proportion of securities to total bank assets has fallen quite substantially as government securities were sold and replaced by loans.[38] From 1935 until 1953 security holdings were larger in total than bank loans although before that, and since then, bank loans were larger than security holdings.[39] Government financial requirements during the depression of the 1930's and the war of the 1940's, together with the increased importance of public activity relative to private activity in those periods, are perhaps sufficient to account for the great gain in the importance of security holdings in bank balance-sheets in those years.[40] A similar development occurred in other banking systems as well. A study of eleven European banking systems, made in 1954, pointed out that "the vastly increased importance of Government paper as an investment for bank funds is perhaps the most spectacular structural change affecting the various

English banks for government securities as an investment for their secondary reserves. (This work is one of the classics among nineteenth-century texts on banking.)

37. Schumpeter, *Business Cycles*, 2, 862–3.

38. Gibson, "The Trend of Bank Loans and Investments in Canada," Chart II, p. 58; "The Postwar Growth in Bank Lending," Sept.–Oct. 1953, p. 3; "The Squeeze on Liquidity," The Bank of Nova Scotia, *Monthly Review*, Apr. 1957, pp. 1–2; Bank of Canada, *Annual Report*, 1960, p. 65, where the percentage of government bonds to total assets are charted; idem, *Statistical Summary*, Financial Supplement, 1956, pp. 18–19, where no ratios are calculated but where the actual figures show a decline for securities and a rise for total bank assets.

39. "The Postwar Growth in Bank Lending," p. 3; Bank of Canada, *Statistical Summary*, Financial Supplement, 1956, pp. 18–19, and Mar. 1961, pp. 139–40.

40. "The Postwar Growth in Bank Lending," pp. 2–3.

banking systems in recent decades."[41] Much the same thing happened to bank balance-sheets in the United States during the 1930's and 1940's as occurred in Canada: holdings of government securities replaced bank loans as the largest bank asset and for much the same reason as in Canada—the increase in the importance of government financing during those years.[42]

More important than the reason for the growth of security holdings in banking is what it represents—namely, the development of excess lending capacity in banking systems.[43] That is, large security holdings by banks reflect banking resources that might have been used to make more loans had the opportunity been present. On this interpretation, investing in securities is seen as a residual activity for the banks, not an activity that competes with loans for a limited supply of banking resources. And indeed there is evidence to suggest that banks do place loans ahead of investment in securities, that loans take precedence over securities.[44]

The residual nature of at least some security holdings, especially short-term government securities, is also reflected in their use to regulate the cash position of the banks. Because the amount of loans outstanding cannot be controlled or regulated precisely by the banks, fluctuations in loan volume relative to cash reserves must be offset by contrary fluctuations in security holdings. Securities—at least government securities—lend themselves to this kind of stabilization treat-

41. Browaldh and Thumholm, *Changes in Bank Balance-sheets, 1938–1952*, p. 15, who give the percentage of government securities to total assets, for select years from 1938 to 1952, for the eleven banking systems studied.

42. "Monetary Policy: Our Changing Economic Environment," Federal Reserve Bank of Philadelphia, *Business Review*, Apr. 1957, pp. 4–5; Whittlesey, "Memorandum . . .," pp. 1194–5; U.S. Congress, *Monetary Policy . . . Public Debt: Compendium*, Pt. 1, pp. 105–6.

43. D. A. Alhadeff and C. P. Alhadeff, "The Struggle for Commercial Bank Savings," *Quarterly Journal of Economics*, 72 (Feb. 1958), 15–16.

44. Schumpeter, *Business Cycles*, 2, 864n1, found that American banks "did not turn to temporary investment in the open market at the expense of their loans to customers when this was more remunerative, as it was in 1929." Winfield W. Riefler, *Money Rates and Money Markets in the United States* (New York, Harper and Brothers, 1930), pp. 62–3, discusses briefly some reasons for banks giving precedence to loans over securities. More recent evidence appears in U.S. Congress, *Monetary Policy . . . Public Debt: Compendium*, Pt. 1, p. 107.

ment, for the buying and selling of securities is a matter that is entirely at the initiative of the banks.[45] Thus, discretionary variations in security holdings may be carried out by a bank to stabilize its cash position in the face of what Boulding refers to as passive changes[46] in the structure of its balance-sheet. Selling securities relieves pressure on the cash position and buying securities takes up any slack that develops. The required cash-reserve ratios of the banks are thus maintained by the individual banks offsetting every passive change in their balance-sheets with active changes in their security holdings.[47] Engaging in security transactions for this purpose may be referred to as carrying out compensating transactions.

The effect of these compensating transactions can be seen in the inverse relationship that exists between fluctuations in bank loans and security holdings.[48] Increases in loans made by the banking system are often followed by decreases in the amount of securities held by the system; conversely, a decrease in loans is often followed by an increase in security holdings. This inverse relationship between loans and securities is not, however, necessarily peculiar to the banking class of lenders. Other lenders working with minimum cash balances and holding constant their liabilities to the public may behave in exactly the same way: buying securities when their loans fall off and selling securities when their loans expand. The mechanics are much the same for both classes of lenders. A bank in buying securities actually spends its cash reserves when it issues its cheque for the

45. Cf. Schumpeter, *Business Cycles*, 2, 644.

46. Kenneth E. Boulding, *A Reconstruction of Economics* (New York, John Wiley and Sons, Inc., 1950), p. 33.

47. Cf. ibid. where a firm that offsets every passive event affecting it by an active event is described as operating under "the pure homeostasis principle."

48. Among the sources that comment on the inverse relationship between bank loans and security holdings are the following: Keynes, *Treatise*, 2, 67; Gibson, "The Trend of Bank Loans and Investments in Canada," pp. 56–7; Whittlesey, "Memorandum . . .," p. 1196; U.S. Congress, *Monetary Policy . . . Public Debt: Compendium*, Pt. 1, p. 107; "Towards a More Stable Money Supply," Federal Reserve Bank of Cleveland, *Monthly Business Review*, Sept. 1954, p. 7; "Monetary Policy: Our Changing Economic Environment," Federal Reserve Bank of Philadelphia, *Business Review*, Apr. 1957, pp. 13–14; Bank of Canada, *Annual Report*, 1956, pp. 54–6, 64.

securities bought, which is exactly what any other lending institution does in buying securities. When the individual bank sells securities and thereby gains cash reserves, it is affected in exactly the same way as other lenders forced to liquidate securities to maintain their cash balances. However, a bank in buying and selling securities may alter its liabilities to the public instead of its cash balance: the non-bank lender does not. And when the banking system buys and sells securities the most likely effect is an alteration in bank deposits rather than a change in cash reserves; asset management in the banking system alters the state of its indebtedness to the banking public. There is thus a difference between the effects of investment activity on the banks as a group and on non-bank lenders when both engage in the same type of security transactions.

THE CONSEQUENCES OF DOMESTIC BANKING OPERATIONS

The separate functions of banks as borrowers, lenders, and investors can now be viewed as a whole for purposes of assessing their net impact on the economy. This is done under the headings of the stability of bank credit, the saving-lending process, and problems of credit control.

The Stability of Bank Credit

Because bank deposits occupy a special place in the economy in that they represent the major part of the money supply, variations in the total are a matter of some importance. It is a serious matter if banks, in carrying out their manifold activities as borrowers, lenders, and investors, cause the total of bank deposits to be unstable; yet it has been charged that bank credit is inherently unstable.[49]

By this it is meant that the demand for bank loans varies with the

49. The charge that bank credit is inherently unstable appears to have originated with R. G. Hawtrey who uses the phrase in his *Trade and Credit* (London, Longmans, Green and Co., 1928), pp. 97, 177. Part of the argument presented there is reprinted in R. G. Hawtrey's "The Trade Cycle," *Readings in Business Cycle Theory*, Blakiston Series of Republished Articles on Economics, 2 (Philadelphia, The Blakiston Company, 1944), p. 344.

state of business, and that the resulting cyclical fluctuations in bank loans cause cyclical fluctuations in bank deposits, which in turn accentuate the business cycle, leading to greater expansions and worse contractions than would occur if bank deposits were more stable.[50] The basic premise of this view is that the unstable behaviour of deposits is the result of the instability of bank loans. Even the critics of the inherent-instability doctrine of bank deposits appear to accept the premise.[51] They then proceed to point out that bank credit is not now inherently unstable because bank loans in themselves are more stable and constitute a much smaller proportion of bank deposits than they used to, and that fluctuations in bank loans are now generally offset by contrary fluctuations in the security holdings of the banks.

It does follow that if bank loans are now more stable in themselves they become a less upsetting factor;[52] the same conclusion may be drawn from the diminished proportion that bank loans bear to de-

50. Whittlesey, "Memorandum . . .," pp. 1192–3; "Towards a More Stable Money Supply," Federal Reserve Bank of Cleveland, *Monthly Business Review*, Sept. 1954, pp. 5–6; U.S. Congress, *Monetary Policy . . . Public Debt: Compendium*, Pt. 1, p. 343; "Money on Good Behaviour," Federal Reserve Bank of Philadelphia, *Annual Report*, 1955, pp. 1–2.

51. However, Whittlesey, p. 1198, makes the ambiguous point that the inherent instability of bank credit fundamentally rests on the deposit multiplier. This seems to make as much sense as would the assertion that instability in incomes is due to the expenditure multiplier. Multipliers, whether they be expenditure or deposit multipliers, determine the amplitude of fluctuations in the related variables, but the fluctuations themselves are due to initial impulses from elsewhere. The deposit multiplier is in principle no different from the expenditure multiplier; there are important differences of detail, however, which are discussed by Procter Thomson, "Variations on a Theme by Phillips," *American Economic Review*, *46* (Dec. 1956), 965–6.

52. The argument is based on the fact that there has been a shift in bank lending away from self-liquidating to longer-term loans based on fixed assets that has tended to make bank loans as a group more stable. "Continuous Borrowing Through 'Short-Term' Bank Loans," Federal Reserve Bank of Cleveland, *Monthly Business Review*, Sept. 1956, pp. 6–7, 10–11; "Money on Good Behaviour," p. 3; "Towards a More Stable Money Supply," p. 7; Whittlesey, "Memorandum . . .," p. 1197. Although the shift has been most marked in the United States, there is reason to believe that the same thing has happened to bank loans in Canada. Cf. Bank of Canada, *Annual Report*, 1955, p. 17.

posits.[53] Furthermore bank deposits are now stable anyway because of the inverse relationship between movements in loans and security holdings in the banking system.[54] Stability is assured, so it is argued, because government debt held by the banks is likely to behave less cyclically than private debt.[55]

These arguments are all valid in their own right but they do not get at the fundamental causes for fluctuations in bank deposits. It is not so much the behaviour of the assets acquired by the banks in creating deposits that is the disturbing factor as the behaviour of cash reserves and cash-reserve ratios. When the amount of cash reserves available to the banking system can be held constant and when the banks can keep their ratio of cash to deposits constant, the total amount of bank deposits will be constant.[56] If total deposits fluctuate in an unstable manner, it is because of destabilizing fluctuations in cash reserves and cash-reserve ratios.

It is perhaps natural to suspect the cash-reserve ratios of banks of rising and falling with the business cycle and thus intensifying

53. Cf. Whittlesey, p. 1198. Robinson, *The Management of Bank Funds*, p. 33, points out that a *ceteris paribus* 10 per cent loan liquidation in 1929 in the United States would have reduced deposits by 7 per cent but that a 10 per cent loan liquidation in 1949 would have reduced deposits by only 3 per cent.

54. Thus, Whittlesey, pp. 1193–4, states it is "the changed relationship between loans and government securities in the portfolios of commercial banks that provides the principal reasons for believing that bank deposits will no longer behave in an inherently unstable manner." Also Henry C. Wallich, "Some Current Features of Bank Liquidity in the United States," Banca Nazionale del Lavoro, *Quarterly Review*, July–Sept. 1951, p. 110, who says that "the total volume of deposits has gained in stability. Instead of being based primarily upon loans, the liquidation of which would cause a general deposit shrinkage, they are now based in good part upon government securities. This part of the deposit structure could shrink only if the securities were sold by the banking system to the public or if the government were to redeem its debt out of taxes."

55. The point is that government debt outstanding is likely to fluctuate counter to the business cycle, not with it. Cf. Whittlesey, p. 1196; "Towards a More Stable Money Supply," p. 7; "Money on Good Behaviour," p. 3.

56. That the total of bank deposits depends on the cash-reserve ratio and the amount of cash reserves was pointed out long ago by W. F. Crick, "The Genesis of Bank Deposits," *Readings in Monetary Theory*, Blakiston Series of Republished Articles on Economics, 5 (New York, The Blakiston Company, 1951), pp. 52–3, which is reprinted from *Economica*, 7 (1927), 191–202.

it.[57] A greater stability in these ratios could then account for any improvement over time in the stability of bank deposits. However, English, American, and Canadian banks (before 1954) at least seem to have a well-established tradition of keeping their reserve ratios stable.[58] With stable reserve ratios[59] destabilizing

57. Polak and White, "The Effect of Income Expansion on the Quantity of Money," p. 422, get an elastic supply curve for bank money by assuming that the cash-reserve ratios of banks fluctuate with interest rates, which they regard as a plausible assumption.

S. C. Tsiang, "Liquidity Preference and Loanable Funds Theories, Multiplier and Velocity Analyses: A Synthesis," *American Economic Review, 46* (Sept. 1956), 556, uses the same assumption in his analysis.

Friedrich A. Hayek in *Prices and Production* (New York, The Macmillan Company, 1932), pp. 99–100, and in *Monetary Theory and the Trade Cycle*, trans. N. Kaldor and H. M. Croome (London, Jonathan Cape, 1933), pp. 169–73, maintains that during an expansion in economic activity bank deposits rise relative to cash reserves. A. C. Pigou, *Industrial Fluctuations*, 2nd ed. (London, Macmillan and Co., 1929), p. 136, also argues that the cash-reserve ratios of banks are variables.

58. Thus, Keynes, *Treatise, 2,* 53, criticized the theory that banks vary their reserve ratios and cited the stability of reserve ratios in the United States. His criticism was perhaps too sweeping, however, for a study of the cash-reserve ratio in eleven European banking systems for several years between 1938 and 1952 found a stable ratio only in England. Browaldh and Thunholm, *Changes in Bank Balance Sheets, 1938–1952,* p. 14.

In Canadian banking the practice of keeping the cash-reserve ratio stable was well established before 1954. W. T. G. Hackett, *A Background of Banking Theory* (Toronto, The Canadian Bankers' Association, 1945), pp. 23–4, 33; A. B. Jamieson, *Chartered Banking in Canada*, rev. ed. (Toronto, The Ryerson Press, 1957), p. 185; Donald B. Marsh, "Canada," *Banking Systems*, ed. Benjamin H. Beckhart (New York, Columbia University Press, 1954), pp. 140–1; Plumptre, *Central Banking*, pp. 259–60.

In the years 1900–13 when the charge against bank credit of being inherently unstable might be thought to have had more validity, the cash-reserve ratios of Canadian banks exhibited considerable constancy. Viner, *Canada's Balance of International Indebtedness*, pp. 173–4.

59. Cash-reserve ratios cannot be completely stabilized, however, because of lags that are inherent in any stabilization process—namely, recognition, administrative, and operational lags. Cf. Milton Friedman, "A Monetary and Fiscal Framework for Economic Stability," *Essays in Positive Economics* (Chicago, The University of Chicago Press, 1953), pp. 145–6, which is reprinted from the *American Economic Review, 38* (June 1948), 245–64. As applied to banking, the recognition lag is a matter of getting current information on the cash-reserve position; the

movements in deposits can only be the result of fluctuations in cash reserves.[60]

A special situation now exists in Canada, however, where changes in cash reserves may cause the observed reserve ratio to fluctuate. This is because the observed ratio in any month, the reserve period, is based on deposits of the previous month, not deposits of the current month. Cash reserves consist of balances held with the Bank of Canada in the current month and Bank of Canada notes held in the previous month.[61] Hence, during any month the only variable in the

administrative lag is a discretionary one, varying with the urgency of the situation; the operational lag depends on the results of the action taken, which cannot always be foreseen: most methods of adjusting the reserve ratio may either affect the cash or the deposits of a bank, and the time it takes to get the ratio back to the norm depends on which result follows the act of adjusting.

60. In the years 1900–13 the Canadian chartered banks were able to maintain constant reserve ratios by using their foreign-exchange assets to adjust their cash reserves to their deposit liabilities; they did not have to adjust their deposits to their cash. Viner, pp. 176–7. From present conditions in the United Kingdom R. G. Hawtrey has concluded that the English banks adjust their cash to their deposit liabilities, and not the other way around, because they can so easily obtain cash by selling Treasury bills, thereby keeping their reserve ratios constant even though deposits fluctuate. R. G. Hawtrey, "Basic Principles and the Credit Squeeze," *The Bankers' Magazine* (London), Dec. 1955, p. 448. Tse Chun Chang, *Cyclical Movements in the Balance of Payments* (Cambridge, At the University Press, 1951), p. 218, noted a marked cyclical variation in the demand liabilities of the chartered banks in Canada for the years 1926–38 matched by corresponding fluctuations in cash reserves that kept the reserve ratio for the banking system nearly constant.

61. Specifically the law specifies that for "the purpose of determining the amount of the cash reserve required to be maintained by a bank during any month (*a*) the amount of its deposit liabilities payable in Canadian currency shall be the average of such deposit liabilities at the close of business on Wednesdays in each of the four consecutive weeks ending with the last Wednesday but one in the preceding month, (*b*) the amount of Bank of Canada notes held by the bank shall be the average holdings of such notes at the close of business on Wednesdays in each of the four consecutive weeks ending with the last Wednesday but one in the preceding month, and (*c*) the amount of its deposit with the Bank of Canada shall be the average amount of such deposit at the close of business on each juridical day of the current month." Canada, Laws, Statutes, *Statutes of Canada*, 1953–54, 2–3 Elizabeth II, c. 48, s. 71 (2).

ratio is the cash balances of the chartered banks with the Bank of
Canada. Therefore, the reserve ratio for any month changes only
when the Bank of Canada permits the cash reserves of the banks to
alter. No matter what action the banks take during the month, they
cannot alter the cash ratio for that month. In the following month
the deposits and till money used in calculating that month's reserve
ratio will reflect what the banks did in the previous month, but
during the month itself the banks will be unable to influence the
ratio in any way. The significance of this is that the cash ratio as now
calculated in Canada for any given month reflects central-bank
policy and not banking policy.[62]

There were undoubtedly possibilities under the gold standard for
cash reserves to fluctuate.[63] Certainly when Canada was on the gold
standard, the chartered banks were able to alter their cash reserves
in response to changes in their loans and deposits. For this purpose
the banks maintained what were called "outside reserves," which
consisted of deposits with foreign correspondents, call loans in New
York and London, and holdings of foreign securities and commercial
paper—mainly of the United States and United Kingdom. These
foreign assets, or outside reserves, could be acquired by shipping and

62. William C. Hood, *Financing of Economic Activity in Canada*, A Study for the
Royal Commission on Canada's Economic Prospects (Ottawa, Queen's Printer,
1959), pp. 393, 395, discusses the Canadian method of setting reserve requirements
entirely in terms of the "lag of required reserves behind current deposit liabilities"
and concludes that this complicates not only the interpretation of the statistics but
also the task of the central bank. He does not consider the implication of the
calculation method for the interpretation of the cash ratio, which may be the
significant one in view of the attention usually focused on that ratio in Canada.

63. Hawtrey, "The Trade Cycle," pp. 341, 348–9, suggests, but in a very loose
manner, that the supply of gold governs the fluctuations of bank credit. However,
Raymond J. Saulnier, *Contemporary Monetary Theory: Studies of Some Recent Theories
of Money, Prices, and Production* (New York, Columbia University Press, 1947), in
his comprehensive review of Hawtrey's writings on the business cycle (pp. 19–108),
which rather strangely makes scarcely any reference to the idea that credit is
inherently unstable, states that Hawtrey explains the turning points of the business
cycle in terms of internal and external flows affecting the cash reserves of the
banking system (p. 74). Saulnier also states that Hawtrey explains the business
cycles in the 150 years before 1914 in terms of "the effect of internal and external
cash flows on bank reserves and credit policy" (p. 81).

selling gold, or they could be liquidated to acquire gold. Hence, when the chartered banks had excess cash reserves—as when their loans fell off—the excess reserves took the form of gold or of Dominion notes, which could be converted into gold, so that excess reserves could be eliminated by shipping gold to acquire additional outside reserves. Likewise, a deficiency in cash reserves could be eliminated by liquidating some of the outside reserves in order to acquire gold.[64] Thus, under the gold standard, fluctuations in bank loans were offset by compensating transactions in outside reserves; however, the consequences were different from those that now follow compensating transactions in securities. In the earlier period, as loans increased so did deposits, but as outside reserves were reduced cash reserves were increased, instead of domestic deposits being decreased. Today Government of Canada securities take the place of outside reserves in the compensating transactions of Canadian banks, and to the extent that compensating transactions no longer influence the cash reserves, there is now greater deposit stability.

In general, if bank deposits are now more stable than they once were, the probable cause is that the cash reserves available to the banking system now fluctuate less than formerly. At least that bank deposits can be stabilized through controlling the cash reserves of the banking system is now an established doctrine in the theory of credit control;[65] fluctuations in bank loans need no longer cause sympathetic movements in bank deposits.

In other words, the answer to the charge that bank credit is inherently unstable should not run in terms of the diminished importance of loans in bank balance-sheets and of the greater stability in loans themselves; these factors are not relevant in the present context. When cash reserves and reserve ratios remain constant, the behaviour and nature of loans do not matter for deposit stability. And

64. Courtland Elliott, "Bank Cash," *Canadian Journal of Economics and Political Science*, 4 (Aug. 1938), 434–5; Viner, pp. 177–82 passim.

65. Keynes, *Treatise*, 2, 225–6, advanced the idea that appropriate management of monetary variables meant control of bank cash by the central bank; this view has been widely held since. Karl R. Bopp, "Central Banking Objectives, Guides, and Measures," *Journal of Finance*, 9 (Mar. 1954), 18, who however advances an alternative guide for central-bank control (p. 21).

the inverse relationship between loans and securities cited by the critics of the instability argument is likewise irrelevant. The inverse relationship is the result of fluctuations in bank loans outstanding which are not accompanied by permissive changes in cash reserves and reserve ratios.

In short, when the banking system has only a given amount of cash reserves to work with and the banks maintain constant cash-reserve ratios, domestic banking operations cannot of themselves result in destabilizing movements in bank deposits.

The Saving-Lending Process

Stability of bank deposits however does not necessarily mean stability of bank loans; the excess lending capacity, represented by large holdings of government securities, now generally a feature of banking systems, permits considerable scope for expanding bank loans even though cash reserves and reserve ratios remain constant. There is some difference of opinion over whether fluctuations in bank loans unaccompanied by fluctuations in bank deposits are a destabilizing influence.[66] Some argue that "it is not self-evident that bank advances are inherently inflationary" since they do not result in an increase in bank deposits because of "the 'scissors movement' between advances and investments that was a normal feature of pre-war banking practice."[67] Others maintain that a loan expansion may be inflationary even though deposits remain constant.[68]

The connection between the level of expenditures and changes in

66. Cf. Harry G. Johnson, "The Revival of Monetary Policy in Britain," *Three Banks Review*, No. 30, June 1956, pp. 16–17.

67. E. J. N. Warburton, "Bank Lending under Directives," *Papers and Proceedings of the First International Credit Conference* (Rome, Associazione Bancaria Italiana, 1953), 2, 190.

68. Warren L. Smith, "On the Effectiveness of Monetary Policy," *American Economic Review*, 46 (Sept. 1956), 604.

Irving Brecher, *Monetary and Fiscal Thought and Policy in Canada, 1919–1939*, Canadian Studies in Economics, No. 8 (Toronto, University of Toronto Press, 1957), p. 45n70, refers to the inflationary effect of chartered-bank operations in the expansion of the late 1920's even though cash reserves remained fairly stable and there was little change in the money supply. Cf. Elliott, "Bank Cash," p. 442.

bank loans, especially increases, determines the role that banks play in the saving-lending process. If, in making new loans, banks create additional loanable funds, they obviously play a different role than if they merely make available to borrowers the loanable funds of others. There are three possibilities in all: in making loans the banks may create new loanable funds, they may simply transfer loanable funds (defined as new and existing savings) from savers to borrowers, or they may do both. Exactly what they do in any given situation by making loans has a bearing on the level of expenditures as well as implications for credit-control policies; the matter therefore merits some consideration.

Existing views are divided on the subject of what contributions the banks, when they lend, make to the stream of payments. The credit-creation school of thought holds that the banks create loanable funds when they make loans. An early representative of this school put the case as follows:

> Banks are, in truth, mostly intermediaries between debtors and creditors—but not in the sense of borrowing funds from one class of customers in order to lend them to another class, but rather in the sense of creating for their borrowing customers funds which may be used by these borrowers as present purchasing power.[69]

A more recent representative refers to

> the well-established fact that commercial banks, in their lending or investing activities, create credit. And from this it has been repeatedly affirmed that the commercial banks do not, indeed cannot, lend out the savings of their depositors.

> .   .   .   .

> Thus it may be said that, in so far as borrowers are accommodated with deposits, the commercial banks originate all funds

---

69. Davenport, *The Economics of Enterprise*, p. 263. Earlier, Henry Dunning MacLeod, *The Theory and Practice of Banking*, 5th ed. (London, Longmans, Green and Co., 1892), *1*, 326, wrote that "the essential and distinctive feature of a '*Bank*' and a '*Banker*' is to *Create* and *Issue Credit payable on Demand*. . . . A bank, therefore, is not an office for *borrowing* and *lending Money*: but it is a *Manufactory* of *Credit*." (Italics are in the original.)

lent. They are not middlemen in the lending process for either depositors or stockholders.[70]

Finally, the following quotation suggests that banks are not in the same class as other financial agencies for

> commercial banks cannot perform the characteristic role of an intermediary in taking loan funds created elsewhere and passing them on to ultimate borrowers. An extension of credit by a commercial bank is not preceded by or contingent upon any private act of saving or of commitment of funds to investment use. If a person saves and accumulates demand deposits, this in no way affects the ability of banks to lend. Banks (in their demand-deposit function) cannot act as a loan-fund broker.[71]

The more traditional view seems to be that banks are only financial middlemen borrowing from one group and lending to another. The view has been put as follows:

> Commercial banks are service institutions whose essential func-

70. L. J. Pritchard, "A Note on the Relationships of Bank Capital to the Lending Ability of the Commercial Banks," *American Economic Review*, *43* (June 1953), 365–6, who also expresses the same views elsewhere as follows: "No correct understanding of the nature of the money supply is possible unless it is realized that the commercial banks do not loan out the savings of the public. . . . It is an established, though apparently not a well-known proposition, that the commercial banks are unique in that they do not loan out the savings of anybody. . . . The commercial banks are not middlemen in the lending process; they create *new* demand deposits as a consequence of their lending activities." Idem, "Toward a More Meaningful Statistical Concept of the Money Supply," *Journal of Finance*, *9* (Mar. 1954), 45n13 (italics in the original). Also cf. his book, *Money and Banking* (Boston, Houghton Mifflin Company, 1958), pp. 263–74, passim.

An early expression (1736) of the argument that banks create credit with the dash of a pen appears in George Berkeley, *The Querist*, ed. Jacob H. Hollander, A Reprint of Economic Tracts (Baltimore, The Johns Hopkins Press, 1910), p. 51, where it is asked whether a person operating a bank has not "a mighty Privilege . . . to be able to create an hundred Pounds with a Dash of his Pen?"

71. J. M. Culbertson, "Intermediaries and Monetary Theory: A Criticism of the Gurley-Shaw Theory," *American Economic Review*, *48* (Mar. 1958), 122. A similar view is expressed by Willis, *The Functions of the Commercial Banking System*, pp. 28, 30.

tion it is to collect the savings of depositors and lend or invest them in the safest and most profitable assets available. In the performance of this function, their role is . . . essentially that of middle men. As middle men they perform services which are such as to induce depositors to transfer command over their real savings to them which, in turn, they distribute among their borrowers.[72]

The same point is argued with some force by Gurley and Shaw in the following terms:

> We take exception to the view that banks stand apart in their ability to create loanable funds out of hand, while other intermediaries in contrast are busy with the modest brokerage function of transmitting loanable funds that are somehow generated elsewhere.
>
> Neither banks nor other intermediaries create loanable funds. That is the prerogative of spending units with surpluses on income and product account. Both banks and other intermediaries have the capacity to create special forms of financial assets that surplus units may accumulate as the reward for restraint on current or

---

72. J. Carl Poindexter, "Some Misconceptions of Banking and Interest Theory," *Southern Economic Journal, 13* (Oct. 1946), 144. Others who view banks as mainly intermediaries are: Westerfield, *Money, Credit and Banking*, p. 174; Thomas, *Our Modern Banking and Monetary System*, p. 53; and Copeland, *A Study of Moneyflows in the United States*, p. 295.

An early statement that lends itself to a similar interpretation is the following: "A bank is a . . . dealer in money. He is an intermediate party between the borrower and the lender. He borrows of one party, and lends to another. . . ." Gilbart, *The Principles and Practice of Banking*, p. 145.

Apparently the intermediary view of banks was widely held in the nineteenth century. Joseph A. Schumpeter, *History of Economic Analysis* (New York, Oxford University Press, 1954), p. 1113, states that a typical economist writing in 1900 would have argued that the existence of banks changes nothing, that the source of all lending is the public, and that banks act only as agents or middlemen who do the actual lending on behalf of the public. In his well-known article of 1921 Edwin Cannan, "The Meaning of Bank Deposits," *Economica, 1* (Jan. 1921), 35, was pleading in part for a "return to the nineteenth century doctrine that banks receive money from one set of people and lend it to another."

A nineteenth-century writer who states the intermediary view in particularly clear terms is Charles Gide, *Principles of Political Economy*, trans. C. W. A. Veditz, 2nd American ed. (London, D. C. Heath and Company, 1907), pp. 367–8.

capital spending. Banks alone have the capacity to create demand deposits and currency, to be sure, but only savings and loan associations can create savings and loan shares: both "create credit," both transmit loanable funds, both enable spending units to diversify their portfolios.

Banks do have a virtual monopoly of the payments mechanism, and only claims upon monetary intermediaries embody the privilege to use this mechanism. The fact that other intermediaries make use of the payments mechanism, which the banks administer, has sometimes been interpreted to mean that other intermediaries have the inferior role of brokerage in loanable funds while the banks have the superior role of creation of loanable funds. Both types of institution, on the contrary, are loanable-fund brokers.[73]

Thus, the controversy seems to be over whether banks are merely financial middlemen like other institutional lenders or whether they differ in being able to create loanable funds.

In a sense, since the non-loan deposits of a bank represent passive borrowing from the public, a bank is an intermediary between lenders (depositors) and borrowers (those to whom it makes loans). However, a true financial intermediary lends the same thing as it borrows: it borrows an asset, usually cash, and lends an asset of a like nature. On this narrow definition a bank is a financial intermediary only when it receives currency on deposit and makes loans by paying out currency. Otherwise a bank does not lend the same thing as it borrows. It borrows cash reserves but usually lends by creating a liability on itself. Thus, those who argue that banks are not true financial intermediaries are technically correct.[74]

73. Gurley and Shaw, "Financial Aspects of Economic Development," pp. 521–2. Also cf. idem, "Financial Intermediaries and the Saving-Investment Process," p. 259.

In *Money in a Theory of Finance*, pp. 202, 243, Gurley and Shaw appear to revise the foregoing views to the extent of granting that all intermediaries, including banks, may create loanable funds.

74. However, Arthur W. Marget, *The Theory of Prices: A Re-Examination of the Central Problems of Monetary Theory* (New York, Prentice-Hall, Inc., 1938), *1*, 165n25, puts the argument for those who insist that an individual bank is an

But the technical difference between a true financial intermediary and a deposit-creating institution does not seem to matter a great deal so far as the final results of the lending activity of either is concerned. In both cases the impact on the economy is much the same although the policy implications differ.

When financial intermediaries are working to minimum cash balances, an expansion in their loans must be preceded or followed by fresh borrowings from the public or by a liquidation of some of their other assets. In this process the intermediaries are in effect transfering funds to borrowers that they have secured from other members of the public. The funds they secure for lending may represent either new savings or existing idle cash balances. Likewise, when all the banks together are expanding their loans, they too must dispose of other assets if cash reserves are held constant; and in liquidating other assets to accommodate the expansion in their loans the banks too are restricted to tapping new savings or existing idle cash balances.

The lending activities of intermediaries and of a banking system with fixed cash reserves depend on savings in a further sense. The greater the level of savings in the economy the more easily lending institutions can dispose of assets (and intermediaries can increase their borrowing from the public) to accommodate an expansion in loans. That is, it is easier in terms of costs, and the lower the cost the greater the elasticity of the response of banks and intermediaries to a given increase in the demand for loanable funds. It is in this sense that an increase in savings is a permissive factor for banks, and for intermediaries too, in expanding loans.

The similarity between the lending consequences of a banking system with fixed cash reserves and of true financial intermediaries can be further brought out by considering how a banking system so placed depends upon savings in expanding its loans. When the banks

---

intermediary as follows: ". . . the individual banker does in fact base the amount of his loans upon the amount of funds deposited with him, is thus in effect an 'intermediary' between lenders (that is, depositors) and borrowers. . . ." The technicality I argue is that a bank may be in effect an intermediary (i.e., the results of its operations are the same as if it did in fact function as an intermediary) but it is not one in terms of operations. Paying attention to this technicality does, I think, clarify what has been an unnecessary point of confusion in banking theory.

as a group increase their loans, new or additional deposits arise, which add to the working balances of borrowers—working balances that will be used to increase expenditures. Then to carry out their compensating transactions in securities the banks induce some members of the public to save—that is, to make new savings by cutting down on their expenditures—or to give up idle balances in order to buy securities from the banking system.[75] The effect is as if savings or idle balances had been tapped for spending, for, if the compensating transactions could not have been carried out, bank loans, and hence spending, could not have taken place. Hence, even though the tapping of the idle balances or new savings comes second in the process of financing increased expenditures through bank loans, the act of tapping is essential to the process. In this sense the banks are acting as middlemen between savers and borrowers, even though what they are doing is creating new deposits and destroying old ones. Every increase in loan deposits must be offset by the destruction of idle deposits (by conversion of existing cash savings into holdings of securities) or of active deposits (by causing new savings, or forced savings if the destruction of active deposits is achieved by calling in loans).[76]

Some of the deposits destroyed by compensating transactions may, of course, have arisen directly from the increased lending activities of the banks. If new loan deposits are rapidly spent and pass into the hands of savers who are induced to buy securities from the banks, the effect is as if the new loans had created the idle deposits destroyed to make the increase in loans possible.[77] The role of the banks in shifting

75. The manner in which the banks can induce the public to change their idle deposits for securities is very well described by Sayers, *Modern Banking*, p. 256. Also cf. John Maynard Keynes, *The General Theory of Employment, Interest and Money* (London, Macmillan and Co., Limited, 1936), p. 197.

76. Cf. Smith, "On the Effectiveness of Monetary Policy," p. 601. D. H. Robertson, *Banking Policy and the Price Level: An Essay in the Theory of the Trade Cycle* (New York, Augustus M. Kelley, 1949), pp. 51–8, discusses the various ways in which savings are converted into loanable funds through the operation of the banking system.

77. This is a plausible possibility because the compensating transactions in securities may follow with a lag the expansion in loans: Banks may try only to make their reserve ratio average a certain figure over the reserve period rather than

funds between savers and borrowers is then not altogether a passive one; even where pre-existing idle deposits are the ones destroyed there may be offsetting additions to idle deposits elsewhere stemming from the increased bank loans.

There need not, however, be any destabilizing effects on the level of expenditures as a result of the banks operating in this manner. Ordinarily there is an initial increase in the level of expenditures when bank loans are increased; unless the compensating transactions of the banks tap new savings (in the form of income diverted from spending on current consumption), the level of expenditures is permanently raised by the increase in bank loans. If the banks do tap new savings with their security sales, expenditures are reduced to their former level even though bank loans outstanding are now greater. There may even be an increase in bank loans without any initial disturbance to the level of expenditures. Furthermore, when there is a change in the distribution of incomes, not accompanied by changes in spending propensities, some groups may have to increase their borrowings from the banking system to maintain their existing level of expenditures. The groups who benefit from the changed distribution in incomes now have additional savings, which may be used to purchase securities from the banking system.[78] Thus, an increase in bank loans may reflect only the fact that the banking system is shifting new savings into the hands of borrowers.

When increased bank loans are accompanied by a permanent rise in expenditures—permanent in the sense that expenditures elsewhere are not reduced within the same income period—the situation is sometimes viewed as representing a change in the proportion of inactive to active balances. This is a little different from saying that funds, in the form of idle deposits, are shifted from savers to bor-

---

attempt to maintain the standard ratio on a daily basis; deviations from the norm may then be permitted, which means that compensating transactions in securities need not be undertaken immediately every time loans expand.

78. The argument is from Erik Lundberg and Bengt Senneby, "Views on an Effective Credit Policy," Skandinaviska Banken (Stockholm), *Quarterly Review*, *38* (Jan. 1957), 6–8, who however neglect the necessary qualification that if the new savers repay bank loans there is no change in the total of bank loans when savings flow from savers to lenders through the banking system.

rowers. When the shift takes place there does occur a destruction of inactive balances and a creation of active balances, and there is, for the moment, a change in the proportion of inactive to active balances; but this is the very short-term effect, it may not be the permanent one, it may not hold true for any length of time. Yet the analysis that runs in terms of the changing proportion of inactive to active balances is a period analysis, for it is linked to velocity, which is a period concept.[79]

Furthermore, the active-balance approach has an identification problem. An inactive balance may perhaps be defined as one from which there are no outflows—there may be inflows—except the final outflow that carries it into the active category. An active balance is one from which there are outflows; its size depends upon the inflows into the account and the outflows from it. An increase in bank loans adds to the stream of inflows into active balances, but as the borrowed funds are spent, outflows from the active balances also rise. Unless the extra spending leads in turn to greater inflows into the original accounts, the final result is that active balances return to their previous level; unless, that is, active balances have been decreased by a speed-up in outflows and additional loans are required to build the balances up again. Although active balances may return to their previous level after the new loans acquired have been spent, the average balance in the account will be higher for the period in which the new loans were incurred; the size of the account relative to the amount borrowed and the period considered determines whether the increase in the average is significant.[80]

79. Sayers, *Modern Banking*, pp. 258–60, who in discussing fluctuations in expenditures in terms of changing proportions between active and inactive deposits, offers his analysis as an alternative to the velocity approach.

80. Smith, "On the Effectiveness of Monetary Policy," p. 602n44, makes income velocity depend on the product of the ratio of active balances to total balances and the velocity of active balances. He regards the latter as being "roughly constant"; in this way he can show that the increase in income velocity that follows from a rise in bank loans (and hence expenditures), when the money supply is constant, is due to an increase in active balances relative to total balances. But there is no more reason for treating the velocity of active balances as a constant than for treating the ratio of active balances to total balances as a constant. The velocity of active balances is derived from a division of expenditures by the average balance

There need not be any significant change in the period ratio of inactive to active balances when bank loans and expenditures rise, although, initially, there is a change in the spot ratio. However, it seems unnecessary to analyze the situation in terms of a changing composition of deposits between active and inactive; all that need be said is that increased bank loans have led to increased expenditures, even though the money supply has remained constant. The important facts are the increase in expenditures and the constant money supply. If other modes of expressing this are wanted, there are the derived concepts of velocity or of relative cash balances.[81]

In short, when the banking system acts as a middleman between savers and spenders it does not thereby necessarily determine the level of idle balances or the division between idle and active balances. This division depends on the needs of the community for working balances. If those needs increase because of higher expenditures, then an expansion of bank loans is accompanied by a rise in active balances; but increased expenditures do not necessarily draw more cash into active circulation.

The lending activity of the banking system, when the system is functioning as a middleman, does not differ in its consequences from that of other lenders. Non-bank lenders also destroy idle balances

---

in active accounts. An increase in bank loans raises the average size of active deposits, but when the new loans are spent expenditures rise by the same amount; the velocity ratio is changed as a result unless the original velocity equalled unity. The velocity of active balances may not be much changed by a marginal increase in balances and expenditures, but then neither may the ratio of active to total balances be much changed by a marginal rise in the average of active balances. One could argue that the ratio of balances remains "roughly constant" and that it is the change in the velocity of active balances that brings about the increase in income velocity. R. A. Musgrave, "Money, Liquidity and the Valuation of Assets," *Money, Trade, and Economic Growth: In Honor of John Henry Williams* (New York, The Macmillan Company, 1951), p. 218n4, uses a formula for income velocity similar in nature to that of Smith and arrives at the same conclusion.

81. Walter S. Salant, "The Demand for Money and the Concept of Income Velocity," *Journal of Political Economy, 49* (June 1941), 405-6, also criticizes an expenditure analysis based on drawing a distinction between active and inactive balances on the grounds that such a distinction appears artificial and is difficult to work with.

through the sale of their assets and (new) liabilities, but they destroy them by transformation. That is, they gain possession of idle balances and convert them, at least temporarily, into active balances through lending. The process may differ slightly between non-bank and bank lenders but the consequences of increased lending by either are the same in these circumstances.[82]

It is when the banking system receives additional cash reserves and expands loans on the basis of the new reserves that the consequences of bank lending depart from that of lending by intermediaries. The additional cash reserves are the results of a discretionary act of the central bank which has the ability to prevent the system from acquiring additional reserves. Given the determination of the authorities to give or permit the system a certain injection of cash reserves, no act of saving, past or present, is required to support the expansion in bank loans that follows. That is, the deposits that bring the additional cash reserves to the banks in the first place need not represent idle balances and may indeed represent active balances. Intermediaries, however, can gain additional cash balances only by inducing people to give up funds in exchange for the debt instruments of the intermediaries, and the funds given up must of course be withdrawn from other uses, either current spending or hoarding.

When increased lending does not depend on new or existing savings, it seems proper to speak of loanable funds being created. In other words, if loanable funds are taken to mean funds withdrawn from some other purpose and made available for lending, then the expansion of bank loans based on a new receipt of cash reserves by the banking system clearly represents a creation of loanable funds, for the expansion of loans does not depend on withdrawing funds from other uses (as it clearly does when cash reserves are constant). The same conclusion applies to any existing total of bank loans outstanding: that part of the total which owes its being to an expansion of bank assets rather than to a transformation of an existing total of bank assets is independent of any act of financial

82. Cf. Warren L. Smith, "Financial Intermediaries and Monetary Controls," *Quarterly Journal of Economics*, 73 (Nov. 1959), 551–2, who argues, however, that the activities of non-bank intermediaries in the United States have not produced significant destabilizing effects in recent years.

saving[83]—those loans were not dependent on funds being withheld from spending.

Whatever the terminology used, increased lending by banks following an increase in cash reserves does have a greater expansionary potential for the level of expenditures than does increased lending by intermediaries based on additional borrowing from the public. Although the cash reserves of the banking system can be rationed directly, the cash balances of intermediaries cannot be directly controlled. This is another point of difference between intermediaries and banks as a group.

Problems for Credit Control

The preceding discussions on deposit stability and the lending role of banks suggest some policy problems for credit control. The solution of one of these problems may require regulating the liabilities of non- ✕ bank lenders. The monetary authorities, by exercising strict control over the cash reserves of the banking system, may regulate the total of bank deposits when banks maintain stable cash-reserve ratios. The liabilities of other lenders, however, could not be controlled in the same way. General control over non-bank lenders would have to depend on their working to a fixed ratio between their cash balances and liabilities to the public; but, since the mechanics of non-bank

83. This does not conflict with the view of D. H. Robertson, *Money*, Cambridge Economic Handbook.—II, 4th ed. (London, Nisbet and Co. Ltd., 1948), p. 90, that existing bank loans are the result of administering "a fund of congealed saving which has been built up in the past." Robertson has in mind real savings, which, as he points out, the making of bank loans may impose or force on the community if the loans add to the level of money expenditures in excess of available resources.

It accords with what MacLeod, *The Theory and Practice of Banking*, *1*, 336, argued when he wrote that it is a complete misconception "of the nature of Banking to say that bankers are merely agents or intermediaries between persons who wish to lend and persons who wish to borrow. This is entirely untrue in the ordinary sense of 'lending' and 'borrowing:' because, in the ordinary case of 'lending,' the lender deprives himself of the use of the thing lent. But when a person pays in money to his banker, he has no intention whatever of depriving himself of the use of it. On the contrary, he means to have the same free command of it as if it were in his own house. The customer, therefore, 'lends' his money to his banker, but at the same time has the free use of it."

C

lending differ from those of bank lending, there is no direct way of controlling the cash balances of non-bank lenders. Non-bank lenders through their own acts can get more cash whereas the banks as a group cannot. Therefore, control of non-bank lenders would have to be applied directly to their liabilities, not to their cash.[84]

Regulating the total liabilities of the banks and other lenders does not solve the problems created by excess lending capacity held by these lenders in the form of government securities. In particular, general control over the liabilities of lenders leaves untouched the problems that arise when lenders can and do substitute loans for government securities in their balance-sheets. Such a substitution carried out on a large scale destabilizes the yield on government securities. When securities are sold by the banks to make way for additional loans, their prices fall and their yields rise; when securities are bought by the banks to take up the slack caused by a reduction in bank loans, the prices of securities rise and their yields fall. The reason for this is that when the banks want to sell or buy large amounts of securities they have to disturb existing market prices to do so. They cannot move as perfect competitors in the securities market. Therefore, in the absence of stabilizing operations by the monetary authorities, large fluctuations in bank loans, which cause the banks to undertake compensating transactions in securities, destabilizes yields on government securities.[85]

84. This differs from the policy prescription of J. G. Gurley and E. S. Shaw, "Reply," *American Economic Review, 48* (Mar. 1958), 137, who suggest that the same type of controls should be applied to the supply function of other financial inter-mediaries as are applied to banks. (The foregoing source is in reply to Culbertson, "A Criticism of the Gurley-Shaw Theory.")

Indirect control over the liabilities of non-bank lenders may be established by regulating their cash needs through the imposition of variable reserve require-ments. If these lenders are forced to hold a large proportion of any new cash gained by issuing their borrowing instruments, they may be induced, through the effect on their profits, to directly reduce their borrowings or to reduce the rates paid for borrowed money, which in turn tends to restrict the amount borrowed.

85. The implication of this for the market in government securities has been commented on as follows: "commercial bank policies . . . have contributed to greater stability of the money supply in a number of ways. But in doing so they have put a heavy burden on the Government securities market. That market has had to be strong and flexible enough to handle smoothly the necessary shifts of

However, the destabilization of security yields by the compensating transactions of the banks may have a stabilizing influence on the fluctuations in bank loans.[86] The dampening influence of movements in security yields on fluctuations in bank loans operates through bank profits; banks become less anxious to add to their loans outstanding in a monetary expansion when security prices are falling, and they become more anxious to increase their loans in a recession when security prices are rising, because they are now buyers of securities rather than sellers.[87] Nevertheless, when security prices fall too rapidly or drastically, central banks become nervous.[88] Yet should they

---

banks in and out of Government securities." "Money on Good Behaviour," Federal Reserve Bank of Philadelphia, *Annual Report*, 1955, p. 14. Cf. Schumpeter, *Business Cycles*, 2, 645.

86. This is a specific instance of the Roosa paradox which is said to arise when an increase in interest rates restrains the supply of loanable funds. The paradox was framed by Sir Dennis H. Robertson, "More Notes on the Rate of Interest," *Economic Commentaries* (London, Staples Press Limited, 1956), pp. 65–70, which is reprinted from the *Review of Economic Studies*, No. 55 (1953–54); also idem, "A Squeak from Aunt Sally," *The Banker* (London), Dec. 1959, pp. 721–2. Attempts to resolve the paradox have been made by Howard S. Ellis, Review of *Economic Commentaries*, in *Journal of Political Economy*, 65 (June 1957), 264. Also cf. John Spraos, "Control by 'Stickiness' of Rates?", *The Banker*, Nov. 1959, pp. 675, 677.

There is no paradox if the argument is not generalized. A rise in security yields may restrict the supply of loanable funds from all lenders who must sell securities to expand their loans at existing rates. Higher yields, however, induce holders of idle balances to buy securities which prevents security prices from falling as far as they otherwise would. At the same time borrowers denied credit by the security-selling lenders may turn to other lenders who are not limited to selling securities to expand and who are induced to expand their loans by the offer of higher rates. These other lenders either reduce their cash balances or activate idle balances of others by offering more attractive borrowing rates, the extra cost incurred being passed on to those who borrow from them. Hence, the supply of loanable funds from certain lenders may be restricted by a rise in security prices at the same time that idle balances are being activated by the rise in yields and other lenders are expanding their loans by activating idle balances.

87. "Money on Good Behaviour," p. 12; cf. Henry C. Wallich, "Some Current Features of Bank Liquidity in the United States," Banca Nazionale del Lavoro, *Quarterly Review*, July–Sept. 1951, pp. 110–11. These topics are dealt with in more detail *infra*, Chapter Two.

88. Concern for rising security yields when banks sell securities as their loans

try to stabilize security yields they thereby destabilize bank cash. The dilemma is particularly troublesome when banks are disposing of securities by the simple process of not replacing maturing issues in their portfolios.

If there is to be no increase in bank cash when banks let the short-term government securities in their portfolios mature without replacing them, new debt must be issued to keep total public debt constant; otherwise the money supply is disturbed.[89] Thus, compensating transactions by the banks raise a problem for debt policy. If compensating transactions are carried out by letting government securities mature, they do not affect security yields when the government permits the actions of the banks to reduce the total debt outstanding. Security yields are stabilized, but the money supply is destabilized. Even if government debt behaves differently from private debt, as is sometimes claimed, increasing in bad times and decreasing in good times, there is no net gain in stability. The counter-cyclical movement in public debt possibly destabilizes bank cash and certainly destabilizes bank deposits other than those of the central government; in an expansionary period the destabilization arises because the central government either retires debt with central-bank money (bank cash) or with cheques drawn upon deposits kept with the banks; the destabilization is of course greater under the former method of debt retirement.

If total public debt outstanding is held constant when the banks fail to replace maturing government securities in their portfolios, the government must meet the compensating transactions of the banks by issuing new debt to the public; the effect is the same as if the banks themselves had sold existing government securities to the public—the distribution of the public debt between the banks and the public is changed in both cases, and security yields are higher.

---

expand is usually expressed as a concern for the maintenance of orderly conditions in financial markets. This is a matter of importance for the Bank of Canada. Cf. Bank of Canada, *Annual Report*, 1956, p. 25.

89. Cf. U.S. Congress, *Monetary Policy . . . Public Debt: Compendium*, Pt. 1, pp. 122–3, Pt. 2, p. 687; D. M. Kennedy, "Loans and Investments in a Tight Money Market," *Burroughs Clearing House* (Detroit), Jan. 1957, p. 94.

Apart from debt policy, it makes no difference to the final outcome whether the banks carry out compensating transactions with expiring securities or with securities still outstanding. If the central bank tries to moderate the fall in security prices by buying securities as the banks sell, the result is a rise in bank cash, which in itself lends additional support to the securities market. Not only is there more buying in the market because of central-bank intervention, but also there is less selling. Banks need not sell as many securities to support a given increase in loans when they effect with their security sales an addition to their cash reserves, rather than a reduction in deposits.

When the monetary authorities become too concerned with security yields and act to relieve their anxieties, they tend to make short-term government securities in the hands of the banks almost perfect substitutes for bank cash. Such securities can be sold with very little movement in their price.[90] When the securities are substituted for bank cash, the central bank will be reluctant to sell securities to reduce bank cash again because of the effect this would have on security yields. The central bank then loses some control over the amount of cash reserves in the banking system. To restore that control and to reduce the scope for compensating transactions by the banks, the central bank, in these circumstances, may require the banks to maintain not only a stable ratio between their cash and deposits but also a stable ratio between their cash plus perfect substitutes for cash and deposits.[91] In other words a secondary as well as

90. The price of short-term securities does not have to fall very much to reflect even large increases in security yields. A 2 per cent one-year security need fall in price only from 100 to 98 to show a rise in yield from 2 per cent to 4 per cent. U.S. Congress, *Monetary Policy . . . Public Debt: Compendium*, Pt. 1, p. 107.

91. The conditions surrounding the adoption of a secondary-reserve ratio in Canada are described in Bank of Canada, *Annual Report*, 1955, pp. 10, 16–17. Some of the advantages and disadvantages of a secondary-reserve ratio and the conditions under which it is needed are listed in U.S. Congress, *Monetary Policy . . . Public Debt: Compendium*, Pt. 1, pp. 123–6, 480–2; and in Erwin Miller, "Monetary Policy in a Changing World," *Quarterly Journal of Economics*, 70 (Feb. 1956), 38–9. Cf. "Commercial Bank Liquidity Ratios Abroad," Federal Reserve Bank of New York, *Monthly Review of Credit and Business Conditions*, Aug. 1957, pp. 111–16.

a primary reserve ratio is required of the banking system.[92] When the banks must maintain a secondary-reserve ratio, they can carry out compensating transactions during a loan expansion only with securities not required to stabilize the secondary ratio. This may mean selling lower-priced securities to support an increase in loans, a condition that may serve to check further loan expansion. At worst it may mean selling non-secondary reserve securities to the central bank and buying from the latter secondary-reserve securities to stabilize the secondary ratio in the face of an increase in loans.

Thus the imposition of a secondary-reserve ratio on the banks may limit the ability of the banking system to carry out compensating transactions; this in turn will mitigate the destabilizing influences of these transactions on expenditures and security yields. But halting the compensating transactions of the banks before they would stop of themselves does not necessarily solve the problems created by a loan expansion. Direct intervention by the monetary authorities may prevent the banks from serving as a medium for transferring funds from savers to borrowers when the banks still have every incentive to continue making loans and carrying out offsetting compensating transactions; but it may make it profitable for other institutions to take over some of the work of the banks in tapping idle deposits for use by borrowers.[93] The level of expenditures can then be made more stable only if others are prevented from taking over the lending function of the banks.

This policy discussion is meant to indicate only some of the problems for credit control caused by domestic banking operations. Most of these are examined at greater length in later chapters. Specifically, Chapter Two deals in detail with the substitution of loans for secur-

92. The Governor of the Bank of Canada and his advisers apparently feel that more than a secondary-reserve ratio is required to restrain the tendency of banks to carry out compensating transactions when bank loans expand. At least this is an interpretation that may be given to a suggestion contained in Bank of Canada, *Annual Report*, 1956, pp. 29–31: a suggestion that the chartered banks might hold against their savings deposits long-term securities, which would not be liquidated to support an expansion in bank loans.

93. Hyman P. Minsky, "Central Banking and Money Market Changes," *Quarterly Journal of Economics*, 71 (May 1957), 171–87 passim, but especially p. 185n2; Smith, "On the Effectiveness of Monetary Policy," pp. 601–3 passim.

ities, and Chapters Six and Seven treat with matters of debt policy and credit control that are just briefly touched upon here.

CONCLUSIONS

Domestic banking operations do create policy problems, but not because of any inherent difference between banking operations and the operations of other financial institutions that function as borrowers, lenders, and investors. The mechanics of banking operations do differ of course from those of other financial institutions, but the results of the operations do little to distinguish an individual bank from an individual financial intermediary. Both are debtors and creditors of the public and both must regulate their financial activities with an eye to their cash position. The banking system, however, differs from any other group of non-deposit financial agencies in its reactions when the monetary authorities permit it to have an injection of new cash reserves; the system may then create loanable funds by expanding deposits in a way that requires neither existing savings nor new savings to be tapped in order to permit bank loans to expand.

When cash reserves are held constant, the banking system is reduced to the same status as other non-bank lenders, except that its liabilities to the public become fixed unless cash-reserve ratios are allowed to vary. But given stable cash-reserve ratios, the banking system cannot by its own acts destabilize total bank deposits; banks then do not cause bank credit to be inherently unstable.

Bank loans can still fluctuate, even though total bank deposits remain constant, when banks have scope for carrying out compensating transactions in securities—that is, for carrying out a substitution between loans and securities. But then the loans of any other type of lender may fluctuate under the same set of conditions, so that the problems created by the compensating transactions of banks are by no means peculiar to banking.

Chapter Two: THE ECONOMICS OF BANKING "OUTPUT"

The reaction of lending firms to changes in the conditions under which they provide funds to the community has been a matter of interest for several years. In the United States discussions on the subject have led to the gradual evolution of a body of thought that is referred to as the "availability doctrine"—a doctrine that provides a theory of the lending behaviour of financial firms and thereby fills a void in economic analysis. However, the availability doctrine does not constitute a complete and systematic theory of lending behaviour, nor does it deal adequately with the specific factors it considers. Such short-comings are perhaps to be expected in a theory developed to justify a particular policy: a policy of flexible monetary control for the rather special circumstances that prevailed in the United States of the late 1940's.[1] Nevertheless the availability doctrine has served the useful purpose of stimulating theoretical interest in the field of lending behaviour and of indicating the need for further analysis of the supply behaviour of lending firms. That analysis is undertaken in this chapter.

The method is to examine the supply behaviour of the banking firm in terms of the general theory of the firm in order to deal with such topics as the following: the effects of changes in cash reserves, in demand for loans, in lending rates, and in security prices on the amount of loanable funds provided by the banking firm; the determination of the allocation of banking resources between loans and

1. The policy problems in the United States that led to the development of the availability doctrine are ably reviewed by J. H. Kareken, "Monetary Policy and the Public Debt: An Appraisal of Post-war Developments in the USA," *Kyklos, 10* (1957), 413, 417, 424.

securities; and the economic basis for the selection of loan applications by the banking system.

The scheme followed in the chapter is to review the availability
doctrine, to describe the general nature of banking output, to consider the questions of willingness to lend and credit rationing, and,
finally, to present the theory of the banking firm. Although the entire
analysis is restricted to the banking firm, it has a wider application
because of the similarity between banking firms and other lenders
noted in Chapter One.

THE AVAILABILITY DOCTRINE

The literature on the availability doctrine is sparse and scattered;
and although elements of the doctrine in significant quantity have
appeared in printed form from 1946 on, full treatment and interpretation was not accorded the doctrine until quite recently.[2] The doc-

2. Two early attempts to give a concise statement of the availability doctrine
were: H. C. Wallich, "The Changing Significance of the Interest Rate," *American
Economic Review*, *36* (Dec. 1946), 765–9; R. A. Musgrave, "Credit Controls, Interest
Rates, and Management of Public Debt," *Income, Employment and Public Policy:
Essays in Honor of Alvin H. Hansen* (New York, W. W. Norton and Company, 1948),
pp. 229–31. The doctrine received some attention in the reply by the Chairman
of the Board of Governors of the Federal Reserve System to the Patman question-
naire (U.S. Congress, *Monetary Policy . . . Public Debt: Compendium*, Pt. 1, pp.
370–3); the gist of that reply is incorporated in "Influence of Credit and Monetary
Measures on Economic Stability," *Federal Reserve Bulletin*, Mar. 1953, pp. 220–3.
One aspect of the doctrine is rather fully dealt with by Paul Samuelson in United
States Congress, Joint Committee on the Economic Report, *Monetary Policy and the
Management of the Public Debt: Hearings before the Subcommittee on General Credit
Control and Debt Management*, 82nd Cong., 2nd Sess., 1952, pp. 693–9, 741. The
thread of the argument contained in the last three sources is summarized by James
Tobin, "Monetary Policy and the Management of the Public Debt: The Patman
Inquiry," *Review of Economics and Statistics*, *35* (1953), 122–4. A brief discussion on
some of the above sources is given by H. C. Wallich, "Recent Monetary Policies
in the United States," *American Economic Review*, *43* (Papers and Proceedings, May
1953), 36–40. A basic source on the availability doctrine is R. V. Rosa (now
Roosa), "Interest Rates and the Central Bank," *Money, Trade, and Economic Growth:
In Honor of John Henry Williams* (New York, The Macmillan Company, 1951), pp.
270–95. Comment on this article is made by Sir Dennis H. Robertson, "More
Notes on the Rate of Interest," *Economic Commentaries*, pp. 64–70. Ira O. Scott, Jr.,

trine analyzes under the general head of "the availability of credit" the reactions of institutional lenders to changes in conditions under which they supply funds to private borrowers. The phrase itself, "the availability of credit," is not clearly defined in the literature, and is sometimes taken to mean the ease with which prospective borrowers can obtain loans, and at other times the willingness with which lenders advance funds.[3]

"Monetary Policy, the Theory of Assets, and the Availability of Credit" (Unpublished Ph.D. dissertation, Harvard University, 1953), pp. 1–79, presents a useful review of some of the literature on the points incorporated into the availability doctrine. W. L. Smith, "On the Effectiveness of Monetary Policy," *American Economic Review*, *46* (Sept. 1956), 588–606, criticizes many of the points raised in the availability doctrine. An excellent synthesis of all the major pieces in the doctrine is made by John H. Kareken, "Lenders' Preferences, Credit Rationing, and the Effectiveness of Monetary Policy," *Review of Economics and Statistics*, *39* (Aug. 1957), 292–302. Ira O. Scott, Jr., "The Availability Doctrine: Development and Implications," *Canadian Journal of Economics and Political Science*, *23* (Nov. 1957), 532–9, reviews the development of the doctrine in economic thought and gives his interpretation of the doctrine. Kareken, "Monetary Policy and the Public Debt," discusses the policy considerations in the United States that led to the development of the availability doctrine, and in "Post-Accord Monetary Developments in the United States," Banca Nazionale del Lavoro (Rome), *Quarterly Review*, Sept. 1957, pp. 322–51, Kareken subjects some of the conclusions arrived at by the availability doctrine to empirical tests.

Jack Guttentag, "Credit Availability, Interest Rates, and Monetary Policy," *Southern Economic Journal*, *26* (Jan. 1960), 219–28, deals with the relationship between credit availability and interest rates. The most comprehensive treatment of all aspects of the availability doctrine appears in Assar Lindbeck, *The "New" Theory of Credit Control in the United States: An Interpretation and Elaboration*, Stockholm Economic Studies, Pamphlet Series I (Stockholm, Almqvist and Wiksell, 1959), all 56 pages of which are devoted to the availability doctrine. His interpretation is based on the statement of the Chairman of the Board of Governors of the Federal Reserve System cited above.

3. United States Congress, Joint Committee on the Economic Report, *Monetary Policy and the Management of the Public Debt: Report of the Subcommittee on General Credit Control and Debt Management*, 82nd Cong., 2nd Sess., 1952, p. 32; Kareken, "Lenders' Preferences, Credit Rationing, and the Effectiveness of Monetary Policy," pp. 295–6, who argues that the phrase "availability of credit" has been over-used and that it has been taken to mean different things. He suggests that it be taken to mean "the willingness of lenders to supply funds in the private market at the expense of holding cash or government securities" (p. 296).

The double meaning attached to the "availability of credit" reflects the two distinct strands of thought that have become associated with the availability doctrine. One strand concentrates on how changing yields for the securities held by lenders may affect the willingness of these lenders to supply loanable funds; the other strand views the reactions of lenders to changes in their supply conditions in terms of the varying ease with which borrowers can obtain funds from the lenders.[4] These two general lines of thought may be briefly summarized, and considered separately for purposes of assessing their adequacy as an explanation of lending behaviour.

In terms of the availability doctrine, increases in the yields of government securities held by large lenders are supposed to restrict the supply of new loanable funds or to shift the existing supply curve to the left. Some even argue that the supply curve not only shifts to the left but also becomes more inelastic.[5] Nor need there be any change in the ability to lend for an alteration in security prices to cause a change in supply. Thus, with no change in cash reserves the banking system may nevertheless be made a less willing lender by increases in security yields, which affect, of course, lending expectations.[6]

In general, however, the supply curve of lenders is shifted because

---

Guttentag, p. 222, defines credit availability as "the complex of noninterest-rate lending terms prevailing in the market at any time."

4. Kareken, "Lenders' Preferences . . .," pp. 295–6, points out how discussions of the availability of credit tend to combine two separate strands of thought and argues that for analytical purposes they must be separated.

Lindbeck, p. 5, divides the different arguments involved in the availability doctrine into five channels of thought but these can be fitted into the two major groups distinguished in the text.

5. Musgrave, "Credit Controls, Interest Rates, and Management of Public Debt," pp. 229–30; Scott, "The Availability Doctrine," p. 536; and Edward C. Simmons, "Consumer Credit Control and Central Banking," *Consumer Instalment Credit* (Washington, Government Printing Office, 1957), Part II, Conference on Regulation, 2, 121 (which forms part of the proceedings of the Conference on the Problem of Consumer Credit Regulation, convened by the National Bureau of Economic Research, at the request of the Board of Governors of the Federal Reserve System), all discuss the availability doctrine in terms of the elasticity of the supply curve as well as in terms of a shift in the curve.

6. Kareken, "Lenders' Preferences . . .," p. 297; Scott, "The Availability Doctrine," pp. 533n1, 535.

the fall in security prices springs a "liquidity trap" that operates in two ways. First, the fall in security prices reduces the market value of the securities held by lenders, especially banks, as a secondary reserve or "liquidity hedge;" this capital-value effect, it is argued, makes lenders less anxious to acquire more private debt from borrowers.[7] And secondly, the "liquidity trap" operates by "pinning in" security holders; the holders can unpin themselves only by liquidating their securities, to make additional loans, at a capital loss.[8] Thus, loans will not be substituted for securities in the balance-sheet of holders because the fall in security prices makes the substitution unprofitable. This may be called a rational "pin-in" to distinguish it from what might be called an irrational "pin-in." The latter arises when lenders allow themselves to be "pinned in" to their security holdings by a reluctance to realize capital losses even though these losses might be recouped eventually by switching now into more profitable loans: that is, a substitution of loans for securities would be profitable.[9] Both types of "pin-in" keep loans from being substituted for securities: the rational type because lending rates are inflexible,[10] and the irrational type because higher lending rates do not appear tempting enough.[11]

7. Kareken, "Lenders' Preferences . . .," p. 294.

8. Ibid.

9. Tobin, "Monetary Policy and the Management of the Public Debt," pp. 122–3, 123n8.

10. That is, when lending rates change less than do security yields so that the differential between them narrows, any incentive to switch from securities to loans is weakened. The change in security prices then provides for a rational pin-in effect. Rosa, "Interest Rates and the Central Bank," p. 290 and n. 29; Henry C. Wallich, "Some Current Features of Bank Liquidity in the United States," Banca Nazionale del Lavoro, *Quarterly Review*, July–Sept. 1951, p. 114; idem, "Recent Monetary Policies in the United States," pp. 37–8.

11. The irrational pin-in clearly depends on flexible lending rates; if rates did not rise there would be no reason for the existence of an irrational reluctance to accept capital losses—it would just not be profitable to incur the capital losses. "The first step in the chain of reasoning for the pinned-in hypothesis is a rise in private yields. Otherwise there would be no motivation for the pinned-in influence to inhibit." Kareken, "Lenders' Preferences . . .," p. 302. It is not clear from the context that just an irrational pin-in is meant, but the quotation has meaning only if it is so restricted.

All these arguments that translate changes in security yields into an alteration in the willingness to lend explain why the supply curve of lenders shifts, but they stop short of explaining the extent of the shift or the determination of the new equilibrium point. Thus, the arguments in the availability doctrine on the impact of changes in security yields on lending behaviour do not explain how far a banking firm will go in expanding its loans by liquidating its securities. The doctrine argues only that any fall in security prices which occurs will moderate the tendency of the bank to substitute loans for securities because of the pin-in effect and of the impact on the liquidity hedge of decreased market values. Unless these effects are absolute, and so prevent any expansion in loans at all, there is nothing in the arguments to indicate at what point the substitution process will be halted.

Likewise, for the banking firm that has lost cash reserves, there is no explanation in the availability doctrine of how the bank will contract. According to the doctrine, any fall in security prices will encourage the bank to liquidate loans rather than securities; but whether liquidation will proceed entirely by way of loans, or only partially, is left unanswered. In other words, the strand in the availability doctrine that concentrates on the consequences of changes in security yields on lending behaviour does not explain how lenders move from one position of equilibrium to another: it only explains why their supply curve for loans shifts.

The other major strand in the availability doctrine considers not so much the effect of changes in supply conditions on the supply curve for loanable funds as the administrative consequences of changing the amount of loanable funds supplied. What is emphasized is how lenders hold their loans in check, and this is discussed under the general head of "credit rationing." It is argued that a reduction in cash reserves may cause the banks to reduce their loans by rationing credit more severely: an increase in cash reserves may cause them to expand their loans by relaxing the degree to which they ration credit. Variations in the availability of credit are therefore viewed as the result of changes in the degree of rationing, induced by changes in security yields.[12]

12. P. A. Samuelson in U.S. Congress, *Monetary Policy and the Management of the Public Debt: Hearings*, p. 697; Wallich, "Recent Monetary Policies in the United

Once again the explanation of lending behaviour is less than complete. Credit rationing is uncritically identified with all excess demand in the loanable funds market, without any consideration of the various causes that might account for the existence of excess demand. All credit transactions, by their very nature, involve some excess demand: there is a margin—a shifting margin—between acceptable and unacceptable loan applications. In addition, limits to lending capacity may be the cause of another form of excess demand—the demand that represents profitable or acceptable business which the lender cannot accept because of limited lending capacity. Finally, some profitable or acceptable loan applications may have to be rejected not because of limited lending capacity, in an absolute sense, but because the cost of making new loans rises faster than lending rates. A full account of credit rationing should therefore take into consideration all these factors.

The availability doctrine then does not provide a complete explanation of lending behaviour,[13] although it does suggest the elements that should be covered in any theory dealing with the subject. Accordingly, the remainder of this chapter is devoted to a fuller and more systematic treatment of those aspects of lending behaviour dealt with in the availability doctrine, with the aim of presenting a more general theory. The discussion is restricted to a banking firm, which is viewed as an economic unit supplying funds or "output" in order to maximize its profits. Therefore, the general nature of banking "output" must be briefly considered next. After that follows a discussion of "marketing" problems that arise from the decisions concerning who is worthy of receiving the funds supplied by the banking firm: this encompasses the "willingness to lend" and credit rationing. With these marketing problems resolved, the full theory of the banking firm can then be presented.

States," p. 37; idem, "The Changing Significance of the Interest Rate," pp. 765–6; Tobin, "Monetary Policy . . .," p. 123; Kareken, "Lenders' Preferences . . .," p. 301; Scott, "The Availability Doctrine," pp. 538–9.

13. Kareken, "Post-Accord Monetary Developments in the United States," pp. 350–1, criticizes the availability doctrine on the grounds that it does not explain what effectiveness monetary policy has had in the United States of the 1950's.

THE GENERAL NATURE OF BANKING "OUTPUT"

Before the theory of the firm can be applied to the banking firm, banking activity must be defined in terms of output and expressed in terms of production functions. Although a banking firm does many things, its main activity is to supply funds to the community. The forms in which it supplies these funds may be taken as its output and the amounts supplied in each form as the measure of its output activity. Since a bank provides funds by making loans and discounts and buying securities, its output may be divided into these two categories, briefly, loans outstanding and securities held.[14] Defining banking output in this way raises two problems.

First, the terms "loans" and "securities" are convenient ones for distinguishing the major categories of banking output but they are not precise. More precise terms are "customer credits" and "open-market credits," and in what follows loans will be understood to mean customer credits, and securities open-market credits. Customer credits consist of all credits which are negotiated directly by the bank with the borrower and which are usually not subject to disposal prior to maturity.[15] Generally, this includes all credits subject to some credit risk: risk of default on principal and interest. Open-market credits refer to all credits acquired in the open-market or on an impersonal basis, and which are held subject to possible resale in that market. In practice, this category generally reduces to special short-

14. Thus, David A. Alhadeff, *Monopoly and Competition in Banking*, Publications of the Bureau of Business and Economic Research, University of California (Berkeley, University of California Press, 1954), p. 108, argues that "like many manufacturing enterprises, banks are multi-product firms. A bank's output can be divided into two main categories: (1) loans and discounts, and (2) investments."

R. E. Speagle and E. Kohn, "Employment and Output in Banking, 1919–1955," *Review of Economics and Statistics*, 40 (Feb. 1958), 23–4, discuss various output concepts for banking, one of which involves lending and investing bank resources.

Also cf. F. Cyril James, *The Economics of Money, Credit and Banking*, 3rd ed., p. 92.

An alternative mode of analysis is to treat the making of loans and the purchase of securities in terms of a bank allocating funds between two different markets.

15. Roland I. Robinson, *The Management of Bank Funds*, p. 12.

term money-market assets and to securities of the central government.[16]

Second, taking banking output to mean only loans made and securities held overlooks the other activities carried on by banks but does concentrate on the two activities responsible for the bulk of bank revenues.[17] How a banking firm adjusts its loans and security holdings has a dominant bearing on its profits.

The total amount of funds that the banking firm can supply to the community by way of loans and securities depends generally on its cash reserves and cash-reserve ratio. Given the amount of cash reserves that it can *retain* (input inventory) and the cash-reserve ratio that it works to, maximum output for the banking firm is fixed.[18] It may not produce this maximum output if it allocates some of its banking resources to other purposes, such as holding real assets, but this qualification can be ignored, without harm, in what follows. In other words the total output of the banking firm is assumed to be always at the maximum possible.

The distribution of that capacity output between loans and securities is another matter. Of special interest in this connection is the amount of available output capacity that is devoted to making loans, for it is in this direction that the special skills of banking lie. (Holding government securities is an activity that requires no specialized skills.) The capacity for total output also sets the absolute limit to the capa-

16. An excellent discussion contrasting open-market and customer credits is given by Robert C. Turner, *Member-Bank Borrowing* (Columbus, Ohio, The Ohio State University, 1938), pp. 59, 61–2.

17. For the fiscal years ending in 1956 the Canadian chartered banks reported total current operating earnings of $513.5 million, of which $314.2 million came from loans and $102.8 million from securities, including trading profits on securities. Bank of Canada, *Statistical Summary*, Financial Supplement, 1956, p. 30, which also gives the annual figures back to 1945. In United States banking, as well, loans and investments provide the major portion of bank earnings. In 1956 insured commercial banks there received more than four-fifths of their income from loans and securities. Federal Deposit Insurance Corporation, *Annual Report*, 1956, p. 38.

18. Cf. J. G. Gurley and E. S. Shaw, "Reply," *American Economic Review, 48* (Mar. 1958), 137, who define production capacity for the banking system in terms of the raw material, "reserves," available to the system and of the input coefficient relating reserves to money output.

city for making loans. This is the limit that sets the ability to lend of the banking firm as distinct from its willingness to lend.[19] However, the effective limit to the output for loans is less than the absolute limit, for the banking firm does not aim at being fully "loaned up." A bank needs some unutilized lending capacity—that is, some output capacity not devoted to making loans—in order to protect its existing level of loans against encroachment from unforeseen losses of lending capacity and to allow for outstanding commitments in the form of unused credit lines.[20] This is more usually expressed by saying that banks have minimum requirements for a liquidity hedge or a secondary reserve.

Convention, sometimes reinforced by legal requirements, determines the amount of output capacity that the banking firm cannot allot to loans. This unused lending capacity is invested in short-term securities suitable for serving the purpose of a liquidity hedge. Requirements for these secondary reserves usually vary with output capacity; they may also vary with security prices, as the availability doctrine argues, but this seems unlikely because of the very short-term nature of the securities held in the reserves. The value of such securities is not much affected by fluctuations in yields so that secondary-reserve requirements based on the market value of the securities held are not much affected. In general, the size of the liquidity hedge will be a function of banking needs and money-market conditions but not of banking profits.[21]

19. The willingness to lend is of course related to the ability to lend, but the ability to lend is only one of the factors that determines the willingness to lend and is not always the decisive one. Joseph A. Schumpeter, *Business Cycles*, 2, 654. This topic is discussed in more detail in the next section.

20. Schumpeter, 2, 641, points out that "while most shopkeepers will normally congratulate themselves whenever they are 'sold out,' the banker does not typically aim at being, and does not congratulate himself if he is, 'loaned up.' On the contrary, this means for him an exceptional and undesirable situation of embarrassment and of danger. . . . Customers' business cannot be handled safely and comfortably unless each bank has a generous allowance of unutilized lending power. Full utilization of that lending power in member banks' business with their industrial and commercial customers is, hence, no equilibrium condition. . . ."

21. That is, the liquidity hedge is not likely to be reduced when bank profits fall, although this is a possibility for a one-product banking firm, which is discussed below.

Hence, the output capacity of the banking firm, less its required liquidity hedge or secondary reserve, sets the effective limit to the total amount of loans the firm can make. When the loan output of the banking firm approaches or exceeds that limit it must begin to restrain its lending activities. In terms of economic contour analysis, the various minima for security holdings at each level of capacity output form a threshold for loans, the purpose of which is to mark off, on the loans-securities profit contours which can be derived for a banking firm, one of the boundaries to the economically relevant area of the iso-profit map. Thus, when the security holdings of the banking firm are measured along one axis and its loans along the other, the threshold locus for minima security holdings is represented by a curve (most likely a straight line) starting at the origin and deviating from the loans axis, indicating that the area between the loans axis and the threshold locus contains values for loans and securities that the banking firm would not freely choose.[22]

Therefore, when the banking firm is providing a quantity of loans that, along with its minimum requirements for securities, defines a point on the threshold locus, it is producing the maximum loan output that it can. It cannot then as a matter of policy expand its loans; it will not deliberately substitute loans for securities. However, when the banking firm is producing less than its possible maximum for loans, the excess capacity for making loans will be invested in securities; it then holds more than its minimum requirement for securities, so that it may, if it chooses, substitute loans for securities by drawing upon its excess capacity for making loans through disposing of some of its security holdings.

When the output activity of the banking firm is viewed as consisting of bank loans and security holdings, two possible cases may be distinguished: the banking firm that is producing at its maximum for loans and so has no excess lending capacity invested in securities; and

22. The threshold locus for minima security holdings is similar to the threshold locus that arises in the contour analysis of consumer behaviour when one of the commodities considered is an indispensable good. Cf. J. A. Galbraith, "Indifference Maps for Indispensable Goods," *Review of Economic Studies*, 20 (1952–53), 153–4. The line OP[1] in Figure 2, *infra*, p. 104, is a threshold locus for security holdings.

the banking firm that is providing less than its capacity output for loans and so has excess lending capacity invested in securities. Any output theory of the banking firm must recognize these two possibilities and deal with each separately. But before proceeding with further analysis of output or production problems in banking, it is necessary to dispose of some problems in distribution. These are problems of selection that arise from decisions, which are an everyday feature of banking, regarding who should get the available banking funds. These problems are discussed next under the heads of "willingness to lend" and "credit rationing."

THE WILLINGNESS TO LEND

The willingness of the banking firm to lend is of course related to its ability to lend. But there is a willingness to lend that is not a matter of ability; it is a willingness that involves a principle of selection: a selection of those whom the banking firm feels are entitled to the loans it can make. This selection principle imposes a non-capacity restraint on loan output, which is discussed in this section under the heads of creditworthiness, uncertainty, credit risks, and the margin of acceptability.

Creditworthiness

The willingness of a banking firm to lend is reflected in the rate at which it rejects, outright or partially, the applications for loans that are presented to it. Among the considerations that influence this rejection rate are the nature and quality of the individual loan applications; it is rejection on these qualitative grounds that determines the willingness to lend which imposes a non-capacity restraint on the volume of loans made by the banking firm. This is the restraint that takes the form of assessing whether or not a particular loan applicant is creditworthy and for how much.

The nature and quality of an application then are the prime considerations in determining its acceptability. This must always be so, for the essence of the lending function in banking is "the underwriting of credit risks."[23] Any underwriting of risks implies a selection

23. Herbert Joseph Davenport, *The Economics of Enterprise*, p. 352.

that excludes all bad risks. Consequently, there cannot be in banking a given set of lending rates at which prospective borrowers can exercise the option of borrowing; each loan has to be individually negotiated between the bank and the applicant.[24] This provides another restraint, in addition to the liquidity hedge, that may prevent the banking firm from being fully loaned-up. The banking firm cannot expand its loans to the utmost permitted by the market available to it simply on the basis of price considerations.[25] Not only the quantity of loan applications but also the quality is important; when the quality is inadequate the volume of loans outstanding may be less than they might be if the banking firm operated only under quantitative restraints.[26]

Selection and rejection on the basis of quality are common to all transactions involving the extension of credit. "Ordinary counsels of prudence" cause suppliers of goods to refuse goods on credit to those with an unsatisfactory credit standing.[27] Although the question of creditworthiness is much the same in trade and bank credit, an important difference arises out of the fact that the trade creditor usually has two sources of revenue from his transactions: that on the transactions themselves and that from any financing charge imposed. The trade creditor can then afford to be less selective in granting credit than can the banking firm.[28]

Yet another distinctive feature associated with the credit selection process in banking is that a loan application may be creditworthy on all other grounds yet rejected because of its general nature: the banking firm may not feel justified in allotting funds

24. Alhadeff, *Monopoly and Competition in Banking*, p. 112.

25. Cf. Schumpeter, *Business Cycles*, *2*, 640.

26. This qualitative restraint perhaps explains the traditional banking view that the volume of bank loans is demand determined—a view that is not inconsistent with the existence of excess demand in the market for bank loans when that demand represents strictly uncreditworthy applicants. The demand view of credit was widely held in Canadian banking circles. Irving Brecher, *Monetary and Fiscal Thought and Policy in Canada, 1919–1939*, p. 38.

27. Arthur W. Marget, *The Theory of Prices*, *1*, 224.

28. Chester Arthur Phillips, *Bank Credit*, p. 3. Also cf. H. L. Severson, "A Survey of the Economics of Allowances for Bad Debts on Loans Held by Commercial Banks," *University of Cincinnati Law Review*, *19* (Jan. 1950), 64.

for the purpose applied for.[29] This consideration resolves itself into the question of whether a given loan proposition is a banking proposition.

Thus, the banking firm, in providing funds, selects the creditworthy from the uncreditworthy. Since there will always be some applications rejected, partially or wholly, for qualitative reasons, there is always some excess demand for bank loans: some of those who want to borrow at the going rates cannot obtain all the financing they would like. The specific economic factors that cause this excess demand to arise and that cause it to vary in size can be examined under the heads of "uncertainty" and "credit risks:" these are the two major aspects of creditworthiness.

Uncertainty

Uncertainty about payment of interest and principal attaches itself in some degree to every loan application made to a bank. This uncertainty is a subjective and individual matter[30]—a matter of opinion and judgement about whether the loan application represents a moral hazard (the borrower will voluntarily default)[31] or a hazard of involuntary default (the borrower will be disappointed in his expect-

---

29. Cf. Henry C. Wallich, "The Changing Significance of the Interest Rate," *American Economic Review*, *36* (Dec. 1946), 768; idem, "Recent Monetary Policies in the United States," ibid., *43* (Papers and Proceedings, May 1953), 39, who refers to the natural dislike of banks for "bad situations" and their inclination to avoid "dubious situations." Loans for speculative purposes, especially in a time of inflation, are likely to be denied otherwise worthy applicants. Cf. Canada, Parliament, House, Standing Committee on Banking and Commerce, *Minutes of Proceedings and Evidence*, 1st Sess., 2nd Parl., No. 9, Feb. 19, 1954, p. 313, evidence of the President of The Canadian Bankers' Association.

30. F. H. Knight, "Interest," *Encyclopaedia of the Social Sciences* (New York, The Macmillan Company, 1930), *8*, 140–1.

31. "A bank always requires that the borrower be a satisfactory moral risk. This is especially important in the case of a small business, in which the success of the firm is so dependent upon the character and reliability of the proprietor(s). A bank does not want to have to police a loan, or seize and sell the firm's assets in order to secure repayment. Therefore, the bank lends only to those in whose integrity it has confidence." Canada, Department of Trade and Commerce, Industrial Development Branch, *Small Business Manual*, 3rd ed. (Ottawa, Queen's Printer, 1959), p. 70.

ations).[32] Thus, although a loan application may appear on the basis of ordinary costs and revenue considerations to offer a profitable opportunity to the bank to extend an advance, the application will probably be rejected if the lending officer entertains strong doubt about the prospects for repayment. If the character of the borrower does not inspire confidence in his honesty, the application will most likely be rejected. Likewise, if there is much uncertainty about the ability of the borrower to profitably employ the borrowed funds, the application is again most likely to meet with disapproval. The uncertainty need not be attached to repayment itself but only to whether repayment can be made on time without involving the lending bank in extra expense and trouble. Much uncertainty on this score will also lead to a loan application being rejected.[33]

Considerations of uncertainty that cause loan applications to be rejected are akin to risk considerations: on all the rejected loan applications it is the risk that the applicant will default which prevents their acceptance. However, there is a distinction between uncertainty of payment for a particular loan application and the risk of bad debts for a given class of loans.[34] Uncertainty is not a measurable quantity and cannot be allowed for as can risk, which is a measurable quantity. The degree of uncertainty varies from loan to loan and no general allowance can be incorporated into costs to allow for a varying feeling of uncertainty about the loan applications on hand. The uncertainty must either be accepted or avoided.

At one extreme the feeling of uncertainty associated with a loan application may be so strong that the application will be rejected. No lending rate, no matter how high, will induce the lender to grant

32. John Maynard Keynes, *The General Theory of Employment, Interest and Money*, p. 144.

33. Roland I. Robinson, *The Management of Bank Funds*, p. 102, points out that "banks must make a quality of loans the majority of which are collectible without extra supervision."

34. The distinction between uncertainty and risk is due to Frank H. Knight, *Risk, Uncertainty and Profit*, London School of Economics and Political Science, No. 16 in Series of Reprints of Scarce Tracts in Economic and Political Science (London, London School of Economics and Political Science, 1948), pp. 19–21, 46. Also cf. Kenneth E. Boulding, *A Reconstruction of Economics* (New York, John Wiley and Sons, 1950), p. 133.

the application; the quality of the application is then completely unrelated to the profit calculus: the application is rejected solely on grounds of quality. At the other extreme the lender feels so sure of being repaid that a feeling of uncertainty does not arise in assessing the loan application. But between these two extreme states—a feeling of certainty that repayment will be forthcoming without trouble and a feeling that it will not—lie varying degrees of uncertainty associated with applications about which the lender is unsure. It is perhaps on this class of application that uncertainty may be reduced to an expense and thus overcome by a sufficiently large payment. That is, a sufficiently high lending rate may induce a lender to accept a higher degree of uncertainty than he otherwise would; the margin between acceptable and unacceptable degrees of uncertainty for a lender may shift with lending rates.[35]

Thus, uncertainty about repayment creates for the lending bank two classes of loan applications: those on which it is prepared to accept the degrees of uncertainty associated with them and those on which it is not. The applications with unacceptable degrees of uncertainty may be further sub-divided into those rejected because of an uncertainty that cannot be reduced to an item of expense, and those rejected because of an uncertainty that reduces to an expense which in relation to lending rates makes the applications unattractive to the banking firm. However, the fact that an application has an acceptable degree of uncertainty does not mean it will be found creditworthy: it may be unattractive on other grounds, to be considered later.

35. This is perhaps what Knight, "Interest," p. 141, had in mind when he wrote that uncertainty is more or less connected with expense and explains the major differences in interest rates found in various sections of the money market.

In short, a premium may be charged for the uncertainty that each loan entails. Some writers refer to such a premium as a premium for the bearing of risks. This is misleading, however, for the premium involved here is in addition to any amount required to cover the estimated likelihood of loss, which is risk proper. Cf. United States, Federal Reserve System, Board of Governors, *Financing Small Business: Report to the Committees on Banking and Currency and the Select Committees on Small Business, United States Congress* (Washington, Government Printing Office, 1958), p. 41.

Uncertainty may also be resolved by the borrower offering more or better collateral, thus reducing the degree of uncertainty.

If the margin between the two main classes of applications is shifted by a change in the structure of lending rates, mainly by raising or lowering the upper limit in the structure, more or fewer applications will be found to have an acceptable degree of uncertainty. With given lending rates, however, a loan application may pass from an unacceptable to an acceptable degree of certainty if the applicant offers more collateral or is willing to accept less than he asked for. A more dynamic factor is represented by an improvement in the credit position of the applicant that causes the bank to be less uncertain about him. The change may be due to an individual betterment of position or it may be the result of a general improvement in business conditions that makes lenders less uncertain about the prospects of borrowers.[36] Thus anything that makes the lending bank feel more or less certain about the loan applications presented to it causes the margin, based on uncertainty, between acceptable and unacceptable applications to shift. It is possibilities for this type of shift in the "uncertainty" margin that explain how the willingness to lend may change relative to the ability to lend: psychological impacts, possibly caused by a change in bank-rate, may change feelings of uncertainty and cause banks to alter their willingness to lend relative to their ability.[37]

Furthermore, variations in the state of business may alter the margin of uncertainty. Some see in this an aggravating factor in the business cycle: banks, so it is argued, become less uncertain in a boom and take on poorer quality loans; in a depression they reverse themselves.[38] How important a factor this is in accounting for cyclical

36. These are changes that affect the quality of the loan applications; they do not affect the lending practice of the banks. For this reason Marget, *The Theory of Prices*, *1*, 225–6, argues that such changes reflect a change in demand even though the change must be registered in the minds of lenders.

37. Cf. U.S. Congress, *Monetary Policy . . . Public Debt: Compendium*, Pt. 2, p. 854; Harry G. Johnson, "The New Monetary Policy and the Problem of Credit Control," Oxford University, Institute of Statistics, *Bulletin*, *14* (1952), 128–9; Wallich, "The Changing Significance of the Interest Rate," p. 765.

38. Cf. R. S. Sayers, *Modern Banking*, p. 237; Albert G. Hart, *Money, Debt and Economic Activity* (New York, Prentice-Hall, Inc., 1948), p. 60. D. S. Thomson, "Changes in Quality of Bank Credit," *Journal of Finance*, *11* (May 1956), 304–5, does not believe that banks become too optimistic in their lending activities during

fluctuations in bank loans is, however, completely obscured by the instability of the demand for loans, which is likely the more important factor in accounting for changes in loan totals.

But given the degree of uncertainty that attaches itself to each loan application at any given moment, the rejection of any single application depends on whether its degree of uncertainty is intolerable. If it is not, the application may still be adjudged not creditworthy because of credit risk, which is a separate element from uncertainty and forms with it the two major considerations in judging the creditworthiness of a loan application. Accordingly, credit risk must be examined next.

Credit Risk

There is a risk of loss that adheres to loans in general and that is apart from the ordinary assessment of individual loan applications. The lending bank cannot tell in advance which loans will turn bad or will cause trouble, but it does know from experience that loans of different classes offer varying possibilities for risk.[39] To provide for these unforeseen losses, it is necessary to incorporate into lending

---

a period of prosperity, but he argues that they are likely to become too conservative following a period of financial difficulty.

A. F. W. Plumptre, *Central Banking in the British Dominions*, p. 213, expresses the opinion that "if one had to choose whether the credit policies of commercial banks were the result or the cause of business fluctuations, it would probably be preferable to consider them the result." And Vernon W. Malach, *International Cycles and Canada's Balance of Payments, 1921–23*, Canadian Studies in Economics, No. 1 (Toronto, University of Toronto Press, 1954), p. 48, found that the Canadian banks were a passive rather than an active factor in the cyclical variations of Canadian business for the years he studied.

39. Cf. U.S., Federal Reserve System, Board of Governors, *Financing Small Business*, p. 437.

George Rae, *The Country Banker: His Clients, Cares, and Work from an Experience of Forty Years*, rev. Ernest Sykes, 7th ed. (London, John Murray, 1930), pp. 33, 273, notes that banking losses are always exceptions; a bank never makes an advance that it expects to become a loss. "It is always . . . the unexpected that happens when a bank makes a bad debt." He further advises that there may be debts on the books of the bank "fair to look at from without, but rotten within."

rates a premium for risk.[40] Thus, credit risk—the risk of bad debts—
or at least the premium charged to provide for credit risk, is one of
the elements in gross interest rates;[41] that is, part of the gross return
from loans is set aside to cover potential bad debts likely to arise in
any given volume of bank loans.

The risk premium that must be charged is a matter of known loss
experience: it is a matter of the portion of each category of loans that
turns bad. Hence, the allowance for risk applies to broad categories
of loans and thus differs from uncertainty, which is an individual
matter. Nevertheless some attempt must be made to assess the risk
inherent in each loan in order to place it in the proper premium
category. The more risky the loan the higher the risk premium it
must bear. However, although risk premiums charged do vary with
types of loans, they vary less than the terms and collateral as the
banking firm adjusts these in each individual case in an attempt to
minimize its losses.[42]

The fact that risk premiums do vary among loans suggests to some
that any loan application, no matter how great its risk, can be accepted simply by charging an appropriate rate to cover the risk.
However, such is not the case; for it is the good borrowers who must
pay for the bad debts that the banking firm incurs. From the amounts
repaid by the borrowers who discharge their debts must come the
funds to cover the losses on defaulting borrowers.[43] Risk-taking is not

40. Cf. Robinson, *The Management of Bank Funds*, p. 125. Canadian bankers have
stressed the assessment of risks as one of the cost components to be covered by
lending rates. Canada, Parliament, House, Standing Committee on Banking and
Commerce, *Proceedings*, 5th Sess., 19th Parl., 1945, p. 284; idem, 1st Sess., 22nd
Parl., 1954, p. 578.

41. Cf. Alfred Marshall, *Principles of Economics*, 8th ed. (London, Macmillan and
Co., Limited, 1920), pp. 585, 590–1; Abba P. Lerner, *The Economics of Control* (New
York, The Macmillan Company, 1944), p. 342.

42. Winfield W. Riefler, *Money Rates and Money Markets in the United States*, pp.
3, 112, found that the influence of credit risk was more in evidence in determining
collateral than the rate charged for bank loans. Also cf. "What Farmers Pay for
Bank Loans," Federal Reserve Bank of San Francisco, *Monthly Review*, Dec. 1957,
p. 172.

43. Cf. Davenport, *The Economics of Enterprise*, p. 398. Joseph A. Schumpeter,
*The Theory of Economic Development: An Inquiry into Profits, Capital, Credit, Interest, and
the Business Cycle*, trans. Redvers Opie, Harvard Economic Studies, *46* (Cambridge,

a matter of individual assessment for purposes of setting risk premiums on each proposition, but rather a matter of organizing large categories of similar risks and of setting a risk premium appropriate for each category; any individual assessment of risk is then a question of selecting that risk category to which the particular application belongs.[44] Thus, for each category of risk that can be organized there is an appropriate risk premium to charge. And it follows that the higher gross lending rates can go, the higher risk premiums can be set and the greater degrees of risk that can be accommodated. Therefore, if there is an upper limit to lending rates, there is a limit to the category of risks that can be accepted.[45]

When loan applications fall into a category for which the risk premium is greater than existing lending rates can allow for, the applications must be rejected as unprofitable; losses from these loans would likely exceed the provisions for bad debts that could profitably be made out of their gross yields. Individually such loan applications may appear sound but collectively they represent too great a risk at existing lending rates. Only higher lending rates would make this class of application acceptable in the short-run; in the long-run a secular improvement in loss experience would lead to the acceptance of loan applications from categories with higher degrees of risk.

Mass., Harvard University Press, 1934), p. 196, states that if it is known from experience that 1 per cent of the loans made are irrecoverable, it can be said that a bank receives the same sum as it lent when it receives an additional 1.01 per cent from all debts that are not bad.

44. Cf. Roland N. McKean, "Liquidity and a National Balance Sheet," *Readings in Monetary Theory*, Blakiston Series of Republished Articles on Economics, 5 (New York, The Blakiston Company, 1951), p. 64, which is reprinted from the *Journal of Political Economy*, 57 (1949), 506–22. Knight, *Risk, Uncertainty and Profits*, p. 46, argues that it is simply a matter of business organization to combine a sufficient number of cases to reduce a determinate uncertainty to any desired limits.

45. Lloyd W. Mints, *A History of Banking Theory in Great Britain and the United States* (Chicago, University of Chicago Press, 1945), p. 276, who argues that banks must refuse credit to poor risks because lending rates are restricted to a small range. Wallich, "The Changing Significance of the Interest Rate," p. 768, also notes that the conventional range for lending rates that usually prevails "limits the maximum risk premiums that can be arranged for."

The Margin of Acceptability

The willingness to lend that is divorced from the ability to lend is thus a function of uncertainty and of credit risk. Uncertainty is a matter of judgement or opinion about whether the particular borrower can use borrowed funds profitably and will make repayment. The banking firm either finds an applicant acceptable for a certain sum or it does not. In addition to the individual fact of uncertainty there exists the fact that all loans entail a credit risk. To allow for this risk the terms and collateral as well as the amount allotted must be adjusted to the conditions of each borrower in order to minimize the risk of loss. The risk that remains can be allowed for more or less by grouping loans into risk categories and applying risk premiums based on known loss experience.

The margin between acceptable and unacceptable loan applications—what may be defined as the margin of acceptability—is then a question of the degree of uncertainty surrounding each loan application and the risk category into which it falls. There may be little uncertainty about a particular loan application, yet the degree of risk associated with the loan category into which it falls may be too great to justify accepting the application at existing rates. Or, the risk associated with an application of a particular class may be very low, yet the uncertainty about the applicant may be sufficiently great to make it necessary to refuse him an advance. In other words, both the risk category into which a loan application falls and the degree of uncertainty the lending bank feels for the application determine whether or not it is accepted.

Thus, given the quality of the demand for bank loans (which includes given economic conditions) and given the loss experience on loans, the margin between acceptable and unacceptable loan applications is set, and set on the strict basis of creditworthiness. This margin will vary autonomously with lending rates, but it is unlikely to vary with changes in lending ability unless, by affecting the thinking of lending officers, such changes alter the quality of loan applications. Thus, rejection or acceptance standards are set for given circumstances, and bank lending activity operates within the context of these standards and without reference to lending ability or capacity. The existence of these credit standards and the rejection of loan applications, partially or totally, at existing lending rates, from considerations of uncertainty and of credit risks, gives rise to excess demand for bank loans. But this is the type of excess demand that cannot be profitably satisfied at existing lending rates: it reflects a willingness to lend that is not related to lending capacity. The excess demand and the willingness to lend that is related to lending capacity are of a different nature and fall under the head of credit rationing.

CREDIT RATIONING

The rejection of loan applications and the trimming of loan requests on the basis of creditworthiness is a normal part of the lending activity of the banking firm. This refusal of loan applications that normally takes place is a function of quality and of lending rates but not of a limitation imposed by lending capacity —a limitation which when it becomes effective may give rise to additional refusals of loan applications. The latter type of refusal is clearly a matter of credit rationing and is the subject of discussion in this section, although how the former type of refusal is related to credit rationing must also be considered. The plan of attack is to deal with credit rationing in terms of views and definitions, nature, lending rates and theory, all in order to offer an explanation of how the banking firm provides loan financing to the community.

Views and Definitions of Credit Rationing

Clear, concise, and comprehensive accounts of credit rationing in banking scarcely exist. Apparently the topic received no analytical treatment in the general banking literature of the nineteenth century although the refusal to grant new loans and the liquidation of existing ones by banks was a common-place occurrence, especially in times of financial crises.[46] Thus, credit rationing must have been a conspicuous

46 Cf. James W. Gilbart, *The Principles and Practice of Banking*, new edition, ed. anon. (London, Bell and Daldy 1871), pp. 222–3, 225.

feature of nineteenth-century banking,[47] especially in North America where the demand for credit exceeded the ability of the early banks to meet it;[48] yet apart from considerable discussion of rationing of credit by the Bank of England,[49] the attention of economists was not drawn to credit rationing until the 1920's. Hartley Withers[50] mentioned briefly, and with approval, an attempt made by the English banks to ration credit in the period following the end of World

47. R. G. Hawtrey, *A Century of Bank Rate* (London, Longmans, Green and Co., 1938), pp. 249–50, explains the effectiveness of bank-rate in the financial history of England as partly due to rationing by the English banks. T. E. Gregory (comp.), *Select Statutes, Documents and Reports Relating to British Banking, 1832–1928* (London, Oxford University Press, 1929), *2*, 104, 128, reproduces material indicating that in times of distress English banks refused to make loans. Elmer Wood, *English Theories of Central Banking Control, 1819–1858: With Some Account of Contemporary Procedure*, Harvard Economic Studies, *64* (Cambridge, Mass., Harvard University Press, 1939), p. 7, alludes to a shortage of reserves causing London banks to restrict credit to traders.

48. Robinson, *The Management of Bank Funds*, p. 93; H. C. Pentland, "The Role of Capital in Canadian Economic Development before 1875," *Canadian Journal of Economics and Political Science*, *16* (Nov. 1950), 472, who argues that the early banks in North America always arose from a shortage of funds, not from a surplus. Harry E. Miller, *Banking Theories in the United States before 1860*, Harvard Economic Studies, *30* (Cambridge, Mass., Harvard University Press, 1927), pp. 184, 210–11, cites American writings which suggest resort to rationing by U.S. banks at various times during the early part of the nineteenth century.

The fact that the demand for bank loans bore heavily upon the limited lending capacity of the banking system gave rise of course to the charge of discrimination in lending against the banks as is indicated by the following quotation: "Favoritism in the discounting of bills was also charged against the banks. . . . it is apparent from the general evidence and from the partial admissions of the bank officers, that the public were not treated with perfect impartiality in the matter of loans. The interests of the banks and of the merchants who held their stocks were still too closely connected to admit of a perfect separation of their interests." Adam Shortt, "The Early History of Canadian Banking: IV. The First Banks in Lower Canada," *Journal of The Canadian Bankers' Association*, *4* (July 1897), 359.

Discrimination differs from rationing in that under the former funds are withheld on the basis of arbitrary considerations or with sinister intent to injure. Alhadeff, *Monopoly and Competition in Banking*, pp. 226–7.

49. The discussion is documented by Jacob Viner, *Studies in the Theory of International Trade* (New York, Harper and Brothers, 1937), pp. 256–7.

50. *Bankers and Credit* (London, Eveleigh Nash and Grayson Limited, 1924), pp. 155, 160–1.

War I.[51] And in 1926 A. C. Pigou[52] referred to credit rationing by banks as a recent development. Others who at that time specifically mentioned credit rationing in their works on banking were Robertson, Hawtrey, and Keynes.[53] Writers who followed them in mentioning credit rationing[54] often failed to provide a satisfactory treatment or definition.

Those who have recently reviewed the literature in an attempt to treat analytically the question of credit rationing in banking have defined credit rationing in terms of excess demand for bank loans at prevailing rates: if a borrower cannot obtain all the bank credit he

51. He attributes to Pigou an unfavourable view of credit rationing which he says (p. 155) is expressed by Pigou in a letter to the *Times* (London), Feb. 12, 1920, p. 10. However, in this letter Pigou argues only for a higher bank-rate and dear money, making no mention at all of credit rationing. R. S. Sayers, *Central Banking after Bagehot* (Oxford, At the Clarendon Press, 1957), p. 69, reports that the U.K. banks were called into conference at the Treasury in Feb. 1920, "to secure sufficient restraint on business by the rationing of credit."

52. *Industrial Fluctuations* (London, Macmillan and Co., Limited, 1927), p. 246.

53. D. H. Robertson, *Money*, pp. 171–4, on the rationing of bank loans remains unchanged from the 1928 edition.

R. G. Hawtrey, *The Art of Central Banking* (London, Longmans, Green and Co., 1932), p. 154, and *Currency and Credit*, 4th ed. (London, Longmans, Green and Co., 1950), p. 93, which to judge by the Preface has not been altered from the 1927 edition, does not specifically mention credit rationing but he does mention regulating the volume of bank loans other than through variations in lending rates.

John Maynard Keynes, *A Treatise on Money*, 2, 365, referred to "an habitual system of rationing in the attitude of banks to borrowers."

54. A select bibliography of recent works mentioning credit rationing should probably include the following: L. V. Chandler, "Monopolistic Elements in Commercial Banking," *Journal of Political Economy*, 46 (Feb. 1938), 21; F. A. Lutz, "The Interest Rate and Investment in a Dynamic Economy," *American Economic Review*, 35 (Dec. 1945), 829; H. C. Wallich, "The Changing Significance of the Interest Rate," *American Economic Review*, 36 (Dec. 1946), 765–6; Hart, *Money, Debt and Economic Activity*, pp. 202–3; H. S. Ellis, "The Rediscovery of Money," *Money, Trade, and Economic Growth: In Honor of John Henry Williams* (New York, The Macmillan Company, 1951), pp. 255–6; P. A. Samuelson in U.S. Congress, *Monetary Policy and the Management of the Public Debt: Hearings*, pp. 695–97; Erik Lundberg, *Business Cycles and Economic Policy*, trans. J. Potter (London, George Allen and Unwin Ltd., 1957), p. 161; J. S. G. Wilson, "Credit Rationing and the Relevant Rate of Interest," *Economica*, 21 (1954), 22–3.

wants at the going rate, credit rationing is said to exist.[55] On this definition the existence of any excess demand for bank loans is *prima facie* evidence of credit rationing, and therefore the definition is not particularly enlightening because it does not recognize the two different categories of excess demand that may exist: namely, excess demand created by considerations of creditworthiness which cause some loan applications to be rejected, and excess demand created by the inability of the banking firm to meet creditworthy demands because of insufficient lending capacity.[56] A better understanding of

55. Kareken, "Lenders' Preferences, Credit Rationing and the Effectiveness of Monetary Policy," p. 295, who defines credit rationing as the non-price rationing of funds; Scott, "The Availability Doctrine: Development and Implications," p. 538.

Guttentag, "Credit Availability, Interest Rates, and Monetary Policy," pp. 220–1, takes a contrary view arguing that credit rationing results from "the application of an array of noninterest rate lending terms" and not from the underpricing of credit.

Kareken's definition of credit rationing has been criticized by Donald R. Hodgman, "In Defense of the Availability Doctrine: A Comment," *Review of Economics and Statistics*, *41* (Feb. 1959), 72, who argues that credit rationing may arise even under an equilibrium price when disappointed borrowers who can offer to pay more are unable to offer "sufficient 'amounts' of non-price factors."

56. R. S. Sayers, "Central Banking in the Light of Recent British and American Experience," *Quarterly Journal of Economics*, *63* (May 1949), 202n1, distinguishes two types of excess demand on the basis of whether or not an increase in cash reserves will lead to a satisfaction of the excess demand. He draws the distinction in interpreting the Keynesian fringe of unsatisfied borrowers.

Wallich, "The Changing Significance of the Interest Rate," p. 766, considers credit rationing as a separate factor from credit risk in causing excess demand for bank loans.

Wilson, "Credit Rationing and the Relevant Rate of Interest," pp. 22–3, recognizes two types of exclusions from the loan market: one due to the need to restrict total loans and the other, to the existence of credit standards.

Pigou, *Industrial Fluctuations*, p. 246, appears to imply that credit rationing is something apart from the rejection of loan applications on the basis of credit standards, but his definition of credit rationing (p. 243) as "the refusal of loans to some people who, at current prices, would like to take them" is all inclusive.

Keynes, *Treatise*, *2*, 365, also appears to imply that rationing of bank credit is divorced from considerations of credit standards. However, he is not explicit on this point, and Marget, *The Theory of Prices*, *1*, 224, has interpreted Keynes' discussion to mean that all credit rationing is merely a matter of applying certain

credit rationing is obtained by distinguishing between these two classes of excess demand and by examining the character of each.

The Nature of Credit Rationing

Excess demand for a commodity arises because the selling price is set too low in relation to the demand, and the commodity must then be rationed in some way. In this sense the refusal of loan applications on grounds of creditworthiness may be thought to represent rationing when the rejection is the result of a limitation in lending rates. Higher lending rates would result in fewer refusals because the lending bank would then be willing to accept a larger proportion of the applications presented to it. However, at the prevailing lending rate, the unsatisfied demand differs from the satisfied demand in that the former does not represent profitable business for the banking firm while the latter does. This differs from the ordinary case of excess demand where the price does not serve to divide buyers into profitable and unprofitable groups, but merely determines the amount that can be profitably supplied. Therefore, in the ordinary case, if more could be supplied at the given price, there would be a ready market for it; in the banking case, however, an increase in the supply ability of the banking firm to expand loans at existing rates would not lead to a satisfaction of excess demand caused by existing credit standards. That excess demand would still remain unprofitable. In other words, excess demand for bank loans that results from excluding loans on the basis of creditworthiness represents a limitation in demand at existing rates and not a limitation in supply.

True rationing means not only excess demand but also a physical limitation in supply: an inability to profitably produce more at existing prices even though additional output could be marketed at those

---

credit standards to borrowers. Ellis, "The Rediscovery of Money," p. 255, appears to take a similar interpretation of Keynes.

Lindbeck, p. 32, in his discussion of credit rationing also draws on the distinction between the exercise of credit standards and credit rationing.

Donald R. Hodgman, "Credit Risk and Credit Rationing," *Quarterly Journal of Economics*, 74 (May 1960), 258–60, 275, 277–8, treats credit rationing in terms of credit ratings which may operate to restrict the amount borrowed even though borrowers offer to pay more.

D

prices. In banking this situation arises when the banking firm is providing all the loans it can on the basis of its existing cash reserves. It then has no excess capacity for making loans and so must truly ration credit in the sense of rejecting any additional loan applications even though they be creditworthy and normally acceptable at existing rates. Higher lending rates would not cause the banking firm to expand its loans in the circumstances—it cannot.[57]

In this view credit rationing results when the banking firm is operating at its effective maximum for bank loans, and when some of the excess demand confronting it represents profitable business at existing rates; a rise in lending rates may reduce this excess demand, but cannot result in the banking firm satisfying any of it. When the banking firm has excess lending capacity, it is not rationing credit simply because it rejects applications for loans that do not represent profitable business at existing rates. Under rationing, as defined here, the volume of bank loans has to be restricted not because additional requests involve an unprofitable extension of loans but because additional requests cannot be met if the amount of loans being carried is at the operational maximum. A *ceteris paribus* increase in cash reserves would enable the banking firm to expand its loans by satisfying some of the profitable excess demand; and, of course, a reduction in its cash reserves would cause it to ration credit to a greater extent.[58]

57. However, both Robertson, *Money*, p. 178, and Pigou, *Industrial Fluctuations*, p. 247, associate credit rationing with a restriction in supply because the price is lower than it would be in a free market. They appear to imply that a higher lending rate would mean a greater volume of bank loans. Banks, however, at existing rates do not make more loans either because they cannot (in which case a higher lending rate has no effect on the volume of loans) or because it is not profitable for them to do so. Under the latter possibility the unprofitability of additional loans is due either to more profitable alternatives for bank funds or to credit standards. In either case the excess demand is not due to capacity limitations but to the unprofitability of the business it represents. Therefore, Pigou and Robertson must have had a notion of credit rationing that involved no more than the rejection by banks of loan applications unprofitable at existing rates.

58. This is apparently what Keynes had in mind when he spoke of a fringe of unsatisfied borrowers that fluctuated in size with the ability of the banking system to make loans, as evidenced by the following quotation: "Thus there is normally a fringe of unsatisfied borrowers who are not considered to have the first claims on a bank's favours, but to whom the bank would be quite ready to lend if it were

Thus, the real test of credit rationing in a banking system is the existence of a state of affairs where bank loans are so close to the feasible maximum that the banks have to refuse to accommodate borrowers who otherwise would represent profitable business. Excess demand is not sufficient evidence of credit rationing; and neither is an inflexibility in lending rates, although a degree of inflexibility is a necessary condition for credit rationing. Hence, rate inflexibility is another dimension of credit rationing that must be explained.

Lending Rates and Credit Rationing

Theoretically, the banking firm that does not have the capacity for expanding its loans could hold in check the volume of loans it makes by letting lending rates rise to whatever level is necessary to eliminate the excess demand from creditworthy borrowers.[59] However, in practice lending rates are not sufficiently flexible to prevent the loans that could be made at prevailing rates from exceeding the capacity of the banking system for making loans. Laws, conventions, and public opinion restrict banks from charging as high a rate as market conditions would sometimes justify, and this is especially so where the political significance of interest rates is greater than their

to find itself in a position to lend more." Keynes, *Treatise*, *2*, 365; also cf. ibid, *1*, 212, 263.

Also Hawtrey's description of the expansion and contraction of bank credit being the result of banks adjusting their resistance to the pressure that they are constantly subjected to by borrowers seems most meaningful when the banking system is operating at maximum "output" for loans and must continually ration credit by refusing accommodation to otherwise creditworthy and profitable applicants. Cf. Hawtrey, *The Art of Central Banking*, p. 155, and *Currency and Credit*, p. 101.

59. Mints, *A History of Banking Theory*, pp. 210–11, reviews some of the literature which in general favours the use of increased lending rates to relieve pressure on the reserves of the banks. However, Robertson, *Money*, p. 169, argues that "it would be little short of a miracle" if the manipulation of lending rates "proved adequate by itself to reduce the stream [of demand for loans] to precisely that volume which week by week, having regard to the size of their reserves, the bankers are prepared to satisfy." He therefore concludes (p. 172) that "there are grounds for suspecting that . . . moderate manipulations of the rate of interest may need at least to be supplemented by some kind of direct rationing of bank loans."

economic significance.[60] Furthermore, there is a frictional lag in adjusting rates, for bank customers are likely to protest frequent changes in lending rates.[61]

Because of the practical limitations and difficulties in adjusting lending rates to the state of demand for bank loans, banks often develop a strong preference for stable rates. Thus, one writer noted that "it has been something of a tradition, even a matter of pride, that the leading institutions [in the British Dominions] should keep their [lending] rates steady in the face of changing circumstances."[62] This observation applies with special force to Canadian banking:

> Canada . . . seems to have evolved a credit control which pivots on a stable rate for money. The chartered banks pay three per cent. on deposits, and charge a basic six per cent. for loans, and they adhere to these rates through shade and shine to an

60. S. N. Sen, *Central Banking in Undeveloped Money Markets* (Calcutta, Bookland Limited, 1952), pp. 35–6; Plumptre, *Central Banking*, p. 212; idem, "The Role of Interest Rates and Bank Credit in the Economies of the British Dominions," *Economic Journal*, *49* (1939), 224.

61. Schumpeter, *Business Cycles*, *2*, 605, who maintains that the frictional lag in lending rates "is intensified on the upgrade by the pressure of public opinion and on the downgrade by risks and fears."

Simple oligopolist considerations—uncertainty by a bank that a rate increase by it will be adopted by other banks as well—may also introduce a lag in the response of rates to a rise of excess demand for loans when there is some doubt about how widespread the excess demand is. Cf. John H. Kareken, "Reply," *Review of Economics and Statistics*, *41* (Feb. 1959), 74. When excess demand is prevalent no bank need hesitate about raising its lending rate simply because of uncertainty as to what other banks will do. Other banks cannot gain business by refusing to raise their rates because they do not have the resources to accommodate any additional business.

62. Plumptre, "The Role of Interest Rates and Bank Credit in the Economies of the British Dominions," p. 222, who cites (pp. 222–3) as follows from p. 3281 of the evidence given before the Royal Commission on Banking and Currency in Canada, 1933: "It has been the aim of the Chartered Banks to maintain rates of interest at a steady level. . . . [as a result] borrowers were enabled to make their commitments without fear of their interest costs being subject to violent fluctuations. . . ."

extent surprising to those accustomed to more fluid and elastic conditions.[63]

In 1929 a Canadian banker expressed the belief that:

The banks in Canada have made in the past and are at the present time making another very important contribution to the Canadian business partnership in that they maintained throughout the whole period of the War [1914–18] very normal interest rates for money when other centers of the world were obliged to pay pretty high rates and even during the past year when rates for time money in New York have reached as high as $9\frac{1}{2}\%$, and call and short loan rates have gone as high as 15 % ... there have been no such fluctuations in money rates in Canada.[64]

As these quotations indicate, there has existed in Canadian banking a strong preference for stable lending rates. That preference shows in the two available statistical series on lending rates—one for the years 1934–43, the other for 1944–53. Through the years 1934–43 of extreme easy money the annual, simple average rate of interest charged on loans outstanding in Canada fell from 5.78 per cent to 4.35 per cent. In the years 1946–53 when the demand for loans underwent a substantial expansion the weighted average of year-end interest charges on loans outstanding rose from 4.22 per cent to 4.70 per cent.[65] Even in the absence of any preference for stable rates, the existence of a legal restriction of 6 per cent on the maximum lending

63. John Percival Day, *Considerations on the Demand for a Central Bank in Canada* (Toronto, The MacMillan Company of Canada, Limited, 1933), p. 55; the part quoted is reprinted from an article by the author in the *Financial News* (London), July 30, 1928. Cf. C. A. Curtis, "Credit Control in Canada," *Papers and Proceedings of the Annual Meeting of the Canadian Political Science Association*, 2 (May 1930), 116.

64. H. B. Henwood, "The Contribution of the Canadian Banks to the Partnership of Business and Commerce," *Journal of The Canadian Bankers' Association*, 37 (Oct. 1929), 107.

65. Canada, Parliament, House, Standing Committee on Banking and Commerce, *Proceedings: Decennial Revision of the Bank Act*, 1st Sess., 22nd Parl., 1954, Exhibit No. 29, p. 773. Interesting comments on the course of lending rates in Canada over the years 1896–1913 appear in Canada, Board of Inquiry into the Cost of Living, *Report* (Ottawa, King's Printer, 1915), 2, 737–8.

rate that Canadian banks may charge reduces considerably the scope for raising bank lending rates in Canada.[66]

When lending rates are not very flexible, loans have to be restricted by means other than rate movements.[67] Thus, one observer noting the stability of lending rates in Canada drew the conclusion that Canadian banks rationed credit.[68] Stable lending rates are likely to create excess demand in that the failure of rates to rise as high as they should causes some loan applications to be unprofitable to the banks; but there need be no rationing of loans among creditworthy borrowers merely because lending rates are not flexible. Stable rates may simply reflect the ability of the banking system to obtain additional cash reserves under conditions of constant costs when the demand for loans from creditworthy sources expands.[69] Thus, when the banking firm is able to draw upon excess lending capacity in-

66. The restriction to a maximum of 6 per cent for bank loans in Canada is imposed by the Bank Act. Canada, Laws, Statutes, *Statutes of Canada*, 1953–54, 2–3 Elizabeth II, c. 48, s. 91 (1).

67. Thus, F. W. Paish, "Bank Policy and the Balance of International Payments," *Readings in the Theory of International Trade*, Blakiston Series of Republished Articles on Economics, *4* (Philadelphia, The Blakiston Company, 1949), p. 39 (reprinted from *Economica*, *3* [Nov. 1936], 404–22) points out that in some countries the rate of interest plays only a minor role in restricting bank loans and that advances have to be arbitrarily refused or reduced to particular borrowers, especially new borrowers.

68. Day, *Considerations*, p. 56. The conclusion that Canadian banks rationed credit receives some support from the evidence of a Canadian banker given in 1910 that when cash reserves came under pressure the defensive reaction was not to raise lending rates but to reduce commitments. United States, National Monetary Commission, *Interviews on the Banking and Currency Systems of Canada* (Washington, Government Printing Office, 1910), p. 51.

69. When this is so, "given a rate of interest, the amount that will be loaned at that rate of interest is largely dependent upon the amount of additional lending power granted to the member banks." Lauchlin Currie, *The Supply and Control of Money in the United States*, Harvard Economic Studies, *47* (Cambridge, Mass., Harvard University Press, 1934), p. 7.

Jacob Viner, *Canada's Balance of International Indebtedness*, p. 176, found that although Canadian banks in the period 1900–13 kept their lending rates almost constant, they never had to refuse accommodation to creditworthy customers; the banks were able to adjust their cash to their loans: in short, credit rationing was not necessary.

vested in some other way, or when its reserves vary naturally with the demand for bank loans, it will be glad to expand its loans at existing rates as demand increases.[70] At existing rates and for given credit standards the amount of bank loans carried by the banking firm may fluctuate with the demand from creditworthy borrowers if lending capacity fluctuates in the same way or if unutilized loan capacity can be drawn into use with no increase in lending costs.

Of course in the face of strong demand for bank loans, limited lending capacity, and unutilized loan capacity that can be drawn upon only at increasing costs, an excess demand for loans is inevitable if lending rates do not rise. Otherwise acceptable loan applications must at first be refused because they cease to be profitable at existing rates; and then, once all unutilized loan capacity is gone, all new applications must be refused for want of lending capacity and credit rationing proper sets in.[71]

70. Schumpeter, *Business Cycles*, 2, 606, who argues that there is "in every neighborhood of equilibrium a positive rate at which banks will in general be glad to expand their loans."

71. This is dramatically illustrated by Canadian experience in 1959 when in the face of an unprecedented increase in loan demand the banks were prevented by the legal ceiling of 6 per cent from raising their lending rates to anywhere near the level justified by market conditions. The lending capacity of the banks was held relatively constant so that at first the banks met the increase in demand for loans by disposing of Government securities. As security prices moved against the banks and they experienced considerable losses in disposing of securities, they began to restrict the supply of credit. An unusual press statement released at the time by the President of The Canadian Bankers' Association, dated in Montreal, May 14, 1959, explained how the banks were going to have "to exercise the utmost care in the handling of their credit facilities, in order to avoid any significant further increase in the over-all total of bank loans." But the demand for loans persisted, the banks were unsuccessful in keeping their loans from rising further and their security holdings from falling lower, and apparently by early August the banks had gone as far as they could in increasing loans by disposing of securities. Another press statement by the President of The Canadian Bankers' Association, dated in Toronto, August 13, 1959, announced that the banks were unable to make any further new loans or "to provide for increases in the amounts already borrowed under existing credits." News stories of these events may be found in the *Financial Post* (Toronto), May 16, 1957, p. 9, and in the (Montreal) *Gazette*, Aug. 14, 15, and 19, 1959, p. 1 in each issue.

This was not the first time that Canadian banks were forced to refuse to lend

Even when lending rates are free to rise, however, credit rationing may exist if lending rates do not rise sufficiently to eliminate the need for rationing. Thus it is noteworthy that, although flexible lending rates have long been a conspicuous feature of English banking,[72] English economists have been most prominent among those who hold that banks cannot rely on the rate of interest charged to keep their loans within appropriate limits. The following quotation illustrates this point of view:

> Banks do not rely exclusively on the rate of interest charged to limit the demands of borrowers; they retain discretion to restrict or refuse advances to any customer. They are in a position to apply direct persuasion or pressure if credit has to be restricted. And when the central bank buys securities, and they find their reserves increased, they will relax these restraints. The rise or fall of bank rate not only reacts on the market rate, but acts as a signal to the bank to apply or to relax restraints on borrowing.[73]

without being able to raise their lending rates. Roeliff Morton Breckenridge, *The Canadian Banking System, 1817–1890*, Publications of the American Economic Association, *10*, Nos. 1, 2 and 3 (New York, Macmillan and Company, 1895), p. 161, argues that the effect of the financial crisis of 1857–63 in Canada was aggravated by the restriction imposed on the lending rate of the banks which left the banks with no recourse but to refuse to lend.

72. The rates charged by the English banks depend on the Bank rate, usually being 1 per cent above it. Walter Leaf, *Banking*, Home University Library of Modern Knowledge, *124* (London, Williams and Norgate, Ltd., [1926]), p. 177; T. Balogh, *Studies in Financial Organization*, The National Institute of Economic and Social Research (Cambridge, At the University Press, 1947), p. 75; A. C. L. Day, *Outline of Monetary Economics* (Oxford, At the Clarendon Press, 1957), p. 178. Great Britain, Chancellor of the Exchequer, Committee on the Working of the Monetary System, *Report*, Cmd. 827 (London, Her Majesty's Stationery Office, 1959), pp. 46–7 (para. 137).

73. Hawtrey, *Currency and Credit*, p. 93. In *The Art of Central Banking*, Mr. Hawtrey writes: "A competitive bank . . . cannot afford to rely exclusively on the rate of interest charged to keep its customers' borrowings within the appropriate limits. It must also be prepared in case of need to limit its loans by refusing some altogether" (p. 154). In *A Century of Bank Rate* he argues that "a high Bank rate leads the commerical banks, not merely to charge correspondingly high rates to their customers, but to keep down the volume of credit by refusing to lend to the less eligible borrowers" (p. 202).

J. M. Keynes[74] also felt that the relaxation and contraction of credit by the banking system did not work through variations in lending rates alone, and apparently it is still not English banking practice to rely exclusively on changes in lending rates to hold loans in check as the following comment suggests:

> It seems to be completely contrary to the tradition of English banking to use the rate of interest to any significant extent as a means of checking the demand for bank advances . . . . In practice, if a bank does not feel justified in lending at the normal rate, it does not feel justified in lending at all. Similarly, when a bank feels obliged to reduce its advances it does not normally raise its charges (except in conformity with changes in Bank rate) either on a total advance or on a marginal proportion of it; it merely asks the customer to make a specified reduction by a specified date. It has thus always been possible for the banks, in times of monetary restriction, to keep the rate charged on advances well below that which customers would if necessary have been prepared to pay.[75]

When lending rates are flexible but do not serve to eliminate excess demand from creditworthy borrowers, movements in them act as the

74. *Treatise*, 2, 364–5. It is noteworthy, however, that the Macmillan committee (Great Britain, Committee on Finance and Industry, *Report*, Cmd. 3987. [London, His Majesty's Stationery Office, 1931], pp. 39, 100), of which Keynes was a member, found in 1931 no evidence to suggest that English banks had to refuse loans because of insufficient lending capacity: the condition necessary to give validity to Keynes' concept of the fringe of unsatisfied borrowers.

Indeed credit rationing because of limited lending capacities cannot be a conspicuous feature of twentieth-century banking in view of the excess lending capacity, held in the form of government securities, that is typical of modern-day banks.

75. R. F. G. Alford and F. W. Paish, "Debate on Monetary Control—Basic Principles and Modern Mechanics," *The Banker*, Aug. 1956, p. 480, who also point out that the reluctance of banks to use lending rates to restrict demand for loans accounts for the confusion about the effects of changes in interest rates on business decisions. Since the rates charged by the banks "are never allowed to fluctuate sufficiently to influence business policy materially, it is not unnatural that business policy is virtually unaffected by their fluctuations" (p. 481).

outward sign of changes in underlying credit conditions:[76] they indicate a change in the degree of credit rationing where credit rationing exists,[77] and a shift in the margin between profitable and unprofitable loan applications. A rise in rates, for example, may reflect not only the restraint imposed by limited lending capacity on the loan output of banks but also a rise in lending costs that makes a larger proportion of loan applications unprofitable business.

In short, the absence of movements in lending rates is no evidence that creditworthy borrowers are being refused bank loans and the

76. W. Randolph Burgess, *The Reserve Banks and the Money Market* (New York, Harper and Brothers, 1927), p. 276; Riefler, *Money Rates and Money Markets*, pp. xv–xvi; P. W. McCracken, "The Present Status of Monetary and Fiscal Policy," *Journal of Finance*, 5 (Mar. 1950), 29; Rosa, "Interest Rates and the Central Bank," *Money, Trade, and Economic Growth*, p. 276. All these writers point out that movements in lending rates are of greater significance than the movements themselves would suggest since they reflect changes not only in the cost of borrowed funds but also in basic credit conditions.

77. P. A. Samuelson in U.S. Congress, *Monetary Policy and the Management of the Public Debt: Hearings*, p. 697, argues that except in the shortest run the degree of credit rationing is kept constant by appropriate changes in lending rates. At one point, however, he appears to view rationing as the result of limited lending capacity (p. 696) while at another point (p. 697) he considers it to be caused by a rise in security yields that makes new loans unprofitable at existing lending rates. On my interpretation rationing does not arise from the fact that it is unprofitable to expand loans, so that an adjustment in lending rates to make an expansion of loans profitable does not constitute a change in the degree of rationing. And when rationing exists because it is profitable to expand loans at a time when expansion is impossible, there is no reason why the degree of the rationing may not vary.

Canadian experience with flexible lending rates in 1956 under conditions of monetary restraint suggests that changes in rates were not sufficient to keep constant the pressure for loans from borrowers who could not be completely satisfied. Thus, when lending rates were raised for the second time in 1956 by the chartered banks, it was reported that "the higher rates would prove a fairer, more feasible way of putting a brake on borrowing than by changing or limiting requested loans." The (Montreal) *Gazette*, Aug. 17, 1956. Hope was high that the increased rates would curb excess demand; it was, alas, not justified. Two months later lending rates went up again, and the statement made this time was that higher rates had not served as much of a deterrent to borrowers, that they were not expected to, and that even with the latest increases the chartered banks would still have to continue refusing or reducing the size of requested loans. Ibid., Oct. 20, 1956; *Financial Post* (Toronto), Oct. 27, 1956, p. 8.

presence of movements in lending rates does not necessarily indicate that excess demand from creditworthy borrowers is being contained. A banking system that is rationing loans among creditworthy borrowers at a given set of lending rates is unlikely to raise those rates freely when demand increases, or to lower them when demand falls. In neither case can the banks expand their loans, because the capacity restraint prevents them from doing so. Their profits suffer when they ration credit more intensely instead of raising rates, but if they are prepared to forego extra profits at one level of excess demand, probably they are prepared to forego those extra profits for all levels of excess demand. Hence, variations in demand for loans from creditworthy sources that occur when the banks are rationing credit may cause more of a change in the degree of credit rationing than in lending rates. Similarly, when demand remains constant but lending capacity is altered, the degree of rationing tends to alter more than lending rates. An expansion in capacity permits some of the unsatisfied demand to be met without rates necessarily having to be raised: a contraction in capacity requires that loans be reduced (because the banking system has no excess lending capacity)—a reduction that is seldom accomplished entirely by a rise in lending rates, so again the degree of rationing is altered.

The failure of lending rates to be completely flexible is thus responsible not only for credit rationing, in the sense of denying credit to creditworthy borrowers, but also for changes in the degree of credit rationing. Thus, another condition of credit rationing is insufficient flexibility in lending rates, and this condition, coupled to that of insufficient lending capacity to meet all creditworthy demand for loans, requires the banks to choose from among a given total of profitable and acceptable loan applications that lesser portion which they can accommodate. To determine how such an allotment might be made, a theory of credit rationing is required.

A Theory of Credit Rationing

Requests for loans from a banking firm at given lending rates divide naturally into two groups: those that represent profitable and acceptable avenues for investment by the banking firm and those that do not. Judgement and opinion about the degree of uncertainty

surrounding each loan application and about the risk category to
which each belongs plays a major part in separating the profitable
and acceptable loan requests from the unprofitable and non-accept-
able. The dividing line between the two shifts for changes in cost
conditions, lending rates, and quality of the given demand. But given
the dividing line, the two categories of loan requests are fixed. One
represents an excess demand for bank loans that cannot be eliminated
at existing lending rates because the banking firm does not find any
of the excluded demand worth granting; the other represents a total
of acceptable demand that the banking firm is willing to satisfy at
existing rates if it can. The problem that must now be solved is what
happens when the total of acceptable loan requests exceeds the operational maximum for loans that the banking firm can make. This is
the problem of credit rationing as it is defined here.

The simplest case is where there is a single lending rate and where
all acceptable and profitable loan requests are homogeneous: that is,
equal in quality and in the net rate of return that they yield the
banking firm. This situation is represented graphically in Figure IA
where net rates of return are measured along the Y axis and loans
along the X axis. The demand for loans from creditworthy borrowers
is represented by the horizontal line rd, the position of which indicates the constant net yield that various amounts of acceptable loan

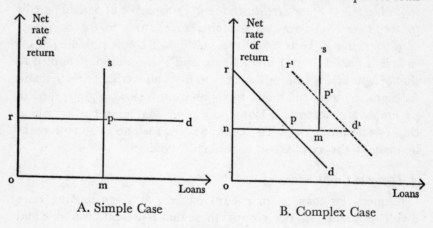

A. Simple Case   B. Complex Case

FIGURE I
DEMAND AND SUPPLY CURVES FOR BANK LOANS

requests produce at the given lending rate. The total amount of loans that the banking firm could make is plotted as the vertical line *ms* placed so as to indicate the fixed maximum capacity that the banking firm has for "producing" loans. If the demand curve defined in the foregoing manner runs through the supply curve, that portion of it which lies beyond the supply curve, *pd* here, represents excess demand from profitable sources that would have to be excluded by rationing. Since the excluded requests would be as profitable to the banking firm as those accepted, rationing here takes place outside the profit calculus. A higher lending rate would do nothing to expand loans, but an increase in cash reserves would.

The rationing situation remains unchanged when variations in the lending costs of loans are allowed for in setting lending rates so as to make the net return on all acceptable loans identical. When the amount demanded exceeds capacity, rationing has to be on grounds other than profitability.

The most complex situation in which rationing may take place arises when all acceptable and profitable loan requests are not equally so to the banking firm. This is the most probable situation since loan applications vary to a greater extent than can be allowed for within the possible range for lending rates. Lending rates charged by banks are normally restricted to a narrow range; there is an upper limit set by either legal restrictions or strong public and political resistance to high rates and there is a lower limit set by cost rigidities.[78] Loans, in

78. ". . . even if pure short-term interest . . . falls so low as to 1 per cent. per annum, the minimum rate which must be charged to the bulk of [bank] borrowers will nevertheless remain at an appreciably higher level than this. In fact the cost of short-term loans to most borrowers falls with the greatest difficulty below 4 per cent." Great Britain, Committee on Finance and Industry, *Report*, p. 103. Keynes, *The General Theory*, p. 208, thought that even if the pure rate of interest fell to zero banks would still have to charge borrowers a minimum of $1\frac{1}{2}$ to 2 per cent.

In Canada the spread in lending rates on ordinary loans is usually of the order of from $4\frac{1}{2}$ per cent to 6 per cent. Canada, Parliament, House, Standing Committee on Banking and Commerce, *Proceedings*, 1954, p. 579. But during the period of monetary restraint in 1956 and 1957 the minimum lending rate was gradually raised to $5\frac{3}{4}$ per cent. The (Montreal) *Gazette*, Feb. 11, 1958, p. 1. Thus the spread of lending rates in Canada was reduced to as narrow a range as from $5\frac{3}{4}$ per cent to 6 per cent, since Canadian banks are prohibited from charging more than 6 per cent for loans. Canada, Laws, Statutes, *Statutes of Canada*, 1953–54, 2–3

contrast, vary greatly in terms of quality and costs. They vary in their specific costs;[79] they vary in terms of their collateral advantages;[80] and they vary in the degree of risks that they present.[81] In view of the extent to which loans may differ among themselves, it seems improbable that variations in lending rates can so take account of the differences as to reduce all loan applications to an equal footing.[82] As a result, at each lending rate the quality of loans made at that rate most likely varies.[83] Consequently all acceptable loan applications may be arranged according to their profitability.[84]

Elizabeth II, c. 48, s. 91 (1), which, with minor exceptions, stipulates that no bank is to charge for a loan "any rate of interest or any rate of discount exceeding six per cent."

79. Canada, Parliament, House, Standing Committee on Banking and Commerce, *Proceedings*, 1954, p. 578, where the President of The Canadian Bankers' Association states that one of the cost items which enters into setting the interest charged for loans is the "work entailed in making and servicing specific types of loan." Also cf. Smith, "On the Effectiveness of Monetary Policy," p. 594n18.

80. That is, some borrowing accounts have a general profitability for the lending bank over and above the profit to be made on lending to such accounts: the size of the balances they carry with the lending bank and the amount of non-lending business (foreign exchange, collections, etc.) that they bring to the bank may make some borrowers more attractive than others to the bank. Cf. Riefler, *Money Rates and Money Markets*, p. 94.

81. Mints, *A History of Banking Theory*, p. 276; McKean, "Liquidity and a National Balance Sheet," *Readings in Monetary Theory*, p. 64, who argues that lenders classify their customers according to risk but that "within a single broad risk-category, *each* borrower presents a different degree of risk . . . since there can hardly be as many interest rates as there are degrees of risk."

82. Knight, *Risk, Uncertainty and Profit*, p. 326, states that "the loan market represents a narrower range of prices according to the grade and kind of the goods than is true of nearly any other market to be named."

83. United States Congress, Joint Committee on the Economic Report, *Monetary Policy and the Management of the Public Debt: Report of the Subcommittee on General Credit Control and Debt Management*, 82nd Cong., 2nd Sess., 1952, pp. 32–3, where it is stated that "the quality of loans on which the same interest rate is quoted varies considerably." This appears to be a crucial premise in the availability doctrine.

84. Musgrave, "Credit Controls, Interest Rates, and Management of Public Debt," p. 230, speaks of "differences in the net returns obtainable from different borrowers."

In this complex situation the curve relating the amount of loans requested by creditworthy borrowers to the net yield at existing lending rates on the various amounts will be a negative-sloping curve, such as *rd* in Figure 1B. For all loan amounts that lie within the capacity of the banking firm to make, the supply curve may be plotted as a horizontal line either coinciding with the loan axis or lying parallel to it at a distance determined by the positive net rate of return the banking firm looks for from loans. (Under certain circumstances, to be explained later, this portion of the supply curve may slope away from the loans axis.) At the point of maximum capacity for loans, however, the supply curve becomes vertical. Such a supply curve is depicted by *nms* in Figure 1B, *nm* representing the loan maximum.

The demand schedule for bank loans, as defined in the foregoing paragraph, may meet the supply schedule at a point before it turns vertical, such as at point *p* in Figure 1B. All creditworthy loan requests are then met, and the uncreditworthy ones that can be assessed entirely in terms of the profit calculus can be represented as an extension of the demand curve below the horizontal supply curve (the segment *pd* in Figure 1B). This extended portion of the demand curve shows that the net yield on the loan requests refused falls below the cut-off rate set by the banking firm: they are excluded because they are not profitable. Accordingly, a rise in lending rates will shift the whole demand curve upwards and will lead to an increase in the amount of loans granted. An improvement in the profitability of some loans at existing rates will alter the slope of the demand curve. A change in cash reserves will shift only the vertical portion of the supply curve and so alter the length of the horizontal part of the curve.

When the point of intersection between the demand and supply schedules for bank loans, as defined here, lies on the vertical part of the supply curve (such as p^1 in Figure 1B), some of the loan requests cut off represent profitable lending outlets because their net yields lie above that net yield at which the banking firm finds loans profitable. Credit rationing must then take place, but it can now be carried out on the basis of profitability. The profitable loan requests excluded can be excluded on the basis of net yields of a lower value than those on loan requests granted. That is, a system of rationing may proceed by meeting those requests yielding the highest returns to the banking firm and by refusing requests with the lowest returns (represented by the segment p^1d^1 in Figure 1B). The exclusion of loan applications from creditworthy sources then takes place on the same grounds as the exclusion of most applications from uncreditworthy sources: namely, on an assessment of the profitability of the proposition. An important difference, however, is that in the case of rationing a rise in lending rates merely shifts the demand curve upwards, if the amount demanded is unaffected by higher rates, without altering the amount of loans made. A change in reserves, however, alters the amount of loans granted.[85]

A partial form of credit rationing may occur when banks in expanding their loans are approaching the limit to their lending capacities. They may then begin to refrain from making certain loans that still offer profitable returns, while continuing to make loans which are more profitable. In other words, banks raise their cut-off rate—the net rate of return for which they are willing to make loans—in the vicinity of the point of capacity output; loan requests that otherwise would be met are refused so that more profitable ones can be accepted. That is, banks lessen the rate at which their diminishing capacity for making loans is used up, in order to ensure that, if total rationing becomes necessary, the requests refused are not of greater profitability than the loans they already have agreed to. A rise in the general level of lending rates does not eliminate this type of partial rationing, and a change in relative rates may alter only the kind of loans that are subject to partial rationing.

The cut-off rate for the net yield on loans set by banks may also rise when the cost of making additional loans increases. This is the situation that occurs when banks have excess lending capacity invested in government securities which they liquidate in order to accommodate an expansion in loans. The cost of making this sub-

---

85. The foregoing theory of credit rationing draws heavily on the theory of capital rationing presented by Joel Dean, *Managerial Economics* (Englewood Cliffs, N.J., Prentice-Hall, Inc., 1951), pp. 586, 596, 598–9.

stitution of loans for securities rises as security prices fall, as they are most likely to when the banking system is selling securities. The net return on the loans made by liquidating securities must then be greater than would otherwise be necessary for it to be worthwhile for the banks to carry out the substitution. Hence, some loan requests are now refused because they are not sufficiently profitable to allow for the extra cost involved in selling securities to accommodate them; but this refusal of loan requests which would have been met but for the fall in security prices does not represent true credit rationing: it represents merely the refusal to accommodate loan requests under unprofitable circumstances.[86] This situation, which is the core of the availability doctrine, is analyzed in greater detail later.

The nature and consequences of credit rationing may now be reviewed. There is always some unsatisfied demand for bank loans because lending rates are not sufficiently flexible to prevent excess demand. But not all excess demand represents credit rationing or the rejection of loans that are profitable and creditworthy but which cannot be accommodated. Some of the excess demand represents business which is unacceptable to the banks for reasons that cannot be incorporated into the profit calculus; and some of it simply represents unprofitable business at existing rates—unprofitable for qualitative reasons (uncertainty and risks) which can be incorporated into the profit calculus, for ordinary cost considerations (e.g. too expensive to administer), or for special cost considerations (such as the cost of drawing on excess lending capacity). Thus, all loan applications can be divided into acceptable and unacceptable, which correspond roughly to profitable and unprofitable. Credit rationing, as defined here, only arises when all the loan applications that fall into the acceptable and profitable category cannot be accommodated because of limited lending capacity. However, in rationing its loans

86. Samuelson, in *Hearings*, p. 697, appears to consider the refusal of a bank to accommodate a borrower at an unprofitable lending rate as credit rationing. If the loan application is unprofitable only because of the cost of getting the additional cash reserves to support the loan, the refusal to grant the loan request is akin to credit rationing when a *ceteris paribus* expansion in cash reserves results in the loan being made. This may happen in certain special circumstances to be analyzed later.

among its creditworthy borrowers, the banking firm may be able to distinguish the more profitable from the less profitable, so that the excluded creditworthy demand represents the least profitable sector of the market.

Thus, the banking firm in making loans distributes its loan "output" in the most profitable manner that it can. Considerations of creditworthiness cause it to restrict its lending in certain directions, and a limitation in capacity forces it to keep its loan output from exceeding a critical amount; but, within these two restraints, it provides what loans it can, and provides them in a manner designed to maximize its profits. How it varies its "output" of loans and securities to maximize its profits is the next topic that must be considered.

THE THEORY OF THE BANKING FIRM

Having dealt with the exclusion of some demand for bank loans from the market, it is now proper to turn to the question of how the banking firm satisfies the demand it does. What must now be considered is how the volume of loans supplied by the banking firm fluctuates in various circumstances. The analysis distinguishes between a banking firm having no excess capacity for making loans and one that does. The former involves no special problems; the latter presents the question of possible different profits goals that such a firm may follow. This question of profit goals must be examined before the "output" behaviour of banking firms is explained, first in terms of an "expansion-path" effect, and then in terms of a substitution effect. The analysis, in short, is an analysis of "output" behaviour in banking, carried out in terms of the theory of the firm.[87]

87. The analysis of general output behaviour in banking must, strictly speaking, relate to an individual bank; but in a banking system where a few large banks predominate, doing the same general kind of business and having similar costs, the analysis of output behaviour could without difficulty apply to a community of banks. The crucial assumption for a community analysis is the assumption of similar costs, which is perhaps not too heroic an assumption to make for a banking system like the Canadian one. The Canadian chartered banks use common costs, prepared by a cost committee of The Canadian Bankers' Association, for such purposes as setting service charges. Canada, Parliament, House, Standing Committee on Banking and Commerce, *Proceedings*, 1954, p. 270, which gives the

The Banking Firm without Excess Lending Capacity

The banking firm that has no excess lending capacity is supplying to the community all the funds it can by way of loans. With its given cash reserves and cash-reserve ratio it cannot expand its loans any further. The government securities and money-market assets that it holds in its secondary reserves are at their irreducible minimum, so that the banking firm cannot, as a matter of policy, plan on substituting additional loans for the securities it is now holding. Thus, the banking firm with no excess capacity for making loans is in effect a one-product firm, for all its discretionary resources are directed towards one output end—the provision of loans.

When the banking firm is carrying all the loans it can and yet is not rationing credit, it is maximizing its profits from loans for a given demand and for existing lending rates. The fact that it is not rationing its credit means that it does not have to turn down loan applications that would be profitable to it at existing rates. As in the ordinary theory of the firm, all additional units of output result in negative marginal returns to total profit. All existing loans yield positive net returns but additional loans would only reduce its total profit.

This banking firm is then in equilibrium in the sense that it is making all the loans it can and for the given demand conditions has no incentive to expand loans. Nevertheless it is not rationing credit. An increase in its cash reserves would not cause it to expand its loans; instead, an increase in reserves would only give it excess capacity for making loans. A reduction in its cash reserves, however, would cause this banking firm to reduce its loans because it no longer has sufficient capacity to support the existing total. The reduction may be carried out directly and immediately, or the reduction may proceed by way of a liquidation of secondary reserves. If the secondary reserves are reduced, then loans are reduced gradually, as opportunity permits, and the secondary reserves restored to the required level.

A fall in demand for loans from the one-product banking firm that

evidence of the President of The Canadian Bankers' Association on the subject of banking costs in Canada.

is in equilibrium gives the firm excess lending capacity; if this does not prompt a defensive change in the lending policy of the bank, it converts the bank into a two-product firm in that its excess lending capacity becomes utilized in some other manner than making loans. A rise in the demand for loans from the banking firm places it in disequilibrium because it cannot meet the additional demand with its present capacity already fully used in making loans. The increase in demand means an increase in loan requests that represent profitable lending opportunities at existing rates. Unless the banking firm raises those rates sufficiently to prevent the appearance of excess demand of a profitable nature, the banking firm has to begin to ration its credit.

So much for the banking firm with no excess lending capacity that does not have to ration credit while providing its maximum amount of loans: now for the one-product banking firm that has to ration credit and so is not in equilibrium. Such a banking firm has to refuse to fully meet profitable requests for loans—requests on which the net return is positive. However, on the basis of the theory of credit rationing expounded in the previous section, all loans that the rationing bank is making have positive net yields and are in excess of the net yields that would be earned on the loan requests which are being refused. In this situation any increase in the cash reserves of the rationing bank will result in an expansion of its loans—an expansion that will continue as capacity increases until the need to ration disappears. Any further increase in reserves beyond this point then converts it into a banking firm with excess lending capacity: that is, it ceases to expand its loans and begins to use its banking capacity or resources in other ways. A reduction in cash reserves only makes the rationing worse: loans must be reduced because of the reduction in capacity, and, unless lending rates are raised, the reduction is carried out by rationing more severely.

The banking firm that is rationing credit may always raise its lending rates in an attempt to eliminate profitable excess demand, but such an increase in lending rates cannot lead to an expansion in its loans, because it is already supplying these to the maximum possible. A fall in the demand for loans from the rationing bank will also reduce the degree of rationing, and if the fall in demand goes far enough, it will eliminate rationing altogether, and may even result in the banking firm developing excess lending capacity. A rise in demand, by giving rise to an increase in the number of profitable applications presented to the bank, will increase the degree of rationing necessary at existing rates.

In summary, the banking firm with no excess capacity for making loans is either not rationing its limited supply of loans among profitable applicants (it is then in equilibrium) or else it is rationing loans. In either case the expansion path for the one-product banking firm— that is, the geometrical representation of the extent to which it will increase or decrease its loans when its lending capacity is increased or decreased—is what has previously been labelled the securities-threshold locus. This is the locus that shows, on the iso-profit map for the loans and securities of the banking firm, the minimum amount of securities the banking firm wishes to hold for each volume of loans. The locus can probably be represented by a straight line (such as OP^1 in Figure 2, p. 104) deviating slightly from the loans axis and towards the securities axis, thus indicating that variations in capacity result mainly in variations in loans outstanding. There is less than a one-for-one correspondence between changes in lending capacity and the changes in loans that follow because of the release and absorption of capacity to meet changing liquidity needs as the loan volume alters.[88]

88. There is a possibility that the threshold locus in this case may not remain invariant for a contraction. The fall in bank profits may cause the contracting bank to reduce the size of its liquidity hedge relative to its total of earning assets by substituting loans for securities. In this way the bank can modify the reduction in its profits, for it can then move to a higher profit contour. Such a reaction would be reflected in a movement of the threshold locus towards the loans axis.

Earl R. Rolph, "Principles of Debt Management," *American Economic Review*, 47 (June 1957), 319, and Joseph Aschheim, *Techniques of Monetary Control* (Baltimore, The Johns Hopkins Press, 1961), pp. 23–4, both argue that a fall in bank income will cause a bank to sacrifice liquidity by shifting out of securities into loans. They explain such behaviour as being motivated by a rise in the marginal utility of income resulting from a fall in total income. Aschheim, p. 41n11, further argues that an increase in returns from loans relative to those from securities induces banks to sacrifice liquidity. This too would cause the threshold locus to move towards the loans axis.

Such reactions only occur in the one-product banking firm, for the bank with

There are no substitution possibilities to consider for the one-product banking firm: it makes all the loans it can, which exhausts its disposable capacity so that there is no question of substituting additional loans for some other form of providing funds to the community. Such a substitution possibility only arises when the banking firm has excess lending capacity—that is, capacity that it is not using for making loans but which may be so used if profitable to do so.

The "Two-Product" Banking Firm

The more usual situation, until quite recently, has been for banking firms to have excess capacity for making loans, the excess capacity being carried in the form of government securities for amounts well in excess of what is required for liquidity hedges. Thus, a banking firm develops excess lending capacity when, after making all the profitable loans it can and allowing for its normal security requirements, it still has capacity for acquiring additional earning assets. The only outlet for the excess lending capacity is likely to be government securities; for at existing security prices, lending rates, and demand conditions, the banking firm has no incentive to utilize any of its excess lending capacity in carrying more loans: the only loan applications that are going unsatisfied are those definitely unprofitable under prevailing conditions. Therefore, the banking firm with excess lending capacity may be treated as a two-product firm for it is providing funds to the community in two forms—by making loans and buying securities. This is not a case of joint products, however. With no restraint on capacity, a banking firm could hold all the securities it wanted without altering its loans; or it could hold all the

---

excess lending capacity need not reduce its liquidity hedge to substitute loans for securities. When a one-product banking firm reduces its liquidity hedge relative to its total earning assets, it means that the bank has reassessed its liquidity needs and feels it can operate with less of a hedge. This is akin to a structural or organizational change induced, as are all such changes, by considerations of profit. As such it is not likely to be a short-run or rapid change and it would probably require more than a marginal change in profits to cause it. For marginal changes in profits, it seems unlikely that a bank would alter its assessment of its liquidity requirements.

loans it wanted without altering its securities.[89] But with a restraint
on capacity, loans and securities become what have been called
alternative products;[90] an increase in the output of one must be
accompanied by a reduction in the output of the other.

The profit goal for the two-product firm, expressed in geometrical
terms, is to reach the peak of the profit mound for the two products
that it produces. At that point the profit from each product is maximized, and of course the joint profit, or total profit from both sources,
is also maximized. This means that each product is being produced
up to the amount at which its marginal profit falls to zero. Although
other firms may achieve this state of bliss, the two-product banking
firm may not. For one thing, the restraint imposed by its limited cash
reserves prevents it from reaching the peak of its profit mound; but
for another, its profit mound does not rise to a single peak of maximum profits for a finite amount of security holdings. That is, the net
yield from government securities does not fall to zero or even become
zero as the banking firm increases its holdings. Thus, the banking
firm unrestricted by a restraint imposed by cash reserves could in
effect expand its holdings of government securities forever, without
suffering a deterioration of profits. What this means geometrically is
that the profit mound for bank loans and government securities never
comes to a peak for any finite value for securities: the point of maximum profit then lies at infinity for securities, but at some finite value
for loans.[91]

89. That is, variations in the amount of loans made have no effect on the costs
of holding securities or on the returns from securities when there is no restraint on
capacity. A relationship of this nature defines products that are technically independent: an increase in the production of one product does not affect the
marginal cost of the other. Sune Carlson, *A Study on the Pure Theory of Production*
(London, P. S. King and Son, Ltd., 1939), p. 83.

90. Dean, *Managerial Economics*, p. 317.

91. An analysis which implies that the profit mound for loans and securities
does come to a peak is offered by Basil John Moore, "The Effects of Counter-
Cyclical Monetary Policy on the Canadian Chartered Banks, 1935–1957" (Unpublished Ph.D. dissertation, The Johns Hopkins University, 1958), Ch. IX, p.
267. (Pagination is that of a privately mimeographed copy and differs from that
of the dissertation. This copy is in the library of The Royal Bank of Canada, other
copies are deposited at the head offices of the various chartered banks in Canada.)

Because the point of maximum profit for both products is un-attainable for the two-product banking firm, it is forced to seek the lesser profit possibilities open to the two-product firm operating under a capacity restraint. Such a firm, if it formulates a precise profit policy under these conditions, is likely either to maximize its joint profit for both products or to maximize its profit in one direction only, foregoing the greater profit obtainable from maximizing joint profits. The nature of each of these profit-maximization goals as they relate to the banking firm requires examination in detail.

The two-product firm operating under a budget or capacity re-straint that prevents it from reaching the peak of its profit mound maximizes its joint profits when the ratio of the marginal net returns from the two products is equal to the marginal rate of transformation between the two products—a familiar equilibrium principle.[92] The marginal net return from either product will be positive and greater than zero. Geometrically, the equilibrium situation in which joint profits are maximized is given by the point where an iso-profit con-tour for the two products is tangent to their transformation curve— the curve that shows at what rate one product can be substituted for

---

Dr. Moore assumes that the marginal cost of funds to a bank rises as it expands, and this, together with falling marginal net returns from securities, means that, at some point, marginal net profit from securities is zero and that beyond this point it becomes increasingly negative. Dr. Moore then argues that to avoid negative marginal net profits from securities a bank will hold excess cash reserves.

The cost of funds, however, does not seem relevant for determining in what form a bank should invest its excess cash—i.e. cash in excess of what it needs to carry for reserve purposes. Given excess cash, the cost of funds is irrelevant. It will always appear to any bank that it can expand its profits by investing any excess cash it has. In investing that excess, of course, it may find its deposits rising, and its cost rising as well, the rise in cost reducing its profits. Its course of action then is not to carry excess cash, but either to refuse additional deposits or to adjust service charges and deposit rates. It is difficult to see, however, how a bank runs into a rising cost of funds in expanding. There is no reason service charges should fall or deposit rates rise (the two components of the cost of funds) as a bank expands by trying to use up excess cash. Thus, with the marginal cost of funds zero, or just not relevant, it is unlikely that marginal net profits from securities would fall to zero or become negative, and so cause the profit mound to come to a peak.

92. Cf. Kenneth E. Boulding, *Economic Analysis* (New York, Harper and Brothers, 1941), pp. 524–5; Carlson, *A Study on the Pure Theory of Production*, p. 98n2.

another.[93] (The point P in Figure 2, p. 104, represents such an equilibrium point.) The iso-profit curve (II in Figure 2) shows the total profit to be earned from the two products, and the slope of the curve represents the ratio of the net returns from the two products. Hence, a movement away from the equilibrium point along the transformation curve (MP¹PS) means that the net revenue given up on the product sacrificed to make the movement exceeds the gain in net revenue from the addition made to the output of the other product.

The application of this geometry to the two-product banking firm requires considerable care because it depends on including in a *ceteris paribus* clause the appropriate parameters, some of a rather complex nature. Care in the selection of these parameters is essential in order to ensure a stable profit mound. The demand for bank loans and lending rates must of course be fixed; but, in addition, the ordering of loan applications must also be fixed, because the order in which the amount lent is built up and altered affects the slope of the iso-profit curves. Security yields must either be held constant or must vary in a known manner, which is incorporated into the iso-profit curves. The ordering of the securities held, acquired, and disposed of must also be fixed, for they are not homogeneous and so a change in ordering securities would also alter the iso-profit curves. Finally, for each total of earning assets there can be two different levels of deposits, depending on whether the combination is reached as a result

---

93. Carlson, ibid. The transformation curve for bank loans and holdings of securities is not, as it is for physical output, an iso-cost curve. That is, the curve does not show what amounts of loans can be substituted for securities for the same total costs but rather shows the rate at which loans can be substituted for securities, given the amount of securities now being held; this rate of transformation is of course a function of the price of securities. Total cost may very well vary along this transformation curve because there is no reason why all the various combinations of loans and securities that a bank can hold should involve the same total cost, especially when the quality of loans is not homogeneous. The nature of the transformation curve for physical output is discussed by R. G. D. Allen, *Mathematical Analysis for Economists* (London, Macmillan and Co., Limited, 1947), pp. 122–3. The transformation curve that is relevant for assets is briefly described by Kenneth E. Boulding, *A Reconstruction of Economics* (New York, John Wiley and Sons, Inc., 1950), p. 61.

of a change in the reserve ratio or in cash reserves. If the cash ratio
is held fixed for all combinations of earning assets, there is only one
deposit total associated with each combination, hence only one deposit cost, and only one profit figure.

Given these parameters, a system of iso-profit curves, which takes
into account the specific costs of making loans and of holding securities, can be derived for loans and securities. (Securities must be
measured in terms of acquisition costs.) The iso-profit curves will
have the usual shape for economic isoquants: the greater the amount
of loans the less the amount of securities needed in order to keep
total profits constant. The qualitative variation in the loans made
gives the contours their curvature. A family of iso-profit curves appears in Figure 2, a typical iso-profit curve being II.

The transformation curve that may be imposed on the foregoing
iso-profit map is the technical possibility curve for the banking firm.
Its intercepts with the axes, which measure amounts of loans and

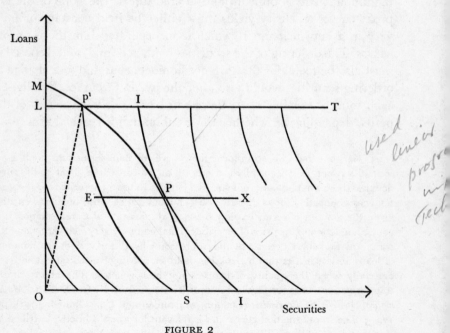

FIGURE 2

PROFIT CONTOUR MAP FOR THE BANKING FIRM

securities, mark on the one hand the maximum amount of loans the banking firm may make on the basis of its given cash reserves, and on the other the maximum amount of securities it could conceivably hold. The rate at which securities may be converted into loans, or loans into securities, is reflected in the slope of the transformation curve (curve MP¹PS in Figure 2), which depends on the prices of the securities acquired or disposed of. The disposal and acquisition policies for securities must be consistent with the iso-profit curves used, and the security prices that give the transformation curve its slope are the prices used in deriving the iso-profit curves. Thus, the amount of securities that can be obtained with the repayment proceeds from, say, a thousand-dollar loan is determined by the prices of the securities bought. Likewise, the amount of securities that must be sold in order to accommodate a given expansion in loans, when cash reserves are held constant, depends on the prices received for the securities disposed of.

Security amounts are measured in terms of acquisition costs so any capital gains or losses realized in disposing of securities are reflected only in the shrinkage of the amount of securities held. That is, capital losses or gains represent a transfer cost: the cost of moving from one combination of loans and securities to another combination containing more loans and fewer securities than the first one. The iso-profit curves do not reflect this transfer cost, which is not essential for assessing whether or not one combination of loans and securities yields a greater net profit per unit of time than some other combination. A capital loss being an absolute amount, and not a flow, does not interfere with the comparison of profitability based on flows: any combination of loans and securities that yields a greater profit than some other combination is the more profitable one, even though a capital loss must be taken to achieve the more profitable combination; for given enough time the differential in profits per unit of time will eventually be able to offset any absolute amount of capital loss. However, under certain circumstances examined further on, capital losses may interfere with making a profitable substitution.

In equilibrium the banking firm maximizes its joint profits for loans and securities by holding that combination of loans and securities which is represented by the point of tangency between its transformation and iso-profit curves for loans and securities—the point P in Figure 2.[94] In theory, any alteration in the ratio formed by the net yields on loans and securities, as when it becomes possible to make new loans at higher net yields than existing ones or when security yields rise, should encourage a substitution between loans and securities in order to keep joint profits at a maximum. Changes that affect the yields on loans alone alter the iso-profit curves and so the point of tangency with the transformation curve; changes that affect the net return from securities alter not only the shape or slope of the iso-profit curves but also the slope of the transformation curve. In addition, a change in the cash reserves of the banking firm alters the size of the transformation curve and so introduces not only the possibility of a substitution effect but also a reserve or capacity effect. Both the substitution effect and the capacity effect are examined in detail later; but first another possibility for profits other than the maximization of joint products must be considered.

The two-product firm operating under a capacity restraint that treats one product as essential or preferred and the other as a by-product or a residual is likely to maximize the profit from its preferred output and to take whatever profit it can from the other. This means that it produces the favoured product up to the point where the marginal net return on it falls to zero; with what output capacity it still has left it produces what it can of the other product. The secondary product is a true residual in that resources for its production represent only those that the firm cannot profitably use in the production of the favoured product: the profit to be earned from the residual product does not influence its production so long as it is positive. Consequently, the total profits earned by the firm that behaves like this is less than the maximum it could earn,[95] and the

94. The geometry of the banking firm, which runs in terms of transformation curves and iso-profit curves and other concepts derived from these, is severely restrictive in view of all the variables that must be fixed in order to get a stable set of curves. However, the limitations of the geometry do not interfere with the analysis in the text, which relies on the geometry to illustrate specific points.

95. An alternative treatment of this situation in which the amount of one product remains fixed while the other varies is suggested by Moore, Ch. IX, 264–6, and Diagram 1, 2, and 3. He uses an average net revenue curve for loans that is kinked at the average return for the prevailing interest rate charged on

production criterion it follows is to produce the preferred product up to the point where its marginal net return falls to zero.[96]

Now a banking firm is not unlikely to view making or carrying loans as a preferred "product" and to treat security holdings in excess of its minimum requirements for secondary reserves as a true residual, variations in which reflect changes in excess capacity for making loans. If banks consider loans their prime regard and treat securities as a residual investment, they do not attempt to maximize their joint profits from loans and securities, but instead, in ordinary times, look mainly to the maximization of their profits from loans.[97] This is not to say that what banks can earn on securities has no implications for lending policies, but lending policies can be altered for other reasons than the pursuit of maximum joint profits.

---

loans. Above the kink the curve is very elastic; below the kink, very inelastic. For the amount of loans at which the kink arises the marginal net return varies over a range of positive and negative values because of the discontinuity in the curve caused by the kink. Thus, the marginal net return from securities may vary, as a result of variations in the quantity of securities held, over a wide range of values, corresponding to the gap between the positive part of the marginal net return curve for loans and the loans axis, and still remain equal to the marginal return from loans. Under this scheme a bank would be carrying the maximum amount in loans, varying its security holdings as a residual, and maintaining a condition of equilibrium.

96. This is similar to the situation of a firm that in using two variable inputs to produce a given product moves up its profit mound by maximizing its profit from the use of one input while using different assigned amounts of the other input. This possibility for the expansion of the firm producing a physical output was apparently first discussed by F. Y. Edgeworth, "Contributions to the Theory of Railway Rates," *Economic Journal*, *21* (Sept. 1911), 367. James Dingwall, "Equilibrium and Process Analysis in the Traditional Theory of the Firm," *Canadian Journal of Economics and Political Science*, *10* (Nov. 1944), 451–2, discusses the same possibility in a little more detail than Edgeworth and independently of Edgeworth's work. B. S. Keirstead, *The Theory of Economic Change* (Toronto, The Macmillan Company of Canada, Limited, 1948), pp. 227–8, presents a useful exposition of Dingwall's discussion of the case under consideration.

97. Breckenridge, *The Canadian Banking System*, pp. 450–1, gives a striking example of Canadian banks, during a period of monetary stringency in 1893, sacrificing very attractive returns from other sources in preference to satisfying the credit needs of their own customers, although they thereby forewent a greater profit.

The policy of maximizing profits from loans alone may be illustrated by use of the ridge line that can be introduced into the iso-profit map of the banking firm. The ridge line marks the peak of the profit mound in the direction of the loans axis; it is therefore the locus of all points where the iso-profit curves turn parallel to the loans axis, because along the ridge line the net return from loans is zero—that is, total profits from loans are a maximum. (In Figure 2 this occurs along the line LP¹IT which is the ridge line for loans.) Furthermore, profits from loans, unlike profits from securities, can be maximized for some finite value because of qualitative variations in loans: net yields on loan applications presented to a banking firm thus vary over a range of positive numbers through zero into negative values. Therefore, from a given total of loan applications the banking firm may select all those amounts that it may lend to yield a positive return, excluding those amounts which represent negative yields. Profits from the applications accepted will then be the largest that can be earned from loans under existing demand conditions. And since the amount of loans for which loan profits are a maximum is independent of the amount of securities the banking firm holds, the ridge line marking the loan values at which net profits for loans is zero lies parallel to the securities axis.

The point where the transformation curve for loans and securities cuts this ridge line for loans defines the equilibrium combination of loans and securities for the banking firm intent on maximizing its profits from loans. When a point on the ridge line is attained with a given lending capacity (such as the point P¹ in Figure 2), it reflects a policy of making all profitable loans that can be made at existing lending rates. When the transformation curve is not large enough to cut the ridge line, the banking firm cannot make all the loans that it wants to, if it is attempting to maximize its profits from loans, and it must ration credit. Loans outstanding then vary as the transformation curve shrinks or expands because of changes in cash reserves; they also vary as a result of changes in demand conditions which shifts the ridge line for loans when this cuts the transformation curve.

So much for the two possible and definite profit goals that might be followed by the banking firm operating with excess lending capacity. These two possibilities lie at opposite ends of the scale for profit values. That is, the banking firm may maximize its joint profits from loans and securities, or it may maximize its profit from loans alone—a smaller profit than maximum joint profits and a profit value that it is most likely to consider as the acceptable minimum. It is most unlikely to hold a combination of loans and securities that yield less than the maximum profit on loans, although it may hold combinations of loans and securities that yield larger profits than the maximum for loans, the limit being the maximum for joint profits. Values for profits between the loan maximum and the joint maximum arise in transitional periods when the banking firm has to compromise in pursuing one of the two definite profit goals. These compromise possibilities are considered later in the discussion of adjustments to lending policies that usually arise when preferred profit goals have to be compromised.

The following two sections deal only with the two clearly defined profit goals discussed fully in this section. The next section considers the nature of the expansion path for the banking firm under both profit goals; the analysis is designed to show how the total amount of loans carried by the banking firm varies as its cash reserves, and so its capacity for making loans, are altered. The section after that considers the nature of the substitution effect and is designed to answer the question of what effect changes in security yields have on loan volume.

Expansion Paths for Banking Firms

Briefly, "expansion path" is the name given to the curve, superimposed on an iso-profit map, that shows how a firm alters its output as its resources are varied. For the banking firm the relevant resources for an expansion-path analysis are cash reserves, of which lending capacity is a function. Variations in its cash reserves then reflect a known variation in the lending capacity of the banking firm; the expansion path must show how changes in this lending capacity affect the amount of loans and securities held. Two classes of expansion path must be distinguished: one for the banking firm maximizing its profits from loans, and one for the banking firm maximizing its joint profits from loans and securities.

The expansion path for the banking firm concerned solely with maximizing its profits from loans must coincide with the ridge line for loans that can be drawn into the iso-profit map. That is, if a firm has excess lending capacity and is maximizing its loan profits, it is meeting all loan requests that yield a positive return; *ceteris paribus* changes in its cash reserves and lending capacity that do not eliminate the excess capacity it has for making loans can only result in a variation in its security holdings. In these circumstances the banking firm is not going to expand its loans when its capacity for making loans is further enhanced, because only unprofitable lending opportunities are open to it; nor is it going to reduce its loans when it loses some of its excess capacity for making loans, for it will then not be maximizing its profits from loans. Rather it will dispose of government securities, the form in which its excess lending capacity is invested, for *ceteris paribus* changes in capacity. In short, changes in the capacity of the banking firm that has excess lending capacity and that maximizes loan profits result only in variations in its security holdings under the conditions for which an expansion-path analysis holds.

The *ceteris paribus* conditions for which an expansion path may be defined for a banking firm are demand, lending rates, and security prices, of which only the first two are crucial for the banking firm intent on maximizing its profits from loans alone. When the demand for bank loans and lending rates are held constant, the ridge line for loans on the iso-profit map for loans and securities is fixed. This ridge line marks the combinations of loans and securities that the banking firm maximizing loan profits will hold under various capacity limitations. In the language of the theory of the firm, the ridge line is an isocline—a locus of all points at which the slopes of the various contour curves are equal—and since the expansion path is only the isocline that marks how a firm moves over its profit mound, the ridge line for loans in this case also represents the expansion path for the banking firm.[98] The locus LT in Figure 2 is such an isocline.

98. For any given iso-profit map there is a whole system of isoclines, each isocline in the system joining all points where the iso-profit curves have equal slopes. A ridge line is a special isocline in that it is the locus of all points where the iso-profit curves turn parallel to one of the axes. The expansion path for the firm that utilizes both of its variables is simply the particular isocline defined for the

With demand and lending rates constant, variations in the lending capacity of the banking firm, as already indicated, result only in variations in its security holdings. As its capacity expands and the banking firm buys more securities, because it cannot profitably expand loans under the stated conditions, its profits also rise, but at a diminishing rate if security prices rise against the buying bank. The net yields from government securities always remain positive, however, so that there is no reason the banking firm, as its reserves and capacity increase, should not go on buying securities exclusively. In a contraction there is no doubt that the banking firm maximizing its profits from loans and carrying more securities than it needs for its secondary reserves (i.e. it has excess lending capacity invested in securities) would liquidate securities as its reserves were reduced if security prices remained constant. In this way the banking firm would keep its loan volume constant and continue to maximize its profits from loans, although total profits would fall as securities were liquidated. The liquidation of securities would proceed as reserves and capacity shrank, until all excess lending capacity was eliminated; at that point the banking firm would be transformed into one without excess lending capacity, and further contraction would proceed mainly by way of liquidating loans, as already explained in a previous section.

However, if in the process of contraction security prices fall sufficiently to make the banking firm incur capital losses in selling securities, its profits will be reduced by more than the revenue foregone on the securities sold. In these circumstances the bank by departing from

---

conditions under which the firm expands or contracts its scale of operations. The relevant isocline is usually fixed by the relative prices for the two variables on which the iso-profit map is based; when these relative prices are held constant to rule out substitution effects, movement over the profit mound that simply represents changes in scale must proceed through points at which the slopes of iso-profit curves remain constant and equal to the given relative prices.

The relationship between isoclines and the expansion path is developed by Carlson, *A Study on the Pure Theory of Production*, p. 36, who also discusses the general nature of expansion paths and isoclines (pp. 31–41). Some refinements to the general analysis of the expansion path appear in J. A. Galbraith, "Extensions of Contour Analysis in Economic Theory" (Unpublished Master's thesis, McGill University, 1950), p. 200.

E

its policy of maximizing loan profits may be able to moderate the fall in profits that naturally occurs as its capacity shrinks: instead of contracting solely by liquidating securities it may contract by withdrawing from some loans as well as from securities. This is a profit-saving move when the capital loss avoided, converted to a time-rate on the basis of the number of periods that the banking firm plans ahead, plus the revenue from the securities that are retained by liquidating loans instead of securities, exceeds the revenue from the loans that are liquidated. The banking firm in departing from the policy of maximizing profits from loans does not avoid a fall in its profits, for such a fall must follow when its cash reserves or lending capacity is reduced, but it does reduce the extent of the fall in profits. The avoidance of a further loss in profits is likely to provide a stronger incentive to depart from a policy of maximizing loan profits than the incentive which always exists under such a policy, that of increasing profits by departing from the policy; that is, the possibility of increasing profits by carrying less loans and more securities is likely to be much less tempting to the banking firm than the possibility of moderating a fall in profits by holding more securities and fewer loans.

When the banking firm departs from a policy of maximizing loan profits during a period of contraction, the situation is represented on the iso-profit map for loans and securities as a movement away from the ridge line for loans along the new and smaller transformation curve resulting from the contraction towards the point at which the curve is tangent to an iso-profit curve. The combination of loans and securities that it holds after the contraction process ceases is represented by one of the points on the transformation curve lying between the point of tangency with an iso-profit contour and the point of intersection with the ridge line. Just where the point of rest will lie on the segment of the transformation curve delineated in the foregoing manner depends largely on how far the banking firm can avoid liquidating securities by withdrawing from loans instead. If it succeeds in reducing its loans, it does so according to the profit criterion: loans are dropped which are no longer profitable because their net revenue cannot compensate for the capital losses and lost security revenue that would occur if securities were liquidated to carry these loans. This withdrawal from loans does not represent credit rationing but merely the giving up of business that is no longer profitable under the changed lending conditions. At the final combination of loans and securities achieved by withdrawing from some loans, total profits will be greater than they would have been had the banking firm continued to maximize loan profits but less than they would be if the banking firm were maximizing joint profits from loans and securities.

The analysis of the expansion path for the banking firm maximizing loan profits may now be summarized. *Ceteris paribus* variations in cash reserves, or lending capacity, lead the banking firm to alter only its holdings of securities; its loans outstanding remain fixed. If the *ceteris paribus* clause is relaxed to permit security prices to vary, the banking firm that continues to maximize loan profits will ignore movements in security prices and continue to respond in the same way to increases in its lending capacity as it does when security prices remain constant. However, when its capacity is being reduced and security prices are falling, there is a strong possibility that the bank will depart from the policy of maximizing loan profits alone and alter its lending policy. Alterations in lending policies, however, lie outside the analysis of expansion paths, and, accordingly, are treated in fuller detail in a later part of this chapter.

Now to turn to the expansion path of the banking firm that maximizes its joint profits from loans and securities. This expansion path is represented geometrically by the isocline formed by the locus of points at which the slopes of the various iso-profit contours are equal to the existing rate of transformation for loans and securities—that is, to the current market price for the securities that would be involved in any substitution process with loans. (The line EPX in Figure 2 is an isocline.) This isocline is the expansion path along which the banking firm would move if security prices remained constant and all other conditions required for a stable profit mound were met. Along that path the ratio of the marginal yields on loans and securities remains constant and equal to the marginal rate of transformation; so that nowhere along the expansion path can banking profits be increased by the bank holding some other proportion of loans and securities that does not define a point on the expansion path. In other words, along the expansion path there is no substitution of loans for securities or vice versa, but only alterations in the totals for loans and for securities, as the capacity for holding loans and securities varies.

To keep joint profits from securities and loans at a maximum when its capacity varies, the banking firm must keep the ratio of net yields from loans to the net yields from securities constant, in order to stay on its expansion path. Therefore, an examination of how net yields from loans and securities may be expected to alter for variations in loans and securities will indicate the nature of the expansion path.

The net yield on loans varies of course with the amount of loans made: the greater the amount of loans granted from a given total of loan applications, the more lower-yielding loan propositions that have to be accepted. Diminishing net yields on loans are a function of the heterogeneous nature of loan applications, but not generally of loans already made. That is, the net yield on additional units of loan "output" is not related to the amount of output already being produced, as is the case in physical output processes. The one exception arises when the principle of increasing risk or uncertainty applies. When that principle applies, an increase in loans of a particular class makes additional loans of the same class less desirable and so less profitable. Furthermore, the net yield on any loan application is independent of the amount of securities held when just the normal cost and revenue of that loan application is taken into account in computing its net yield.

Likewise, the net yield on securities is unaffected by the amount of loans held; indeed the net yield on securities is not even affected by the amount of securities held, when security prices are held fixed, as they are for expansion-path analysis. The gross yield from securities then remains a constant for variations in security holdings so long as the composition of the securities held does not change. The cost (on a yield basis) of investing available funds in securities is likewise probably a constant; either there is no marginal cost or there is a constant marginal cost for a given composition of securities. At least there are no input factor prices that should vary when security holdings are increased, and hence there is nothing to induce diminishing returns and so rising marginal costs. The net yield from securities then should never fall to zero.

If the net yield on securities does remain invariant for changes in security holdings, the ratio of net yields on loans to net yields on securities remains a constant for all movements over the loans-securities profit contours parallel to the securities axis. In other words all the isoclines for the profit contours lie parallel to the ridge line for loans (LIT in Figure 2) and to the security axis, indicating that the iso-profit curves are parallel to each other in the direction of the security axis.[99] The expansion path, which is a particular isocline such as EPX in Figure 2, then lies parallel to the security axis indicating that a *ceteris paribus* change in cash reserves and lending capacity results only in the banking firm changing its holdings of securities. Its volume of loans outstanding remains fixed and is not disturbed so long as only capacity effects are involved, unless excess capacity is eliminated by a contraction in overall capacity.

In actuality, net yields on securities may not remain exactly constant for all changes in security holdings, but no significant variation in net yields is likely to occur so long as security prices and the composition of security holdings remain fixed. (Variations in security holdings are dealt with in the following section.) However, when a banking firm obtains increased capacity, it may in adding to its security holdings alter its investment policy, thus changing the composition of securities held and in a way that causes a significant change in net yields. An alteration in investment policy will usually not cause the net yields earned on additional securities acquired to fall—the banking firm can avoid this by merely maintaining the existing composition of its securities. Thus, the only movement in net security yields, when the banking firm expands its holdings on the

99. This is the situation that arises in contour analysis when the mound from which the contours are derived comes to a peak or ridge for finite values in one direction, but rises continuously in the direction of the other axis without coming to a peak for any finite values. In consumer analysis this possibility is represented by the indifference map for two commodities, the demand for one of which is not capable of saturation. This means that the marginal utility of the insatiable good never falls to zero and can indeed be taken as a constant, which when the insatiable good is money provides the geometrical representation of the Marshallian assumption of the constant marginal utility of money. Cf. J. A. Galbraith, "Indifference Maps for Indispensable Goods," *Review of Economic Studies, 20* (1952–53), 152–3, and "Extensions of Contour Analysis in Economic Theory," pp. 97–8.

basis of increased lending capacity, is an upward movement: the banking firm utilizes its new capacity to acquire securities yielding more than its existing holdings. Theoretically the banking firm maximizing joint profits should substitute securities for loans because relative yields on loans and securities now favour such a substitution. In fact such a substitution is improbable, for the possibility of carrying out such a substitution existed before but was not adopted. It is as if the banking firm decided upon the volume of loans it wanted to make at existing security prices; it is unlikely to change that decision in favour of fewer loans when all that has changed is lending capacity. The decision to make the new addition to excess capacity yield more than the existing excess capacity is therefore unrelated to lending policy; only a change in net yields from securities that is independent of investment policy reacts on lending policy and induces a substitution effect.

Hence, when the lending capacity of a banking firm that is maximizing its joint profits from loans and securities expands, the path of expansion is likely to be outwards across the profit contours in a direction running parallel to the security axis. The banking firm continues to maximize joint profits on the basis of the old lending and investing policies, but it takes advantage of a change in capacity to alter its investment policy independently of its lending policy, in order to reap still further profits.

When lending capacity is contracted, however, the nature of the reaction may differ from the simple policy of just altering security holdings to the extent necessary. The forced liquidation of securities that the banking firm must undertake, when it suffers a loss of lending capacity, may also cause a change in the composition of the securities that it holds, which eventually reacts on lending policy. Thus, during a contraction process, in which security prices are held constant, the banking firm may, for a while, restrict the loss on security income to about the average of what it can earn on its poorest loans, or to less than this, by liquidating low-yielding securities. But, if the contraction proceeds far enough, it may find itself liquidating securities on which the net yield exceeds what is being earned on some of its loans because it has to begin liquidating higher yielding securities. When that occurs, the banking firm can only continue to maximize its joint profits, and incidently to moderate the fall in its profits, by liquidating lower-yielding loans in place of higher-yielding securities. Where this is possible, the banking firm contracts by reducing both securities and loans. However, there is another possibility in this situation. The banking firm may maintain the practice of liquidating securities only and raise lending rates instead of trying to reduce loans, protecting its profits in this way; this possibility is considered in greater detail later.

In short, the expansion path for the banking firm that maximizes joint profits may be parallel to the security axis for all expansions and for small contractions in capacity, but for larger contractions the adjustment path may deviate from the parallel position, or else lending policy may be altered.

Substitution Effects in Banking

In addition to adjusting its loans and securities in response to *ceteris paribus* changes in capacity, the banking firm may also make adjustments in response to price changes: that is, changes in security yields and lending rates. Changes in these variables may induce a substitution effect between loans and securities. Since changes in security yields are the more prominent and common, they are considered first and in some detail, and then, more briefly, movements in lending rates are discussed.

Changes in security yields and the substitution effect that they may cause are closely associated with the capacity or resource effect just analyzed. The capacity effect not only alters size but also may lead indirectly to a substitution effect when the banking firm buys additional securities on the basis of increased capacity and security prices rise as a result. Likewise, a contraction in capacity not only reduces the size of the banking firm but also, in causing it to liquidate securities at possibly falling prices, may give rise to a substitution effect. As the capacity effect has already been examined, only the substitution effect caused by a change in security prices need now be dealt with. This is done by considering the effects of a rise in security prices, first, on the loans and securities held by a banking firm that maximizes its joint profits, and then on those held by a banking firm that maximizes its loan profits. The effects of a fall in security prices on loans and securities held are also considered for the same two categories of banking firms.

A rise in security prices definitely favours a substitution of loans for securities when the banking firm is maximizing joint profits from loans and securities. It is as if the point of tangency between the transformation curve and an iso-profit curve moved in a direction favouring a larger loan volume, either because the slope of the transformation curve had been altered simply by an autonomous change in security prices, or because in buying securities on the basis of new reserves received the banking firm moves the price of securities up. In the first instance, the banking firm will find it profitable to sell some of its existing securities and use the proceeds to accommodate an increase in its loans; in the second instance, it will be using some of the additional capacity to acquire more loans. It is even conceivable that, for a large enough rise in security prices when the banking firm is expanding on the basis of new cash reserves, the substitution effect may outweigh the capacity effect; the amount of securities held is then actually reduced, some of the existing securities being liquidated to increase loans even further, because a higher point on the profit mound can be reached in this manner.

However, when the banking firm is following the policy of maximizing profits from loans alone, a rise in security yields with or without an accompanying expansion in capacity does not affect the volume of loans carried. Such a banking firm cannot increase its loans further without reducing profits because it is making all the profitable loans it can; it must continue to hold its existing total of loans no matter how high security prices go in order to keep its profits from loans at a maximum.

A fall in security prices does not affect the net yield on existing securities, and so does not alter the slope or position of the iso-profit curves for loans and securities; the fall in prices does, however, change the slope of the transformation curve. Consequently the point of tangency between the transformation curve and an iso-profit curve is shifted by the fall in security prices, and shifted in a direction that favours a reduction in bank loans, since securities now have a higher net yield than the lowest yielding loans. By giving up all loans that yield less than securities now do, and by taking on more securities in place of the loans given up, joint profits can be increased: the addition to net revenue from the increase made to security holdings more than offsets the revenue foregone on the loans that had to be given up. The banking firm that wishes to maximize its joint profits must clearly substitute securities for loans when security prices fall.

When the fall in security prices is accompanied by a reduction in reserves, or is the consequence of a reduction in reserves, the banking firm attempting to maximize its joint profits must reduce not only its security holdings but also its loans, in order to preserve equality between the rate of transformation and the relative net yields of loans and securities. To what extent loans are reduced in such a situation depends on how much the slope of the transformation curve is altered—a function of the change in security prices—and on the volume of low-yielding loans that the bank is carrying. In addition to the fall in loans that the substitution effect itself calls for, a further reduction in loans may result, if the banking firm runs into capital losses while liquidating securities and reacts in a manner that causes it to become "pinned-in" to securities—the pin-in effect of the availability doctrine that is analyzed in greater detail in the next part of this chapter. Here the qualification needs to be made that the banking firm, when it must contract, may try to avoid taking capital losses by liquidating more loans and less securities than it otherwise would on the basis of pure profit considerations.

And of course it is only through capital losses that the banking firm maximizing loan profits alone is affected by falling security prices; as already explained, the realization of capital losses as it liquidates securities following a contraction in capacity may lead the banking firm to depart from the policy of maximizing profits from loans alone.

The other factor besides a change in security prices that may induce a substitution effect between loans and securities is a change in lending rates. When a banking firm that is maximizing joint profits raises its lending rates, it causes some loan requests previously refused because of net yields below those on securities to become more profitable than securities. The point of tangency between the transformation curve and an iso-profit curve moves in favour of a substitution of loans for securities; the rise in rates brings this about by shifting the iso-profit curves, unless the higher rates affect the demand for loans sufficiently to shift the iso-profit curves in the contrary direction so that there is no net shift. In general, a substitution of loans for securities will follow a rise in lending rates if the point of tangency representing the equilibrium position for maximum joint profits is shifted in the direction of greater loan volume by higher rates; if the tangency point is shifted the other way in favour of securities, it is more probable that lending rates would be reduced again than that securities would be substituted for loans.

Lending rates are unlikely to be lowered and kept lowered if the only effect is to provide an incentive to substitute securities for loans. Even though a banking firm treats securities as of equal importance to loans, it is not going to risk offending public opinion by initiating action that would cause it to restrict loans. Therefore, it will normally only reduce its lending rates when the demand for loans is sufficiently interest-elastic to bring forth loan applications on which the yields exceed what can be earned from securities. Profits at the new combination of loans and securities for lower lending rates must of course be greater than profits at the old combination for the higher lending rates if the banking firm is to benefit from the rate reduction.

When lending rates are raised, the banking firm that just maximizes loan profits is encouraged to expand its loans, which it can do if it has excess lending capacity and the rise in rates does not reduce significantly the flow of loan applications presented to the banks. The rise in rates will convert some loan applications previously refused because of negative returns into positive-yielding propositions. Given the policy of meeting all requests for loans that provide a positive net yield, the additional applications made profitable by a rise in rates will be accommodated by liquidating securities. The situation may be described as an outward movement in the ridge line for bank loans caused by the rise in rates, with the banking firm moving up its transformation curve, selling securities and making new loans, until the point is reached where the transformation curve cuts the ridge line in its new position. In Figure 2, p. 104, this would be the point P^1.

The banking firm maximizing loan profits that reduces its lending rates may cause some of its existing loans to become unprofitable; unless this movement is offset by the appearance of other positive-yielding loan applications stimulated by the fall in rates, the banking firm should reduce its loans and acquire securities in order to continue maximizing its loan profits. It is as if the ridge line for loans had moved downwards towards the security axis on the iso-profit map for loans and securities. However, if the effect of reduced rates is to cause the ridge line to move in this manner, the banking firm will probably not carry out the substitution of securities for loans that is now called for, but will raise lending rates again.

The foregoing discussion of the substitution effect that a change in lending rates creates ignores possible changes in security prices that may result when the substitutions are actually made. Any change in security prices that does follow an attempt to carry out a substitution between loans and securities encouraged by a change in lending rates will in general dampen the tendency to do so. Thus, a rise in lending rates that prompts a substitution of loans for securities will be moderated if security prices fall as securities are sold. In short, it is the change in lending rates relative to security yields that provides the incentive for any substitution effect that occurs following a rate adjustment.

CHANGES IN LENDING CONDITIONS AND POLICIES

The adjustments that the banking firm with excess lending capacity makes in its holdings of loans and securities, when output capacity is altered, the demand for loans constant, and when security prices and lending rates change, have now been examined in terms of the expansion path and of a substitution effect. In this section the adjustments that are made when the demand for bank loans changes are examined first; after this, the defensive and offensive measures that the banking firm can take to protect its profit position when this is threatened during periods of credit expansion and contraction are examined in detail under the general head of "changes in lending policies."

Changes in Demand

What occurs to the loans outstanding of the banking firm with excess lending capacity when the demand for bank loans changes is best examined by assuming constant cash reserves or lending capacity; the examination must allow for both an expansion and a contraction of demand for each of the two definite profit policies that the banking firm may adopt. The analysis, however, is worked out mainly for the banking firm that maximizes loan profits, for this is where the most difficult problems lie. The reaction of the banking firm maximizing joint profits to changes in demand for loans presents no problems.

A banking firm maximizing loan profits finds additional loan applications profitable when the demand for bank loans expands. This banking firm follows the policy of accepting all loan applications that promise it a positive net yield, and an expansion in demand increases the amount that the bank can lend at positive net yields. To expand its loans, however, the banking firm, when its cash reserves remain fixed, must draw upon its existing excess lending capacity, invested in securities. It does this by selling securities; but as it sells, security prices are likely to fall, especially if other banks are also selling. The fall in security prices means that more income-yielding units of securities have to be given up to accommodate a given increase in loans. For example, when the price of a security falls from 100 to 50, 2,000 income units of the security must be given up to accommodate an increase of 1,000 in loans. The profitability of the substitution depends on whether or not the income from the 2,000 in securities given up is less than the income earned from the additional 1,000 made in loans. When the revenue foregone on the securities liquidated exceeds that earned on the additional loans made, bank profits deteriorate and the deterioration is accelerated if capital losses are realized in the substitution process.

If deterioration in profits occurs because security prices fall when the banking firm is substituting loans for securities following an expansion in the demand for loans, the banking firm may, as a defensive move to protect its profits, halt the substitution process before it has satisfied all the additional loan applications on which the yield is positive. It then departs from the policy of maximizing loan profits; how far it departs depends largely on how rapidly security prices fall. If security prices do not fall at all, the substitution can be carried further without profits suffering; but even here profits begin to decline after rising at first. During the early stages of the substitution the revenue from the new loans may exceed that on the securities given up; but as the substitution proceeds, loan applications with lower yields than securities appear. Accepting these lower-yielding loans will cause profits to fall again, although total profits may still remain above what they were before the loan expansion started.

The general solution for the problem of when the substitution of loans for securities will come to a halt can be illustrated by the geometry of the banking firm. Before the loan expansion, the equilibrium position for the banking firm maximizing loan profits is represented by the point of intersection of its transformation curve with the ridge line for loans, which is the point P^1 on the iso-profit map of Figure 2, p. 104). The expansion in the demand for bank loans gives rise to a new system of iso-profit curves[100] in which the ridge

100. A new system of iso-profit curves results because all loan applications must be re-ordered in the light of the new demand facing the bank. Both loans outstanding and new applications are arranged in order of descending profitability. If all loans and applications that yield a positive net return are acceptable to the banking firm, and it makes the volume of loans indicated by this consideration, there is no policy problem. However, if the banking firm departs from the policy of making all loans that yield a positive return, and sets the cut-off rate above zero, the situation becomes more difficult; for it may be that some of the low-yielding lending propositions that are now excluded include those previously met by the bank. In this case, some high-yielding new applications have replaced loans previously made but now too low-yielding to be carried. That is, the banking firm has rearranged its loan portfolio, dropping some business no longer profitable, and replacing it with more profitable new business.

For the banking firm that wants to make the largest amount of loans it can without reducing existing profits, the foregoing behaviour is rational. If the banking firm cannot drop any of its existing loans, it is reduced to carrying its existing loans and adding only those new loans that, on the average, yield a zero net profit, when account is taken of the income foregone on the securities liquidated in making the loans. All the new loans made in themselves will yield a positive net return, but the total profit on them will just equal the total loss on the securities sold. Beyond this point no additional loans can profitably be made whose net yield is not sufficient to offset the loss of income and of capital value on the securities that would have to be liquidated.

In the geometrical illustrations used in what follows in the text, the assumption is implicitly made that the banking firm is not hampered by the restraint of maintaining all existing loans: it can replace some of them with new loans when this is profitable and leads to a greater expansion of loans.

line for loans lies above the old ridge line: that is, it lies parallel to the security axis, but at a higher loan value than the old ridge line. (It is as if LP¹IT in Figure 2 were raised higher.) The banking firm should therefore move up its transformation curve until it meets the new ridge line (which would be at some point between P¹ and M on MP¹PS) if it adheres to the policy of maximizing loan profits. However, if total profits at the new point of equilibrium for the loan-maximization policy is less than at the old equilibrium position, and the banking firm has sufficient warning of this, it may try to protect its profits by halting the substitution of loans for securities before the new equilibrium point is reached. Just where it does halt depends on the size of the recognition and administrative lags. When these are zero, the substitution may be halted at the point on the transformation curve where it is cut by the new iso-profit curve that represents the same total profit as the old equilibrium point.[101] This position always lies between the two equilibrium points (the old and the new) for a loan-maximization policy when total profit at the new equilibrium position is below that at the old. When there are lags, the substitution process may be carried beyond the point at which profits would be no less than before. Beyond that point profits are definitely less, and depending on the adjustment lags, the substitution process will be halted somewhere beyond that point but, if possible, before the new equilibrium position is reached.

The substitution of loans for securities will be fully completed voluntarily in the foregoing situation only when the new equilibrium position for a loan-maximization policy provides at least the same total profit as the old equilibrium position. It is in this connection that the behaviour of security prices is significant for the analysis. The further prices fall for the securities that the banking firm is liquidating the less steep is the slope of its transformation curve with reference to

101. That is, it is willing to make a larger amount of loans for the same total profit, so long as all its costs, including provisions for bad debts, are fully allowed for. This represents plausible behaviour because the banking firm maximizing loan profits is not motivated to maximize total profits. It is attempting to maximize its total profits from loans subject to the restraint of maintaining existing profits. So long as total profits do not fall, it is not attracted by the possibility of greater profits to be had from holding fewer loans and more securities.

the securities axis—the greater the amount of securities, measured in terms of acquisition costs, that have to be given up to increase loans by a given amount. It therefore follows that the lower the level of security prices, and the lower prices fall, the sharper the path of the transformation curve towards the loan axis. This means that profits fall off faster for a movement along the transformation curve towards the loan axis, because the closer an iso-profit curve is to the loan axis the less profit it represents compared to that represented by an iso-profit curve further from the loan axis. Thus, a movement across the iso-profit map for loans and securities, towards the loan axis and parallel to the security axis, cuts curves representing a descending order of total profits. Hence, the less slope the transformation curve has with reference to the security axis, the less possibility there is that its intersection with the ridge line for loans, when this has been shifted by an expansion in demand, will represent a more profitable position than the old equilibrium point. In other words, the more security prices fall the sooner it is likely that the substitution of loans for securities, stimulated by a rise in demand, will come to a halt. Indeed, a fall in security prices that means taking capital losses perhaps prompts a quicker reaction of the banking firm to the possibility that its profits may fall if it carries on the substitution process too long: the fall in security prices then serves as a signal that operates to cut down the adjustment lags involved in taking action to protect profits.

The realization of capital losses, however, may restrict the substitution process even more than would be called for by a simple comparison of the transformation curve with a system of iso-profit curves. These geometrical concepts, as previously indicated, do not take into account explicitly capital losses. One combination of loans and securities that is more profitable than another, capital gains and losses excluded, remains more profitable regardless of what capital losses are involved in moving from the less profitable to the more profitable combination. The profit differential, being an amount per period of time, can offset any fixed sum such as a capital loss. Hence it is theoretically profitable for the banking firm to move away from an old equilibrium combination towards the new one along its transformation curve, stopping short of the point where total profits fall to the same level as at the old equilibrium position. However, considerations regarding capital losses, discussed further on, may cause the banking firm to stop even before that point is reached.

The reaction of a banking firm maximizing loan profits to a fall in the demand for bank loans may be more briefly dealt with. Unless it changes its terms and conditions of lending, the banking firm has no recourse but to watch its loans contract, and to invest in securities the capacity now freed from making loans. Profits may rise, fall, or remain constant as a result of this involuntary substitution process, depending on the nature and extent of the loan contraction and on the movement in security prices that takes place. If profits do fall, the banking firm may attempt to reverse the involuntary substitution of securities for loans that it is forced to take when demand contracts— an attempt that takes the form of trying to keep the amount of loans outstanding as high as possible. What this means is discussed in the next section, but it does not mean departing from the policy of maximizing profits from loans: a contraction in demand, unlike an expansion, is unlikely to force an abandonment of this policy.

Now to analyze the effects of a change in demand for bank loans for the banking firm that maximizes joint or total profits from loans and securities. This analysis can be brief for there are no difficulties here. A reduction in the demand for bank loans forces upon this type of banking firm also an involuntary substitution of securities for loans —a process that continues as long as loans contract. At the end of the process the banking firm will still be maximizing its joint profits for the new demand conditions, but it is much more likely, in this case, that total profits in the new equilibrium position will be much less than in the old one. Many of the loans paid off may have been more profitable than the securities acquired to take their place. An increase in the demand for loans from the banking firm means a profitable opportunity to substitute loans for securities; the substitution process is carried to the point at which total profits under the new demand conditions are at their maximum, and this will always be at a higher level than it was in the old position of equilibrium. Lower-yielding securities can now be replaced by higher-yielding loans. However, capital losses here as well may interfere with the profit goal that the banking firm seeks to achieve. That is, the banking firm may stop short of the point at which total profits are at a maximum because in moving towards that point by selling securities it begins to realize capital losses.

The possibly inhibiting effects of capital losses represent a refinement to the general analysis of the consequences for the banking firm of an expansion in the demand for loans. If the banking firm is reluctant to take capital losses, it may cease to substitute loans for securities following a rise in demand for bank loans, even though a further substitution is called for on the basis of its current profit policy. Thus, if it is following a policy of maximizing its loans subject to the restraint of maintaining existing profits, it may stop short of this goal because it runs into capital losses. In view of the fact that profits will probably be higher as a result of stopping short, the behaviour of the banking firm cannot be considered irrational. However, when the banking firm is pursuing a policy of maximizing its total profits from loans and securities and stops short of this goal, accepting a lower level of profits in order to avoid capital losses, its behaviour may be thought irrational.[102] But this is not necessarily so. The bank may, it is true, make a net addition per unit of time to its

102. As previously indicated, the reluctance of lending firms to realize capital losses is one argument found in the availability doctrine to explain how a fall in security prices may prevent lenders from substituting loans for the securities they now hold. This pin-in effect is said to be irrational if it takes hold when it is still profitable to make the substitution. Both C. R. Whittlesey, "Monetary Policy and Economic Change," *Review of Economics and Statistics, 39* (Feb. 1957), 36, and Smith, "On the Effectiveness of Monetary Policy," pp. 589–93, discount the idea of an irrational pin-in, arguing that when it is profitable for lenders to switch they will do so.

Some argue that the pin-in effect is weakened when banks are able to offset capital losses against current income for income tax purposes as can be done in the U.S. where the tax saving amounts to 52 per cent of the capital loss. Eugene A. Birnbaum, "The Growth of Financial Intermediaries as a Factor in the Effectiveness of Monetary Policy," International Monetary Fund, *Staff Papers, 6* (Nov. 1958), 398–9; Howard S. Ellis, "Limitations of Monetary Policy," *United States Monetary Policy: Its Contribution to Prosperity without Inflation* (New York, The American Assembly, Columbia University, 1958), p. 152; Paul A. Samuelson, "Reflections on Monetary Policy," *Review of Economics and Statistics, 42* (Aug. 1960), 268n3.

profits by substituting more loans for securities, but it may be that the net addition to profits would be so small in relation to the capital loss that the banking firm feels it would take too long to offset the loss. In addition uncertainty about keeping the additional loans made outstanding at existing rates long enough to offset the capital loss may make it appear more profitable not to make the loans.

Hence the reluctance of the banking firm to realize capital losses, when in the long run it is profitable to take the losses and carry more loans and securities, is explainable in terms of uncertainty about the permanency of the new demand for bank loans. This reluctance is a function of the length of time it would take to offset the capital losses and of the state of the inner reserves of the bank. The larger the inner reserves against which capital losses can be applied the more willing the bank will be to take capital losses for a long-run benefit, since current profits can be protected from the impact of the capital losses.[103] When the bank is reluctant to take capital losses, there exists a special situation in which an increase in cash reserves would result in an expansion of bank loans. The provision of extra lending capacity at normal banking costs, such as can be provided by central-banking operations, permits granting loans that are profitable when capital losses do not have to be taken.[104]

103. Until Jan. 1957 the chartered banks in Canada were permitted to value their security holdings at market value and to maintain tax-free inner reserves against these holdings. Hence, capital losses incurred in liquidating securities could at times be hidden in these reserves. However, in Jan. 1957 an order-in-council was passed (SOR/57–18, *Canada Gazette*, Pt. II, Jan. 23, 1957, p. 139) requiring the banks to value their Government of Canada and provincial-government securities at not more than amortized value. Since amortized value may exceed market value, the banks may no longer carry tax-free inner reserves against these securities to write them down to market value. With the elimination of tax-free inner reserves on this class of securities it is now more difficult for Canadian banks to protect their profits from capital losses incurred in selling securities to make loans. Cf. A. B. Jamieson, *Chartered Banking in Canada*, p. 414A; *Financial Post*, Jan. 19, 1957, p. 38.

104. This is explicit in the following quotation: "If the volume of loans is being held back by difficulties of the chartered banks . . . in the cost and difficulty of selling bonds in order to make room for loans, then loans are being held down below where they otherwise would be by reason of monetary tightness. In such circumstances, if the public interest seems to call for it, the Bank of Canada by

Changes in Lending Policies

Thus changes in the demand for bank loans as well as changes in security yields and capital losses, to say nothing of changes in cash reserves, may all react on bank profits to cause the banking firm to depart from its general lending policy. The consideration likely to cause deviation from a given lending policy is the desire to at least maintain existing profits, or, if this is not possible, to minimize any shrinkage in existing profits. Any event that threatens existing profits, such as a reduction in reserves or a fall in demand for loans or a change in security prices, is likely therefore to cause the banking firm to alter its lending rates and to alter the degree to which it may refuse loan applications.

Perhaps the easiest and most natural reaction for the banking firm faced with a situation in which its profits are threatened is to avoid making unprofitable loans or carrying loans that have become unprofitable because of a change in lending conditions. Thus, when an expansion of bank loans becomes unprofitable under conditions of constant reserves, rising demand, and falling security prices, the banking firm may start refusing all new and additional requests for loans that are not profitable under the prevailing supply conditions. This approach is feasible if net yields on loan applications differ significantly within each lending-rate bracket. The new applications that do not yield a sufficient amount to compensate for the loss of income on the securities that must be liquidated if the applications are granted can be singled out for refusal; those new applications that still represent profitable business at the going rates after allowing for substitution or transformation costs can of course be accepted.

When bank profits are falling because a reduction in cash reserves forces the banking firm to reduce its earning assets, the defence of profits may take the form of withdrawing from some loans when this is less unprofitable than liquidating securities. Again the banking firm introduces a greater degree of exclusion into its lending activities, but

---

increasing the chartered banks cash reserves can make it easier and more practical for them to increase their loans." Canada, Parliament, House, Standing Committee on Banking and Commerce, *Proceedings*, 1954, p. 141, evidence of the Governor of the Bank of Canada.

the greater exclusion is due to a shift in the margin between profitable and unprofitable loans; it cannot be considered a form of credit rationing proper, for profitable loans need not be denied so long as the banking firm continues to have a choice between liquidating securities or liquidating loans.

When, instead of a reduction in cash reserves, a contraction in the demand for bank loans causes profits to fall, the problem will be the exact opposite in that the banking firm will now be looking for ways of becoming a more lenient lender. It is the involuntary substitution of lower-yielding securities for higher-yielding loans occasioned by the fall in demand that is the cause of the difficulty. Therefore, if the banking firm can halt or reverse the substitution, it will moderate the fall in profits. Where the banking firm has previously been refusing loan applications that would provide positive net yields, it may now welcome applications from such sources. But when there is no scope for lowering the degree of rejection, because loan applications that offer the prospects of some positive yield are not currently being refused, the only recourse available is a general reduction in lending rates. If the rate reduction reacts unfavourably on profits, the banking firm has in reserve another defence—a reduction in its deposit rate, which reduces its fixed charges and so helps protect profits.

An alteration in lending rates may be a necessary step to defend banking profits; it may of course also be an alternative to changing the degree of rejection applied to loan applications.[105] Thus, when the banking firm, with fixed cash reserves, meets an additional demand for loans by liquidating securities, it may find after the event that its profits are falling. With loan demand still rising, the banking firm may attempt to prevent a further deterioration in profits by making an upward adjustment in lending rates. New borrowers may be placed in higher-rate categories than they normally would; if

105. Cf. U.S. Congress, Joint Committee on the Economic Report, *Monetary Policy and the Management of the Public Debt: Report*, p. 33, where it is stated that "lenders . . . are not likely indefinitely to pass up opportunities to raise their rates, nor—in the opposite situation—are they likely to refrain indefinitely from cutting them when this is necessary to secure business. Therefore, if any change in the underlying demand and supply situation (as affected by monetary policy) persists, it will come to be reflected more-and-more in the actual cost of borrowing money. . . ."

there is a fixed maximum for lending rates, new borrowers to whom the bank would lend only at the maximum rate must now be refused accommodation altogether. Requests for additional advances from regular borrowing customers may be met at higher rates applied to the extra sums they want to borrow. Again if there is a set maximum lending rate, existing borrowers at the maximum rate cannot have their requests for increased borrowings met.

Such rate adjustments would provide an element in lending rates, levied on the additional loans, to cover the extra cost of expanding loans;[106] these partial rate adjustments would not, however, do anything to make up for the depletion of profits that has already occurred. But rate adjustments of this nature do not seem to be a part of general banking practice. Banks may have some notions of a "just" price that inhibits them from asking a higher rate from a borrower than they ordinarily would; certainly if a bank does not feel justified in lending an additional amount to a borrower at his existing rate, either it does not lend him more or it charges him a higher rate on his total advance: differential rates are not levied on any individual borrower.[107] Rate adjustments, then, when they come, are general— either for all classes of borrowers or for specific classes. Partial rate adjustments that apply just to new loans or to additions on existing loans are not one of the defences employed by the banking firm to protect its profits.

Thus, alterations in lending rates usually take the form of a general movement, and may be upwards when the profitability of loans and

106. Thus, if the extra cost is a capital loss on liquidating securities to make loans, lending rates have to be raised by some small amount to offset this capital loss. Smith, "On the Effectiveness of Monetary Policy," p. 591, presents some calculations that show, under certain restricted conditions, how much a rate on a given debt instrument has to be raised to compensate for a known capital loss.

107. "It is conceivable that a bank might lend additional amounts at increasing rates, e.g. the first £5,000 at 5 per cent p.a., the next £3,000 at 7 per cent, and a further £2,000 at 10 per cent—but as a matter of practice, an English banker never would. Once he has decided on the amount of finance necessary to cover a proposition acceptable to him, he will lend the whole amount at a flat rate." Wilson, "Credit Rationing and the Relevant Rate of Interest," p. 231n.

The same sentiment is expressed by Alford and Paish, "Debate on Monetary Control—Basic Principles and Modern Mechanics," p. 480.

loan applications are falling, and may be downwards, as previously indicated in the discussion on declining demand, when loans become more desirable than securities. Any event that affects banking profits may evoke a change in lending rates, but of particular interest is the relationship between security yields and lending rates. It appears that when banks hold a large amount of securities for which prices fluctuate, the resultant fluctuations in yields are accompanied by similar changes in lending rates.[108] It has certainly been the experience in Canada that more flexible security prices have been accompanied by more flexible lending rates.[109]

108. The (Montreal) *Gazette*, Nov. 28, 1957, p. 14, in reporting on a general reduction to be made in lending rates of the chartered banks from $5\frac{3}{4}$ per cent to $5\frac{1}{2}$ per cent stated that the planned reduction was related to decreases in security yields that had occurred; it further commented that previous increases in lending rates, of which there had been four within a two-year period, had been caused primarily by increases in security yields.

109. A greater degree of flexibility in the lending rates of the chartered banks than had hitherto been exhibited developed after the Bank of Canada rediscount rate itself became more flexible in 1955, when it began to rise from $1\frac{1}{2}$ per cent until, within two years, it reached a peak of over 4 per cent. Within that two-year period of a rising bank-rate the chartered banks raised their prime rate on loans from $4\frac{1}{2}$ per cent to $5\frac{3}{4}$ per cent. The *Financial Post*, Feb. 2, 1957, p. 3; the (Montreal) *Gazette*, Aug. 23, 1957; Bank of Canada, *Annual Report*, 1955, pp. 7, 10; idem, 1956, pp. 45–6. C. A. Curtis, "Credit Control in Canada," p. 117, forecast these developments in 1930 when he suggested that a central bank in Canada with a changeable discount rate might make the lending rates of the chartered banks more flexible.

The more flexible bank-rate in Canada, of course, was reflected in greater movements in yields on government securities. When changes in bank-rate ceased to be discretionary, however, and were made automatic by linking the rate to the average yield on thirteen-week Treasury bills at the weekly tender, the emerging association of changes in lending rates and bank-rate broke down. E. P. Neufeld, "The Bank of Canada's Approach to Central Banking," *Canadian Journal of Economics and Political Science*, 24 (Aug. 1958), 343. The change in the method of setting bank-rate was made on Nov. 1, 1956; the press release announcing the change is reproduced in Bank of Canada, *Annual Report*, 1960, pp. 63–4.

The 6 per cent limit on the lending rate of banks in Canada restricts, of course, upward flexibility. This was dramatically illustrated in Aug. 1959 when bank-rate rose above 6 per cent, the banks being of course unable to raise their lending rates to the level that such a bank-rate justified. Cf. Press Statement, President of The Canadian Bankers' Association, Toronto, Aug. 13, 1959.

The link between security prices and lending rates lies in banking profits, and for the banking firm that maximizes total profits the link is perhaps more direct than for the firm that maximizes only profits from loans. When total profits are being maximized, a *ceteris paribus* rise in security yields may prompt the banking firm to raise lending rates instead of substituting securities for loans. The banking firm does this if it feels under a restraint to maintain its existing level of loans. It then forgoes the opportunity of substituting securities for loans but tries to maximize total profits under the new circumstances by raising lending rates. In terms of the geometry of the banking firm, it attempts to keep the point of tangency between its transformation curve and an iso-profit curve at the point representing its existing holdings of loans and securities. Since a rise in security yields alters the system of iso-profit curves in one direction, the rise in lending rates must shift them in the opposite direction for the banking firm to succeed in keeping the tangency point where it wants. Whether or not the iso-profit curves react in the desired manner depends of course on the interest-elasticity of the demand for bank loans.

A fall in security yields may react on the lending rates of the banking firm maximizing joint profits from loans and securities in the following manner. A contraction of bank loans which results in an involuntary substitution of securities for loans by the banks causes bank profits to fall and security prices to rise. As a defensive measure the banks lower their lending rates in an attempt to enlarge their volume of loans outstanding or to prevent at least the volume from falling further. There is then a sympathetic movement in security yields and lending rates.

The banking firm that maximizes only its loan profits is not so likely to alter its lending rates as a result of unrelated movements in security prices, but when changes in security prices bear on bank profits, lending rates may well begin to move in the same direction as security yields. Indeed, downward revisions in lending rates when security yields rise are more to be expected when a banking firm is pursuing a policy of maximizing loan profits than when it is maximizing total profits. This is only so however when the demand for loans is contracting and the contraction causes bank profits to fall;

the only counter action that the banking firm maximizing loan profits can take in this situation is to reduce lending rates to revive demand. Since security yields have probably fallen as the result of banks buying securities to replace loans paid off, security yields and lending rates both move in the same direction.

An expansion in the demand for bank loans from the banking firm that maximizes loan profits causes a substitution of loans for securities. And, as already explained, such a substitution, in which security yields rise, carried through to the point where the banking firm is still maximizing loan profits probably causes total profits to fall below their previous level. If the banking firm wishes to adhere to the policy of maximizing loan profits but is unwilling to see total profits fall below existing levels, it may raise lending rates in an effort to keep to the same lending policy without profits suffering.[110]

In the preceding analysis of changes in lending policies prompted by events that react on bank profits, changes in lending rates are treated apart from changes in the degree of ease with which loan applications are met. However, in the every-day world of modern banking the two types of policy changes usually occur together, and furthermore in almost all cases the prime mover is a change in the demand for bank loans. A period of monetary stringency generally starts with an expansion in the demand for loans which banks accommodate by liquidating securities. In a large bank into which there is a constant flow of loan applications, the process of expanding

110. Thomas Wilson, "The Rate of Interest and Monetary Policy," *Oxford Economic Papers*, 9 (Oct. 1957), 249–50, asks himself, as though it could hardly be possible, if English banks raise their lending rates, when the demand for loans expands, not to check demand but to maintain the incomes of the banks.

Alhadeff, *Monopoly and Competition in Banking*, pp. 147–8, concludes that any parallel movements between security yields and lending rates charged by banks are the result of both responding to a common set of forces. He goes on to point out that when securities are purely marginal for banks, in the sense that only truly surplus funds are invested in securities, changes in security yields can have no *direct* effect on lending rates since there is then no competitive interaction between lending rates and security yields. However, the only indirect relationship he recognizes between the two is one provided by anticipations: changes in security yields by affecting anticipations lead to changes in lending rates. He overlooks the more obvious link provided by profits—the link between lending rates and security yields that is emphasized here.

loans and then selling securities is almost automatic since the functions of credit assessment and cash adjustment are two distinct and separate functions handled by different officers. The impact on profits shows up after the event: there is no prior calculation of the profitability of the over-all substitution. If profits have fallen or have given signs of falling, ways and means are sought to defend the profit position. The types of new loans that are being made are examined to assess which types are tending to make the substitution process unprofitable, and those types found unprofitable under the existing expansionary conditions, which include falling security prices, begin to be excluded from further loan accommodation, unless a moderate rise in rates makes them profitable propositions again. Hence, lending rates are likely to be raised to restore the profitability of some classes of loans, while those loan categories that the permissible rate increase cannot make profitable in the existing circumstances are excluded.[111] In this situation greater exclusion of loan applications goes hand-in-hand with higher lending rates.

When the demand for bank loans contracts, the order of events is just the opposite. As the banks involuntarily substitute securities, probably at rising prices, for loans, they suffer a drop in profits. They

---

111. Smith, "On the Effectiveness of Monetary Policy," pp. 595-6, discusses briefly the order of events as they affect the banking system during a loan expansion. He sees the banks as first becoming more reluctant lenders and then raising their lending rates, although he makes this separation of reactions mainly for purposes of exposition and not because the two reactions necessarily occur separately. However, he does speak of the banks meeting loan demands that they had previously refused during the initial phase of the credit expansion before lending rates were raised. This seems unlikely because it would be administratively difficult for a large bank to decide not to make certain classes of loans and then to reverse itself afterwards when lending rates were raised. And of course there is no question of a reversal in policy of this nature when both higher lending rates and a greater degree of exclusion are introduced at the same time, as most likely they would be.

H. C. Wallich, "Recent Monetary Policies in the United States," *American Economic Review*, 43 (Papers and Proceedings, May 1953), 40, suggests that the more careful selection of loan applications that occurs during a credit expansion makes a limitation of supply appear as a limitation of demand, and from this interpretation he draws the conclusion that banks have less incentive to raise rates than they otherwise would.

then seek out creditworthy borrowers more carefully and may at the same time lower lending rates to encourage a greater supply of satisfactory borrowers. Again, rates and the willingness to lend move in the same general direction.

✓ CONCLUSIONS

The main conclusions of this chapter may now be summarized. An approach that provides a more complete and comprehensive explanation of banking behaviour than does the availability doctrine is one that treats the "output" behaviour of the banking firm within the context of the general theory of the firm. Treating banks as firms providing an output of funds in different forms has some special features not usually associated with the analysis of physical output. For one thing a banking firm operates under a capacity restraint set by the amount of its cash reserves and its reserve ratio. The existence of this restraint makes it necessary to distinguish between a banking firm that has excess capacity for engaging in its main activity—making loans—and one that has no excess capacity, because "output" behaviour in banking differs in these two situations. The capacity restraint also introduces different profit policies when the banking firm has excess lending capacity, and these have to be considered in analyzing how a banking firm reacts to a change in supply and market conditions.

Account must also be taken of the fact that financial "output" differs from physical output in that the quality or nature of the buyer is an important consideration in providing the output. This is true of course of most transactions involving the use of credit. In banking, qualitative considerations associated with lending resolve into degrees of uncertainty about repayment prospects and into classification of risks. There are degrees of uncertainty and classes of risks that are acceptable and there are those that are not. The division between the two corresponds roughly to the division between profitable and unprofitable. However, lending expenses relative to revenue, not connected with uncertainty or risks, may also lead to a division of loan applications into profitable and unprofitable.

Excluding loan applications and requests on the basis of profitability is common in banking. Although such exclusion creates excess demand, because it operates through a refusal to lend rather than through the quoting of a rate sufficient to eliminate the undesirable demand, the exclusion does not have all the characteristics associated with rationing. In particular, the refusal to lend has a rational basis and is not the result of a limited supply at quoted prices being insufficient to meet the demand. True rationing arises in banking only when lending capacity is too small to support all the profitable loans that could be made at existing rates. Rationing in this sense is rare in modern banking systems.

The banking firm that does not have to ration its credit most likely has excess lending capacity which it invests in government securities. Changes in security yields are thus added to changes in cash reserves and in the demand for loans as factors that influence loan "output" and "output" behaviour in general. Usually, a variation in reserves, when everything else remains constant, disturbs mainly the security holdings of the banking firm: there is little if any effect on loans. Changes in security yields and in the demand for loans may induce or inhibit substitutions between loans and securities and may in addition cause the bank to alter its lending conditions. Any changes in lending conditions may be interpreted in terms of defending profits. And in general, as the analysis of the whole chapter argues, the amount of loans and securities that a bank holds under given conditions, and changes in those amounts, can be explained almost entirely in terms of the profit calculus.

Chapter Three: COMPETITION, PROFITS, AND THE CAPITAL ACCOUNTS

The major questions dealt with in this chapter are why banks compete for deposits among themselves and with outside competitors, how profits in banking are affected by monetary policy and by the way in which monetary control is applied to the banking system, how bank profits differ from those in other fields, and what connection exists between retained revenues and the capital position in banking. Despite their seeming diversity, these questions are closely related, and their answers bring out certain special effects of banking activity on bank balance-sheets. The analysis runs mainly in terms of the banking system as such, all banks taken together, rather than in terms of the individual bank.

COMPETITION IN BANKING

The Competition for Deposits

Banks place great stress on getting and keeping deposits. The continual striving for deposits is a common and conspicuous feature of a competitive banking system, reflected in the prevalent banking attitude that deposits are the lifeblood of a bank.[1] Economists sometimes find this attitude puzzling because deposits are merely liabilities of the banks which the banks themselves can create simply by going into greater debt to the public. Of course, what banks are really competing for are not the deposit liabilities but the cash items that can be obtained from the public by incurring the deposit liabilities.

1. Cf. A. B. Jamieson, *Chartered Banking In Canada*, p. 203.

Deposits of currency and of cheques and monetary instruments of a like nature drawn on other banks provide the receiving bank with additional cash. Receipts of cheques and monetary instruments drawn on the receiving bank, including those issued by the bank itself, do not directly provide the receiving bank with extra cash; but they do prevent that bank from losing cash, which it would lose if the items received were deposited elsewhere.

A bank wishes to take in all the cash it can and to hold on to as much of it as possible because the more it has and can retain the more funds it can supply to the public. That is, the more cash a bank has the greater its output capacity. And because a bank always utilizes its output capacity to the full in supplying funds, it follows that the more output capacity the bank has and uses the greater its profits are likely to be. Hence, the competition for deposits is really a competition for greater output: banks compete for deposits in order to become larger and thus to be able to supply more funds to the public.

However, such financial growth as follows from the competition for deposits is profitable only if the bank does not incur exceptional expense to get and keep cash, and if it makes good use of what cash it gets. A bank can always offer exceptional inducements—such as special services to depositors or higher interest rates on deposits—but such devices may not be profitable. Or a bank in growing on the basis of cash received may make poor loans or investments, which do not turn out well, and fail to increase its profits as a result.

The day-to-day competition for funds, or cash deposits, is a matter of trying to attract and to retain deposits within the existing establishments of the bank. A bank tries to gain cash at the expense of other banks, to get cash from the public by offering deposits in exchange for currency, and above all, to keep what cash it already has. An alert policy, good service, and astute advertising can do much to bring cash to a bank and to keep it there. But over a longer period of time a bank may find that this is not enough, and that to hold its own in the struggle for deposits it must expand its banking offices in order to trap and to retain its share of the deposit business. In other words a bank may have to grow physically in order to remain an effective competitor for funds.

The fact that a bank may actively create deposits, or that the volume of deposits may be altered as a result of internal entries, does not make the competition for deposits any less meaningful. For instance, most bank loans are made by giving the borrowers deposits. Hence, when loans are made, an increase in deposits occurs without anyone bringing a cash item to the bank. Likewise, various internal entries, such as service charges and interest on savings balances, alter the amount of deposits without cash items passing between the bank and the public. Thus, fluctuations that are not directly related to the competition of the bank for deposits occur in the amount of deposits held by a bank. The competition for deposits is not a competition to actively alter deposits, which banks can do, but a competition to get and to retain deposits, for a bank competes for the deposits that it actively creates on the same basis as it competes for the deposits that it does not create. This it must do because the deposits a bank creates could easily be lost to other banks or to currency withdrawals. Hence a bank competes for the deposits it creates in order to retain them and so to preserve its cash position.

So far the discussion has been in terms of an individual bank competing with other banks for deposits. However, banks also compete with other types of deposit-receiving institutions, and the initial effect of this competition on the banking system depends on what the non-bank deposit institutions do with any cash they gain from the banking system. If the non-bank depositories, which gain cash as a result of bank customers transferring bank deposits to them, place the cash they gain in accounts or deposits maintained with the banking system, the banks as a group lose neither cash nor deposits: total deposits in the banking system remain constant, although their ownership is rearranged. The banking system would lose cash and deposits if the non-bank depositories placed their cash gains in accounts kept with the central bank. This would only be a temporary loss, however, for when the non-bank depositories utilized their new cash receipts, cash and deposits would flow back to the banking system. Still, the return flow could be less than the initial outflow, for the non-banks may wish to keep higher cash balances with the central bank when their deposit liabilities are higher. There is then a net loss of cash and deposits to the banking system.

As a rule, non-bank depositories do not keep balances or deposits with the central bank.[2] They may add to their currency holdings, though, when their deposit liabilities expand.[3] They gain cash from the banks, convert some of it into currency to hold, and utilize the rest to expand their earning assets. The additional currency held by the non-bank depositories comes from the banks and so reduces both the cash and the deposits of the banking system. The loss will not be great, for the non-banks will not add to their currency holdings more than the minimum required for working purposes. Thus, even though rival deposit institutions gain deposits at the expense of the banks, banks as a group will not lose deposits to any significant extent. Consequently, most deposit competition between banks and non-banks is unlikely to affect in any significant way the amount of deposits held by the banking system.

Competition from Non-Bank Sources

Although for the individual bank it may appear necessary and profitable to compete for deposits with non-bank depositories, for the banking system such competition may appear wasteful and unprofitable when it does not directly affect the amount of deposits held by the banking system. If that competition leads to higher interest rates paid on deposits, it would seem that all banks are accomplishing is to raise the cost of providing deposits.[4] Despite the absence of any immediate impact on total bank deposits, however, there may be sound

2. In Canada two savings deposit institutions—the Montreal City and District Savings Bank and The Quebec Savings Bank (La Banque d'Economie de Québec) —in the Province of Quebec carry some of their cash reserves with the central bank, but they are the only private domestic institutions, other than the chartered banks, from which the Bank of Canada may accept deposits. Canada, Laws, Statutes, *Bank of Canada Act*, office consolidation (Ottawa, Queen's Printer, 1955), ss. 18 (1) (1)–(n).

3. Cf. Deane Carson, "Bank Earnings and the Competition for Savings Deposits," *Journal of Political Economy, 67* (Dec. 1959), 583n9.

4. Cf. David A. Alhadeff and Charlotte P. Alhadeff, "A Note on Bank Earnings and Savings Deposit Rate Policy," *Journal of Finance, 14* (Sept. 1959), 405, 408–9; Warren L. Smith, "Financial Intermediaries and Monetary Controls," *Quarterly Journal of Economics, 73* (Nov. 1959), 544n7; Carson, "Bank Earnings and the Competition for Savings Deposits," pp. 583–7.

long-run reasons for the banking system meeting outside competition. The validity of these reasons depends on the nature of that outside competition.

The real competition that a banking system may face from outside arises when other financial units compete for the same type of earning assets as the banking system holds. That is, non-bank financial firms may buy and hold the same type of open-market securities as banks, and they may make the same kind of customer loans or ones that are close substitutes for bank loans. In this connection any financial arrangements or instruments that enable potential bank borrowers to obtain loanable funds outside the banking system compete with the activities of the banks by affecting the return on the earning assets of the banks. The stronger the demand of lending firms for the same type of assets, the lower the rate of return. If outside competition reduces the demand for bank loans when the banks are not fully loaned up, it results in the banks carrying less loans and more open-market securities: a shift in the composition of bank assets that is likely to be from high-yielding to low-yielding assets. Hence, outside competition can reduce bank profits in the short-run, by affecting the composition of bank assets and the return on those assets, even though total deposits remain fixed.[5]

In the longer run, outside competition, unless checked, may indirectly affect the size of the banking system. If outside competition grows and so provides more financing of the type banks can provide, there is less need for growth in the banking system. Indeed, if the total-financing needs of an economy do not grow over time, and outside competition meets more and more of those needs, the banking

5. The composition of bank deposits may also be altered as a result of outside competition, with the banking system being left with fewer savings deposits and more demand deposits. In banking systems where reserve requirements against demand deposits are higher than against savings deposits, the system may be forced to contract. The central bank could, of course, offset the effects on cash requirements of such a change in the composition of deposits, but it may not if it concentrates its attention on the behaviour of demand deposits instead of total deposits. The point is discussed further by William G. Dewald, "Bank Earnings and the Competition for Savings," *Journal of Political Economy*, 69 (June 1961), 281–2, and by Deane Carson, "Bank Earnings and the Competition for Savings: A Reply," ibid., p. 287.

system will have to be reduced in size, in the interest of stability.[6] If the central bank restricts the growth of the banking system to what is necessary to meet the demands of the economy for bank financing, it follows that the less outside competition grows the greater will be the prospects for growth of the system.

The above growth effect of outside competition arises when the size of the banking system is closely regulated, but when there is no attempt to regulate the outside competition. The problem is accentuated in a period of restrictive monetary policy. Then the banks are prevented from doing all the financing business they could; the amount of financing carried out may continue to mount, however, if other financial firms can still get funds to lend, or if funds otherwise find their way from lenders to borrowers. In the interest of stability the monetary authorities have to bear down on the regulated sector—

6. There may, of course, be a range over which total financing may increase without resulting in an undesirable expansion of economic activity as a whole, but what the monetary authorities must guard against is too great an increase for the maintenance of stability. Cf. Robert V. Roosa, "The Changes in Money and Credit, 1957–59," *Review of Economics and Statistics, 42* (Aug. 1960), 261.

In "Are the Banks Losing Deposits?," *The Bankers' Magazine* (London), June 1961, pp. 461–3, it is argued that although banks do not lose deposits to non-bank depositories who are customers of the banking system banks could lose ground to outside competitors "in financing the whole economy." The argument, however, is pushed only to the point of showing that any addition to the amount of financing provided by non-banks, bank financing remaining constant, lowers the ratio of bank financing to total financing. This is not carrying the argument far enough to prove any disadvantage to the banking system. Unless the additional financing provided by the non-banks is in some way at the expense of financing that might have been done by the banks, there is no disadvantage to the banking system.

An early statement of the view that the size of the banking system can be affected by the intensity of financial competition is given by J. G. Gurley and E. S. Shaw, "Financial Intermediaries and the Saving-Investment Process," *Journal of Finance, 11* (May 1956), 261–2. Their argument, however, runs in terms of the demand for money, as a financial asset to hold, being reduced by financial competition, thus giving rise to an excess supply of money which the central bank then eliminates. But the reduction in the demand for money is only the first step in the process. It provides non-bank lenders with the means of expanding their financing activities and it is the expansion in these activities as such, not the reduction in the demand for money, that leads to counter-action by the central bank.

F

the banking system—to offset the expansionary effects of the un-regulated sector—the outside competition of the banks.

All outside competition has the foregoing effects on the profits and the growth prospects of the banking system regardless of how the funds are obtained that provide the outside competition. The way in which the funds are raised, however, does have some bearing on the strength of the competition. That is, the form of the instrument used may determine the ease with which competitors can get funds for competing with the banks. It may be that the use of the deposit form of borrowing may enable competitors to get more funds than can be raised by non-deposit forms.

If non-bank financial firms, like banks, can issue demand deposits, they may be able to get funds for expansion, by inducing bank customers to transfer working or transaction balances from banks to them, or to convert idle balances with banks into working balances with them. If competing financial firms cannot issue demand de-posits, they are restricted in their borrowing possibilities to tapping idle balances with the banks or to enticing holders of working bal-ances to convert them into a non-working form. As far as the conse-quences are concerned it does not matter whether or not this is done by issuing deposits. In short, the significance of the type of liabilities issued by non-bank competition in obtaining funds lies entirely in the effect on the amount of funds that can be raised, and not in any similar-ity, as such, between the type of liability used and bank deposits.[7]

The only action banks themselves can take against the effects of outside competition is to raise the effective rate of interest they pay on deposits or reduce their charges for loans. Outside competition when it does not operate on the basis of providing demand deposits becomes possible only when there is a sufficient gap between the

7. An exception may arise when non-bank financial firms provide demand deposits or deposits that count as part of the money supply. The monetary author-ities may react to the total money supply, defined to include non-bank deposits, by manipulating the part supplied by the banking system. Then if non-bank deposits expand at a time when the central bank is trying to stabilize the total money supply, official action designed to keep total money supply constant may force banks to contract their deposits. It can then be said that the form of the liabilities issued by non-banks have a direct bearing on the position of the banking system.

deposit rate and the loan rate of the banks. If this gap is large enough, non-bank lenders doing the same financing business as banks may be able to operate profitably by paying a little more for borrowed funds than the banks and by lending at the same or a slightly lower rate. Or non-bank lenders using bank financing may be encouraged by too wide a deposit-loan rates differential to borrow directly from the public, paying more than the deposit rate but less than the loan rate they previously paid. Finally, too wide a spread between the deposit and loan rates may encourage bank borrowers in general to negotiate directly with deposit holders for funds within the limits set by the two bank rates. All these possibilities can be discouraged by narrowing the spread between deposit and loan rates, for competitors cannot pay more for funds than banks, and then pass the higher rates on in higher lending rates when banks are providing funds to the same market at a lower rate.

Financing activity then that is competitive with bank financing can be checked by appropriate movements in bank deposit or lending rates when the banking system is able to meet all the demands made upon it. Financing activity that is not competitive with bank financing cannot be so checked. In this case outside lenders are acquiring earning assets that the banking system does not desire to hold. Accordingly, these non-bank lenders are not restricted in their lending charges by what banks charge; these lenders may attract funds by paying more than the deposit rate of banks and recover the extra cost by charging more to their borrowers. If the banks were to try to restrict the activities of these lenders, not by bidding for their borrowing customers, but by trying to reduce their supply of funds through a rise in deposit rates, the non-bank lenders could meet the challenge by raising their own borrowing rates and adding the extra cost to their lending charges. Any check to the activity of these non-bank lenders then depends on the price-elasticity of the demand for their financing services.

There may or may not be an advantage to the banking system in trying to restrict the activities of those not competing for the same type of assets as the banks. If non-bank financing activity is restricted here, the banks will not wish to do the financing now foregone by others. Under normal conditions the drop in financing means less spending and a lower level of activity, and it could mean a higher yield on financial assets. The central bank might as a result be induced to permit more growth in the banking system in an attempt to stimulate the economy. There could be a net gain for the banking system. Under inflationary conditions, however, there is a definite advantage to the banks in discouraging the financing activities of those who normally are not competitors of the banking system. If these non-bank lenders are expanding when the banking system is being restricted, their activities will contribute to the inflationary conditions that the central bank is reacting against, and so may cause the central bank to increase the degree of restraint imposed on the banking system. Thus, the more these non-bank lenders expand in these circumstances the more the banking system is restricted.

In general, the banking system suffers certain undesirable effects from outside competition, defined as all lending activity that encroaches upon the field of bank financing. The banks may be able to avoid most of these effects by meeting the competition, but this involves certain costs too. Clearly, it pays the system to meet outside competition up to the point where the extra costs offset the long-run benefits to be gained from such competition, namely, a faster growth or larger size and a higher return on assets.[8] There may also be a gain to be had by reacting against the financing activities of those who do not compete with the banks for earning assets, but again the potential benefits must be set off against the cost of so reacting.

PROFITS IN BANKING

Monetary Policy and Bank Profits

Bank profits are affected not only by deposit competition but also by counter-cyclical monetary policy. To consider the effects of the

8. Walter A. Morton, "A Zero Deposit Rate," *American Economic Review*, *30* (Sept. 1940), 547–9, concludes that the banking system would have higher profits if it paid no interest at all on deposits. The savings on interest payments, he argues, would exceed the loss of income from lower yields on earning assets resulting from the increase in outside competition that would follow the elimination of the deposit rate. He does not, however, take into account the longer-term effect of increased outside competition on the growth prospects or size of the banking system.

latter on bank profits it is necessary to construct a scheme for relating types of monetary policy to bank profits. Such a scheme is provided by a system of iso-profit curves for the banking system, defined for interest rates and the amount of loanable funds that the system is able to provide by way of loans or security holdings.

Figure 3 (p. 148) shows a set of iso-profit curves for a banking system. Interest rates are measured along the vertical axis and the amount of loanable funds supplied by banks, along the horizontal axis. Interest rates may be measured in terms of an index or some representative rate that reflects the average yield on bank assets. The amount of loanable funds is simply the total of earning assets that the system can carry, which is a function of monetary policy. Any one iso-profit curve is the locus of all combinations of interest rates and loanable funds that produce the same total profit for the banking system. Each iso-profit curve approaches the interest-rate axis asymptotically, but cuts the loanable funds axis for some finite value. The less loanable funds the system is able to supply, the greater interest rates (or yield in bank assets) must be to maintain bank profits at a given level. With interest rates constant, it is obvious that bank profits rise as loanable funds expand, so that the further an iso-profit curve is from the interest axis in Figure 3 the higher the level of profits it represents. Less obvious, perhaps, is that with the same amount of loanable funds bank profits rise with interest rates. The effect of higher interest rates on profits is gradual, for it depends on lower-yielding assets being replaced by higher-yielding ones; but as between two points of time marking off a significant time interval, bank profits will be higher at that point for which interest rates are higher, the amount of loanable funds being the same in the two instances.[9] Capital losses

9. Paul A. Samuelson, "The Effect of Interest Rate Increases on the Banking System," *American Economic Review*, 35 (Mar. 1945), 23, reasons that banks are made better off by a rise in interest rates, but apparently on grounds that this enhances their net worth. Basil John Moore, "The Effects of Counter-Cyclical Monetary Policy on the Canadian Chartered Banks, 1935–1957" (Unpublished Ph.D. dissertation, The Johns Hopkins University, 1958), pp. 169–74, offers an excellent critique of the Samuelson argument and concludes that the argument does not bear on the profits of the banking system. (Pages cited are those of a privately mimeographed copy of the dissertation, the pagination of which differs from that of the dissertation itself.)

may be realized of course when interest rates rise, but such losses do not reduce profits when the losses are only realized in moving to a more profitable distribution of earning assets.

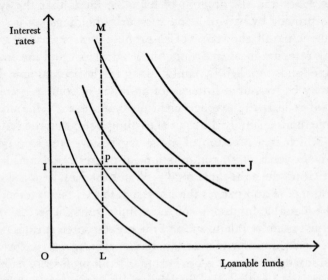

FIGURE 3

ISO-PROFIT CURVES FOR A BANKING SYSTEM

The cost conditions underlying Figure 3 are such that while a rise in interest rates may raise the cost of funds to the banking system they do not raise costs as much as they do revenues. Likewise, any rise in costs caused by an expansion in loanable funds is assumed to be less than the rise in revenues.

The effects of counter-cyclical monetary policy on bank profits can now be examined with the aid of Figure 3. For defining ease and tightness in monetary policy a point may be selected which represents the interest rates and loanable funds that exist when the economy is in a satisfactory state of equilibrium. Such a point is P for which interest rates are OI and the amount of loanable funds supplied by the banking system is OL. Monetary policy is not reacting against either an expansion or a contraction in the level of activity in the economy. Bank profits are at a level indicated by the iso-profit curve on which P lies.

Tightness in monetary policy may now be defined as any combination of higher interest rates and less loanable funds than prevails at the point P. That is, all points to the left of PM and above IP in Figure 3 reflect a tighter monetary policy than exists at P. Thus, monetary policy may reduce the amount of loanable funds supplied by the banking system below OL and raise interest rates above OI. Higher, lower, or constant bank profits can clearly be associated with such a move, for the new combination of loanable funds and interest rates may lie on the same iso-profit curve as P, or it may lie above or below it. Therefore, when a restrictive monetary policy takes the form of reducing the size of the banking system, it does not necessarily follow that bank profits will fall.

Restrictive monetary policy may, however, also be associated with an increase in the size of the banking system as well as with an increase in interest rates. That is, the monetary authorities in trying to restrain an expansion of the economy may only succeed in restricting the growth of the banking system instead of causing the system to contract.[10] Tightness in monetary policy would then result in a combination of interest rates and loanable funds lying to the right of PM and above PJ in Figure 3. In that area bank profits are definitely higher than at P.

An easing in monetary policy from that associated with the point P may lead to lower interest rates and more loanable funds from the banking system. Such a combination would lie to the right of PL and below PJ. Again, bank profits may be higher, lower, or the same as at P. It is also quite possible that an easy monetary policy could result not only in lower interest rates but also in a smaller banking system. This occurs in a contracting economy when bank loans fall off and the banking system makes use of the excess cash so provided to acquire securities from the central bank. The result is a combination of loanable funds and interest rates, lying in the area OIPL, which produces less profit than P.

This analysis suggests that a tightening of monetary policy to restrain an expansion in the economy is more likely to raise bank

10. Canadian experience with central banking has been that the lending resources of the banks have never been "decreased by any significant amount for any significant period." Bank of Canada, *Annual Report*, 1960, p. 18.

profits than to reduce them. Indeed, if a restrictive monetary policy never succeeds in reducing the size of the banking system, bank profits will always be raised by such a policy. An easing in monetary policy seems more likely to reduce bank profits than to raise them, although the latter possibility cannot be ruled out.[11]

Monetary Control and Bank Profits

Bank profits may also be affected by the way in which monetary control is exercised, and here there are two general possibilities: alterations in the supply of cash reserves and alterations in the legal reserve requirements of the banking system. In either of these ways the authorities can make the amount of cash in the banking system exceed or fall short of system requirements, and so upset the general equilibrium of the banking system, which requires balance between cash needs and cash supplies.

Control exercised through the supply of cash reserves can be carried out by affecting the amount of reserves borrowed or purchased from the central bank by the banking system; by not offsetting fortuitous changes in cash reserves caused by such things as currency flows between the banks and the public, or deposit transfers by the public between the central bank and the banking system; or by effecting net payments between the general public and the central bank. The last represents open-market operations proper. For purposes of analysis open-market operations only will be used to contrast control through the supply of cash reserves with control exercised through variations in legal reserve requirements.

The comparative effect on bank profits of these two methods of control depends on the immediate operational aims of the control authorities. They may emphasize the level of bank deposits and induce contraction or expansion in order to produce a given change in

11. Moore, "Counter-Cyclical Monetary Policy," in examining the effects of counter-cyclical monetary policy on Canadian banks, found (p. 238) that in every period of expansionary policy he examined the ratio of bank profits to total assets fell, but that in periods of restrictive policy the ratio rose substantially. He found the relationship between absolute profits and policy less clear (p. 239). In periods in which he classified monetary policy as restrictive profits either rose or remained constant; for expansionary policies, profits either fell or remained constant (Table 23, p. 243).

deposits. Or, they may concentrate on the amount of earning assets held by the banking system and induce banking expansions and contractions in order to produce a given change in earning assets. Finally, they may be less specific and simply operate in terms of generating a given cash excess or deficiency in the system. The two contrasting methods of monetary control may be assessed in terms of each of these aims.

First, a given increase in deposits may be achieved by an appropriate increase in cash reserves with reserve requirements constant, or by an appropriate reduction in reserve requirements with cash reserves held constant. It follows that for a given rise in deposits earning assets rise less when cash reserves are increased instead of being held constant. Hence, bank profits are lower when open-market operations, instead of reductions in reserve requirements, are used to expand deposits.[12] By similar reasoning it can be shown that earning assets, and so bank profits, fall less when a given reduction in deposits is produced by open-market operations instead of by a rise in reserve requirements. Also, for given variations in deposits, the volume of earning assets held by the banking system varies less if the deposit variation is induced by open-market operations, rather than by changes in reserve requirements. Therefore, if the immediate control aim is regulation of the deposit volume, it would seem preferable to exercise control through open-market operations, for this involves less variation in bank earning assets and bank profits.

Second, a given increase in bank earning assets may be achieved by increasing bank cash, reserve requirements unchanged, or by lowering reserve requirements while keeping cash reserves constant. It follows, therefore, that bank deposits are raised more for a given increase in earning assets induced by open-market operations than by a reduction in reserve requirements, because cash is increased by the former but not by the latter. If costs rise with deposits, bank profits are lower under open-market operations than under reduced reserve

12. Cf. U.S. Congress, Joint Economic Committee, *Employment, Growth, and Price Levels: Hearings*, 86th Cong., 1st Sess., 1959, Pt. 6A, "The Government's Management of its Monetary, Fiscal, and Debt Operations," p. 1254, memorandum by John H. Kareken.

requirements.[13] For a given fall in earning assets, bank cash also falls under open-market operations, so that deposits fall by that much more than they do when an increase in reserve requirements, which leaves bank cash constant, is used to produce the same fall in earning assets. Thus, bank profits here may fall less under open-market operations than under reserve reductions. Also, monetary control directed at producing given variations in bank earning assets will produce smaller variations in bank deposits if carried out by varying reserve requirements.

Third, it may be that monetary control is more a matter of creating cash excesses and deficits in the banking system for purposes of regulating the direction and rate of movement of the system. For a given cash excess the expansion in earning assets is greater when the excess is generated by lowering the reserve ratio instead of by open-market operations. The smaller the reserve ratio the larger the lending multiplier which combines with the given excess to determine the expansion in earning assets. Similarly, for a given cash deficit the contraction in earning assets is less when the initial deficit is produced by raising the reserve ratio instead of by open-market operations, for the larger the reserve ratio the smaller the lending multiplier. Most likely bank profits are highest when earning assets are highest, which they are when variations in reserve requirements are used for both contraction and expansion. Bank deposits may be higher or lower under open-market operations, depending on whether or not the generation of the cash impulse affects bank deposits.[14]

13. Total revenue from earning assets is the same in the two situations so that any difference in net profits between the two must arise from the difference in deposits. John H. Kareken, "On the Relative Merits of Reserve-Ratio Changes and Open-Market Operations," *Journal of Finance*, *16* (Mar. 1961), 65n1, 69–70, assesses the impact on bank profits in this situation in terms of the effect on the ratio of earning assets to total assets.

14. For example, cash in the banking system may be altered without affecting deposits, as occurs when securities are traded between the banks and the central bank. Or bank cash may be altered in a way that alters deposits to the same extent, as occurs when the central bank trades securities with the general public. Richard Goode and John G. Gurley, "Open-Market Operations *versus* Reserve Requirement Variation: Comment," *Economic Journal*, *70* (Sept. 1960), 617n1, come to the opposite conclusion for what seems to be the same circumstances. They

When the art of monetary control consists of providing impulses to the banking system for contraction and expansion, it is perhaps best served by promoting expansions through reductions in reserve requirements or ratios and contractions through open-market operions. When expansion is desired, it makes good sense to couple the impulse fed into the banking system with the largest multiplier possible, and this is what is achieved by lowering the reserve ratio[15] so that more expansion is induced and encouraged by lowering reserve ratios.[16] When contraction is desirable, however, open-market oper-

state that "the same initial reserve deficiency" produced by open-market sales causes deposits to fall more than would the same deficiency produced by higher reserve requirements, while the decline in earning assets caused by the higher requirements might equal, exceed, or fall short of the decline produced by open-market operations. It seems to be just the other way about.

15. Warren L. Smith, *Debt Management in the United States*, Joint Economic Committee: Study of Employment, Growth, and Price Levels: Study Paper No. 19 (Washington, Government Printing Office, 1960), p. 142, sees as an advantage in using reductions in reserve requirements in providing for secular growth of the banking system the larger banking multipliers that would result. He believes, however, that cyclical and short-run changes in the banking system are better achieved by open-market operations than by changes in reserve requirements, because of the greater flexibility of the former.

16. Joseph Aschheim, *Techniques of Monetary Control* (Baltimore, The Johns Hopkins Press, 1961), pp. 29–31, argues that open-market purchases encourage expansion more than a reduction in reserve ratios, for when the purchases take securities from the member banks this reduces bank earning assets. Therefore, the marginal utility of income for banks is higher under open-market purchases than under reduced reserve requirements, and so the incentive to expand is correspondingly greater. The comparison made here, however, is not valid. For one thing, if open-market purchases are made entirely with non-bank security dealers, a banking system that gets the same amount of excess reserves through a reserve reduction is in exactly the same position as a system that gets the excess as a result of open-market purchases. If the excess is generated by the banks selling securities, they are obviously selling to make a profit on the transaction and not to raise cash. They will, therefore, want to reinvest the proceeds immediately so as not to lose income. Once they have replaced the securities sold to the central bank they hold the same amount of earning assets as before: their incentive to expand further depends on what excess cash they have left, and they are in exactly the same position as banks who hold the same amount of earning assets and get an equivalent amount of excess cash through a reduction in reserve requirements.

ations serve better for they couple the necessary impulse with a larger multiplier than would a rise in reserve ratios,[17] and hence contraction is greater under open-market operations.[18]

In summary, the operating aims of monetary control determine, when choice is possible, which is the more desirable technique of control to use, and the technique used, in turn, determines the effect of monetary control on bank profits. For variations in deposits or earning assets induced by control, banks fare better under open-market operations for a contraction, and under reserve reductions for an expansion. When control is applied by altering the amount of excess cash in the banking system, however, banks are better off when variations in reserve requirements are used for both expansion and contraction.

17. This is perhaps the theoretical justification for the Federal Reserve policy in the post-accord period of only lowering reserve ratios and never raising them—a policy that is criticized by Kareken, "On the Relative Merits of Reserve-Ratio Changes and Open-Market Operations," p. 71.

18. There is another argument advanced against using a rise in reserve ratios to induce a contraction. The higher the reserve ratio the less the relative cash loss to other banks when a bank loses deposits to them, assuming that reserve requirements are based on current or spot deposits. Hence, higher ratios dampen down possible adverse losses of cash required for reserve purposes and so lessen the need to hold liquid assets for cash adjustment purposes. With higher cash ratios a smaller proportion of liquid assets can be carried and a higher proportion of less-liquid assets. Cf. Aschheim, p. 24; Earl R. Rolph, "Principles of Debt Management," *American Economic Review*, 47 (June 1957), 319; Richard C. Porter, "Open-Market Operations *versus* Reserve Requirement Variation: Comment," *Economic Journal*, 70 (Sept. 1960), 619–20, and "Reply" by Joseph Aschheim, ibid, p. 622.

This liquidity consideration which induces a shift between loans and securities is not likely to be a short-run consideration that follows immediately every rise in reserve ratios. It is an adjustment more likely to follow only after banks have had some experience with clearing losses at the higher ratios.

An income effect is produced in a contraction by both open-market sales and higher reserve requirements, and where this is greater for higher reserves there may be an impact on liquidity as noted in Chapter Two. If, however, it takes more than a marginal change in bank income to affect liquidity needs, as well it might, open-market sales must produce no more than a marginal drop in income and higher reserve ratios must produce a more than marginal drop in income for higher reserve ratios to have a greater effect on liquidity needs. Even then it is an effect that most likely follows, with a considerable lag, the initial adjustment made in response to a rise in reserve ratios.

The Nature of Bank Profits

Another interesting analytical aspect of bank profits is the form they assume, or the way in which they are realized. This feature of banking profits is most noticeable when banks are considered collectively and their balance-sheets are consolidated into one statement covering the entire banking system.

On this consolidated basis, bank profits appear in a different form and have a different effect than do profits in other fields of business. Profits of other businesses usually show up, initially, in additions to cash balances and accounts receivable. Later, of course, profits retained in the business may assume other forms as the cash generated by profit-taking is used to acquire other assets or to pay off liabilities to the public.

The chain of events is different in banking. Usually, the realization of profits in banking does not generate additional cash for the banking system; instead, it reduces banking liabilities to the public—that is, deposits. The reason for this is that most items of bank expenses and revenues do not involve cash receipts or cash losses for the banking system, because most of the profit-and-loss transactions pass through the deposit accounts rather than through the cash accounts. Although an individual bank may gain cash as a result of making profits, that cash will come from other banks which thereby suffer a loss of deposits. The net effect is that in the banking system the amount of cash is not usually disturbed when profits are made, but the amount of deposits is reduced. An examination of how revenues are collected and expenses are paid in the banking system will help to explain the connection between banking profits and deposits.

Banks meet their expenses largely by issuing their own cheques or other similar monetary instruments, or by making credit entries to customers accounts. An example of such credit entries occurs when interest is paid on savings accounts; the interest is automatically credited to the account of the depositor. Thus, internal credit entries passed through the accounts of customers in payment of bank expenses have an immediate and direct effect on bank deposits. Paying expenses in this way increases bank deposits. Bank deposits are also increased when banks pay their expenses with cheques and the recipients pay these into their own banks. Therefore, the fact that banks issue their own cheques and vouchers in payment of expenses usually means that an expansion of bank deposits occurs somewhere in the banking system. Bank expenses paid with currency do not, of course, affect deposits directly, although a large loss of currency in this manner would require the banking system to contract. However, only a very small portion of all bank expenses are paid with currency, and most of this is probably offset by revenues received from the public in the form of currency.

Similarly, most items of bank revenue reduce the amount of deposits held by the banking system. Thus, a large part of bank revenue is collected in the form of cheques drawn on accounts held in the banking system. Bank deposits are therefore directly reduced when bank revenues are collected in this fashion. The same effect is achieved when banks collect revenues by debiting the accounts of their customers directly, in accordance with prior agreements, for amounts owing to the bank. Service charges are a familiar example of this procedure. Some items of revenue, as already noted, may be collected in the form of currency, but these constitute an insignificant portion of all revenue items collected. Thus, the general statement holds that the collection of bank revenues from the general public reduces bank deposits.

It follows from the reasoning of the two preceding paragraphs that when bank revenues exceed bank expenses, the amount of deposits in the banking system is reduced by roughly the amount of profits made. And if some of the expense items are internal to the banking system— such as are depreciation charges—deposits are further reduced by the amount of these retained expense items. These statements apply mainly to the banking system rather than to individual banks, although they apply to a certain extent to the latter when the system is made up of a few large banks. An individual bank is more likely to lose cash than to gain deposits when it pays its expenses. Likewise, it may gain cash instead of losing deposits when it collects revenue. However, these tendencies are modified by the practice of business reciprocity, which is no more prevalent in banking than it is in other fields. Business reciprocity refers to the tendency of firms to deal with each other, to buy from those who buy from them. In accordance with this practice a bank may distribute its expenditures for various items among its own customers so that as a result a good part of its expenses are paid to its own depositors.[19] And of course a large part of its revenue is collected from its own depositors. Hence, a large bank in its profit-and-loss transactions may affect its own deposits, just as profit-taking in the banking system affects deposits.

When bank profits show up as a reduction in bank deposits, which is the usual situation when only transactions with the public are involved, no extra cash is generated in the banking system. But the ratio of cash to deposits is raised above its equilibrium value by the fall in deposits. This means that the system is in a position to expand. The acquisition of additional assets by the banking system increases bank deposits again because what the banks spend for those assets is probably deposited with the banks again. This increase in deposits restores the ratio of cash to deposits to the level prevailing prior to the making of profits. Thus, deposits fall at first when profits are made by the banks, then as the banking system expands deposits are restored to their previous level. This effect depends on the central bank not reacting to the adjustment process and so not changing bank cash.

The end result is that profits earned from serving the general public fulfil the same function in banking as in other businesses: when retained they enable the organization to expand its assets. The main difference is that the growth of other firms financed from profits proceeds first by an increase in current assets, mainly cash, followed by a shift into other assets; in banking, profit-induced growth may proceed first by reducing liabilities to the public, and then by expanding them again as additional assets are acquired.

The assets that the banking system are most likely to acquire when profits are realized are open-market assets. The acquisition of open-market assets represents the quickest and surest method of expansion

19. Reciprocity in U.S. banking is discussed by Richard L. Kraybill in "Are Bankers Artless Buyers?," *Banking* (Journal of the American Bankers Association), Apr. 1960, p. 62, and in "We are Skillful Buyers . . . But!," ibid., June 1960, pp. 55, 125. It is more briefly noted by G. W. Stocking and W. F. Mueller, "Business Reciprocity and the Size of Firms," *Journal of Business, 30* (Apr. 1957), 79, and by Melvin Mandell, "Reciprocity," *Dun's Review and Modern Industry* (Chicago), Sept. 1960, p. 32.

and the easiest way to restore the cash-reserve ratio to its normal
level. And this procedure is likely to be followed even if all the profits
earned are not retained but are paid out eventually in dividends. In
this latter case, the banking system invests its profits in short-term
securities. Then when dividend payments are made, the system
liquidates its short-term securities to keep the ratio of cash to deposits
at the appropriate level. As in other businesses, it is only the retained
revenues that permit a permanent increase in the assets of the banking system to follow from profit-making activities.

The foregoing analysis is based on the assumption that profits
generally do not expand the amount of cash in the banking system.
A minor exception is profits realized in the form of currency. A more
important exception may arise from transactions with the central
government. There are no complications if the government pays its
receipts into accounts kept with the banks and meets its expenses by
drawing on such accounts. When the banks pay taxes and other
expense items to the government, government deposits are raised;
and when the government pays interest or other items of revenues to
the banks, government deposits are reduced. In short, profit-and-loss
transactions between the banks and the government merely affect
deposits as do most other transactions of a like nature.

The situation is entirely different when the government banks with
the central bank. Banks as beneficiaries of government expenditures
then receive additional cash because the government cheques they
receive are drawn on the central bank which must give the banks
cash in exchange for the cheques. Similarly, when the government
deposits its revenues with the central bank, the banks lose cash in
making payments to the government. The cheques the banks issue to
the government are not re-deposited with the banks, but are deposited with the central bank to which the banks must give up cash.
The cash the banks pay to the central bank, or that they receive from
it, takes the form of debits and credits to the accounts that the banks
keep with the central bank.

When the banking system does gain cash as a result of making
profits, the system is in a position to utilize that cash directly to
acquire additional assets just as any other group of firms would be.
However, the banks can acquire assets to a greater extent than the

amount of profits earned in the form of cash, because as the banks attempt to utilize this new cash the amount of deposits left with the banking system expands. That is, the capacity of the banking system for supplying funds to the community is enlarged so that the amount of earning assets that the banks can hold expands more than by the amount of profits realized in cash form. This effect of cash profits is peculiar to banking, but it depends on the central bank doing nothing.

THE CAPITAL ACCOUNTS

Retained revenues, defined as revenues not paid out to the public or to the government as expenses, dividends, or income taxes, affect in a very broad way the capital position of the banking system in the sense that retained revenues must show up somewhere in the consolidated balance-sheet of the system. Retained revenues represent the amounts set aside out of total revenues for depreciation allowances, bad debts, and additions to inner and outer reserves. The total of these retained revenues together with all external expense payments, dividend payments, and payments for income tax exhausts the gross earnings of the banking system. They could of course exceed the gross earnings but this would be exceptional; usually the total of the foregoing items will be equivalent to gross earnings. The retained revenues themselves are equivalent to the earnings retained in the banking system plus the allowances for internal expenses, such as depreciation, bad debts, and additions to inner reserves.

The retention of revenues by the banking system is preceded mainly by a reduction of deposits in the banking system. This permits the system to expand, and the expansion is placed on a permanent basis by the retention of revenues. If revenues are not retained, the banks cannot make a permanent addition to their earning assets by making profits. The form in which revenues are retained has no bearing on the expansion that follows, but the allocation of retained revenues to the various categories does determine the effect on the consolidated balance-sheet of the banking system.

There are two main categories of accounts to which retained earnings may be allocated: they may be allocated to inner reserves or to

outer reserves. Inner reserves include all those accounts used to reduce the book values of bank assets.[20] Usually such accounts are not
shown separately, but are applied to the assets affected to show the
latter at depreciated or reduced values. In this sense depreciation
allowances on buildings, machinery, and equipment may be classed
with the inner reserves. Such allowances are usually deducted from
the book value of the fixed assets, which are thus shown at their
depreciated values in bank balance-sheets. Hence, the allocation of
retained revenues to depreciation reduces the value of the fixed assets
held by the banking system. However, the revenues from which the
depreciation allowances were taken have previously reduced bank
deposits and thus enabled the banking system to acquire other assets.
This expansion which follows the realization of revenues prevents
total assets in the banking system from being reduced by the act of
depreciating the fixed assets. What is taken off the fixed assets gets
added on to other assets. That is, total assets remain constant when
revenues are used to write down fixed assets, the act of depreciating
merely keeping that portion of the revenues used in the process from
showing up in a corresponding increase in banking assets.

Provisions for bad debts and additions made to inner reserves
proper also prevent the revenues used for these purposes from showing up in an expansion in the value of banking assets. Provisions made
for bad debts are used to reduce the book value of loans to their true
value, that is to the amount that appears likely to be repaid. The
inner reserves proper are made up of additional amounts set aside
to allow for unexpected lending losses. These reserves are also used
to reduce the book value of loans. Thus, the balance-sheet figures
for loans exclude not only all known bad debts but also a further
amount for loans now thought to be good but which may turn bad
later.

However, the acquisition of earning assets that follows from the
realization of the revenues allotted to provisions for bad debts and additions to inner reserves will be at least sufficient to keep the balance-

20. The different types of inner reserves carried by Canadian banks are classified
and defined in Canada, Parliament, House, Standing Committee on Banking and
Commerce, *Proceedings*, 1954, p. 775, and some aspects of them are discussed on
pp. 180-2, 475-7.

sheet total for banking assets from falling. Of course the banking system now holds more assets in terms of book values than it did before, but the additional funds thus supplied to the public depend on the specific inner reserves for loan depreciation only to the extent that the existence of such reserves leads to a greater retention of revenues than otherwise would take place. It is the retention of revenues in itself that enables the system to supply more funds to the community.

Retained revenues not distributed to the various inner reserves are allotted to the outer reserves, namely, to the rest account and to undivided profits.[21] Additions to these accounts do not reduce the value of bank assets; instead they lead to an expansion of bank liabilities (and assets), even though the revenue added to the outer reserves may have reduced bank deposits. The banking system has expanded its deposits again following any reduction in deposits caused by banking profits. Thus, after the banking system has digested the income it has earned, bank deposits are no less than they were before. Therefore, the additions made to the outer reserves from banking income represent a net addition to total bank liabilities, and total bank assets are correspondingly larger. Furthermore, the addition to the outer reserves of the banks, like the addition to the inner reserves, is related directly to the growth of the banking system only because such additions reflect the retention of revenues, which permits additional funds to be supplied to the public.

Thus, retained earnings enable the banking system to acquire additional assets. And as in other fields of economic activity, retained earnings may be used to acquire additional fixed or physical assets as well as additional financial assets. There is this difference, however, that the banking system may be deprived of enjoying the benefits of its retained earnings through central-banking operations. The central bank could, if it wanted to, so reduce bank cash that the banking

21. Outer reserves of Canadian banks may also be increased by transfers from inner reserves and from premiums realized on the sale of new capital stock. A large part of the existing outer reserves originated with premiums realized on the issue of capital stock; retained earnings after provisions for all inner reserves have been the second largest source of outer reserves. Ibid., p. 774; Bank of Canada, *Statistical Summary*, Financial Supplement, 1956, p. 30.

system would be unable to expand on the basis of its retained revenues.

When the banks are permitted to expand on the basis of their retained revenues, they most likely acquire additional financial assets at first, even though they may be planning eventually to acquire new fixed assets. The acquisition of new fixed assets could follow immediately upon the realization of retained revenues, but generally open-market assets are bought first to offset the effect of retained revenues on the balance-sheet. Then when fixed assets are acquired, the banks issue their cheques to pay contractors and suppliers. As a result, somewhere in the banking system bank deposits are raised by the issue of these bank cheques, and raised relative to the amount of cash in the banking system. Consequently, some banks in the system will find that they have to liquidate some of their open-market securities until the ratio of cash to deposits in the system is restored to the equilibrium level. The end result is that new fixed or capital assets now appear in the consolidated balance-sheet for the banking system as a partial or full offset to retained earnings.

If new capital expenditures run ahead of retained earnings in the banking system, the banks in the system must dispose of open-market securities in excess of the amount of earnings retained. The new fixed assets acquired thus completely offset retained earnings and displace some additional financial assets from the balance-sheet.[22]

Banks can of course finance their capital expenditures by issuing new capital stock. The effect of such issues is mainly to reduce deposits in the banking system, for the majority of the purchasers of the new stock will draw upon their bank deposits in payment.[23] The reduction in deposits is relative to the amount of cash in the system so that the cash-deposit ratio is raised above its usual level. As a

22. Of course when retained earnings run ahead of capital expenditures the result is a gain in earning assets relative to deposits. Cf. Lauchlin Currie, *The Supply and Control of Money in the United States*, Harvard Economic Studies, 47 (Cambridge, Mass., Harvard University Press, 1934), p. 50.

23. Leland J. Pritchard, "A Note on the Relationships of Bank Capital to the Lending Ability of the Commercial Banks," *American Economic Review*, 43 (June 1953), 364, who also mentions currency payments and gold flowing from other countries to buy new bank stock as minor qualifications to the generalization that new capital issues by banks only reduce deposits in the system.

result the banking system can acquire additional assets until the ratio of cash to deposits is restored to its normal level, most of the restoration being caused by an inflation of deposits as the banks buy up new assets. Thus, the raising of new capital has the same effect on the balance-sheet of the banking system as does the retention of earnings: it enables the banking system to acquire new assets when the central bank does not intervene.

CONCLUSIONS

Banks are generally competing in order to increase their capacity for carrying earning assets, and to this end they compete for cash reserves with each other and with other deposit institutions. This almost continuous struggle for cash reserves appears as a competition for deposits: a competition to get deposits away from other institutions and to keep what deposits the individual bank actively creates itself. The size of its deposits reflects the success of the bank in attracting new deposits and retaining old ones.

Competition for deposits by the banking system makes sense even if the short-run effect is to raise costs and to leave total deposits unchanged. Longer-run benefits may follow if the bank competition sufficiently restricts the growth of non-bank lenders to require the central bank to permit the banking system to grow at a faster rate in order to meet the financing needs of the economy. The greater growth thus gained may more than compensate the banks for the cost of competing for deposits with non-bank lenders.

Banking profits are also affected by counter-cyclical monetary policy. There is no reason for a definite relationship to exist between changes in bank profits and in monetary policy but theoretical considerations suggest that bank profits may be increased by a restrictive monetary policy and reduced by a policy of easing. The converse, however, cannot be ruled out.

Profit-taking by the banks initially affects the level of deposits. That is, expenses incurred by banks usually increase bank deposits, and revenues earned by them decrease bank deposits. The consequence of this is that when the banks as a group realize a net profit bank deposits are reduced. However, the action that the banks take to keep their cash-reserve ratios stable results in a restoration of deposits in the banking system when these are upset by profit-taking, so long as the central bank does not decide to alter the supply of cash reserves.

Profits retained by the banks may be used to increase either the outer or inner reserves of the banks. When retained profits are used to increase the outer reserves, the final effect of profit-taking on the consolidated balance-sheet of the banks is an expansion in assets equal to the retention of earnings. That is, the reduction in deposits relative to cash reserves that the retention of earnings causes enables the banks to add that amount to their assets. When retained earnings are added to the inner reserves, the results are slightly different. An addition to inner reserves reduces bank assets, but the reduction in bank deposits relative to cash reserves that also results enables the banking system to acquire new assets to the amount of the reduction. Hence, retained earnings add to the capacity of the banks for carrying earning assets, and it is the retention of earnings, not their specific allocation, that causes this favourable effect. In the end, however, it is the central bank, through its control of bank cash, that has the final say on what effect retained earnings have on total bank assets.

Chapter Four: INTERREGIONAL BANKING TRANSACTIONS AND OPERATIONS

The present chapter considers some geographical or regional aspects of domestic banking operations not touched upon in the previous chapters. Specifically, the chapter deals with the connection between banking activity and geographical movements in bank deposits. The nature and meaning of interregional movements of funds are discussed and related to banking and financial activity in general. Then the relationship between banking structure or organization to the mobility of funds is examined, mainly by comparing branch banking and unit banking. Finally, special attention is directed to branch banking and the mobility of funds, for here existing doctrine is, if not confused, at least misleading.

THE INTERREGIONAL MOVEMENT OF FUNDS

The interregional movement of funds within a country arises for a variety of reasons. These must be classified and the meaning of the expression "movement of funds" clearly stated in order to analyze the connection between banking activity and the geographical distribution of bank deposits. Following this some attention is given to the difference between banking activity and the activities of other financial institutions as it bears upon the movement of funds.

Definition and Classification

A few elementary considerations help to frame a general definition for the movement of funds. First, the concept "funds" is simply a short expression for currency and deposits. Thus it is movements of currency and deposits that are involved here, and more exactly movements of currency and of deposits that are geographically significant. Geographical significance need not be defined precisely for present purposes; it is sufficient to say that when a large country can be divided into a few economic regions, which can be done with the United States and Canada, a movement of funds from one of these economic regions to other domestic regions constitutes a significant geographical movement of funds.

Deposits are more likely to be moved than currency because they are a much larger component of the money supply than currency (and so more payments are made with deposits than with currency). Also it is generally easier and more convenient to move them over long distances. Hence, the discussion of the movement of funds can be mainly restricted to a discussion of geographical movements in bank deposits, and in what follows a movement of funds will mean a movement of deposits, unless otherwise stated. The mobility of funds is an alternative expression that will be used to refer to a movement of funds or of deposits.

The expression "movement of funds" strictly speaking must apply to funds already in existence, because movement can only refer to moving something already owned or, less exactly, to transferring an existing item to someone else. Thus, a movement of deposits means in an exact sense the geographical redistribution of a given total of deposits. The ways in which such a geographical redistribution may be effected serve to distinguish different types of deposit movements. Three different types of event can cause deposits in one region to fall while deposits elsewhere rise by a like amount so that total deposits remain constant.

One type of event that causes a change in the geographical distribution of a given total of deposits is a movement of deposits by their owners from one banking point to another without any change in ownership: a movement of deposits in the strictest sense of the term. This is the type of movement that only the owners of deposits can effect; banks cannot on their own initiative move the deposits of the public. Movements of deposits without a change in their ownership may occur for various reasons. The geographical movement of individuals and firms, reflecting a changing population distribution and industrial structure, may cause a corresponding interregional movement of deposits.[1] Changes in the distribution of banking offices may also be a source of interregional deposit movement; when new banking offices are opened, deposits may be shifted to them from outside branches. Or, the closing of old branches may lead to the transfer of deposits from a region. These kinds of geographical movements are the result of long-term and slow-moving changes.

Less dependent on long-term considerations are deposit movements that occur because depositors decide to redistribute their funds among existing branches; they change their point of banking. Thus, some businesses that obtain bank loans and maintain deposits in outside regions[2] may decide to switch their banking to branches within their home area; there is then a lump-sum, once-for-all interregional shift of deposits. The same applies if businesses in a given area decide to transfer working or saving balances to financial centres outside their home area. These changes in points of banking, however, do not represent economically significant movements of funds, unless they bring about a change in regional spending patterns. Whether or not a spending unit maintains deposits with branches in its home area is not an important economic fact—the significant thing is its spending in the area. If the unit maintains deposits outside the area in which it spends, its spending gives rise to an interregional flow of funds; if it then decides to shift its deposits to branches within the spending area without changing its pattern of spending, the result is a once-for-all transfer of funds that replaces a stream of payments previously flowing between residents of the area and the spending unit with the outside deposit account.

The second and more usual type of event that causes a geographical movement of deposits is associated with interregional payments. Interregional payments employing only deposits involve in effect a

1. Cf. "Deposits on the Move," Federal Reserve Bank of Philadelphia, *Business Review*, Mar. 1957, pp. 19, 21.

2. Cf. ibid., p. 20, where it is pointed out that many large firms in the United States obtain loans from banks outside the regions in which they operate. Also cf. "The Interregional Flow of Bank Loans," Federal Reserve Bank of Boston, *New England Business Review*, July 1959, pp. 5–7.

transfer of deposits: that is, a geographical movement of deposits in which the ownership of the deposits is altered. Such movements arise from interregional spending and transfer payments. Thus, an unbalance on all other accounts in the interregional balance of payments of an area with other regions is accommodated by a change in the volume of deposits in the area, offset by a corresponding change in deposits elsewhere. The movement in deposits that results, like the first type of movement discussed, requires the bookkeeping services of the banking system, but it cannot be initiated by the banks themselves.

Finally, banking activity that alters the geographical distribution of deposits without changing the total for deposits creates the same effect as a movement of funds undertaken by the banking public. In the widest sense of the term there has been a movement of deposits because the geographical pattern of an existing total of deposits has been altered. However, a major characteristic of this type of movement is that it involves no movement: the change in the geographical distribution of deposits is not the result of moving deposits from one point to another. Furthermore, two transactions, not one, are required to bring about the redistribution.

This situation arises when the central bank encourages the banks to maintain deposits at some given level. Then any events that cause total bank deposits to deviate from the given total will be countered by the banks with discretionary acts that restore deposits to the permitted level. Thus, a change in the demand for bank loans that causes deposits in some regions to fall leads to offsetting action by the banks affected. If the impact of this offsetting action is felt mainly in other areas, there will be a rise in deposits in those areas. In other words, the geographical impact of events that cause deposits to move in one direction may differ from the geographical impact of the compensating transactions that restore deposits to their previous level. When the adjustments are over, the geographical distribution of deposits differs from what it was before, partially as a result of banking activity. The redistribution is the result of the banks, with the co-operation of the banking public, creating new deposits in some areas and destroying existing deposits elsewhere.

Thus when the mobility of funds is simply equated with any change in the geographical distribution of deposits, it follows that the greater the ability of a banking system to create deposits where they are needed, within the limitations imposed by given cash reserves and reserve ratios, the greater the mobility of deposits is likely to be in that banking system. This raises the question of the relationship of banking structure to the movements of funds, but before that matter can be dealt with a more detailed examination is necessary of the connection between banking in general and the mobility of funds.

Banking and the Mobility of Funds

From what has already been said, it is clear that banks cannot initiate a movement of deposits in the stricter senses of the expression. That is, a bank cannot move the deposits of anyone from one locale to another on its own initiative: it can only do so on the instructions of the owners, and a bank is not the owner of the deposits on its books. Banks take part in an actual movement and transfer of funds only in their capacity as providers and operators of the payments mechanism.

Not every movement of funds by the public requires the services of the banking system. Currency may move from one region to another without any help from the banking system. However, the usual way in which the public effects a movement of funds is to use cheques and similar monetary instruments rather than currency. The banks act as agents in effecting the movement of funds in this case by giving deposits in exchange for monetary instruments drawn on other deposit accounts; any change in the geographical pattern of deposits is the result of the payment activities of the public. The banking system in carrying out the transfer orders of the public may not have to transfer any funds itself. If deposits move simply from some branches of a bank to other branches of the same bank, the bank need transfer none of its own funds. When a movement of funds by the public requires net payments among the banks, settlement is effected by means of transfers on the books of the central bank: the existing total of deposits kept by the banks with the central bank is simply redistributed among them. In general, then, when the public make net interregional payments using their deposits to do so, the only type of transfer effected by the banks on their own behalf is a transfer of cash reserves among themselves.

The banks that gain cash reserves as a result of the payment activities of the public expand their earning assets, but at the same time the banks that have lost cash reserves are contracting. It is possible for these banking adjustments following a redistribution of cash reserves among the banks to cause a further change in the geographical distribution of bank deposits. The possibility arises because the expanding banks most likely increase their deposits somewhat unless they fail to retain any of their excess cash reserves; the contracting banks most likely lose some deposits in the process of contraction. A difference in the geographical location of the new deposits created and the old deposits destroyed as banks adjust to the redistribution of cash reserves among themselves is sufficient to alter the geographical distribution of deposits.

However, the greater possibility for banking activity itself to alter the geographical pattern of deposits arises not as a result of a simple redistribution of cash reserves among the banks, but as a result of the banks altering the composition of their earning assets. The banks first acquire additional earning assets and then, if cash reserves remain constant, they dispose of other assets in order to make room for the new assets. Or the procedure may be reversed: the banks lose some of their earning assets without suffering a loss of cash reserves and then take up the slack by acquiring other assets. Such changes in the composition of the earning assets held by the banks result in the creation of new deposits and the destruction of old ones, but the overall level of bank deposits remains constant. Therefore, if the deposits destroyed have a different geographical pattern from that of the deposits created, the overall effect of the substitution process is a changed geographical distribution of the given total of deposits: in a wide sense, there has been a movement of funds. Whether such a "movement" occurs as the result of substitutions between loans and securities in the banking system depends on the regional demand for bank loans and on the location of those who trade securities with the banks.

It is only in the foregoing manner that a banking system has much opportunity for altering the geographical distribution of bank deposits; and in doing so it does not move deposits or funds at all. There is a special situation, however, in which the banks themselves do make a geographical transfer of funds. This arises when banks in some areas in paying out currency raise the money supply in those areas, and when, at the same time, banks in other areas in receiving currency reduce the money supply in the currency-reducing areas. There is then a geographical redistribution of the money supply which may in this case be accompanied by the banking system moving currency from the banks taking it in, to the banks losing it. The movement may be direct, from the surplus banks to the deficit banks; but more likely it is indirect, with the surplus banking offices shipping their redundant currency to their local supply depots, and the deficit banking offices ordering additional supplies of currency from their local supply depots.

Banking activity may alter not only the geographical distribution of a given total of deposits but also the existing total of deposits. The latter possibility is worth considering although it really does not represent a deposit movement. The possibility arises when the cash reserves available to the banking system are altered. When the reserves are expanded new deposits are created: when reserves are contracted some old deposits must be extinguished. Both the creation of the new deposits and the destruction of the old deposits may change the existing geographical pattern of deposits. This geographical change does not, however, constitute a movement of deposits in any sense, because it is a change brought about by altering total deposits, not by altering the composition of an existing total. The expansion and contraction of deposits that occurs generally requires no movement of funds, only bookkeeping entries to write-up or write-down the deposits of the banks with the central bank. The sole exception results when currency flows are responsible for the alteration in cash reserves: currency shipments between the central bank and the individual banks may then take place.

Other Financial Institutions and the Movement of Funds

Other financial institutions that borrow from some segments of the public in order to lend to other segments may cause a movement of funds. They may borrow more funds in some areas than they lend, and may lend more funds in other areas than they borrow.

If these institutions keep their cash balances with the central bank, they cause bank deposits to be destroyed in the areas in which they borrow from the public. There is no movement of funds from the area as a result of the borrowing, just a transfer of claims on the books of the central bank as the borrowing institutions gain cash from the banks. When these other financial institutions make loans by issuing cheques on their central-bank deposits, their borrowers most likely deposit the cheques with the banks. Bank deposits are thereby increased, but again there is no movement of funds, only a transfer of balances on the books of the central bank between the banks and the other lending institutions. Thus other financial institutions that keep their working balances in the form of deposits with the central bank may cause a change in the geographical distribution of bank deposits through their normal operations but without actually moving deposits, in much the same way as the banking system does.

If these other financial institutions keep their working cash balances with the banks, as they normally will, they cause a movement of deposits between themselves and the public whenever they borrow from the public or lend to them. If these borrowing and lending operations alter the geographical pattern of deposits, it is because the financial institutions have actually transferred deposits between regions. This differs from the way in which a geographical change in funds is caused by banking activities. Here deposits are borrowed—not destroyed—and get paid away—not created—as part of a genuine transfer of funds.

In general, financial institutions other than banks may, in their activities as borrowers and lenders, cause a movement of deposits in a way that the banking system cannot, because banks differ from other financial institutions in being the suppliers of the funds moved. The banks only take part in a genuine movement of funds when, as operators of the payments mechanism, they effect transfers of funds ordered by the deposit owners.

BANKING STRUCTURE AND THE
MOVEMENT OF FUNDS

Analytical discussions of the mobility of funds usually relate the topic to banking structure, structure being identified with the relationship of existing banking offices to each other. The two extremes in banking structure are the banking system in which each banking office represents an independent bank, and the banking system in which all the banking offices are controlled by one bank. A less striking contrast, although still a sharp one, is provided on the one hand by a banking system with many banks but few branches—and these all in the same general locality—and on the other hand by a banking system with few banks but many branches widely distributed; or more simply, the contrast between branch banking and unit banking. This section considers such differences in banking structures in order to examine the effect of structure on the mobility of funds. Three themes are considered: the collection and utilization of cash reserves; regional variations in banking activity; and banking response to interregional deposit movements. All three themes are related, of course, to the subject of banking structure and the movement of funds.

Cash Reserves and Deposit Mobility

The banking system that maximizes its cash reserves and which keeps these reserves most fully utilized does a better job of supplying funds to the community than banking systems that are less efficient at these tasks. Efficiency in these matters may be related to banking structure, but it has nothing to do with the mobility of funds unless ability to supply funds is considered a matter of mobility. However, discussions of the mobility of funds under branch and unit banking seem to imply that mobility is a function of collecting and utilizing cash reserves. To relate the mobility of funds to the cash reserves of the banking system may seem to have little relevance for an analysis of present-day banking, in which the determination of the volume of cash reserves lies outside the control of the banks, and in which most banks are equally capable of keeping their reserves fully utilized. However, arguments are still current about banking structure and

its effect on the mobility of funds that imply some relationship between moving funds and the cash reserves of the banking system. The
current arguments are a carry-over from earlier days of banking
when banks had more scope for influencing the total amount of cash
reserves in the system. When the banking habit was less developed
than now, and the banking system formed a smaller part of the
payments mechanism, banks could add quite considerably to the
total amount of cash reserves by inducing the public to hold deposits
in lieu of legal-tender money. Success of course depended on the
monetary authorities being unable to offset the increase in reserves,
a not unlikely situation given the undeveloped state of central banking. Thus, considerable pools of potential cash reserves for the banks
existed in the economy, and could be tapped by cultivating the
deposit habit in the public through existing banking offices, and
through opening new banking offices in areas where savings were
being held in the form of idle currency hoards.[3]

In adding to cash reserves through attracting currency and specie
out of idle hoards, banking structure may have some bearing on the
amount of cash reserves obtained. One type of banking structure may
be more effective than another in getting cash reserves from a given
economy and so may acquire a larger amount of cash reserves to work
with. Thus it may be that the propensity of the public to hold deposits instead of currency may vary directly with the size of the
banks. Hence a greater degree of concentration of banking units in
the system may mean a greater volume of deposits and so a greater
amount of cash reserves.[4]

But if the ability to tap idle funds in the form of currency is
independent of banking structure, the amount of cash reserves in the
banking system will not vary with the nature of the units forming

3. Thus, H. M. P. Eckardt, *A Rational Banking System: A Comprehensive Study of
the Advantages of the Branch Bank System* (New York, Harper and Brothers, 1911), pp.
102–3, in arguing the case for branch banking speaks of a branch banking office
collecting in its community idle funds formerly kept in "iron safes, in bureau
drawers, old stoves, under rag carpets, and in people's pockets," and thus providing
its head office with additional cash reserves to support banking business elsewhere.

4. James W. Gilbart, *The Principles and Practice of Banking*, p. 82, in listing the
advantages of a branch bank over a local private bank included greater ability to
attract deposits.

that system. And if cash-reserve requirements are also independent of banking structure—that is, if a large bank or a branch bank does not have different reserve requirements from a small bank or a unit bank—the maximum volume of bank deposits that can be supported will be independent of banking structure.[5] Banking structure only has a bearing on the level of deposits in a banking system when the confidence of the public in the banks is related to structure, and when one type of banking structure permits a fuller use of cash reserves than another. The confidence factor requires no further comment, but the utilization of cash reserves does.

The full utilization of cash reserves is only related to the mobility of funds in the sense that additional cash reserves gathered from an area, but which cannot be fully used in that area, are employed in expanding deposits elsewhere. There is supposedly a movement of funds when a banking system acquires additional deposits in an area that gives it additional cash reserves and these cash reserves are used to expand deposits in other areas: the collection of deposits in one area permits the expansion of deposits in others. An early argument in favour of branch banking held that it had an advantage over single-office banking in being able to employ the surplus funds of one area in other areas where they could be profitably used.[6] From this argument the suggestion naturally followed that branch banking developed in order to link together areas with surplus funds and areas deficient in funds.[7]

But collecting cash reserves in one place and using them to create new deposits elsewhere is a question not of moving funds but of being able to avoid excess reserves. A banking system that gains an addition to its cash reserves by its activities in some regions, and then is unable to employ its new cash reserves fully by creating sufficient new de-

5. A small bank, however, may not consider it worth the cost to watch its reserve ratio carefully, preferring instead to carry excess reserves, varying in size to some extent.

6. Gilbart, pp. 82–3, saw as a merit in branch banking over unit banking the ability of the former to make better use of its cash reserves or what he referred to as banking capital.

7. R. G. Hawtrey, *A Century of Bank Rate*, p. 55, briefly mentions branch banking developing in England "to link together districts where there was an excess of deposits and districts where there was a deficiency."

G

posits anywhere—or more exactly, is unable to expand its earning assets to the possible maximum—accumulates excess cash reserves. In other words the argument about banking structure and using the surplus funds of one area in other regions is an argument, not about which banking system gives greater mobility to funds, but about which banking system best avoids excess cash reserves. This argument is best examined by considering what would prevent banks from always fully using their cash reserves, and relating this to banking structure.

Market imperfections could prevent a banking system dependent on market organization and reliable market information from always effectively using its cash reserves. Thus a single-office bank, or a single-district bank, that acquired excess cash reserves which it could not use in its home district might for lack of market knowledge hold excess reserves. Or it might hold excess reserves, even though it is aware of outside investment opportunities, because the excessiveness in its reserves is only temporary, and existing market organization does not allow sufficient scope for temporary investment. In the opposite situation, when its reserves come under pressure because, for example, of an increase in the demand for bank loans, the single-office bank may have to refuse to allow its loans to expand for want of knowledge of where it can borrow reserves or dispose of assets for cash, or for want of market organization that provides funds on a sufficiently temporary and flexible basis.

A banking system made up of a number of multi-office banks covering a wide geographical area is not so dependent on external market organization, or so limited in knowledge as smaller, more local banks. A nation-wide bank has the opportunity and possibility of matching excess reserves caused by its activities in some areas against deficiencies in reserves caused by activities in other areas; and a temporary slack in some parts of its organization may serve to relieve temporary strains at other parts. When such a bank acquires excess cash reserves it has a better idea of where new earning assets can be acquired, and so is better able than a local bank to keep its reserves fully utilized.[8] Thus, in an economy where there is a lack of

8. Gilbart, p. 83, discusses situations in which a local bank would be bothered by an excess or a deficiency of reserves but in which a branch bank would not.

external organization that interferes with the effective utilization of cash reserves, branch banking, by providing an internal organization for making use of cash reserves, would overcome the deficiency.

In the absence of market imperfections, however, any banking system would be able to avoid excess reserves, but always of course at some cost. Whenever excess cash reserves arose in the banking system they would be employed somehow and somewhere in adding to the earning assets held by the system. A unit bank would have to employ excess cash reserves in its own area or pass them on through the money market to some other bank. If the bank is not rationing credit in the sense of having to deny creditworthy and profitable borrowers, it will most likely have to place its funds in the money market, adding to its balances kept with other banks or buying money-market assets.[9]

Local banks in need of funds can then borrow from the money-market centre to which the excess reserves of surplus areas have flowed. Under banking conditions of an earlier day, and with perfect market organization, there might actually be a flow of funds as excess reserves accumulated in some areas were used in accommodating

9. This was the situation in England before branch banking became fully developed there. Excess cash reserves, in the form of specie, converged on London to be employed by the bill-brokers. Cf. Gilbart, p. 322; Hawtrey, *Bank Rate*, pp. 10, 51; Walter Bagehot, *Lombard Street*, p. 12; R. S. Sayers, *Central Banking after Bagehot* (Oxford, at the Clarendon Press, 1957), p. 13.

The use of discounting in English banking in the nineteenth century to redistribute cash reserves among the banks of the system is brought out by the evidence of the Governor of the Bank of England before the Select Committee of the House of Commons on the Bank Acts, 1858, as reproduced by T. E. Gregory (comp.), *Select Statutes, Documents, and Reports Relating to British Banking, 1832–1928* (Oxford, University Press, 1929), 2, 78–9.

The role of organized money markets in enabling local banks to keep fully invested at all times is also discussed in Bank for International Settlements, Monetary and Economic Department, *Credit and its Cost* (Basle, the Bank, 1957), pp. 30–2.

The correspondent system in the United States produced the same concentration of surplus funds in the financial centers as did the English system of discounting. Cf. John M. Chapman, *Concentration of Banking: The Changing Structure and Control of Banking in the United States* (New York, Columbia University Press, 1934), p. 308.

additional banking business elsewhere. This would or could be so when excess reserves took the form of specie. Specie would flow to the money-market to be lent out. In this way it would get into the hands of banks requiring cash reserves, which would either import it from the money-market to add to their till money, or leave it in the money-market centre to add to their clearing balances. Under a system of centralized reserves and a well-developed banking organization, however, surplus reserves in some parts of the banking system show up as increased clearing balances, either absolutely or relative to deposits; there is in this case no physical movement or geographical transfer of funds when the excess reserves become available through the money-market to banks needing them.

Thus market organization would enable any type of banking system to fully utilize its cash reserves, excess reserves anywhere in the system being placed in the money-market centre to be drawn upon by other banks to expand their loans or to add in turn to their money-market investments. Hence, when there are no market imperfections, banking structure has no bearing on the ability of the system to effectively use all the cash reserves in the banking system.

Although, in the absence of money-market imperfections, different types of banking structure may be equally successful in employing their cash reserves, the cost of doing so may vary with structure. When overall cash reserves are adequate for meeting existing loan demand but regional variations in the pressure on banks exist, a unit banking system has to bear the cost of transferring reserves from banks where they are redundant to banks where reserves are under pressure. Thus unit banks, to avoid carrying excess reserves, often will be compelled to lend to other banks—for example, carry increased balances with correspondents—or to invest in the money-market at lower rates than they would obtain on loans; and unit banks needing reserves have to meet the cost of drawing them from other banks. Branch banking, by placing a larger proportion of existing cash reserves under the ownership of the same bank, avoids some of this cost.[10] More specifically, under present-day conditions of excess

10. In earlier days of banking when cash reserves mainly took the form of specie, the avoidance or elimination of excess cash reserves often meant a movement

lending capacity invested in government securities, the cost avoided by a nation-wide system of branch banking in adjusting to offsetting regional differences in reserve pressure is the cost of trading in securities. Unit banks in a particular area coming under reserve pressure sell securities to adjust their cash position; if at the same time other banks are in the market for securities in order to take up a slack in their cash position, their buying as the other banks sell likely prevents any movement in security prices. Only a trading cost is involved in this adjustment situation: a cost, however, that branch banking avoids. Even when this cost is entirely internal to a banking system made up of unit banks, so that banking costs in the aggregate do not

---

of specie had to be made. Under unit banking the specie would move to the money market, and then perhaps move from there to a district where it was needed. Under branch banking the specie would move directly between the two points involved, thereby by-passing the money market. Gilbart, p. 322, saw as the main effect of branch banking in England the diminution of rediscounting bills in London. He described (p. 496) the Scottish system of branch banking which enabled the banks in it "to transfer the surplus capital of the agricultural districts to the manufacturing and commercial districts, without going through the process of rediscounting their bills." The advantage of this, he thought (p. 497), lies in the fact that "there is no occasion for the intermediate party, the bill-broker." The practice of rediscounting fell into disrepute in England after the crisis of 1857. Sayers, *Central Banking after Bagehot*, p. 14.

W. Stanley Jevons, *Money and the Mechanism of Exchange* (New York, Appleton and Co., 1875), p. 253, seems to see the advantage of branch banking in keeping cash remittances to a minimum. Each branch need settle accounts only with its head office which thereby acts like a clearing house or bankers' bank.

Roeliff Morton Breckenridge, *The Canadian Banking System, 1817–1890*, Publications of the American Economic Association, Vol. X, Nos. 1, 2 and 3 (New York, Macmillan and Company, 1895), pp. 376–7, argued that an advantage of branch banking in Canada was that "the collection and distribution of loanable capital from and to different parts of the country are accomplished at the minimum of expense and with the maximum of thoroughness. When the instrument of both the services is a single organization such as a large bank with numerous branches, the task is better performed, it would seem, and certainly at less cost than when two or more banks are necessary to the same series of services and each must be rewarded for its part." In current usage what Breckenridge meant is that branch banking is able to utilize its cash reserves at lower cost than a less concentrated banking system.

differ from that of a branch-banking system,[11] the extra cost may still affect banking activity. The individual unit banks bearing the internal cost of getting needed reserves from surplus banks may charge higher lending rates or find fewer loan applications profitable than a branch bank.

Thus, under branch banking, lending rates, so it is argued, tend to be more uniform across the country than under unit banking.[12] Under branch banking excess reserves can be used to expand deposits in a great many places at no extra cost; under unit banking excess reserves may lead to the same expansion in deposits, but only at extra costs. If the extra costs are covered in lending rates, then it does follow that there is likely to be more difference in lending rates among regions under unit banking than under branch banking. This could mean a greater volume of bank loans would exist under branch banking than under unit banking even though both systems create and maintain the same amount of deposits. And in turn this means that the unit banking system would carry more open-market assets and fewer negotiated credits than the branch system.[13] The same conclusions follow if the extra adjustment cost the unit system has to bear shows up not in rates but in a higher rejection standard for loan applicants; the extra cost of meeting loan demand in certain circumstances makes some loan applications unprofitable to a unit system that would be profitable to a branch system.

Banking structure may also bear on the number of banking offices in a country or area and when it does it reflects imperfections in financial markets. Thus, it is argued that an independent bank office is less likely to be established than a branch office in an area where deposits would greatly exceed loans or loans deposits.[14] If the area is profitable for banking, however, and if a branch office has no cost

11. Gilbart, pp. 321–2, also thought that branch banking would have an absolute cost advantage over a system of local banks.

12. Chapman, *Concentration of Banking*, p. 304, argues that lending rates will be more uniform under branch banking.

13. Hawtrey, *Bank Rate*, pp. 55–6, saw as a consequence of the development of branch banking the elimination of the need "to embody credit in a negotiable instrument."

14. Cf. "The Growth of Branch Banking," Federal Reserve Bank of Boston, *New England Business Review*, Apr. 1959, pp. 3–4.

advantage over a unit office, it must be a limitation in financial markets that enables a branch office to be established when a unit office would not. If the area is an excess-deposits one, market limitations must restrict the ability of a unit bank to find profitable investment outlets outside the area. If the area is an excess-loans one, the limitation must restrict the ability of the unit bank to borrow on a continuing basis outside the area. Under these conditions branch offices could arise when unit ones could not. Branch banking is then one way of overcoming market limitations and in so doing adds to the convenience of the banking public by providing more offices. It does not now, however, add to the total amount of bank deposits or bank assets. These aggregates are determined by monetary policy and any addition to the number of banking offices simply distributes the permitted totals over a larger number of units.[15]

Regional Variations in Banking Activity

Banking structure and the mobility of funds is usually discussed not only from the point of view of collecting cash reserves and using them but also from the point of view of meeting regional needs or demands for bank loans as they arise. This is closely related to the matter of using cash reserves to the full. Ability to cope with regional changes in the demand for bank loans is usually analyzed in connection with compensating variations in the pressures on the existing amount of cash reserves in the banking system. In such a situation the overall

15. A branch office opened in an excess-deposits area either attracts deposits that were being carried at other banks for want of a local banking office or attracts funds from currency hoards, held for want of a local depository. In the former case, existing deposits are simply redistributed. In the latter case, bank deposits and cash reserves rise. If bank deposits were at an appropriate level before, they are now too high and presumably monetary policy will act to reduce deposits. The same reasoning applies to a branch opened in an excess-loans area. Either borrowing is transferred from elsewhere or additional loans are made at the new office, with monetary policy taking offsetting measures to keep total bank assets at their previous level. In the latter case the most that can happen is a redistribution of the composition of bank assets without any significant change in the total.

A qualification to the foregoing is where an increase in the number of banking offices reduces the growth of competing non-banks to such an extent that monetary policy permits the banking system to grow at a faster rate, in accordance with the analysis of Chapter Three.

level of bank deposits may not change, but in some areas deposits are rising because of an expansion in loan demand while in other areas they are falling because outstanding loans are being repaid. The problem this poses is proportional to the degree of decentralization of the banking system. For a large-scale branch-banking system, the situation of compensating regional variations in the pressures on cash reserves scarcely matters; for unit banking the situation may create a problem.

The example usually given to illustrate the problem is that of a seasonal increase which occurs in the demand for loans in some districts as loans are falling seasonally in other districts. With constant cash reserves, banking activity in some districts is releasing cash reserves just as activity in other districts is absorbing reserves. If the banks in the districts affected are independent of each other, it means that while the reserves of the banks in the expanding districts are coming under pressure, banks in the contracting districts are accumulating excess reserves. When there is no market organization for getting the temporary surplus of reserves from the banks having them to the banks needing them, the existing level of cash reserves in the banking system is not being used to best advantage. Branch banking on a nation-wide scale easily, almost automatically, accommodates itself to this type of situation.[16] Deposits fall in the districts where loans are being repaid, but rise in districts where there is a seasonal increase in the demand for loans. If the seasonal increase in loans in some districts matches the seasonal decrease in others, total deposits in the banking system remain unchanged, and the total for loans is also stable. Thus, a nation-wide branch-banking system easily maintains a stable reserve ratio in the face of compensating seasonal variations in loans and deposits. A system of unit banks, on the contrary, has to take specific steps to get seasonally excess reserves from banks having them to banks requiring them. If the unit-banking system cannot effect the necessary transfer of reserves, banks in the district with the seasonal expansion in demand for loans will have to ration credit, while banks in the seasonally contracting districts will

16. Cf. Chapman, *Concentration of Banking*, p. 297; Shirley Donald Southworth, *Branch Banking in the United States* (New York, McGraw-Hill Book Company, Inc., 1928), p. 105.

be carrying excess cash reserves. Of course some borrowers may move from district to district by issuing negotiable credit instruments.

The advantage of branch banking is not so marked when there is only a unilateral change in loans on a regional basis. For instance, when the demand for loans increases in a district, without compensating changes in loans occurring elsewhere, the extent to which loans are expanded at existing rates depends on the unutilized lending capacity that the banking offices in the district affected can draw upon. If the excess capacity for making loans was equal in all cases, banking structure would have nothing to do with the results that followed. However, it would be natural to hold that unit banks would have less excess lending capacity than branch banks. It might appear that a branch banking office could draw upon greater excess lending capacity that a unit banking office when both banks have the same proportion of their assets in loans. But this is purely a matter of size. Where the unit bank is as large as the branch bank, taking into account all the branches of the latter, the unit bank will have as much scope for expanding its loans as a branch of the branch bank—both banks being equally loaned up. Only when the branch bank represented in the given district is larger than the unit bank will the former have more excess lending capacity to draw upon than the latter and so be better able to meet an increase in the demand for loans in the district. Then unit banking may result in a lower level of loans in the district, and perhaps in higher lending rates.

In general the pattern of loans in an economy may differ according to the banking structure, at least in the short run. If cash reserves do not move easily from surplus banks to deficit banks, unit banking may result in areas of credit rationing co-existing with areas of excess reserves or excess lending capacity. Such co-existing areas could arise even if cash reserves were easily transferable among the banks; the unit banks in an area with an expanding demand for bank loans might use up their excess lending capacity before all legitimate demands had been met and while some banks elsewhere still had excess lending capacity. This would not happen in a system of nation-wide branch banking for all excess lending capacity would be exhausted before the expansion in loans in a particular district would be brought to a halt.

In short, in a situation where cash reserves have to be transferred among banks under a system of unit banking but not under a system of nation-wide branch banking in order to fully employ cash reserves, branch banks have an obvious advantage over unit banks. Such situations arise when the regional demand for loans alters or the overall pressure on cash reserves alters geographically. Unit banks then have to trade securities or engage in other types of transactions in order to redistribute existing cash reserves to meet the altered geographical conditions facing the banking system; under branch banking no such transactions are generally necessary.

Banking Response to Interregional Deposit Movements

What now has to be considered is how the response of the banking system to interregional deposit movements varies with banking structure.[17] The geographical movement of deposits by the public means a fall in deposits in one area and a gain in deposits in other areas. If all banking offices were but branches of the same bank, movements of deposits would not require the bank to make any external adjustments. However, if every banking office were a separate bank, all geographical movements of deposits would cause a redistribution of cash reserves among the banks. Therefore, the smaller the number of banks for a given number of banking offices the less transferring of cash reserves there will be for any given geographical movement of funds. Thus the degree of external adjustment required by a banking system as a result of a flow of deposits is related to its structure. Two cases may be selected for examination: where the banking structure is such that a geographical movement of deposits usually causes a net transfer of cash reserves among the banks; and where the structure is such that a movement of deposits does not usually result in a redistribution of existing reserves.

A geographical movement of deposits results in no net transfer of cash among banks when the banking offices gaining and losing the

17. An early argument in favour of branch banking was that it made it easier for the public to transmit funds. Cf. Gilbart, p. 321. But under modern banking conditions ease in transmitting funds is no longer a monopoly of any particular type of banking structure.

deposits are branches of the same bank. The gaining branches do not expand on the basis of the deposits received nor do the losing branches contract; the cash reserves and total deposits of the bank to which these branches belong remain constant so that the overall cash-reserve ratio remains undisturbed. There is no reason for any external banking adjustment, and therefore there are no secondary repercussions.

The case where the geographical movement of funds causes a redistribution of cash reserves of a like nature is a little more complicated. The banks gaining deposits are placed in a position to expand; how they expand depends on whether they are rationing credit, or whether they have excess lending capacity and are not restricting loans because of high cost in freeing their excess lending capacity. If the deposit-gaining banks are rationing credit, they probably expand loans; and the expansion is probably local. If these banks are not rationing credit, they most likely buy securities.

How the deposit-losing banks contract following a geographical movement of deposits that drains them of reserves also depends on the situation facing them. If the contracting banks have excess lending capacity, they can sell securities and at little change in security prices if the deposit-gaining banks are buying securities at the same time. There is a possibility that the contracting banks may have securities to sell at the same time that the expanding banks are banks which have been rationing credit or banks now faced with an increased demand for bank loans. This means that while one group of banks will be trying to sell securities another group of banks, instead of trying to buy securities with the new reserves coming to them, will be expanding loans. Consequently, security prices tend to move against the contracting banks so that they sell fewer securities than they otherwise would and somewhat reduce loans.

As a result of these banking adjustments that follow a transfer of cash reserves among unit banks when deposits are moved geographically by the banking public, there may be secondary repercussions on the regional pattern of deposits. The usual effect is for deposits to increase further in the areas to which deposits moved, as the banks there expand on the basis of their new reserves, and for deposits to

decline further in the deposit-losing areas, as the banks there contract. A less probable situation, but a possible one, occurs when the
expanding banks fail to retain all their newly acquired excess cash
reserves and are therefore unable to expand deposits further. This
may be a direct result of the manner of adjustment by which the
reserve-gaining banks lend reserves to the reserve-losing banks. The
effect is the same as that achieved by nation-wide branch banking:
the only change in the geographical distribution of deposits is that
caused by the payment acts of the public, banking adjustments not
producing any secondary changes in deposits.[18]

In general, the effects of a regional change in deposits on the
banking system will differ less with banking structure when there is
no overall credit rationing and excess lending capacity is common.
The effects differ most when the pressures upon the banks for accommodation show the greatest regional variations: branch banking
tends to even out these pressures; unit banking, to vary its regional
resistance to them.

Internal Banking Debt

In a unit banking system in which each banking office represents
an independent bank, deposit movements between banking offices
require each office to make an external adjustment because each
banking office maintains a cash-reserve ratio that it supposedly stabilizes. In a branch-banking system no individual banking office makes
an external adjustment as a result of deposit movements; any adjustments required are effected by head office. The individual
banking office that gains deposits from other branches gains a
claim on them or on head office, and receives a credit instead of
cash reserves, which it does not carry except for currency. The
banking office that loses deposits goes into debt to other branches

18. Douglas Hellweg, "Comments on Task Force Report," *Record of the Federal
Reserve System Conference on the Interregional Flow of Funds* (Washington, Federal
Reserve System, 1955), III-(6)-3, discusses the adjustment difficulties faced by
unit banks when there is a geographical movement of deposits and points out how
their response to inflows and outflows of deposits is "conditioned by the need to
maintain legal reserve ratios and by the desire to avoid accumulations of excess
reserves."

or to its head office.[19] This gives rise to what might be called branch indebtedness.

The nature of branch indebtedness is worth examining in detail because the subject is not fully discussed elsewhere, and because it appears to be a cause of misunderstanding in analyses of branch banking and the mobility of funds. Theoretically, branch indebtedness at any given moment of time measures the sum total of all net claims outstanding that a branch has against all other branches of the same bank and against its head office. These net claims may constitute either a credit or a debit. If they constitute a credit, it means that the rest of the bank of which it is a part is in debt to the branch; if the net claims constitute a debit for the branch, it means that the branch is in debt to the rest of the bank. The claims that make up branch indebtedness are for funds owing on various monetary instruments, for funds collected for various purposes, for amounts due as a result of the acquisition or the disposal of non-loan assets, and amounts due as a result of branch profits.

The clearing of cheques among branches is a major source of branch indebtedness. Cheques drawn on a branch by its depositors and falling into the hands of other branches give those branches claims the given branch—claims that are reflected in branch indebtedness. And cheques received by a branch that are drawn on other branches give to the receiving branch claims on the rest of the bank. This exchange of cheques issued by depositors, when it involves branches of the same bank, simply gives rise to reciprocal indebtedness among the branches involved. Cheques drawn on branches of other banks received by a branch, or cheques drawn on the branch that pass into the hands of branches belonging to other banks, create an indebtedness between the branch and its head office, or between the branches it clears with and head office.

Besides cheques issued by depositors that may be exchanged among branches, there are monetary instruments of a like nature—such as

19. Items received by a branch on other banks are cleared by it to the clearing branches for its bank, so that the receiving branch gets a credit with other branches of the same bank. But the clearing branches must clear to the clearing branches of the other banks, so that they get a credit or debit with their head office for the net clearings they make.

money orders and bank drafts—issued or sold by branches, and which may be responsible for some branch indebtedness. Collections made by a branch for other branches also give rise to branch indebtedness, as do cheques issued by a head office. The receiving branches in the latter case receive credits either with their head offices or with any clearing branches engaged in settling these items. Government cheques and post office money orders paid into branches give the receiving branches a claim on the clearing branches and the clearing branches a claim on head offices. Branch profits, which represent a return on the investment in branches by head office, are settled by means of changes in branch indebtedness. Non-loan assets —such as currency, securities, and foreign exchange—acquired or disposed of by branches are treated as head-office assets gained or lost, for which the branches receive credits or debits to their accounts with head office. Thus, branches that acquire assets for head office are given a credit with head office, and branches that dispose of head-office assets settle with head office through the branch-indebtedness account. Branch loans are not, however, considered to affect the debtor relationship of branches with each other or with head office. That is, a branch in carrying out its lending activities does not have to settle with head office or other branches for the loans it makes or receives repayment for.

As a result of all the foregoing types of settlements there exists in branch banking an indebtedness between a branch and each of the other branches of the same bank with which it exchanges claims for funds. This indebtedness represents a purely inter-branch debt. Then, in addition, there is an indebtedness between each branch and its head office resulting from the various items and transactions requiring settlement between head office and the branches. This indebtedness is a pure branch–head-office debt. However, because head offices act as clearing centres for their branches, all amounts owing by a branch to all other branches may be treated as an amount owing to head office, and all amounts due the branch from other branches, as an amount due from head office. Thus, all branch indebtedness may be reduced to the category of debt between head office and each of its branches.

The reduction of all branch indebtedness to a branch–head-office debt serves the useful accounting purpose of indicating which branches owe funds to head office—to which branches head office has supplied funds—and to which branches head office owes funds—which branches have advanced funds to head office. The general measure of branch indebtedness adopted for this purpose is the difference between the loans and deposits on the books of a branch. That is, the difference between its loans and deposits is considered to measure the outstanding indebtedness between a branch and the rest of the bank, as represented by head office. If its deposits are in excess of its loans, the branch is looked upon as supplying funds to head office: the branch has excess deposits. If its loans are in excess of its deposits, the branch is considered to be the recipient of funds from head office: the branch has excess loans. On this view some head offices allow interest to those branches having excess deposits and charge interest to branches having excess loans.[20]

The loan-deposit differential is a fairly satisfactory measure of branch indebtedness because most of the transactions requiring settlements between branches or between branches and head office affect branch deposits. Thus cheques received as deposits and drawn on other branches add to the deposits of the receiving branch and so alter its loan-deposit differential in keeping with the change in its debtor position to the rest of the system. The same holds for cheques drawn on a branch and presented to other branches: the cheques are cleared back to the branch drawn upon, which then reduces its deposits relative to its loans—a change in its loan-deposit differential that reflects the change in its debtor position with the rest of the bank.[21] The exchange of other monetary instruments between a

20. In Canadian banking this interest is referred to as head-office interest and is calculated on the difference between average deposits and average loans over the interest period. Cf. A. B. Jamieson, *Chartered Banking in Canada*, pp. 195–6; E. L. Stewart Patterson, *Canadian Banking*, rev. ed. (Toronto, The Ryerson Press, 1941), p. 267. John M. Chapman and Ray B. Westerfield, *Branch Banking: Its Historical and Theoretical Position in America and Abroad* (New York, Harper and Brothers, 1942), pp. 176–9, discuss some of the considerations that enter into the question of paying interest on branch indebtedness.

21. When cheques drawn on a branch represent overdrafts, however, the effect of receiving such cheques in the clearings is to increase the loans of the branch rather than to decrease its deposits, but the results in terms of its loan-deposit differential are the same.

branch and other parts of the banking system—for example, as a result of collections for other branches, transactions in non-loan assets, and branch expenses and revenues—may affect branch deposits; when it does, the change caused in the loan-deposit differential of the branch reflects also the change in the debtor position of the branch caused by the deposit-altering events. As a general rule, then, anything that causes the deposits of a branch to change relative to its loans makes its indebtedness with the rest of the banking system vary by a like amount.[22]

Consequently, variations in branch loans which produce corresponding variations in branch deposits—as when a branch writes up deposits in making loans or when borrowers repay loans from deposits accumulated with the branch—do not affect the indebtedness of the branch to head office or to other branches as far as the loan-deposit differential is concerned: the differential is not affected when loans are made by creating deposits or when loan repayments reduce branch deposits.

Furthermore, all the events that alter branch indebtedness need not alter branch deposits: they may instead alter currency holdings. Cheques drawn on other branches may be presented for currency, collections for other branches may be received in currency, transactions in non-loan assets may be settled in currency, and so forth. The alteration in branch holdings of currency may be viewed as an alteration in a head-office asset so that a branch gaining currency becomes a creditor of head office, and a branch losing currency becomes a debtor. However, when the gain in currency results from collections made for other branches, disposing of non-loan assets, or similar actions which place the branch in debt to the rest of the system, there is an immediate offsetting of claims: the gain in cur-

---

22. This covers the situation where advances are made by way of discount; an increase in bank loans then gives rise to a less than corresponding increase in deposits, and the differential between loans and deposits changes by the amount of the discount taken. This qualification is pointed out by Jacob Viner, *Canada's Balance of International Indebtedness, 1900–1913*, p. 185, who uses the loan-deposit differential as a rough measure of foreign borrowing by Canadians. Since the discount taken is an item of profit owing to head office, the deviation it causes between loans and deposits reflects the increase in branch indebtedness to head office; discounts on loans then cause no trouble for measuring branch indebtedness.

rency neither affects the loan-deposit differential of the branch nor reflects any net change in the indebtedness of the branch. Similarly, a loss of currency occasioned by incurring claims on the rest of the system forms part of a total transaction that alters neither branch indebtedness nor the measure of branch indebtedness.

Alterations in the currency holdings of a branch as a result of loans made or repaid in currency, or as a result of currency deposits or withdrawals, unlike the previous currency transactions, affect the loan-deposit differential of the branch. But such alterations in currency holdings also reflect changes in branch indebtedness. When the currency holdings of the branch become unduly depleted, they have to be restored by ordering more currency from the supply depot; and when currency holdings become unduly large, the excess is shipped off. These adjustments in the currency holdings of a branch effected through the physical movement of currency must be recorded in the internal accounts of the bank, the branch being credited for all currency it ships out and debited for all shipments of currency it orders. These debits and credits are not reflected in the loan-deposit differential,[23] which takes no account of physical movements of any kind or of changes in total branch assets relative to branch deposits. These are events that affect the capital investment of head office in the branch, and hence the loan-deposit differential, in not measuring such events, does not take into account changes in the capital investment of head office in its branches. In short, the loan-deposit differential measures only the intra-bank debt arising from current operations of each branch, and does not incorporate either the initial investment in branches or changes in that investment.

Furthermore, the loan-deposit differential of a branch at any moment of time measures the sum total of all operations that have

23. The balance in the internal account of a branch in which its debits and credits with the rest of the bank are entered should equal approximately the difference between its loans and deposits except for items in "float;" physical shipments of money parcels, recorded in the clearings account of branches but not reflected in the loan-deposit differential; and monetary instruments issued by a branch without affecting its deposits which get paid into other branches. Cf. Patterson, *Canadian Banking*, pp. 269, 281.

affected the indebtedness of the branch since the moment it opened for business; any existing figure for the indebtedness of a branch, therefore, may be the result of past operations rather than of current ones. Branch indebtedness caused by current operations is measured by the change in the loan-deposit differential over the current period and not by the absolute size of the differential at the end of the period. Thus it is possible for a branch to be heavily indebted to the rest of the banking system because of operations long since a part of its history, and yet to be a large creditor as a result of current events.[24]

What is of greatest interest here, however, is not the branch indebtedness of individual banks but the total indebtedness between branches and their head offices in a branch-banking system. That total indebtedness is measured by the difference between total loans and total deposits in the banking system. If that differential were zero—loans equalled deposits—it would indicate that the amounts owing by the debtor branches of each bank were exactly matched by amounts due to the creditor branches of the same bank. However, loans do not equal deposits in most banking systems; indeed they fall far short of such an equality.[25] Therefore in a branch banking system, where loans fall short of deposits, head offices must be net debtors of their branches. In the terminology of bank

24. There is no satisfactory, simple account of the accounting system used to record inter-branch transactions in Canadian banking. Brief sketches of the system used, on which the foregoing paragraphs in the text are based, appear in James Holladay, *The Canadian Banking System* (Boston, Bankers Publishing Company, 1938), pp. 127–9; Patterson, *Canadian Banking*, pp. 268–76, 281; Jamieson, *Chartered Banking in Canada*, pp. 176, 195, 199. The history and development of accounting for inter-branch clearings in Canada are dealt with in Victor Ross, *A History of The Canadian Bank of Commerce: With an Account of the Other Banks Which Now Form Part of Its Organization* (Toronto, Oxford University Press, 1922), 2, 530–9.

25. In the Canadian banking system deposits now exceed loans by such a wide margin that just about every branch in the system must be a creditor of head office—that is, must have an excess of deposits over loans. At December 31, 1956, total bank loans in Canada amounted to $5.4 billion and total Canadian dollar deposits, $11.2 billion. Bank of Canada, *Statistical Summary*, Financial Supplement, 1956, pp. 17, 19. D. B. Marsh, "Canada," *Banking Systems*, ed. B. H. Beckhart (New York, Columbia University Press, 1954), p. 136, notes that in one large Canadian bank as many as 98 per cent of the branches may have excess deposits.

accounting, the branches are net suppliers of funds to their head offices.[26]

How this net indebtedness between branches and head offices in a branch-banking system may vary is subject to misinterpretation. For constant cash reserves, any movement in deposits initiated by the public or resulting from banking action would, so long as total bank loans outstanding remained constant, alter the distribution of branch indebtedness among branches, but would not alter the total, as measured by the difference between total loans and total deposits. Variations in total loans, however, with cash reserves fixed, would alter the amount of branch–head-office indebtedness because the differential between total loans and total deposits would be altered. Some of the change in branch indebtedness might also reflect a gain in cash reserves for some banks and a loss in reserves for other banks. This does not impair the analysis, however, because total deposits will not thereby be changed and total loans will be much the same whether or not the events that transpire cause a transfer of cash reserves.

Any expansion in cash reserves would also cause deposits to rise by a like amount, assuming that the additional cash reserves come to the banking system as a result of the public depositing cash-reserve instruments. When cash reserves do come to the banking system in this

26. The conventional way of explaining this state of affairs is to say that the head offices of the banks have invested the excess deposits of their branches in securities. At least this interpretation is given in *Historical Outline of Canadian Banking Legislation and Some Features of the Present Working of the Canadian Banking System* (Presentations by J. A. McLeod, President, The Canadian Bankers' Association, before the Royal Commission on Banking and Currency, at Ottawa, 1933 [n.p., n.n., n.d.]), p. 26, and is accepted by the Royal Commission on Banking and Currency in Canada, *Report* (Ottawa, The King's Printer, 1933), p. 31, and by D. B. Marsh, "Canada," p. 137. However, it is a moot point whether the excess deposits lead to the security purchases or the security purchases to the excess deposits. Each is the result of the other. Strictly speaking, security purchases by head offices are based on excess cash reserves. Once the excess reserves are in existence, it is difficult to separate the security purchases based on excess reserves from the effect of the purchases on deposits. That is, the security purchases based on an addition to cash reserves lead to increased deposits, and the increase in deposits, because they represent a retention of cash reserves by the banking system, leads to further security purchases, and so on until the excess reserves are eliminated.

way, total branch indebtedness is raised at the same time. If loans outstanding now expand on the basis of the new reserves, there is no further change in total branch indebtedness because deposits and loans go up together. However, if, on the basis of the new reserves, security holdings are expanded instead of bank loans, there results an expansion of bank deposits relative to loans that reflects a growth in the general indebtedness of head offices to their branches. This result is produced by the head offices spending excess cash reserves by issuing cheques for securities. These head-office cheques are deposited with the branches and as a result total branch indebtedness increases. The deposits gained by the branches do not represent an addition to the cash reserves of the banks but merely a conservation of existing cash reserves. This conservation of existing reserves means that it takes several rounds of spending by head offices to eliminate excess reserves. That is, the branches by gathering in as deposits the cheques of head offices determine the rate at which excess cash reserves can be worked off.

The chain of events here describes how the general indebtedness of head offices to their branches that is now prevalent in modern branch-banking systems came about. The prevalence of deposits over loans that now exists is the product of head-office investment activities, which grew in importance over the years because cash reserves increased to a greater extent than they could be utilized in making loans. Head offices were therefore compelled to use their excess reserves in acquiring securities if they wished to keep a constant reserve ratio; such security purchases by head offices, however, increased bank deposits relative to bank loans.

In unit banking the difference between loans and deposits reflects mainly the receipt of cash-reserve deposits by the independent banking offices used in acquiring non-loan earning assets. This is what any excess of deposits over loans reflects in the consolidated position of any bank. Thus, when the position of a branch bank is consolidated, the differential between loans and deposits that may be computed from the consolidated balance-sheet bears the same interpretation it would if the banks had no branches. The internal indebtedness in branch banking that is measured by the difference between loans and deposits has a significance because it makes accounting sense, in viewing the relationship between head office and its branches, to separate the lending and deposit activities of the latter from other banking activities, which can be assigned to head office. The same effect could be achieved in a unit bank by treating loans and deposits as the property of one department of the bank, and by assigning to another department responsibility for all other banking assets. This other department could then be viewed as borrowing excess deposits or lending an amount equal to excess loans to the department carrying the loans and deposits.

However, an internal indebtedness achieved in this way and measured by the loan-deposit differential is not truly analogous to branch indebtedness because it lacks the geographical feature of the latter. A closer resemblance to branch indebtedness in unit banking is provided by bank indebtedness or inter-bank debt. This arises when a bank receives claims on another bank, and instead of calling for settlement converts the claims into balances with the other bank. A transfer of cash reserves between the banks concerned is then avoided. Inter-bank debt in a unit bank system thus serves much the same function as branch indebtedness in branch banking. The main difference between the two types of debt, reflecting the fact that one is external and the other internal, is that inter-bank debt is unlikely to be available to the same extent as is inter-branch debt.[27]

BRANCH BANKING AND THE MOBILITY
OF FUNDS

The reason for considering in detail the concept of branch indebtedness is that the concept forms the basis for the existing view of branch banking and the mobility of funds. That view, it is argued

27. F. W. Paish, "Banking Policy and the Balance of International Payments," *Readings in the Theory of International Trade*, Blakiston Series of Republished Articles on Economics, *4* (Philadelphia, The Blakiston Company, 1949), p. 38, reprinted from *Economica*, *3* (Nov. 1936), 404–22.

Considerations affecting inter-bank debt and its use as a substitute for country-wide branch banking are discussed in American Bankers Association, Economic Policy Commission, *Member Bank Reserve Requirements* (New York, the Association, 1957), pp. 102, 104. Also cf. Katherine Finney, *Interbank Deposits: The Purpose and Effects of Domestic Balances, 1934–54* (New York, Columbia University Press, 1958), pp. 97–8.

here, is misleading if not erroneous. Therefore in this part the traditional view of branch banking as it relates to the mobility of funds is presented, followed by an examination of the arguments on the merits of branch banking that are based on it. These arguments are considered first from the point of view of the interregional activities of the banks, and then from the point of view of the interregional payment activities of the public.

Existing View

The existing view is that branch banking adds mobility to funds by utilizing excess deposits at the branches that accumulate them, either in supporting loans at branches where loans exceed deposits or in acquiring other earning assets. This view springs naturally enough from the concept of branch indebtedness under which head office is seen as a debtor of branches having excess deposits, and as a creditor of branches having excess loans. The clearest Canadian expression of this view appears in a statement presented in 1933 by The Canadian Bankers' Association to the Royal Commission on Banking and Currency in Canada which stated it as follows:

> If the deposits of a branch should be in excess of the loans which it has made together with the amount of cash required by that branch, the excess of deposits is credited to Head Office; and the funds are used at other branches where the loan requirements exceed the deposits; or else they are invested by Head Office in bonds, or otherwise employed to the best advantage; credit for the use of such funds being given to the branch from which they are drawn.
>
> If the loans to be made by a branch, together with the amount of cash required in the till, exceed the deposits locally received by that branch, the necessary funds are drawn from other branches by Head Office, and made available to the branch requiring them; and that branch is accordingly debited for the use of the funds so borrowed.[28]

28. *Historical Outline of Canadian Banking Legislation and Some Features of the Present Working of the Canadian Banking System*, p. 26. This view is also quoted in full in Canada, Royal Commission on Banking and Currency in Canada, *Report*, p. 31, pars. 91–2.

The notion that a branch-banking system transfers excess deposits between branches is also found in general texts on money and banking, as well as in specialized texts on branch banking.[29] Thus it seems to be established doctrine that under branch banking head office borrows excess deposits from its branches in order to employ them itself, and to lend them to other branches having excess loans. This seems to accord with the accounting conventions in which excess deposits represent a head-office debt to branches and excess loans a branch debt to head office. However the purpose of the accounting is to assess the profitability of individual branches, not to explain banking behaviour in wider terms; and indeed the accounting does not offer a suitable basis for interpreting the regional impact of branch banking.

Excess loans and excess deposits reflect unsettled financial claims. They may also reflect a movement of funds, but if they do, it will not usually be a movement initiated by the banks. An inquiry into the nature of excess deposits will serve to indicate what foundation there is for the existing view of branch banking mobilizing excess deposits. That view took shape when banks could hope to add to their cash reserves by attracting currency and specie from the public. Excess deposits at certain branches then might well reflect the collection of physical assets, currency and specie, as opposed to the collection of financial claims on other banking offices.

Branches receiving large deposits of currency and specie in excess

---

The same sentiment, expressed in less detail, may also be found in United States, National Monetary Commission, *Interviews on the Banking and Currency Systems of Canada* (Washington, Government Printing Office, 1910), pp. 31–2, from an interview with Henry C. McLeod, General Manager of The Bank of Nova Scotia. Also cf. H. M. P. Eckardt, *Manual of Canadian Banking*, 4th ed. (Toronto, Monetary Times, [1913]), p. 150; and remarks by the Canadian minister of finance, W. T. White, in the course of the debate on the second reading of the Bank Act bill of 1913 before the Canadian parliament, quoted in The Canadian Bankers' Association (comp.), *Bank Act Revision Proceedings: Extracts from and Synopses of Debates in the House of Commons and Proceedings and Discussions of and Evidence Received by the Select Standing Committee on Banking and Commerce . . . in the Years 1913, 1923, 1924 and 1928* ([Montreal], The Canadian Bankers' Association, 1933), p. 407.

29. Cf. Ray B. Westerfield, *Money, Credit and Banking*, p. 950; Chapman and Westerfield, *Branch Banking*, pp. 139, 172, 174–5.

of their working needs are thus able to ship away the excess to head office or to other branches in cash clearing centres for use there. In the days when banking was less developed than now movements of this nature were most likely quite common because so much of the means of payment lay outside the banking system. But with the gradual replacement of physical money by bank money, the physical movement of cash reserves in branch banking has become of minor importance, as book entries serve to effect changes in the cash reserves of the system. That is, branches now receiving deposits of cash-reserve money that add to the cash reserves of the banking system as well receive them mainly in the form of central-bank and government cheques, not in the form of specie and currency as previously, which require no physical movement of funds and no movement of excess deposits.

But excess deposits may indicate the movement of deposits by the public rather than an expansion in the cash reserves of the banking system. When the geographical distribution of deposits is altered by the public, there is likely to be a redistribution in branch indebtedness among the existing branches. Deposits move relative to loans, for the branch distribution of loans is unlikely to be altered by the movement in deposits, especially if there is no credit rationing in the banking system because of limited reserves. The change in the deposit-loan differentials at the various branches merely reflects this movement of deposits by the banking public; it does not reflect any movement of deposits or funds by the banks themselves. At most, there may be a redistribution of existing cash reserves among the banks, effected by means of transfers on the books of the central bank. Thus, in the present context the growth in excess deposits at some branches reflects a movement of deposits from other branches. When the deposits come from other branches of the same bank, the excess deposits represent no net gain in the cash reserves of the bank; when they come from branches of other banks, the excess deposits do represent an addition to the cash reserves of the receiving bank. The second case is exactly similar to what occurs under unit banking in the same situation; the first is unique to branch banking, of course, but it requires no action by the bank: no transfer of excess deposits, no utilization of excess deposits, just some bookkeeping entries to balance the books. And the bookkeeping only records what has taken place and does not lead to further action by the particular bank.

Interregional Banking Activities

Nevertheless, it is what the banks themselves do that receives emphasis in discussions of branch banking and the mobility of funds; and what the banks do is supposedly based on the excess deposits and excess loans of their branches. Thus, those who approve of branch banking consider one of its advantages to consist in its ability to shift excess deposits from where they accumulate to where they can be used. A typical statement of this thought is the following:

> A marked advantage of a system of branch banking on a wide geographical area is its capacity to shift funds from regions of plethora to regions of relative dearth. In part this means from older regions, where deposits are not absorbed by local credit needs, to the newer, more rapidly developing regions, where the demand for loans is great and the accumulated deposits are too scant to meet that demand. In the newer regions loans may for a long period exceed deposits. Branch banking has been highly serviceable, for instance, in the expansion of the western provinces of Canada, for they could plant branches there far in advance of the accumulation of capital necessary to support a unit bank and could shift funds thither in large volume and continually for years, for lending to the nascent industries. The excess resources of the eastern Maritime Provinces have been utilized in the Prairie Provinces.[30]

Of course the idea of a banking system taking excess deposits from a region for use elsewhere causes the opponents of branch banking to

30. Chapman and Westerfield, *Branch Banking*, p. 236. The same thought is expressed by Benjamin Haggott Beckhart, "The Banking System of Canada," *Foreign Banking Systems*, edited by H. Parker Willis and B. H. Beckhart (New York, Henry Holt and Company, 1929), pp. 411–12; idem, "Banking, Commercial, Canada," *Encyclopaedia of the Social Sciences* (New York, The Macmillan Company, 1930), 2, 445; E. L. Stewart Patterson, *Canadian Banking*, p. 64; idem and Franklin Escher, *Banking Practice and Foreign Exchange*, Modern Business, Canadian Edition, 8 (New York, Alexander Hamilton Institute, 1914), pp. 65–6.

cry exploitation and denudation,[31] which is not surprising considering
that the advocates of branch banking make so much of its efficiency
in draining areas of excess deposits.[32] A modern statement of the
criticism is the following:

> The funds of a community, received by branch banks as de-
> posits, are sent to financial centers for investment, and so are not
> devoted to local economic development. While it is true that this
> concentration of funds in large centers occurs under the corres-
> pondent bank system, it is more pronounced when local banks
> are mere branches operated by a central office that may be more

31. The denudation argument in Canada is almost as old as Canadian banking
itself. Adam Shortt, "The Early History of Canadian Banking: IV. The First
Banks in Lower Canada," *Journal of The Canadian Bankers' Association*, 4 (July
1897), 359–60, reports that in the 1820's the Quebec branch of the Bank of
Montreal was said to be only partially lending out its deposits in Quebec City and
to be sending the rest to Montreal for use there. The charge, however, may have
had no basis in fact; early Canadian banks, as banks in general at that time, were
established not to obtain cash reserves by way of deposits but to issue bank-notes.
It seems most unlikely that Canadian banks in the 1820's received from the public
any substantial amount of deposits that provided them with cash reserves. Walter
Bagehot, *Lombard Street*, p. 85, states that up to 1830 and for some years after
English banks treated deposits as very minor matters and depended mainly on
their note circulation.

Therefore, before bank deposits became an important form for acquiring earning
assets, banks relied on paying out bank-notes in exchange for earning assets.
Presumably bank-notes might be paid out in exchange for specie and legal-tender
currency, but it is unlikely that banks acquired much cash reserves in this way.
Bank-notes outstanding, then, reflected the acquisition of earning assets, and in
issuing bank-notes the banks were contributing funds to the community. Aside
from the fact that where the banks issued their currency helped determine the
geographical distribution of the money supply, there was nothing in the mechanics
of note-issue as such that involved any notion of the banking system draining funds
away from some areas to utilize them elsewhere. Only the failure to issue notes in
some areas, in order that cash reserves might be otherwise utilized, could be
charged against note-issuing banks.

32. Chapman and Westerfield, *Branch Banking*, p. 189, dismiss the denudation
argument as "the flimsiest of arguments," expressing amazement at how frequently
and universally it is used, although their analysis of the mobility of funds in a
branch-banking system certainly invites the charge.

interested in making large loans and investments from the main office.[33]

The criticism that branch banking drains funds from surplus areas has meaning only in the context of cash reserves gathered in these areas being used to acquire earning assets elsewhere. And the criticism itself is valid only if the reaction of branch banking to excess cash reserves anywhere differs from the reaction of unit banks. Specifically the criticism implies that a unit bank gaining excess cash reserves will utilize these reserves in expanding its activities locally, whereas a branch bank may not.

Excess deposits may accumulate in an area because of a movement of deposits into the area from elsewhere, or because of the expansion of cash reserves in the banking system which takes place in the area under consideration. In the first case where deposits move interregionally, the banks in the deposit-receiving area gain cash reserves as a group, if the deposits are being shifted from banks not represented in the area to the same extent as they are represented in the deposit-losing areas. Under a nation-wide system of branch banking an interregional movement of deposits is unlikely to result in the banking offices in the receiving area gaining cash reserves. At least, under branch banking there is less likelihood that excess deposits accumulating in an area, as a result of a geographical movement of deposits by the public, reflect a net gain in the cash reserves of the banks represented there. When excess deposits in an area do not mean

33. Major B. Foster et al, *Money and Banking*, 4th ed. (New York, Prentice-Hall, Inc., 1953), p. 301, who, however, merely state the arguments for and against branch banking without necessarily approving of any or all of them. H. Parker Willis, "Branch Banking," *Encyclopaedia of the Social Sciences*, 2, 679, considers branch banking as raising "the question as to the extent to which the banking organization can safely be trusted with the function of shifting at will the fluid capital of the community from one locality to another," and he presents the arguments on branch banking as they bear on this point. His conclusion is that "the essential quality of branch banking is that of providing an easier flow of funds from one community to another." Other expressions of this criticism are voiced by Joseph French Johnson, *The Canadian Banking System*, National Monetary Commission (Washington, Government Printing Office, 1910), p. 91; and John Evans, in the Canadian House of Commons, 1923, quoted in The Canadian Bankers' Association (comp.), *Bank Act Revision Proceedings*, p. 413.

a gain in cash reserves, the existence or accumulation of excess deposits calls for no action by the banks: they do nothing. When the excess deposits represent a gain in cash reserves, the situation is similar to the case of unit banks.

Unit banks gaining excess deposits as the result of a movement of deposits to them from elsewhere do gain cash reserves. They expand on the basis of their new reserves, acquiring what earning assets they can. Deposits in the area of the expanding banks may rise further to the extent that the unit banks can retain any of their newly acquired excess cash reserves. The additional earning assets thus acquired by the unit banks may take the form of more loans, if loans in the area were previously being restrained by a shortage of cash reserves or by the high cost of acquiring reserves to support additional loans. When the foregoing conditions do not apply, more than likely the unit banks expand by buying securities. But in either case any expansion in deposits, and any expansion in bank loans, that occurs in the surplus area is at the expense of the deposit-losing areas, where a contraction is necessary because of the loss of reserves. In other words, unit banking adds a secondary or repercussions effect to the basic movement of deposits, unless unit banks make lending and borrowing arrangements that prevent cash reserves from moving with the movement of deposits. If they do this, they achieve the same effect as branch banking.

There would seem to be no benefit to having secondary banking repercussions every time deposits move geographically; indeed a basic unbalance in interregional balances of payments may only be made worse by such secondary repercussions. Hence branch banking by minimizing transfers in cash reserves within the banking system, when the public alters the geographical distribution of deposits, perhaps makes a greater contribution to the economy as a whole than unit banking. The excess deposits that, under branch banking, may accumulate in certain areas as a result of deposit movements, thus, do not cause any banking reaction, and so lead to no drain of funds from the areas.

The denudation argument can therefore only apply to cases where excess deposits in an area are the result of the banks there gaining cash reserves. If the banks do not use the newly acquired cash reserves in expanding loans and deposits within the area but employ them elsewhere, there may be some basis for the denudation charge; the charge could be levied whether the banks were unit banks or branch banks. The presumption of the charge, however, is that branch banks behave differently from unit banks.

Given similar reserve ratios and reserve policies, bank deposits will expand to the same extent following a net gain in cash reserves for the banking system regardless of banking structure. What is in question, however, is whether the geographical distribution of the new deposits will differ with banking structure. When bank loans are being restrained, because of inadequate cash reserves or because of high costs in freeing reserves for supporting loans, branch banking may lead to a different distribution of loans and deposits than unit banking when cash reserves are increased. Branch banking will expand loans where the demand is most intense, which may not be in the area from which the new cash reserves come. Unit banking will expand loans in the area in which the new cash reserves are gained. Under such a set of conditions branch banking is guilty not of taking funds away from the area giving it cash reserves but of employing the excess cash reserves acquired to expand deposits elsewhere. In using its excess cash reserves in this way, branch banking actually only transfers something from the area of excess deposits when the cash reserves it gains there take a physical form; otherwise, the cash reserves take the form of claims on the central bank and there are no funds to be transferred: just deposits to be created, at the receiving banks and at the central bank. The drain of funds that branch banks are accused of causing consists of not using cash reserves in expanding in the areas in which the cash reserves were gathered.

Furthermore, this drain occurs under the special circumstances of bank loans being restrained. If the banking system is able to make all the loans it wants to, an addition to the cash reserves of the system is unlikely to result in a reaction that varies with the structure of the banking system. Unit banks and branch banks in this case expand in the same manner: mainly by buying securities, and possibly by increasing loans if security prices fall. Securities are bought in central markets so that the consequences of the purchases for the regional distribution of funds to the community by the banking system are unlikely to differ significantly for the type of banking unit buying the securities. And if loans are expanded, the expansion in the excess-deposit area is not likely to differ with banking structure: branch banks will be as anxious to expand loans in the area as unit banks. Thus, if excess deposits accumulate in an area because the banking system is gaining cash reserves, bank loans not being restricted in any way, branch banking does not lead to different results from unit banking; the reaction of either may cause deposits to expand elsewhere, or to expand partly or fully in the excess-deposit area. When the expansion is not by way of increasing bank loans, excess deposits may be further increased in the area being considered, and the area can only be viewed as being drained of funds in the loose sense that some of the cash reserves gathered in the area are employed in supporting additional deposits elsewhere.

The other argument about denudation in branch banking concerns the concept of excess loans. Now loans in excess of deposits are a peculiarity of branch banking, for a unit bank will seldom have more loans than deposits.[34] Excess loans usually arise at branches that have few deposits other than those they actively create, and which lose a large portion of their created deposits. Such branches in making loans simultaneously increase their deposits; then as their borrowers pay away these deposits, the branches lose deposits and so are left with loans in excess of deposits. The branches do not have to make any adjustments for their loss of deposits but their head offices do, unless the lost deposits show up at other branches of the same bank. Excess deposits elsewhere then offset the excess loans. However, the condition, excess deposits equal excess loans, does not mean that the excess deposits have been employed to accommodate the excess loans, even in an accounting sense. A bank bases its "output" behaviour on the relation of its total deposits to its cash. When neither of these

34. Even in branch banking, however, the fact that a proposed branch would be mainly a lending branch might weigh against establishing the branch. At least it has been argued that "no bank would open a branch simply to make loans; deposits or other collateral advantages must be present or in prospect. That the loans at a branch may exceed the deposits does not alter the principle." Patterson, *Canadian Banking*, p. 247. Banking officers report that branches where loans exceed deposits are usually found in smaller towns having a large enterprise that makes most of its payments outside the local area.

changes, it takes no action. Any further accounting that it does by way of computing excess loans and excess deposits it does solely for the purpose of assessing the contribution of each branch to the state of equilibrium achieved, and not for determining banking policy.

A condition of excess loans then merely reflects the fact that pressure is being exerted on the cash position of the banks concerned. Even if branches expand their loans and retain the deposits thus created, so that they do not show an excess of loans over deposits, such branches still subject the cash reserves of their banks to strain because deposits have risen relative to cash reserves.

In neither case, however, does the expansion in loans require any transfer of funds to the branches which are adding to their loans. If the branches do not lose any of the new deposits they create, their indebtedness to head office does not change. Head office, however, has to adjust for the expansion in deposits. It sells securities, and somewhere in the banking system deposits must fall. If they fall at the branches that have expanded loans, those branches become indebted to head office on that account, but the excess loans that these branches now show do not depend on the accumulation of new excess deposits at other branches. If deposits fall elsewhere when head offices sell securities to accommodate an expansion of loans by branches in a particular area, the indebtedness to head office of the branches at which deposits fall changes in favour of the head offices. In this situation branches in the expanding area show more loans and deposits and no change in branch indebtedness, while branches elsewhere show a fall in deposits relative to their loans and so a deterioration in their debtor relationship with head office. In other words the situation cannot be explained in terms of a loan expansion in one area based on head offices of branch banks borrowing funds from their branches in other areas.

In short, when loans expand regionally in a branch-banking system and the banks sell securities to accommodate the additional loans, the resulting impact on the geographical distribution of bank deposits cannot be explained in terms of excess deposits at some branches being employed by head offices to carry excess loans at other branches.

Interregional Savings and Capital Movements

Confusion about the nature of branch banking is also caused by the tendency to identify excess deposits with savings. As a result, branch banking is often seen as transferring the surplus savings of some regions to those deficient in savings. In short, branch banking is considered to initiate or undertake interregional capital movements. The interpretation is clearly seen in the following quotation:

> In Canada, with its banks with forty and fifty branches, we see the deposits of the saving communities applied directly to the country's new enterprises in a manner nearly perfect. One bank borrows money from depositors at Halifax and many points in the maritime provinces, where the savings largely exceed the new enterprises, and it lends money in Vancouver or in the Northwest, where the new enterprises far exceed the savings. Another in the same manner gathers deposits in the unenterprising parts of Ontario, and lends the money in the enterprising localities of the same. The result is that forty or fifty business centres, in no case having an exact equilibrium of deposits and loans, are able to adjust the excess or deficiency of capital, the depositor obtaining a fair rate of interest, and the borrower obtaining money at a lower rate than borrowers in any of the colonies of Great Britain, and a lower average rate than in the United States, except in the very great cities in the East.[35]

35. B. E. Walker, *A History of Banking in Canada* (Toronto, [n.n.], 1899), p. 85. The same point is made, in more general terms by another early writer, Charles A. Conant, *A History of Modern Banks of Issue: With an Account of the Economic Crises of the Present Century* [2nd ed.], (New York, The Knickerbocker Press, [1896]), p. 572, who wrote as follows: "The system of branches has resulted in Scotland and Canada in the ready transfer of the savings of the agricultural sections to the manufacturing cities, while the branches in the cities have stood ready to furnish capital for the farming districts on the less frequent occasions when it has been needed. The transfer of capital in this way has been carried on to some extent in England by the practice of rediscounting. . . ." For a similar view cf. Patterson, *Canadian Banking*, p. 65. Perhaps in the same category is the statement by Paish, "Banking Policy and the Balance of International Payments," p. 37, that "it is well known that certain areas, especially residential areas, habitually lend large amounts to industrial areas through the medium of the banks."

This is not always considered in a favourable light as the following comment indicates:

> While the branch system has assisted greatly in the development of the new areas, it has been somewhat at the expense of others. There is little doubt that some sections, such as the Maritimes, have contributed a great deal of capital to the development of the other sections of the country. This has doubtless been to the benefit of the country at large but not necessarily to the part contributing the capital.[36]

Thus, it seems to be accepted that branch banking utilizes the savings of thrifty areas to promote the development of industrious ones. This conclusion stems from the older concepts of banking that regard deposits as accumulating from the thrift and industry of the community, and which hold that banks only lend the funds of others.[37] When deposits are equated with savings, it follows that areas where excess deposits exist have surplus savings and areas where loans exceed deposits are deficient in savings. If branch banking then functions by transferring excess deposits to areas where there are excess loans, it is easily established that branch banking is responsible for interregional movements of savings and capital.

The fallacy of the conclusion lies in overlooking the fact that any interregional movement of savings and capital is related to the interregional payments of the regions concerned and not to the concepts of excess deposits and excess loans, which only reflect the net effect

36. C. A. Curtis, "Banking," *Encyclopedia Canadiana* (Ottawa, The Canadiana Company Limited, 1957), *1*, 303, who expresses himself in the same way in "History of Canadian Banking," *Readings in Money and Banking*, ed. Elizabeth M. Rosengren (Toronto, University of Toronto Press, 1947), pp. 33–4, reprinted with revisions from the *Encyclopedia of Canada*. A similar criticism is briefly discussed in S. A. Saunders, *The Economic History of the Maritime Provinces*, A Study Prepared for the Royal Commission on Dominion-Provincial Relations (Ottawa, [King's Printer], 1939), p. 99. A more detailed criticism appears in Johnson, *The Canadian Banking System*, pp. 92–3.

F. Cyril James, *A Colloquy on Branch Banking: Contemporary Questions and Answers* (New York, American Economists Council for the Study of Branch Banking, 1939), p. 16, also accepts the view that Canadian banks have "drawn money from the wealthier East to the developing West" but considers this in a favourable light.

37. J. Brooke Willis, *The Functions of the Commercial Banking System*, p. 26.

H

of interregional payments. The matter is set straight by considering how savings may influence interregional payments and capital movements.

When regional differences in savings cause an interregional movement of funds, it is the effect of savings on interregional payments that causes the movement, not the banking system. Thus, savings in an area may reflect a level of spending that is not sufficient to maintain equilibrium in the external accounts of the area. The area exports more to other regions than it imports from them so that in the absence of offsetting capital movements other regions must make a net payment to the savings area. The net payment takes the form of a transfer of deposits to the savings area, the movement of deposits serving as an accommodating item in the interregional accounts of the area. Hence deposits rise in the savings area and, because the rise is relative to loans, branch indebtedness in the area changes in favour of the banking branches there. Although from the banking point of view branches in the savings area are supplying funds to their head offices, funds are not being withdrawn from the area— quite the contrary: funds are flowing into it.[38] There is no question of excess deposits in the gaining area being used elsewhere. Despite the growth of excess deposits in the savings area there is no exploitation of the area by the banking system; neither are other regions beneficiaries of the banking system, because, since they are losing deposits, deposits fall relative to loans within those areas.

Of course interregional movements of deposits caused by regional differences in savings and spending cannot persist in one direction indefinitely. With total deposits in the economy fixed, one region cannot gain deposits continuously from other regions: the temporarily accommodating movements of deposits must at some time give way to other adjustments if the paying areas are not to lose all of their money supply.[39] The banking system, however, is neither the maker

38. Excess deposits here measure the net payment made between the area and all other areas. A. Hagger, "Movements in Tasmania's 'International Reserves'," *Economic Record*, *36* (Apr. 1960), 242, uses excess deposits in estimating net money payments on interregional account for Tasmania.

39. Income changes and factor movements constitute the main avenues through which disturbances in the system of interregional payments may be countered.

nor the cause of the adjustments required to halt a movement of deposits to a given region, although the system may be affected through a loss of branches or banks.[40]

Implicit in the foregoing analysis is the fact that if the level of savings in various regions does not react on the interregional balance of payments, there can be no connection between savings in one area and development elsewhere. The banking system cannot utilize the savings of one area for the benefit of another. And when regional differences in savings do cause an interregional movement of deposits, the movement will take place regardless of the banking structure involved; but the repercussions of that movement may well differ with banking structure.

Savings in an area may, however, lead not to a temporary unbalance in interregional payments but to equilibrating interregional capital movements. Specifically, a high-savings area may be a net purchaser of securities sold by residents of other regions: the result is an interregional movement of capital. If an inflow of deposits into the savings area on current account in the interregional balance of payments is exactly matched by the purchase of securities from sellers outside the region, the long-term capital movement can persist indefinitely. The increase in deposits in the savings area from unbalanced interregional trade is used up by the net purchase of securities outside the home area. There is no geographical

---

Penelope Hartland, "Interregional Payments Compared with International Payments," *Quarterly Journal of Economics*, *63* (Aug. 1949), 393, 407, who argues that in the United States "the most important determinant in the maintenance of regional balance-of-payments equilibria . . . has been the mobility of productive factors, especially that of capital."

Bertil Ohlin, *Interregional and International Trade*, Harvard Economic Studies, *39* (Cambridge, Mass., Harvard University Press, 1933), pp. 399–404, discusses the adjustment process involved in restoring balance to interregional trade.

40. That is, an outflow of deposits may cause the banking offices affected to be closed. This was the experience of banks in the Ninth Federal Reserve District of the United States after World War I. A large unfavourable clearing position developed against the banks in the District as a result of a large outflow of deposits from the District, and many of the banks, lacking easily disposable earning assets, failed. Hellweg, "Comments on Task Force Report," pp. III-(6)-3-4.

redistribution of the money supply, and no change in branch indebtedness.[41]

Thus, when the capital movement equals the export surplus from the savings area, it prevents the region from temporarily gaining deposits from other regions. However, if the capital movement diverges from the export surplus, there is a net flow of deposits, either out or in depending on the direction of the divergence. This short-term flow of deposits gives rise to a change in branch indebtedness, but it is the actual transfer of deposits rather than the change in branch indebtedness[42] that serves to balance the temporary divergence between the long-term capital movements and the export surplus. Branch indebtedness merely prevents the divergence from having more drastic effects than it otherwise would; it divorces short-term flows of purchasing power from cash reserves, so that the accommodating balancing item in the interregional balance of payments is represented by a transfer of deposits and not by a transfer of cash reserves.

The banking system only becomes actively involved with interregional capital movements, as well as with regional savings, when it buys and sells securities as a counterpart to its lending operations. Loans may be expanded in some areas, and the securities that must be disposed of to accommodate the loan expansion may be sold in different areas. In effect, the areas buying the securities are supplying funds to the expanding areas, for the purchasing areas, by providing

41. James C. Ingram, "State and Regional Payments Mechanisms," *Quarterly Journal of Economics, 73* (Nov. 1959), 626, 628, suggests that the "existence of a large stock of financial claims, readily transferable from place to place" is the chief reason that interregional balances of payments are of little concern in the U.S. Discussion of how long security transactions between regions may serve to accommodate interregional balances of payments appears in Richard L. Pfister, "State and Regional Payments Mechanisms: Comment," *Quarterly Journal of Economics, 74* (Nov. 1960), 645, 647, and in James C. Ingram, "Reply," ibid., p. 651. Tibor Scitovsky, "The Theory of the Balance of Payments and the Problem of a Common European Currency," *Kyklos, 10* (1957), 26–8, also points out how an integrated capital market within a country encourages interregional capital flows and so prevents interregional balance-of-payments difficulties.

42. Ohlin, p. 400, appears to identify short-term capital inflows in interregional trade with changes in bank indebtedness rather than with movements in deposits.

a demand for the securities that the banks must sell, contribute to the ease with which borrowing areas can get additional accommodation from the banks. Indeed, it makes little difference whether the residents of an area purchase securities directly from residents of other areas, or whether they buy them from the banking system when the latter is selling to accommodate an increase in bank loans elsewhere. In the one instance, deposits flow directly from one area to another; in the other, deposits are destroyed in one place and created in the other, through the medium of the banks. Banking structure is not particularly relevant in either case.

In short, the contribution of regional savings to development elsewhere and to interregional capital movements has little to do with the kind of banking system that exists. A branch-banking system accommodates any interregional capital movements that arise, as well as movements in interregional trade induced by changes in regional savings; but the accommodation does not take the form of transferring savings from an area for the profit of other regions; neither does it take the form of inducing capital movements.

Nevertheless, branch banking does make a contribution to the mobility of funds in an economy. Without branch banking, interregional deposit movements mean a corresponding movement of cash reserves in a geographical sense that is significant. In a centralized branch-banking system cash reserves may also be redistributed among the banks when deposits are shifted by interregional payments, but the redistribution of reserves has no geographical significance. In branch banking the volume of deposits in an area does not depend on any notion of the amount of cash reserves held by banking offices in the area. As a result unbalanced interregional payments that give rise to accommodating interregional movements of deposits call for less abrupt and smoother readjustments than under unit banking: areas losing or gaining deposits do not thereby necessarily lose or gain cash reserves.[43] Consequently, gains and losses in regional deposits can go uncorrected for a longer time than would be possible if cash reserves were also being altered. A branch-banking system does not have to make banking adjustments for deposit movements be-

43. Scitovsky, "The Theory of the Balance of Payments and the Problem of a Common European Currency," p. 21.

tween areas by expanding in one area on the basis of cash reserves received there and contracting elsewhere. Branch indebtedness serves in place of these specific geographical adjustments. Thus, the contribution of branch banking to the mobility of funds in an economy lies in easing the adjustment process in interregional payments. This, not the shifting of excess deposits by head offices, nor the tapping of surplus funds somewhere, nor the imposition of involuntary capital movements, is the real economic contribution represented by branch indebtedness.

CONCLUSIONS

The mobility of funds in an economy, as it relates to banking, involves the regional distribution of bank deposits and changes therein. Mobility in this sense may result from the activities of the banking public which cause the geographical distribution of deposits to change. Banking activity itself may cause a change in the geographical pattern of deposits, as when the banking system makes loans and creates new deposits in some areas, and sells securities and reduces deposits in other areas. And since any existing geographical distribution of deposits is very largely the result of the way and direction in which the system uses its cash reserves, the mobility given to funds by the banking system may be said in a very wide sense to rest on its ability to create deposits where they are needed.

This was once thought to be a major advantage of branch banking over unit banking: that branch banking could more easily employ its cash reserves and prevent excess reserves from accumulating anywhere. The argument had some force when money-market organization was deficient and bank loans represented the only available outlet for banking activity. But under present-day conditions of large security holdings by banks and of well-organized security markets, the effective utilization of cash reserves is unlikely to be much affected by banking structure. Banks, whether they be branch banks or unit banks, now regulate their cash position by buying and selling securities.

Likewise, when banking action alters the geographical distribution of deposits, the nature of the banks concerned has little to do with the results. Thus, if bank loans expand in one area, the banking system has to sell securities to accommodate the expansion when cash reserves remain constant. It makes little difference to the final effects whether the banks selling the securities are branch banks or unit banks. Branch banking only has an advantage over unit banking when extra pressure on cash reserves from one region is accompanied by a reduction in pressure on reserves from other regions. A typical example is provided by compensating changes in the regional demand for loans: as the demand increases seasonally in one area, it falls seasonally in another. Branch banking on an interregional scale can meet this situation passively because total deposits are not affected. The branch bank need make no adjustment because a fall in its deposits in one area is offset by a rise elsewhere. In a unit-banking system, however, there have to be adjustments, and this imposes on the system an adjustment cost not present under branch banking.

The advantage of branch banking over unit banking, in relation to the mobility of funds, is most marked when the public is redistributing its deposits geographically. When such a movement of deposits takes place, it usually means a movement of cash reserves in a unit-banking system, seldom a significant transfer of cash reserves in a branch-banking system. The transfer of cash reserves in unit banking as a result of deposit movements most likely means that secondary effects are imposed on the primary movement as a result of the deposit-receiving banks expanding and the deposit-losing banks contracting. Branch banking avoids such secondary effects by substituting branch indebtedness for transfers of cash reserves. This makes for a smoother adjustment to unbalance in interregional payments.

In general, branch banking did not develop, as has been argued, to link together areas of excess deposits and areas of excess loans. It developed because it had cost and operating advantages over unit banking, and its main contribution today to the mobility of funds in an economy lies in the smoothness and ease with which it can accommodate an interregional movement of funds initiated by the public. Yet the view persists that branch banking is more active than this in mobilizing funds within an economy. In particular, it is held that branch banking is governed by an incentive to mobilize excess deposits at some branches for use at branches with excess loans or for use elsewhere. This is not so, and the behaviour of branch banking cannot be explained in these terms.

Excess deposits and excess loans at branches reflect only what has happened as the result of a geographical shift in deposits caused by the public or by banking action. And any contribution that branch banking makes to the mobility of funds depends, not on transferring excess deposits to branches having excess loans or on head office utilizing excess deposits, but on ability to accommodate with a minimum of disruption a regional shift in funds by the public, to perhaps meet a regional increase in the demand for loans more readily, and to possibly insure a smoother and more rapid response to an increase in cash reserves injected into the banking system.

Chapter Five: INTERNATIONAL BANKING TRANSACTIONS AND OPERATIONS

International transactions and operations involve more than one banking system, and involve one banking system in more than one unit of account. These complications require an analysis of the foreign-exchange operations of banks and the foreign-banking operations of domestic banks. They are discussed under the first major heading of this chapter, and are introduced by some considerations on points of similarity and difference between interregional and international transactions.

International payments and transactions do not involve, at least in any prominent fashion, movements of deposits in any of the senses discussed in Chapter Four, but they do have distribution effects on deposits—distribution effects that concern residents and non-residents. These distribution effects of international transactions are thoroughly examined under the second major heading of this chapter, the examination being related to short-term capital movements, international savings, and international investment.

The final section of the chapter deals, for the sake of completeness, with official operations in foreign exchange and with gold movements.

BANKING AND INTERNATIONAL TRANSACTIONS

Interregional and International Payments

One obvious point of difference between interregional and international payments is that the former involve payments between regions using the same unit of account for financial transactions, while the latter involve transactions between regions using different units of account. Different units of account prevent direct transfers of purchasing power from being made between international regions such as can be made between national regions; a deposit cannot be transferred from one country to another in the same way as it can be from one region to another within the same country.

A usual corollary of the fact that units of account differ among international regions is a different banking system for each region, unless a single banking system covers more than one national region.[1] When banking systems are restricted to a single country, banking operations in loans and securities do not alter the distribution of deposits among international regions as they may among regions within the same country. That is, banks do not make loans in one country and sell securities in another to accommodate the expansion in loans. Thus, there is no sense in which a banking system confined to one country can be said to have altered in any active way the distribution of deposits among international regions as it can be said to do in certain instances among regions of the same country. Any shifts in deposits that result from international payments can arise only from the initiative of bank customers; the banks are passive media for any deposit shifts that do occur.

Furthermore, the shifts in deposits that result from international transactions are of a different order from those that result from inter-regional payments; with the latter there is an actual movement of purchasing power from one region to another, which cannot take place when international payments are made. So long as the banks and the monetary authorities do not take a position in foreign exchange, the residents of a country can only acquire foreign exchange in the exchange market from other residents who have holdings of foreign exchange, or from non-residents who are willing to hold home currency. Therefore, international payments by residents of the home country in foreign currency mean they either use their own foreign

1. Where one banking system covers more than one national region, money settlements for transactions between those regions are no different from inter-regional settlements, even though units of account may differ between the regions. Ida Greaves, "Colonial Trade and Payments," *Economica*, 24 (Feb. 1957), 48.

balances or else give up domestic deposits to other residents or to non-residents in exchange for foreign balances. Neither method of settlement causes a movement of deposits between countries, and the second method, the acquisition of foreign exchange through the market, only causes either a redistribution of domestic deposits from the residents buying exchange to the residents selling it, or else a shift in domestic deposits from residents to non-residents, without deposits leaving the country. Thus, the characteristic feature of the movement of deposits that accompanies international payments is a shift in deposit ownership internal to the countries affected; there is no shift of deposits across national borders and no loss or gain of purchasing power in any national region. In contrast, interregional payments are marked by actual movements of deposits and flows of purchasing power from one region to another.[2]

Despite this difference in the nature of short-run deposit movements in interregional and international payments, both movements may operate upon the level of expenditures to adjust any disequilibrium in the balance of payments. Under interregional payments the actual shift in purchasing power between regions has an obvious bearing on regional expenditures; under international payments the adjusting effect on expenditures arises from a shift of domestic deposits between residents and non-residents, without a movement of deposits from the country, and a shift of deposits from the importers to the exporters of a country.

The geographical immobility of deposits for settling international transactions, which results from the existence of different national units of account, adds to the adjustment process an element not

2. J. E. Meade, *The Balance of Payments*, Vol. I of "The Theory of International Economic Policy," issued under the auspices of the Royal Institute of International Affairs (London, Oxford University Press, 1951), pp. 251–2, in discussing differences between the balance of payments for regions and for countries, gives as one difference the flow of cash reserves that arises from international disequilibrium but not from interregional disequilibrium. Movements of cash reserves, however, arise only when national banking systems have common cash reserves, or when, in a special sense, exchange rates are fixed. Under flexible rates and with different kinds of cash reserves in use among national banking systems, international settlements no more require the mobility of cash reserves than do interregional settlements.

present in interregional payments—an exchange rate for currencies. Where the rate of exchange is permitted to fluctuate with market conditions, it not only may facilitate or quicken the exchange of deposits within a country but also may react directly on prices and incomes.

The absence of mobility in the deposits used in settling international transactions also serves to relegate to a minor role the use of branch indebtedness; indeed, branch indebtedness has little to do with international transactions, for the geographical movement of deposits within a national area is not a conspicuous consequence of international transactions. There are one or two situations where branch indebtedness may arise in connection with international operations, however, and these are discussed in their place.

In summary, different national units of account and separate national banking systems mean that international settlements differ from interregional settlements in the nature of deposit mobility and in the role of branch indebtedness. Because international settlements do not require deposit mobility, branch indebtedness is not needed for effecting them; and because there is no branch indebtedness, there is no settlement by a geographical movement of deposits. The absence of branch indebtedness would normally call for the movement of cash reserves to effect settlement, but since there is no deposit mobility there can be no movement of cash reserves either. Therefore, the immobility of cash reserves is a feature common to both international and interregional settlements in a branch-banking system. What is peculiar to interregional settlements is the geographical mobility of deposits; what is peculiar to international settlements is the exchange of domestic deposits among residents, and between residents and non-residents all within the same country. There are thus more points of difference than of similarity between the banking effects of international and interregional payments.[3]

3. Meade, pp. 251–3, and F. W. Paish, "Banking Policy and the Balance of International Payments," *Readings in the Theory of International Trade*, Blakiston Series of Republished Articles on Economics, *4* (Philadelphia, The Blakiston Company, 1949), pp. 37–8, discuss briefly some differences between the nature of interregional balances of payments and that of international balances of payments; their points of view differ slightly in some aspects from that given here.

Banks and the Foreign-Exchange Markets

Although banks are not active agents in effecting the redistribution of deposits that constitutes one part of the process of making international payments, they nevertheless do perform an essential function in the sphere of international settlements—the conversion of currency, which is primarily a banking function. The banking system by buying and selling foreign exchange provides for the conversion of home currency into foreign currencies and of foreign currencies into home currency. But not all international settlements require the banks of the home country to provide this conversion function; they do not all involve a foreign-exchange operation for the home country.

International settlements made in the currency of the home country require only a transfer of domestic deposits between residents and non-residents on the books of the home banks—there is no conversion of currencies. Thus, if Canadians receive payment in Canadian currency for goods and services sold to others, they do not need foreign exchange even though some of their sales are to non-residents: if they pay for purchases with Canadian currency, they do not engage in a foreign-exchange transaction themselves even though they buy from non-residents.[4] What occurs as a result of these payments is a change in the Canadian deposits of residents, accompanied by an offsetting change in the Canadian deposits of non-residents.[5]

Warren L. Smith, "Areas of Regional Research," *Record of the Federal Reserve System Conference on the Interregional Flow of Funds* (Washington, Federal Reserve System, 1955), III-(7)-21, lists six points of difference between the system of domestic interregional payments that exists in the United States and that of the international gold standard in the classic form.

4. Cf. William S. Shaterian, *Export-Import Banking: The Documents and Financial Operations of Foreign Trade*, 2nd ed. (New York, The Ronald Press Company, 1956), p. 226.

5. At December 31, 1956, non-residents had $349 million in Canadian currency on deposit with the chartered banks; about $100 million represented deposits of foreign banks. Bank of Canada, *Statistical Summary*, Financial Supplement, 1956, p. 35; Canada, Department of Finance, *Statement of the Assets and Liabilities of the Chartered Banks of Canada*, December 31, 1956, liability item 3 less asset item 5. This statement is compiled monthly from returns that the chartered banks make to the Minister of Finance and is published as a supplement to the *Canada Gazette*, Pt. I.

There is no change in the total Canadian money supply, unless the shift in deposits is between the chartered-bank deposits of Canadians and the Canadian deposits of foreign central banks with the Bank of Canada. In that case payments for international purchases reduce deposits and cash reserves in the banking system by the amount that deposits of the foreign central banks are increased at the Bank of Canada. Likewise, payments for Canadian exports made from the Canadian deposits of foreign central banks with the Bank of Canada increase the deposits and cash reserves of the chartered banks.[6]

Even international settlements made in currencies other than the home currency may not constitute a foreign-exchange operation for the home banks. Residents may maintain foreign-currency deposits with the home banks or with foreign banks; they may deposit their receipts of foreign exchange in these accounts and make international

---

When the chartered banks grant overdraft facilities in Canadian currency to foreign banks, the overdraft is treated as a reduction in foreign-bank Canadian dollar deposits; granting the overdraft, and its use by a foreign importer, has the same effect, then, as a shift in Canadian deposits from non-residents to residents. When the overdraft is repaid, presumably with Canadian-currency receipts from Canadians, there is a shift the other way since cancellation of the overdraft results in an increase in the Canadian deposits of foreign banks.

6. Foreign central-bank deposits in Canadian currency with the Bank of Canada cannot be very large; at December 31, 1956, the Bank of Canada held Canadian deposits, excluding chartered bank and Government of Canada deposits, of only $31 million. This could represent not only deposits by foreign central banks but also deposits by the two Quebec savings banks, the Bank for International Settlements, the International Monetary Fund, the International Bank for Reconstruction and Development, and the Industrial Development Bank. Bank of Canada, *Annual Report*, 1956, Financial Statement; Canada, Laws, Statutes, *Bank of Canada Act*, Office Consolidation (Ottawa, Queen's Printer, 1955), ss. 18 (1) (l)-(m), 19 (e); idem, *Statutes of Canada*, 1944–45, 8 George VI, c. 44, s. 24 (d). The Bank of Canada buys and sells foreign exchange on behalf of other central banks and foreign governments, and if these pass through the accounts of the Bank of Canada, they have an effect on the cash reserves of the chartered banks. Where the foreign customer does not have an account with the Bank of Canada, however, the transaction is usually carried out on an agency basis without affecting Bank of Canada accounts. Cf. Sidney Turk, "Foreign Exchange Market in Canada," *Canadian Chartered Accountant, 63* (Aug. 1953), 66.

payments from them.[7] International receipts and payments that flow through the foreign-currency deposits of the home banks affect their foreign deposits and assets but not their domestic deposits; the domestic money supply remains unaffected. This conclusion holds whether the foreign-currency deposits are held by residents or non-residents.[8] However, the use by residents of foreign-currency deposits held with foreign banks outside the home country does not affect the domestic banking situation; unbalance in international settlements involving these outside deposits of residents means that a non-bank short-term capital movement accommodates the unbalance.

Only receipts and payments in foreign currency that are converted into domestic deposits, or from domestic deposits, by the home banks require a foreign-exchange banking operation in the home country. Receipts of foreign exchange are then converted into domestic deposits and domestic deposits into foreign exchange by the banks. The sale of foreign exchange to the home banks therefore increases domestic deposits, and at the same time increases the foreign balances of the home banks. The sale of foreign exchange by the home banks reduces their domestic deposits and their foreign balances. Unless the home banks take steps to stabilize their foreign balances, their sales and purchases of foreign exchange may not balance, with the result that their foreign-exchange operations destabilize their domestic deposits.

The impact of a net flow of international payments on a banking system that takes no neutralizing action—and where there are no cash-reserve effects from shifts in deposits between the central bank and the commercial banks—may be summarized as follows:

7. Resident firms having many receipts in foreign exchange may accumulate them in a foreign-currency deposit for conversion later, or for meeting future foreign-payment obligations. Some details on the nature of these deposits and their handling in Canada are given by Sidney A. Shepherd, *Foreign Exchange in Canada: An Outline* (Toronto, University of Toronto Press, 1953), pp. 92-3.

8. It is not unusual for non-residents, especially foreign banks, to carry foreign-currency deposits with Canadian branches of the chartered banks, either to meet payments in Canada in foreign currency or because higher interest rates can be paid on such deposits in Canada than elsewhere. Canadian banks also receive foreign deposits from non-residents at their foreign branches.

1. Equal changes in the domestic deposits and foreign balances of the home banks.
2. Equal changes in the foreign-currency deposits and foreign balances of the home banks.
3. A shift in domestic deposits between residents and non-residents, and between the importers and exporters of the home country.

All three effects may occur at the same time, although they need not be in the same direction. Even when the international receipts and payments of a country cancel out or balance, there may be offsetting movements in the foregoing categories.

Covering Operations in Foreign Exchange by Banks

Only the first effect in the summary causes a change in the foreign-exchange position of the banks. That is, when the domestic deposits and foreign balances of the home banks are altered at the same time by foreign-exchange activities, the foreign balances of the banks are thereby altered relative to their foreign liabilities, and they have an uncovered foreign-exchange position. One of three possibilities may then exist: the banks may simply let their foreign-exchange position fluctuate, taking no further action; the banks may have to keep their foreign-exchange position constant because of exchange controls; or the banks may undertake voluntarily to stabilize their foreign-exchange position by engaging in covering operations in the exchange market.

Permitting the foreign-exchange position to vary is only a sound policy for banks when countries are on a common currency standard and there are no exchange controls. Exchange rates are then stable, and there is unrestricted convertibility between the national currency and the accepted international means of payment, which can be used or substituted for cash reserves in more than one banking system. Under such conditions there is little exchange risk, and foreign balances provide a domestic banking system with a useful form of secondary reserves; banks can regulate their cash-reserve ratios by letting their foreign balances fluctuate, as Canadian banks used to when Canada was on the gold standard. The result of this banking policy is to stabilize exchange rates, but to destabilize domestic deposits when there is a net flow of international payments; depending on the direction of the flow, home banks become either net sellers or net buyers of exchange. The effect of the resulting fluctuations in domestic deposits on the cash-reserve ratios of the banks is offset by an appropriate substitution of foreign balances for international reserves, or vice versa, by the banks, since international reserves represent cash reserves or claims for cash reserves. Conditions that would permit modern banking systems to follow this course of action no longer exist; therefore they need no further discussion in the present context.

Under exchange controls, banks are compelled to maintain a more or less constant position in foreign exchange. They are required to sell any foreign exchange purchased in the market to the control authorities, and to meet selling orders by drawing upon the official supplies of foreign exchange. In other words, the banks act as buying and selling agents for the control authorities; they cannot, to any extent, take a position in the market themselves. Hence, the initial impact of a net flow of international payments on the banking system is to alter bank deposits and cash reserves in the same direction.

When exchange rates may fluctuate, even within narrow limits, there is an exchange risk that discourages banks from altering their foreign-exchange position. Under flexible exchange rates, banks are more likely to prefer a constant foreign-exchange position.[9] Consequently they attempt to cover any exposed exchange position by

9. The preference of Canadian banks for a stable foreign-exchange position extends back to the early 1930's, or to the beginning of unstable exchange rates; at least the literature on the subject at that time refers to the policy of Canadian banks in avoiding taking positions in foreign exchange. R. F. Knight, "Foreign Exchange from a Practical Viewpoint," *Journal of The Canadian Bankers' Association*, *39* (July 1932), 450; Canada, Royal Commission on Banking and Currency in Canada, *Report* (Ottawa, King's Printer, 1933), p. 34. Recent statements are unanimous in pointing out that Canadian banks try to balance their foreign-exchange position. Turk, "Foreign Exchange Market in Canada," p. 62; Shepherd, *Foreign Exchange in Canada*, p. 32; A. B. Jamieson, *Chartered Banking in Canada*, p. 334. New York banks also try to balance their purchases and sales of foreign exchange. "The New York Foreign Exchange Market," Federal Reserve Bank of New York, *Monthly Review of Credit and Business Conditions*, Nov. 1957, p. 151; Dec. 1957, p. 165.

undertaking offsetting or covering operations in the market. This means the banks try to balance their purchases of foreign exchange with their sales; they try to avoid being net buyers of foreign exchange when the flow of international payments is inwards, and they try to avoid being net sellers when it is outwards. Under this policy the banking system does not absorb the impact of net flows in international payments; consequently the domestic money supply is not destabilized by the foreign-exchange operations of the banks.

The banking policy of covering operations in foreign exchange is worth considering in detail because it is a policy that is pursued by banks operating under a system where there is some flexibility in exchange rates, as in Canada, and because it is a policy that requires initiating action by the banks as principals, unlike the situation that exists under exchange controls.

Under a policy of covering operations in foreign exchange, whenever the banks buy foreign exchange from their customers they try to sell it again, and whenever they sell exchange they try to buy a like amount. In this way they prevent their foreign balances from fluctuating as a result of their conversion activities in foreign exchange. When there is an inward flow of international payments, the banks avoid becoming large net buyers by lowering their buying and selling prices for foreign exchange; the reduction in buying price slows down sales to the banks by inducing some residents to postpone their conversion of current receipts and some non-residents to postpone buying domestic currency. The reduction in selling price influences non-residents to convert some of their holdings of domestic currency into foreign currency and some residents to switch from domestic to foreign currency. Hence, price adjustments work to slow down sales to the banks and to speed up purchases from them.

When the purchases and sales of the banks balance, the only effect on the books of the banks is a change in the distribution of deposits among their customers; the domestic deposits of exporters and other sellers of exchange are higher because of the foreign exchange sold to the home banks, while the domestic deposits of importers and other buyers of exchange are lower because of their foreign-exchange purchases. Also the banks by selling to non-residents foreign exchange acquired from residents bring about a shift of domestic deposits from

non-residents to residents. Hence, a consequence of covering operations in foreign exchange by the banks is a shift in domestic deposits
among residents, and between non-residents and residents: the same
type of distribution effects as would follow if the banks did not deal
in foreign exchange and the original buyers and sellers had to deal
among themselves. These distribution effects on deposits do not disturb the total, so long as accounts with the central bank are neither
increased nor decreased by the operations in the foreign-exchange
market—not too severe a condition to meet.

Although covering operations are undertaken to isolate the foreign
balances of the banks from the effects of foreign-exchange transactions, complete isolation is not always possible; activities of the
banks in the foreign-exchange market usually cause some fluctuations
in their foreign balances. Various lags make it impossible to exactly
balance sales of foreign exchange with purchases; items in transit, or
"float," temporarily affect the size of the foreign balances held, as
when exchange is bought by cable and sold by bank draft.[10] Forward-
exchange operations are also sometimes a source of variations in the
foreign balances of the banks.[11] Aside from these possibilities, cover-

10. Jamieson, *Chartered Banking in Canada*, p. 334. Banks usually consider themselves to be in a balanced position in foreign exchange if their total purchases and
sales of exchange are equal, regardless of the dates of maturity. Paul Einzig, *The
Theory of Forward Exchange* (London, Macmillan and Co., 1937), p. 137. This
attitude, of course, enables banks to undertake covered interest-arbitrage operations on their own behalf, despite the restraint imposed by a policy that prohibits
the deliberate carrying of a position in foreign exchange.

11. For example, when a customer buys foreign exchange from his bank for
forward delivery, payment as well as delivery is postponed till some future date.
Since the bank is committed to deliver a given amount of foreign exchange on the
final date, it usually buys foreign exchange immediately to cover that future
obligation. Its foreign balances are thereby increased for the present. Normally,
the bank then tries to return to its original position by selling foreign exchange now
in accordance with an agreement to buy it back later—a combination spot sale and
forward purchase made at one and the same time and with the same party. Such
a swap operation, as it is called, keeps the foreign balances of the bank constant
and also ensures that it has the exchange available to meet its forward commitment
on the agreed date. If the swap cannot be done, and it can not always be done,
the bank is left with an increase in its foreign balances, as a result of its initial
purchase, for the duration of its forward contract. On the expiration of that
contract and the delivery of the forward exchange the foreign balances of the bank

ing operations in foreign exchange by the banks mean that bank activities in the foreign-exchange market seldom destabilize either the foreign balances or the domestic deposits of the banks.[12]

Of a different nature from the ordinary foreign-exchange transactions carried out by banks for their customers are those transactions that banks initiate in order to gain and use foreign balances for domestic purposes. In such transactions the banks sell spot foreign exchange from their foreign balances and buy it back in the forward market. Foreign balances of the banks are reduced over the period of the forward contract but the exchange risk is covered. When the spot sales are made to depositors of the banking system, the effect of the transaction is to reduce domestic deposits in the banking system for the duration of the forward contract. There is, of course, no effect on the total cash reserves of the banks. What a banking system gains by drawing upon its foreign balances in this way depends on the context in which the transactions are carried out. There are four possibilities here: the foreign balances of the banking system are stationary; foreign balances are rising because banks borrow foreign exchange from some of their customers in lieu of buying it outright from them; foreign balances are rising because, in addition to normal purchases of foreign exchange, the banks attract deposits of foreign exchange, and bank customers are being persuaded to give up some domestic deposits to hold foreign-currency deposits.

When foreign balances are stationary, a spot sale of foreign ex-

---

are restored to their previous level. Shepherd, *Foreign Exchange in Canada*, pp. 32, 44; Paul Einzig, *Foreign Balances* (London, Macmillan and Co., Limited, 1938), p. 62. Canada, Dominion Bureau of Statistics, *Canada's International Investment Position, 1926–1954* (Ottawa, Queen's Printer, 1956), p. 54, reports that Canadian banks have at times held foreign exchange temporarily to meet forward obligations.

12. To have domestic deposits remain undisturbed in the face of foreign-exchange operations, however, requires the banks to stabilize their foreign balances, the monetary authorities to do likewise, and the central bank to offset any cash-reserve effects resulting from transactions in foreign exchange. A very clear statement of the conditions under which international payments have no effect on total domestic deposits is made by Einzig, *Foreign Balances*, pp. 118–19, 138. Recognition of the fact that international transactions need not disturb the domestic money supply under conditions such as now prevail in Canada appears in Bank of Canada, *Annual Report*, 1956, p. 19.

change to depositors of the banking system, covered with a forward purchase, simply reduces the foreign balances and the domestic deposits of the banking system. If the system is then able to restore deposits to their previous level by expanding domestic earning assets, the system gains additional domestic assets for the duration of the forward contract, although all of the additional assets are at the expense of reduced foreign assets. Total assets of the banking system remain constant. The effect, which is only a temporary one, however, is similar to a sale of securities by the banks: one type of asset replaces another type in the balance-sheet of the banks.[13]

Banks may be able to increase their foreign balances by inducing their customers to leave foreign exchange on deposit with the banks instead of selling it. The exchange if sold would be sold to the banks, who would in turn sell it to other depositors of the banking system, so that the position of the banking system would be left unaffected by the exchange transactions. If, however, the banks borrow the foreign exchange, instead of buying it, they add to their foreign assets and liabilities, and hence the size of the banking system is increased. The new foreign assets, or that portion of them not required as reserves against the additional foreign liabilities, may be sold spot against a forward purchase. This reduces domestic deposits initially, but if total domestic deposits in the banking system are permitted to remain constant, the banks can carry more domestic earning assets than they otherwise could.[14] They are able to do this because they have ex-

13. Paul Einzig, "Dollar Deposits in London," *The Banker* (London), Jan. 1960, p. 27, suggests that London banks might convert their holdings of dollars into sterling "when money is tight and the banks concerned are reluctant to withdraw funds from the money market or to realize investments." He goes on to argue that, in the absence of intervention by the monetary authorities, the banking system could not improve its liquidity in this way, but he appears to overlook the effect on liquidity of the reduction in deposits that results from the conversion of dollars into sterling.

14. Alan R. Holmes and Fred H. Klopstock, "The Market for Dollar Deposits in Europe," Federal Reserve Bank of New York, *Monthly Review*, Nov. 1960, p. 201, mention the swapping of dollars into sterling by British banks in order to expand loans at home. Probably in this process the granting of the loans comes first. Domestic deposits are expanded by the amount of the new loans, and the swapping of dollars for sterling reduces domestic deposits to their previous level, thus preserving the cash and liquidity ratios.

panded their total assets in the first place by borrowing foreign exchange through accepting foreign-currency deposits. The spot sale and forward purchase of foreign exchange is then just a means of adjusting the composition of their new total of assets. The effect on domestic earning assets remains as long as the banks can keep their foreign-currency liabilities outstanding and can renew their forward contracts in foreign exchange.

Banks may in addition to their ordinary purchases of foreign exchange from customers attract foreign-currency deposits at their domestic branches. This is new business that adds to the assets and liabilities of the banking system in the same way as in the previous case. The banks are then in a position to convert foreign assets into domestic assets by selling exchange spot and buying it back forward.[15] Domestic deposits are reduced, which enables banks to hold more domestic assets when cash reserves and requirements remain constant.

Finally, banks may offer holders of domestic deposits an incentive to switch into a foreign-currency deposit. It may be possible to offer such holders a higher rate of return on foreign-currency deposits because there is a profit to be made on the covering exchange transaction, or because there is a convention that limits the rates that can be paid on domestic deposits but not on foreign-currency deposits. The effect on the banking system is to reduce domestic deposits and increase foreign liabilities. When there are no reserve requirements against foreign liabilities,[16] the banking system can expand its domestic earning assets to restore domestic deposits to their previous

15. This type of operation as practiced by London banks is described in "Dollar Deposits in London," *The Economist*, July 11, 1959, pp. 109–10; by Einzig, "Dollar Deposits in London," p. 23; and idem, "Some Recent Changes in Forward Exchange Practices," *Economic Journal*, 70 (Sept. 1960), 494–5.

16. Canadian law does not specify what cash reserves the chartered banks should maintain against their foreign-currency liabilities; the Bank Act merely states that a "bank shall also maintain adequate reserves against liabilities payable in foreign currencies." *Statutes of Canada*, 1953–54, 2-3 Elizabeth II, c. 48, s. 71 (4). Of course when Canadian banks operate in countries that require banks to maintain a certain cash-reserve ratio, the Canadian banks are bound to comply for the deposits they hold in that country. However, for the foreign-currency deposits they hold in Canada, the chartered banks are not subject to any legal requirements for cash reserves against those deposits.

level. The total assets of the banking system are greater by the amount of increase in the foreign liabilities assumed.[17]

No foreign-exchange operation need be carried out to achieve the foregoing effect. The depositor who accepts a foreign-currency deposit to earn a higher rate normally wants domestic funds again on termination of his deposit contract. A bank that grants a foreign-currency deposit in exchange for domestic funds thus need pay out only domestic funds to extinguish its foreign liability at the end of the contract. A bank may, nevertheless, go through the market in switching the domestic deposits of a customer temporarily into foreign deposits. The bank then buys foreign exchange spot to cover its new foreign liability, and sells forward to provide for the domestic funds the customer will want at the end of the contract. The bank then sells the foreign exchange spot and buys it back forward, which places the bank in exactly the same position as if it had never gone into the market at all.

All four methods of using foreign balances for domestic purposes have the effect of reducing domestic deposits. This means that if monetary policy does not interfere banks can expand their domestic earning assets, at least temporarily, by drawing upon their foreign balances. In those cases where foreign liabilities are also increased, the total assets of the banks rise by the same amount as domestic earning assets.

Foreign-Banking Operations of Domestic Banks

Covering operations, however, need not mean that the foreign balances of banks are committed to varying only by the net income

17. Harry C. Eastman, "Aspects of Speculation in the Canadian Market for Foreign Exchange," *Canadian Journal of Economics and Political Science*, 24 (Aug. 1958), 370–1, suggests that beginning in 1956 "Canadian banks encouraged their clients to keep funds in United States dollar account," and that this economized on bank cash, mitigated the restrictive effect of Bank of Canada action on the money supply, and added to the lending ability of the banks. Actually, domestic deposits are reduced by such behaviour, and the Bank of Canada could have surely prevented deposits from rising again by appropriate action on bank cash. In other words, there is nothing in the nature of the transaction to interfere with central-bank control, for the central bank need not accommodate such transactions as they might transactions in which a sale of securities is involved.

earned on them; this would be the case only if ordinary operations in the market represented the sole source of foreign exchange for banks. This is not the case, however: most banks attract some foreign-currency business to their domestic banking offices, and many large banks operate offices in foreign countries. Both possibilities represent sources of foreign exchange for the banks concerned.

The acceptance by banks of foreign-currency deposits has developed greatly in the last few years with the growth in Europe of active markets for dollar and sterling deposits (Euro-dollar and Euro-sterling deposits). Foreign-currency deposits, of course, are simply deposits held with banks in currency other than that of the country of the receiving or accepting banks. The depositors may be other banks or non-banks, and they may be residents of the country whose currency is used, residents of the country of the accepting banks, or residents of some third country. These deposits may arise for political reasons, the depositors preferring to hold deposits of a certain currency in countries other than the country of the currency.[18] Or, such deposits may arise because the accepting banks can offer higher rates for the deposits than can the banks in the country whose currency is being deposited.[19] Foreign-currency deposits may be the only area in

18. "The original impetus for the postwar development of the continental dollar market is believed to have arisen from the desire of several banks in Eastern Europe to leave their dollar balances with their correspondents in France and England rather than carry them in their own name in the United States." Holmes and Klopstock, "The Market for Dollar Deposits in Europe," p. 197. Einzig, "Dollar Deposits in London," pp. 24–5, suggests that many European holders of dollars prefer not to carry them in the U.S. in order to keep the knowledge of such deposits from their own taxation authorities.

19. The banks in a particular country may be prohibited from paying more than a certain rate for deposits in their currency, which is the case in the United States where maximum rates of interest that may be paid on deposits are prescribed for member banks. Board of Governors of the Federal Reserve System, *Regulation Q: Payment of Interest on Deposits*, sect. 3. During 1959 and 1960 the maximum rate that U.S. member banks could pay on deposits was less than non-U.S. banks could pay for U.S. dollar deposits kept with them, with the result that the amount of dollar deposits held outside the U.S. expanded greatly. Holmes and Klopstock, "The Market for Dollar Deposits in Europe," p. 197; New York Clearing House Association, *A Study of Regulation Q as it Applies to Foreign Time Deposits: Report to the Board of Governors of the Federal Reserve System* ([n.p.], [n.n.], 1960), p. 15;

which the banks of some countries can compete for new business in terms of price,[20] and this tends to raise the rate paid on such deposits. The accepting banks may also have exceptional opportunities for investing the resulting foreign balances,[21] or for relending the foreign balances, either to other banks or to non-banks.[22]

The acceptance of foreign-currency deposits has no effect on the cash reserves of the banking system accepting the deposits unless the foreign balances acquired are turned over to the monetary authorities. The general effect is to raise the foreign balances and the foreign liabilities of the accepting banks, the banks having, in effect, borrowed foreign balances. If these foreign balances are then lent to non-banks, there is simply a substitution of loans in foreign currency for foreign balances. A less liquid foreign-currency asset replaces a more liquid one. Much the same effect results if the foreign balances are lent to other banks, except that foreign balances due from one bank replace foreign balances due from another bank. A third possibility is that the banks themselves invest the foreign balances in securities of the country of the currency. Again, the effect is to replace a liquid asset with a less liquid one. The possibility that the banks may convert foreign balances into domestic ones for use at home was covered in the previous section.

The banking system of the country whose currency is used in

Einzig, "Dollar Deposits in London," p. 24; and "Dollar Deposits in London," *Economist*, p. 109.

20. This appears to be the situation with Italian banks which are large users of Euro-dollar deposits. A rate agreement for lira credits restricts inter-bank competition in Italy, but lending in dollars, which requires accepting or gaining U.S. dollar deposits, has opened a way for Italian banks to compete in terms of price for new customers. Holmes and Klopstock, "The Market for Dollar Deposits in Europe," p. 200; New York Clearing House Association, p. 14.

21. Canadian banks are said to be in an advantageous position to employ U.S. dollars, borrowed from European holders, in the New York money market. Holmes and Klopstock, "The Market for Dollar Deposits in Europe," p. 261. Also cf. New York Clearing House Association, p. 12.

22. London banks are said to be in an excellent position to serve as intermediaries between lenders and borrowers of dollar deposits because of their "unexampled network of correspondent banks and agencies." "Dollar Deposits in London," pp. 109–10.

foreign-currency deposits also experiences no effect on its cash reserves or total deposits as a result of transactions in such deposits, unless the deposits pass into the hands of those who hold the foreign balances they represent with the central bank, or who use them in settling transactions with banks in the country of the currency in question.[23] If these banks have foreign branches, they may accept deposits in their own currency at these branches;[24] this reduces deposits at home but not the total of deposits held in the currency of the country, counting the deposits held both at home and at the foreign branches.

Excess deposits or excess loans in foreign currency on the books of a domestic branch measure its indebtedness to the rest of the banking system on foreign operations, just as its domestic loan-deposit differential measures its indebtedness on domestic operations. Thus when domestic branches accept deposits of foreign exchange, the actual exchange flows into accounts maintained abroad by the head offices, so that the accepting branches obtain foreign funds for head offices. When, however, foreign-currency deposits on the books of domestic branches are drawn down, foreign funds must be supplied from the foreign balances of the head offices: the head offices place the branches in foreign funds. And when foreign-currency loans are granted by domestic branches and the deposits that result therefrom are drawn upon, the foreign balances of head offices have to be drawn upon. When the foreign loans are repaid, however, head offices are placed in foreign funds again by the lending branches.

Excess deposits or excess loans in foreign currency on the books of domestic branches represent situations in which the branches are adding to the foreign funds of their head offices, or are drawing upon them; the foreign-currency, loan-deposit differential at domestic branches therefore measures an indebtedness between head office and its branches arising from the foreign-currency business of the latter.

23. Cf. Holmes and Klopstock, "The Market for Dollar Deposits in Europe," pp. 198–9; C. Gordon Tether, "Dollars—Hard, Soft, and Euro," *The Banker* (London), June 1961, pp. 399–400.

24. Foreign branches of U.S. banks have attracted large amounts of Eurodollars. Holmes and Klopstock, "The Market for Dollar Deposits in Europe," p. 201.

The indebtedness on this account represents a closer approximation to the interpretation that branches advance funds to head office, or are placed in funds by head office, than does the indebtedness on domestic account. Although excess deposits or loans on foreign account may be interpreted in this way—as lending foreign funds to head office or borrowing them from head office—they cannot also be represented as a drain of purchasing power from the excess-deposit area, or as an augmentation of purchasing power in the excess-loan area. Unlike their domestic counterpart, excess foreign deposits at the branches of area banks do not mean an increase in purchasing power for spending on area resources. The deposist are held for spending or making payments abroad. Hence a loss of these deposits, and a condition of excess loans in foreign funds, does not represent a loss of purchasing power for the area.

In short, domestic branches may have two categories of branch indebtedness from their operations—one in domestic currency and one in foreign currency. They are dissimilar in their consequences and interpretations and they are handled separately by the banks. Thus when head-office interest is paid on excess deposits or charged for excess loans the rates applied may differ between the domestic and the foreign categories.

A home banking system that operates banking offices[25] in other countries has an additional source of foreign-currency deposits and of foreign assets in the form of loans, securities, and cash reserves. However, to tap this source of foreign business an initial direct investment in fixed and working capital in foreign countries must be made by the home banks; most if not all of this investment requires the use of foreign exchange. The investment does not mean, however, that a

25. Frank M. Tamagna and Parker B. Willis, "United States Banking Organization Abroad," *Federal Reserve Bulletin*, Dec. 1956, pp. 1284–92, discuss the organizational structures used by American banks in carrying on a foreign-banking business. Some details on the operations of the foreign branches of Canadian banks appear in *Historical Outline of Canadian Banking Legislation and Some Features of the Present Working of the Canadian Banking System*, Presentations by J. A. McLeod, President, The Canadian Bankers' Association, before the Royal Commission on Banking and Currency, at Ottawa, 1933 ([n.p., n.n., n.d.]), pp. 37–9. Canadian banks operate mainly unincorporated branches abroad, but some of the banks have incorporated branches.

home bank has to take an exchange position and use its domestic banking resources for the purpose of establishing branches abroad. The home bank may have acquired sufficient foreign balances from deposits of foreign currency at its branches in the home country to cover the foreign investment. It may simply convert the asset form of the foreign-currency deposits of its branches from foreign balances and securities into the less liquid form of investments in foreign branches. The financing aspects are similar to those, discussed in Chapter Three, of domestic capital expenditures financed, indirectly, by liquidating domestic earning assets.

Thus the direct investment in foreign branches by home banks need not represent a drain on domestic banking resources, but in that case it represents the investment of existing foreign balances in a less liquid form. However, when the foreign branches make profits, the head office is provided with a return in foreign currency on its investment, which it can use to augment its foreign balances or, by conversion, its domestic resources. The effects in either instance work through the cash-reserve ratio. Thus profit-taking by a foreign branch has the same initial impact as profit-taking by domestic branches: it reduces branch deposits and thereby destabilizes the cash-reserve ratio. With foreign branches of course it is foreign deposits that are reduced and foreign cash-reserve ratios that are destabilized. The foreign excess reserves created by profit-taking may be used to expand foreign earning assets, just as domestic excess reserves are used to expand domestic earning assets. Or excess foreign reserves may be converted through the foreign-exchange market into domestic funds. If the latter course is adopted, it means that excess reserves abroad are converted into excess reserves at home, since the sale of foreign exchange by the banks for domestic funds reduces domestic deposits. The foreign profits of the home banks then lead to the expansion of domestic earning assets; the stabilization of foreign cash-reserve ratios following profit-taking and the conversion of profits into domestic funds temporarily destabilizes the domestic cash-reserve ratio. Thus the transfer mechanism for banking profits earned abroad and converted into home currency works to stabilize foreign cash-reserve ratios at the expense of the domestic reserve ratio.

In addition to yielding foreign exchange to their head offices through profits, foreign branches also provide a source of foreign balances when their deposits exceed their loans. When their loans exceed their deposits, foreign branches impose a drain on the foreign balances of their head offices; if the foreign balances cannot stand the drain, foreign branches then impose a drain on domestic banking resources. These consequences of excess deposits and excess loans of foreign branches do not necessarily give rise to an actual movement of funds between the branches and their head offices. Fluctuations in the non-loan deposits of the foreign branches of home banks, considered as a unit, in a foreign country mean corresponding fluctuations in the cash reserves of those branches, because they constitute only a part of the banking system in the country. Hence an increase in their deposits relative to their loans generally means an increase in their cash reserves, and a decrease in their deposits relative to their loans generally means a decrease in their cash reserves. Fluctuations in their loans reflected in *pari passu* fluctuations in their deposits mean no change in their cash reserves, only a change in the reserve ratio. It is the change in deposits relative to loans and the resulting change in the cash-reserve holdings of the foreign branches that represent for head office a change in its foreign balances. The excess reserves of its foreign branches represent a gain in the foreign assets of head office when the extra reserves are retained in cash form or converted into securities; so long as the branches do not utilize the reserves in making loans, head offices have additional foreign balances. Likewise, if the foreign branches suffer a loss of cash reserves—diminishing excess deposits—their head offices suffer a loss of foreign balances. When the loss of cash reserves at foreign branches is so great that the local resources of the branches are insufficient to make good the loss, then and only then do head offices actually transfer funds to their foreign branches.

In general foreign branches may accumulate or may lose foreign cash reserves in the course of their ordinary banking activities, and in doing so, they acquire and lose head-office assets. As a result their indebtedness to head office varies accordingly, the variation in indebtedness being reflected in changes in the differential between loans and deposits. At first it may appear that an excess of loans over deposits at foreign branches represents a movement of funds from their head offices to the branches and that an excess of deposits over loans represents a movement of funds from the branches to their head offices. In other words the existing view of branch banking advancing funds to branches with excess loans and transferring funds from branches with excess deposits can be applied to foreign branches as well as to domestic branches. The usefulness of such an application may be assessed by considering what may happen when foreign branches acquire excess cash reserves.

Excess cash reserves at foreign branches, as already explained, provide free or disposable foreign balances for the banks affected. If the excess reserves are used in the countries in which they arise, there is no movement or transfer of funds from the branches to their head offices. In the process some of the excess reserves are paid away in acquiring earning assets and the rest are absorbed in supporting additional deposits. When loans are acquired, a rise in loans relative to deposits at the foreign branches is likely. Branch indebtedness thus moves against the branches, indicating that they have tied up and lost foreign balances, which are considered to be head-office assets. When loans are not expanded in the process of using excess cash reserves within the country in which they arise, deposits likely rise relative to loans at the foreign branches. The increase in head-office indebtedness to foreign branches, which the foregoing change in their deposit-loan differential indicates, shows that the foreign branches have been able to add to foreign non-loan earning assets. But the branches do not supply head office with funds that it can employ elsewhere.

The excess reserves of the foreign branches, instead of being used within the country in which they arise, may be converted into exchange at a financial centre in another country. That is, the foreign branches buy foreign balances for head office in some money-market centre in a third country, instead of buying assets within the country in which they operate. The foreign branches may buy foreign balances for their head offices in two ways. They may simply buy foreign exchange outright with their excess reserves, as when they acquire the foreign exchange from the central bank that holds their cash reserves. Or the foreign branches may buy the foreign exchange by expanding their deposits on the basis of their excess cash reserves. When the foreign branches add to their deposits by buying foreign exchange, they build up their credit with head office; in contrast, when they reduce their cash reserves, they do not alter the state of their indebtedness with head office, for they have only converted existing head-office assets into another form.

From the view-point of the head offices, there has been a movement of their foreign funds, in the sense that foreign balances belonging to them in the countries where their branches have accumulated excess cash reserves have been used, either directly or through credit creation, to buy elsewhere foreign balances, which can be used in any way the head offices see fit. In the same way foreign branches provide their head offices with foreign funds that can be employed elsewhere, and the provision of those funds is accompanied or preceded by a change in the deposits of the foreign branches relative to their loans. This change in branch indebtedness occurs, however, as a result of the branches accumulating excess reserves—because they acquire deposits of cash reserves, because their loans outstanding are reduced, or because they sell other assets for cash or for a reduction in their deposits. It is what is done with the excess reserves that determines whether head offices are placed in foreign funds in the sense that there is a movement or transfer of funds. And then a movement or transfer is required only because a conversion or purchase transaction is carried out.

If a head office has branches in more than one country, it may be able to use the excess reserves of branches in one country to make up a deficiency in cash reserves at branches in other countries. Excess reserves in one country may be used to acquire balances in a foreign money-market centre; these foreign balances may then be sold to acquire cash reserves, or reduce deposits, on behalf of branches, in some third country, that need to build up their cash-reserve ratios. The fact that foreign branches with excess cash reserves will have increased their deposits relative to their loans, and that foreign branches deficient in reserves will have experienced a fall in their deposits relative to loans, makes it possible, in such a situation, to interpret the action of head office in terms of transferring excess deposits from its branches in one country to its branches having excess loans in other countries.[26] A better interpretation, or a less confusing one, however, is the more direct one running in terms of excess cash reserves of branches in one country being used through the foreign-exchange market to bolster up the cash-reserve ratios of branches in another country. In short, what head office is doing is using its foreign balances in some common money-market centre to stabilize the cash-reserve ratios of its banking offices in different countries. To the extent that such a policy is successful, domestic banking resources are not employed in the operations of foreign branches; the foreign operations overall are self-supporting.[27]

DISTRIBUTION EFFECTS ON DEPOSITS OF INTERNATIONAL PAYMENTS

The more significant banking effects of international operations lie not in the scope they offer the banks for manipulating foreign balances, but in their distribution effects on domestic deposits and foreign balances. Under such effects the banks become less the actor and more the medium acted upon; but despite the passive role of the banks in the redistribution process generated by international payments, the changes in deposits that result are worth consideration. Accordingly, the effects of international payments on the distribution of domestic deposits are analyzed here, from the point of view of flexible exchange rates and covering operations by the banks in foreign exchange. Possible interregional deposit changes are discussed first, then the type of deposit changes that arises in connection with the balance of international payments.

26. *Historical Outline of Canadian Banking Legislation*, pp. 37–8, describes the cash-reserve management of foreign branches of Canadian banks in the 1930's in terms of the excess deposits of branches in one country being applied to offset the excess loans of branches in another country, the operation being carried out either through the London or the New York money market.

27. This appears to be the case in Canadian banking. C. A. Curtis, "History of Canadian Banking," *Readings in Money and Banking*, ed. E. M. Rosengren (Toronto, University of Toronto Press, 1947), p. 32, and idem, "Banking," *Encyclopedia Canadiana* (Ottawa, The Canadiana Company Limited, 1957), *1*, 301, expresses the opinion that the outside business of the Canadian banks is in general self-supporting and draws capital neither to nor from Canada.

Interregional Distribution Effects

One possible effect of international settlements on domestic deposits may be a regional or geographical change in their distribution. The possibility arises from the activity of the banking system in the foreign-exchange market. Purchases and sales of foreign exchange for domestic currency by branches may produce a regional change in deposits, or the covering operations in foreign exchange carried out by the trading departments of the head offices may have a like effect.

When the sales and purchases of foreign exchange by branches in the banking system are in balance, not only overall but also within each region, the existing geographical distribution of domestic deposits is not disturbed by the foreign-exchange business of the banks. When branches in all areas are all net sellers or all net buyers of foreign exchange, and to the same degree, then any change in the geographical pattern of deposits depends on the impact of the covering operations undertaken by the head offices. Any regional redistribution of deposits that arises under these conditions must be due to the failure of covering operations to stabilize deposits in some areas. Thus if branches are net purchasers of foreign exchange—their domestic deposits rise—head offices must become net sellers of foreign exchange, and their sales reduce deposits somewhere. Head-office sales may not be evenly distributed among depositors, and therefore, a redistribution of deposits between regions is brought about through the covering operations of head offices. The situation is analogous to that discussed in Chapter Four, where compensating transactions in securities, undertaken by head offices to offset fluctuations in loans at some branches, cause a regional change in deposits.

If branches in one region are net buyers of foreign exchange and branches in all other areas are net sellers, or if the situation is the exact reverse, so that overall branch sales and purchases of exchange balance, there are no covering operations, but there is a natural redistribution of deposits among regions. Hence deposits are reduced in one area because residents there are net purchasers of foreign exchange from area branches; meanwhile deposits rise elsewhere by a like amount because bank customers there are net sellers of foreign

I

exchange. Total deposits remain constant but their geographical pattern is altered.

The fact that the purchases and sales of foreign exchange by area branches are balanced or unbalanced is no assurance that deposits in the area will or will not fluctuate because of foreign-exchange operations by the banking system. An unbalanced position may be exactly countered in the area by head-office covering operations, and a balanced position may be upset by covering operations. Thus any geographical change in the distribution of domestic deposits that results from the activities of banks in the foreign-exchange market is most likely the resultant not only of branch purchases and sales but also of head-office transactions.

The changes in branch indebtedness that result from the transactions of domestic branches in foreign exchange may be thought, at least under Canadian conditions, to involve the branches in an actual movement of funds. Under Canadian conditions all purchases of foreign exchange by the branches flow into accounts held abroad, and all sales by branches are made from these same accounts. Because these accounts are carried as assets on the books of the head offices, branches acquire a debt to their head offices for sales made from the accounts, and obtain a credit for exchange bought for these accounts.[28] In these cases the branches appear to be actually placing the head offices in funds or drawing upon head-office funds. In balance-of-payments language, there is a capital movement or flow when branches buy and sell foreign exchange. However, a rise in domestic deposits relative to loans because branches are net purchasers of foreign exchange does not improve or preserve the cash position of the head offices as it might when the rise is the result of branches receiving domestic-exchange items on deposit. Just the reverse happens: the domestic cash position of the banks is put under pressure when the branches buy foreign exchange. And, when branches sell foreign exchange, their deposits most likely fall relative to their loans, but this reflects not a deterioration in the cash position of head offices, but an improvement. In other words, the purchase

28. A few details on the accounting aspects of the foreign balances held by Canadian banks are given by E. L. Stewart Patterson, *Canadian Banking*, pp. 260-1, 263-4; Turk, "Foreign Exchange Market in Canada," p. 62.

and sale of foreign exchange by branches do not differ in their effect from the purchase and sale of any other asset by the branches. Such purchases and sales, unless settled with currency, may be interpreted as causing net changes in head-office assets—changes that are accompanied by changes in branch indebtedness contrary to the effect on cash reserves. That is, a rise in head-office assets, whether foreign or domestic, in this context means a rise in head-office indebtednesses to branches although a deterioration in the cash position. Thus it is not useful to interpret branch purchases and sales of foreign exchange in terms of funds being acquired and disposed of for head offices, because the acquisition of foreign funds in this way does not really improve the over-all cash position of the banks, nor does the disposal of foreign funds worsen the cash position. Branch transactions in foreign exchange affect the distribution of domestic deposits, but because of the policy of covering operations, do not provide a basis for expansion and contraction.

International settlements that do not make use of the exchange market, and so do not call upon the domestic banks to exercise a foreign-exchange function, may nevertheless, just like domestic settlements, cause a regional shift in domestic deposits. This only occurs when domestic deposits are used in international settlements; when residents of the home country use their own holdings of foreign exchange in international settlements, there are no regional effects on domestic deposits. The main effects are reflected in the foreign loan-deposit differential of the domestic branches.

The geographical effect on domestic deposits, arising from their use in settling international transactions, is a possibility because settlement in domestic currency means a transfer of domestic deposits between residents and non-residents. If non-resident holdings of domestic deposits are more heavily concentrated in one area or centre than are the deposits of residents, general shifts in domestic deposits, between residents and non-residents in settlement of international transactions, are very likely to be accompanied by a changing geographical distribution of deposits. Branch indebtedness plays the same role in accommodating this regional change as it does in other cases.

Thus, aside from international settlements effected entirely with home-owned, foreign-exchange holdings, international transactions require the use of domestic currency somewhere in the payments process; and whenever domestic deposits are activated, interregional distributive changes are possible. Geographical distributive changes may result from the exchange of domestic deposits between residents and non-residents, from covering operations in foreign exchange by the banks, or simply from the ordinary purchases and sales of foreign exchange by branches.

Deposit Changes and International Payments

However, the geographical aspects of the deposit changes that accompany international payments are of less importance than their other aspects, among which the main one is perhaps the accommodating role they may play in the balance of international payments. The nature of that role must now be considered, first with respect to the balance of payments in general, and then with respect to short-term and long-term capital movements.

The current account in the balance of international payments is the most common source for the changes in deposits that result from international settlements. The current account is made up of all imports and exports of goods and services that generally require international payments, or payments between residents of one country and those of another. There are some imports and exports that do not require international payments, and, in addition, there are capital-account transactions that either require or displace international payments. However, for the purpose of showing the relationship between deposit movements and the current account, other capital movements, which include non-cash items, can be ignored for the time being, and all imports and exports assumed to be settled for in cash. The omitted items are introduced later as complicating factors in the basic analysis.

Ignoring the use of circulating currency, residents of the home country may pay for imports in three general ways: by drawing on their holdings of foreign-currency deposits; by using their domestic deposits to buy foreign exchange, through the banking system (which undertakes covering operations), from other residents, or from non-residents; or by paying foreign exporters in domestic funds. Each of these payment methods represents a short-term capital flow into the home country, either by way of a reduction in resident holdings of foreign deposits, or by way of an increase in non-resident holdings of domestic deposits. Hence, if the international transactions of the home country consisted only of imports, its balance of international payments would show total imports balanced by a net short-term capital inflow of a like amount.

Similarly, residents of the home country may receive payment for exports in three general ways: they may be paid in foreign funds which they add to their holdings of foreign deposits; they may give up their foreign-exchange receipts, through the banking system, to other residents or non-residents in exchange for domestic deposits; or they may accept payment from foreign importers in domestic funds. Each of these methods of settlement represents a short-term capital outflow from the home country, which takes the form either of an increase in resident holdings of foreign deposits or of a decrease in domestic deposits held by non-residents. Thus, if the home country had no other items but exports in its international transactions, its balance of international payments would show total exports completely balanced by a net short-term capital outflow, represented by increased holdings of foreign deposits of residents and by reduced holdings of domestic deposits owned by non-residents.

Therefore, when exports equal imports and everything is paid for in cash, there are no net capital movements in the balance of international payments: the capital inflows that accompany imports are offset by the capital outflows that accompany exports. It is unlikely that any significant change occurs in the foreign deposits of residents and non-residents as a result of international payments when trade between their countries is in balance, but a change is possible. For example, residents may accumulate their foreign-exchange receipts, or otherwise add to their holdings of foreign deposits; however, if the trade balance is not to be upset, non-residents must at the same time be adding to their holdings of home-country deposits so that no net capital movements in deposits take place. This possibility is discussed in greater detail later; the example is offered here only to illustrate that, when exports equal imports and when there are no other capital movements, distributive changes in deposits from international causes may still result.

However, a more natural way for changes in non-resident holdings of national deposits to occur is through an unbalanced trade account. Thus if exports exceed imports in a country, the excess represents a net capital outflow made up of an increase in the foreign deposits of residents and a reduction in domestic deposits held by non-residents. That is, because of the trade surplus, residents of the home country are likely to receive more foreign-exchange receipts than are required to pay for imports, so that the excess receipts go to increase resident holdings of foreign exchange; likewise, the receipts of home-country currency by foreigners are probably less than they need to pay for imports from the home-country, and so they must draw upon some of their holdings of home-country deposits. Where only one currency is used for international settlement in the trade of the home country concerned, however, changes occur only in non-resident holdings of the national currency used.

Or, as a result of decisions independent of the trade balance, residents of the trade-surplus country may decide to increase their holdings of foreign balances, thus enabling foreigners to increase their holdings of deposits in the trade-surplus country despite their trade deficit with that country. Their gain in such deposits, however, when subtracted from the increased foreign balances held by the trade-surplus country, must equal the export-import differential. In this case a capital outflow in deposits from the home country overwhelms a capital inflow in deposits so that a net capital outflow is produced to accommodate the trade balance. This situation, however, is a special one that is discussed later. Usually residents of the home country alter their holdings of foreign deposits through an unbalanced current account—that is, by buying a greater or lesser amount from foreigners than foreigners buy from them—accompanied generally by an opposite, but not necessarily equal, change in non-resident holdings of domestic deposits.

Non-resident holdings of national currencies may also vary because of transactions outside the current account—that is, because of capital transactions. Thus the sale of fixed capital assets, new or old, or of financial assets, new or old, by the residents of one country to those of another, settled in cash, must give rise to changes in deposits that represent capital outflows from the selling country. The sales are then similar to exports from the selling country in their effect on non-resident holdings of national deposits. Likewise, purchases of fixed assets or financial assets, by the residents of one country from those of another, paid for in cash, give rise to changes in deposits that represent capital inflows into the purchasing country. The purchases are similar to imports in their effect on non-resident holdings of domestic deposits. The nationality of the capital item traded in does not matter so long as the item is traded between residents of different countries. Thus, residents may sell domestic securities or foreign securities to non-residents in order to increase their holdings of foreign balances. It is the nationality of the buyers and sellers that matters. When residents buy and sell foreign securities among themselves, international transactions or payments are not generated even though a foreign item is the subject of trade; nor are they when non-residents trade in domestic securities among themselves.

Transactions in capital items may be either long-term or short-term in nature, corresponding roughly to whether their direct effects are permanent or temporary. The transactions may also represent either absolute changes in the amount of foreign assets held by residents or simply a change in the composition of the foreign assets held. Thus, residents may sell some foreign securities to add to their holdings of foreign deposits: a conversion process that does not add to the total of their foreign assets, and a process in which a decision to alter the size of foreign cash balances initiates an international transaction in securities. However, a conversion-type transaction is just as likely to follow from a change in total foreign holdings caused by basic trade conditions. Thus, a current-account deficit that reduces resident holdings of foreign deposits may prompt residents to sell foreign securities in order to restore their foreign cash balances to their previous level.

Cash loans granted to foreigners or obtained from them, in other ways than by new security sales and purchases, represent still another cause of international deposit changes. Thus, a straight loan of domestic deposits to non-residents, or the borrowing of foreign balances by residents from non-residents represents a very direct and personal way of altering the amount of foreign balances through international capital transactions.

Most of the deposit changes associated with the type of international transactions mentioned—current-account transactions, transactions in capital assets, securities, and other international indebtedness—are passive, serving to accommodate the balance of international payments where necessary. Thus, where the trade account alone is unbalanced, changes in non-resident holdings of national deposits passively occur to accommodate the unbalance. If, however, changes in foreign-held cash balances give rise to international security transactions, international investment, or other international lending, foreign balances may be stabilized and the unbalanced current account accommodated by non-deposit type capital movements. These other capital movements may exist or occur no matter what is happening to non-resident holdings of deposits; when they are not sufficient to restore balance to the current account, passive changes in deposits constitute the balancing item required.

The accommodating role of deposit changes in the balance of international payments may be supplemented or aided by the use of trade, or non-cash, credit. Thus, commercial credit granted by exporters, or advanced to importers, eliminates the need for immediate payment, so that changes in the foreign deposits of residents or in the domestic deposits of non-residents do not occur when exports and imports move on credit. The results are the same when capital transactions move on non-cash credit. Deposit changes are temporarily inhibited by credit transactions; that is, the need for deposit changes to accommodate international transactions is postponed, with the result that deposit changes follow sales and purchases with a lag— often a varying lag. Although there must eventually be deposit changes when the credit granted is paid off, in the meanwhile the credit granted represents a capital movement that may serve the same accommodating function as deposit changes in the balance of international payments.

Short-term capital movements, such as deposit changes and changes in trade credit granted,[29] serve, however, only as a temporary

29. The three major categories of short-term capital movements in the Canadian balance of international payments are short-term transactions in securities (stat-

means of accommodating the balance of payments. A change in trade credit is a temporary measure that eventually gives way to deposit changes. Hence, to indicate the temporary nature of short-term capital movements as equilibrating factors in the balance of payments, only deposit changes need be considered. The deposit changes on which all international transactions eventually rest cannot continue indefinitely in one direction in order to support a fundamental unbalance in international payments; one-way movements in resident holdings of foreign deposits and in non-resident holdings of domestic deposits have restricted scope, set on the one hand by the size of existing stocks, which determines what the run-off can be, and on the other hand by the willingness of non-residents to accumulate increasing amounts of national currencies. Small one-way movements in deposits may give way to long-term international borrowing and investment; thus, any imbalance in international payments may eventually be corrected by long-term capital movements. The increasing resistance that international deposit changes run into—to reductions on the one hand and to increases on the other—is the only hope for an automatic corrective.

The resistance to involuntary changes in foreign deposits that unbalanced international settlements tend to generate first exhibits itself in movements of exchange rates, where these are free to move. Rate changes directly affect foreign expenditures: they do not work through changes in foreign deposits. When a change in exchange rates encourages an increase in foreign spending, foreign deposits are not first increased and then spent: the increased expenditures are made and then the exchange is acquired when purchases are paid for

---

istically defined as transactions in securities outstanding), changes in commercial credit, and changes in bank deposits. Cf. R. A. Radford, "Canada's Capital Inflow, 1946–53," International Monetary Fund, *Staff Papers*, 4 (1954–55), 218; Samuel I. Katz, *Two Approaches to the Exchange-Rate Problem: The United Kingdom and Canada*, Essays in International Finance, No. 26 (Princeton, International Finance Section, Department of Economics and Sociology, Princeton University, 1956), p. 8; Canada, Dominion Bureau of Statistics, *The Canadian Balance of International Payments, 1956, and International Investment Position* (Ottawa, Queen's Printer, 1957), pp. 25–6. Short-term capital transactions in securities are dealt with in the next section of the text on arbitrage transactions.

in foreign funds. Likewise, a rate change that discourages foreign spending, discourages expenditures directly, and not by first prompting a reduction in foreign deposits. The expenditure-effect of movements in exchange rates directly alters expenditures, which in turn produce secondary effects on holdings of foreign deposits; the decision to alter expenditures precedes the effect on foreign deposits.

The point of the foregoing paragraph may perhaps be made clearer by considering the effect of a movement in exchange rates on foreign deposits in various countries when the rate movement is in favour of the home country—its imports become cheaper, its exports more expensive. The rate movement in favour of the home country may cause its international receipts to exceed its international payments.[30] Home-country foreign deposits are tending to rise despite a disinclination to accumulate foreign exchange, reflected in the movement of the exchange rate in favour of the home country which results from pressure to convert unwanted foreign-exchange receipts. At the same time foreigners are reluctantly running down their balances of home-country currency to help finance their import surplus; the rate movement reflects that reluctance because the movement is in a direction to encourage foreigners (that is, to inhibit their reluctance) to reduce their foreign balances, and to discourage them from replacing depleted balances.

However, where the rate movement encourages the home country to import more, the home-country residents have need for some of their excess foreign-exchange receipts; they stop trying to convert them into home funds and spend them instead. When spent the receipts pass to foreigners in whose hands they represent domestic holdings; the tendency for foreign balances to increase is thereby dampened—inhibited altogether if the increase in import demand is sufficiently great. Also, the rate movement in favour of home-country

30. Joan Robinson, "The Foreign Exchanges," *Readings in the Theory of International Trade*, Blakiston Series of Republished Articles on Economics, *4* (Philadelphia, The Blakiston Company, 1949), pp. 87–94, shows that a movement in the exchange rate may affect the balance of trade in any one of the three possible ways depending on the various supply and demand elasticities. Also cf. Donald Bailey Marsh, *World Trade and Investment: The Economics of Interdependence* (New York, Harcourt, Brace and Company, 1951), pp. 204–6.

imports may discourage exports from the home country; foreigners then reduce their foreign spendings and thus save their balances of home-country deposits from further depletion. Hence rate movements that have a direct, equilibrating effect on exports and imports tend to inhibit changes in foreign deposits in the countries affected.

However, the autonomous shifts in exports and imports that the rate movement causes may not be sufficient to place the balance of international payments in equilibrium; exports and imports might have to be particularly sensitive to rate changes to produce sufficiently immediate responses without foreign deposits having to change. That is, even if rate changes could influence exports and imports sufficiently to restore balance, thereby inhibiting deposit changes altogether, the rate changes may have to be so great and sharp that before they can reach their equilibrating levels deposit changes themselves might occur to inhibit further rate movements. Steeply falling exchange rates in terms of the home currency may induce home-country residents to hold their foreign-exchange receipts off the market, or may induce other home-country speculators to acquire foreign deposits. There is a speculative rise in foreign deposits held by residents that represents a temporarily accommodating capital outflow from the home country. Foreigners may also come under the speculative influence and reduce their holdings of home-country deposits by accelerating and anticipating their foreign payments. Foreign deposits fall in the home country, the fall representing another accommodating capital outflow from the home country. Thus, where movement in exchange rates causes speculative responses, changes in foreign deposits are induced, which accommodate the balance of payments and inhibit further rate changes if the deposit movements are in the right direction. The adjustment process stimulated by the initial unbalance may proceed partially by way of exchange-rate movements, and partially by way of accommodating changes in foreign deposits; rate movements cause a partial adjustment in exports and imports that inhibit some deposit movements, and the changes in deposits that actually arise inhibit further rate movements and eliminate the remaining unbalance on international settlements.

Where deposit changes are necessary to accommodate the balance of payments, however, the accommodation can only be temporary, and if full equilibrium is to be restored to the balance of payments, there must be further movements in exports and imports that eliminate the accommodating deposit movements. The deposit changes must therefore have an expansive influence on the home country and a contractive one on foreign countries. That is, the speculative increase in the foreign deposits of the trade-surplus country and the decrease in foreign holdings of its own deposits must expand the home economy so as to induce a further increase in its imports; and at the same time corresponding deposit changes for the trade-deficit countries must represent contractive influences which induce further reductions in their imports from the home country.

The expansionary influence in the home country is most easily seen in the shift of domestic deposits from non-residents to residents; the shift represents an acceleration of income payments by non-residents to residents. Under the circumstances, the increase in home-country foreign deposits is also probably expansionary; accretion of foreign deposits in the hands of the original recipients has a wealth effect, and the acquisition of foreign deposits by other home-country speculators is undoubtedly financed from idle domestic deposits that pass into the hands of resident and non-resident spenders in the home country. In the trade-deficit countries the drain of domestic deposits into idle foreign balances and the reduction of non-domestic deposits held in the trade-surplus country, seem clearly deflationary.[31]

31. The role of deposit changes in the adjustment process for international payments thus differs from that in interregional payments. Unlike the interregional case, the deposit movements under international payments do not affect the level of purchasing power in the countries involved. That is, there is no change in the money supply in the home country or other countries because of unbalance in international transactions, so long as official reserves of foreign exchange are held constant, as is assumed throughout this analysis. There is no flow of deposits between countries—there cannot be because the deposits of each country are expressed in different units—and there is no flow of bank cash between the countries either, because this too differs for each country. In contrast, unbalance in interregional settlements is met by a definite movement of deposits from the deficit to the surplus area.

Irving Brecher and S. S. Reisman, *Canada-United States Economic Relations*, A Study for the Royal Commission on Canada's Economic Prospects ([Ottawa, Queen's Printer], 1957), p. 150n28, suggest that, since capital inflows do not disturb total deposits under a flexible exchange rate, the impact of capital inflows

In short, where exchange-rate movements do not result in autonomous shifts in exports and imports of sufficient magnitude to produce balance-of-payments equilibrium, accommodating deposit changes fill the gap. Should the deposit changes then lead to equilibrium in the balance of payments, it must be through expenditure effects that induce equilibrating changes in exports and imports. The initial unbalance is thus eliminated partially by autonomous changes in exports and imports and partially by induced changes. The degree of expansion and contraction involved is reflected in the induced trade changes required, and is measured by the accommodating deposit changes that take place: the greater the deposit changes the greater the destabilizing effect on expenditures. Flexible exchange rates inhibit deposit changes on the one hand, but induce them on the other; only where the net change in deposits is less than it would be do flexible exchange rates contribute to the stability of foreign deposits. They so contribute when they cause exports and imports to move in an equilibrating direction.

The expenditure effects that follow from the accommodating movements in foreign deposits are considered again later; the main point of the present analysis is that changes in foreign deposits are an accommodating feature of every international transaction settled with cash. Thus, exports, capital assets, and securities sold by residents to non-residents for cash are accompanied by increases in resident holdings of foreign deposits, and by reductions in non-resident holdings of domestic deposits, both of which represent capital outflows. Likewise, imports, capital assets, and securities sold by non-residents to residents for cash are accompanied by decreases in resident holdings of foreign deposits and by increases in non-resident holdings of domestic deposits, both of which represent capital inflows. Cash loans by residents to non-residents, or vice versa, also give rise to deposit changes that represent international capital movements. In addition, the use of trade credit in international trans-

on domestic stability must be analyzed in terms of its effect on velocity. This seems to me a less useful approach than that of assessing directly the impact of capital inflows on the level of domestic expenditures: the effect on velocity is then the outcome of the effect on expenditures.

actions represents capital movements, which, however, are temporarily at the expense of deposit changes. Thus, aside from the use of commercial credit, deposit changes are an inseparable part of international settlements; any imbalance in international transactions remaining after a rate movement has taken effect is automatically offset by an appropriate change in foreign deposits in the countries concerned.

Deposit Changes and Short-Term Capital Movements

Deposit changes, however, are not always passive elements in the balance of payments; apart from the effect of movements in exchange rates on foreign deposits, deposit changes may be an active factor. Thus, the balance of payments may remain in equilibrium when, conceivably, residents of one country decide to alter the absolute level of their foreign assets by altering the level of their foreign deposits. If non-residents at the same time decide to alter in the same direction, and by the same amount, their holdings of deposits in the initiating country, there is no balance-of-payments effect. But when non-residents do not decide to alter their holdings of foreign deposits to the extent necessary to permit residents of the initiating country to express without disturbance their changed preference for foreign balances, either the preferences of the latter are involuntarily changed, or a balance-of-payments effect arises. If the residents of a country desire merely to change the composition of their foreign holdings between deposits and other assets, the alteration in deposits induces its own offsetting capital transaction. Therefore, except when residents and non-residents decide to alter their foreign balances in the same direction and by the same amount, holdings of foreign balances vary only when accompanied by net transactions in current-account items, in security transactions, or net changes in international debt;[32] it matters not whether the net transactions are the cause of the changes in foreign balances, as is usually the case, or whether they are the result of deposit changes, as may sometimes be the case.

The main aspects of international deposit changes of interest for the present analysis are the expenditure effects generated by the deposit changes. However, one type of movement in foreign deposits

32. Einzig, *Foreign Balances*, pp. 138–41, covers all these ways in which foreign balances may be altered.

is of interest in itself, because of the general lack of understanding that appears to exist about its immediate effects. The movement in question is that which results from covered interest-arbitrage transactions.[33]

Covered interest-arbitrage transactions may take place when it becomes profitable to shift short-term funds from a money market in one country to a money market in another. The profitability of covered interest-arbitrage transactions is assessed by comparing the differential between interest rates in the two countries with the cost of covering the exchange risk, which is given by subtracting the spot from the forward rate of exchange for the currency to be invested in, and expressing the difference as a percentage of the spot rate. When the cost of the forward covering operation, applied against the difference in yields,[34] shows a net return in excess of a certain critical amount,[35] short-term changes in foreign deposits may take place as a result of arbitrage transactions.

33. Uncovered interest-arbitrage transactions have no complicating features for the analysis of their effects on deposits; they are exactly similar to other international transactions in financial assets. A related problem, beyond the scope of this study but worthy of attention, is the relationship between interest differentials and exchange rates under which uncovered international transactions in securities may arise. The problem is particularly relevant for Canada where large borrowers continually must decide whether to borrow at home or abroad, depending partly on relative interest costs for new security issues. C. G. Bale, "On the Exchange Risk Involved in Borrowing Abroad," *Canadian Journal of Economics and Political Science*, 27 (Feb. 1961), 98–100, derives a formula to show what change in the exchange rate will eliminate the incentive to borrow abroad resulting from a given interest-rate differential.

34. This is the usual rule-of-thumb applied to determine when arbitrage is profitable. The precise formulation compares the cost of cover with the differential in interest rates divided by one plus the interest rate in the country in which investment is contemplated. S. C. Tsiang, "The Theory of Forward Exchange and Effects of Government Intervention on the Forward Exchange Market," *International Monetary Fund, Staff Papers*, 7 (Apr. 1959), 79–80.

35. John Maynard Keynes, *Monetary Reform* (New York, Harcourt, Brace and Company, 1924), p. 139, sets the critical amount at $\frac{1}{2}$ per cent. M. N. Trued, "Interest Arbitrage, Exchange Rates, and Dollar Reserves," *Journal of Political Economy*, 65 (Oct. 1957), 405n7, sets it at $\frac{1}{2} - \frac{3}{4}$ of 1 per cent. Einzig, "Some Recent Changes in Forward Exchange Practices," pp. 486–8, argues that the critical minimum is now much less than $\frac{1}{2}$ of 1 per cent and may even fall below $\frac{1}{16}$ of 1

The arbitrage transactions may be effected by holders of deposits in a low-interest country exchanging those deposits for funds in a high-interest country—a spot foreign-exchange transaction, the sellers of the spot exchange then sell forward their newly acquired foreign funds at the current forward rate. This fixes for the arbitrageurs the entire cost of the operation, eliminates the exchange risk, and places them back in their original funds at the end of the investment period. The arbitrage transactions may also be effected by non-resident holders of funds in the high-interest country keeping them there for interest-arbitrage purposes when otherwise they would normally convert into other exchange. All that such holders need do to engage in a covered interest-arbitrage operation is to sell their foreign funds forward and thereby eliminate the exchange risk.

The movement of foreign funds to high-interest countries, or the retention of foreign funds in high-interest countries, for interest-arbitrage purposes, when the exchange risk is covered, ceases when the profitability of the movement is eliminated. The movement may become unprofitable because the spot and forward exchange rates diverge, thus increasing the cost of the covering operation. This divergence in the rates comes about naturally, because the arbitrage operations themselves will alter the forward rate, and the spot rate too, unless this is fixed or the spot and forward sides of the operations are handled as a single transaction, in which case only the forward rate is affected. Interest-arbitrage operations, depending on their size, may also narrow the yield differentials between international money markets, and this too helps to halt the flow of arbitrage funds.[36] When interest-arbitrage movements are large, they most certainly affect yields. However, the markets in foreign exchange are often more sensitive than money markets so that the main effect of arbitrage is on exchange rates. And if the spot rate is fixed, the forward rate bears the brunt of the arbitrage.

---

per cent. Gairdner and Company Limited, *Short Term Money Market Letter* (Toronto), Oct. 22, 1959, state that "a favourable spread of at least 0.40% or 0.50% is necessary to cause much foreign short term investment."

36. Cf. Tsiang, "The Theory of Forward Exchange and Effects of Government Intervention on the Forward Exchange Market," p. 79.

The foregoing is a brief sketch of the nature and mechanics of covered interest-arbitrage transactions. A more detailed discussion of these aspects is not necessary for the present analysis as they are adequately covered in other sources.[37] Less adequately covered are the effects on foreign balances of arbitrage transactions.

When conditions for covered interest-arbitrage transactions between two countries arise and are exploited by the residents of the

37. The first adequate theoretical treatment of covered interest-arbitrage transactions, which still serves as a model today, was contributed by J. M. Keynes, "The Forward Market in Foreign Exchanges," *Journal of The Canadian Bankers' Association*, 29 (July 1922), 453–64, reprinted from the *Manchester Guardian Reconstruction Supplement*, Sec. I, Apr. 20, 1922. The discussion is repeated in his book, *Monetary Reform*, pp. 133–41. Many aspects of the theory of covered arbitrage transactions are discussed by Einzig, *The Theory of Forward Exchange*, pp. 149–246. A good short account of the subject appears in Marsh, *World Trade and Investment*, pp. 183–5. Trued, "Interest Arbitrage, Exchange Rates, and Dollar Reserves," p. 404, gives a very good example of a typical arbitrage transaction, and the rest of his article covers many of the technical details. "Foreign Money and the Reserves," *The Banker* (London), June 1955, pp. 335–40, discusses the movement of arbitrage funds to London, but an otherwise good discussion is marred by conclusions that are too general for the analysis to support. (The point is noted later.) "Foreign Money in London," *The Economist*, June 4, 1955, pp. 867–8, ably discusses the subject, but unfortunately at a critical point makes a careless slip in analysis that leads to an erroneous conclusion. (This is also cited in more detail later.) Some discussion of the movement of arbitrage funds from Canada to London in 1955, when such movements were highly profitable, appears in Canada, Dominion Bureau of Statistics, *The Canadian Balance of International Payments, 1955, and International Investment Position* (Ottawa, Queen's Printer, 1956), pp. 25–6. A type of arbitrage operation that American parent companies of Canadian subsidiaries engage in by borrowing U.S. dollars and advancing Canadian dollars as temporary financing to their subsidiaries, when the cost of forward cover is less than the difference in lending rates between the two countries, is described by G. H. Chittenden, "The New York Foreign Exchange Market," *Canadian Banker*, 65 (Spring 1958), 81.

Other recent literature dealing with the subject includes Einzig, "Some Recent Changes in Forward Exchange Practices," pp. 485–95; Tsiang, "The Theory of Forward Exchange and Effects of Government Intervention on the Forward Exchange Market," pp. 78–86; Alan R. Holmes, *The New York Foreign Exchange Market* (New York, Federal Reserve Bank of New York, 1959), pp. 36–48; Peter B. Kenen, *British Monetary Policy and the Balance of Payments, 1951–1957*, Harvard Economic Studies, *116* (Cambridge, Mass., Harvard University Press, 1960), pp. 138–42.

low-interest country (the home country in this analysis),[38] the arbitrage movement may be imposed upon an already balanced position in international transactions. The problem is to determine where the arbitrage funds are to come from. The arbitrageurs need foreign funds, yet the international-payments situation is not providing additional funds for this purpose: all foreign-exchange receipts are needed for other international payments. The arbitrageurs may get other residents to give up their foreign balances, or use some of their own existing foreign deposits, so that total foreign balances (defined as foreign deposits and securities) of home-country residents do not change. It is unlikely, however, that the existing working balances in foreign funds of residents can be diverted to arbitrage purposes without disturbing the trade balance. Thus, the only way in which foreign funds for arbitrage may be obtained without disturbing a balanced-trade position is by increasing total foreign balances held by home-country residents by persuading foreigners to hold more home-country deposits. In this case, as resident holdings of foreign funds increase so do non-resident holdings of home-country funds; it is as if residents and non-residents had exchanged balances.

The possibility is not remote. Since arbitrageurs cover their arbitrage investments through forward sales of foreign funds, they enter into transactions with buyers who thereby become involved in a forward sale of home-country funds. If the buyers of the forward exchange are non-residents, they may seek to acquire additional home-country funds immediately to provide initial cover for their forward commitments. Therefore, if the forward sales of foreign currency by the arbitrageurs are made to non-speculative, non-residents who are not hedging on other accounts, foreign balances of home-country residents are increased at the same time as non-residents are increasing their holdings of the home-country currency. In addition, non-residents may decide to increase their holdings of funds in the

38. Conceivably arbitrage funds could move from high-interest to low-interest countries if the cost of forward cover is negative and in favour of the high-interest country. There is then a profit on the forward transaction that exceeds the loss on interest. Marsh, *World Trade and Investment*, pp. 184–5. The analysis of the text deals only with the more usual situation of money flows from low-interest to high-interest centres.

currency of the arbitrageurs independently of forward transactions, and this independent decision also enables foreign funds to be obtained for arbitrage without disrupting the balance of payments.

However, some incentive may have to be provided, most likely in the form of rate movements, to get non-residents to increase their holdings of balances in the country of the arbitrageurs. To leave the trade balance unaffected the rate movement must encourage changes in foreign deposits only, and must leave exports and imports unaffected. Under these circumstances, international arbitrage movements bring about an increase in foreign balances in both the high-interest and low-interest countries. At the end of the arbitrage period, the withdrawal of the arbitrage funds must result in a corresponding reduction in the foreign balances of both countries if the trade balance is still to be undisturbed.

Usually, arbitrage movements imposed upon a balanced-payments position temporarily unbalance the trade account in favour of the home country; residents of the home country are then provided with foreign funds for arbitrage purposes through an excess of foreign receipts over foreign payments. The saving out of net foreign-exchange receipts by residents of the home country to provide arbitrage funds is probably at the expense of foreign expenditures; non-residents are likely to be encouraged as much to increase their spending or payments in the home country as to accumulate additional home-country funds. These effects could stem from changes in exchange rates and from the expenditure effects of the deposit movements. The net result is that while the arbitrage transactions lead to some increases in foreign balances (here defined widely as deposits and other short-term liquid assets) held by both countries, they also unbalance the trade account and other transactions in favour of the home-country from which the arbitrage funds flow.

However, the effect on the trade balance is only temporary: once the foreign funds for arbitrage have been acquired, the exchanges revert to their previous position—unless a permanent change in preferences has occurred during the transition period—and the various accelerating and decelerating influences gradually work themselves out until balance is restored in all international transactions. At the end of the arbitrage period, arbitrageurs give up their arbitrage funds in keeping with their forward-exchange commitments, and all holdings of foreign balances revert to what they were previously. No lasting effect has occurred.

The preceding discussion of arbitrage movements deals with the subject under conditions of balance in international payments made and received: the analysis that follows deals with the subject under conditions of an unbalanced payments position. Indeed, the most common situation is for arbitrage movements to be imposed upon an unbalanced position in international transactions. Residents of the home country, for example, are gaining funds, either domestic or foreign, from non-residents because of the unbalance in international payments. Under such circumstances interest rates in the foreign country are apt to be higher than in the home country, especially if the unbalance is the result of inflationary conditions in the foreign country, and of less inflationary conditions in the home country. Home-country residents then, as a group, are induced to hold or obtain foreign-exchange receipts, which are accruing to them in excess of their other needs, for interest-arbitrage purposes. Thus, the effect of the unfavourable balance-of-payments position on the exchange rate of the foreign country is mitigated by the demand for arbitrage funds.

If the main effect of the unbalanced position was previously manifesting itself through residents of the high-interest country (A) reducing their foreign balances to finance their trade deficit, the demand for arbitrage funds from the low-interest country (B) will arrest or reverse this tendency. Residents of the home country (B) will be seeking to exchange their domestic funds for foreign funds, so that residents of (A) can then, indeed must, build up their holdings of funds in (B). The effect of the arbitrage transactions in this case is not so much to alter the spot exchange rate as it is to prevent the residents of the high-interest country (A) from losing their holdings of balances in the low-interest country (B).

However, both effects are temporary. Once the arbitrage movement has ceased, the previous trends in the exchanges reappear. Residents of the home country (B) stop accumulating foreign balances; at the end of the arbitrage period their foreign balances drop back to the previous level, and the residents of (B) no longer want or need additional foreign funds. The residents of (A) must then begin to finance some of their unbalanced trade by running down their foreign balances. Thus, arbitrage has only postponed for the residents of (A) a reduction in their holdings of non-domestic balances, and for the residents of (B) the conversion of some of their foreign-exchange receipts into domestic currency. Unless arbitrage movements have started an adjustment process, the unbalanced situation in international payments remains at the end of the arbitrage period.

A less favourable situation for arbitrage exists when the net flow of payments is in the direction in which arbitrage is profitable, say from a low-interest country to higher-interest ones.[39] The foreign balances of residents of the low-interest country are being depleted, making it more difficult for them to obtain foreign funds for arbitrage. At the same time non-residents find their balances in the low-interest country rising, at a time when it is profitable to reduce them for arbitrage purposes. Thus, both residents and non-residents are trying to move out of balances in the low-interest country into balances in high-interest countries. Unless the monetary authorities in the high-interest countries are willing to accumulate balances in the low-interest country, and the monetary authorities in the low-interest country are willing to reduce any foreign balances they have in exchange for home balances, funds will not be available for arbitrage. In the absence of official intervention the spot exchange rate moves against the low-interest country, possibly discouraging non-residents from reducing their foreign balances for arbitrage. For those who wish to cover their exchange risk, the movement in rates would most likely make arbitrage unprofitable.

This examination of the consequences of a movement of arbitrage funds from the home country to the foreign country does not take account of the investment form assumed by the arbitrage funds: actually they could take the form of interest-bearing deposits, but they are more likely to move into short-term securities. The form,

39. This was the situation that prevailed in the United States in 1960 when the net flow of payments was outwards from the U.S. and interest rates were higher abroad than in the U.S. A flow of arbitrage funds from the U.S. was then imposed on the basic net flow of payments. Cf. Board of Governors of the Federal Reserve System, *Annual Report*, 1960, pp. 12–13.

however, that the arbitrage investment takes does not affect the conclusions reached; they stand whether the foreign deposits employed in arbitrage remain as deposits or are put into short-term foreign securities.

Nothing is changed either when the arbitrage movements are viewed from the side of the recipient country. Foreign arbitrageurs have to build up their balances in the recipient country (now taken as the home country). This need may be accommodated by home-country residents building up their foreign balances—the balanced-payments situation. It may accommodate itself by temporarily unbalancing the trade position because home-country residents are induced to buy more from foreigners, and foreigners to buy less from the home country. Or, foreigners may use or acquire the home-country funds obtained from an existing trade deficit for arbitrage purposes in the home country. The first two possibilities influence the spot rate of exchange between the currencies involved; the third temporarily prevents the current trade situation from affecting the spot rate. The spot rate is not disturbed by arbitrage so long as an appropriate unbalance in trade provides the arbitrageurs with the foreign funds they need, either from the excess foreign-exchange receipts of the low-interest country, or by acquisition from the residents of the high-interest country who are now anxious to acquire the domestic deposits of the arbitrageurs because their own foreign balances have been depleted. When, however, the arbitrage movement is in the same direction as the net flow of payments, the spot rate of exchange for the country from which funds are flowing is depressed on two accounts: the basic flow of payments and the arbitrage movement.[40]

40. These conclusions on the effect of arbitrage transactions are similar to those arrived at by Trued, "Interest Arbitrage, Exchange Rates, and Dollar Reserves," p. 411, who suggests that movements of covered interest-arbitrage funds generally "firm the spot rate for a currency, depress the forward rate, and add to total official and private holdings of foreign currencies." He fails, however, to point out that the gain in holdings of foreign balances for the recipient country is only temporary, and in the circumstances under which arbitrage usually arises the "gain" represents merely the postponement of impending depletions. Nor does he distinguish between those cases in which the spot rate is actually raised by arbitrage transactions and those in which it is merely prevented from falling. These qualifications do not, however, limit the general usefulness of Mr. Trued's article.

The discussion so far has been without reference to the forward-exchange part of the arbitrage transaction and without reference to the banking systems. These may be considered together, for it is through forward transactions that banks necessarily take part in the movement of arbitrage funds: the spot exchange transactions that may arise from arbitrage movements need not alter the position of the banks, which can cover themselves through offsetting transactions in the foreign-exchange market. However, forward transactions may place the banks in a changed position, and when this happens the foregoing analysis is modified. The situation is best considered by keeping separate the spot and forward exchange transactions associated with covered arbitrage even though they may arise simultaneously. The various possibilities are worked out for two cases: balance in the payments accounts and unbalance in favour of the country doing the arbitrage.

The arbitrageurs sell their forward exchange to banks which, in turn, seek non-bank buyers. These non-bank buyers may expect to need the foreign funds that they have bought forward, or if the funds they have bought forward are domestic funds to them, they are selling forward what is for them foreign funds—they may be selling forward in anticipation of receipts, or they may just be speculating. In none of these cases does their demand for forward exchange alter the previous analysis. However, when the exchange market cannot absorb all the forward exchange, placed on the market by arbitrageurs, at profitable prices to the banks which bought the exchange as middlemen, the banks become unwilling net buyers or holders of forward exchange.

One situation is that the banks in the country from which the flow of arbitrage funds takes place have made net purchases of forward exchange from arbitrageurs at given rates. On buying foreign funds forward from the arbitrageurs, the banks sell foreign exchange spot as an initial step in covering their forward-exchange commitments. They may have sold spot and bought forward in one transaction, if arbitrageurs acquire their foreign funds for arbitrage from the same bank that buys their forward exchange; but whether or not the two transactions are simultaneous does not matter. The banks have bought forward and sold spot, and to return to their original position they must do a swap by buying spot and selling forward. But this is exactly the direction in which the market wants to go, and the banks, in trying to go in the same direction, may so move the rates against themselves that a swap becomes unprofitable. They then remain over-sold in spot because this covers their forward commitment to buy spot at the end of the arbitrage period; at that time their spot position returns to its normal level. The banks still lose money on the trans-action, however, for they are forced into holding less foreign balances when it is profitable to hold more.[41]

In the interim, the home banks lower their buying quotes for forward exchange, which of course has a tendency to choke off the arbitrage demand; also in the interim the home banks carry reduced foreign balances so that home residents can build up their foreign balances for arbitrage purposes. The consequences depend again on the availability of foreign funds for arbitrage purposes. The arbi-trageurs may not have to buy foreign funds in the market: they use their own existing foreign balances. If this does not direct funds from the foreign-exchange market, no other disturbances follow; but this is an unlikely situation. Usually there will not be idle foreign balances that their holders can employ in arbitrage; it is more likely that foreign funds must be held off the market or bought in the market in order that their holders or buyers may engage in arbitrage. What happens to the spot rate of exchange for foreign funds then depends partly on the trade position. Where this is in balance and foreign funds are held off the market by residents who undertake arbitrage transactions, buying pressure for foreign funds increases; this however is matched by pressure from the home banks which are selling, in keeping with their position as net forward buyers of foreign funds. The net result is likely to be no change in the spot rate. Hence, arbitrage transactions by home-country residents are accommodated in this situation by the home banks running down their foreign bal-ances while arbitrageurs run up theirs. However, the action of the banks in lowering their buying rates for forward exchange serves to bring the arbitrage movements to a halt by making arbitrage un-profitable.

A modification of the above case is provided for when the arbi-

41. Cf. Kenen, *British Monetary Policy and the Balance of Payments*, p. 146.

trageurs have to acquire foreign funds for arbitrage by buying in the market. Since usually the arbitrageurs are more willing to buy than the banks are willing to sell, although the banks must sell as a matter of course, the spot rate for foreign funds rises. In other words, the banks still give up their foreign balances so that arbitrageurs may have funds to speculate with, but they give them up only at increasing costs. The upward movement in the spot rate helps to make arbitrage less profitable; it may also unbalance the trade position, probably in a direction that causes the spot rate to rise even more.

The home banks may also be net forward buyers of foreign funds, because swap operations are unprofitable, when the payments position is unbalanced in favour of the home country. The excess foreign-exchange receipts accruing to the home country are taken up by the arbitrageurs; and the excess supply of foreign funds yielded by the favourable trade balance may be matched by the extra demand generated by the arbitrageurs, so that the spot rate for foreign exchange does not move. However, the home banks as net buyers of forward foreign funds have to sell spot foreign funds to cover themselves; this lowers the spot rate for foreign funds, which tends to make arbitrage even more profitable. But the lower spot rate may also improve the trade balance, which tends to slow down the reduction in spot rate. The banks still lower their forward buying rate for foreign funds, and it is this action by the banks that causes arbitrage to become unprofitable.[42]

The home banks may avoid engaging in arbitrage transactions if the foreign banks become the net buyers of the forward exchange sold by the arbitrageurs, when it is not profitable for the banks to carry out swap transactions. The foreign banks as net purchasers of the funds (in their own currency) sold forward by the arbitrageurs have forward commitments to pay out funds in the home-country currency (that is, the currency of the arbitrageurs); they must then buy home-country funds spot as the initial step in stabilizing their foreign position. Their next step is to sell their newly acquired hold-

42. Trued, "Interest Arbitrage, Exchange Rates, and Dollar Reserves," p. 408, briefly considers the case where the home banks buying the forward exchange from the arbitrageurs cannot do a swap transaction, but his conclusions are less general and exhaustive than those of the text.

ings of home-country currency spot and to buy them back forward all in one swap transaction. But this is the same direction as others in the market for these funds wish to move; the attempt by the foreign banks to move in the same direction as the market may move the rates against them, making it unprofitable for them to do the swap. They then hold their newly acquired home-country funds as the only offset they now have to their position as net sellers of forward home-country funds. Consequently, the foreign banks have increased their holdings of home-country funds so that, in effect, residents of the home country could have foreign funds for arbitrage purposes. These are the effects on foreign balances in both countries, whether the foreign banks purchase the forward exchange in isolated acts or whether their purchases are tied to spot sales of the currency of their own country.

The consequences of these movements in foreign balances depend on a set of circumstances similar to those discussed in the cases where home banks were the net buyers of the forward exchange. Thus, where trade is balanced and the arbitrageurs already have foreign funds, the spot rate of exchange is only altered by the arbitrage operations when the retention of foreign funds by non-residents for arbitrage purposes does not disturb the foreign-exchange rate. The foreign banks must buy home-country funds spot to cover their net position in forward exchange. Unless the diversion of foreign funds for arbitrage results in a greater demand for foreign funds by home-country residents, the spot rate of exchange for the home currency rises. The spot rate may fall if the arbitrageurs have to sell home-country funds to get foreign funds, as they are likely to be more eager sellers than the foreign banks are buyers of home currency. A fall in the spot rate for home funds works against arbitrage movements in this case; a rise, for arbitrage movements. However, if the trade balance reacts in a stabilizing way to changes in the spot rate, a rise in the rate generates an unfavourable trade balance for the home country, which checks the rise in the rate. If a fall in the rate generates a favourable trade balance for the home country, the fall in the rate is checked. But whichever way the spot rate moves, if it moves at all, the forward selling rate for home-country funds rises because the foreign banks are unwilling sellers: they are unwilling sellers either because swap operations are unprofitable or because it is unprofitable to cover by holding additional home-country balances, since interest rates are lower in the home country. The effect of a rise in the forward rate here is to lessen the profitability of arbitrage transactions.

Where the payments position is unbalanced in favour of the country of the arbitrageurs (the home country), the spot rate of exchange for the home-country currency is likely to be raised by the foreign banks being net buyers of the forward exchange sold by the arbitrageurs. Although the arbitrage demand for foreign funds tends to restrain the rise in the spot rate for home currency caused by the favourable trade balance, the foreign banks are forced into being net buyers of spot home-country currency in order to cover their forward position. The effect on the spot rate is the same if the foreign banks buy the spot exchange from the arbitrageurs at the same time as the forward contracts are negotiated. When the spot and forward transactions are simultaneous, the exchange market is prevented from feeling the impact of the demand for foreign funds from the arbitrageurs; the spot rate moves as it would have moved had there been no arbitrage.[43] In this case the spot rate for the home currency is moving up, arbitrage or no arbitrage, and this, if it tends to correct the trade balance, restrains the upward movement. The upward movement of the spot rate for the home currency favours arbitrage

43. Trued, "Interest Arbitrage, Exchange Rates, and Dollar Reserves," pp. 405–6, in analyzing the case where foreign banks cannot do a swap, concludes that the spot rate of exchange for the home currency will be lowered as a result—the foreign currency is strengthened. However, he does not indicate that this conclusion holds only in a balanced-trade situation, in which the arbitrageurs are more willing as buyers of foreign funds than the foreign banks as sellers.

Both "Foreign Money and the Reserves," *The Banker*, June 1955, pp. 338–9, and "Foreign Money in London," *The Economist*, June 4, 1955, p. 868, conclude that the spot rate is unaffected by arbitrage transactions. They fail, however, to make clear that this conclusion holds only when the trade position is unbalanced and the foreign banks cannot do swaps. *The Economist*, furthermore, reaches its conclusions by reasoning that by leaving out a step makes its analysis entirely misleading and most unclear.

Mr. Trued (p. 406n8) implies that the conclusions of *The Banker* and *The Economist* are wrong, but the conflicting conclusions among these sources can be resolved by a careful distinction of the various possibilities, as is indicated in the foregoing.

movements, but the foreign banks are very likely to raise the forward selling rate for home-currency funds faster than the spot rate rises, and this tends to restrict the opportunities for arbitrage.

Thus, the consequences of covered interest-arbitrage movements depend on whether or not the banks can do swap transactions. But in all cases the consequences are temporary, only delaying or altering during the arbitrage period basic trends that re-assert themselves after the arbitrage movements are over, unless preferences themselves are altered by the very act of arbitrage. The more lasting effects of activities in international savings and investments are associated with uncovered capital movements of a longer term; these are discussed in the two sections that follow.

International Savings

Residents of a country may draw upon the savings of other countries in a more lasting manner, than through attracting covered arbitrage funds, by selling securities to foreigners or by borrowing on long-term from foreigners. The following analysis examines the effects of such transactions in long-term securities, portfolio investment, on foreign balances and monetary stability in the borrowing country, to determine how a borrowing country may draw upon the savings, financial and real, of other countries. For that reason the analysis of portfolio investment is restricted to security sales by the borrowing or selling country. Sales of new securities are considered first, followed by a brief treatment of sales of outstanding securities.

The sale of new securities by residents to non-residents may reflect the transfer of domestic deposits from savers to spenders; and as the savers are non-resident, there may be a problem of converting foreign savings into domestic savings. That problem does not arise, however, where non-residents buy the securities by drawing upon their holdings of deposits in the currency of the borrowing country, and where the proceeds of the sale are used entirely for expenditures within the borrowing country. This is the situation that may arise when the new security issues are not directed specifically to foreign investors and where the domestic projects they are to finance require no imported materials. There is then a direct transfer of domestic deposits from non-residents to residents. This may represent merely the activation of idle domestic deposits held by non-residents, who, by buying the new issues, simply change the composition of their foreign assets. The security issuers are only drawing upon the foreign financial savings of non-residents; there is no change in real savings. However, the reduction in non-resident holdings of the deposits of the borrowing country may represent new savings by non-residents at the expense of production in the borrowing country: non-residents reduce their spending and deposits in the borrowing country so that they may buy the new securities. There is a reduction in the exports of the borrowing country that is offset by new home expenditures financed from the proceeds of the new security issues. Despite the movement of the trade account against the borrowing country, there is no drawing on the real resources of the lending country; real savings are made by foreigners, but these savings are made in the resources of the borrowing country. Furthermore, the fact that the trade balance moves in favour of the lending country means that that country cannot reduce its foreign balances; its trade surplus makes up for the initial reduction in its foreign balances.

The new securities may also be paid for by non-residents in their own currency: particularly if the issues are expressed in the currency of the foreign investors. In this case some of the proceeds may be used to pay for imports required for the domestic projects being financed by the security sales. This possibility may be deferred until later and the assumption retained for the present that the entire proceeds of the issue are used to finance expenditures within the borrowing country.

Non-residents may pay for the new securities bought in their own currency and yet still save in the resources of the borrowing country; they switch their purchases from the goods to the securities of the borrowing country. The consequences are exactly the same as when foreigners reduce their imports and save on the currency of the borrowing country in order to buy its securities. The trade balance moves against the borrowing country, but there is no effect on the exchange rate because the total of exchange transactions is not in the least altered. The real savings tapped by the security issues are again savings in the resources of the borrowing country, even though the saving is done by non-residents.

It is unlikely that foreigners typically save on imports from the borrowing country to buy the new securities paid for in their own funds; if they increase their savings to buy the securities, they are more likely to save at the expense of production in their own country. Since, under present assumptions, the security proceeds are all converted into the currency of the home country, the spot rate of exchange for the foreign currency comes under pressure and the currency of the borrowing country appreciates. As a result exports and imports may be altered in a way that restrains the appreciation of the rate so that at least some of the security proceeds must be used to finance the increase in imports relative to exports in the home country. If the trade balance does not become sufficiently unfavourable to use up all the security proceeds, the excess proceeds (in foreign funds) may pass into the hands of residents of the borrowing country who add them to their foreign savings; or the excess proceeds may be acquired by non-residents, who thereby dissave in foreign assets to save in the assets of their own country.

Where the security proceeds in excess of those required to finance any change in the trade balance are acquired by residents of the borrowing country, two possibilities emerge: the residents may save on home production to acquire foreign exchange to put into foreign financial assets; or the residents may dissave in domestic form to save in foreign form. Under the first possibility the foreign security sales are accompanied by real savings by residents of the borrowing country; under the second there are no real savings, only the financial savings of residents have been tapped by the security sales.

Where the excess security proceeds are sold to non-residents, the transactions tap the foreign savings of foreigners who give up deposits of the borrowing country for deposits in their own currency. There are no real savings here either.

Assuming that all possibilities are present, when foreigners save on their real resources to purchase the new securities issued by the borrowing country, the consequences are as follows: there is some saving in the resources of the borrowing country by foreigners, measured by the drop in exports to foreigners due to expenditure and exchange-rate effects; some saving in the resources of the debtor country by its residents, measured by the extent to which they increase their imports at the expense of domestic resources; some further saving in the resources of the debtor country by its residents, who reduce their domestic expenditures to acquire foreign funds to hold or invest; and some financial dissavings of debtor-country funds by residents and non-residents, unaccompanied by any real savings. Thus, the issue of new securities to foreigners in this complex case taps both the real and financial savings of residents and non-residents alike, all savings being in the resources and financial assets of the debtor country, even though foreigners have increased their savings in the resources of their own country to finance their security purchases. The financial counterpart of the increased savings in the lending country is represented either by the securities bought or, if lending-country residents acquire the excess security proceeds in the exchange market, by an increase in the idle deposits of residents within the lending country. The real savings in the lending country are indirectly converted into real savings in the borrowing country through the expenditure-effects on exports and imports that the savings produce.

However, there need be no increase in real savings in the lending country when its residents buy foreign securities; there may be only dissavings in the financial assets of the lending country by its residents. Nevertheless, the consequences are the same as when the purchase of securities is accompanied by increased real savings in the lending country, except that the effect on the trade balance may be weaker because the expenditure-effects from increased real savings are now missing. All the conclusions of the foregoing paragraph apply, with the proviso that real savings now occur only in the borrowing country.

Account may now be taken of the fact that some of the proceeds from the securities sold may be required directly to finance additional imports for the domestic projects associated with the new security issues. Only the consequences of the import content of the security issues need be considered, as the non-import content has consequences similar to those of issues where all the proceeds are spent at home. If the new securities are bought with new savings in the lending country, the import content of the proceeds represents the direct use by the borrowing country and the transfer to it of real savings in the lending country. Where the securities are bought with existing savings in the lending country, the import content of the proceeds does not represent new real savings; resources of the lending country are directly tapped, causing forced savings there or else stimulating production. The same conclusion applies if foreigners dissave in the financial assets of the borrowing country to acquire the securities, except that the use of the proceeds to pay for imports prevents any permanent or lasting reduction in the foreign balances of the lending country. If, however, the foreign investors save on the resources of the debtor country to buy the securities, the import content of the security proceeds has a double effect on the trade balance: resources are drawn from the lending country at the same time that real savings increase in the borrowing country. The wider gap thus created in the balance of international payments must be closed by appropriate changes in foreign balances.

However, where new security sales directly affect exports and imports they generally produce an equilibrating effect on the balance of international payments because the security sales tend to be offset immediately by the appropriate movement in the current account. The indirect effects of security sales, working through the exchange rate, may also move the trade balance against the borrowing country so as to offset the security sales in the balance of payments. But after all the effects of the security sales on the trade balance have been taken into account, there may still remain a gap, between the trade balance (assumed initially to be zero) and the security sales, that can be closed only by a change in foreign balances. That is, to the extent that the security sales exceed the current-account deficit of the issuing country, after all the direct effects of the sales on the trade balance have been taken into account, the excess proceeds must result in a reduction in the foreign balances of the lending country and in an increase in the foreign balances of the borrowing country. One extreme case is where non-residents purchase all the securities bought by reducing their foreign balances without reducing their other foreign spending; there is no immediate impact on the trade balance, and international security sales are entirely offset in the balance of payments by a change in foreign balances. The other extreme case is where the security proceeds are used directly and entirely to finance additional imports, and where investors have saved on the production of the borrowing country to buy its securities; the current-account deficit of the debtor country exceeds the amount of the securities sold to foreigners by precisely 100 per cent. There is no immediate impact on foreign balances other than the change in balances that will be induced by the trade deficit.

When net new security sales are a continuing feature in the balance of payments of a country, equilibrium requires that eventually the current-account deficit of the borrowing country exactly match the net amount of its security sales. Thus, wherever the initial effect of security sales is to leave the deficit at less than sufficient to offset the sales, further changes in exports and imports must be induced to achieve an equilibrium. This can only come about through expenditure effects generated by the short-run deposit changes that accommodate the balance of payments during the adjustment period. Therefore, whenever new security sales are accompanied by changes in foreign balances, because the current-account deficit of the issuing country does not immediately match its security sales, the sales themselves are likely to have a net expansionary effect on the debtor country—an expansionary effect that is needed to induce a further increase in its imports and decrease in its exports. In the special case where the current-account deficit exceeds the amount of securities sold to foreigners, both because the proceeds come from investors saving on the resources of the issuing country and because they are used to finance imports directly, a contractive effect must be generated to reduce imports, and possibly increase exports, until the current-account deficit is reduced to the size of the security sales.

In short, the eventual offset of net security sales to non-residents by an excess of imports over exports does not guarantee that such sales are not expansionary or even contractionary; they are likely to be expansionary or contractionary when some of the current-account deficit has had to be induced by a change in expenditures rather than directly brought about by shifts in the export and import functions.

The foregoing analysis is in terms of new security issues; but little of it need be changed when transactions in existing securities are introduced. The transfer possibilities are the same for old securities as for new ones, and so are the equilibrium conditions: the trade deficit in the selling country must match its net sales of securities. The

K

adjustment process, or the movement towards equilibrium, however, has an additional element of uncertainty not present when only new securities are involved; in the latter case it is almost a certainty that all the proceeds from the new security sales will be spent, a certainty that is lacking in the case of old security sales. The lower the propensity to spend the proceeds of old security sales, the smaller the direct expenditure effect on the debtor country: and the smaller the direct effect on its imports. The expansion needed to restore equilibrium in the balance of payments may have to be imported; that is, because of expenditure effects in the lending country, the adjustment may proceed more through a reduction in exports than it does when new security sales are the disturbing factor.

Another common form of long-term capital movement, which does not differ in its effects in any way from transactions in new and old securities, is direct investment in the existing physical assets of a country by foreigners. In this special case of direct investment, the interest of the investor is not in the financial asset acquired but in the actual control or ownership gained over some existing fixed asset located in the borrowing country. But this difference in the form of the investment does not affect the analysis of the transfer problem or of the monetary consequences of the transactions: the analysis is the same as for securities.

International Investment

Direct investment in new fixed assets in a given country by non-residents is a different matter; it raises the question of new physical investment in a country by foreigners. In this section the interest lies in the consequences of international investment in the physical sense and not, as in the previous section, in the transfer and utilization of foreign savings.

Direct investment that represents new construction and new machinery and equipment put in place in the home country by non-residents forms part of total net investment in the home country. An extreme example of foreign participation in domestic investment results when the new fixed assets sponsored by foreigners are created entirely from non-resident resources: physical imports then provide the offsetting entry for direct investment in the balance of international payments. No short-term capital flows are generated by the direct investment; the foreign investors simply use funds in their own currency to buy the necessary imports. Aside from displacement effects, which are considered later, there is an autonomous increase in net investment in the home economy offset by an autonomous rise in imports. (It is as if all the income generated by the direct investment was spent outside the country.) There are no investment-multiplier effects in the home country.[44] The multiplier situation is similar to that in which domestically-inspired investment has an import content; only the non-import content of any increase in domestically-initiated investment provides an expansionary stimulus for the economy.[45]

Another extreme example is direct investment made entirely from domestic resources: the direct investment then has no import content. This type of direct investment definitely has investment-multiplier effects on the home economy differing in no respect from the multiplier effects of domestically-financed investment with zero import content. The short-term capital movements in deposits accompanying this direct investment are similar to those that accompany commodity exports; they are eventually replaced by a trade or current-account deficit as the multiplier effects on incomes and expenditures in the debtor country induce the appropriate changes in exports and imports.

Between these two extreme examples of direct investment falls the

44. There may be an export-multiplier effect, however, if the imports from the direct-investment country induce an increase in its imports from the recipient country. Cf. Fritz Machlup, "Period Analysis and Multiplier Theory," *Readings in Business Cycle Theory*, Blakiston Series of Republished Articles on Economics, *2* (Philadelphia, The Blakiston Company, 1944), p. 227, as reprinted from *Quarterly Journal of Economics*, *54* (Nov. 1939), 1–27; Marsh, *World Trade and Investment*, p. 254.

H. W. Arndt, "Overseas Borrowing—The New Model," *Economic Record*, *33* (Aug. 1957), 253, also concludes that direct investment financed entirely by capital imports leaves internal balance in the home economy unaffected at a higher level of investment and imports.

45. Cf. A. C. L. Day, *Outline of Monetary Economics*, p. 378. There may be, however, offsetting short-term capital movements to the import content of domestically-inspired investment not present for the import content of foreign-inspired investment.

more usual class represented by direct investment that draws partly on imported resources and partly on domestic resources.[46] The investment-multiplier effects and short-term capital movements attach themselves only to the non-import content of the investment.

The discussion of the consequences of the three basic types of direct investment can be given greater generality by taking into account displacement aspects. Thus, new direct investment may displace a like amount of other spending, by residents and non-residents, on the resources of the debtor country; the import content of the direct investment then exerts a deflationary influence on the home economy.[47] Where there is no import content, the displacement effects of direct investment are neither expansionary nor deflationary,[48] unless the investment induces changes in exports by altering export markets in the lending country. However, direct investment that stimulates rather than displaces other domestic investment which uses some domestic resources is clearly expansionary, even though it uses only imported resources. In short, when new investment that is stimulated by new direct investment by foreigners exceeds the increase in imports relative to exports caused by the direct investment, the new investment has an expansionary multiplier effect on expenditures for the resources of the debtor country.

Therefore, the condition for the absence of expansionary effects from direct investment in the country receiving it is met when the increment in new investment generated by the direct investment

46. Day, pp. 425–6, considers the classes of direct investment mentioned here, but he considers the external effects without specific examination of the internal effects.

47. Arndt, "Overseas Borrowing—The New Model," p. 253, appears to take the view that because total investment is not reduced when direct investment, all import content, displaces domestic investment, there is no change in total domestic spending. This overlooks the negative multiplier effects of reduced spending on domestic resources when domestic investment is displaced by foreign investment from imported resources. Negative multiplier effects may also arise from a reduction in exports if the direct investment displaces some foreign spending on domestic exports; the external balance of the home country is then also affected.

48. Marsh, *World Trade and Investment*, p. 69, makes the qualification that international investment tends to expand output and employment in the recipient country only if it is not a substitute for other investment or for consumption expenditures.

directly creates a current-account deficit in the home country to match the increased investment. That is, when the import content of the increase in investment generated by direct investment is sufficient to produce a current-account deficit equal to the increase in investment, there are no net multiplier effects; but this is a rather restricted case. Usually the import content of all new investments associated with direct investment will, after allowing for any direct increases in exports, produce a current-account deficit that falls short of matching either the direct investment itself or the total increment in new investment. Multiplier effects are then set in motion which may eventually restore external balance by altering the current-account deficit until it is brought into equality with the amount of direct investment made. But the fact that imports are made eventually to exceed exports by exactly the amount of new direct investment is no assurance that the direct investment has not been expansionary; whether it has depends on how external balance is achieved, a matter that merits attention because of the common belief that foreign investment in a country offset by a current-account deficit is non-expansionary under all circumstances.[49]

49. R. A. Radford, "Canada's Capital Inflow, 1946–53," International Monetary Fund, *Staff Papers*, *4* (1954–55), 250n25, summarizes this point of view as follows: current-account deficits financed by a concurrent inflow of capital are non-inflationary; this holds whether the capital inflow has an import content or whether "the capital receipts are spend locally and the foreign exchange equivalent is used to finance increased imports of goods and services of all kinds resulting from a generalized expansion of domestic activity."

C. S. Tsiang, "Balance of Payments and Domestic Flow of Income and Expenditures," International Monetary Fund, *Staff Papers*, *1* (1950–51), 278, makes the general statement that if the investment expenditures associated with direct investment and direct borrowing "are on domestically produced goods and services, but are offset by additional imports in other sectors of the economy, the impact and multiplier effects on income still cancel each other out."

The foregoing statements are too general; whether foreign investment is inflationary, deflationary, or neutral depends on how external balance is achieved. In this connection Hal B. Lary, "The Domestic Effects of Foreign Investment," *American Economic Review*, *36* (Papers and Proceedings, May 1946), 682–3, disagrees with "the common and undiscriminating treatment of an export surplus as expansionary, an import surplus as deflationary, and balanced trade as neutral." Lary argues that this depends on the causal sequences and relationships involved.

Some of the changes in imports and exports that help achieve external balance in the face of direct investment may result from the impact on foreign trade of the direct investment itself. This is most clearly seen when the direct investment, and the other domestic investment that it affects, have an import content; there is then a direct impact on imports. There is also a direct impact on exports when the direct investment displaces other foreign spending by the lending country in the debtor country. This may be countered in time, however, if the import content of direct investment stimulates the lending economy, and, in turn, its imports. The net effect of these two offsetting tendencies on the imports of the lending country gives the impact effect of direct investment on the exports of the recipient country; obviously its exports may decrease, remain constant, or increase. A positive impact effect on exports has income-creating properties;[50] a positive impact effect on imports has income-destroying properties, in the sense that the larger the import content of a given amount of direct investment the less the spending on the domestic resources of the debtor country that results from a given direct investment.

In addition to the direct or impact effect of direct investment on exports and imports, there may be an indirect effect working through the exchange rate. That is, the direct investment may alter the exchange rate, and this may cause a further change in exports and imports. The change in exports resulting from the rate movement has an income effect depending on the extent to which current production is immediately affected. The change in imports produced by a movement in the exchange rate has income effects depending on how the change affects domestic spending. With relative prices and incomes given, a movement in the exchange rate most likely causes not only a substitution effect between current domestic spending and imports but also a substitution effect between savings and imports. It is only the change in imports related to domestic spending that has any effect on incomes.

50. Some of the increases in exports must represent sales from current production for the increase to have an income-creating effect. Cf. F. D. Holzman and A. Zellner, "The Foreign-Trade and Balanced-Budget Multipliers," *American Economic Review, 48* (Mar. 1958), 74.

When all the changes in imports and exports associated with direct investment have been taken into account, there may still be a balance-of-payments gap. It would be a very special case where the impact effect of direct investment on exports and imports and any concurrent exchange-rate effect produce exactly the required current-account deficit. The gap in the balance of international payments that results when the trade deficit is less than the direct investment is filled by short-term capital movements in foreign deposits; the international receipts of the debtor country exceed its international payments so that its residents build up their foreign deposits, and non-residents reduce their holdings of the domestic deposits of the debtor country. The existence and direction of these deposit changes represent an expansionary influence for the debtor country —an influence that must operate to inflate the debtor country, to induce a further change in its imports relative to its exports, in order to restore external balance. The expansionary influence is the result of the multiplier effects stemming from the excess of the new investment over that portion of the trade deficit which is income destroying. The portion of the trade deficit which is income destroying is less than the full deficit by the extent to which income-induced changes in imports and movements in the exchange rate cause a substitution between savings and imports.

Thus, as is the case with security sales, foreign borrowing that is eventually matched by a current-account deficit may be expansionary; it all depends on how external balance is achieved. When the foreign borrowing shifts the import and export functions sufficiently to produce external balance, internal balance may still be upset if the income-altering properties of the imports differ from those of the exports, as they may. And clearly, where direct investment, or foreign borrowing, does not shift the import and export functions sufficiently to give the debtor country a large enough trade deficit to balance its foreign borrowing, the deficit can be enlarged further only by an increase in expenditures within the debtor country. Expenditures must rise if imports are to increase further relative to exports, but this induced rise in imports does not in any way nullify the expansionary effects of increased expenditures. The induced rise in imports represents only a leakage; the significant thing is not that imports rise, but that the faster they rise, relative to expenditures, the less expenditures must rise to achieve external balance. (The higher the marginal propensity to import, the less expansionary the situation.) In other words, the more expenditures must rise to induce the necessary increase in imports, the more expansionary the foreign borrowing. Only when the induced rise in expenditures is no more than the induced increase in imports—the marginal propensity to import is one—is foreign borrowing not expansionary in this situation. Thus, the excess of direct investment over the trade deficit that directly arises from it has expenditure-multiplier effects; the working out of the effects of the multiplier induces the necessary changes in imports and exports for restoring external balance.

In short, to assess whether a given trade deficit that exactly offsets new direct investment or foreign borrowing for new investment represents a neutral or expansionary situation, it is necessary to separate autonomous changes in the trade deficit from induced changes.[51] Autonomous changes contributing to the trade deficit generally represent a deflationary impulse; induced changes reflect the working out of an expansionary impulse. Whether the net autonomous change in the trade deficit is deflationary depends mainly on how imports have been altered. Given exports, a trade deficit due to an autonomous rise in imports is deflationary only to the extent that the additional imports are at the expense of domestic spending. Any autonomous change in imports financed from savings is of course neutral.[52] Thus, it is the autonomous increase in imports that comes

51. The distinction between autonomous and induced changes in foreign trade is drawn by Fritz Machlup, *International Trade and the National Income Multiplier* (Philadelphia, The Blakiston Company, 1943), pp. 12–13, and by Hugo Hegeland, *The Multiplier Theory*, Lund social science studies, no. 9 (Lund, Sweden, G. W. K. Gleerup, 1954), p. 168.

52. Traditional multiplier analysis assumes that any autonomous change in imports is accompanied by an equal and opposite change in spending on domestic production. Holzman and Zellner, "The Foreign-Trade and Balanced-Budget Multipliers," pp. 76–7. However, some writers assume that autonomous changes in imports affect only savings and thus have no effect on domestic income. This is the position adopted by P. A. Samuelson, "The Simple Mathematics of Income Determination," *Income, Employment and Public Policy: Essays in Honor of Alvin H. Hansen* (New York, W. W. Norton and Company, 1948), p. 148.

at the expense of domestic production (because it represents a substitution, or because it reduces the domestic content of new investment) which gives a trade deficit its deflationary impact. When this autonomous increase in imports is sufficient to offset the direct investment and any increase in exports that results, foreign borrowing for new investment of itself is not expansionary. But if external balance cannot be achieved in this way and so requires an autonomous increase in imports financed from savings and an income-induced rise in imports to accommodate the balance of payments, then the final trade deficit represents not a neutral but an expansionary situation.

When direct investment stimulates other investment in the debtor country, and both types of investment have high import contents, the direct increase in imports relative to exports may exceed the direct investment but still fall short of the total rise in new investment resulting from the direct investment. Imports then exceed exports by more than the foreign borrowing, which means that the trade deficit must be reduced to achieve equilibrium in the balance of international payments—deflation is required to induce a reduction in imports relative to exports—but since the new investment associated with the foreign investment exceeds the increase in the income-destroying trade deficit, the debtor economy comes under the influence of positive multiplier effects. Expenditures rise and the trade deficit becomes worse. The changes in the rate of exchange and in holdings of foreign balances that follow from the worsening trade position must affect the basic spending propensities if external balance is to be achieved.

The analytical implications of direct investment, or of foreign borrowing in general, for domestic monetary stability may now be summarized. If the balance of payments for the debtor country in a given period discloses foreign borrowing in excess of a current-account

W. Stopler, "Notes on the Dollar Shortage," *American Economic Review*, *40* (June 1950), 289, recognizes that imports may have two effects: deflationary if they represent spending abroad that otherwise would have been made at home; neutral if made out of income that would otherwise have been saved. Holzman and Zellner, pp. 76–7, discuss these two possibilities but consider the general case to be that in which an autonomous increase in imports is accompanied by a decrease in spending on domestic production as well as by a decrease in savings.

deficit, the foreign borrowing is definitely expansionary; if the net foreign borrowing is observed to be less than the current-account deficit, the borrowing may still be expansionary, depending on how much the borrowing has stimulated other domestic investments. Finally, if balance is observed between the foreign borrowing and the current-account deficit, it does not necessarily indicate that the foreign borrowing has not been expansionary; more than likely it has been.

OFFICIAL OPERATIONS AND INTERNATIONAL PAYMENTS

Most of the analysis of this chapter, especially the previous part, is in terms of constant domestic cash reserves or of no net intervention by the monetary authorities in international payments. But even when exchange rates are flexible there may be official intervention in the foreign-exchange market, or exchange transactions by the authorities that disturb the cash reserves of the banking system. These are now considered, first under the head of "official operations in foreign exchange," then under the head of "gold movements".

Official Operations in Foreign Exchange

Interest here is not in the necessary or non-discretionary operations of the central government or monetary authorities in the foreign-exchange market, but in the discretionary operations that are carried out for policy reasons: non-discretionary acts can be either neutralized or harnessed to a particular policy. Discretionary intervention in the foreign-exchange market by the authorities is primarily for purposes of influencing the exchange rate. Even where the policy is to permit the rate to fluctuate, there may be intervention for smoothing purposes.[53] Even though they consist of no more than smoothing

53. When it was Canadian policy to permit the external value of the dollar to be determined by market forces alone, the exchange authorities used to intervene in the market to smooth out fluctuations. Turk, "Foreign Exchange Market in Canada," p. 66; Canada, Parliament, House, *Debates*, 2nd Sess, 22nd Parl., 1955, 5, 2729, statement by the Minister of Finance on the exchange-rate policy of the Canadian government. The intention to depart from that policy by intervening

operations, discretionary acts have consequences for banking and monetary systems, and merit analysis.

Discretionary selling of foreign exchange by the monetary authorities occurs when there is buying pressure in the exchange market tending to depreciate the home currency. The extent to which discretionary selling is carried out depends partly on the selling pressure, partly on the preference of the authorities for stable rates; it also depends on the international reserves the authorities have available for selling. Reserves become a limiting factor when the authorities attempt to maintain the rate above the market or to keep it from falling as fast as it otherwise would.

When only foreign balances are disposed of by the monetary authorities to influence exchange rates, one necessary result is a transfer of foreign balances from official holdings to residents and non-residents in exchange for domestic deposits.[54] Consequently, in the home country private deposits are reduced and public deposits increased, with the proceeds from the official sales of foreign exchange being deposited either with the central bank or with the commercial banks. To deposit the proceeds with the central bank is of course to transfer deposits from the commercial banks to the central bank, thereby depleting the cash reserves of the banking system. Therefore, when the exchange authorities have a choice they are likely to prefer accumulating the proceeds from foreign-exchange sales with the commercial banks because there is then no cash-reserve effect on the banking system. Decisions about the division of public funds between the commercial banks and the central bank can be made independently of foreign-exchange operations, and as a part of the existing policy towards the cash-reserves of the banking system.

The accumulation of public deposits with the commercial banks as a result of sales from the official reserves of foreign exchange is apt to be deflationary or, at most, neutral. However, governments seldom

---

in the foreign-exchange market specifically for purposes of lowering the external value of the Canadian dollar was announced on June 20, 1961, in the budget speech of the Minister of Finance. Canada, Parliament, House, *Debates* (daily edition), 4th Sess., 24th Parl., June 20, 1961, pp. 6643, 6649.

54. Einzig, *Foreign Balances*, pp. 138–9, discusses the distribution effects on foreign balances of official buying and selling in the exchange market.

accumulate large holdings of domestic deposits with the banking system—large idle balances offend against accounting respectability. Hence, usually, disposing of the domestic proceeds from official sales of foreign exchange becomes a cause for further government action.

The proceeds, if not required to pay off government debt or meet current expenditures, may be invested in existing government securities or used to retire maturing ones. Where securities held by the banks and the public are bought or retired, private deposits are restored to their previous level. This is obvious and direct when securities and deposits exchange hands between the government and the public; it is less direct when the government buys securities from the banks. The banks in turn must buy securities from the public to preserve their cash-reserve ratio, and in doing this they fill the void left by the depletion of public deposits on their books with private deposits. Thus, in this case, the official sale of foreign exchange starts a chain of events that ends up as a transfer of domestic deposits from the private buyers of foreign exchange to the private sellers of securities, with total private deposits and bank cash reserves remaining unchanged. Security yields, however, are reduced or kept low by this process of transfer.

Buying or retiring securities held by the central bank, of course, has deflationary effects on private deposits and cash reserves; the transfer of government deposits from the commercial banks to the central bank to finance the security transactions reduces the cash reserves of the banks and prevents private deposits from being restored to their previous level.

Where the proceeds of the exchange sales are used to pay off the bank advances of the government, the effect is the same as government purchases of securities from the banks. Private deposits are restored to their previous level because the banks buy securities from the public to stabilize their total deposits when the government repays its bank loans from deposits held with the banking system. The effect on security yields is weaker than in the previous example because fewer securities are sold.

Finally, the government may use the proceeds from its sale of exchange to finance expenditures in excess of revenues; this too restores private deposits to their previous level, and in a definitely expansionary manner.

So much for discretionary selling of foreign exchange by the exchange authorities, now for discretionary buying. Such buying is most likely when there is selling pressure in the foreign-exchange market with the authorities buying to moderate the tendency of the home currency to appreciate. In this case the question of financing purchases arises.

Financing is no problem when the exchange authorities hold large balances in idle deposits. The idle deposits are simply reduced and private domestic deposits in the hands of residents and non-residents are increased, as residents sell some of their foreign balances and non-residents some of their national currency to the official buyers of the home country. Where both the public and private deposits are carried with the commercial banks, the transfer from one category of deposit to the other has no effect on the cash reserves of the banking system. However, where public deposits are carried with the central bank, the payment from public deposits into private deposits not only increases total bank deposits but also expands the cash reserves of the banks. Spending from idle balances by the government is likely to be expansionary or at least neutral, unless the government is running a surplus in its budgetary accounts during the current spending period. There may then be a net deflationary effect as a result of financing purchases of foreign exchange from surplus revenues.

Exchange authorities having neither existing idle balances nor a current surplus to draw upon may have a supply of securities to dispose of, or they may be able to issue new securities. The financing of foreign-exchange purchases by selling securities reduces domestic deposits and increases public deposits, but the effect is then reversed or cancelled when the exchange authorities make their purchases of foreign exchange. The final outcome is an indirect transfer of private deposits from the buyers of securities to the sellers of foreign exchange. In the process security yields are raised.

Borrowing from the banks to finance official purchases of foreign exchange has effects identical to those arising from the sale of securities by the exchange authorities. In this case, however, the banks have to sell securities, in order to accommodate the government loan; hence security yields are still raised. Total private domestic deposits remain undisturbed, but there is, as before, in effect a transfer of domestic deposits from security purchasers to foreign-exchange sellers. When the exchange authorities borrow from the central bank, there is of course a cash-reserve effect.

Thus, the discretionary selling and buying of foreign exchange by the exchange authorities create financial problems for the government that may be solved in various ways.[55] Most of the solutions do not cause any change in total domestic deposits; and where public funds may be deposited with the commercial banks, the cash reserves of the banking system need not be disturbed by the operations of the authorities in the foreign-exchange market. Thus the banking system may not be much affected by official exchange transactions; the same cannot be said for the economy as a whole.

To examine the effects of official exchange transactions on the economy requires establishing the conditions under which discretionary buying and selling of exchange by the authorities arise. Specifically, the effects depend on whether the home currency is depreciating or appreciating and on whether the home economy is in an inflated or deflated state.

The home currency may be appreciating at the same time as the home economy is inflating. To analyze the effects of official intervention in the exchange market, it is convenient to assume that the excess of foreign receipts over foreign payments forcing the exchange up also represents a positive income-generating impulse from abroad. If an appreciating exchange rate for the home currency reduces the size of the net income impulse received from abroad, by inhibiting foreign receipts and encouraging foreign payments, a free market rate serves the interest of both internal and external balance. Discretionary buying of foreign exchange by the home authorities in this case prevents the home currency from appreciating as much as it otherwise would; therefore, the expansionary impulse received

55. Some discussion on the financing of official purchases of foreign exchange in Canada appears in Samuel I. Katz, "The Canadian Dollar: A Fluctuating Currency," *Review of Economics and Statistics*, 35 (Aug. 1953), 237, and in the Bank of Canada, *Annual Report*, 1950, pp. 8–9.

from abroad by the home economy remains larger than it would be under a free rate. When the exchange rate is not permitted to rise, external balance must depend entirely on inflation in the home economy. Hence, the more deflationary the financing method adopted by the authorities in handling their exchange purchases, the greater the interference with the adjustment process for restoring external balance. Using idle domestic deposits thus interferes least with the adjustment process; borrowing and security sales may retard the adjustment process, mainly because they produce higher security yields; and using a government surplus to finance exchange purchases may most counteract the movement towards external balance, but to the benefit of internal balance.

If, in the foregoing case, the home country is deflating instead of inflating, the home currency still appreciating, a rate appreciation that reduces the expansionary impulse received from abroad works against internal balance. Official buying of the home currency, however, by checking the appreciation of the currency, requires more expansion to restore external balance. In this case, however, the more expansion the better; and the more expansionary the financing methods adopted by the government for its purchases of foreign exchange, the quicker the return to external balance and the quicker the improvement in internal balance.

Of course, if a rate appreciation has a perverse effect on the flow of international payments, as it might, it will work against external balance but in favour of internal balance. Official intervention in the exchange market will then not be in the best interest of internal balance.

When the home currency is depreciating, it may be assumed that as a result of unbalance on external account the home economy is subject to a deflationary impulse from abroad. If the home economy is inflated, a depreciating currency that favours external balance reduces the deflationary impulse from abroad and so works against internal balance. Official intervention in the exchange market then keeps the economy exposed for a longer time to the deflationary impulse from abroad and so works in the interest of internal balance. Furthermore, the more deflationary the method of handling the proceeds from the official sales of foreign exchange the better. Thus, accumulating the proceeds of exchange sales in idle government deposits is most desirable; other methods of disposing of the proceeds are less desirable and become even more so, the more expansionary they become.

If instead of being inflated the home economy is deflated, a depreciating currency that works towards external balance and so reduces deflationary impulses from abroad is in the interest of internal balance. Official intervention in the exchange market prevents these benefits from arising. External balance can only be achieved by the economy continuing to deflate. Hence, the authorities least interfere with the adjustment process when their disposal of the proceeds from exchange sales are most deflationary. Thus, accumulating the proceeds in idle deposits represents the minimum of interference; debt retirement and security purchases may go against the deflationary trend because they lower security yields; and financing a government deficit from the sales proceeds halts the move towards external balance, but in the interest of internal balance.[56]

Thus, in all cases of government intervention in the foreign-exchange market, official intervention is likely to interfere with the process of restoring external balance, unless movements in exchange rates are not equilibrating. However, in some instances official intervention is beneficial for internal balance.

Gold Movements

Gold, as well as foreign balances, may form a part of the international reserves of a country; hence, it may enter into international transactions not only as a commodity but also as a means of international payment. Thus, although the international gold standard as such no longer exists, gold movements may still have an impact on monetary systems.

Two classes of gold movements may be distinguished: movements

56. Fritz Machlup, "The Theory of Foreign Exchanges," *Readings in the Theory of International Trade*, Blakiston Series of Republished Articles on Economics, *4* (Philadelphia, The Blakiston Company, 1949), pp. 138–44, reprinted from *Economica*, *6* (Nov. 1939), 375–97, discusses official intervention in the foreign-exchange market in a slightly different manner and arrives therefore at slightly different conclusions.

of non-monetary gold and movements of monetary gold. The former arise from new gold production and all other movements of gold not part of the monetary stocks of gold; monetary-gold movements are then movements of gold that are already in monetary stocks, usually in the hands of official holders.

Non-monetary gold movements are most significant in gold-producing countries, such as Canada. New gold production is the source of most non-monetary movements in gold, and so the influence of such movements on the monetary system is mainly a matter of how new production is marketed in the producing country. New gold may be handled in the same way as most other commodities: sold to private dealers at home and abroad.[57] When marketed privately, gold does not affect the banking system any more than transactions in any other commodity do. Only when non-monetary gold is sold to foreign official sources, who pay in the producer's currency by drawing upon a central-bank account in the producing country, does it disturb the banking situation. And when new gold is marketed through official sources in the producing country, there is likely to be a monetary effect; the mines sell their output to the monetary authorities and are paid with government cheques drawn on the central bank—gold production then increases the cash reserves of the banking system.[58]

57. This possibility has been available to Canadian gold mines since early 1956. Canada, Dominion Bureau of Statistics, *The Canadian Balance of International Payments*, 1956, p. 14.

58. In Canada most of the newly produced gold is sold to the Government through the Royal Canadian Mint, and is paid for, like other items of government expenditure, from government deposits with the Bank of Canada. Canada, Department of Finance, *Report of the Master of the Royal Canadian Mint*, 1955, p. 7; Bank of Canada, *Statistical Summary*, Financial Supplement, 1956, p. 68. From these two sources it can be calculated roughly that less than 10 per cent of new gold production in Canada in 1955 was sold other than to the Mint. The purchasing dominance of the Mint in the Canadian gold market exists because gold producers who wish to receive the government subsidy paid to eligible producers must sell all their output to the Mint. The terms of assistance and the regulations surrounding it are summarized in Canada, Department of Mines and Technical Surveys, Mineral Resources Division, *Summary Review of Federal Taxation and Certain Other Federal Legislation Affecting Mining, Oil, and Natural Gas Enterprises in Canada* (Ottawa, Mineral Resources Division, Apr. 1957), pp. 12–13. The payment of government

Monetary gold is usually part of the official stocks of international reserves, held partly in the home country and partly abroad, where it is earmarked for the home country, and kept in the vaults of a foreign central bank. Sales from these stocks to non-residents—sales to residents are unlikely—may be made either from the earmarked supplies held in other countries or from domestically located supplies. Sales from domestically held supplies may mean only earmarking the portion sold for the account of the foreign buyer; there need be no physical shipment of gold from the selling country when it sells from its monetary stocks. Likewise when a country purchases gold it may simply add to its earmarked supplies abroad, or reduce the earmarked supplies held by foreigners in the buying country, without any physical shipments taking place.[59]

Sales of monetary gold by a country usually result when total international payments by its residents exceed the total international receipts of its residents, and the authorities are supporting the exchange rate for the home currency. Non-residents must then accumulate balances of the home currency, or residents of the home country must reduce their foreign balances as an initial step in accommodating the net flow of international payments from the home country. If the currency of the home country is a key currency, non-residents usually will be willing to accumulate balances in it initially. Most of the accumulation is likely to be carried out by official non-resident holders, for private holders will have little need to add to their working balances or holdings in this situation of a stable rate and a flow of funds in favour of non-residents. Official holders may prefer, however, to add to their reserves of gold rather than their holdings of foreign exchange and accordingly may convert at least

---

subsidies to gold mines means that gold in Canada has through these transfer payments another though indirect monetary effect on the banking system.

59. Some interesting details on the mechanics of gold transactions are given by Ed Tyng, "Significant Changes in the World Gold Market," *Burroughs Clearing House*, Mar. 1956, pp. 42–3, 105–6. The handling of gold in Canada is briefly discussed by J. A. Terrace, "The Lure of Gold," *Canadian Banker*, 60 (Winter 1953), 54–7. Also cf. Miroslav A. Kriz, *Gold in World Monetary Affairs Today*, Essays in International Finance, No. 34 (Princeton, International Finance Section, Department of Economics and Sociology, Princeton University, 1959), pp. 5–14.

part of their increased holdings into gold by purchase of gold from the home country. The monetary authorities then sell gold to official non-resident holders of home currency in exchange for home currency. The effect on the banking system in the home country depends on the banking arrangements.

If official non-resident holders of home currency have accumulated their funds with the home-country central bank, a cash-reserve effect occurs at the time the official holders acquire the funds. At the time of the gold transaction the home authorities gain balances with the central bank and lose gold, and there is no further cash-reserve effect, unless the authorities pay out to the public the funds they have taken in from the sale of gold or otherwise transfer the funds to the commercial banks.[60]

If the country experiencing an adverse flow of international payments is not one with a key currency, its residents probably are running down their holdings of foreign balances carried in the key currencies, and drawing upon the official holdings of such currencies held by their authorities. The authorities thereby accumulate domestic balances which, if carried with the home central bank, reduce the cash reserves of the home banking system. To replenish official home holdings of key foreign currencies the authorities will then sell gold to the authorities having the key currencies. No cash-reserve effect on the banking system results in the home country from such a sale of gold.

There may be a cash-reserve effect, however, on the banking system of the country buying the gold, for the authorities in that country add to a central-bank deposit in the name of the selling country, and subsequent spending from that account could add to the cash reserves of the banking system.

Purchases of monetary gold arise from an overall excess of inter-

60. In the United States a sale of gold by the Treasury does not normally add to Treasury balances because the Treasury uses the proceeds from the sale of gold to buy an equal amount of gold certificates held by the Federal Reserve banks. Hobart C. Carr, Madeline McWhinney, and Kathleen N. Straus, "Gold and Foreign Account Transactions: Their Effect on Member Bank Reserves," *Bank Reserves: Some Major Factors Affecting Them* (New York, Federal Reserve Bank of New York, 1953), pp. 23–4.

national receipts over international payments when the authorities are maintaining the exchange rate for the home currency and are unwilling to hold all of the foreign balances that come to them. The authorities then convert excess foreign balances into gold. The purchase of gold has no effect on the cash reserves of the home banking system, although there may have been such an effect initially when the authorities acquired the foreign balances.

Hence gold movements, monetary and non-monetary, may still have cash-reserve effects on banking systems, especially where new gold production moves into the official holdings of producing countries or where official gold purchases from non-residents are paid for from the government account with the central bank. Sterilization may be necessary, but it may come about almost automatically when reductions in the government account with the central bank, caused by gold purchases, are offset by shifting government deposits from the commercial banks to the central bank.[61] There is then no net effect on bank cash or bank deposits; only an indirect shift from government deposits to other deposits on the books of the commercial banks. Therefore, gold movements need not be destabilizing.

CONCLUSIONS

International payments impose upon banking systems a different pattern of reaction and behaviour than interregional payments. Different monetary units of account and separate banking systems explain the difference in effect produced by international payments. The main consequence of the difference is that in international payments deposits do not move from country to country as they do from region to region in interregional payments within the same country.

Banks may become involved in international transactions or foreign business by conducting foreign-banking operations. They may do

61. Government deposits at the commercial banks may have to be built up by security sales to the public, or by budgetary surpluses, in order to carry out the sterilization. Both methods, used in conjunction with the transfer of government deposits from private banks to the central bank, have been employed in the United States to sterilize government gold purchases. Carr et al, "Gold and Foreign Account Transactions: Their Effect on Member Bank Reserves," p. 24.

this at their domestic branches by accepting foreign-currency deposits and granting foreign-currency loans, and banks may also actually operate foreign branches. The foreign business of branches, both domestic and foreign, gives rise to branch indebtedness in the same way as does their domestic business. Domestic branches may have excess deposits or excess loans in foreign currency. Because foreign-currency deposits at domestic branches are more independent of banking action than domestic deposits, excess foreign deposits and excess foreign loans reflect, in the one case, the accumulation of foreign funds by branches that their head offices can utilize and, in the other case, the drawing upon the foreign funds of head offices by branches. Excess deposits of foreign branches reflect excess cash reserves which can be converted into other currencies and used elsewhere. Here the traditional explanation of excess deposits at foreign branches in one country being sent to foreign branches in another where loans exceed deposits fits less well. A better explanation is that excess cash reserves of branches in one country are utilized, through the foreign-exchange market, to bolster cash reserves at branches in other countries.

Banks also take part in foreign transactions without carrying on any foreign business themselves, through performing the basic banking operation of converting foreign currencies into home currencies and vice versa. This banking activity in the foreign-exchange market does not disturb the money supply when banks undertake covering operations in foreign exchange. Such operations consist of matching purchases and sales of foreign exchange, and are usually carried out when there are no exchange controls and exchange rates are flexible. Covering operations stabilize the foreign balances of the banks and make it unnecessary for the banks to undertake compensating transactions in securities to hold domestic deposits constant in the face of foreign-exchange activities.

The main impact of the conversion activities of the banks then is not on total deposits but on the distribution of that total. The distribution changes occur within the country and may have a geographical aspect, with international payments shifting deposits between regions of the country. But the more significant aspects of deposit changes induced by international settlements show up as alterations in non-resident holdings of domestic deposits in the countries having international transactions. Changes in these non-resident holdings, or foreign deposits, are an intimate part of the balance of international payments. Indeed cash payments on international accounts cannot be made without affecting foreign deposits somewhere; hence any unbalance in cash transactions in the balance of payments is automatically accommodated by appropriate changes in foreign deposits. Non-cash credits and movements in exchange rates supplement the temporary role of deposit changes in accommodating the balance of international payments, and eventually, in the final equilibrium position, all net deposit changes must vanish from the balance of payments.

All deposit changes in the balance of payments are not, however, passive in nature; some initiate changes in the trade and capital accounts. This is most readily seen in covered interest-arbitrage transactions, but the various effects that these produce are only temporary and pass away after the arbitrage ceases.

More lasting effects are produced on national economies by transactions in international savings and investment. The former are represented by sales of new securities to foreigners and are of particular interest because of the possibilities they offer for tapping foreign savings, but the savings they tap are usually savings in the real resources of the debtor country. Where sales of new securities do not directly produce a large enough trade deficit to accommodate the capital movement, the sales have an expansionary effect on the debtor country even though in final equilibrium the trade deficit matches the amount borrowed.

The same holds for new direct investment by foreigners in the debtor country: direct investment in excess of the autonomous (income-destroying) trade deficit that accompanies it is definitely expansionary. Even though it is less than its accompanying trade deficit, direct investment may still be expansionary if it stimulates sufficiently other new domestic investment in the debtor country. Finally, balance between new direct investment and the trade deficit is no guarantee that the former has not been destabilizing; it all depends on how the balance has been achieved.

Official intervention by governments in the foreign-exchange market, or official transactions in gold need not disturb the money supply. Gold transactions can be easily sterilized, but official intervention in the foreign-exchange market can create difficulties. In some cases the intervention may be beneficial for internal balance, but it is quite likely to interfere with the adjustment process for restoring external balance.

Chapter Six: GOVERNMENT
FINANCIAL OPERATIONS

This chapter is a departure from previous ones in that it singles out for separate treatment one specific category of bank customer—the central government. There are of course good reasons for according the central government special treatment in an analysis of banking operations. The central government is usually the largest financial entity in the country by virtue of the size of its budget and of its outstanding debt. Furthermore, the central role occupied by government debt in the financial assets of a country often makes the financial activities of the government the most important single influence in the money market. Finally, unlike other users of the banking system, national treasuries usually carry their active working balances with the central bank; hence government financial transactions can have a more disturbing impact on the banks than the transactions of other bank customers.

A central government comes into contact with the banking system in three ways: through its regulation and supervision of the banking system; through its sponsorship, in some way, of the financial activities of ordinary bank customers; and through its own financial activities.[1] This chapter is concerned only with the last—the financial operations of the government itself—and examines how these operations affect the banking system and the community at large.

THE NATURE OF GOVERNMENT FINANCIAL
TRANSACTIONS

The financial transactions of the central government include the handling of cash balances, the administration of any other financial

1. F. Cyril James, *The Economics of Money, Credit and Banking*, p. 486.

assets the government may hold, and the management of the public debt. All these aspects of government financial transactions are discussed in the succeeding parts of this chapter, but they cannot be properly discussed without first considering that concept of the government budget which is significant for government financial transactions.

The relevant budget is the budget of the central government including all its agencies and extensions but excluding special government accounts or investment funds. These funds are fed by special levies, such as unemployment insurance contributions or by other special but voluntary payments such as those from deposits left with a postal savings bank or from premiums paid for government insurance. When the funds collected from these special sources are not combined with the ordinary working funds of the government, the operations of special funds are more conveniently analyzed apart from the ordinary financial operations of the government.

Of most interest for financial analysis is what might be called the financial budget and not the accounting or income budget. This is the budget made up of all the non-financial expenditures and receipts of the government. The expenditures include those for currently-produced goods, for subsidies and other transfer purposes, and for existing real assets including goods in inventories. They exclude acquisitions of financial assets, including government securities, and debt retirement, including reductions in payables. The receipts include those from taxes and other assessments, from the sale of currently-produced government goods and services, and from the sale of existing government non-financial assets, including those in government stockpiles.[2]

A deficit in such a budget may be financed by a reduction in cash balances, by selling securities from the government portfolio, and by

2. This is the flow-of-funds budget of Morris A. Copeland, *Trends in Government Financing*, A study by the National Bureau of Economic Research (Princeton, Princeton University Press, 1960), pp. 24–5, 32. It differs from the cash budget in that it excludes all purely financial transactions but includes transactions that do not result in the immediate payment of cash. It differs from the national-accounts budget in that it includes transactions on capital account as well as those on income account, and excludes tax accruals.

an increase in debt (including payables). A surplus may be disposed of by letting cash balances rise by acquiring other financial assets (including receivables), and by debt retirement. Balance in the budget means that any variation in the total of financial assets of the government can only result from a corresponding variation in its financial liabilities. Likewise, any change that occurs in the composition of its financial assets is independent of the budget.

If receivables and payables are small or do not vary greatly, and if other financial assets and public debt are held constant, the full impact of an unbalanced financial budget falls on cash balances. It is convenient to analyze the effect of the budget on cash balances in these terms, reserving till later the impact on other financial assets and on the public debt. Proper assessment of the cash-balance effect of the budget, however, requires taking into account what impulse it provides for the expansion or contraction of incomes in the economy. This requires rearranging and combining the various non-financial receipts and payments of the government to form three main categories: net transactions in capital assets, net tax receipts, and all other government expenditures on current production.

Thus, all transactions in capital assets and non-current production between the government sector and all other sectors can be grouped to form one set of net transactions. Subsidies and transfer payments made by the government may be treated as a deduction from tax receipts; and non-tax receipts not arising from the sale of specific goods and services by the government may be added to tax revenues. Hence, net tax receipts here refer to all government receipts, less gross sales of specific items, less subsidies and transfer payments. Receipts from the sale of government goods and services currently produced may be offset against the factor purchases made by the government in producing the goods and services sold. Net sales on this account are similar to certain types of taxes and so may be added to tax revenues.[3] Government purchases of currently-produced goods

3. This is on the assumption that what other sectors buy from the government does not affect spending for privately-produced goods and services. Net purchases by the public of government-produced goods and services are similar to indirect taxes in the national-income equation: they must be deducted from total spending to arrive at the factor cost of national income.

and services for resale in excess of the amount sold may be treated as straight government purchases, and these, added to all other government expenditures on current goods and services, form the third category of non-financial transactions in the budget.

To summarize, the three major parts of the financial budget consist of net transactions in capital assets and non-current production, net tax receipts including net sales of government-produced goods and services from current government production, and all other government expenditures on current production including net purchases of items for resale.

Payments and receipts in foreign currency may be segregated from the above accounts. They represent direct transactions between the government and non-residents and so do not directly influence the domestic economy. Such payments and receipts affect the foreign deposits of the government (ignoring payables), and since fluctuations in these are likely to be borne by the official reserves, there is no immediate impact on the domestic financial system. Hence, foreign-currency transactions can be excluded, and the analysis of the financial budget and its components restricted to transactions settled in domestic currency.

Of course some domestic-currency transactions may represent direct government payments to non-residents or government receipts coming directly from non-residents. These receipts and payments cause shifts between government deposits and deposits of non-residents held in domestic currency. Such shifts are not a significant consequence of the financial budget of the government so domestic-currency transactions between the government and non-residents may be safely ignored. This leaves only government payments and receipts in domestic currency which result from transactions with residents in the three categories of the financial budget already distinguished: net transactions in capital assets, net tax receipts, and

---

G. L. S. Shackle, "The Deflative or Inflative Tendency of Government Receipts and Disbursements," *Oxford Economic Papers*, No. 8 (Nov. 1947), p. 51, treats government purchases of goods and services for resale as an offset to their sales proceeds because "the two parts of the transaction form a unity, of a character which would be entirely altered if one part were performed without the other."

expenditures on currently-produced goods and services for the government's own use.

All transactions in these categories affect government deposits; and while this effect is of primary interest for this chapter it cannot be considered without reference to the impact of the transactions on income generation. This impact is measured by the net impulse that the total budget provides for the expansion or contraction of income-expenditures in the economy. The net impulse is measured by applying to each category of the budget the coefficient which represents the extent to which amounts in that category add to or subtract from autonomous income expenditures. The algebraic sum of the product of the various budget amounts and their coefficients yields the net impulse or multiplicand for the regular income-expenditure multiplier.[4]

The size of the various income-creating and -destroying coefficients used depends on the nature of the various items in the budget. Thus, government expenditures on current production purchased from residents add to autonomous income expenditures to the extent that basic spending propensities remain undisturbed and the expenditures represent factor purchases.[5] Because of the import content in some of the goods bought, however, not all government expenditures on current production represent factor purchases; thus the income-generating coefficient of government purchases varies with the import content of the items purchased and will be less than one. Money income increases initially by the amount of government purchases multiplied by their income-generating coefficients when elasticities of supply are infinite. If supply elasticities are finite, prices will rise

4. The idea of applying to each item of government expenditure an "income-creating coefficient" and to each item of revenue an "income-destroying coefficient" is developed by Ralph Turvey, "Some notes on Multiplier Theory," *American Economic Review*, *43* (June 1953), 284–5. William H. White, "Measuring the Inflationary Significance of a Government Budget," International Monetary Fund, *Staff Papers*, *1* (1950–51), 359–69 passim, discusses the nature of adjustments that must be made to various revenue and expenditure items in government budgets in order to arrive at the size of the impulse they provide for the economy.

5. John F. Due, "Government Expenditures and Their Significance for the Economy," *Fiscal Policies and the American Economy*, Kenyon E. Poole, editor (New York, Prentice-Hall, Inc., 1951), p. 202.

as well as money incomes, unless the rise in prices restricts private spending sufficiently to keep money incomes from rising. But the general likelihood is that government expenditures for domestic factor purchases will raise money incomes.

Tax receipts that reduce autonomous income expenditures have income-destroying coefficients with negative values. The value varies with the individual features of the tax, but will in general lie between minus one and zero. The autonomous part of direct taxes (the part not dependent on income) reduces autonomous income expenditures in accordance with the propensity to spend the taxed funds. Thus, direct taxes paid out of incomes reduce disposable incomes and leave less for private spending; the propensity to spend the taxed funds determines the income-reducing coefficient of direct taxes and is usually assumed to be the same as the propensity to spend funds after taxes. Taxes on asset transactions—such as gifts and inheritances— may have zero or very low income-reducing coefficients. Indirect taxes paid at the time of spending income reduce autonomous income expenditures by the full amount if money illusion is present; their income-destroying coefficient is less than one, however, if there is no money illusion.[6]

Where the initial impact of a tax is to not only reduce money incomes but also cause prices to fall, other spending may be stimulated; the deflationary impulse provided by the tax item is thereby reduced, but it is unlikely to be completely eliminated. It becomes more difficult to apply multiplier analysis here because the actual

6. Money illusion exists, for example, when money expenditures of consumers depend solely on money disposable income. The consumer spends a fixed amount on consumer goods regardless of price; hence an indirect tax applied to such goods reduces real spending but not money spending, so that the tax collections represent payments made entirely from funds that would have been spent on current production. No money illusion means that real consumption depends on real disposable income; if prices rise, real consumption falls, but not by as much as it does under money illusion. Thus, an indirect tax when applied causes some increase in money expenditures so that its collection does not represent a full substitution of tax payments for income expenditures: income expenditures fall by less than the amount of the tax collections. E. Cary Brown, "Analysis of Consumption Taxes in Terms of the Theory of Income Determination," *American Economic Review*, 40 (Mar. 1950), 76–7, 81–2.

working out of the process may disturb prices more and give rise to offsetting expansionary impulses. The main point is, however, that items of taxation bearing on any part of autonomous income expenditures provide an initial deflationary impulse, and they are likely to have a net deflationary effect after all repercussion effects have been exhausted.

The category of government transactions involving capital assets and non-current items of production mainly affects asset prices and the composition of assets held outside the government sector. If a net flow of funds from the government on these accounts increases autonomous income expenditures, however, the transactions have an income-creating coefficient in excess of zero. Similarly, if a net flow of funds to the government on these accounts reduces autonomous income expenditures, the transactions have a negative income-destroying coefficient.

The application of income-creating and income-destroying coefficients to determine the net impulse provided by the financial budget is restricted to the autonomous part of the budget—that is, the items that exist and occur independently of income-expenditures in the economy. Therefore, to determine the impulse effect of the budget, it is necessary to distinguish between the autonomous components and the income-induced ones and to exclude the induced components.

The non-financial receipts of the government tend to have some income-induced components. Many taxes are geared to incomes and economic activity so that tax yields vary directly with changes in national income. Transfer payments, considered here as negative taxes, usually vary inversely with national income so that a part of net tax revenues is probably income-induced. Consequently, items of government expenditures that generate income also generate some of their own financing—that is, each item of disbursement has its own inherent tax yield at existing tax rates.[7] Therefore, changes in income and government expenditures will usually induce changes in total tax revenues even though the tax structure remains constant. Income-induced changes in tax revenues do not represent deflationary impulses when they are positive or expansionary ones when negative;

7. Shackle, "The Deflative or Inflative Tendency," p. 51.

such induced changes are merely reflections of other deflationary or expansionary forces at work in the economy.

The same conclusion applies to income-induced changes in government expenditures, which, however, are usually considered to be completely independent of national income—that is, government expenditures are usually treated as being solely income-determining, having no income-determined component.

The existence of income-induced components in the financial budget means that a deficit in the autonomous parts of the budget may be exactly offset by a surplus in the induced parts. The income-expenditures that the autonomous deficit generates, along with other components of autonomous spending, induce a sufficient increase in government receipts to produce a balance in the *ex post* or observed budget. Another likelihood is that balance among the autonomous items in the budget is associated with an overall budget surplus. In short, the final or observed position of the budget is the result of both autonomous and induced effects, with the latter modifying the former. Thus, autonomous government receipts and expenditures produce a given budget position which is modified to the extent that additional government receipts have been induced by income. Any variation in income caused by changes in the various components of national income affect the observed budget position by affecting tax revenues. For this reason the observed state of the financial budget does not reflect the degree to which the budget has exerted an expansionary or deflationary influence on the economy.[8]

It is, of course, the autonomous elements in government expenditures and revenues, not the income-induced ones, that provide income impulses for the economy; the income-induced components are

8. Cf. White, "Measuring the Inflationary Significance," p. 355; Paul A. Samuelson, "The Simple Mathematics of Income Determination," *Income, Employment and Public Policy: Essays in Honor of Alvin H. Hansen* (New York, W. W. Norton and Company, Inc., 1948), p. 145, who points out that for a change in investment only a budget deficit decreases, or a surplus rises, as income increases, giving a negative pseudo-deficit multiplier.

John G. Gurley, "Fiscal Policies for Full Employment: A Diagrammatic Analysis," *Journal of Political Economy*, 60 (Dec. 1952), 526, presents a useful diagram that can be adapted to illustrate differences between autonomous and induced budget changes, and to show the separate results of the two.

entirely passive.[9] In terms of multiplier analysis the autonomous elements are impounded in the multiplicand and the induced elements are provided for in the multiplier itself;[10] induced taxes, therefore, are a leakage and their marginal rates affect the size of the multiplier. The higher the marginal rates of taxation the smaller the income multiplier[11] and the greater the effect of an autonomous change in spending on the budget balance.[12]

9. White, pp. 374, 376, discusses income-induced tax changes as leakages from the flow of purchasing power of the same order as leakages into savings and imports; and he argues for the exclusion of induced tax changes from the observed deficit in order to assess the impact of the budget on income.

10. Cf. Fritz Machlup, *International Trade and the National Income Multiplier*, pp. 12–13; Donald Bailey Marsh, *World Trade and Investment: The Economics of Interdependence*, pp. 235, 237.

11. Cf. A. C. L. Day, *Outline of Monetary Economics*, p. 216.

12. Although it is generally recognized that induced deficits and surpluses do not represent expansionary or contractionary impulses for the economy, this is often overlooked. The most glaring neglect is evident in the stabilizing budget policy proposed by the Committee for Economic Development. The gist of the proposal is that if a budget is balanced at a full-employment level of income it will become automatically over-balanced when income rises above that level, and under-balanced when income falls below the desired level. That is, in inflation a surplus automatically appears, and in depression, a deficit, as a result of the income-induced component in tax revenues. Such induced deficits and surpluses do nothing directly to modify the destabilizing impulses that give rise to the fluctuations in income; the induced change in tax revenues cannot equal the amount of the initial destabilizing impulse unless marginal tax rates are 100 per cent. As a result disposable income changes and the multiplier is greater than one because of the changes induced in spending based on disposable income. Walter W. Heller, "CED's Stabilizing Budget Policy After Ten Years," *American Economic Review*, 47 (Sept. 1957), 634–51, takes a critical view of the stabilizing budget, but fails to point out the above-mentioned fallacy in the policy consisting of identifying any deficit or surplus with a stimulating or depressing impulse. Alvin H. Hansen, *Monetary Theory and Fiscal Policy* (New York, McGraw-Hill Book Company, Inc., 1949), pp. 176–80, likewise criticizes the stabilizing budget without any reference to its fundamental weakness in basing stability on income-induced changes. Milton Friedman, "A Monetary and Fiscal Framework for Economic Stability," *Essays in Positive Economics* (Chicago, The University of Chicago Press, 1953), pp. 140–1, who also advocates a stabilizing budget, argues that induced deficits and surpluses prevent spending from fluctuating as much as it otherwise would. The point is correct but overlooks the more essential point that fluctuations in spending are not thereby eliminated and countervailing forces set in motion.

Thus, it is both useful and necessary to distinguish between induced and autonomous surpluses and deficits. Autonomous surpluses and deficits are not directly observable; they are produced by the autonomous components in government spending and tax structures. Induced surpluses and deficits spring from changes in national income and are also not directly observable when they follow autonomous changes in the tax structure or in government expenditures: autonomous surpluses and deficits then merge with the induced ones to produce the observable budget position. Hence, autonomous variations in government spending, given tax rates and the tax structure, produce smaller variations in the observable deficits and surpluses because of income-induced changes in tax collections. In this case the observed surplus that results from a reduction in government expenditures understates the extent of the deflationary influence of the budget; likewise, the observed deficit understates the expansionary influence of an increase in government expenditures. The same conclusions follow when government revenues vary autonomously while government expenditures remain constant; the resulting deficits and surpluses are less than the autonomous changes in tax receipts at the initial level of national income, and hence they understate the influence of the budget on the economy.

The observed or overall position of the financial budget is, of course, the relevant one for the analysis of government financial transactions. If the position is one of balance, the budget has no effect on government cash balances or deposits. Whether such a balanced budget provides a net impulse for income expansion or contraction depends on the autonomous part of the budget. If this is balanced,[13] the impulse effect depends on a comparison of the average

---

A stabilizing budget is, of course, an improvement over old-style budgets in which government expenditures were made a function of revenues and the tax structure was subject to deflationary changes when national income fell. But more is required for true stability than independence between government expenditures and revenues: an inverse relationship is required.

13. A balanced autonomous budget and a balanced overall budget are possible only when the level of income which prevails when the autonomous budget is balanced induces an equal amount of government receipts and expenditures. The induced portion of the budget is then in balance as well.

L

income-generating coefficient of the expenditure side with the average income-destroying coefficient of the receipts side. Equality between the two means no impulse effect, whereas a larger income-generating coefficient means a positive impulse and vice versa,[14] the impulse being given by the product of total expenditures and the differential in the coefficients. When the autonomous part of the budget is not in balance, the impulse it provides is then given by the algebraic sum of the two average coefficients weighted by their corresponding variables. The result could well be a negative net impulse associated with an autonomous deficit and a positive net impulse, with an autonomous surplus. More likely, however, an autonomous surplus would be found to provide a positive net impulse and an autonomous deficit, a negative net impulse.

In general, the impulse provided by a deficit, surplus, or balance in the overall financial budget of the government depends on the position of the autonomous part of the budget and on the relevant income-creating and income-destroying coefficients. Any particular overall budget position may be associated with a nil, expansionary, or contractionary income impulse.

These possibilities must be taken into account in order to assess the general impact of money flows between the government sector and all other sectors. The more specific impacts which government payments and receipts have on the distribution of income and the al-

---

14. The possibility of a negative income effect when the autonomous budget is balanced is discussed by Day, p. 221n4. A balanced autonomous budget results in income expenditures equal to the amount of total government expenditures (one version of the balanced-budget theorem) when the inequality between the two mpulse-determining coefficients is positive and equal to the reciprocal of the multiplier. Cf. Turvey, "Some Notes on Multiplier Theory," p. 285. A deficit in the autonomous budget associated with an overall balanced budget will also produce total income expenditures equal to the amount of government expenditures when the net impulse provided by the budget is equal to the product of government expenditures and the reciprocal of the multiplier. This is another version of the balanced-budget theorem. This possibility of a deficit in the autonomous budget, balance in the overall budget, and a budget multiplier of unity is analyzed by William A. Salant, "Taxes, Income Determination, and the Balanced Budget Theorem," *Review of Economics and Statistics*, *39* (May 1957), 156–8.

location of resources[15] are ignored, however. Such matters as these are more appropriate for a study on public finance than for one on the monetary consequences of government financial operations. Thus, essentially non-financial consequences of government budgets are generally ignored in the analysis that follows. Also neglected are the possible effects of government transactions on the geographical distribution of the money supply; this is a topic that seems to provide little scope for theoretical analysis—it requires mainly an empirical approach.[16]

The following sections of this chapter, then, present a theoretical analysis of government financial operations from the point of view of managing government deposits and the public debt. Since budget policy plays a crucial role in the management of public funds, a discussion of deposit management follows the preliminary remarks on cash budgets. Asset and debt management, which supplement deposit management, are examined after government deposits.

THE MANAGEMENT OF GOVERNMENT
DEPOSITS

Deposit management in the government sector is much like deposit management in any other sector; that is, the mechanics are the same. However, there is a policy dimension to government deposit management that is not present elsewhere; government deposits must be managed not only with an eye to the financial needs of the government but also with an eye to the monetary policy of the moment. Deposit management must attempt to minimize possible conflicts with monetary policy. It is this aspect of the management of government deposits that is emphasized here. However, for a full assessment of deposit management it is necessary to also take into account the

15. Due, "Government Expenditures and Their Significance for the Economy," p. 226.

16. One aspect of the problem, illustrating the statistical methods involved, is considered for the United States, by Selma J. Mushkin, "Distribution of Federal Expenditures among the States," *Review of Economics and Statistics, 39* (Nov. 1957), 435–50.

other consequences of fluctuations in government deposits for the private sector.

Closely allied with deposit management is asset and debt management. Governments by buying and selling existing securities through the operation of special investment accounts can alter the size of their deposits, and the same thing can be accomplished through altering the total public debt outstanding. However, deposit fluctuations can be considered separately, for one of the advantages of such fluctuations is that they permit the separation of budget policy from debt management.[17] Accordingly, asset and debt management are considered separately in the following section; the present section deals solely with the administration of government deposits, aside from asset and debt management, and from the points of view of mechanics, policy possibilities, and consequences.

Administrative Aspects of Government Deposits

In handling its domestic-currency cash receipts and payments, the central government probably operates only one general or active account, making all disbursements from it and placing most or all of its receipts directly into it.[18] The universal practice among governments seems to be to carry their operating account with the central bank and to use that institution as the main government banker.[19] Cash receipts in domestic currency accruing to the central government flow into a government account with the central bank, and all government disbursements flow from there. These receipts and payments may pass through the banking system however.

This is especially so in countries where the government uses the commercial banks as initial depositories for tax receipts and other

17. Cf. Earl R. Rolph, "Principles of Debt Management," *American Economic Review*, 47 (June 1957), 305, who points out that government debt outstanding need not fluctuate with government deficits and surpluses if government deposits are allowed to fluctuate.

18. The use of vault cash or till money by the central government and possibel variations in the amount so held is ignored as a refinement to the analysis not worth considering. Brief mention of the possibility is made by Leland J. Pritchard, *Money and Banking*, pp. 407–8.

19. R. S. Sayers, *Modern Banking*, p. 135; Day, *Outline of Monetary Economics*, p. 153.

payments due the government. Government officials in different parts of the country receiving public funds may deposit them with the commercial banks for, in effect, transmission to the seat of government where the receipts are deposited to the government account with the central bank. Government payments made by cheques also flow through the banking system, when the recipients deposit them with the banks and the latter process the cheques, returning them to the treasury. Processing government cheques involves considerable paper work for the banks, as the central government is undoubtedly the largest issuer of cheques and monetary instruments in the country.[20] A large portion of government expenditures—those associated with the national debt—are made without the use of cheques, with the banks again accommodating the payments. Thus, bond coupons detached from government securities get deposited with the banks, who forward the coupons to the central bank; the latter as manager of the national debt makes direct payment to the banks, and then draws down the government account by the amount of the payment.

The details of handling government funds vary from country to country—the preceding sketch approximates Canadian conditions[21]

20. In Canada the chartered banks during 1953 cashed 48 million government cheques, 38 million post office money orders, 17 million government bond coupons, and made 889 thousand remittances to the treasury for government funds paid into their branches. Canada, Parliament, House, Standing Committee on Banking and Commerce, *Proceedings: Decennial Revision of the Bank Act*, 1st Sess., 22nd Parl., 1954, p. 153, evidence of the Deputy Minister of Finance.

21. Further details on handling government deposits in Canada may be gleaned from W. C. Clark, "Financial Administration of the Government of Canada," *Canadian Journal of Economics and Political Science*, 4 (Aug. 1938),407–10; H. R. Balls, "Budgetary and Fiscal Accounting in the Government of Canada: Part II," *Canadian Tax Journal*, 4 (Mar.–Apr. 1956), 138; A. E. Buck, *Financing Canadian Government* (Chicago, Public Administration Service, 1949), pp. 114–15, 120; E. L. Stewart Patterson, *Canadian Banking*, rev. ed. (Toronto, The Ryerson Press, 1941), p. 117. In the last-mentioned source it is stated that most balances of the Government of Canada are carried with the Bank of Canada: this is no longer so—most of the government balances are carried with the chartered banks, although the main working account is carried with the Bank of Canada.

Brief mention of recent changes in handling government funds in Canada is made in Bank of Canada, *Annual Report*, 1957, pp. 28, 45, and J. S. G. Wilson, "The Canadian Money Market Experiment," *Banca Nazionale del Lavoro* (Rome), *Quarterly Review*, Mar. 1958, p. 23n6.

—but the common element seems to be the use of the central bank as a depository for the main government account.[22] And it is the use of the central bank as a depository for public funds that may lead deposit management to impinge on monetary policy: the ordinary financial transactions of the government with the private sector may disturb the amount of cash reserves in the banking system. Thus an excess of government receipts over outlays increases the government deposit at the central bank at the expense of the cash reserves of the banks; the excess receipts of the government, in the form of cheques on bank deposits, give it a net claim on the banks that is settled on the books of the central bank, which acts as banker for both the government and the banks. The banking system in this instance loses in cash reserves and deposits. When government outlays exceed receipts, the results are an increase in the deposits of the private sector with the banks, a like increase in the cash reserves of the banking system, and a reduction in government deposits with the central bank. That is, net government payments to the private sector give the banks a net claim on the government that is convertible into cash reserves.

In general, when the government makes net payments to the private sector, or receives net receipts from it—that is, when the government does not stabilize its deposits with the central bank—its transactions have a cash-reserve effect. Balance in government payments generally mean balance in the government deposit with the central bank, but not necessarily so. Transactions between the central bank and the government—such as lending and borrowing operations—cause movements in government deposits that do not reflect cash-reserve effects. And where transactions between the central bank and the government stabilize government deposits when they would otherwise fluctuate, cash-reserve effects from the cash budget are not thereby eliminated.

22. Cf. *Relations between the Central Banks and Commercial Banks*, Lectures delivered at the Tenth International Banking Summer School, Garmisch-Partenkirchen, Germany, Sept. 1957 (Frankfort on Main, Fritz Knapp Verlag, for Bundesverband des privaten Bankgewerbes e.V., 1957), pp. 35–6, 53, 77, 87, 104, where brief mention is made of the practices followed in some European countries in depositing public funds.

However, when government deposits at the central bank are stabilized without the aid of transactions between the government and the central bank, government financial activities have no net cash-reserve effects. Nevertheless, the stabilization of government deposits is unlikely to come about naturally and continuously; there are bound to be at least erratic and random deviations between overall government receipts and expenditures that produce corresponding fluctuations in the cash reserves of the banking system. Therefore, when it is desirable or necessary to offset these cash-reserve effects discretionary action is necessary. Within the context of government financial operations, and outside the realm of central banking proper, the government may take discretionary action to stabilize its deposits by entering into counteracting transactions in securities, akin to the compensating transactions in securities carried out by the banks to stabilize their cash reserves. In some countries this is the only recourse available to the government for stabilizing its central-bank deposits;[23] in other countries, however, government deposits with the central bank may be stabilized by carrying public funds with the commercial banks and letting these accounts bear the brunt of the fluctuations in total government deposits. Failing other methods to stabilize government deposits with the central bank, offsetting action—in the form of open-market operations—must be carried out by the central bank when it is desirable to eliminate the cash-reserve effects of government financial transactions.

Because fluctuations in government deposits with the central bank are similar to open-market operations in their effect on cash reserves, they may at times be permitted to leave their impact on the banking system in order to further the efforts of monetary policy. To be used in this way the fluctuations in government deposits must occur at the right time and in the right direction. Such a fortuitous conjunction

23. In the United Kingdom Treasury bills are used to stabilize government deposits with the Bank of England, their issues and maturities being manipulated for this purpose. Sayers, *Modern Banking*, 135–8 passim; "The Financial Machinery," *Barclays Bank Review* (London), Nov. 1956, pp. 73–4; Great Britain, Chancellor of the Exchequer, Committee on the Working of the Monetary System, *Principal Memoranda of Evidence*, *1* (London, Her Majesty's Stationery Office, 1960), p. 82 (Memorandum of evidence submitted by H.M. Treasury).

is most likely to happen when deliberate deficits and surpluses are being incurred. Discretionary surpluses and deficits are then accompanied naturally and automatically by cash-reserve effects that supplement budget policy, and which do the work of open-market operations. The cash-reserve effects may not, however, be of the right amount so that even here they may have to be modified or supplemented by open-market operations. Induced surpluses and deficits, as well, through their impact on government deposits have an open-market effect that produces counter-cyclical variations in cash reserves.

Nevertheless, simple fluctuations in government deposits at the central bank, reflecting the net impact of ordinary government financial transactions with the private sector, do not offer a very fine tool for monetary policy; all that can be expected from them are reinforcing movements. By themselves they are seldom wholly adequate; debt operations and open-market operations are more than likely to be required to give the proper magnitude to deposit fluctuations.

Deposit management has more scope for supplementing monetary policy, or for avoiding conflicts with it, when public funds are carried at the commercial banks as well as with the central bank; there is then the possibility of shifting government deposits between the central bank and the commercial banks simply for their cash-reserve effects. Because this method offers a slightly different kind of weapon for monetary policy than other available techniques, and since it differs from the simple passive policy of letting government deposits at the central bank fluctuate with the fiscal position of the government, it is worth considering in some detail.

The Policy of Einlagen-Politik

The policy followed in depositing public funds, when commercial banks may be used as depositories, is referred to in German banking law as the policy of *Einlagen-Politik*. *Einlagen-Politik* expresses the idea that the monetary authorities may pursue monetary aims by altering the allocation of public funds between the central bank and the commercial banks.[24] Thus any decision on the distribution of govern-

24. K. Klasen, "Relations Between the German Central Banking System and the Commercial Banks," *Relations Between the Central Banks and Commercial Banks,*

ment deposits between the banks and the central bank that is influenced in any way by considerations of the consequences for cash reserves represents a use or form of *Einlagen-Politik*. On this definition a decision not to shift government funds between the two types of depositories because of cash-reserve considerations is as much a use of *Einlagen-Politik* as is a decision to so shift funds to affect cash reserves.

The purest form of *Einlagen-Politik* is a shift of government funds between the banks and the central bank made solely for its effects on cash reserves and without regard to the cash position of the government. Certain restraints, however, may restrict the use of *Einlagen-Politik* in its purest form. Possible restraints are: the need to carry a minimum of deposits with the commercial banks to compensate them for the work involved in handling government funds; the need to maintain a minimum balance in the working account with the central bank;[25] and the reluctance of central governments to maintain for any length of time deposits much in excess of their operating needs.

Where public funds are carried by the government with the commercial banks, one of the prime motives for doing so is generally to compensate the banks for services provided to the government.[26]

Lectures delivered at the Tenth International Banking Summer School, Garmisch-Partenkirchen, Germany, Sept. 1957 (Frankfort on Main, Fritz Knapp Verlag, for Bundesverband des privaten Bankgewerbes e.V., 1957), p. 35.

25. Cf. H. C. Carr, "The Treasury and the Money Market," *The Treasury and the Money Market* (New York, Federal Reserve Bank of New York, 1954), p. 6; "The Treasury's Deposit Balances and the Banking System," Federal Reserve Bank of New York, *Monthly Review of Credit and Business Conditions*, Apr. 1958, p. 52.

26. The primary purpose of leaving public funds on deposit with the chartered banks in Canada appears to be to compensate the banks for the banking services they provide to the Government of Canada, especially for cashing Government cheques without charge as required by the Bank Act. Canada, Parliament, House, Standing Committee on Banking and Commerce, *Proceedings*, 1954, p. 153, where the Deputy Minister of Finance further comments that the Government "should keep working balances in the banks equal to about one week's disbursements . . . [so that] each bank will always be in funds to meet cheques presented to them for payment. For short periods balances may drop to $50,000,000 or less, but normally they are around $100,000,000."

Therefore financial or accounting considerations influence decisions regarding the placement and management of public funds with the banks; governments are likely to feel compelled to maintain balances of a certain amount with the banks, although concern for the level of cash reserves may temporarily inhibit the compensation motive.[27] These considerations suggest that shifts of government funds from the banks to the central bank, when total government deposits are constant or falling, are restricted in scope. In the opposite situation the government is under a restraint to maintain a certain minimum working balance with the central bank, for purposes of efficient operations; hence, shifts of government deposits from the central bank to the commercial banks may not be able to proceed very far when the

------

The public funds left with the chartered banks in Canada are distributed among them "in accordance with a formula worked out in co-operation with the banks, which reflects, generally speaking, the relative amount of work done for the government by each bank." Balls, "Budgetary and Fiscal Accounting in the Government of Canada," p. 138.

The system of compensating Canadian banks for services to the government by giving them a share of the government deposits has a long history in Canada; it was employed before there was a central bank and when the main government deposit was carried with the chartered bank acting as the chief fiscal agent for the government. H. M. P. Eckardt, *A Rational Banking System: A Comprehensive Study of the Advantages of the Branch Bank System*, p. 285. Also cf. Harold G. Villard and W. W. Willoughby, *The Canadian Budgetary System*, The Institute for Government Research, Studies in Administration, No. 5 (New York, D. Appleton and Company, 1918), pp. 145–7, and the sources cited therein.

27. Thus under the Canadian system of deposit management for public funds, a former Deputy Minister of Finance, Clark, "Financial Administration of the Government of Canada," p. 409, has stated that, although public funds are allotted to the chartered banks on the basis of the amount of banking work they do for the Government, "the division of funds between the Bank of Canada on the one hand and of the chartered banks on the other hand must take into account general considerations of monetary policy." The very same view is expressed by a present official of the Department of Finance, Balls, "Budgetary and Fiscal Accounting in the Government of Canada," p. 138. This carefully guarded statement of policy may mean that when a re-allocation of existing public funds is called for on accounting or financial grounds the re-allocation is postponed if it would produce an effect on cash reserves contrary to the aims of current monetary policy; on this interpretation the allocation of public funds in Canada is hardly an active policy of monetary control.

total deposits of the government are constant or falling. The only way to free *Einlagen-Politik* from the restrictions imposed by minimum requirements for balances is for the government to carry excess deposits with both the commercial banks and the central bank.[28] Government deposits can then be shifted between the two types of depositories without immediately running into the limitations imposed by minimum requirements for balances. Given sufficiently large excess deposits it is unlikely that these minima would exercise a restraint on shifting government deposits since shifts continuously in one direction are unnecessary in the marginal application of *Einlagen-Politik* for which it is best suited.

However, excess deposits are not a characteristic of the financial position of modern governments; the policy of *Einlagen-Politik* is reduced to some sort of relationship with what is happening to the cash balances of the government. The closest relationship is represented by the use of *Einlagen-Politik* to stabilize government deposits with the central bank. Fluctuations in total government deposits are then reflected entirely in the balances kept with the commercial banks. Thus, when the government is incurring an overall cash deficit so that its central-bank deposit is falling, with cash reserves rising, public funds might be shifted to the central bank; this would reverse the cash-reserve effect and restore the working balance of the government with the central bank to its previous level. Or, a cash surplus may be transferred from the central-bank account to the balances kept with the commercial banks, thereby annulling the cash-reserve effect of the surplus. These extreme examples illustrate the value of leaving public funds on deposit with the banking system for minimizing the disturbance of government financial transactions on cash reserves; and where public funds are carried with the commercial banks, they are likely to be utilized for this purpose.[29] Complete stabilization of

28. Cf. Earl C. Hald, "Monetary Aspects of Changes in Treasury Cash Balances," *Southern Economic Journal*, 22 (Apr. 1956), 455.

29. The primary purpose of keeping some public funds on deposit with the commercial banks in the United States appears to be to isolate the cash reserves of the banking system from the effects of financial operations by the government. Norris O. Johnson, "United States Treasury Operations and Functions," *American Financial Institutions*, Herbert V. Prochnow, editor (New York, Prentice-Hall, Inc.,

government deposits at the central bank through the manipulation of deposits maintained at the commercial banks, however, encounters the same restraints as does the purest form of *Einlagen-Politik*. Only for surpluses and small deficits will it generally be possible to use *Einlagen-Politik* to eliminate the cash-reserve effects of the government budget.

However, *Einlagen-Politik* may still be an effective policy even if discretionary shifts in government deposits do not or cannot bear a one-to-one relationship to changes in total government deposits. Shifts in government deposits between the banks and the chartered banks when smaller in magnitude than the corresponding fluctuations in the cash balances that prompt the shifts may still represent an effective policy of *Einlagen-Politik*. Thus, a discretionary surplus, reflecting an anti-inflationary policy by the government, causes a reduction in cash reserves equivalent to the size of the final surplus; if this is a larger reduction in cash reserves than is required to support the chosen policy of deflation, an appropriate shift from the government balances with the banks will give the required effect. Should the effect of the surplus on cash reserves not be sufficient, the effect can be supplemented through *Einlagen-Politik* only by making a pure transfer of government funds, for which the scope, as previously noted, is quite limited.

The possibilities of combining a policy of *Einlagen-Politik* with a discretionary deficit are less than with a discretionary surplus. A discretionary deficit, engineered as part of an inflationary policy, reduces the government deposit with the central bank and at the same time increases cash reserves. If the increase is too large for correcting the deflation, it may be reduced to the required size by shifting government deposits from the commercial banks to the central bank. Such a shift helps to restore the depleted balances of the government with the central bank, but only at the risk of reducing government balances with the commercial banks below their mini-

---

1951), p. 515; *The Treasury and the Money Market* (New York, Federal Reserve Bank of New York, 1954), pp. 1–15, which consists of three essays dealing specifically with government deposit management in the United States and with the use of the commercial banks as special depositories.

mum. In contrast, a surplus naturally generates the excess deposits needed for pursuing an effective policy of *Einlagen-Politik*.

The foregoing remarks apply also to induced surpluses and deficits. A purely income-induced surplus is the result of an income-inflation in the private sector; to regulate the expansion, *Einlagen-Politik* can be pressed into service to provide, alone or with assistance, a suitable cash-reserve effect. A purely income-induced deficit results from income-deflation in the private sector and produces an effect on cash reserves in the right direction; but the possibilities of modifying or tailoring that effect to the needs of monetary policy through the use of *Einlagen-Politik* run into the limitations mentioned in connection with the discretionary deficit.

The implication of the argument to this point is that, without carrying excess deposits, *Einlagen-Politik* in its purest form—shifts of government funds between public and private depositories solely for their effects on cash reserves and independent of changes in total government deposits—is generally not a feasible policy. A policy of *Einlagen-Politik* is then likely to show up in a redistribution of government deposits when the total is changing, either to eliminate or reduce the effect of an unbalanced government budget on cash reserves. Even here there is most scope for the policy when the budget is in surplus. If *Einlagen-Politik* were restricted to this context, government deposits at the banks and the central bank would fluctuate together and in the same direction. However, the transfers of deposits may vary not only in amount from the fluctuations in total government deposits but also in timing—that is, a lead or a lag may be introduced between the realization of a surplus or deficit and its impact on cash reserves.[30] This is accomplished by accelerating or delaying the withdrawal of government funds from the banks, and by accelerating or delaying the deposit of surplus funds with them.

Thus, government deposits with the banks may be shifted to the central bank in anticipation of future requirements; or such a shift

30. The policy of *Einlagen-Politik* in the United States apparently takes the form of leads and lags in withdrawing public funds from the commercial banks, although variations in amounts as well as timing are employed. "U. S. Treasury Tax and Loan Accounts," *Readings in Money and Banking*, ed. Charles R. Whittlesey (New York, W. W. Norton & Company, 1952), p. 90.

may be delayed or lagged behind government expenditures, and government balances with the central bank allowed to fall below their usual level for a short period. In this way government deposits are managed so as not only to accommodate the spending needs of the government but also to obtain a temporary reduction or expansion in cash reserves. Likewise, government funds may be shifted from the central bank to the commercial banks in anticipation of an increase in receipts; or surplus funds that would normally be transferred to the commercial banks may be allowed to accumulate at the central bank for a short period before being shifted. Again a temporary effect is produced on cash reserves, within the larger framework of administering government deposits in accordance with the financial needs of the government.

Large-scale debt operations offer more scope than do ordinary budget transactions for the lead-and-lag technique of applying a policy of *Einlagen-Politik*. Thus, when new debt is incurred through the net issue of government securities to the private sector, the proceeds, in contrast to ordinary receipts, are likely to be accumulated with the commercial banks.[31] The issue then has no effect on cash reserves; the proceeds may be shifted to the central bank as required to meet expenditures or the shifting may be timed relative to the expenditures to induce a temporary change in cash reserves. When debt is to be retired, the funds earmarked for that purpose may be accumulated with the banks until required for meeting the maturing securities; the act of debt retirement then causes no fluctuations in cash reserves. This is the use of the lead-and-lag method to offset the disturbing effects of government debt operations on the cash reserves of the banks, but it may be modified to provide for a more active policy of *Einlagen-Politik*.

In conclusion, *Einlagen-Politik* is a discretionary weapon of mon-

---

31. In Canada cheques issued by the public in payment for new securities issued by the Government are handled differently from ordinary government receipts. The proceeds of a new issue are not deposited with the Bank of Canada as are ordinary receipts, but rather are deposited with the chartered banks on which the cheques are drawn. Canada, Parliament, House, Standing Committee on Banking and Commerce, *Proceedings*, 1954, pp. 154–5, evidence of the Deputy Minister of Finance.

etary policy, but it has limited scope. It is most feasible when the government is running a surplus on its cash budget, or has new debt proceeds accruing to it as a result of security sales to the private sector. Otherwise, unless the government adopts the practice of carrying deposits in excess of its needs, *Einlagen-Politik* is at best a short-run supplementary device of credit control; it thus becomes relegated to the relatively passive role of minimizing the impact on cash reserves of the financial operations of the government.[32] *Einlagen-Politik* is likely to remain just another means for offsetting the effects of the budget on the cash reserves of the banking system until governments adopt the procedure of carrying excess deposits for the prime purpose of monetary policy. Perhaps the day will come when government deposits will be regarded primarily as an instrument of monetary policy rather than as a financial medium.[33] Until then all the benefits

32. Carr, "The Treasury and the Money Market," p. 5, states that in the United States very little scope has been found for manipulating public funds so as to actively support monetary policy; in practice the shifting of government deposits between the commercial banks and the Federal Reserve Banks has been limited to minimizing the disturbing effects of government financial activities on the money market.

A recent change in the technical procedure for handling government funds in Canada has, however, eased the task of monetary management at the year-end. Previously, at each year-end the central bank had to buy large amounts of securities in the open market to offset the restrictive effects on cash reserves of the pre-Christmas drain of currency from the banks into circulation. But during the month of December, 1957, the Bank of Canada, instead of engaging in the usual open-market operations for the foregoing purpose, paid over to the Government, in instalments, its profits, which are required to be paid to the Government at the end of the year. These profits when transferred from the Government account with the Bank of Canada to the Government accounts with the chartered banks have the same effects on cash reserves as open-market operations. Bank of Canada, *Annual Report*, 1957, p. 29.

33. E. P. Neufeld, *Bank of Canada Operations: 1935-54*, Canadian Studies in Economics, No. 5 (Toronto, University of Toronto Press, 1955), pp. 45-6, briefly discusses the policy of *Einlagen-Politik* in Canada with the implication that it is a more active instrument of policy than I acknowledge it to be. In support of his contention he cites the views of W. C. Clark, quoted in *supra* n. 27, from which I draw a slightly different conclusion. Neufeld also gives a useful compilation for the division of government deposits between the Bank of Canada and the chartered banks (Appendix B, pp. 158-64), for the end of each month, 1935-54, along with

of a policy of *Einlagen-Politik* could be obtained, and all the limitations avoided, by the central bank carrying deposits with the commercial banks. These central-bank deposits could be manipulated in the same way as government deposits to serve monetary policy.

Consequences of Deposit Management

Until government deposits are treated less as an accounting variable and more as a policy variable, the major consequence of deposit management in the government sector will remain a disturbance in the cash reserves of the banking system. Hence, the cash-reserve effects of government budgets should be discussed under the heading of the consequences of deposit management; but the matter of alterations in cash reserves fits more conveniently into the discussion on central banking in the next chapter. This section, therefore, considers only the consequences of deposit management under a policy of *Einlagen-Politik* that completely eliminates cash-reserve effects.

Under such a policy government deposits with the central bank are stabilized, and all fluctuations in government balances occur in those held with the commercial banks. The effect of an unbalanced government budget is to produce a shift in deposits between the government sector and the private sector. Accordingly, an excess of government receipts over government outlays results in a shift in bank deposits from the public to the government on the books of the banking system: a deficit in the cash budget of the government results

---

monthly changes and percentages. Data such as this are difficult to interpret. When deposits at the two different types of depositories move in an opposite manner, the movement may represent a shift in public funds carried out for the purposes of monetary policy without regard to the budget position; it may, however, also represent the less ambitious use of leads and lags in meeting the financial needs of the government. Again, if the deposit movements are both in the same direction, the similarity may represent the skilful use of *Einlagen-Politik* to achieve a cash-reserve effect of a desired size; or it may represent the failure to stabilize completely government deposits at one place or the other when such stability might be called for. Furthermore, special transactions cause the government deposit with the Bank of Canada to fluctuate without inducing any corresponding change in government deposits with the chartered banks; paramount among these special transactions are purchases of new government securities by the Bank of Canada and the retirement of maturing government securities held by the Bank.

in a shift of bank deposits the other way. Because cash reserves remain constant under the circumstances postulated, bank deposits do not change in total: only the composition of that total between public and private ownership varies with alterations in the net budget position of the government.

A change in ownership of a given total of bank deposits within an economy is only of significance when the change covers groups of a radically different nature—as lenders and borrowers, savers and spenders. Even then it is the underlying transactions themselves, such as the lending and borrowing operations or the redistribution in incomes, that are of first importance, the shift in deposits being merely an accompanying consequence. Thus, in considering the economy *in toto*, a shift in deposits between the public and the government is of no great significance in itself if the government behaves much like any other unit in the economy.

However, when sectoring is introduced for the purpose of examining transactions between the sectors identified—as between national geographical areas or as between countries—a shift in deposits between sectors becomes more significant. (The discussions in Chapters Four and Five serve perhaps as an illustration of this statement.) It is self-evident then that what one sector gains by way of deposits from other sectors is a gain for it and a net loss for the others, and, as long as the sectors are treated separately, the net gains and losses are not cancelled out as they are when all sectors are consolidated and treated as a group.

Hence, when the government sector is considered apart from the rest of the economy, as in this chapter, for purposes of assessing the impact of its financial operations on the economy, shifts in deposits between the government and private sectors become important. A surplus in the government budget reduces the money supply of the private sector while a deficit increases it, even though the total money supply, including government deposits, may remain constant. These conclusions are valid whether or not the total money supply is defined to include government deposits with the banking system; the results stem from sectoring, not from definitions.

Sectoring is necessary for the purpose at hand and perhaps requires no further justification than that; but if further justification is sought, it may be found in the observation that the government sector reacts differently from the private sector to fluctuations in its cash position. The difference lies not so much in the administration of cash balances as in the treatment of spending and collection plans. A modern central government is unlikely to alter its spending plans in response to a change in its financial position in the same way as private spending units; nor is a central government apt to alter its tax rates and output of revenue-producing assets in response to fluctuations in its deposits. That is, non-structural or cyclical fluctuations in the cash position of a central government are not likely to prompt it to make correcting changes in its expenditure and receipt programmes.

Governments do react to changes in their cash positions, but that reaction is mainly in the form of asset and debt management. The nature and consequences of this reaction are considered later; for the present only the effect on the private sector of a change in the cash position of the government is dealt with.

The effect on the private sector of changes in government deposits with the banking system may be assessed in terms of the type of budget unbalance causing the deposit change. For this purpose both a deficit and a surplus are considered for two types of budgets: those that contain an income impulse and those that do not. The deficit is linked with an overall financial budget that contains or provides a positive income impulse, and it is assumed that over the period to which the observed deficit applies the effect of the impulse has worked itself out: that the equilibrium level of income has been achieved. In other words a portion of the income that prevails can be attributed to the influence of the budget. The analysis of a surplus is restricted to a budget containing a negative income impulse, the influence of which on the equilibrium level of income can be expressed as the amount by which income is reduced below what it would be if the budget contained no income impulse.

In all four cases (two with income impulses and two without) the main point of interest is the effect of changes in the money supply of the private sector caused by the observed deficit or surplus. Of particular interest is the change in money supply that is autonomous in the sense that the total of assets within the private sector is altered by the amount of the change. For autonomous changes in money supply there are no offsetting changes in holdings of other assets such as there are when money supply is altered by open-market operations. The autonomous change in money supply will be equivalent to the observed deficit or surplus when the non-financial *asset* transactions in the budget balance out. When these asset transactions do not balance out, a deficit in them causes a non-autonomous increase in money supply, for it raises money supply in the private sector by reducing holdings of other assets in the sector. Similarly, a surplus in asset transactions reduces money supply in the private sector but increases asset holdings by a like amount. In both cases total asset holdings remain unchanged. The more interesting changes in money supply are the autonomous ones so in what follows it is assumed that asset transactions in the budget cancel out. The effect of unbalanced asset transactions is analyzed separately, after autonomous changes in money supply have been considered.

Given an observed deficit in an overall financial budget which is making a positive contribution to the equilibrium level of income, the full consequence of the budget must be worked out in terms of its contribution to the level of income and to the increase in the money supply of the private sector. The addition to money supply is equivalent to the amount of the deficit and all of the addition is assumed to be autonomous.

The consequences of the increase in the money supply and the addition to total wealth caused by the deficit depend on arbitrary assumptions about how much of the additional money supply is absorbed into transactions balances.[34] When the increase in the money supply resulting from the deficit is insufficient for meeting the extra transactions demand for cash caused by the addition to incomes attributed to the budget, the situation is similar to that of income being expanded without a rise in the money supply: interest rates tend to rise and to check increased spending—the increase in the

34. Frank P. R. Brechling, "A Contribution to the Liquidity Preference Theory of Interest," Banca Nazionale del Lavoro, *Quarterly Review*, Dec. 1957, p. 431, who because of the arbitrary nature of the assumptions required does not incorporate into his analysis, which is at a higher level of abstraction and refinement than the analysis presented here, a change in the money supply caused by unbalanced government budgets.

money supply merely prevents the tendency from being as great as it otherwise would be.[35]

When the incomes attributable to a budget deficit do not absorb the entire increase in the money supply in transactions balances,[36] idle balances in the private sector tend to rise, reflecting initially an increase in the discretionary disposable wealth of the sector. Theories are not wanting to relate changes in money balances, liquid assets, or even total wealth, to changes in spending,[37] all of which would apply to the situation being considered. The free or discretionary cash balances, the liquidity, and the total wealth of the private sector are all increased as a result of a government deficit putting additional funds into the sector in excess of the needs for transactions balances; further spending is likely to be stimulated, independently of any effects produced through changes in interest rates.[38] There is, in short, a wealth effect that stimulates additional spending. The wealth effect takes hold because the initial recipients of the increment in

35. Laurence S. Ritter, "Some Monetary Aspects of Multiplier Theory and Fiscal Policy," *Review of Economic Studies*, *23* (1955–56), 127; Ralph Turvey, "Mr. Ritter on Monetary and Fiscal Policy," ibid., *24* (1956–57), 71. Mr. Ritter's analysis incorporates into the multiplier formulae changes in the money supply and interest rates; however his formulae indicate that, in his model, changes in the money supply affect income (spending) only through interest rates: he introduces no wealth effect, which, since it involves a change in spending propensities independent of interest rates, does not belong in his analysis. Mr. Turvey supplies some corrections and critical comments to Mr. Ritter's equations.

36. John Maynard Keynes, *The General Theory of Employment, Interest and Money*, p. 200, thought that an increase in the money supply caused by government expenditures would not be entirely absorbed into transactions and precautionary balances by the higher income emanating from a government deficit.

37. James Tobin, "Asset Holdings and Spending Decisions," *American Economic Review*, *42* (Papers and Proceedings, May 1952), 110–13, presents a concise summary of the various hypotheses relating spending to various concepts of asset holdings.

38. Laurence S. Ritter, "Functional Finance and the Banking System," *American Journal of Economics and Sociology*, *15* (July 1956), 401, mentions the possibility of a wealth effect caused by deficit financing, although he attributes to the autonomous increase in the money supply resulting from a deficit not only a wealth effect but also a liquidity effect. This seems an unnecessary and confusing distinction to make just to point out that the composition of the wealth-increase may also be important in determining the reaction of spending to increased wealth.

money balances, which for them represents an increase in their discretionary disposable wealth, distribute it in accordance with their preferences for goods, services, and liquidity, including different savings forms. Thus, the new disposable balances directly finance some additional spending on goods and services, and only a portion of them leaks away to be exchanged for real assets or securities, or to be held idle.

The additional spending generated by the wealth effect absorbs some more free cash into transactions balances and continues to do so until it works itself out. When all spending processes are completed, expenditures are higher, transactions balances larger, and asset prices higher because of the wealth effect than they would be simply as a result of an addition made to the level of income without an increase in money supply. Furthermore, some of the additional money supply flows into idle balances, to stay there or to be exchanged for real assets or securities, with the asset or security sellers, after satisfying their needs for transactions funds, becoming the final holders of the new idle balances. Since the increase in idle balances is measured after all needs for transactions cash have been met, the new idle balances are exchanged for real assets or securities purely on a speculative basis—these transactions in real assets and securities are over and above those already carried out in order to get additional transactions cash. In short, the increase in idle balances is relative to the existing supply of real assets and securities so that asset and security prices are forced up and interest rates down. This change in interest rates provides a separate influence in favour of expansion over and above that provided directly by the wealth effect.

The main consequence of an observed deficit in the overall budget of the government sector, which contains a positive income impulse, is an addition to incomes accompanied by an increase in the money supply of the private sector that helps meet the increased demand for transactions cash. If any of the additional money supply is left after the initial demand for transactions cash has been met, there is a wealth effect that tends to stimulate increased spending. This increased spending, however, is not likely to prevent the total of idle balances from rising. There is then a further effect on interest rates tending to lower them, which in turn stimulates further spending.

A deficit in a budget that provides no direct impulse for altering the level of income also produces an increase in the money supply of the private sector, but the increase takes place in circumstances different from those of the previous case. Here the government sector provides the private sector with an addition to its stock of money, and so total wealth, without contributing to the level of incomes in the sector. If none of the additional money is required for transactions balances, and none will be so required if the private sector is not expanding, idle balances are increased initially by the full amount of the increase in money supply. Hence, not only is there an absolute growth in disposable wealth, but also there is a tendency for interest rates to fall because of the accumulation of idle balances, some of which are acquired indirectly through an exchange of securities within the private sector. On two counts then, the deficit on a budget with a nil income impulse, by increasing the money supply in the private sector, sets in motion forces to expand the economy. It is only through these secondary monetary effects rather than through its fiscal effect that such a deficit has counter-cyclical influence; the fact of being a deficit is not in itself sufficient to give it any stimulating properties.

An observed surplus in a budget that contains an impulse which keeps income lower than it otherwise would be reduces the private money supply at the same time as it depresses the transactions demand for cash. When the transactions demand for cash is reduced by the same amount as the money supply, no secondary monetary repercussions are likely to follow from the deficit. When all the cash released from transactions balances is not eliminated, some remains for influencing interest rates in a downward direction. Although total wealth is reduced, it is not sufficiently reduced to offset the expansionary effects that the change in the composition of wealth has on interest rates. The negative effect of a straight reduction in total wealth is more than offset by a positive composition effect resulting from a shift of funds from transactions balances to idle balances.

The negative wealth effect asserts itself, however, when the amount of cash released from transactions balances by a reduced level of incomes is less than the amount by which the budget surplus reduces the money supply. In that event there is a further fall in expenditures, which draws idle funds into active circulation when expenditures do not fall enough to eliminate excess demand for transactions balances; interest rates then tend to rise. It is under these last-mentioned conditions that the surplus produces its strongest anti-inflationary effects.

A surplus in a budget that contains no income impulse simply draws funds from the private sector. If the private sector is not releasing funds from transactions balances, and it will not be if incomes are stable or rising, the reduction in the money supply of the sector will tend to raise interest rates. Furthermore, the reduction in total wealth within the private sector resulting directly from the reduction in the money supply has, aside from interest-rate considerations, an independent effect on total spending. Again, these secondary monetary consequences are the only contributions that a surplus in a budget without an income impulse makes towards deflation in the private sector.

It remains to analyze the consequences of a deficit or surplus on transactions in existing real assets between the government and private sectors. The unbalance in asset transactions may be as much the doing of the private sector as of the government sector so both possibilities must be considered. In both there is a shift of deposits between the government and private sectors, but the variation thus produced in the money supply of the private sector is not autonomous because it does not represent a corresponding fluctuation in the total wealth of the private sector. For example, a government surplus on capital account—still excluding debt operations—reduces the money supply of the private sector, but at the same time increases its holdings of non-monetary assets: private deposits are exchanged for government-owned assets. Likewise, a deficit on capital account increases the money supply in the private sector, but reduces holdings of other assets: government deposits are exchanged for privately-held assets. Therefore, the only direct monetary consequence of unbalance in the capital transactions of the government is a change in the composition of the wealth of the private sector that makes the sector either more or less liquid.

The main consequence of the change in wealth composition produced by net government transactions in asset items is of course price changes for the assets traded. Where the price-changing transactions are initiated by the government sector, the price changes themselves may react on the spending behaviour of the private sector.[39] But the change in the composition of wealth held in the private sector may be self-initiated: the sector takes the initiative in carrying out net capital transactions with the government sector. The change in asset prices cannot then be used to explain the changed behaviour of the private sector.[40]

The preceding discussion covers the consequences of government deposit management for the private sector when it is assumed that the government does not react in any way to fluctuations in its total deposits. No reaction by the government means primarily that the government does not engage in asset or debt operations in order to stabilize or modify the fluctuations in its deposits. Reaction by the government to changes in its cash balances is examined in the discussion of government asset and debt management that follows.

GOVERNMENT ASSET AND DEBT MANAGEMENT

Governments are unlikely to permit their deposits, either at the commercial banks or the central bank, to fluctuate without limit. There is, of course, a lower limit below which total government deposits cannot fall without impairing the financial operations of the government. Although there need be no upper limit for government deposits, central governments do seem to be generally reluctant to hold large or excessive balances—a reluctance that may spring from both accounting and political considerations. Whatever the reason, large government surpluses are seldom disposed of by being impounded in idle balances. It is at the upper and lower limits, admittedly flexible, for government deposits that asset and debt man-

39. Tobin, "Asset Holdings and Spending Decisions," pp. 122–3, feels that the composition of wealth makes itself felt on the level of spending through the structure of interest rates and asset prices rather than through its effect on the size of particular components in total wealth.

40. Ibid., p. 115, where it is argued that "an explanation of spending decisions must relate the spending of a household to determinants outside its control."

agement come into play to supplement ordinary deposit management. The nature of the asset and debt management that is prompted by fluctuations in government deposits must now be considered, and then the impact of asset and debt management is analyzed from the point of view of the banking system, of deficit financing, and of debt retirement.

The Nature of Asset and Debt Management

Asset and debt management within the government sector refer here to the manipulation of government accounts and outstanding debt in the course of administering to the financial needs of the government. Asset management is considered first, then debt management.

Asset management involves handling the non-deposit financial accounts of the government in accordance with the specific financial purposes for which the accounts are established. Two different types of accounts may be distinguished: general purpose or investment accounts, and special investment accounts.

General investment accounts are usually established for the purpose of stabilizing government deposits. Thus when a government has a temporary accumulation of funds for which it has no immediate need, it may use them to buy some of its existing securities to hold in a general investment account—a step it may take in lieu of adjusting its short-term debt. Then when government deposits are being depleted, the government may sell some securities from its investment account to replenish its deposits. The absorption of government securities by the investment account is a form of debt retirement, and the release of securities from the account is akin to new security issues.[41] At least the absorption and release of government securities in this way serve the same purpose as incurring new debt and retiring old debt: regulating the size of government deposits. When the investment-account technique is employed, the government can avoid, even temporarily, accumulating excess deposits, and can immediately counter any reduction in its balances. An investment account thus

41. Cf. Warren L. Smith, *Debt Management in the United States*, Joint Economic Committee: Study of Employment, Growth, and Price Levels: Study Paper No. 19 (Washington, Government Printing Office, 1960), pp. 40-2.

enables the government sector to carry out a form of compensating transactions in government securities.[42]

An investment account may also be used to influence cash reserves by introducing a lead or a lag effect into the fluctuations in government deposits that induce the government to carry out compensating transactions in securities—for example, securities may be bought in anticipation of a surplus or sold in anticipation of a deficit. Government purchases and sales of its own securities in the open market in this case have the same effect as open-market operations by the central bank. However, the operation of a general investment account by the government is designed primarily, not for monetary purposes, but for stabilizing government deposits.[43] The non-cash reserve effects of transactions by the account are then of more interest than are their cash-reserve effects; the former are similar to those stemming from deficit financing or from the use of government funds to retire debt, and so are covered by the subsequent discussion of those topics.

Special investment funds, in contrast to the general investment account, are less subject to discretionary control. The moneys accruing to them are generally specifically earmarked for that purpose, and their disbursement and investment are usually rigidly prescribed

42. The Government of Canada maintains a "securities investment account" that represents the investment of idle cash balances by the Government in its own securities. Canada, Parliament, House, Standing Committee on Banking and Commerce, *Proceedings*, 1954, pp. 144, 172.

43. There seems to be little intent in Canada for the Government to operate its securities investment account for purposes other than investing its surplus funds. In 1954 the Canadian Deputy Minister of Finance reported on the policy as follows: "We have . . . what is known as the securities investment account in which we invest from time to time part of the government cash balances. The securities investment account does not operate in any way with the intention of influencing the market. We merely employ idle funds by buying varying types of government bonds. The Bank of Canada acts as our agent in the acquisition and disposition of these. All we do is decide how much from time to time we should have in interest bearing securities rather than idle balances in the banks." Ibid., p. 172. Neufeld, *Bank of Canada Operations*, pp. 46, 114, mentions the securities investment account as a tool for attaining central-bank objectives and argues that the account has so been used. His discussion indicates that the operations of the account have in the past aided monetary policy in Canada, but the account appears to have done so only by functioning in the manner for which it was designed.

by enabling legislation. The funds are established for specific insurance or trust purposes—such as pension, annuity, and insurance payments[44]—and receipts in excess of current needs of the funds are usually not available to the government for general purposes, but, instead, must be invested in government securities. Since these special funds in general pay out—by way of ordinary disbursements and security purchases—to the private sector about as much as they collect from it, they have no cash-reserve effects unless their receipts and disbursements follow with a lag.[45] When they run a surplus, the operations of the special accounts are similar in their financial aspects to debt retirement, and therefore their impact on the private sector is considered under that topic.

As well as special and general investment funds, other miscellaneous accounts within the government sector may hold government securities.[46] But open-market purchases and sales of securities for these accounts are akin to debt issues and retirements, and their consequences come under the general discussion of debt operations.

As indicated, the general nature of asset management requires no more than carrying out transactions in outstanding government securities for certain specific financial purposes. Debt management, in contrast, deals with new and maturing issues and is closely affected by restraints imposed by the government budget and by monetary policy.[47]

The budget restraint on debt management operates through fluctuations in government deposits that alter the amount of government debt outstanding—that is, government deposits may be stabilized through destabilizing total debt outstanding by floating new issues in excess of retirements or by letting retirements exceed new issues. Variations in outstanding short-term debt, such as treasury bills, may

44. Some of the special funds operated by the Government of Canada are mentioned and discussed by Balls, "Budgetary and Fiscal Accounting in the Government of Canada," p. 133.

45. Cf. "Federal Investment Funds in the Money Market," Federal Reserve Bank of Kansas City, *Monthly Review*, Nov. 1956, p. 13.

46. A list of government accounts in Canada appears in Bank of Canada, *General Public Holdings of Certain Liquid Assets*, Research Memorandum (Ottawa, The Bank, 1953), p. 11.

47. Cf. Henry C. Murphy, "Debt Management," *Fiscal Policies and the American Economy*, Kenyon E. Poole, editor (New York, Prentice-Hall, Inc., 1951), p. 158.

be used to smooth out temporary fluctuations in government deposits; more permanent changes may be countered with operations in longer-term debt. In general, formal debt retirement follows any increase in deposits that proves to be more than temporary; and net new issues are likely to be made when working balances become permanently depleted, or have to be raised to a higher operating level as a result of a growth in transaction needs.

Monetary policy imposes restraints upon the methods or mechanics of debt retirements and new issues: because of their size these operations would create considerable disturbance in the cash reserves of the banking system if they were not checked in some way. Net new issues may be prevented from interfering with cash reserves, when this would conflict with monetary policy, by depositing the proceeds of the issues with the commercial banks until they are needed; they can then be drawn upon as expenditures are made so that cash reserves are not disturbed in any way by government borrowing to finance its expenditures. Where this *Einlagen-Politik* technique is not available to a government, the same end may be accomplished by having the central bank initially take up the new issue; then the central bank may dispose of the securities in the open market as the government spends the deposits created for it by the central bank.[48]

Debt retirement may also be combined with a policy of *Einlagen-Politik* so as to minimize the effects on cash reserves, or it may be handled by having the central bank and other government accounts acquire the maturing issues at the same time as the government is accumulating the debt-retirement funds in its deposits with the central bank. There are of course no cash-reserve effects under these conditions: at maturity date the retirement takes place mainly within the government sector as deposits and security holdings there are simultaneously cancelled.[49]

---

48. This, or something similar to it, appears to be the technique followed in the United Kingdom in handling new government issues. "Government Debt Policy and the Banking System," *Midland Bank Review* (London), Feb. 1958, p. 4; Great Britain, Chancellor of the Exchequer, Committee on the Working of the Monetary System, *Principal Memoranda of Evidence, 1,* 107–8.

49. This, too, is similar to the method of debt retirement followed in the United Kingdom. Ibid.

The disturbing effects of debt operations on cash reserves may not, or need not, of course, be offset. It becomes a matter of deliberate policy to let debt operations influence cash reserves, and manipulation of the total debt outstanding for this purpose is similar to open-market operations, which are discussed in the next chapter. Even when deprived of its effects on cash reserves, however, debt management may disturb the stability of the private sector. Its potentiality for disturbance is similar to that of government transactions in outstanding securities; hence, in the following discussion of debt management no distinction is made between dealings in new or maturing debt and outstanding debt. The subject is treated within a context that rules out cash-reserve effects, and from the following points of view: impact on the banking system, deficit financing, and debt retirement.

The Banking System and Debt Operations

Taking government debt operations to include all government transactions (excluding central-bank transactions) in its own securities, the impact of these operations on the banking system is now considered when the transactions are entered into directly with the banks. For purposes of this analysis, the security transactions that fall under debt operations may be separated into those involving debt retirement, refunding, new issues, and existing securities.

When bank-held government debt is retired with government deposits held with the banks, the initial effect is to reduce by equal amounts bank holdings of government securities and bank deposits. However, since there is no loss of cash reserves, the banks restore their cash-reserve ratio by replacing the matured government debt with other earning assets, and government deposits with private deposits. It does not necessarily follow, however, that these substitutions made possible and necessary by debt retirement favour loan expansion.[50] Debt retirement only favours loan expansion when the

---

50. Richard A. Musgrave, "Debt Management and Inflation," *Review of Economics and Statistics, 31* (Feb. 1949), 29n8, appears to consider a probable outcome of retiring debt held by the banks an expansion of bank loans that would otherwise not occur.

retired securities are either higher yielding than alternative loans, or the securities, prior to maturity, were disposable only at prices that made it unattractive for the banks to sell them in order to accommodate additional loans. Neither condition holds likely for maturing government securities. When the banks have profitable opportunities for expanding their loans, they will take advantage of them without waiting for government securities to be retired, as the analysis of Chapter Two on the subject of substituting loans for securities bears out. The only connection between loan expansion and debt retirement arises when the banks have already taken on more loans than their cash reserves can support; the retirement of some of the government securities held by the banks may then make it unnecessary for the banks to dispose of other earning assets to accommodate the additional loans. In general, however, retirement of bank-held securities will lead the banks to replace their lost earning assets with other securities, most probably government securities. Yields on government securities are thereby lowered, non-bank holdings of government securities reduced, and private deposits correspondingly increased. These conclusions are valid, of course, only when cash reserves are not affected by government debt retirement; the conclusions that apply when cash reserves are affected appear in the next chapter.

The situation is a little different when the government does not retire debt at maturity but refunds it instead. If the banks take the same share of the refunding issue as they held of the maturing issue, nothing is changed. When they take a smaller share it means that the non-bank public and the government must increase their holdings of government securities.

When the non-bank public increases its holdings of government securities under these conditions, government debt is, in effect, shifted from the banks to the rest of the private sector. As a result of this shift which takes place through the refunding issue, the banking public makes a net payment to the government, while the government makes a net payment to the banks. That is, the banking public takes more of the refunding issue than it previously held of the maturing issue and so must make a net payment for the difference; the banks buy less of the refunding issue than they had held of the maturing issue and so receive a net payment from the government. If all payments pass through the books of the banks, the result is a reduction in private deposits without a change in government deposits with the banks. The banks are affected in the same way as they are by debt retirement: their total deposits and holdings of government securities are both reduced. In the present case, however, the banks refrain from replacing a loss of government securities in their portfolios, indicating that they have already expanded into higher yielding assets, and that they are therefore letting their maturing debt run off to restore their cash-reserve ratios. In the final position, after the refunding operation has been completed, private deposits and government deposits with the banks are left at the same level as they were before the refunding process started. This same conclusion applies when all government receipts and payments pass through a central-bank account.

When the government sector increases its holdings of government securities because the banks do not replace all of their maturing securities with the refunding issue, a net payment must be made to the banks by the government. This may take the form of a reduction in government deposits with the banks or with the central bank. The former possibility is similar to what may occur when government debt held by the banks is retired; under the latter possibility cash reserves in the banking system are increased.

When a refunding issue is floated, the banks may take more of the issue than they held of the maturing issue. Government debt is then shifted from the non-banking public, and from the government sector to the banks. When the banks take a smaller share of the refunding issue, the banking effects are just the reverse of those analyzed. The action of the banks in this case is likely prompted by a fall in alternative investment and lending outlets that reduces their private deposits and creates a slack in their cash-reserve position.

Treasury bills, which are short-term government debt instruments regularly refunded, offer the greatest opportunity for producing a redistribution of government debt among the banks, government sector, and banking public. At each issue date for new treasury bills the banks have a limited opportunity for divesting themselves of government debt, and the central bank has an opportunity for influencing cash reserves by altering its share of the total bills held.[51]

Transactions between the government and the banks in existing government securities offer no complications. The banks only enter into these transactions in order to regulate their cash position: the transactions alter either cash reserves or government deposits with the banks, thus helping the banks to stabilize their cash-reserve ratios. The banks do not engage in security transactions with the government sector to any significant extent on the basis of price considerations; rather, they are mainly motivated to enter into such transactions by their need to carry out compensating transactions. Thus, bank loans and deposits are not directly affected by government operations in existing government debt, so long as the operations do not take on the characteristics of central-bank open-market operations. They may be indirectly affected by the impact government operations in the bond market have on security yields; the cost of converting securities into loans is thereby disturbed so that the loans-securities substitution possibility is altered.

The purchase of new government securities by the banks does not differ in effect from the purchase of existing government debt. So long as the government deposits the proceeds of security sales with the banks, the sales do no more than take up a slack in the cash position of the banks—if this were not so, the banks would not be the final holders of the new government issue.[52] The banks may take up a new government issue, however, even when they have no excess

51. This technique, as practiced in Canada, and the nature of Canadian Treasury bills, is discussed in Bank of Canada, *Annual Report*, 1956, pp. 46–8. A good short account of the use of treasury bills in the United States is "The Bill Market: Its Nature and Structure," Federal Reserve Bank of Philadelphia, *Business Review*, Sept. 1955, pp. 3–14. The Treasury-bill procedure in the United Kingdom, as it existed in 1955, is described in "How the Bill Tender Works," *The Economist* (London), June 11, 1955, pp. 953–5. More recent information is given by A. Rudd, "Changes in Lombard Street," *Bankers' Magazine*, Apr. 1957, pp. 316–19.

52. Thus it appears most unlikely that the government sale of public debt to the banks would result in a contraction of private debt held by the banks. The possibility that it would is mentioned by R. A. Musgrave, "Money, Liquidity and the Valuation of Assets," *Money, Trade, and Economic Growth: In Honor of John Henry Williams*, p. 234n31.

reserves, if the central bank undertakes to supply the banking system with the necessary supporting cash reserves. The central bank then buys a small amount of government securities to enable the banking system to buy a larger amount of new government securities.

The impact of government debt operations on the banking system is not great, especially when cash reserves are held constant throughout the operation. In what follows the banking system can be ignored, and the consequences of government transactions in securities on the private sector of the economy considered, without regard to banking effects, under the headings of deficit financing and debt retirement.

Deficit Financing

The connection between asset and debt management and deposit management is most clearly seen in the case of deficit financing. Large deficits that reduce government deposits below the minimum required for efficient operations raise a financing problem. There are three general solutions to this financing problem: to borrow from the central bank; to borrow from the commercial banks; to sell securities —either from existing holdings or by floating new issues. Borrowing within the government sector may be ignored for present purposes: it is the equivalent of deposit creation—the modern form of printing money, long a prerogative of governments. Borrowing from the banks may also be ignored for it differs in no way from selling securities to the banks, which already has been discussed. This leaves the sale of securities by the government to finance a deficit; and here it is only necessary to discuss sales to non-banks in the private sector.

The analysis of security sales to the private sector may be taken in two steps. First, their consequences are assessed when the sales are viewed as an isolated act; then their consequences are assessed when the combined operation of spending and financing is considered as a unit. When considered in isolation the security sales have a cash-reserve effect if the proceeds are paid into the central bank; however, when the financing is considered as but part of a combined operation, cash reserves are not affected. It is therefore best to treat the isolated case as minus cash-reserve effects, which can be done quite simply by assuming that the proceeds of the security sales are deposited by the government with the commercial banks.

M

Under these conditions a shift of bank deposits from the private sector to the government sector follows the sale of government securities. Consequently the private sector holds more government securities and fewer deposits than previously, indicating a change in the composition of assets held within the private sector that lowers the liquidity of the sector. Given stable preferences, the change is accompanied by rising interest rates and falling bond prices. The fall in bond prices stimulates the demand for bonds, mainly at the expense of idle balances, but partly at the expense of other goods and services.[53] Hence, expenditures on current production in the private sector are reduced. The rise in interest rates depresses capital values, and if spending is a function of the capital value of asset holdings,[54] there is a further tendency for expenditures to fall. The hypothesis seems valid. No one is encouraged to increase his spending by the fall in the market value of his assets, and those in whom the precautionary motive runs strong may well be prompted to reduce current expenditures in favour of increased savings. Lenders certainly lend less under falling bond prices, for at existing rates it is less profitable for them to substitute loans for securities. Thus, expenditures that depend on outside financing may be curtailed, although the main influence works to prevent an expansion in lending activities. And any spending that is directly a function of interest rates is lowered by the rise in rates.[55]

53. This is the contention of Earl R. Rolph, "Principles of Debt Management," p. 307.

54. This proposition is developed in some detail by Earl R. Rolph, *The Theory of Fiscal Economics*, Publications of the Bureau of Business and Economic Research, University of California (Berkley, University of California Press, 1954), Ch. 5, "Monetary Basis of Fiscal Theory," pp. 82–122. Don Patinkin, *Money, Interest, and Prices: An Integration of Monetary and Value Theory* (Evanston, Ill., Row, Peterson and Company, 1956), p. 205, makes the demand for commodities depend partly upon the real value of bond holdings in the private sector. Tobin, "Asset Holdings and Spending Decisions," p. 122, concludes his survey of the various hypotheses relating spending to asset holdings with the comment that "changes in the interest rate alter the real value of wealth and may affect spending by this route." Also cf. Franz Gehrels, "Government Debt as a Generator of Economic Growth," *Review of Economics and Statistics, 39* (May 1957), 183–4.

55. Rolph, "Principles of Debt Management," p. 306, rejects the approach that links debt changes to spending through the rate of interest.

In short, an increase in the amount of government debt held by the private sector decreases expenditures there, and is therefore deflationary.[56] But this deflationary impact of government borrowing must now be set off against the effect produced by the government deficit it finances. Deficits may arise in a number of ways but only three need be considered here to indicate the net impact of deficit financing on the private sector. These are deficits on budgets containing positive income impulses, and on those containing no impulse; and then there is the separate possibility that there may be a deficit in government transactions in real assets.

The effects of a budget deficit associated with a positive income impulse and financed by letting government deposits fall were analyzed in a previous section of this chapter. The probable effects include a higher level of incomes, an increase in the private money supply, a wealth effect, and more idle balances, all contributing to more spending and lower interest rates. The new element to be introduced into this situation now is the sale of securities by the government to restore government deposits to the pre-deficit level. If the restoration of government deposits takes place in the accounts from which withdrawals were made in financing the deficit, there is no net change in the cash reserves of the banking system.

The sale of securities works against the tendency for interest rates to fall as a result of the monetary effects of the deficit. Interest rates will not fall as far as they otherwise would, and could be inhibited from falling or even raised, depending on the extent to which the deficit adds to idle balances relative to the volume of security sales. Although the sale of securities eliminates the addition made to the money supply by the deficit, the increment added to the total wealth of the sector by the deficit remains unaltered in value. The form the

56. Rolph, "Principles of Debt Management," pp. 305–6, claims this conclusion follows from the elementary fact that the open-market sale of government securities by a central bank is deflationary. This is misleading for the more deflationary effects of open-market sales surely follow from their impact on cash reserves. Rolph's conclusion that an increase in government debt is deflationary does not, however, depend on any cash-reserve effect.

Abba P. Lerner, *Economics of Employment* (New York, McGraw-Hill Book Company, Inc., 1951), p. 132, also maintains that government borrowing, considered as an isolated act, is deflationary, because of the effect it has on interest rates.

wealth increment takes, however, is altered from a money to a security form by the security transactions. Nevertheless, the value of the previous stock of financial assets held is prevented from having as high a capital value as it would in the absence of the deficit-financing security sales, which have an upward effect on interest rates. Hence, there is both an interest-rate and wealth effect on expenditures to be offset against those produced by the deficit itself.

It seems unlikely that the expenditure-reducing effects of the increase in the government debt in the private sector would be as great as the expenditure-increasing effect initiated by the deficit. The two offsetting effects would balance under the following conditions: the sale of securities actually raises interest rates, more than offsetting the fall induced by the deficit; the resulting loss in capital values exactly compensates for the addition made to total wealth by the deficit; higher interest rates reduce income expenditures by the amount that the government budget contributes to income. It seems improbable that either condition would be realized or that any combination of these conditions would occur that would make the net effect of deficit financing neutral or deflationary.[57]

Therefore, a deficit, in a budget providing a positive income impulse, financed by security sales to the public remains an expansionary act; it is, of course, a less expansionary act than meeting a deficit from existing government deposits.[58] Furthermore, because a constant but continuing deficit causes a steady growth in the wealth—money supply and holdings of government securities—of the private sector, unless it is accompanied by a continuous fall in security prices that produces nullifying changes in capital values, the deficit generates increased expenditures long after the ordinary multiplier has spent its force.[59]

A deficit in a budget that contains no income impulse provides

57. Cf. Smith, *Debt Management in the United States*, pp. 113–14.

58. Gehrels, "Government Debt as a Generator of Economic Growth," p. 188, who incorporates government debt into the formula for the income multiplier, concludes that the existence of a wealth effect slows down the multiplier process and reduces the size of the final income change.

59. Ibid., pp. 186, 188. Cf. Walter S. Salant, "A Note on the Effects of a Changing Deficit," *Quarterly Journal of Economics*, 53 (Feb. 1939), 303–4.

only a favourable wealth effect, adding as it does to the total wealth of the private sector through its effect on the money supply there. The conversion of the increased wealth from a money to a debt form through the sale of securities by the government does not eliminate or reduce the wealth effect produced by the deficit. It does, however, tend to make interest rates higher, although the effect on interest rates of security sales in this case is probably weaker than in the previous one, for the level of idle balances is likely to be higher here, the level of income lower. Only if the financing of the deficit by the sale of securities raises security yields more than the deficit tends to reduce them is there a possibility that the deficit financing could be deflationary. The changes in capital values and any fall in expenditures resulting from the rise in interest rates must then overwhelm the positive effects of the addition to wealth made by the deficit. Such a drastic result seems improbable. The increase in the government debt occurs at a time when idle balances are increasing so that government security sales are more likely to inhibit an advantageous fall in interest rates than to cause a disadvantageous rise in them. Hence, the overall monetary effect of deficit financing remains slightly expansionary; it would be even more so if the government did not have to sell securities.

Every deficit that appears in government transactions in real assets does not produce a change in the total wealth of the private sector. It does, however, make that sector more liquid by changing the composition of its existing assets from non-financial assets to money. The sale of securities restores the composition of wealth in the private sector to a less liquid form. The first change in the composition of wealth raises the prices of the non-financial assets disposed of by the private sector, and may add to idle balances in that sector. If the latter happens, government security sales may not alter interest rates because more idle funds are now looking for securities. The market value of existing holdings of securities would then not fall. Even if the market value did fall, because interest rates are altered, the fall might quite easily be more than offset by the gain in market values of the non-financial assets raised in price by the deficit expenditures of the government. Hence, a deficit in the real-asset transactions of the government is at worst neutral; at best, slightly inflationary.

Debt Retirement

Budget surpluses pose a less pressing problem than do budget deficits; indeed, the only problem they raise is what to do with the increase in government deposits. The question arises when government deposits get conspicuously large, and generally results in the deposits being disposed of in some way. The only ways of disposing of excess deposits, without altering government spending and revenue plans on non-debt account, are to buy existing government securities or to retire outstanding debt. The adoption of either of these is referred to here simply as debt retirement.

The analysis of debt retirement, like that of deficit financing, may be confined to transactions with the non-bank private sector and dealt with in two steps—the first step taking security purchases as an isolated act, and the second step combining them with the act of accumulating the funds used to make the purchases.

Government purchases of securities from the private sector, paid for from government balances with the commercial banks, shift bank deposits from the government sector to the private sector without disturbing cash reserves. A rise in bond prices must take place, or a fall be prevented or moderated, in order to bring about the resulting change in the composition of the wealth of the private sector away from securities and towards deposits. According to the asset theory of spending, the rise in bond prices stimulates the demand for other goods and services and leads to increased spending. Spending theories based on the quantity of money and liquidity also lead to the foregoing conclusion that debt retirement increases expenditures. The fall in interest rates raises capital values so that, again on the asset theory of spending, an increase in spending is also encouraged. And any spending directly related to interest rates is of course stimulated by a reduction in rates. On all counts, then, a decrease in the amount of government debt in the hands of the private sector leads to increased expenditures there. Debt retirement of and by itself is expansionary.[60]

However, the expansionary effect of government security pur-

60. This is the conclusion reached by Rolph, "Principles of Debt Management," p. 306.

chases must be set against the deflationary effect of the accumulation of the purchase funds; only in this way can the net effect of the combined operation that makes up debt retirement be assessed. That assessment, as in the case of deficit financing, distinguishes three possibilities: a surplus on a budget that provides a negative income impulse; a surplus on a budget that provides no impulse; and, as a separate consideration, the qualifications caused when the surplus arises out of transactions in real assets.

The budget with a negative income impulse makes for lower incomes and expenditures in the private sector, and the surplus reduces the money supply of the sector by reducing its total wealth. The accumulation of debt-retirement funds is clearly deflationary in this case. Now debt-retirement restores the money supply of the private sector to its previous level, but only by reducing other assets in the hands of the public—total wealth is not thereby restored to its pre-surplus level, and the composition of its post-surplus level is altered. The security purchases are unlikely to provide any kind of direct positive income impulse, certainly no impulse of a size sufficient to offset the negative impulse of the budget itself.[61] Therefore, unless government security purchases, through changes in interest rates and capital values, can stimulate sufficient spending to offset the negative contribution of the budget to income, the net effect of debt retirement is deflationary. Offhand, it would appear that the effect on income of the budget should be stronger than the indirect effects of security purchases on expenditures.[62] Nevertheless, even though debt retirement may be, on balance, deflationary, it is still not so deflationary as doing nothing with the funds accumulated from an autonomous surplus.[63]

61. Cf. Alvin H. Hansen, "Comments (Symposium—How to Manage the National Debt)," *Review of Economics and Statistics, 31* (Feb. 1949), 30. Lawrence S. Ritter, "A Note on the Retirement of Public Debt During Inflation," *Journal of Finance, 6* (Mar. 1951), 67, gives a slightly different account of the process of debt retirement but does emphasize that the deflationary impact of debt retirement lies in the budget surplus that precedes it.

62. Cf. F. W. Paish, "Monetary Policy and the Control of the Postwar British Inflation," *United States Monetary Policy: Its Contribution to Prosperity without Inflation* (New York, The American Assembly, Columbia University, 1958), pp. 124–5.

63. Cf. Smith, *Debt Management in the United States*, pp. 114–15, who argues, however, that debt retirement in inflationary periods makes more difficult the task

A surplus on a budget that provides no income impulse is not associated with any budget effect on incomes and expenditures. The overall effect is restricted to a drop in the money supply and so in the total wealth of the private sector. This drain of money from the private sector, and the consequent reduction in private-sector wealth that it represents, is not directly reversed by government purchases of securities. Such purchases restore the money supply of the private sector by reducing its holdings of government securities. The impact of the negative wealth effect can only be countered through debt retirement by the effect this has on capital values and interest rates. The interest-rate effect is not likely to be very strong, however, for under the circumstances government security purchases may well work to prevent interest rates from rising rather than cause them to fall. So debt retirement in this situation may be deflationary, although the effect is undoubtedly mild since it only works through a reduction in total wealth.

A surplus in government transactions in real assets, considered in isolation, does not even produce a change in the total wealth of the private sector. The consequences of debt retirement in this situation are a fall in certain asset prices, because of net government sales of these assets to the private sector, and a rise in security prices, because of net government purchases effected through retiring debt. Clearly, the final result may be expansionary, deflationary, or neutral, and any disturbance is probably small.

These are some of the possibilities for debt retirement; a special case is provided by the operations of the various special investment funds maintained by the government. The impact of the investment activities of these funds is similar to that of a budget surplus used to retire debt. The analysis of debt retirement may therefore be applied to the operations of these funds.

---

of applying monetary restraint. The government is absorbing securities when banks and others, pressed hard by restrictive monetary policy, are selling securities to finance private spending. Debt retirement here may actually aid the monetary authorities for it may help prevent deterioration of the bond market without adding to the cash reserves of the banking system. If the government were not buying up debt, the monetary authorities might have to become reluctant buyers of securities to prevent bank selling from upsetting the market.

The receipts of these funds have all the characteristics of other government revenues: some represent non–income-reducing payments; some, autonomous income-reducing payments; and some, income-induced payments. The ordinary disbursements from these funds also range over the various types of government expenditures. When these disbursements fall short of receipts, and so produce a surplus that must be invested by the funds in government securities, the funds differ in their impact on the economy from that of the ordinary flow of funds through the government sector.[64] Indeed, when the investment of their surplus receipts is lagged, the funds resemble, in their effect on the economy, central-bank open-market operations, but only for a transitional period.[65] The investments of the funds may also be used to influence interest rates, but there seems little scope for utilizing them either for this purpose or for open-market operations.[66] Furthermore, since the funds most likely operate as perfect competitors in the securities markets—their security transactions not being large enough to disturb the market—their net withdrawals of money from the private sector, and their investment of it in government securities, which is similar to a debt-retirement operation, little disturb incomes and expenditures in the private sector.

The conclusion to this analysis of government asset and debt management is that when the central government reacts to fluctuations in its deposits by resorting to debt transactions, the initial impact of the ordinary financial transactions of the government is modified in varying degrees, depending on the circumstances surrounding the transactions. And this is so even when cash-reserve effects are ruled

64. It is therefore slightly misleading to suggest that the transactions of special investment funds are no different from the collection of taxes and the subsequent disbursement of the proceeds, as is implied by "Federal Investment Funds in the Money Market," Federal Reserve Bank of Kansas City, *Monthly Review*, Nov. 1956, p. 13.

65. Ibid., p. 15.

66. The limitations of using special investment funds in the United States for purposes of monetary policy are noted by W. N. Peach, "Treasury Investment Funds and Open-Market Operations," *Journal of Finance*, 6 (Mar. 1951), 51–2, and by Helen J. Cooke, "Marketable Issues of the United States Treasury," *The Treasury and the Money Market* (New York, Federal Reserve Bank of New York, May 1954), p. 31.

out. Indeed, the main effect of debt retirement or deficit financing, as it is defined here, is to modify the initial effects of budget surpluses and deficits on the private sector of the economy, but not to reverse them.

CONCLUSIONS

The financial operations of a central government not only may produce income effects in the private sector of the economy but also may in addition alter the money supply within the sector as well as the amount of cash reserves in the banking system. Where the fiscal transactions of the government alter the cash reserves of the banking system in accordance with the current needs of monetary policy, budget policy supplements monetary policy. When the government budget produces a cash-reserve effect not in accordance with the needs of monetary policy, the effect has to be corrected, perhaps even offset. The correction or offsetting may be carried out as part of the financial operations of the government. A suitable policy of *Einlagen-Politik*—moving government funds between the commercial banks and the central bank—may be employed for the purpose, or where this is not possible, the same results may be accomplished through asset and debt management.

When the cash-reserve effects of an unbalanced budget are eliminated through *Einlagen-Politik*, there still remains a deposit effect which affects the money supply in the private sector and thereby alters other variables as well. If the deposit effect as well as the cash-reserve effect of an unbalanced budget are eliminated through asset and debt management, the impact of the government budget on the private sector is less severe—but an impact of some sort remains.

Chapter Seven: CENTRAL BANKING[*]

The transactions of the central bank that bear directly on the position of the member banks[1] are the subject of this chapter. They include not only transactions between the member banks and the central bank but also those between the central bank and non-bank members of the private sector. These transactions are analyzed mainly within the context of open-market operations and bank-rate policy because these two aspects of central banking are of prime importance in influencing the activities of the member banks. Although administrative techniques are also important, they are not analyzed here because they do not give rise to transactions; and this study is concerned only with the economics of banking transactions. Transactions between the central government and the central bank and transactions in foreign exchange are excluded from this chapter, either because they do not directly affect the banking system or because they have been discussed in a previous chapter.

Hence, the core of this chapter is an analysis of open-market operations and bank-rate policy. Preceding the discussion of these, central banking is defined and the general nature of central-bank transactions examined. And the chapter ends with an analysis of the manner in which central banks may exercise control over a banking system.

---

1. The term "member bank" is taken from J. M. Keynes, *A Treatise on Money*, *1*, 9, who uses it to distinguish the commercial banks in a banking system in which there is also a central bank.

* See Postscript, p. x, regarding the original source of the material in this chapter.

THE NATURE OF CENTRAL BANKING

Defining a Central Bank

A central bank[2] is any banking institution that, if it holds cash reserves at all, permits its reserve ratio to fluctuate in order to influence the financial environment of the country in the national interest.[3] A central bank cannot therefore use profits as a guide for its behaviour; for if it carries reserves, it must carry more at one time than at another, thereby interfering with the maximization of its profits. Furthermore, acting as a central bank often calls for doing just the opposite of what other banks are doing: building up the reserve ratio when other banks are running theirs down, and reducing the reserve ratio when other banks are increasing theirs. Thus, the central bank is the bank that does not keep step, but which by breaking step may cause all other banks to change direction.

2. In 1829–30, in one of a series of lectures expounding the creed of the Saint-Simonians, the term "central bank" was used in the sense of a bank operating to control a banking system. The relevant passage is quoted in Charles Gide and Charles Rist, *A History of Economic Doctrines from the Time of the Physiocrats to the Present Day*, trans. R. Richards, 2nd English ed. (London, George G. Harrap and Company Ltd., 1948), p. 230n1. The idea expressed in the quotation given there is attributed to Barthélemy-Prosper Enfantin, *Le Producteur*, Vol. III, p. 385. This appears to be the first occurrence in the literature of the term "central bank." F. A. v. Hayek, "The Counter-Revolution of Science," *Economica*, *8* (May 1941), 145n1.

3. H. Parker Willis, "Central Banking," *Encyclopaedia of the Social Sciences* (New York, The Macmillan Company, 1930), *2*, 302, points out that the term "central banking" is of recent origin, not widely used before the beginning of the twentieth century. He adds that variations in meaning persist, but that general usage now limits the description "central" to "those banks which have a distinctly public purpose, that is, banks which transact business not primarily for the purpose of making profit but rather for the sake of the ulterior effects upon the money market and upon the banking structure in general." Also cf. idem, *The Theory and Practice of Central Banking* (New York, Harper & Brothers Publishers, 1936), pp. 5, 115; R. S. Sayers, *Central Banking After Bagehot* (Oxford, At the Clarendon Press, 1957), p. 1; M. H. de Kock, *Central Banking*, 3rd ed. (London, Staples Press Limited, 1954), p. 25.

A similar definition is put forward by C. A. Thanos, "The Definition of a Central Bank and Its Practical Implications," *Economia Internazionale*, *11* (Feb. 1958), 113.

To-day the central bank is the banking institution that does not keep any cash reserves at all, need not keep them because it is the source and creator of all banking reserves, and may conduct its affairs unrestricted by any cash-reserve requirement. Such an institution, however, is the central bank not because it need keep no reserves but because it acts to influence the financial environment in the national interest: it lets its deposits vary relative to its zero reserves. The distinguishing characteristic, then, of a central bank is the fluctuation that occurs in its liabilities to the public relative to its cash reserves, including the case of zero reserves. In other words, a central bank does not attempt to maximize its assets as do member banks.[4]

If the distinguishing characteristic of a member bank is its stable reserve ratio, the distinguishing characteristic of a central bank is its unstable reserve ratio.[5]

It is this difference in the behaviour or nature of the reserve ratio that sets a central bank apart from a member bank. Otherwise, to judge by their balance-sheets, central banks appear much like member banks.[6] Both have deposits and security holdings; both have capital and reserves. However, a central bank is not likely to have time deposits and a member bank is not likely to have note liabilities. If a central bank has any cash that cash will generally differ in kind from the cash held by member banks and a central bank will tend to hold much more cash relative to its liabilities than do the member banks. In addition, a central bank generally has fewer loans outstanding and is more liquid than member banks. Yet these minor accounting differences are not sufficient to turn a banking institution into a central bank. Unless the institution operates without regard to its reserve position, it is similar to other banks; for if it worked to a more or less stable reserve ratio, it would just expand and contract with the other banks.

---

4. Cf. Gordon W. McKinley, "The Federal Home Loan Bank System and the Control of Credit," *Journal of Finance*, *12* (Sept. 1957), 330, who points out that an institution which keeps fully invested does not exercise any control over credit.

5. Keynes, *Treatise*, *2*, 285, in noting points of contrast between member banks and a central bank lists as one the greater willingness of a central bank to vary its reserve ratio.

6. A. F. W. Plumptre, *Central Banking in the British Dominions*, p. 29.

So defined, the pre-1914 Bank of England was not a central bank. That institution stood apart from its contemporaries, in size, influence, function, and make-up, but in the crucial sphere of management it operated much as they did. Throughout the pre-1914 period the Bank was managed primarily with regard to its reserve; the main objective was the maximum economy of reserves—that is, the maximum banking profit consistent with the maintenance of the convertibility of its notes.[7] The aim of the Bank "was to keep its banking operations within the limits appropriate to its reserves;" whenever it acted in a given situation it "was guided not primarily by evidence of the state of business but by the state of the reserve."[8] It appears then that the Bank of England was managed much like any other bank attempting to regulate its reserves.[9] Of course being a large bank with special privileges it did feel it had some general responsibilities; it did have some awareness that it should not operate in the same way as other banks. But given this feeling that responsible management of any large and specially placed banking institution would tend to have, there apparently remained sufficient scope for profit-making to be the deciding influence in the affairs of the Bank.[10]

7. Jacob Viner, *Studies in the Theory of International Trade*, p. 270, who also notes (p. 254) that "the evidence available warrants the verdict that during the period from about 1800 to about 1860 the Bank of England almost continuously displayed an inexcusable degree of incompetence or unwillingness to fulfill the requirements which could reasonably be demanded of a central bank."

8. R. G. Hawtrey, *A Century of Bank Rate*, pp. 40, 64.

9. Walter Bagehot, *Lombard Street*, p. 36, maintained that the Bank of England was not managed like other banks because "they keep an altogether different kind and quantity of reserves;" this is not, however, a sufficient condition to make a banking institution a central bank. The credit policy of the Bank of England prior to 1914 was "directed mainly by the strength or otherwise of its reserves," and in this respect it differed in no way from the behaviour of other banks. Sir Cecil H. Kisch and W. A. Elkin, *Central Banks: A Study of the Constitutions of Banks of Issue, with an Analysis of Representative Charters*, 4th ed. (London, Macmillan and Co., Limited, 1932), p. 107, for the thought quoted in the foregoing sentence.

10. R. S. Sayers, "The Bank in the Gold Market, 1890–1914," *Papers in English Monetary History*, T. S. Ashton and R. S. Sayers, editors (Oxford, At the Clarendon Press, 1953), p. 145, notes that it was not until after World War I that the Bank of England obtained its reputation "of considering the public interest alone, to the entire exclusion of possible effects on its own profits."

Indeed, considering the philosophy of the nineteenth century gold standard it is doubtful if any banking institution could have operated as a central bank proper.[11]

However, it might be argued that a bank in reacting to its reserve proportion, or gold reserves, in a manner which helps correct the cyclical difficulties of its country, is performing in fact as a central bank, even though it is reacting mechanically to indices relevant to its own situation without regard for the national interest.[12] But the question is not whether what the so-called central banks of the nineteenth century did conformed to the general interest of their countries, but their motive. That self-interest serves the national interest is not enough to make a bank a central bank. Motive, then, is really what distinguishes a central bank from member banks.[13]

Central banking in the sense in which that term is now understood emerged only after 1919 when central banks began to depart "from that mechanical subservience to reserve proportions which had previously been supposed essential to the art of central banking."[14] Wider considerations than the state of the reserves began to influence central banks; the evolution was formally recognized, albeit hesi-

11. "According to nineteenth-century doctrine gold reserves governed credit policy. The duty of the central bank was to preserve the gold standard by maintaining convertibility of the currency into gold. . . . The tack might be described as the maintenance of adequate gold reserves." R. G. Hawtrey, *The Art of Central Banking*, p. 257.

Viner, *Studies*, pp. 393–5, lists four possible objectives that a central bank may pursue under a gold standard. All but one imply acting on the basis of reserves without regard to wider considerations of general business conditions. The exception is the objective of exploiting what possibilities there are under the gold standard for stabilizing the internal economy. However Viner notes that this objective "does not seem ever, at least during the nineteenth century, to have been a formally adopted and consistently applied aim of central bank policy" (p. 394).

12. This is the argument put forth by Joseph A. Schumpeter, *Business Cycles*, 2, 652.

13. In short, "a central bank is a bank exercising discretionary control over the banking system in the interests of economic stability." R. S. Sayers, "The Dilemma of Central Banking," *Journal of the Institute of Bankers* (London), June 1958, p. 161.

14. Hawtrey, *The Art of Central Banking*, pp. 208–9. Kisch and Elkin, *Central Banks*, pp. 107–8, note that in the 1920's other considerations than the amount of reserves held began to influence central-bank behaviour.

tantly and cautiously, in 1923 when the Federal Reserve System noted in its now famous report for that year the inadequacy of reserve ratios as guides to policy for central banking.[15] The modern central bank may be said to have been born in that year, and its growth and development were greatly assisted when Keynes and the Macmillan committee condemned central banking based on any concept of a reserve ratio.[16] The reserves of a country, which were formerly the exclusive concern of the central banking institution, are still an important fact for monetary policy; but they are removed from the banking sphere and relegated to a less influential position; at least other considerations as well as the reserves now serve to guide and influence monetary policy.

Thus, if the function of a central bank is to regulate and influence credit conditions, that function can be carried out by any large bank that is willing to alter its reserve ratio. No other qualifications are necessary for a banking institution wishing to serve as a central bank. Above all, it need not be a cash-creating institution—that is, an institution that issues legal tender notes and creates deposits which serve as the cash reserves of other banks. So long as it regulates its banking business primarily to take cash from other banks or to give cash to them when this means letting its own cash-reserve ratio fluctuate widely, it is a central bank. Simply by altering its loans and securities, the claimant to the role of central bank can, just as may an ordinary bank, expand its operations and lose cash to other banks, or it can contract and gain cash from them. Now this is exactly what an ordinary bank does, but there is a most important difference between doing this as a member bank and doing it as a central bank. The member bank expands its operations because it has excess cash and not because it wishes to augment the cash reserves of other banks; likewise, it contracts its operations in order to gain cash, but its main concern in doing so is to augment its own reserve position, not to influence other banks to contract.

15. United States, Federal Reserve Board, *Annual Report*, 1923, pp. 30, 38. Also cf. W. Randolph Burgess, *The Reserve Banks and the Money Market*, pp. 187–8.

16. Keynes, *Treatise*, 2, 262–3, 268, 272; Great Britain, Committee on Finance and Industry, *Report*, Cmd. 3897 (London, His Majesty's Stationery Office, 1931), p. 122.

There are certain obstacles in the way of a member bank trying to act as a central bank. So long as a bank has earning assets, it can dispose of them—reducing its loans and selling its securities—thereby gaining a favourable clearing balance with other banks and so influencing them to contract. But its influence is limited by its stock of earning assets. Likewise, an ordinary banking institution serving as a central bank may incur an unfavourable clearing balance with other banks by buying securities and increasing its loans to give other banks cash with which to expand. Here it runs into the limitation set by the size of its cash balances—the same limitation as is faced by central banks operating under an international metallic standard. However, these obstacles to a member bank serving as a central bank do not rule out the possibility; they merely place limits on the degree to which it can so serve.

When a central bank does no ordinary banking business, its loss or gain in the clearings is absolute. But when a central bank carries on a regular banking business, some of the cash it loses may return to it when other banks expand on the basis of the cash gained from the central bank. The expansionary influence of the central bank is thereby moderated for the time being; however, this scarcely constitutes an argument against a central bank doing ordinary banking business.[17] An ordinary bank may do a full banking business and still serve, within the limits already noted, as a central bank, so long as it is able to subordinate its ordinary business to the general credit conditions of the country.[18]

Since the main purpose of a central bank is to influence credit and monetary conditions within a country—not to control other banks, as is sometimes erroneously implied—a one-bank system in which the

17. If customer credits are relatively inflexible, however, so that they cannot be easily altered, they are not suitable business for an institution that wishes to act as a central bank.

18. Competition between a central bank and member banks for ordinary banking business need not be a source of friction between them. When the central bank takes business away from the member banks through aggressive competition for purposes of increasing cash reserves, the member banks are really being placed in a better position. Of course, when the member banks take business away from the central bank, the member banks may feel happier, but they will actually be worse off if their successful competition results in a loss of cash reserves.

lone bank acts as a central bank is not at all ludicrous or meaningless. A lone bank can, through its ordinary banking business, regulate its reserve ratio so as to expand its deposits relative to its cash when this appears to be in the interest of the country; it may likewise contract its deposits when this appears to be in the general interest.[19] Whether or not other banks exist is not important for central banking; if they do exist, the central bank then works through them and with them to influence credit conditions.

A central bank, in fact, usually has several unique attributes, none of which are essential to its function as a central bank; yet the attributes possessed by central banks are usually mistaken for the qualities necessary to the role. The attributes of a central bank may be stated as follows: creator of cash; bankers bank; government banker; lender of last resort; restricted commercial business; and public ownership or control.[20] Whether any of these attributes is really essential depends on how it is related to the fundamental requirements for a central bank, of size and a willingness to carry more idle cash than other banks, and to alter its cash ratio, quite drastically if necessary, in order to influence general credit conditions.

A central bank clearly does not need to be a cash-creating institution.[21] An institution that does not create cash but which carries the same kind of cash as other banks may still function as a central bank. Legal tender money may be provided by some separate entity that supplies both the member banks and the central bank. The central bank need not issue bank-notes at all, in that case; or if it does, it need not have the right of sole issue. Since bank-notes are only a substitute for deposits, a multiple note issue does not interfere with credit control by the central bank.

If a central bank need not be a cash-creating institution in order to function as a regulator of the monetary economy, it need not be

19. Cf. R. S. Sayers, *Central Banking in Undeveloped Countries*, Fiftieth Anniversary Commemoration Lectures (Cairo, National Bank of Egypt, 1956), pp. 7–8, who argues that central banks are universally necessary.

20. Cf. Great Britain, Committee on Finance and Industry, *Report*, p. 16; Plumptre, *Central Banking*, p. 15; S. N. Sen, *Central Banking in Undeveloped Money Markets*, pp. 1–2.

21. Willis, "Central Banking," p. 303, argues otherwise.

a bankers bank; that is it need not hold the reserve balances of the other banks.[22] Each bank would hold its own reserves:[23] either there would be no bank of final settlement, or the banks could arrange to maintain clearing funds at some accepted place other than at the central bank,[24] and the central bank could join them there. An ability to shift these clearing balances between the central bank and all the other banks is all that is required for central-banking purposes.[25]

Nor is there anything inherent in central banking that requires the institution exercising that function to be the government banker.[26]

22. Serving as a bankers bank in the past was not an uncommon function for otherwise ordinary banks; in the United States several banks through correspondent relationships acquired considerable balances from other banks in the nineteenth century and thus served as bankers banks. Lloyd W. Mints, *A History of Banking Theory in Great Britain and the United States*, p. 126. W. Stanley Jevons, *Money and the Mechanism of Exchange* (New York, Appleton and Co., 1875), p. 251, applied the term "bankers bank" to any bank appointed to hold the cash of other banks to permit debits between banks to be settled by means of bank credit instead of by cash payments.

Commercial banks in Portugal are not compelled to hold deposits with the central bank, although they must maintain reserves; as a matter of convenience, however, they keep part of their required reserves on deposit with the central bank to facilitate the clearing of cheques. H. W. Auburn (ed.), *Comparative Banking* (London, Waterlow & Sons Limited, 1960), p. 66.

23. Bagehot, *Lombard Street*, pp. 67–9, thought that the natural system of banking was one in which all banks carried their own reserves and that the single-reserve system only arose in England because of government intervention with the banking system.

24. This was the system that prevailed in Canada from 1927 to 1935 before there was a central bank. W. W. Duncan, "Clearing House," *The Canadian Banker*, *64* (Winter 1957), 150.

25. Hawtrey, *The Art of Central Banking*, p. 284, implies that any bank to which other banks entrust their reserves by that fact becomes a central bank; this is central banking by election, not by choice of the bank concerned. Sen, *Central Banking in Undeveloped Money Markets*, p. 3n2, severely criticizes the concept of bankers bank, claiming that the operation of central banks in undeveloped countries has been hampered by adherence to the concept.

26. Great Britain, Committee on Finance and Industry, *Report*, p. 16, argued that the central bank should be the government banker in order to prevent uneven flows of government expenditures and receipts from disrupting the money market. Hawtrey, *The Art of Central Banking*, p. 266, shows what a "palpable misconception" this is.

The role of lender of last resort is perhaps the attribute of a central bank considered most crucial for the proper performance of the central-banking function. According to this concept the central bank should always accommodate the money market when accommodation is not available elsewhere at any price; the role is thus an emergency one. However, the role as such is not an independent or separate function of a central bank in the true sense. Any banking institution that conducts its affairs so as to regulate the monetary environment in the best interest of the country will, as a natural part of its operations, be acting as a lender of last resort, accommodating the market in the interest of orderly conditions and in the interest of avoiding financial panics and crises. If the Bank of England had behaved as a true central bank in the nineteenth century, there would have been no need to frame the concept of lender of last resort; that concept would have been an inherent and indistinguishable part of the Bank's general policy, and but one of many operating rules.

Lastly, an institution may be a central bank whether it be privately- or publicly-owned or controlled; not the facts of ownership or control but the facts of behaviour are the determining conditions. If a privately-owned institution can ignore profits in order to regulate the financial system in the general interest, then a private banking institution can be a central bank. And if it has all the usual attributes of a central bank, it will be a profitable organization even though it is banned from maximizing its profits, for central banking under present conditions is highly profitable.

To argue that all the attributes usually possessed by a central bank are not necessary to turn a banking institution into a central bank is not to say that such attributes do not facilitate central-banking operations; all the attributes mentioned greatly ease the task of the central bank in regulating the monetary economy. Central banks today have all these attributes and may have additional rights and prerogatives that enhance their ability to function as central banks; yet to identify a central bank with the attributes it possesses is to overlook the essential nature of central banking, which is to regulate whatever banking business it does for the sole aim of furthering whatever seems best for the economy.

Central-Bank Transactions

Before considering how central banks behave so as to influence the monetary environment, it is useful to discuss briefly the nature and importance of central-bank transactions for monetary policy.

Central-bank transactions may be divided into domestic and foreign transactions, with domestic transactions further divided into transactions with non-bank members of the private sector who are not depositors of the central bank, transactions with member banks, transactions with the central government, and transactions with all others who are also depositors of the central bank.

Domestic transactions between the central bank and non-bank members of the private sector affect the domestic deposits of the central bank, just as the deposits of the member banks are affected by transactions with the general public. However, in the case of the central bank the deposits on its books that are affected are not usually those of the public with whom the transactions are carried out but rather the central-bank deposits of the member banks. The non-bank public, who are generally not depositors of the central bank, deposit cheques received from the central bank with a member bank which in turn deposits the cheques in its central-bank account; likewise, payments are made to the central bank by cheques drawn on deposits kept with the member banks which settle with the central bank by drawing upon their central-bank accounts.[27] Hence, the deposits of

27. In Canada the practice is for central-bank cheques coming into the hands of the banks and the member-bank cheques falling into the hands of the Bank of Canada to be exchanged generally at the nine cash clearing-house centres where the Bank of Canada has agencies. These clearing houses are central or cash clearing houses, so called because settlement among the members of each of these clearing houses is effected by means of entries on the books of the Bank of Canada. The Bank of Canada is a member of the clearing house at each cash-clearing centre where it has an agency, and like the other members, it has a net balance each banking day owing to the clearing house or a net balance due from it at each centre. The total amount owing to any one clearing house by the members at the end of a clearing is of course equal to the total amount due from the clearing house to other members. For all members other than the Bank of Canada, the amount owing to a central clearing house is deducted from their accounts with the Bank of Canada; the amount due from the clearing house to the members other than the Bank of Canada is settled by crediting the amounts to the members' accounts

the central bank are affected by its transactions with the general public, not directly, but indirectly through the medium of the member banks, who thereby have their cash reserves disturbed.

Domestic transactions between the central bank and the member banks are similar in their payment aspects to those carried out between the central bank and the general public. The main technical difference is that in this instance cheques are exchanged directly between the member banks and central bank as principals to the main transactions; central-bank deposits are then affected without any disturbance to the deposits on the books of the member banks.

Domestic transactions between the central bank and the government have the same general effects on the balance-sheet of the central bank as do its transactions with the general public or with the member banks. The total deposit liabilities of the central bank are generally affected, but in this case the specific deposit category is not a deposit account of a member bank but the deposit account of the government. Thus central-bank transactions with the government have no immediate effect on the cash reserves of the banking system. Nor do domestic transactions between the central bank and any other depositors it may have besides the government and member banks. These transactions too leave unaffected the central-bank deposits of the member banks. Of course, transactions between the other central-bank depositors and the member banks alter the distribution of a given total of central-bank deposits and so change the cash reserves of the banking system without the central bank being a part of the transactions.

---

with the Bank of Canada. The Bank of Canada makes the appropriate entries on its books as instructed by the central clearing houses. The settlement between the Bank of Canada and each central clearing house is automatically taken care of in the process; for when the Bank of Canada credits more to the accounts of the member banks than it debits them for, or vice versa, as a result of the daily clearings, it is automatically altering the total of its own deposit liabilities—and the amount of the alteration represents the indebtedness between the Bank of Canada and the clearing house. In short, when the Bank of Canada pays out more than it receives, or vice versa, it has an overall unfavourable or favourable clearing balance. Cf. A. B. Jamieson, *Chartered Banking in Canada*, pp. 342–3; The Canadian Bankers' Association, By-laws, Dec. 1956, Art. 24, Rule 12, with amendments to date supplied by the office of the Association, Montreal.

Foreign transactions (transactions in a foreign asset or liability, or both) of the central bank may be entered into with the same categories of customers as are domestic transactions. The foreign transactions may, like domestic transactions, affect the domestic deposit liabilities of the central bank; in which case they also affect its foreign assets or foreign profit-and-loss account. They may, however, affect the foreign liabilities of the central bank, in which case either its foreign assets or domestic assets may be affected. And when the transactions are with the member banks or the general public the likelihood is that domestic cash reserves are affected.

Profit-taking by a central bank has similar effects to that of member banks: deposits are altered. Thus, central-bank income reduces its deposits and central-bank expenses increase them. Since all but an insignificant amount of central-bank revenue is from interest earned on the government securities it holds,[28] central-bank profits reduce mainly government deposits. In contrast, central-bank expenses are incurred largely with non-bank members of the private sector—employees and suppliers. Hence, central-bank expenses increase mainly member-bank deposits at the central bank. Therefore, since most of its revenue comes by way of reductions in government deposits and most of its expenses show up as increases in member-bank deposits

28. In 1953 all but $87 thousand of the $54 million in income received by the Bank of Canada was earned from interest and discount. Canada, Parliament, House, Standing Committee on Banking and Commerce, *Proceedings: Decennial Revision of the Bank Act*, 1st Sess., 22nd Parl., 1954, Exhibit No. 1, p. 734, which classifies the income and expenses of the Bank of Canada for the years 1945–53. Similar data are not available for more recent years. Since all but an insignificant amount of the interest-earning assets held by the Bank of Canada are Government of Canada securities and since the lending business of the Bank is very small, its interest and discount income must represent almost entirely interest on Government securities. Cf. Bank of Canada, *Annual Report*, 1953, Statement of Assets and Liabilities, p. 20.

In the United States in 1956 the twelve Federal Reserve Banks had total current earnings of $596 million of which $572 million was earned on U.S. Government securities. Another $23 million was earned on loans to member banks. United States, Board of Governors of the Federal Reserve System, *Annual Report*, 1956, p. 80. Over the period 1914–50 about two-thirds of the total earnings of the Federal Reserve Banks have come from their holdings of U.S. Government securities. U.S. Congress, *Monetary Policy . . . Public Debt: Compendium*, Pt. 1, p. 315.

with the central bank, the profit-and-loss transactions of the central bank have a cash-reserve effect; that is, the process of profit-taking actually increases member-bank cash reserves even though total central-bank deposits are reduced.

The disposal of central-bank profits does not change this situation. Most of the profits are distributed to the government as owner or major shareholder. Government deposits with the central bank are thereby built up again, but not completely since net income is less than gross income—earned mainly from the government—and since not all net income is distributed as dividends to the government: permanent additions may be made to various inner reserves. None of these allocations affect cash reserves; they merely prevent the restoration of the total deposits of the central bank to their previous level. And the central bank, unlike member banks, does not automatically take steps to make good any reduction in its total deposits. In other words, the central bank does not attempt necessarily to expand its earning assets when it makes a net profit.

Nor does a central bank have to contract or take any steps when it operates at a loss instead of a profit. In the absence of institutional requirements to the contrary a central bank can operate at a loss indefinitely. It requires no financial aid, from the government or elsewhere, in order to do this. Losses simply expand the deposit liabilities of the central bank which can be balanced by a corresponding reduction in its capital accounts, or by an increase on the asset side in an account set up to register the deficit. Central banks are unlike ordinary firms in that losses do not normally drain cash from them and so make retrenchment necessary.

The policies that central banks may actually adopt in the management of their transactions can be discussed and analyzed under the headings of open-market operations and bank-rate.

OPEN-MARKET TRANSACTIONS

Open-market operations are to central banking what compensating transactions are to commercial banking. The subject is therefore a broad one and encroaches upon such topics as liquidity preference and policies of monetary control. In this part the general nature of

open-market transactions and their relationship to liquidity preference is considered; in the following part various open-market policies
are analyzed.

Open-Market Operations

Open-market operations may be defined in a very general way as
the acquisition or liquidation of marketable financial assets by the
central bank, on its own initiative or as a result of market forces,
which has an immediate effect on the cash reserves of the banking
system. The assets dealt in may be foreign exchange, government
securities, or other securities so long as the dealings in securities are of
the nature of investment transactions, and not of loan transactions,
carried out on an impersonal basis without regard to any consideration of customer-banker relations. This excludes all lending transactions, including repurchase agreements which represent the accommodation of particular customers. It also excludes all transactions that leave cash reserves unaffected, such as the investment of
foreign balances in foreign securities by the central bank, or the
purchase of securities from the government which results in an addition to government deposits carried with the central bank. The net
redemption by the issuer of securities held by the central bank,
whether or not it results in an increase in bank cash, is also excluded
by the foregoing definition of open-market operations because it corresponds to a repayment of a loan rather than to an investment
transaction by the central bank.

Open-market operations as defined may be carried out specifically
for their cash-reserve effects, or they may simply reflect the attempt
by the central bank to make markets for the assets dealt in. Transactions may be conducted in markets for existing assets or for issues
of new assets. If the latter, purchases must not be of the nature of
private placements, or be entered into with customers of the central
bank, for they do not then represent open-market operations as defined here. The refunding of an existing security issue part of which
is held by the central bank may involve the central bank in open-
market operations, voluntarily or involuntarily. If the central bank
does not take up any of the refunding issue, it engages in open-market
operations to the extent that customers of the banking system take

over the share of the issue previously held by the central bank. Cash reserves of the banking system are then increased as a result of the failure of the central bank to renew its holdings of the securities refunded. In general, any deviation between the share of the new issue and of the refunded issue held by the central bank represents open-market operations by the central bank. Variation may be partly involuntary if the central bank gets less of a refunding issue than it had bid for. This covers, in particular, the situation where the central bank is bidding for Treasury bills issued to refund existing bills: the bank may then find itself taking up more or less of the bills than it had planned. Zero open-market operations in this situation require the central bank to hold as much of the new issue as it held of the refunded issue.

The instruments most generally used in open-market transactions are government securities.[29] The market for these securities is generally an open market in the sense of not being formally organized, of being broad and competitive, and of being open to many buyers and sellers;[30] hence, central-bank transactions in the government-securities market are referred to as open-market operations even though only a very few buyers and sellers actually trade with the central bank.[31]

Open-market operations may be undertaken for the specific purposes of affecting the cash reserves of the banking system or interest rates. Open-market transactions that alter cash reserves change both the total assets and liabilities of the central bank; transactions designed to hold cash reserves constant are in the nature of sterilization

29. Cf. de Kock, *Central Banking*, pp. 182–3.

30. "Market," and "Open Market," *Encyclopedia of Banking and Finance*, comp. Glenn G. Munn and F. L. Garcia, 5th ed. (Cambridge, Mass., The Bankers' Publishing Company, 1949), pp. 385, 513.

31. In the early 1950's in the United States the open-market transactions of the Federal Reserve System were carried out with only ten dealers in government securities, including five banks. U.S. Congress, *Monetary Policy . . . Public Debt: Compendium*, Pt. 1, p. 623. In 1956 the number of dealers appears to have been seventeen of which still only five were banks. Robert V. Roosa, *Federal Reserve Operations in the Money and Government Securities Markets* (New York, Federal Reserve Bank of New York, 1956), pp. 28–9.

The names of these dealers, along with sketches of the non-bank dealers and some discussion of their method of operation, appear in "Dealings in Governments," *Business Week*, July 12, 1958, pp. 100–1, 103–4, 106, 108, 110.

operations: they offset the effects of independent changes in the accounts of the central bank that disturb cash reserves.

Open-market operations carried out to influence the structure of interest rates have the net effect of changing the composition of central-bank assets without changing the total: the central bank sells securities of one class and buys an equal amount of another.[32] There is no net effect on cash reserves from this type of transaction. This is not so when open-market operations are undertaken to influence the general level of security yields. The motive for such transactions is usually to moderate fluctuations in security yields, which means that the central bank usually has to buy when the market wants to sell, and vice versa. The transactions are then at the initiative of the market so that the central bank has no control over the volume of cash reserves.

Open-market operations that make bank-rate effective are generally considered as a separate category, but this is not a useful classification. Although there is a connection between central-bank loans and open-market operations, which is discussed later, open-market operations nevertheless constitute an independent policy weapon whose primary effect is on cash reserves and security yields; any reaction on central-bank loans is secondary.

As a weapon of monetary policy open-market operations have reached a state of full development only in the United Kingdom, the United States, and Canada: elsewhere their use is much more restricted.[33]

England is generally considered the birth-place of open-market operations because in the nineteenth century, especially prior to 1833,[34] the Bank of England used transactions in securities to adjust

32. These have been called switching operations; they have been carried out in Canada. Plumptre, *Central Banking*, p. 233. This type of open-market operations has also been conducted by the Bank of England. Great Britain, Committee on Finance and Industry, *Report*, p. 152, which also lists other types of open-market operations that the Bank of England has undertaken.

33. Peter G. Fousek, *Foreign Central Banking: The Instruments of Monetary Policy* (New York, Federal Reserve Bank of New York, Nov. 1957), p. 31.

34. Hawtrey, *A Century of Bank Rate*, p. 256; Viner, *Studies*, pp. 257–61. Charles Rist, *History of Monetary and Credit Theory: From John Law to the Present Day*, p. 313, says open-market operations were practiced in eighteenth century England and cites

its reserve position. Security transactions, however, do not seem to have been an important instrument of policy for the Bank in the nineteenth century;[35] they appear more like the compensating transactions of commercial banks than the open-market operations of a central bank. Security transactions by a banking institution only take on the characteristics of open-market operations in the modern sense when the transactions are carried out primarily not to regulate the reserve position of the transacting bank but to regulate the activities of other banking institutions; on this interpretation the Bank of England did not exercise open-market operations until the 1920's when these were first used for other purposes than regulating the reserves of the Bank.[36]

Deliberate use of open-market operations on a continuing basis as a means of influencing the general credit situation dates from 1923 when the policy was formulated by the monetary authorities of the United States. This was a real innovation in central-bank practice,[37]

Cantillon to prove his point. Richard Cantillon, *Essai sur la Nature du Commerce en Général* [London, 1755], edited with an English translation by Henry Higgs and reissued for the Royal Economic Society (London, Frank Cass and Company Ltd., 1959), pp. 321, 323, however, merely discusses the tactics of the Bank of England in buying up government stock at the request of a "Minister of State" in order to raise the price of the stock. Apparently these early transactions in securities were merely an attempt to manipulate the price of the securities for the benefit of the treasury.

35. Elmer Wood, *English Theories of Central Banking Control, 1819–1858: With Some Account of Contemporary Procedure*, pp. 5, 86–7, dates the origin of open-market operations in the modern sense of the word from about 1830 when the Bank of England begun buying government stock on its own initiative. He maintains that such open-market operations were never carried out on a very large scale and that the operations were not a very important instrument of policy.

Sir John Clapham, *The Bank of England: A History* (Cambridge, At the University Press, 1944), 2, 295–8, discusses the market operations of the Bank of England during the nineteenth century and shows that, although they were no novelty, they were not a frequent occurrence.

36. Cf. Keynes, *Treatise*, 2, 231.

37. Hawtrey, *A Century of Bank Rate*, p. 256, holds it was not an innovation, but he argues from the fact that the Bank of England engaged in security transactions in the nineteenth century. De Kock, *Central Banking*, pp. 180–1, traces the evolution of open-market operations prior to their complete adoption by the Federal Reserve

and it marks the origin of open-market operations as a genuine weapon of monetary policy. Security transactions by the Federal Reserve Banks commenced on a large scale in 1922 and were carried out for the purpose of providing the Banks with earning assets at a time when their loans to member banks were being repaid from the proceeds of the large gold inflows into the United States. In 1923 the policy was formulated that henceforth security transactions should be carried out with primary regard to the general credit situation.[38] And so open-market operations were born.

In Canada the central bank—the Bank of Canada—has been an active trader in government securities since its founding in 1935.[39] But its early activities as a trader seem to have been prompted more by the desire to develop and broaden the market for government securities than to actively engage in open-market operations. Furthermore, the easy-money policy of the 1930's required little more than accommodating the market when the market wanted to sell.[40] The practice adopted in May 1938 of submitting to the market a daily list of bids and offers on all issues that the Bank of Canada would trade[41] was merely a technique for accommodating the market. Under such an arrangement open-market operations depend entirely on the reaction to the daily lists of those with whom the central bank

System. Arthur I. Bloomfield, *Monetary Policy under the International Gold Standard: 1880–1914* (New York, Federal Reserve Bank of New York, 1959), pp. 45–6, found only a few examples of central banks, between 1880 and 1914, deliberately using open-market operations as an instrument of policy.

38. United States, Federal Reserve Board, *Annual Report*, 1923, pp. 11–16, 18. Keynes, *Treatise*, 2, 255, based his discussion of the evolution of open-market operations in the United States on this Report. Further details on the development of open-market operations in the United States are given in U.S. Congress, *Monetary Policy . . . Public Debt: Compendium*, Pt. 1, pp. 214–33, 279–93, Pt. 2, pp. 669–72. Also cf. the New York Clearing House Association, *The Federal Reserve Re-Examined* (New York, the Association, 1953), pp. 56–7.

39. Canada, Parliament, House, Standing Committee on Banking and Commerce, *Proceedings*, 1954, p. 13, evidence of the Governor of the Bank of Canada.

40. Cf. Sen, *Central Banking in Undeveloped Money Markets*, p. 67, who points out that it does not require a high state of financial development to carry out open-market operations when the market is in need of funds.

41. E. P. Neufeld, *Bank of Canada Operations, 1935–54*, p. 70. This procedure is now being used in West Germany. Fousek, *Foreign Central Banking*, p. 38.

trades. The interest stabilization policy of the 1940's further inhibited the full development of open-market operations in Canada;[42] but a step towards that fuller development was taken in January 1948 when the Bank of Canada ceased issuing its daily list of bids and offers, indicating that the securities market had become sufficiently active to make the technique of the daily list no longer necessary.[43] The date on which open-market operations finally came of age in Canada is perhaps October 17, 1950, when bank-rate was raised, from the rate set in 1944, thus marking the formal ending of the interest-stabilization policy of the 1940's.[44]

Open-market operations in Canada are still restricted by such considerations as developing the market for government securities and maintaining orderly conditions in that market,[45] but despite these restraints the Bank of Canada now has some scope for carrying out more than passive transactions in government securities. It can be more active in its regulation of the market and the banking system than previously.

As indicated earlier, open-market transactions are usually conducted by the central bank with only a few security dealers, including member banks.[46] Of course the banks and other dealers who trade securities in the same circle as the central bank do not necessarily trade in the securities market for the specific purpose of trading with

42. Cf. Neufeld, *Bank of Canada Operations*, pp. 101, 125.

43. Ibid., p. 70; Bank of Canada, *Annual Report*, 1947, p. 9.

44. Bank of Canada, *Annual Report*, 1950, pp. 12–13; Neufeld, *Bank of Canada Operations*, p. 125.

45. Bank of Canada, *Annual Report*, 1956, pp. 49, 52; Canada, Parliament, House, Standing Committee on Banking and Commerce, *Proceedings*, 1954, p. 13; idem, *Minutes of Proceedings and Evidence*, 3rd Sess., 22nd Parl., No. 10, May 22, 1956, p. 380.

46. During the 1950's only five banks in the United States were participating directly in the open-market operations of the Federal Reserve System. *Supra*, n. 31. In Canada, because of the small number—eight at present—all the banks may trade with the Bank of Canada; and in the United Kingdom all the London clearing banks probably transact security business with the Bank of England. Actually the Bank of England does not trade itself, but executes its operations through established brokers in the market. Hence, in particular transactions the market may not know until after the event whether or not it is trading with the central bank. Fousek, *Foreign Central Banking*, p. 35.

the central bank. The central bank is merely one trader in that market and the other traders in the routine of operating their securities business simply approach the central bank as a matter of course. That part of the market which deals with the central bank is then taking the initiative. However, the central bank may itself take the initiative and approach the dealers and banks with whom it trades. The technique then is for the central bank to get bids or offers from the dealers and to accept the best.[47]

The impact or extent of open-market operations depends on the immediate state of those traders linked with the central bank. It depends on their needs to buy and sell to adjust their own position or to meet the orders of their clients, or on the possibilities for influencing their clients to buy or sell. In the one instance the pressure for transactions is transmitted from the wider market to the inner circle enclosing the central bank; in the other, the pressure works out from the central bank through the inner circle to the wider market.

47. This is the method usually employed in the United States, where it is referred to as a "go-around," to effect open-market operations. On occasion, however, open-market operations may be carried out without making a go-around simply by accepting bids and offers volunteered by the market in the course of routine calls. Roosa, *Federal Reserve Operations*, p. 82; United States Congress, Joint Economic Committee, Subcommittee on Economic Stabilization, *Hearings*, 84th Cong., 2nd Sess., Dec. 10–11, 1956, p. 152.

In Canada open-market operations are more usually carried out by letting the market come to the Bank of Canada than by the Bank of Canada taking the initiative in approaching the market. This policy has been described by the Governor of the Bank of Canada as follows: "The central bank does not ordinarily take the initiative to increase or decrease the cash reserves of chartered banks. That is to say, it does not step out and bid for securities if it thinks an increase in cash reserves is desirable, or step out and offer securities in the market, if it thinks a decrease in cash reserves is desirable.

"At any rate, not usually. For the most part there are transactions going on in the market all the time. People are making offers to buy or to sell, and the central bank is usually in a position to be able to respond to offers to buy from others rather than to take the initiative to make offers itself." Canada, Parliament, House, Standing Committee on Banking and Commerce, *Minutes of Proceedings and Evidence*, 3rd Sess., 22nd Parl., No. 9, May 15, 1956, p. 349.

Some details on the method of conducting open-market operations in Canada appear in J. S. G. Wilson, "The Canadian Money Market Experiment," Banca Nazionale del Lavoro (Rome), *Quarterly Review*, Mar. 1958, pp. 42–3.

This pressure is exerted in either direction by inducing exchanges between securities and money. Thus, an exchange of securities and money takes place between the central bank and the private sector as a direct result of open-market operations. A further exchange of a like nature may take place between the member banks and the non-bank private sector if the banks undertake compensating transactions in securities as a result of the change in their cash reserves. The consequences of open-market operations depend largely on how these substitutions or exchanges between securities and money come about; since this is the subject matter of liquidity-preference theory, open-market policy can best be analyzed in terms of liquidity preference. Accordingly, a liquidity-preference model is developed in the following section for application to the analysis of open-market policy.

Open-Market Operations and Liquidity Preference

The concept of liquidity preference best serves for analyzing open-market operations when it is restricted to the non-bank private sector. The net assets of this sector consist of cash (currency plus bank deposits), government debt, and real assets. All its financial liabilities, except bank loans, are internal to the sector and so cancel out.[48] When bank loans are held constant along with the amount and attractiveness of real assets and the transactions demand for cash, the preference of the private sector for holding its remaining wealth in the form of cash (idle balances) and government debt represents liquidity preference.

For an individual this liquidity preference for idle balances and government debt can be represented by a system of indifference curves referred to a pair of axes along which idle balances are measured in one positive direction and the number of government bonds in the other positive direction. The indifference curves will be convexed to the origin of these axes because idle balances and govern-

48. Ralph Turvey, "Consistency and Consolidation in the Theory of Interest," *Economica*, 21 (Nov. 1954), 302–5, who discusses the type of sectoring necessary for applying a simple liquidity-preference theory of interest to the non-bank private sector. The cancellation of private debt other than bank loans implies there is no borrowing from the government sector.

ment bonds are not perfect substitutes for each other.[49] That is, the more idle balances an individual has the less willing he is to give up bonds for still more idle balances; and the more bonds he holds the less willing he is likely to be to acquire still more bonds by reducing his idle balances.[50] Speculative and precautionary motives are perhaps sufficient to explain this foregoing relationship between bond holdings and idle balances.[51]

Given the amount of wealth the individual has to divide between idle balances and government bonds—all his other propensities and spending plans being fixed—the division of that wealth between bonds and balances will depend on his liquidity preference, as reflected by his indifference curves, and on the price of bonds.

The possible choices may be illustrated by interposing a straight line on the liquidity-preference map for bonds and balances to make a positive intercept with the idle-balance axis for the amount of idle balances the individual could hold if all his liquidity-preference wealth was held in that form, and a positive intercept on the bond-axis for the amount of bonds he could hold if all his liquidity-preference wealth was put into government bonds at the given bond price. One such line is SL in Figure 4 (p. 368) which shows two indifference curves of an individual for idle balances and bonds. This line may be called

49. Earl R. Rolph, "Principles of Debt Management," *American Economic Review*, 47 (June 1957), 307, argues that government debt and cash are not perfect substitutes because "people do not shift altogether out of holding cash and into holding debt as the result of a slight reduction in the prices of debt. Rather they are found to hold both debt and cash in the face of large variations in the prices of debt."

50. Cf. Frank P. R. Brechling, "A Note on Bond-Holding and the Liquidity Preference Theory of Interest," *Review of Economic Studies*, 24 (June 1957), 190.

51. The speculative motive alone is not sufficient to explain the convexity of the curves, however. If people's expectations about the course of bond prices alone determined their preferences for cash and bonds, they would be found to be holding either bonds or cash exclusively, but not both together. Borjie Kragh, "The Meaning and Use of Liquidity Curves in Keynesian Interest Theory," *International Economic Papers*, No. 5 (1955), pp. 161–2. Richard M. Davis, "A Re-examination of the Speculative Demand for Money," *Quarterly Journal of Economics*, 73 (May 1959), 327–38, argues that in the absence of certainty there will be a range of expected prices for bonds which results in varying combinations of bonds and balances being held at different current prices.

N

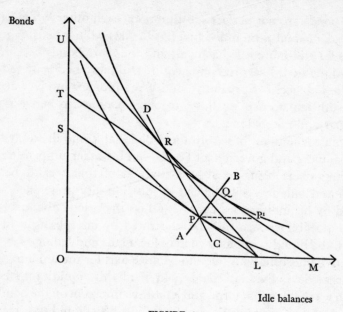

FIGURE 4

LIQUIDITY PREFERENCE MAP FOR BONDS AND BALANCES

a wealth-restraint line, the slope of which reflects the given price for bonds. For the wealth-restraint line SL in Figure 4 the price for bonds is given by the inverse of the slope SL.[52] At that price and for the given wealth-restraint, the combination of idle balances and bonds the individual desires to hold is represented by the point P.

Given the preference of the individual for bonds and balances (that is, given a stable set of indifference curves), a change in his expenditures for real assets, or a change in his demand for transactions cash, shifts the wealth-restraint line without changing its slope. Thus, an increase in the funds allotted to satisfying the preference for bonds and idle balances is allocated between the two in the proportion indicated by the point of tangency of the wealth line with an indifference curve. A withdrawal of wealth from this preference map is at the expense of both bonds and idle balances, preferences unchanged, and proceeds according to the wealth isocline—the locus

52. Cf. Davis, "A Re-examination of the Speculative Demand for Money," p. 329.

of all points of tangency between the indifference curves and a shifting wealth-restraint line of a given slope. These possibilities are illustrated in Figure 4 where TM is another wealth-restraint line and AB, which passes through the tangency points P and Q, is a wealth isocline.

A demand curve for bonds may be derived from the preference map for balances and bonds in the standard manner by letting the wealth-restraint line rotate through the various price ranges for government bonds. In Figure 4 the wealth-restraint line SL, rotated by using the point L as pivot, traces out a demand curve for bonds, a segment of which is shown as CD in the figure. As with the demand for commodities, a change in the price of bonds produces both a substitution effect and a wealth effect.[53] Thus, when the price of bonds falls from that reflected in the slope of SL to the lower price reflected by the slope of LU, the wealth effect is measured by the movement from P to Q, and the substitution effect by the movement from Q to R.

The substitution effect simply reflects the fact that bonds are substituted for idle balances when bond prices fall, and that idle balances

53. Brechling, "A Note on Bond-Holding and the Liquidity Preference Theory of Interest," pp. 190-1, discusses the wealth effect and the substitution effect associated with the demand curve for bonds, and points out how they correspond to the substitution effect and income effect in the general theory of the demand for goods. He does not, however, derive his demand curves for bonds and money from indifference curves, and his interpretation of his demand curves is slightly confusing because he maintains that they are drawn on the assumption of constant wealth (p. 195) whereas they do take into account the wealth effect resulting from a change in bond prices (p. 191n4). The confusion arises because there are two wealth effects—one arising from a change in total real wealth (due to a change in savings, say), and one arising from a change in the price of assets. This is similar to the two income effects in ordinary demand theory, in which one is incorporated into the demand curve and the other is not. Cf. Milton Friedman, "The Marshallian Demand Curve," *Essays in Positive Economics* (Chicago, The University of Chicago Press, 1953), pp. 63-4, reprinted from the *Journal of Political Economy, 57* (Dec. 1949), 463-95.

Mr. Brechling also deals with the substitution effect and wealth effect in the demand for bonds in "A Contribution to the Liquidity Preference Theory of Interest," Banca Nazionale del Lavoro, *Quarterly Review*, Dec. 1957, p. 425. (This second article is a further development of his first, not only covering the same ground but also adding other material.)

are substituted for bonds when bond prices rise. The wealth effect means that with a fall in bond prices the individual can acquire more bonds with his given allotment of funds, and so becomes better off in terms of interest-income earned. The fall in the capital values of his existing holdings of bonds does not directly influence his transactions in bonds because he is holding them as a store of wealth, not as a means of payment. The fall in capital values may, however, cause him to reduce his expenditures, thereby freeing some cash from transactions duties and thus pushing his wealth restraint line outward.

From the demand curve for bonds derived in the foregoing manner, it is a simple matter to calculate for each rate of interest the amount of idle balances the individual will be holding at that rate.[54] In this way a demand curve for idle balances may be derived in terms of a rate of interest; this is the curve that is sometimes referred to as the liquidity-preference curve. The significant feature of this curve is that the number of bonds varies along it so that an increase in the amount of idle balances demanded, as reflected by a movement along the curve, means a reduction in the number of bonds held, and vice versa.[55]

The community demand curve for idle balances within the non-bank private sector has the same properties as the individual demand curve. The *ceteris paribus* clause associated with the former must impound the following: asset preferences; the distribution of wealth within the private sector; the composition of the government debt held by the private sector, although the total may vary, so that one interest rate remains representative; the amount and attractiveness of real assets; bank loans to the private sector; and the non-asset spending of the private sector, or else the transactions demand for

54. The rate of interest may be derived from Figure 4 by multiplying the slope of any wealth-restraint line with the annual amount of contractual interest paid on the bonds held. Cf. Davis, "A Re-examination of the Speculative Demand for Money," p. 328.

55. This follows from the manner in which the curve was derived from the indifference map. The customary interpretation of the demand curve for any good does not hold the quantities of other goods constant, but lets them vary for different points on the demand curve. Cf. Friedman, "The Marshallian Demand Curve," pp. 49–50.

cash.[56] But these conditions are sufficient to define a unique set of market-behaviour curves for the private sector which are similar in shape and function to the indifference curves expressing the preference of an individual for idle balances and government securities.[57] Each market-behaviour curve helps determine the proportion in which a constant total real wealth (in bonds and idle balances) will be divided between bonds and idle balances at each bond price.

Associated with each community demand curve for idle balances is a unique set of market-behaviour curves reflecting the community choice for idle balances and government securities. A change in interest-rate expectations or in non-speculative preferences shifts these behaviour curves and so alters the demand curve based on them.[58] If this change in preference occurs when neither the amount of idle balances nor the number of bonds in the private sector is being altered, a change in interest rates must nevertheless follow; the wealth restraint line must rotate so as to remain tangent to the be-

56. All these conditions are specified by Turvey, "Consistency and Consolidation in the Theory of Interest," pp. 301, 303–5, who gives them as the conditions necessary to identify a demand curve for money in a simple scatter diagram for cash and a rate of interest.

57. James Edward Meade, *A Geometry of International Trade* (London, George Allen and Unwin Ltd., 1952), p. 9n, states that a unique set of community market-behaviour curves exists for any two goods whose relative prices depend only on the total amounts of the two goods available on the market for consumption; he credits Mr. Turvey for pointing out this condition.

The market behaviour curves are similar to community indifference curves; but since they do not purport to measure welfare, they get around the difficulty that makes it impossible to draw a unique set of community indifference curves. Tibor de Scitovszky, "A Reconsideration of the Theory of Tariffs," *Readings in the Theory of International Trade* (Philadelphia, The Blakiston Company, 1949), p. 366n10, reprinted from the *Review of Economic Studies*, 9 (1942), 89–110.

58. Price changes for securities do not alter the behaviour curves because, for a given set of curves, expectations are assumed as given; price changes only have an effect on the curves if they change expectations, but this possibility is ruled out by assuming constant expectations. The connection between price changes and shifts in preference curves is briefly discussed by Kenneth Boulding, *A Reconstruction of Economics*, pp. 82–3. Constant expectations is one of the *ceteris paribus* items that Turvey, "Consistency and Consolidation in the Theory of Interest," p. 304, appears to postulate as necessary for the derivation of a stable liquidity-preference function.

haviour curve passing through that point representing the fixed combination of bonds and idle balances held.[59] If the amount of idle
balances is altered at the same time as preferences change, there may
be no need for the price line to change its slope; it is shifted to a new
position and at the final combination of idle balances and bonds held
it may be tangent to the behaviour curve passing through that
point.[60]

The community wealth-restraint line may be shifted by a change
in expenditure plans that releases or absorbs funds for transactions
purposes. But a community itself can only alter the amount of its idle
balances by shifting them between the active and the inactive sphere.
It cannot alter by itself its total holdings of government securities—
these are fixed for it. Thus, a shift of the community wealth-restraint

---

59. This supports the conclusion that "shifts in people's preferences about the
mere *form* in which they want to hold their savings can make interest rates change,
even though the propensity to save and the attractiveness of investment remain
unchanged." Leland B. Yeager, "Interest Rates and Total Spending," *Southern
Economic Journal*, *24* (Jan. 1958), 289.

It also covers the similar point made by J. M. Keynes, *The General Theory of
Employment, Interest, and Money*, p. 198. He argued that when an item of news
affects everyone's expectations about interest rates "in precisely the same way, the
rate of interest . . . will be adjusted forthwith to the new situation without any
market transactions being necessary.

"Thus, in the simplest case, where everyone is similar and similarly placed, a
change in circumstances or expectations will not be capable of causing any displacement of money whatever;—it will simply change the rate of interest in
whatever degree is necessary to offset the desire of each individual, felt at the
previous rate, to change his holding of cash in response to the new circumstances
or expectations; and, since everyone will change his ideas as to the rate which
would induce him to alter his holdings of cash in the same degree, no transactions
will result."

60. This represents the situation where individuals who hold their liquidity-
preference wealth exclusively in the form of idle balances decide to alter their
total wealth holdings, and where other individuals who hold both idle balances and
bonds alter their preferences for the two by adjusting their total wealth through
a transfer of balances between the active and inactive spheres. The amount of idle
balances can then be altered without affecting interest rates. Cf. Dennis H.
Robertson, "Mr. Keynes and the Rate of Interest," *Readings in the Theory of Income
Distribution* (Philadelphia, The Blakiston Company, 1946), pp. 445–6, reprinted
from *Essays in Monetary Theory* (London, P. S. King and Son, Ltd., 1940), pp. 1–38.

curve—because of a shift between active and inactive balances—that occurs without a change in community preference for bonds and idle balances usually alters the slope of the wealth-restraint line—that is, the bond price.

For example, if Figure 4 is interpreted as holding for a community rather than for an individual, a shift in the community wealth-restraint line from SL to TM, caused by the community reducing transactions balances to add to idle balances, enables the community to move only from P to P^1 on TM. At P^1 the number of bonds held is the same as at P. Since P^1 represents the new equilibrium combination of idle balances and bonds held by the community, the slope of the wealth-restraint line, TM, must alter until it is tangent to the behaviour curve passing through P^1.

In other words, the community, unlike the individual, cannot divide a given increment to its liquidity-preference wealth between balances and bonds, nor withdraw funds by partly drawing on existing balances and partly liquidating securities; all net additions or withdrawals must be reflected entirely in idle balances. The public by attempting to liquidate securities and withdraw idle balances only succeeds in altering the ratio of idle balances to securities held within the private sector; and with constant preferences the ratio can only be altered by changing the bond price. Therefore the community in which liquidity preference remains constant cannot shift its wealth-restraint curve without altering its slope.

The only way in which the community can alter its holdings of government debt is to trade with the banks or the public sector. With everything else constant, such trading takes place along the community offer curve for money and bonds. In Figure 4 a community offer curve can be represented by CD. Along that curve bonds and cash exchange for each other at varying bond prices. Through such an exchange the amount of security holdings and idle balances in the private sector is altered, and the community demand curve shows the relationship traced out between the amount of idle balances held in the private sector and the rate of interest.[61] Thus, the private sector

61. Because the community demand curve for money reflects an exchange between securities and idle balances carried out between the non-bank private sector and the banking system, the curve does not become flat for some critically

may alter its ratio of idle balances to bond holdings not only by shifting funds between active and inactive balances but also by trading with the banks or the public sector. However, transactions with the banks and the public sector disturb the bond price more than does a shift of similar magnitude between active and inactive balances.[62]

---

low rate of interest; the community gives up securities for idle balances as the rate of interest falls, and continues to do so as long as it has securities to sell. When its supply of securities is exhausted, its demand curve for money stops or ends at that point. Cf. Kragh, "The Meaning and Use of Liquidity Curves in Keynesian Interest Theory," p. 158, who also concludes that the demand curve for idle balances comes to a stop when the private sector no longer holds bonds. A more detailed argument against the demand curve becoming flat is given by Don Patinkin, *Money, Interest, and Prices: An Integration of Monetary and Value Theory*, pp. 146–9.

The kind of community-preference map that exists when the community does reduce its holdings of bonds to zero for some minimum rate of interest is derived by R. C. O. Matthews, "Liquidity Preference and the Multiplier," *Economica, 28* (Feb. 1961), 38–9. He shows that the preference curves must be parallel to each other in a vertical direction when bonds are measured along the vertical axis. Then, for the same money balances all the curves have the same slope. Furthermore, the curves must become straight lines when they acquire the slope which corresponds to the slope of the wealth-restraint line at the minimum interest rate for which bonds are given up entirely. All points of tangency or contact with the highest behaviour curve that can be reached, traced out by the wealth-restraint line for lower rates of interest, then fall on the pivotal point on the money axis around which the wealth-restraint line rotates.

62. This conclusion follows from the geometry of the market behaviour curves. A given increase in idle balances caused by a shift of funds from transactions balances does not alter the number of bonds held by the community. Therefore, a higher behaviour curve is reached on the preference map for bonds and idle balances when idle balances are increased by reducing transactions balances than is reached when idle balances are increased by selling securities to the banking system. The higher the behaviour curve the less its slope is likely to be with reference to the securities axis, given the amount of idle balances. And since this slope represents the bond price, it follows that the less the slope the lower the bond price. Hence, an increase in idle balances effected through open-market operations leads to a point on the preference map for bonds and idle balances where the slope representing bond prices is larger than at the point that would be reached by a similar increase in idle balances effected by reducing transactions balances. Therefore, open-market operations disturb the bond price more. The same conclusion is

OPEN-MARKET POLICIES

The foregoing discussion of the community demand curve for money and of the community behaviour curves associated with the demand curve can now be applied to assessing the consequences and effects of open-market policies adopted by central banks. For this purpose open-market policies may be classified as initiating, accommodating, and refraining. These are purely expository distinctions, because any particular open-market policy is apt to represent a mixture of central-bank reactions. That is, a policy of one class may serve the needs of other policy classes at the same time. For example, an open-market policy that is accommodating may also at the same time be fulfilling the role of an initiating policy. However, the three-fold classification adopted here does provide a useful division of the analysis of open-market policy. In what follows the consequences and effectiveness of open-market operations are discussed on the assumption that member banks are unable to offset or nullify the cash-reserve effects of the open-market operations. This is the traditional approach which assumes that where open-market operations alter the cash reserves of the banking system a multiple contraction or expansion of bank deposits and assets takes place.

Initiating Open-market Policy

Initiating open-market operations is a policy that assumes its

---

reached, but in different ways, by Brechling, "A Contribution to the Liquidity Preference Theory of Interest," p. 436, and by Patinkin, *Money, Interest, and Prices,* p. 208.

Turvey, "Consistency and Consolidation in the Theory of Interest," p. 301, assumes that a *ceteris paribus* increase in the quantity of idle balances will lower the rate of interest.

There will be no effect on the rate of interest as a result of a shift from active to idle balances only when the marginal propensity to hold idle balances is one. Brechling, "A Contribution to the Liquidity Preference Theory of Interest," p. 435. In terms of liquidity-preference geometry the foregoing condition means that the isoclines of the preference map are all parallel to the axis along which idle balances are measured, meaning that the demand for idle balances is not capable of saturation while the demand for bonds is.

purest form when the economy is in a state of rest, but at a level which the central bank considers inappropriate. Open-market operations are then initiated by the central bank in an attempt to move the economy to what is considered a more appropriate state of activity. This policy poses two questions for analysis. How is the change that it is decided to make in the cash reserves of the banking system brought about? What secondary effects or consequences follow from the change in reserves?

The first question concerns getting the market to trade with the central bank. When the economy is in a state of rest (as it is assumed to be for purposes of analyzing initiating open-market policy), the member banks are attempting neither to expand nor to contract; that is, they are not trying to substitute other earning assets for securities or securities for other earning assets. On their own account then the banks are neither net buyers nor net sellers in the securities market at a time when the central bank wants to operate in the market. Some banks, however, do operate a trading portfolio, over and above their investment portfolio, which is managed with the aim of maximizing profits on trading securities. Within the limits imposed by the funds allotted to the trading department, the operations of a bank trading account are carried out without regard to the cash position of the bank.[63] Operations of any size in the trading portfolio force the bank to carry out compensating transactions in securities for its investment account. Thus, the central bank can absorb or release a certain amount of cash reserves by inducing the banks that it trades with to alter their position in securities by having them quote the prices at which they will trade and accepting those quotes. When the central bank buys in this way it forces the investment departments of the banks in turn to buy securities from the wider market, because the sales made by the trading departments of the banks provide the banks with excess cash; likewise, central-bank sales to the trading departments of the banks force the investment departments in turn to sell securities in the larger market. The selling

63. A brief discussion of the practices and policies of Canadian banks in operating their trading portfolios in securities appears in Canada, Parliament, House, Standing Committee on Banking and Commerce, *Proceedings*, 1954, pp. 246–7, evidence of the President of The Canadian Bankers' Association.

or buying pressure initiated by the central bank is thus forced out into the larger market. But sales or purchases between the central bank and the member banks initiated by the former do not depend on the capacity of the banks to carry out security transactions; rather they depend on the resources each bank is willing to devote or allot to its trading department; and the amount of cash reserves that a central bank can create or destroy through such transactions is accordingly restricted.[64]

The non-bank traders with which the central bank deals directly also take a position in government securities, and likewise take advantage of any invitation from the central bank to submit offers or make bids in order to accomplish a profitable change in their position. Unlike the bank traders, however, the non-bank traders seldom use their own resources to finance their position. That is they have neither idle resources of their own that they can use to extend their position by buying, nor do they by reducing their position free their own resources. Rather, the non-bank dealers rely heavily upon funds borrowed from a variety of sources;[65] the result is that when they buy securities their indebtedness goes up, and when they are net sellers of securities their indebtedness goes down.[66] Thus, the initial reaction of

64. The Governor of the Bank of Canada stated in 1954 that he would be glad to see the Canadian banks expand their security-trading operations. Ibid., p. 13.

65. They may borrow from banks, non-banks, and even the central bank. The borrowing activities of U.S. non-bank security dealers is discussed by Roosa, *Federal Reserve Operations*, pp. 29, 47–8. The financing of security dealers in Canada is discussed by R. M. MacIntosh, "Broadening the Money Market," *The Canadian Banker, 61* (Autumn 1954), 66–72 passim, and by Brian Land, "How Canada's Money Market Keeps Idle Cash at Work," *Canadian Business* (Montreal), Feb. 1958, pp. 104–6.

66. When the central bank is initiating open-market operations for the purpose of altering the level of economic activity in the domestic economy, bank financing of non-bank traders may not be either available or necessary. This may be the situation when both the banks and non-banks are buying or selling in response to the trading opportunities offered by the central bank. Thus, when the non-banks are buying and need financing, the banks themselves are buying and are not in a position to finance the dealers. Likewise when the dealers are selling, they are in a position to repay the banks, at a time when the banks themselves are selling securities to the central bank and so are in a position to advance funds to the dealers.

these traders to inducements to change their position is reflected not necessarily in their outright trading business but in their borrowing account. So the change in cash reserves that the central bank can effect through this channel is determined partly by the borrowing position of the non-bank dealers. In some circumstances it may even be necessary for the central bank to provide financing for the dealers in order to get them to take up the amount of securities the central bank wishes to place on the market.[67] When the central bank does this it is in effect lending securities to the dealers, who must then find buyers for the securities they have borrowed.[68] The dealers may also look for other buyers and sellers as well, either at the same time as they adjust their position, or after they have exhausted all possibilities for adjusting their position.

The amount of cash reserves that the central bank can then influence through the non-bank dealers depends partly on the ability

---

Alterations in the sources of funds for financing dealers in government securities and alterations in their demand for funds now constitute the basic dynamic element in the short-term money market, replacing activity in stock-market loans and commercial-paper transactions in that role. A discussion of how the New York money market has changed along these lines appears in Harold V. Roelse, "The Money Market," *Money Market Essays* (New York, Federal Reserve Bank of New York, Mar. 1952), pp. 6–7, and in R. S. Sayers, "The New York Money Market Through London Eyes," *The Three Banks Review*, Dec. 1955, pp. 22–3. Parker B. Willis, *The Federal Funds Market: Its Origin and Development* (Boston, The Federal Reserve Bank of Boston, 1957), pp. 8–9, discusses briefly the changing importance of various instruments in the money market between the 1920's and the present, and provides a useful comparative table of the results.

67. Select security dealers in the United States and Canada borrow from the monetary authorities under repurchase agreements. Under these agreements the authorities acquire securities from the dealers and advance them funds, the dealers agreeing to buy back the same securities within a stipulated period at the purchase price plus a specified rate of interest. Repurchase agreements are especially important in the United States in facilitating open-market purchases and sales. Roosa, *Federal Reserve Operations*, pp. 25, 83; MacIntosh, "Broadening the Money Market," p. 72; Land, "How Canada's Money Market Keeps Idle Cash at Work," pp. 30–1, 105; Wilson, "The Canadian Money Market Experiment," p. 25.

68. In this case the effect of open-market sales of securities on cash reserves is delayed until the dealers find buyers among the general public, at which time bank deposits and cash reserves are reduced.

of these dealers to find outside buyers and sellers.[69] This imposes a time restriction on open-market operations initiated by the central bank; if the central-bank operations are large, they must give the dealers time to find outside buyers and sellers or the securities market will be completely disrupted. Given time, then, central-bank selling gives rise in turn to selling by the non-bank traders, and central-bank buying likewise gives rise to security purchases by the dealers. So here too the pressure set up by the central bank is transmitted to the outer reaches of the market through the medium of the traders.

Thus, the central bank in initiating open-market operations brings about a change in cash reserves by inducing the bank and non-bank traders it deals with to alter their position in government securities and initiate further transactions with the smaller operators in the securities market. The more the traders can alter their own position and initiate transactions with others the more securities the central bank can move in its open-market operations. The scale of the movement also depends on the extent to which the central bank is willing to see security yields change. The lower the price at which the central bank is willing to sell, or the higher the price at which it will buy, the more open-market operations it can initiate.

Thus, the central bank effects a given change in the cash reserves of the banking system through open-market operations by exchanging cash for securities, or securities for cash, with the banks and non-bank traders that it usually deals with. This is the first step in the policy of initiating open-market operations, and in many ways the least interesting step. At least it poses no interesting aspects for analysis. Given an active and broad market in government securities, the central bank by altering its buying and selling prices for securities produces the desired change in cash reserves. The much more interesting question is what happens as a result of the change in the cash reserves of the banking system.

The non-bank dealers, through whom cash reserves to the banking system may be altered, may be briefly dismissed. Payments between them and the central bank constitute part of the change in cash

69. Cf. D. I. Fand and I. O. Scott, Jr., "The Federal Reserve System's 'Bills Only' Policy: A Suggested Interpretation," *Journal of Business, 31* (Jan. 1958), 12–13.

reserves produced by open-market operations, but the payments themselves call forth no special reaction from the dealers. The non-bank dealers may be prompted to greater activity in the market as a result of the transactions with the central bank, but the effect of this is only to spread through the market the price changes initiated by the central bank.

It is the reaction of the member banks that provides the special effects of open-market operations initiated by the central bank. As has been indicated, the first phase of the operations accomplishes little: security prices are altered, the banks hold a different amount of cash reserves, and the non-bank private sector holds a different combination of government securities and deposits; but all this occurs within a rather limited and specialized circle of economic units. More significant effects result when the banks react to the change in their cash reserves.

The first point to consider is the effect on bank loans outstanding of the change in cash reserves produced under a policy of initiating open-market operations. An increase in cash reserves will serve to illustrate. The increase in reserves of and by itself provides the banks with a resource effect, which enables them to hold more loans and securities than they could before. Since the increase in reserves comes at a time when the economy is in a state of rest at a lower level of activity than seems desirable—the reason for increasing the cash reserves of the banks—it is likely that the resource or capacity effect of the increase in resources works entirely in favour of increasing the security holdings of the banking system. It is not altogether surprising that an increase in cash reserves which occurs when the demand for bank loans is constant does not in itself lead to any change in bank loans. Prior to the expansion the banks were making all the loans they cared to and the change in resources does not in itself change the profitability of the circumstances under which they can make loans; the increase in reserves then represents excess lending capacity, which is used in expanding bank holdings of securities[70] in the manner analyzed in Chapter Two.

70. A. J. Brown, "The Liquidity-Preference Schedules of the London Clearing Banks," *Oxford Economic Papers*, No. 1 (Oct. 1938), pp. 68–9, suggests that when banks receive extra cash they will find it easier to increase their holdings of securities than to expand their loans, for expansion of the latter must await new

However, the increase in cash reserves is accompanied by a rise in security prices that may produce a substitution effect between securities and loans. If low security prices were previously discouraging the banks from making all the loans that they otherwise would have made, some expansion in bank loans will follow the rise in security prices. The substitution effect also works in favour of loan expansion, even though security prices were not previously an inhibiting force, if the banks pursue the policy of maximizing their joint profits from loans and securities rather than just their profits from loans; there is then scope for an increase in loans to follow an increase in security prices because it becomes less costly to make the substitution of loans for securities. In the situations mentioned, the greater the increase in security prices that follows from open-market operations the greater the expansion in bank loans; but any expansion in bank loans that does follow stems entirely from the change in security yields and not from the change in cash reserves.

The same conclusions apply more or less when cash reserves are reduced. With a given demand, any reduction in bank loans caused by a policy of initiating open-market operations is the working of the substitution effect. That is, any reduction in bank loans outstanding depends on the effect of open-market operations on security prices, unless banks are rationing credit, in which case a reduction in reserves means a reduction in loans.[71]

Any cash reserves acquired by the banks from open-market operations that are not absorbed in making additional loans are used in purchasing securities from the non-bank private sector, it being assumed that the central bank refrains from selling securities to the banks so as not to eliminate the cash reserves previously supplied.

---

loan applications. The American Bankers Association, Economic Policy Commission, *Member Bank Reserve Requirements* (New York, the Association, 1957), p. 26, maintains that in most circumstances large U.S. banks would respond to a reduction in legal reserve requirements by buying government securities and not by making additional loans. The results of a survey of several hundred banks on this question are offered as evidence.

71. A. C. L. Day, *Outline of Monetary Economics*, pp. 140–1, assumes that open-market operations will alter the amount of bank loans outstanding, but he does not elaborate.

Since the economy is in a state of rest, the community demand curve for idle balances remains stable, especially if there has been little expansion in loans following from the open-market operations. The banks then buy securities from the public in accordance with the conditions represented by the demand curve for idle balances. That is, the banks exchange deposits for securities with the public, and the effect on interest rates is shown by the demand curve. The demand curve then represents the open-market operations curve for the banks (as well as for the central bank);[72] it shows how much of an increase in deposits the public will accept for a given drop in interest rates.

The very act of exchanging securities for idle balances by moving along that curve may shift it, especially if expectations are upset by the fact that the banks are buying securities. The curve is also shifted if the change in interest rates and capital values affects expenditures and the transactions demand for cash; and the same effect follows when the new loans finance additional expenditures that create a change in the transactions demand for cash differing in amount from the accompanying increase in loan deposits.

The effectiveness of open-market operations initiated by the central bank for purposes of stimulating an economy that is in a state of rest depends almost entirely on the effects produced, directly and indirectly, on security yields. Thus, what effects the operations have on bank loans depend on the change in security yields; what other effects they have on expenditures depend on how changes in security yields influence expenditures determined partly by interest rates and expenditures determined partly by changes in capital values.[73] The

72. Turvey, "Consistency and Consolidation in the Theory of Interest," p. 302, refers to the demand curve for idle balances as an open-market operations curve. Cf. Brechling, "A Note on Bond-Holding and the Liquidity Preference Theory of Interest," p. 196.

73. Lloyd W. Mints, *Monetary Policy for a Competitive Society* (New York, McGraw-Hill Book Company, Inc., 1950), p. 202, argues that open-market operations are unlikely to have any immediate effect on aggregate demand because the buyers and sellers of government bonds will be mainly banks and institutional investors. Consequently, the cash balances of consumers and of business firms will not be immediately affected, but there may be some delayed influence, Mints maintains, on consumer demand if rising values for bond holdings induce bond holders to spend more liberally.

multiple effect on deposits is a secondary factor that only plays a role in the stimulating process through helping to determine the effect on security yields: the greater the deposit multiplier the greater the effect on interest rates. Or, what is the same thing, given the deposit multiplier, the greater the open-market operations the greater the effect on security yields.[74]

If the economy is heading down at the time that the open-market operations are undertaken, the effectiveness of open-market operations may be even further weakened. Bank loans will be falling off and any substitution effect prompted by rising security prices may not be sufficiently strong to prevent some decline in total loans outstanding. It is unlikely that open-market operations in this instance bring about any change in bank loans outstanding. Offsetting the absence of stimulating effects from loans, however, is the fact that the fall in interest rates will be greater than in the case where the economy is in a state of rest. The amount of idle balances in the non-bank private sector is rising relative to bond holdings as a result of the fall in expenditures releasing cash from transactions balances; the outward shift in the wealth-restraint line of the community, as already explained, must lower interest rates. The open-market purchases of the central bank and member banks lower interest rates in addition to this. Any stimulation must therefore come entirely from the effects on interest rates.[75]

When the economy is operating at a level that is considered to be too high, open-market operations may be initiated to reduce activity.

74. Brechling, "A Contribution to the Liquidity Preference Theory of Interest," pp. 431–3, presents an analysis of open-market operations that differs in content from that given here. He emphasizes that open-market operations change the composition of wealth-holdings in the private sector without changing the total; he is not concerned with assessing the general effectiveness of open-market operations. If open-market operations must depend for their effectiveness on their interest-rate effects, as it is argued here that they must, it would seem important that open-market operations be carried out so as to have as widespread an effect on interest rates as possible.

75. As Keynes, *General Theory*, pp. 197–8, points out, however, open-market operations may affect interest rates not only directly but also indirectly by affecting expectations. A change in expectations, of course, changes liquidity preference and so shifts the demand curve for idle balances.

The reduction in the cash reserves of the banks causes them to liquidate some of their security holdings. The liquidations proceed according to the community demand curve for money and are effected by the exchange of securities for deposits with the non-bank private sector. Interest rates rise as the money supply is reduced. Bank loans may be reduced through any substitution effect that arises from the effect of open-market operations on security yields; and when loans are reduced, the reduction of the money supply that accompanies the loan repayments may differ from the amount of transactions cash released by the fall in loan-financed expenditures— there is then a shift in the demand curve for money that either adds to the general tendency for interest rates to rise or else moderates the tendency. In any case the deterrent effects of open-market operations in the present illustration depend entirely on the impact on security prices that they generate.

If the economy is expanding, instead of remaining in a state of rest at too high a level, it may be even more difficult for open-market operations to be effective. Bank loans are likely expanding at a time when the banks are already selling securities. The substitution effect, which favours securities at the expense of loans, that accompanies the reduction in cash reserves may offset the effects of a greater demand for bank loans and so keep total loans from growing; the chance of reducing the total will be even less than it is when the economy and the demand for bank loans is stable. The demand curve for money is shifting because of rising expenditures, which moves the wealth-restraint line of the community to the left in the community preference map, causing a rise in interest rates. The open-market operations of the central bank and member banks add to the upward movement of interest rates so that any restraining influence generated by open-market operations must again come from their direct and induced impact on security prices. That is, restraint comes not from the multiple contraction of the money supply in itself but from the impact of the change on interest rates.

Accommodating Open-market Policy

An accommodating policy of open-market operations arises in its purest form when cash reserves are not being disturbed by autonomous factors and the domestic economy is in a state of transition or flux. If expenditures are rising under these conditions, securities are more than likely being sold for financing reasons. The banks are selling securities to accommodate additional loans, and the public in general is trying to liquidate some of its security holdings, with the result that security prices are falling. When the level of expenditures in the domestic economy is falling the situation is just the reverse. Funds are being released from transactions balances with some of them becoming available for investment in securities; the general public then tries to increase its holdings of government securities. The banks also become net buyers because, as their loans fall, they resort to security purchases to take up the slack in their reserve ratios. Under the circumstances security prices are rising, yields are falling.

In either of these circumstances, the central bank is apt to feel some obligation to support or to accommodate the market. Such a step may be necessary to maintain orderly conditions in the market, or it may be that the central bank is a too important member of the market to be able to withdraw from it.[76]

The circumstances surrounding an accommodating policy of open-market operations has been aptly described by the Governor of the Bank of Canada in the following words:

> When there is a need for more money in the country, you probably find some people—you are certain to find some people —are selling securities in order to raise cash. If there is a need for

76. Accommodating the securities market is the modern version of the classic role of lender of last resort, a role that present-day central banks seem as willing to play as their nineteenth-century ancestors were reluctant to accept. Indeed, central banking today is more likely to be regarded as a means of accommodating the market than of initiating independent action. Thus, a recent newspaper account of Bank of Canada operations viewed the situation as one in which the Bank of Canada "face the choice between buying government bonds, when banks or others want to turn them into cash, and refusing to buy them. If they buy, they increase the money supply. If they refuse to buy, they send the bond market down—and interest rates up.

"Always from day to day they must weigh the consequences of the two alternatives. Their day-to-day answer is nearly always a compromise. . . ." "Bank Interest Rate Hike Symbol of Ottawa Stand," *Financial Post* (Toronto), Aug. 18, 1956.

more money as indicated by that fact, the central bank can buy some of those securities that are being offered, and thereby provide the cash. It will probably do so at prices which progressively decline as the strength of the selling pressure keeps up, so that you will probably find rising interest rates at a time when there is a demand for more money.

The rise in interest rates, of course, would be much greater if the central bank took no action at all. If we simply stood still interest rates would rise until sufficient buyers were found among the general public to balance the sellers among the general public. So, on the other side of the picture too, when, for a lack of other opportunities to invest, people are interested in buying government securities on an increasing scale, the tendency will be for the central bank to provide some of those government securities and sell them, and in that way dampen the fluctuation, which in that case would be a rise in government security prices, and a decline in interest rates. Generally speaking the central bank tries, and I think certainly should try, to foster orderly conditions in markets, and to dampen fluctuations, but not necessarily to prevent fluctuations if they represent real changes in supply and demand.[77]

Later in response to questioning the Governor added:

I cannot be more precise than to say that under normal circumstances when we feel through the market that the total demand for credit is rising or falling, we yield somewhat to that demand. If the total demand for credit is rising, we provide for some of that demand by buying government bonds. Under those circumstances people are trying to sell government bonds but we do not necessarily stand there and buy them at a fixed price. If people continue to sell government bonds, we normally back away and buy tomorrow at a lower price than we did today. But we do, to some extent, meet the demand for more credit.[78]

77. Canada, Parliament, House, Standing Committee on Banking and Commerce, *Minutes of Proceedings and Evidence*, 3rd Sess., 22nd Parl., No. 9, May 15, 1956, p. 349.

78. Ibid., No. 10, May 22, 1956, p. 383. Similar sentiments are expressed in Bank of Canada, *Annual Report*, 1956, pp. 49, 52.

In short, a purely accommodating policy of open-market operations provides an increase in cash reserves when security prices are falling and a reduction when security prices are rising. In the first instance the domestic economy is expanding; in the second, it is contracting. That is, the central bank by resisting changes in security prices stabilizes security yields but at the cost of destabilizing cash reserves. Hence the emphasis in a policy of accommodation is on interest rates, unlike an initiating policy where the emphasis is on cash reserves. Therefore the problem becomes not one of trying to effect a given change in cash reserves, with interest-rate changes being one of the accompanying consequences, but rather one of trying to moderate the movement in interest rates, with the changes in cash reserves being one of the secondary consequences.

The cash-reserve effects that accompany the accommodating policy of the central bank are more inhibiting than stimulating. Their exact nature depends on the banking situation. When the economy is expanding the banks are increasing their loans and then selling securities to stabilize their position. In the first step of that process they have temporarily expanded their assets and deposits so that in the succeeding step they must liquidate securities in order to reduce their earning assets and deposits to the level appropriate for the amount of cash reserves they have. But if while the banks are in the act of carrying out the second step of the substitution process—that is, liquidating securities to reduce their deposits—the central bank expands the amount of cash reserves in the banking system by adopting an accommodating policy, the banks need not liquidate to the full extent of their initial over-expansion. They need not complete the second step in the substitution process because they can now carry more loans and securities than they could before. Hence the deposit reduction caused by the second step in the substitution process is halted earlier than it otherwise would be; interest rates are prevented from going as high as they would have and the banks may be encouraged to undertake a further substitution of loans for securities.

If the banks are buying securities instead, because their loans are being repaid, the cash-reserve situation is the exact reverse. The banks find their deposits and earning assets shrinking; so they sub-

stitute securities for the loans their customers do not renew, thereby
building up their earning assets and liabilities again. While the banks
are in the midst of doing this, the central bank may accommodate
the market by selling securities: the result is then to halt the expansion
process that the banks have started. The banks do not succeed in
replacing all of their repaid loans with securities because they lose
some cash reserves as a result of the accommodating policy of the
central bank. Security yields are also prevented from falling as low as
they otherwise would, and the banks are encouraged to resist further
reductions in their loans by lowering their lending rates and in other
ways becoming more liberal lenders.

An accommodating policy may not be altogether the creation of
the central bank. Such a policy may be more or less forced upon the
central bank by its role as manager of the public debt; in this role it
may be obliged to alter its security holdings in the financial interest
of the government at a time when it might prefer not to alter its
security holdings at all. This conflict threatens whenever the government debt is refunded.

If government debt is refunded at a time when the private sector
is selling securities to finance an increased level of expenditures, the
banks and other debt holders may simply let their maturing government securities go without replacing them from the refunding issue.
If the government refunding issue is not to fail, the central bank must
take up what the private sector does not. There is then a shift of
government debt from the private sector to the central bank and a
shift of central-bank deposits towards the member banks. The overall
effect is similar to an open-market purchase of securities by the
central bank.[79]

The situation is the reverse when the private sector takes up a
larger share of the refunding issue than it held of the maturing one.

79. Central-bank accommodation of government financing in this fashion arises
most often with treasury bills that are issued regularly and frequently. Of course,
the treasury-bill system of government financing offers the central bank another
point of entry into the securities market. The central bank by adjusting its bidding
for new treasury bills may alter their distribution between the public and private
sectors to achieve a given cash-reserve effect. Cf. Bank of Canada, *Annual Report*,
1956, pp. 47–8.

There is then a shift in public debt from the central bank to the private sector and a reduction in cash reserves. The accommodation by the central bank here consists of not outbidding the private sector on the refunding issue, either knowingly or unwittingly.

The central bank is not, however, likely to be completely accommodating: in moderating fluctuations in security yields it is most unlikely that the resulting changes in cash reserves will be sufficient to make it unnecessary for the banks to carry out compensating transactions to offset fluctuations in their loans. The compensating transactions the banks still have to carry out will be less than under an initiating policy, for the same change in cash reserves, but they will not necessarily be negligible.

At the same time as the banks are carrying out what compensating transactions they have to, the community demand for money is changing. When expenditures in the private sector are undergoing change, the amount of funds allotted by the sector to idle balances and bonds will also be subject to change; that is, the community wealth-restraint line applicable to liquidity-preference analysis is shifting. Furthermore, preferences for bonds and idle balances may also be altering. Consequently, the demand curve for idle balances is shifting so that the banks cannot exchange securities for deposits or deposits for securities according to a given demand curve. The actual open-market operations curve—the curve that traces out the relationship between idle balances and the interest rate—for the banks and the central bank is given by the various amounts of idle balances and the particular demand curve for idle balances that holds for each moment of time and for each value of idle balances. In other words, the shifting demand curve and the changing value for idle balances trace out a curve showing the reaction of the rate of interest to the changes occurring.[80]

80. Brechling, "A Note on Bond-Holding and the Liquidity Preference Theory of Interest," pp. 194–5, calls the curve that results when the amount of idle balances and the demand for money change simultaneously an interest-reaction curve. However, he derives his interest-reaction curve by considering only autonomous changes in idle balances; these increase total wealth and thereby shift the demand curve for money. In his later article on the subject ("A Contribution to the Liquidity Preference Theory of Interest," pp. 434–5) he distinguishes between idle and active balances, and obtains a wealth effect from a transfer of funds

Thus, the banks (and the central bank) in attempting to change the composition of private wealth held in idle balances and bonds, move from demand curve to demand curve instead of along a fixed demand curve, as they do when open-market policy is initiating. That is, the total amount of wealth devoted to holding idle balances and bonds is being altered at the same time as the banks are attempting to induce the sector to alter the composition of its liquidity-preference wealth—the banks are then faced with the task of inducing an alteration in the composition of a changing total. Consequently, an accommodating open-market policy has a less active effect on interest rates than does an initiating open-market policy. An accommodating policy does not force the banks to carry out compensating transactions in securities: it minimizes the compensating transactions that they have to carry out because of the changing demand for bank loans. Fluctuations in interest rates are therefore bound to be less, but the fluctuations in bank deposits will be greater. If the accommodating policy of the authorities does no more than this—particularly if it does not change lending policy or expectations—its cyclical influence on expenditures stems from the change in security prices that it prevents; expenditures related to interest rates and capital values rise and fall with the business cycle more than they otherwise would.

Open-market Policy of Refraining*

Refraining from open-market operations is the easiest type of open-market policy to identify and describe. It is effected by holding con-

---

between idle and active balances that shifts the demand curve for idle balances. Without the division of the money supply into active and inactive balances, changes in the expenditures of the private sector would not cause a wealth effect and so would not cause a shift in the demand curve that faces the banks when they trade in securities with the public. Cf. George Horwick, "Money, Prices and the Theory of Interest Determination," *Economic Journal*, 67 (Dec. 1957), 637, who points out that he obtains a wealth effect in his model only if the money supply is dichotomized.

Turvey, "Consistency and Consolidation in the Theory of Interest," p. 301, derives a set of interest-reaction curves, which he calls *ceteris paribus* curves, but he seems to imply that these curves only exist for autonomous changes in idle balances.

* See Postscript, p. x, regarding the original source of the material in this section.

stant the security holdings of the central bank—the bank simply abstains from either buying or selling securities in any substantial amounts. Such a policy does not mean, however, that cash reserves will remain constant. Other, non-security transactions passing through the books of the central bank may cause changes in cash reserves independently of open-market operations; these changes in cash reserves may be referred to as autonomous changes.

The question of refraining or not refraining from open-market operations is most likely to arise at just such times as autonomous changes in cash reserves are occurring.[81] Autonomous changes in cash reserves may occur at the right time, for the right amount, and in the right direction. Under such a fortuitous conjunction the central bank need only refrain from open-market operations and so avoid offsetting the cash-reserve effects that have arisen. However, if the timing, direction, or amount of the autonomous changes in cash reserves is wrong, the changes have to be corrected, modified, or eliminated. The corrections may be made by anticipating the autonomous changes and taking initiating action to offset them; a policy of initiating open-market operations is then more or less forced upon the central bank. Or the central bank may wait until the autonomous changes create pressures in the securities market and then take accommodating action. Hence, the opposite to a refraining open-

---

81. In the United States open-market operations are undertaken most often to offset wholly or partially inappropriate changes in cash reserves caused by other factors. "Monetary Policy and Bank Reserves," Federal Reserve Bank of Cleveland, *Business Trends*, Dec. 26, 1954, [p. 2]. That this is also true of Canada is indicated by the remarks of the Governor of the Bank of Canada in which he points out that open-market operations are "not something that one uses only when serious trouble has developed, it is something which is used from day to day and we try to keep it moving, at any given time, in the right direction. The most important thing about open-market operations is that they take place on practically every business day of the year." Canada, Parliament, House, Standing Committee on Banking and Commerce, *Minutes of Proceedings and Evidence*, No. 10, May 22, 1956, p. 381.

Because so many other factors are continuously at work on cash reserves, the observed changes in the security holdings of the central bank are a poor indicator of open-market policy, even a misleading one. Cf. Roosa, *Federal Reserve Operations*, pp. 100–3; Karl R. Bopp, "A Flexible Monetary Policy," Federal Reserve Bank of Philadelphia, *Business Review*, Mar. 1958, p. 5.

market policy—not refraining from open-market operations—is either an initiating policy or an accommodating policy.

Refraining from open-market operations is therefore a policy that calls for a decision about whether to refrain or not to refrain in the face of autonomous changes in cash reserves. The decision once made requires no more analysis than that already devoted to it here; but the consequences of that decision depend on the nature of the autonomous changes in cash reserves that have called for the decision. Accordingly, the remainder of this section is devoted to analyzing the consequences of refraining from offsetting various types of autonomous changes and comparing the effects with those that would be produced by open-market operations. For this purpose two general classes of autonomous changes in cash reserves may be distinguished: changes that represent corresponding changes in the total money wealth of the non-bank private sector, and changes that do not.

Autonomous changes in cash reserves that also represent changes in the total wealth of the non-bank private sector result from unbalanced income transactions between the private sector and the public sector. The transactions may be the outcome of official foreign-exchange operations or of government fiscal operations, but they must be on income account; if they are on non-income account, they do not represent a change in the total wealth of the private sector, only a change in the composition of its existing wealth—and in this respect they are no different from open-market operations. It is therefore the effect on total wealth that makes this category of autonomous changes in cash reserves differ in its impact from ordinary open-market operations.

Thus, an autonomous change in cash reserves that reflects a change in total wealth may thereby alter the level of expenditures; since open-market operations do not alter total wealth they cannot alter the level of expenditures through that avenue. This is the really significant difference between the two, but they are usually compared on the basis of being alternative methods of altering cash reserves and the money supply. Indeed, the autonomous change attracts attention for its effect on cash reserves and the money supply, not for its direct income effects from which the alteration in total wealth flows.

The two—autonomous, wealth-altering changes in cash reserves and open-market operations—also differ in their effects on interest rates. The autonomous change affects the rate of interest less than do open-market operations of an equivalent amount because the former only affects the rate of interest by altering the amount of idle balances relative to a given quantity of bonds whereas the latter alter idle balances and the quantity of bonds in an inverse manner.[82]

Some writers argue that this difference in the effect on interest rates creates an important distinction between changes in the money supply produced by open-market operations and autonomous changes in the money supply that alter total wealth.[83] The cash-reserve component in the two types of money-supply changes does differ in its effect on interest rates in the two cases; but the cash-reserve component is by far the smallest part of the change in the money supply that follows the change in cash reserves. When the expansion in deposits is the same in the two cases, it follows that the larger the deposit multiplier the less the difference between a change in the money supply caused by open-market operations and one caused by an autonomous, wealth-altering change in cash reserves. The change in interest rates associated with either still differs between the two ways of altering the money supply, but the difference is due entirely to the way cash reserves are changed, so that the larger the induced change in the money supply relative to the change in cash

82. *Supra*, n. 62. A further reason for the greater effect of open-market operations here on the interest rate is that while all the change in cash reserves produced by open-market operations goes to alter the amount of idle balances only a portion of the autonomous change in cash reserves represents a change in idle balances, the remainder going into active balances.

83. Lloyd A. Metzler, "Wealth, Saving, and the Rate of Interest," *Journal of Political Economy, 59* (Apr. 1951), 97, refers to changes in the quantity of money that take place through open-market operations and those that take place without any off-setting changes in private holdings of other assets as "two fundamentally different types of increase or decrease in the quantity of money," because of the difference in their effects on interest rates.

Ralph Turvey, "Mr. Ritter on Monetary and Fiscal Policy," *Review of Economic Studies, 24* (1956–57), 72, also sees an important distinction in the way that the quantity of money is altered in the effect it has on interest rates; for this reason he differentiates between open-market operations as a way of altering the quantity of money and other methods that alter total wealth as well.

reserves the less significant becomes the difference in interest-rate effects.

However, there is a special case of an autonomous change in the money supply where the interest-rate effect may differ significantly from that produced by open-market operations; this is provided by a government income deficit or surplus that, by letting the surplus or deficit affect only government deposits on the books of the member banks, changes the money supply without changing cash reserves; there is then a change produced in the money supply of the private sector without any change in cash reserves. All of this change in the money supply—or at least that part of it which alters liquidity-preference wealth—affects interest rates differently from the same change produced in the quantity of money by an open-market change in cash reserves. The differences in the effects on interest rates of the two changes in the quantity of money here is greater than when the open-market increase in the money supply is compared with an auto-nomous change that applies just to cash reserves and not to the total alteration in the money supply.

There are a wide variety of autonomous changes in cash reserves that fall into the category of changes which do not represent a net change in the total money wealth of the non-bank private sector. These may be divided into two sub-groups: those that involve the private sector and those that do not. In the first group may be placed the following transactions: a conversion of deposits into currency or currency into deposits made by the public; unbalanced income trans-actions between those who bank with the member banks and those who bank with the central bank; and changes in non-bank borrowing from the central bank.[84] The second group includes the following: administrative shifts of government deposits between member banks and the central bank; changes in member-bank borrowing from the

84. Similar to these in that cash reserves are altered without changing liquidity-preference wealth is the case where cash-reserve changes do reflect changes in the total money wealth of the private sector, but where the entire change in wealth is accounted for by corresponding changes in the transactions demand for cash. This case arises most likely when expenditures are altering in the right direction and amount to cause the transactions demand for cash to alter by the given change in the quantity of money.

central bank; and changes in legal reserve requirements. All of these ways in which cash reserves may be changed autonomously have in common the fact that the change in reserves themselves is effected without altering interest rates; these reserve changes therefore differ from those produced through open-market operations, which do have an effect on interest rates. For all but two of the above-mentioned ways of altering cash reserves autonomously, the change in reserves reflects an equal change in bank deposits, which means that the deposit multipliers applying to them are the same as apply to open-market changes in cash reserves,[85] and that the volume of transactions in interest-earning assets resulting from the multiplier process is the same for the autonomous changes in cash reserves as it is for open-market operations.

Changes in member-bank borrowing from the central bank and changes in reserve requirements, however, produce cash-reserve effects that have different earning-asset multipliers from those of the other autonomous factors mentioned in the previous paragraph. In fact they have the same earning-asset multiplier as open-market operations carried out with the banks. For instance, member-bank borrowings of cash reserves from the central bank to the amount of 10, or open-market security purchases by the central bank from the member banks of 10, or a lowering of cash-reserve requirements that give the banks excess cash reserves of 10, means that all of the 10 can go towards supporting the deposits generated in buying additional earning assets. But when the change in cash reserves is accompanied by a corresponding change in deposits some of the cash is immediately impounded into required cash reserves to support the reserve-creating deposits and only the unimpounded cash reserves remaining are

85. Changes in the preference of the public for currency and deposits are sometimes considered separately as a special factor operating on cash reserves, but it seems unnecessary here to distinguish them from other autonomous changes in cash reserves. They differ from them in that not only do they provide a positive or negative multiplicand for the various banking multipliers but also they alter the size of the multiplier itself. In this respect they are similar to changes in required reserve ratios. Effects of changes in the currency ratio and in required reserve ratios on the various banking variables are tabulated by Procter Thomson, "Variations on a Theme by Phillips," *American Economic Review*, *46* (Dec. 1956), 969–70.

available for expanding earning assets.[86] Hence, since autonomous changes in the cash-reserve position of the banks resulting from changes in reserve requirements and bank borrowing from the central bank have the same earning-assets multiplier as cash-reserve changes caused by open-market operations,[87] they also have the same effect on interest rates. Thus in this case autonomous changes in cash reserves produce results identical to open-market operations.

Autonomous changes in cash reserves, however, are more often than not accompanied by open-market operations that either nullify or modify them; therefore a truer comparison of actualities lies not between pure autonomous changes in cash reserves and open-market operations, but between autonomous changes corrected by open-market operations and some pure form of open-market operations.

One possibility is for an autonomous change in cash reserves to be completely offset by open-market operations;[88] there is then no change in cash reserves, but this constancy is maintained only by altering interest rates. This is just the opposite of what occurs under an accommodating open-market policy designed to keep interest

86. In the simplest multiplier cases, the earning-asset multiplier applied to a change in cash reserves not offset by a corresponding change in deposits is given by the reciprocal of the reserve ratio; for a change in cash reserves accompanied by a change in deposits, the earning-asset multiplier is the reciprocal of the reserve ratio, minus one.

James W. Angell and Karl F. Ficek, "The Expansion of Bank Credit," *Journal of Political Economy*, 41 (1933), 17, 22–5, present more complicated multipliers for earning assets, which however still show that they differ depending on the manner in which cash reserves are altered.

87. That is, borrowed reserves and reserves released by a lowering of reserve ratios take the same earning-asset multipliers as reserves created by open-market operations between the member banks and the central bank. Reserves that come to the banks as a result of open-market operations between the central bank and the public take a smaller earning-asset multiplier. But when the open-market operations of the central bank with the public are combined with the earning-asset expansion or contraction of the banks, the total transactions in earning assets between the public and the banking system are equal to those undertaken on the basis of borrowed reserves or reserves released from legal requirements.

88. Of course discretionary autonomous changes in cash reserves, represented by changes in cash-reserve requirements and administrative shifts in government deposits between the member banks and the central bank, will not be offset; the discussion here applies only to non-discretionary autonomous changes.

rates constant: the constancy of interest rates there is achieved by letting cash reserves vary.

More likely, autonomous changes in cash reserves are only partially offset by open-market operations so that some net change in cash reserves remain. The residual change in cash reserves, however, will be associated with a different interest-rate effect from that of a similar change in cash reserves produced directly by initiating open-market operations. The interest-rate effect is weaker in the complex case, it may be nil there, or it may even be of opposite sign from that of the interest-rate effect produced by pure open-market operations. The difference in signs arises when the partially offsetting open-market operations have a stronger interest-rate effect than the autonomous change in cash reserves, so that the residual change in cash reserves becomes associated with an interest-rate movement contrary in direction to that of simple open-market operations producing the equivalent change in cash reserves.

In the same way accommodating open-market operations may result in a given change in cash reserves being associated with an observed change in interest rates that is opposite in sign to that which initiating open-market operations would have produced. Instead of an increase in cash reserves being accompanied by a fall in interest rates, just the opposite occurs when a fall in interest rates is met by open-market purchases that do not prevent rates from falling.

The general conclusion of this section must be that in view of the wide number of possibilities it does not seem useful to differentiate changes in the quantity of cash reserves and money according to the changes in interest rates that accompany them. Indeed, there is little to choose between the various autonomous changes in cash reserves that do not alter total wealth and open-market operations; both lead to much the same change in interest rates and in the quantity of money. It is a different matter with wealth-altering cash-reserve changes: the less these affect liquidity-preference wealth the more they affect expenditures and the transactions demand for cash; hence the more effective they are when used to regulate expenditures. Even when their cash-reserve effects must be offset by open-market operations, they still exert an influence to the extent that they have altered expenditures; open-market operations cannot offset the change in total wealth that the autonomous changes have produced and which is the cause of their influence on expenditures. But the stronger influence of these cash-reserve changes over open-market operations lies not in their different effects on interest rates but in their effects on expenditures.

BANK-RATE POLICIES

A central bank may come into contact with the financial system through its activities as a lender as well as a trader in government securities. Thus, lending transactions offer a central bank another policy means for exercising its function as a regulator of the monetary environment. How a central bank may use lending transactions as a policy weapon is considered here first in the abstract; then the method, as a policy weapon, is compared with open-market operations. This leads naturally into a discussion of bank-rate. Then the question of how bank-rate policy evolved is taken up, and the section concludes with an examination of the nature of present-day bank-rate policies.

Central-Bank Lending

It has long been recognized that a central bank may regulate, or at least influence, credit conditions through its lending activities. That regulation or influence may work through two devices: lending policy and lending rates.

The lending policy of the central bank may operate in much the same way as that of member banks to determine who may or may not have central-bank credit; within such scope as it has for determining who may borrow from it, the central bank may set its standards in terms of collateral, maturity dates, and borrowing limits. By altering these terms then, the central bank can influence the volume of its loans outstanding. Since a central bank is not influenced by the state of its reserves, it would never have to refuse to lend as member banks might have to do because of limited resources or considerations of cost. It would, in short, be a lender of last resort, but not necessarily a lender of last resort at unchanging terms and rates.

If a central bank holds terms and rates constant and does not

engage in open-market operations, its volume of loans outstanding
will vary naturally with conditions in the money market. As the
market tightens and the demand of borrowers exceeds the ability of
the banking system to meet it at existing lending rates, the excess
demand converges on the central bank. Similarly, when the demand
for loans falls off and the banking system acquires excess reserves, the
loans of the central bank naturally tend to fall off, and the tendency
is accelerated if the member banks lower their lending rates.

A central bank is unlikely to hold its lending attitude and lending
rate (bank-rate) constant in the face of fluctuating demand for accommodation. When its loans seem to be rising too fast, it may
become a less accommodating lender: it might narrow its definition
of worthy borrowers, and it may raise bank-rate. And, when its loans
are falling, the central bank may offer some resistance by lowering
its bank-rate and becoming more ready to lend.

The central bank may, independently of conditions in the market,
take the initiative in an attempt to alter the volume of its lending
business. When a central bank is a large and continuous lender,
decisions by it to alter the amount of its loans have a direct bearing
on the cash reserves of the banking system. Every change in its loans
to member banks or to depositors of member banks causes a direct
and immediate change in cash reserves; every change in its loans to
borrowers who deposit with it does not immediately affect cash reserves, but may eventually do so when these borrowers engage in
transactions with customers of the member banks. It follows that a
central bank will be most effective in bringing about an alteration in
cash reserves through variations in its lending policies when its borrowing clientele is largest and its depositing clientele smallest.

The effectiveness of changing cash reserves through altering central-bank lending attitudes and rates also depends of course on how
borrowers react. The alteration in rate must have some effect on the
amount borrowed, and the change in lending attitudes will be most
effective when the demand schedule is not shifting. Otherwise, variations in the number of worthy borrowers may offset changes in
lending standards, as when a shift in demand brings forth more
borrowers who are eligible for loans, even at the higher standards.

The reaction of the member banks to changes in lending conditions

o

at the central bank is also important in determining the effectiveness of central-bank action in this field. This reaction, however, is only important when the member banks borrow directly from the central bank, or when there is a class of borrowers who may deal with either the member banks or the central bank. Borrowers who deal only with the central bank are unaffected by what the member banks do, and borrowers who deal only with a member bank are not directly affected by changes in central-bank lending conditions.

The most important central-bank borrowers are probably those who can borrow either from the member banks or the central bank. A change in central-bank lending terms relative to those of the member banks bears directly on this class of borrower and causes them to shift between the two sources of bank credit open to them. Hence a change in cash reserves follows.

The effect on cash reserves is not necessarily a significant accomplishment. For instance, when a central bank tightens its credit conditions relative to those of the member banks some of its borrowers will find it worthwhile to borrow from the member banks; accordingly they switch, borrowing from the member banks and repaying the central bank. Cash reserves are thereby reduced. If the member banks are very liquid, nothing is changed except the liquidity of the system, the member banks converting their liquid assets into cash to maintain their cash-reserve ratios. If the banks are fully loaned-up, a reduction in their reserves forces contraction on them; but in this situation they are not going to remain more willing lenders than the central bank. They would therefore reverse their lending standards when the central bank did so. No redistribution of lending business would follow as a result of the change in central-bank credit conditions. Any restraint on credit then works through the changed borrowing conditions, not through the cash reserves.

It might be the same if the central bank relaxed its lending conditions; if the member banks were not fully loaned-up and could lower their standards too, especially their lending rates, the banks would react to the tendency for borrowers to leave them for the central bank by matching the lower credit conditions of the latter. Again, there would be no shifting of borrowers, no effect on cash reserves, and complete dependence of credit control on the reaction of borrowers to the changed lending conditions. Only when the member banks do not respond to the more liberal lending policies of the central bank, because of limitations on lending capacity or rigidities in costs, does the central bank succeed in altering cash reserves in this manner.

Generally, then, central-bank lending policy does not seem to be a device of credit control that works through the cash reserves of the banking system; at least, in the abstract, it seems more likely to work through its effect on the borrower. Indeed, when the central bank acts as a lender of last resort, it must accommodate the market during a credit expansion, thereby losing control over cash reserves—it can only influence the costs of additions to those reserves, with the market itself deciding on the amount of additional reserves that will be created. In downswings too the market may have the deciding voice on the extent to which cash reserves are liquidated through paying off central-bank loans. Even when the central bank attempts to take the initiative by altering its lending conditions relative to market rates, it may find the banks following it so that lending conditions in general change rather than cash reserves.[89]

These conclusions apply most fully when the central bank is a continuous and large lender; they are less apt when it is an infrequent lender. Nevertheless, the abstract considerations from which the conclusions are drawn serve to illustrate the nature of central-bank lending as a weapon of monetary policy and provide a basis for comparison with open-market operations.

Central-Bank Lending and Open-market Operations

Credit control exercised through central-bank lending works mainly through lending rates in contrast to credit control applied through open-market operations, which works through altering cash reserves; but open-market operations also have a price effect. Open-

---

89. Keynes, *Treatise*, *1*, 216, appears to imply that a change in bank-rate to be effective must be accompanied by some change in cash reserves. On this view a bank-rate change that altered other lending rates without changing cash reserves would not be considered effective. However, Keynes does hold that the important effect of bank-rate changes is on other lending rates, the change in cash reserves being secondary (ibid., p. 200).

market operations obviously produce their effects on cash reserves by altering central-bank buying and selling rates for government securities; bank-rate policy works through a variation in the price at which the central bank will buy non-government debt—that is, make loans —and the buying rate can also be a selling rate, because for some sufficiently large rate borrowers can be induced to repay loans—that is, buy non-government debt from the central bank. The central bank can also effect a change in its loans outstanding by altering its lending standards; the comparable act for open-market operations would be a change in trading standards—that is, decisions about what types of securities to buy or sell.

Another difference sometimes cited between open-market operations and central-bank lending is that the former are supposedly at the initiative of the central bank while the latter is at the initiative of the borrower.[90] This is analogous to commercial banking where security transactions are initiated by the banks and lending transactions, by the borrowers. Central banking is different, however, unless the central bank actually refuses to deal in government securities at any price when it does not want to—that is, it does not accommodate the market. But so long as the central bank feels any concern for orderly conditions in the securities market it is as likely to accommodate the market through its security transactions as it is through its lending transactions; the initiative then rests with the borrowing and trading public even if securities are traded with the central bank and indebtedness to the latter altered.

In other words the central bank has to set prices for securities as well as set rates for its loans, and given these prices and rates, it is up to the public what use is made of central-bank offers to trade and lend. It might be thought that even here there might be a difference because it is easier to induce a trading operation than a borrowing one, but such is not the case in the present context. A good selling price for securities will induce purchases from the central bank, but so will a high bank-rate, when the central bank has many loans outstanding, cause a withdrawal of loans and repayments. Likewise, a good buying price will induce security sales to the central bank and

90. Cf. Day, *Outline of Monetary Economics,* p. 148.

a low bank-rate will attract borrowers away from other lenders and may induce as well an overall increase in borrowing.

The last two statements require elaboration and qualification to bring out the true difference between bank-rate policy and open-market operations. The central bank as a trader in securities is not a destabilizing influence; it does not subject the market to additional pressure. When it is accommodating the market, it is buying when others want to sell and selling when others want to buy. It does not initiate security transactions when the market is under pressure: other traders do not resist its entry by altering their bids and offers so as to frustrate the attempts of the central bank to either buy or sell securities. This contrasts with what may occur when the central bank attempts to alter its position as a lender. The central bank then enters into direct competition with other lenders who therefore tend to resist the efforts of the central bank to change its loans outstanding; they do this by altering their lending rates in accordance with changes in bank-rate. It is a different matter, however, when the central bank is merely serving as an accommodating lender instead of an initiating one; borrowers welcome an additional lender because other lenders cannot accommodate them.

In short, open-market operations are generally not a competitive factor in the market calling forth defensive reactions from others, although lending policy may sometimes be a competitive force causing other lenders to react to preserve their positions.

Since there is so little difference between open-market operations and bank-rate policy in terms of actual mechanics, the two may conflict if bank-rate does not keep a proper relation to the rates at which the central bank is buying and selling securities. The possibility for conflict arises because those who borrow from the central bank nowadays often have a choice between altering their holdings of government securities and altering their indebtedness to the central bank. Aside from non-economic considerations—such as a reluctance to borrow—there is no significant difference between selling a security, to the central bank or in the market, and borrowing from the central bank on the basis of the security. Which is done, aside from custom and other frictions, turns on costs and needs. When cash is required temporarily, it may be cheaper to borrow than to sell securities only to have to buy them back later. Even when cash is needed permanently it may be cheaper to borrow if security prices are expected to rise soon.

Thus, when the market requires accommodation, the central bank can decide in what form that accommodation should be provided by altering the relative cheapness of the two ways in which it can provide accommodation—buying securities or making loans—so long as it is as ready to make loans as it is to hold securities.

In an initiating context the two devices become complements. Thus, when central-bank indebtedness is general, a variation in the price or cost of that indebtedness may cause borrowers to alter their security holdings. For example, a rise in bank-rate as part of an initiating policy by the central bank may cause the borrowing traders to sell securities in order to repay their central-bank loans; this occurs when the banks are not in a position to accommodate the traders at a more favourable rate than that of the central bank—hence there will be no shifting of loans between the central bank and the member banks. Open-market policy then reinforces bank-rate policy in this situation if the central bank refrains from open-market operations, by quoting prices on securities that are in a proper relation to the new and higher bank-rate.

When the central bank lowers bank-rate, it may encourage traders to expand their operations and to finance their additional purchases by borrowing from the central bank; again, refraining from open-market operations reinforces bank-rate policy in getting reserves into circulation, or, if borrowing from the central bank does not alter, in bringing about a reduction in lending rates.

Reinforcing bank-rate policy in this way through an open-market policy of refraining depends on central-bank borrowers being also holders of government securities so that they are borrowing either to finance their security holdings or to avoid having to sell securities. The situation differs from that of the pure model where the borrower was assumed not to be borrowing to hold securities, or not to have the alternative of financing by selling securities.

The opposite case, where policy changes are initiated through open-market operations, is perhaps more common. The central bank sells securities, and the market borrows from the central bank to carry the securities purchased, or the banks borrow to replenish temporarily their cash reserves. Or the central bank may buy securities, and the market then repays its indebtedness to the central bank. In either situation the whole point of open-market operations is lost since cash reserves are not altered, but both possibilities for frustrating open-market policy arise only because of inappropriate bank-rate policies.

It is sometimes argued from the concept of lender of last resort that open-market sales will be followed by increased borrowing from the central bank, and that open-market purchases will be followed by a reduction in indebtedness to the central bank; the conclusion is then drawn that initiating open-market operations are merely an appendage to bank-rate policy and not an independent policy weapon.[91] This is, however, a rather misleading conclusion; it leads to the further inference that open-market sales, by forcing the market to borrow from the central bank at a bank-rate previously above market rates, are merely a device for making bank-rate effective.[92]

But the fact that open-market sales are followed by an increase in central-bank indebtedness is proof of the effectiveness of open-market operations, and it is as much the function of bank-rate to retain that effectiveness as it is for open-market operations to make bank-rate effective. It is true that if there were no access to central-bank credit open-market sales would exert a contractionary influence; the reaction of the market would be to sell securities if necessary. If central-bank loans were available, the market would resort to them only when bank-rate was not too high. Thus, a high enough bank-rate would discourage borrowing that offsets the cash-reserve effects of the open-market operations. Only when the market has no recourse but to borrow from the central bank does bank-rate become the effective instrument of control; cash reserves then remain unchanged but lending rates rise. Open-market operations have worked through bank-rate to raise lending costs, and they have worked directly to lower security yields. But under present conditions where borrowers

91. Cf. Keynes, *Treatise*, 2, 250–1, who criticizes the argument.

92. Great Britain, Committee on Finance and Industry, *Report*, p. 152, lists as a separate device of monetary policy the use of open-market operations to force the market to borrow from the central bank.

usually possess disposable securities, it is the level of bank-rate, providing it is set high enough, that prevents borrowing, so that the cash-reserve effects of open-market operations remain.

When the market is in debt to the central bank, open-market purchases may simply result in a reduction in that debt. But the nullifying effect of debt repayment on cash reserves can go on only for as long as the market is in debt to the central bank; once the market is out of debt the cash-reserve effects of open-market operations assert themselves in a more positive direction. The effectiveness of open-market operations in this situation then depends on their amount, not on the level of bank-rate.

In short, open-market purchases of sufficient size can be effective even though central-bank indebtedness is reduced. Open-market sales are also effective: directly so if no one, as a result, borrows from the central bank; indirectly through the rise in lending rates that likely follow the rise in bank-rate. Therefore, given an appropriate level of bank-rate, open-market operations are in general an independent weapon of monetary control, except in a money market where central-bank borrowers are not large holders of government debt.[93]

The Effectiveness of Bank-Rate

The effectiveness of bank-rate depends not only on the level at which bank-rate is set but also on the conditions under which borrowing from the central bank may take place. Such borrowing may occur for reasons of profit or of need and may reflect both non-bank and bank borrowing. For purposes of analysis non-bank borrowing is separated from bank borrowing.

Non-bank borrowing from the central bank arises when there exist borrowers who may obtain loans from the central bank as well as

93. Keynes, *Treatise, 2,* pp. 251–2, argues that although bank-rate policy and open-market policy cannot be carried on along different lines they nevertheless represent different techniques of control.

Paul A. Samuelson, "Reflections on Monetary Policy," *Review of Economics and Statistics, 42* (Aug. 1960), 266, points out that there is no evidence of a unit change in open-market operations inducing an offsetting change in borrowing from the central bank. Therefore, he argues, it is not difficult to allow for changes in central-bank indebtedness in carrying out open-market operations.

from the member banks. When cost or profit considerations alone determine from which source funds will be obtained, these borrowers may meet all their needs for bank financing from the central bank rather than from the member banks. When these borrowers are in debt to the banking system but not to the central bank, it is because they find it more profitable to borrow from the member banks than from the central bank. If it becomes more profitable to borrow at the central bank, say because bank-rate falls, these borrowers will shift their borrowing from the member banks to the central bank, unless member banks reduce their lending rates to keep bank loans the most profitable source of funds. A fall in bank-rate is then effective in reducing bank lending rates. Other lending rates may fall as well, especially if the borrowers themselves are carrying on a lending business. If, however, central-bank borrowing has become more profitable because the banks have come under pressure and so have raised their lending rates—bank-rate remaining fixed—there is an actual shift of borrowers from the member banks to the central bank. Bank-rate, by being maintained at its existing level, is then effective in expanding the cash reserves of the banking system.

When non-bank borrowing from the central bank exists because borrowing from the member banks is more costly, borrowers will shift from the central bank to the member banks when it becomes profitable to do so as a result of bank-rate rising relative to bank lending rates, or of bank lending rates falling relative to bank-rate. Here, an increase in bank-rate will be effective in reducing the cash reserves of the banking system if the banks have excess capacity for accommodating more borrowers at existing rates. If the banks have no excess capacity, they can protect themselves against a shift of borrowers to them by raising their lending rates. Bank-rate is then effective in raising lending rates.[94]

Non-bank borrowing from the central bank based on need reflects a situation where borrowers cannot obtain additional funds from the member banks. Such borrowing may not be unprofitable but to be genuine need-borrowing it must be undertaken with reluctance and with a desire to repay at the earliest opportunity. Under such con-

94. When it brings about changes in other lending rates bank-rate is effective in the classical sense. Cf. Sen, *Central Banking in Undeveloped Money Markets*, p. 31.

ditions the level of bank-rate perhaps has little relevance. The higher it is, of course, the less profitable recourse to the central bank will be and the more drastic is likely to be the action taken by borrowers to get out of debt.

Bank borrowing for profit from the central bank raises two separate questions for analysis: the effect of bank-rate on bank profits and the effect on the amount borrowed by the banks. The effect on bank profits depends partly on the extent to which the banking system can expand its earning assets on the basis of a given amount of borrowing from the central bank. When the asset multiplier for the banking system exceeds unity, bank profits could be raised by bank borrowing from the central bank even when bank-rate stands above the average yield on bank earning assets. A given amount of borrowed cash enables the banking system to hold a greater amount of earning assets, the difference in these two amounts more than compensating for the higher rate paid for the borrowed cash. Hence, the greater the asset multiplier of the banking system, the more bank-rate must be above the yield on bank earning assets to prevent bank borrowing from the central bank resulting in an expansion in bank profits.[95]

An individual bank, however, in a multi-bank system cannot expand its earning assets to the same multiple of the amount borrowed as can the banking system. Each bank gets only its share of the expansion in earning assets that results from some bank adding to the cash reserves of the banking system by borrowing from the central bank. Nevertheless, the individual bank that borrows and expands may find that its earning assets have expanded by more than the amount borrowed. Borrowing could raise bank profits even though bank-rate is above the yield on the additional assets acquired.

Some writers appear to conclude that bank-rate fails to restrict bank borrowing for profit from the central bank when bank-rate is not high enough to keep profits of the borrowing bank from rising

95. Keynes, *Treatise*, 2, 244–7, in effect examines the relation between bank profits and bank-rate in a banking system which can expand by borrowing reserves from the central bank. He shows that when the ratio of the yield on bank assets to bank-rate is kept constant as bank-rate varies bank profits are increased by a rise in bank-rate.

when such borrowing occurs.[96] The restraint imposed by bank-rate, however, depends not on the ultimate effect of such borrowing on the profits of a borrowing bank, but on how the bank assesses the profitableness of the borrowing transaction. Borrowing that might raise bank profits might very well appear unprofitable to the individual bank. To take a highly simplified, and unlikely, situation, a bank that is in equilibrium may be confronted with the possibility of acquiring a given block of earning assets. It may assume that the acquisition of these assets will cost it an equal amount of cash. If it does, it will not consider it worth the effort to acquire the assets if it has to borrow cash from the central bank at a rate no lower than the yield on the assets to be acquired. A higher bank-rate is only necessary to make the proposed acquisition appear unprofitable if the bank assumes the acquisition will partly expand its deposits and partly reduce its cash. The bank is unlikely, however, to take any account of the cash that will flow back to it as the result of expansion by other banks based on cash gained from the borrowing bank. Hence, the bank will overestimate the cash it will need and this may make the proposed transaction appear unprofitable even though it would not be.

96. At least that is the implication given when the profitableness of borrowing from the central bank is calculated in terms of how much the borrowing bank can expand on the basis of the new reserves so obtained. This is done by Chester Arthur Phillips, *Bank Credit: A Study of the Principles and Factors Underlying Advances Made by Banks to Borrowers*, pp. 115–16, who, because he gets an asset multiplier of only 1.22 for the individual bank, concludes that a bank-rate only slightly in excess of bank lending rates would check the tendency for banks to borrow.

J. S. Lawrence, "Borrowed Reserves and Bank Expansion," *Quarterly Journal of Economics, 42* (Aug. 1928), 622, assigns a higher value to the multiplier of the individual bank, and argues from this that bank-rate has to be at least 1.79219 times as high as bank lending rates in order to keep banks from borrowing at the central bank.

Keynes, *Treatise, 2,* 248–9, in his definitive treatment of the subject appears to accept the view that the value of the asset multiplier enters into the decision of banks about borrowing.

Ray B. Westerfield, *Money, Credit and Banking,* p. 675, who also points out how high bank-rate must be to make borrowing unprofitable, suggests that banks do not take advantage of a lower rate to add to their profits by borrowing because they do not understand the process of multiple expansion that such borrowing would set in motion.

The more usual context in which the profitableness of bank borrowing from the central bank arises is one in which a bank is faced with eliminating an existing deficiency in its cash reserves.[97] The cost of borrowing is then compared with the cost of raising cash by disposing of earning assets. If bank-rate is above the yield on the lowest yielding asset that can be disposed of, it will appear to be cheaper to the adjusting bank to dispose of the asset rather than borrow.[98] If the bank does not have any immediately disposable assets so that it must borrow to eliminate a cash deficit, a bank-rate above the yield on its earning assets will strike the bank as being at an unprofitable level. It might then react by restricting its acquisition of earning assets, by raising its lending rates, or by trying to work off what earning assets it can as the opportunity arises.

Bank-rate, then, is effective in restricting the amount of bank borrowing for profit from the central bank when it is above the yield on the disposable assets used by banks in adjusting their cash positions. Under such conditions a fall in bank-rate below money-market rates will cause profit borrowing by banks to expand; a rise above money rates will cause borrowing to contract. Here bank-rate can be used to vary the amount of profit borrowing and so the cash reserves and size of the banking system. Where banks do not have money-market assets to dispose of, bank-rate must rise above bank lending rates to contract profit borrowing. If lending rates rise with bank-rate, however, the only check on profit borrowing, so long as banks are free to borrow, is the price elasticity of the demand curve for bank loans.

Banks may borrow from the central bank solely for reasons of need. When they do, it is with reluctance and for no more than they have to. The level of bank-rate is then of secondary importance. Such borrowing will be paid off as soon as possible even though a borrowing bank might find it profitable to stay in debt. Thus, need borrowing represents a temporary means of adjusting to a cash deficit. If

97. Cf. Robert C. Turner, *Member-Bank Borrowing*, pp. 14–15.

98. Keynes, *Treatise*, 2, 249; U.S. Congress, *Monetary Policy . . . Public Debt: Compendium*, Pt. 1, p. 393.

It is perhaps for this reason that a bank-rate set just above money-market rates has come to be viewed as a penalty rate that discourages borrowing from the central bank. Cf. Fousek, *Foreign Central Banking*, p. 18.

banks resort to need borrowing to avoid a heavy loss that an immediate cash adjustment through some other means would bring, it follows that the higher the bank-rate the fewer the occasions on which resort to need borrowing will help avoid or postpone incurring adjustment losses.

Need borrowing and profit borrowing by banks may exist side by side in the same banking system, but only when profit borrowing arises first, or when some banks are borrowing for profit and some for need. Once all banks are borrowing for need, they will not add to such debt by borrowing for profit.[99]

Bank-rate, then, is a significant variable when the central bank is willing to lend to those who find it profitable to borrow from the central bank. Bank-rate can be made effective in the sense of regulating the amount of central-bank loans outstanding or of causing alterations in other lending rates by manipulating the rate with reference to the lending rates of the banks and to money-market rates. When borrowing from the central bank in cases of need is permitted, the level of bank rate is not particularly relevant although the amount so borrowed might be mildly sensitive to the rate.

The Evolution of Bank-Rate Policy

The present attitude towards bank-rate policy is shaped by how it evolved and was supposed to function in the United Kingdom. Therefore, to establish a foundation on which to build a critique of present-day bank-rate policies, some discussion of the historical background of bank-rate policy is necessary.

Bank-rate policy developed in nineteenth-century England from the practice adopted by the Bank of England for regulating its reserves through manipulation of its lending or discount rate—a practice that dates back to about 1839.[100] That is, early bank-rate policy was

99. An analysis that attempts to explain the existence of both need and profit borrowing is given by Murray E. Polakoff, "Reluctance Elasticity, Least Cost, and Member-Bank Borrowing: A Suggested Integration," *Journal of Finance*, 15 (Mar. 1960), 3–8. The difficulty of identifying in practice the borrowing that is for need and that which is for profit is clearly stated by Turner, *Member-Bank Borrowing*, pp. 67–8.

100. Keynes, *Treatise*, 1, 186–7. Also cf. Sayers, *Central Banking after Bagehot*, p. 61. A. C. Pigou, *Industrial Fluctuations* (London, Macmillan and Co., Limited,

designed more to safeguard the reserves of the Bank of England than to regulate the general state of credit and business within the country. If the reserves were being threatened, up went bank-rate; if the reserves became redundant, down went bank-rate. On these grounds it might be argued that until bank-rate policy became divorced from the state of the reserves and came to be applied with broader views in mind, bank-rate policy in the United Kingdom was not an independent weapon of monetary control. This would date the use of bank-rate policy as an instrument of general credit control only from the 1920's.[101]

Borrowing from the Bank of England in the pre-1914 era was by means of discounting commercial paper. Normally suppliers sold their bills to the banks or discounted them, sometimes using the service of bill brokers. When trade was expanding the supply of bills increased relative to the lending capacity of the banking system; the excess bills that the banking system could not handle converged on the Bank of England.[102] The Bank would buy up the bills and would as a consequence suffer a rise in its liabilities—notes and deposits— relative to its reserves. This was usually a prelude to a loss of reserves by the Bank, because increased activity in the country would lead to an internal drain of gold into circulation and to an external drain for increased imports. When gold began to flow from the Bank of England, or possibly in anticipation of its flow, the Bank would raise its bank-rate in an attempt to preserve its gold reserves.

The rise in bank-rate was a signal for other lending rates to rise as

---

1927), p. 255, refers to this practice of regulating the reserves by means of bank-rate adjustments as the reserve-discount policy, which he suggests was a policy of self-interest. Bloomfield, *Monetary Policy under the International Gold Standard*, p. 38, refers to this practice of central banks varying the bank-rate inversely with their reserve ratios and concludes that on the whole over the business cycle it tended to have a stabilizing effect.

101. Hawtrey, *A Century of Bank Rate*, pp. 32, 37, 40, 64, 68, 223, 242.

102. Merchants frequently took their new bills directly to the Bank of England for discounting; it was not until 1890 that the Bank of England accepted discount houses as the principal channel through which bills came to it for discount. London banks never offered bills to the Bank of England after 1825. Ibid., pp. 36–7. W. T. C. King, *History of the London Discount Market* (London, George Routledge & Sons, Ltd., 1936), p. 38.

well, with the general result that it became more expensive for suppliers to discount their bills. Supposedly the suppliers reacted by holding on to their bills until maturity and improved their asset position by postponing their own purchases—in effect running down their inventories. Hence bank-rate reacted directly on borrowers, reducing their demand for accommodation and thereby relieving the pressure on the banking system and on the reserves of the Bank of England.

But bank-rate also had another effect: it tended to produce a rise in deposit rates because of a practice that tied such rates to bank-rate.[103] The circumstances under which bank-rate would be raised were such that deposit rates were tending to rise anyway because of the drain on cash from the banks and the competition among them to retain or attract offsetting primary deposits; the convention tying deposit rates to bank-rate was therefore merely one of convenience. The higher deposit rates tended to attract foreign depositors as well as domestic depositors, with the result that both the internal drain and external drain might be slowed down or perhaps even reversed. The pressure on cash reserves and Bank of England reserves would thereby be alleviated. Bank-rate would then be lowered whether or not the inflationary influences that had caused the initial rise had passed over.[104]

Therefore, in so far as bank-rate policy had anything to do with credit control, that control was supposed to work through the ultimate borrower, causing him to reduce the supply of bills he brought forward for discounting: costs, not cash reserves, were the restraining factor.[105] Checking an inflation depended on interest rates. It was the

103. King, *History of the London Discount Market*, p. 173.

104. Keynes, *Treatise*, *1*, 190, points out that a bank-rate policy which protects the reserves through regulating gold flows interferes with credit control; and Hawtrey, *Bank Rate*, p. 253, indicates how unreliable a guide for monetary policy the reserves were since the attraction of gold to England by a high bank-rate often resulted in a premature relaxation of credit.

Schumpeter, *Business Cycles*, *2*, 673 and n. 2, also points out that cyclical increases in bank-rate not only had restrictive effects but also had relieving ones; he thought the latter were the more important.

105. Keynes, *Treatise*, *1*, pp. 187–91, examines three traditional views on the manner in which bank-rate was thought to operate: viz., through changes in cash

same in a deflation. If the supply of private bills coming forward for discount was falling off because of reduced demand, excess lending capacity developed in the banking system, and gold flowed into the banks from internal and external sources because of reduced domestic needs and a current-account surplus on international transactions. The gold reserves of the Bank of England would therefore be rising; and if the Bank expected the increased reserves to remain with it, it would lower bank-rate in an attempt to expand its earning assets. The fall in market rates was supposed to increase the supply of bills and to check the inflow of gold, thereby countering the tendency to redundancy of reserves.

However, if the Bank of England thought that the increase in its reserves was only temporary and would soon be drawn away, the Bank would not lower bank-rate and so would not follow market rates down. It might, in an attempt to diminish the potential demand on its reserves, sell securities in the open market so as to reduce its note and deposit liabilities. This was known as making bank-rate effective, because the move was usually followed by a rise in market rates; this was the forerunner of open-market operations.[106]

In general then, bank-rate policy in pre-1914 England evolved as a tool for regulating the gold reserves of the Bank of England. As such it was a poor tool of monetary policy, and one that did not come to have a wider application until the 1920's. The policy apparently worked through changes in lending rates, the reaction of the borrower being all important. However, the situation could not have been quite like this, and further analysis is required to see exactly how

---

reserves, through regulating gold flows, and through influencing interest rates. He argues that any credit control inherent in bank-rate policy must attach itself solely to the interest-rate effect.

106. Hawtrey, *Bank Rate*, pp. 68–70, who, however, views this procedure in more modern terms as a deliberate attempt to regulate the cash reserves of the member banks; but a narrower view of the operations as merely an attempt to safe-guard the reserves of the Bank of England seems justified from the more general analysis presented elsewhere in Mr. Hawtrey's book.

Peter B. Kenen, *British Monetary Policy and the Balance of Payments, 1951–1957*, p. 57, takes the view that open-market operations by the Bank of England in the nineteenth century were "the handmaiden of its discount policy."

restraint must have worked in those days; this requires focusing attention on the reaction of lenders, especially banks.

In nineteenth-century England the banking system must never have
been very far from fully-loaned.[107] Some elasticity in the system was
provided by call loans to the money market, which could be liquidated
for cash when the demand for loans expanded; the liquidation of
call loans forced the money market to turn to the Bank of England,
and in this way the cash required by the banks to support the expansion in loans was provided. But once all call loans were liquidated,
the banks would be unable to meet any additional demands for loans.
The excess demand for accommodation then had to turn to the Bank
of England, which would accommodate the market at a rising bank-
rate. The rise in bank-rate would keep bank-rate above market rates,
but apparently it was never sufficient to discourage all borrowers
because the Bank always did provide some accommodation. This
gave the banks additional cash reserves to satisfy business previously
turned away. For a mild expansion one rise in bank-rate, coupled
with the increase in other lending rates associated with it and with
the increase in cash reserves, might suffice to check some demand and
enable the banks to meet the remaining new demand. However, in
a more dynamic situation one rise in bank-rate might not suffice; the
drain of gold for exports and into circulation might increase to such
an extent that much of the extra cash reserves provided by the Bank
of England in accommodating the market might flow right through
the banking system. The banks would then experience little increase
in lending capacity so that the pressure of excess demand on the Bank
of England would continue to weigh heavily. In this scheme of things
the Bank of England, as a lender of last resort, had no control over

107. If the banks had been always fully-loaned, there would have been continuous borrowing from the Bank of England. Bagehot, *Lombard Street*, pp. 114–15,
stated that in ordinary times there was never enough money to discount all the
bills in Lombard Street without taking funds from the Bank of England. Hawtrey,
Bank Rate, p. 70, however, argues that the normal situation was one in which the
Bank of England did no discounting for the market at all. (Also, cf. Keynes,
Treatise, 2, 227.) If that were the case, any fall in bank loans below their normal
level would not result in an automatic reduction in cash reserves through the
repayment of indebtedness by the market to the Bank of England. Thus, some
excess lending capacity likely developed when the economy was not fully extended.

the volume of bank cash except by way of costs; there would be no halt to the spiral except through increasing bank-rate and other lending rates.

This system would seem to call for extreme fluctuations in bank-rate and lending rates in the face of large movements in the demand for bank loans; yet apparently the Bank of England was able to contain any credit situation through small changes in bank-rate. One possible explanation is that small changes in lending rates were sufficient to discourage the supply of private paper coming forward for discount;[108] in a dynamic situation this can only mean that small changes in bank-rate had a stabilizing effect on the demand curve, moderating significantly its shiftability by altering expectations.[109] But in a dynamic situation it is just as likely for a change in bank-rate to have a perverse effect, a rise being taken as a signal that inflation is developing; everyone then adjusts his position accordingly, which only adds to the strength of the inflationary forces.[110]

It seems much more likely that in nineteenth-century England what control over credit there was depended greatly on special reactions by lenders, mainly in the form of credit rationing. Mild fluctuations in lending rates would be explained if the banks raised their lending rates only to cover increased lending costs, such as a rise in the rate of pure interest in the economy. Such a pricing policy would not always be sufficient to choke off a rising demand for accommodation.

108. W. Manning Dacey, "The Floating Debt Problem," *Lloyds Bank Review*, Apr. 1956, pp. 30–1, argues that credit control in England used to work through higher rates discouraging the supply of private paper coming forward for discounting.

109. Hawtrey, *Bank Rate*, p. 249, in an attempt to explain the apparent effectiveness of small changes in bank-rate gave as one reason the adverse effect on the expectations of traders that checked the tendency of the demand curve for loans to move out.

110. Paul A. Samuelson, "Recent American Monetary Controversy," *Three Banks Review*, Mar. 1956, p. 10n1, argues that changes in bank-rate may induce perverse reactions in a dynamic situation; a rise in bank-rate is interpreted as a confirmation that the economy is inflating, and vice versa, with every one adjusting his position so as to aggravate the developing situation. W. L. Smith, "The Discount Rate as a Credit-Control Weapon," *Journal of Political Economy*, 66 (Apr. 1958), 174, also concludes that the effects of bank-rate changes on business expectations are likely to be destabilizing, or at best neutral.

Therefore, rationing must have been necessary, in what was a fully-loaned banking system, to exclude business that was still profitable; furthermore, some of the rationed demand must have been of the variety that could not shift to the Bank of England. Hence, only some of the excess demand created by the limited lending capacity of the banking system found its way to the central bank; the rest, having no alternative source of credit, went unsatisfied.[111] Rationing, then, is sufficient to explain the effectiveness of bank-rate policy over the trade cycle without undue movements in bank-rate.

111. During the nineteenth century the practice of financing internal trade by advances and overdrafts began to replace financing by discounting bills of exchange. The resort to less negotiable credit instruments must have made for greater dependence of borrowers on the banks and to have diminished the importance of alternative means of financing.

Hawtrey, *Bank Rate*, pp. 249–50, implies that one reason small changes in bank-rate were effective in regulating credit conditions in nineteenth-century England was that a rise in bank-rate caused the banks to restrict their lending. In an earlier work, *The Art of Central Banking*, p. 154, Mr. Hawtrey definitely argues that English banks resorted to rationing. Also cf. his *Currency and Credit*, 4th ed. (London, Longmans, Green and Co., 1950), p. 93, where he states that a change in bank-rate reacts not only on market rates but also on the willingness of the banks to lend. In an appendix to *Lombard Street* by Walter Bagehot, the evidence of an official of the London and Westminster Bank before an 1858 parliamentary committee is reproduced in which he stated (pp. 338–9) that his bank definitely refused to make some loans when its cash reserves were under pressure. And John Stuart Mill, *Principles of Political Economy*, rev. ed. (New York, The Colonial Press, 1899), 2, 158, mentions briefly in his discussion of commercial crises that at such times banks raise their lending rates and "withhold their customary advances."

James W. Gilbart, *The Principles and Practice of Banking*, pp. 222–3, speaks of banks refusing accommodation in "seasons of pressure," thus implying that in his day credit rationing was a normal part of banking operations.

Keynes, *Treatise*, *1*, 267, held that a change in the cash reserves of the banking system would directly alter bank loans outstanding; based on his observations of the English banking system, this conclusion only holds when banks must ration credit.

If the discussion in the nineteenth century about the duty of the Bank of England to act as a lender of last resort was a reflection of the general feeling that the Bank should behave differently from other banks, the implication is that other banks must have restricted their lending. In other words, there would have been no need for the concept of lender of last resort if the other banks had always been willing to provide accommodation at some price.

If the foregoing interpretation is valid, credit control in nineteenth-century England rested, not on control of the cash base,[112] but partly on the reaction of borrowers to changes in lending rates and partly on changes in credit rationing by the banks. The role of lender of last resort imposed on a reluctant Bank of England took direct control of the cash reserves out of the hands of the Bank;[113] fluctuations in the reserves of the banking system then were the net results of changes in indebtedness to the Bank of England and of gold flows into and out of the banks.

Bank-Rate Policy Today

Bank-rate policy today, where it has evolved into a genuine instrument of credit control is an entirely different creature from its nineteenth-century counterpart. No longer is bank-rate policy merely an automatic response to changes in the banking reserves of a country; it now functions, at least in the United Kingdom, as a truly dis-

112. Wood, *English Theories of Central Banking Control*, pp. 3, 178.

113. That the Bank of England should always act as a lender of last resort was the major policy prescription in Walter Bagehot's *Lombard Street*; after he wrote in 1873, the responsibility of the Bank of England as the lender of last resort became unequivocally recognized. Cf. Hawtrey, *The Art of Central Banking*, p. 126.

At the time that Bagehot wrote, banking opinion seemed generally against the unqualified view that the Bank of England should always be a willing lender (*Lombard Street*, pp. 168–70), an opinion that did not prevail against the arguments of Bagehot. Undoubtedly Bagehot had to state his case strongly in a day when financial crises were both frequent and disastrous; there was definitely a need for some agency to assume responsibility for orderly conditions in the money market. Yet perhaps those who opposed the views of Bagehot were not completely wrong in the light of today when it appears that central banks have heeded only too well Bagehot's advice, and become as a result, at times, all too accommodating. It might have been better for the development of central banking had Bagehot not won so decisive a victory; a less urgent concern for orderly conditions in the market might have led in recent years to a more vigorous check to inflation through control of the cash reserves of the banking system.

Cf. Friedrich A. Hayek, *Prices and Production* (New York, The Macmillan Company, 1932), p. 100, who sees the role of lender of last resort imposing on the central bank the duty of accommodating trade and expanding credit as increasing demands require. As long as the general opinion holds that this is the proper duty of central banking, he argues, it is utopian to expect central banks to contract the reserve base when this is clearly called for.

cretionary instrument designed to influence the general credit situation.[114]

Furthermore, bank-rate now works in a different environment; government debt, not private debt, is most likely to be the main borrowing instrument for obtaining advances from the central bank. Although the demise, or at least the diminished importance, of private negotiable debt in England and its replacement in the bank-rate mechanism by government debt has weakened the link between lending rates and bank-rate, some vestige of the link still remains. But a more important price effect of bank-rate now, in view of the greater holdings of government debt by money-market and bank lenders, falls on government debt. A rise in bank-rate causes the money market to lower buying prices for the main assets dealt in, namely government debt. The fall in security prices directly affects lenders: to expand their loans they are faced with the prospect of selling securities at a capital loss when they have no excess liquid assets to dispose of. If lenders cover a fall in security prices with an offsetting rise in lending rates, the situation becomes similar to that before 1914; bank-rate policy works entirely through lending rates. Should lending rates not rise sufficiently to compensate for the cost of selling securities to accommodate categories of loans previously profitable to the banks, applications for new money on such loans may be refused. The reaction of lenders is then added to that of borrowers to slow down the expansion in new credit. Thus, if security yields prove more flexible than lending rates, a new element is added to bank-rate policy that was not present in the nineteenth century.

A rise in bank-rate that lowers security yields still may attract foreign funds as in the old days but, unlike the old days, any effect the inflow of foreign funds may have on cash reserves is likely to be offset or sterilized.

A bank-rate policy still works best in an accommodating role when the domestic economy is expanding or contracting and security prices are moving down or up; bank-rate movements are then closely

114. Cf. Great Britain, Chancellor of the Exchequer, Committee on the Working of the Monetary System, *Report*, Cmd. 827 (London, Her Majesty's Stationery Office, 1959), para. 441, p. 153, where, however, it is suggested that bank-rate works as an instrument of monetary control because of the tradition behind bank-rate.

geared to open-market policy and are a reflection of the buying and selling attitudes of the central bank as well as of its lending attitude. A change in bank-rate that places it above market rates when the market is not seeking accommodation from the central bank either as a borrower or as a seller of securities is apt to be impotent unless reinforced by open-market policy.

Aside from these changes and qualifications, however, a modern bank-rate policy that is in the tradition of the nineteenth century would work through its reaction on lenders and borrowers. It would work by altering the cost at which loanable funds are obtainable—an influence it can effect whether or not the market borrows from the central bank. In other words, the effectiveness of bank-rate would depend not on keeping the market from making use of central-bank credit except as a last resort in an emergency sense, but on altering the cost of reserve funds and of loanable funds in general.

Bank-rate policy as it is practised in the United States and Canada today is not in this tradition of the nineteenth century; it does not depend on making cash reserves more expensive and discouraging borrowers or even lenders. Rather its effectiveness is judged by its success in restricting the use of central-bank credit facilities to the minimum and to strictly emergency conditions. In both countries bank-rate policy has thus been reduced to the level of a technical financial device—an extremely valuable one that aids the banks in the often difficult task of adjusting their cash position, but nevertheless a device that has no connotations for monetary policy.

Such a device is a necessary element in the financial environment of both Canada and the United States where cash-reserve ratios are prescribed by law. If the banks are to keep their cash reserves close to the minimum level, it is essential that they have access to immediately available cash; otherwise they must carry excess reserves or be exposed to the constant danger of breaking the law.[115] In both

115. Both Joseph Aschheim, *Techniques of Monetary Control*, pp. 92, 98, and Milton Friedman, *A Program for Monetary Stability*, The Millar Lectures, No. 3 (New York, Fordham University Press, 1959), pp. 44–5, suggest that breaking the law and paying the penalty rate imposed for so doing provides sufficient escape for banks trying to keep their reserves to a minimum. It seems hardly likely that banks would countenance breaking the law even if it meant only a payment of a penalty

countries the most satisfactory safety device—in terms of ease, convenience and need—is the advance from central banks; under emergency conditions there are no perfect substitutes for central-bank credit, only close substitutes.[116] Restraining the use of central-bank credit facilities then cannot depend on price alone, and administrative restraints are required to restrict access to borrowed reserves; these restraints operate to restrict borrowers to very short-term loans for rigidly prescribed purposes.[117]

These administrative restraints are designed to restrict the use of borrowed reserves to those emergency occasions on which a bank has no recourse but to borrow. Such an occasion arises when reserve ratios are legally prescribed and the cash of a bank falls below the legal requirements towards the end of the reserve period; there may then be no other method of meeting the reserve requirement except by borrowing from the central bank.[118] Since the need for such finan-

---

rate. They would be much more likely to prefer holding excess reserves so as to avoid deficiencies at all costs.

116. Thus, both Samuelson, "Recent American Monetary Controversy," p. 11, and Roosa, *Federal Reserve Operations*, p. 24, describe the rediscount facility available to member banks in the United States as a necessary and important safety valve.

In Canada the only method by which the banks can acquire cash reserves on the same day is by borrowing from the Bank of Canada. No other methods yield cash reserves until at least the next day. Cf. R. M. MacIntosh, "Broadening the Money Market," *Canadian Banker*, *61* (Autumn 1954), 67–9.

117. The conditions under which Canadian banks may borrow from the Bank of Canada are discussed in Bank of Canada, *Annual Report*, 1956, pp. 44–5; the corresponding American conditions are contained in Regulation A of the Board of Governors of the Federal Reserve System, the latest revision of which is reprinted in "Advances and Discounts by Federal Reserve Banks: Regulation A Revised," *Federal Reserve Bulletin*, Jan. 1955, pp. 8–14.

118. This is particularly so in a unit-banking system where the flow of cash reserves between banking offices is more complex and causes more difficulty than in a branch-banking system where reserves are concentrated. Thus, in the United States borrowing from the central bank is absolutely necessary to "give each of the thousands of independent unit banks a supplemental source of temporary reserves to help meet the sudden and often unexpected reserve drains that may at any time strike any of them." Roosa, *Federal Reserve Operations*, p. 15.

Winfield W. Riefler, *Money Rates and Money Markets in the United States*, pp. 28–33, discusses the circumstances under which a member bank might borrow from a Federal Reserve Bank in the United States.

cing generally results from unexpected cash losses that occur too late in the reserve period to be offset in any other way, the borrowing is not related to lending activities of the borrowing bank as such or to the pressure of demand for bank loans. The rate charged for such emergency accommodation cannot be much in excess of the cost of accumulating excess reserves towards the end of each reserve period or else the banks will habitually resort to precautionary measures of this nature (involuntary "window-dressing") rather than borrow. Thus the emergency bank-rate is closely related to the yield on the nearest cash-substitute asset available to the banks, because it is the yield on this asset that measures the cost of holding excess reserves for precautionary purposes.

A rate for emergency loans from the central bank that is low enough to discourage the deliberate accumulation of excess reserves is not high enough however to discourage non-emergency borrowing. The demand for such non-emergency borrowing depends on the volume and relative prices of the substitutes for advances from the central bank. The higher the level of bank-rate the greater the number of assets a bank will have that are substitutes for borrowed reserves; the lower the level of bank-rate the fewer such substitutes that will be available.[119] When bank-rate is just above the yield on the most liquid assets held by the banks, as it is in Canada and the United States,[120] the avoidance of non-emergency borrowing from the central bank depends on the member banks carrying excess liquid

119. Edward C. Simmons, "A Note on the Revival of Federal Reserve Discount Policy," *Journal of Finance*, *11* (Dec. 1956), 420, argues that the use of the discount mechanism in the United States does not depend on "choice among alternatives resting on cost-profit calculations," but his criticism is too sweeping. Within the context in which borrowing from the Federal Reserve System is permitted, decisions to borrow will take into account the profitability of doing so when close substitutes for borrowing are available as they often will be. It is only when borrowing is not absolutely essential but profitable that non-profit considerations play a large part in determining the extent of borrowing from the central bank.

120. In the United States the discount rates of the Federal Reserve Banks tend to be above the rate on treasury bills, but below that on prime market paper. U.S. Congress, *Monetary Policy . . . Public Debt: Compendium*, Pt. 1, p. 396. In Canada the practice was introduced in 1956 of automatically setting bank-rate at $\frac{1}{4}$ of 1 per cent above the average tender rate on accepted tenders at the weekly auction for three-month treasury bills. Bank of Canada, *Annual Report*, 1956, p. 46.

assets, or on non-economic restraints on advances from the central bank.

Where bank-rate is moved independently of market rates so as to encourage non-emergency borrowing at one time and discourage it at another, bank-rate serves a wider purpose; but the rate is not so used in Canada or the United States, and the general reluctance of banks to take advantage of central-bank lending facilities at present weighs against its use in this manner.

Despite the obviously restricted nature of bank-rate, it is sometimes argued that it serves the ends of monetary policy in the United States because there are usually some borrowed reserves in existence there, the volume of which fluctuates. The general argument is that by regulating the extent to which the banks are in debt to the Federal Reserve System the authorities can influence the amount and kind of lending that the banks do.[121] Given the limited conditions under which banks may borrow, the main way of regulating their indebtedness to the System is through open-market operations. Taking away reserves through open-market operations may cause some banks to borrow during the transition period while the reserve effects are being worked out. But it is the loss of the reserves itself, not the borrowing reflecting the reserve-loss, that influences the lending behaviour of the banks. If the member banks go further into debt to the central bank, it is because they have sustained unexpected reserve-losses; they are not then in so favourable a position to meet additional demands from customers for funds. Likewise, if banks were previously borrowing to cover an unexpected loss of cash, they are not in so favourable a position to extend loans as when, because of open-market operations, they suddenly gain cash that enables them to pay off their borrowings. In short, variations in member-bank indebtedness to the central bank reflect the changing state of the money market, and it is conditions in the money market, not the volume of indebtedness, that is the causal force influencing bank-lending policies.

Bank-rate policy, then, under North American conditions of rationing and other limitations on central-bank credit, is not an active

121. U.S. Congress, *Monetary Policy . . . Public Debt: Compendium*, Pt. 1, pp. 283, 396. Also cf. Simmons, "A Note on the Revival of Federal Reserve Discount Policy," p. 417; Burgess, *The Reserve Banks and the Money Market*, pp. 214-15.

weapon of monetary policy. Bank-rate borrowing is merely an emergency device, useful within the limited sphere of the money market for making the financial machinery run a little more smoothly. Bank-rate is set with the idea of restricting bank and non-bank borrowing from the central bank as much as possible to need borrowing, without making the cost of such borrowing onerous. Given this limited objective, the question arises whether bank-rate should be changed as required by discretionary acts of the authorities, as it is at present in the United States, or allowed to vary automatically with some market rate, as it is in Canada.[122]

The argument for letting bank-rate vary automatically with some market rate of interest is that it prevents changes in bank-rate from being interpreted as reflections of policy.[123] Discretionary changes in the rate are always likely to be interpreted as representing changes in monetary policy even when they do not. That is, under North American conditions, bank-rate will often have to be adjusted when market rates are changing, in order to hold constant the degree of restraint being applied to the banking system. If bank-rate were not changed, the changing relation between it and market rates might cause a change in the amount of borrowing from the central bank and so in the degree of pressure on the cash position of the banks. Hence, bank-rate may have to be changed at times when no change in policy is contemplated.[124] At other times, when a change in bank-rate does reflect a change in policy, the correct interpretation of this by the general public may induce perverse reactions and so aggravate the situation that the authorities are attempting to correct. Therefore, if bank-rate is allowed to vary with market rates in accordance with some impersonal or non-discretionary formula, it will not be possible to take bank-rate as a signal of the intent of the authorities, and the difficulties that such attempts create will be eliminated.[125]

122. Bank-rate in Canada varies weekly with the average yield on new three-month treasury bills. Cf. *ante*, n. 120. Canada now has a fixed bank-rate as well.

123. Bank-rate in the U.K. was often viewed as an index of economic prospects. Sayers, *Central Banking after Bagehot*, p. 64.

124. Cf. Friedman, *A Program for Monetary Stability*, p. 40.

125. A general defence for the use of a non-discretionary bank-rate is advanced by the Bank of Canada, *Annual Report*, 1960, pp. 58–64.

The case for making discretionary changes in bank-rate rests on the need for some signal of intent from the monetary authorities which such changes can provide, and with much greater effect than mere statements or declarations. If there is no need for such a signal, then there is clearly nothing to favour discretionary changes in bank-rate when automatic changes can provide the level of bank-rate required for holding in check borrowing from the central bank.

There are two general conditions under which a signal of intent from the authorities is unnecessary. No signal is really necessary if monetary policy is not being used as a flexible instrument for stabilizing the economy in the face of short-run fluctuations in economic activity. Significant short-run expansion or contraction in the size of the banking system is not called for and so no signal is necessary. A signal serves a useful function only when monetary policy is trying to regulate the size of the banking system for short-run stabilization purposes. It may make sense then, may even be essential, to have a signal to inform the system that has to be controlled the direction in which it is expected to move.[126]

Even here a signal will not be necessary if the monetary authorities have complete and perfect control over the banking system. Any desired change or movement in the banking system can be completely produced by the central bank and there is no possibility of the position of the banking system being anything other than what the central bank wants. A signal is then unnecessary for the central bank can

126. An argument that might appear to rule out use of a signal of intent is presented by Robert V. Roosa, "The Radcliffe Report," *Lloyds Bank Review*, Oct. 1959, pp. 10–11, who maintains that a certain amount of uncertainty in the market is necessary for successful open-market operations and that announcements of policy would eliminate any uncertainty.

A signal of intent, however, need not disclose the full market plans of the central bank. Such a signal can indicate direction of movement without disclosing with what amounts and at what prices the central bank will deal. When the central bank wishes the banking system to move in a given direction, it cannot hope to hide this information; and, indeed, it should not try to hide the information if it wishes its action to be effective. Here, a signal of intent given as the central bank carries out any market transactions required for its policy, or after it has completed its market transactions, will ensure a faster reaction by the banking system than otherwise. In such cases the market will know only which side of the market the central bank is on but no more.

manoeuvre the banking system into any desired position whether or not the system is fully aware of the direction in which it is being moved by the authorities.

Where, however, control of the banking system is less than complete so that the response of the system to application of pressure by the central bank may vary, a signal becomes an important tool of monetary policy. If the central bank is easing up, a signal to this effect will indicate to the banks that the ease they are experiencing is something more than temporary or accidental; the system is then likely to respond faster to the plodding of the central bank. Likewise, when the central bank is tightening up, the banks will be quicker to respond in the desired fashion if a discretionary rise in bank-rate is used to indicate to them that contraction of the system is to be vigorously enforced.

A signal is also useful in situations when central-bank control is not so complete that accidental degrees of ease or tightness cannot be avoided. On such occasions a discretionary bank-rate can serve to counter the incorrect impression of policy that the immediate experience of the banks conveys. For example, the system may suddenly become easy with cash at a time when the central bank does not intend to ease up, but imperfect control of the system has not enabled it to maintain the degree of cash tightness desired. A high or increased bank-rate might then serve to indicate the intention of the authorities to pursue a tight policy.

Use of a signal of intent to get the banking system to react in the manner desired more quickly than it might otherwise, or to compensate for imperfect control of the cash base of the banking system, still runs into the problem of inducing perverse reactions. This problem, however, is common to all stabilization policies and will exist whether or not a signal is used by the monetary authorities. If the monetary authorities are successfully attempting to restrain the banking system in an inflationary situation, they will be unable to hide the fact from the markets. Knowledge of the restrictive policy will be conveyed through the reaction of the banking system to the policy and so feed any perverse reaction likely to arise. A signal spreads the knowledge faster, perhaps, but it also hastens the desired response from the banking system.

Where a signal has a useful role to play, it can be conveyed by discretionary changes in bank-rate. Such changes will be most effective as a signal if restricted to changes meant to convey a message about policy. They should not be mixed up with changes required to keep bank-rate in a proper relation with market rates at times when matters of policy are not at stake. In ordinary circumstances setting the rate by means of a formula meets the operational needs served by bank-rate. Departure from the formula setting of the rate can then be introduced by the authorities when it is necessary to issue a signal of intent to counteract or reinforce the impressions of the market about the course of monetary control. When the signal has served its purpose, a return to formula setting of the bank-rate will be possible. In short, discretionary changes in bank-rate imposed upon a bank-rate normally set by an impersonal formula are perhaps the best way to use bank-rate as a signal of intent; discretionary and non-discretionary changes in bank-rate can then both be utilized to best advantage.

THE "MODUS OPERANDI" OF MONETARY CONTROL

The whole point of open-market operations and of bank-rate policy, when used as a device for monetary policy, is to exercise some control over the banking system. Hence, the discussion of central-bank transactions raises the broader topic of the basis for central-bank control of the banking system. This matter is treated here, first by dealing with the general situation in which excess cash forms the basis for control of the banking system; then by considering, in turn, the problems or complications introduced by the existence of liquidity ratios and of provisions for averaging cash requirements.

Control Through Excess Cash

Control of the banking system may be defined as regulating the size of the system in some way, as by fixing the size, changing it, affecting its rate of change, or simply influencing its direction of change. This can be done by upsetting the equilibrium of the system or by altering its state of disequilibrium. In the least complicated situation the general equilibrium of the banking system depends solely on how much cash is in the system and on the amount of cash required and desired by the system. When these two amounts coincide, the system can be said to be in equilibrium. There is then no excess cash in the banking system, and for the combination of earning assets and cash held by the system there is no desire to adjust cash relative to earning assets.

Therefore, positive (non-zero) "excess cash" defines a state in which the system has too much cash relative to earning assets, and the tendency of the system is then to restore equilibrium by expanding. When excess cash is negative, there is too little cash relative to earning assets and the tendency of the system is to reach an equilibrium by contracting. Thus, any non-zero excess cash will cause a reaction in the system to restore equilibrium and, under appropriate conditions, the reaction takes the form of a substitution between cash and earning assets with consequent effects on the size of the system. For excess cash to have this effect, however, all earning assets must be homogeneous in regard to the effect on the banking system of variations in their amounts. That is, regardless of what kind of earning assets banks acquire or dispose of the effect on the size of the banking system is the same.[127]

Hence, if monetary policy can bear upon the amount of excess cash in the banking system, or in any financial system, it can control that system. The possibilities of affecting excess cash depend on influencing its determinants, which consist of the cash demands of the system and the quantity of cash available to the system. Thus, each of these components must be examined in order to explain how excess cash may be manipulated to control a banking system.

The cash demands of a banking system, or of any financial system, may be represented by a function that describes all combinations of earning assets and cash for which there is no desire to alter cash relative to earning assets. For any given level of earning assets this demand function shows the amount of cash just right for those assets. This cash quantity may be styled the cash demand of the system at the given level of earning assets.

127. The need for this restriction is made clear by the analysis of the problems associated with the existence of a liquidity ratio, which are discussed under the next heading.

This cash demand is determined partly by the liabilities of the system and partly by the possibilities for carrying out a substitution between earning assets and cash. For a banking system minimum cash needs are likely to be positive and to vary directly with deposit liabilities.[128] At any given level of earning assets there will be a certain amount of deposits outstanding and consequently a basic need for cash, set by working needs and possibly by legal or conventional requirements. Any change in liabilities relative to earning assets alters, of course, the basic amount of cash required for the given level of earning assets. Additional cash, in excess of basic needs, may be held because the possibility of substituting earning assets for cash is not present, not desired, or not profitable. These restraints are a function of such things as speculative considerations, uncertainties, money-market imperfections, interest rates, and costs.[129] Together

128. For non-banking financial systems cash requirements may be zero if members of the system can operate without cash balances. According to J. Brooke Willis, *The Functions of the Commercial Banking System*, pp. 32–3, cash requirements of a banking system will disappear only when clearance among banks is perfect and when the public never attempts to redeem deposits for currency.

129. These things are all related to one another. Thus, speculative considerations and money-market imperfections may combine to cause banks to hold additional funds idle. When instruments with a short enough maturity are not available and interest rates are expected to rise shortly, it may appear unprofitable to invest new cash receipts immediately. Walter S. Salant, "The Demand for Money and the Concept of Income Velocity," *Journal of Political Economy*, 49 (June 1941), 419–20, explains bank holdings of idle reserves in terms of low interest rates and uncertainty about future rates. He argues that below a certain rate it will appear more profitable to wait in hope of acquiring assets at a lower price.

Uncertainties about the course of clearings in combination with the size of balances held and money-market rates may result in cash being held to meet unexpected clearing losses. The lack of suitable money-market instruments for the investment of temporary cash receipts may also cause extra cash to be held at times. Keynes, *Treatise*, 2, 54, gives as a reason for banks holding idle reserves the absence of earning assets "the liquidity of which is beyond question."

Interest rates and the cost of administration may combine to make it unprofitable to reduce cash balances further even though working needs would permit it. "Reserve Adjustments of City Banks," Federal Reserve Bank of Kansas City, *Monthly Review*, Feb. 1958, p. 3, observes that large banks have an advantage over small ones in keeping their reserves to a minimum because "while the day-to-day fluctuations of reserves are relatively small in percentage terms, the amount is

with the basic cash needs they determine the minimum level of cash that the banking system will want to hold for a given level of earning assets. When cash is at this minimum no attempt will be made to carry more earning assets and less cash; and of course there will be no attempt to reduce earning assets and carry more cash for this would only reduce profits to no end.

The cash available to a banking system includes all cash firmly held and which either will continue to be held or will be used for other purposes. Two problems arise here, however: one caused by cash borrowed from the central bank, and the other by the use of both central bank and bank money as bank cash.

Profit borrowing by member banks from the central bank adds as effectively to available cash as does cash from any other source. Its amount is fixed at any moment of time either by physical limitations or by profit considerations: additional earning assets are not available for acquisition, and borrowing is at the permissible maximum, or it is not profitable to borrow more to add to earning assets. Whatever the nature of the restraint it is always effective in that the borrowing is as large as the restraint permits. Variations in the strength of the restraint then result in variations in the amount borrowed.

The situation is different, however, for need borrowing. It gives rise to a compulsion to repay when cash becomes available from other sources regardless of whether or not this is the most profitable use for new cash. Consequently, in computing the amount of cash available for meeting cash demands, such borrowing is deducted from cash on hand. That is, in making up cash positions banks, in effect, set aside cash to offset need borrowing and in this way arrive at what additional cash they require to satisfy their ordinary cash demands.[130] Thus, available cash is taken net of need borrowing, which means that the banking system is never in equilibrium when

---

large enough to justify special action to gain earnings on these transitory balances." "Some Observations on Excess Reserves of Member Banks," Federal Reserve Bank of St. Louis, *Monthly Review*, Oct. 1960, p. 6, states that "some smaller banks keep a comfortable reserve position to avoid the costs of making daily calculations and the necessary asset adjustments required of a bank which is always almost fully invested."

130. Cf. Turner, *Member-Bank Borrowing*, p. 151.

need borrowing is outstanding, for such borrowing is inconsistent with zero excess cash.[131] Need borrowing does, however, enable a system to operate with a combination of earning assets and cash firmly held, that is not an equilibrium combination, until some way can be found to restore equilibrium. It follows that variations in need borrowing do not alter available cash or the extent of the final adjustment that must be made to restore equilibrium.

Banks may hold as cash both central-bank money and bank money —balances due from banks within the system—but it may well be that the equilibrium of the system depends on central-bank money alone. This is the case when bank demand for central-bank money varies directly with the size of the system, as it is likely to because of vault needs and legal or conventional requirements. Bank money does not provide a means of meeting the cash needs of a system whose equilibrium has been upset. For example, the acquisition of more earning assets based on intra-system borrowing, which increases bank money, requires more central-bank money. Yet any attempt by the system itself to get more central-bank money will only nullify the original acquisition of earning assets. Likewise, if a system draws down its bank money in acquiring more earning assets, it will find itself with insufficient central-bank money; the attempt to eliminate the deficit will again nullify the expansion in earning assets.[132] The available cash used in computing the excess cash of a banking system should then consist of central-bank money only.

Given the cash available to a banking system, or to any financial system, and the cash demands of the system, the amount of excess cash in the system at the existing level of earning assets is arrived at by subtracting the cash demands from the available cash. If the excess is greater than zero, the system has too much cash relative to earning assets; if excess cash is negative, the system has too little cash

131. If excess cash is zero when there is some need borrowing outstanding, it means that available cash less need borrowing is equal to cash demands. But then there is sufficient cash to meet all demands and to pay off the need borrowing. There is no reason for the need borrowing.

132. When bank-money absorbs some central-bank cash, because reserves are required against deposit liabilities owing to banks, a reduction in bank money reduces the need for central-bank money and so allows some of the previous expansion in earning assets to remain.

P

relative to earning assets. The system may restore balance between cash and earning assets in one of two ways: by changing available cash, without affecting earning assets, through variations in profit borrowing; or by a substitution between earning assets and cash. Thus, when profit borrowing remains constant, excess cash greater than zero will cause the system to expand by acquiring earning assets; negative excess cash causes the system to contract by liquidating earning assets. The substitution comes to a halt when excess cash becomes equal to zero.[133] Hence, when profit borrowing is fixed, a system can be held to a given level of earning assets by keeping its excess cash zero for that level of assets. Or, a system can be made to expand or contract by making its excess cash greater or less than zero, again so long as profit borrowing does not vary. If a system is already expanding or contracting, its reaction can be modified by changing the excess to which the system is reacting. Therefore, if there is some way in which the monetary authorities can act upon the excess cash of a banking system, or of any financial system, they can regulate the size of the system.

There are, in fact, three distinct ways in which the authorities may manipulate excess cash: by direct alteration of available cash; by direct action on cash demands; and by changing the terms and conditions under which cash is made available to the system.

Excess cash may be manipulated by directly altering available cash when a well-developed money market exists, and limits can be imposed on the amount of cash that the banking system can obtain by borrowing from the central bank or by converting earning assets

133. There are three possibilities here. (1) The substitution of earning assets for excess cash causes no direct loss of cash. Excess cash is eliminated only by a rise in cash demands, because the addition to earning assets increases deposit liabilities by a like amount. This describes a banking system from which there is no leakage of cash to currency in circulation. (2) The substitution of earning assets for excess cash causes a complete loss of cash. This describes either a non-bank financial system in which the acquisition of earning assets has no effect on the liabilities of the system, or a banking system that acquires all its additional earning assets from the central bank. (3) The substitution causes some direct loss of cash and some rise in cash demands. This describes a banking system in which the acquisition of earning assets adds to deposits by a lesser amount because of the leakage of cash to currency in circulation.

into cash. A well-developed money market ensures that any extra cash supplied to the banking system can be invested so that cash need not be held for lack of earning assets: cash demands are then independent of changes in available cash. Effective limits to profit borrowing[134] or asset conversion[135] ensure that reductions in available cash will not be offset by increased borrowing or by liquidating assets for cash.

Given these conditions and restraints, excess cash can be set at any value simply by altering the cash supplied to the banking system. A reduction in available cash below cash demands at the prevailing level of earning assets produces a negative "excess" and causes the banking system to contract. If cash demands happen to be falling autonomously at the same time, the negative excess can still be maintained by further reducing available cash. Likewise, a positive "excess" can be injected into the system by a sufficient rise in available cash so that expansion of the system follows. If cash demands are rising at the same time, available cash need only be increased by a larger amount in order to maintain the desired excess. In short, complete control of the supply of cash to the banking system means that the monetary authorities can manipulate excess cash at will, by acting on available cash alone, and thus the authorities can control the banking system by maintaining control over its cash.[136]

134. No limit to need borrowing is necessary because need borrowing is not a satisfactory way of meeting a loss of cash. Profit borrowing may be limited by rationing, or by setting rates high enough to make borrowing unprofitable.

135. Running off liquid assets to meet a loss of cash can be restricted, at least partially, by prescribing liquidity ratios, which reduce the amount of liquid assets available for conversion into cash. The whole question of liquidity ratios is considered under the next heading.

136. In this context the demand for cash is immaterial—so long as what demand there is is independent of supply. When there is this independence, supply can always be altered to offset any fluctuations in demand and to achieve any desired degree of excess cash. When expansion or contraction has proceeded far enough the excess may be eliminated, again by an appropriate change in supply.

Thus, given perfect control over the supply of bank cash, monetary control of the banking system does not require the maintenance of a fixed reserve ratio by banks. It does not even require the imposition of legal reserve requirements, a condition usually laid down as essential for monetary control. Cf. "The Functions of Reserve Requirements," Federal Reserve Bank of New York, *Monthly Review of*

P*

A direct attack on the cash demands of the system is another way of manipulating excess cash, which works when cash requirements specified by the authorities are effective. Such specified requirements are effective if a rise in requirements causes a banking system to hold more cash than it otherwise would and if a reduction in requirements would cause it to hold less cash.[137] A well-developed money market is also necessary to make lower requirements effective, for without such a market banks may not be able to use the cash freed by the fall in legal requirements. Restrictions on profit borrowing and the turn-

---

Credit and Business Conditions, June 1952, p. 81; U.S. Congress, Senate, Committee on Banking and Currency, *Member Bank Reserve Requirements: Hearings*, 86th Cong., 1st Sess., 1959, pp. 102, 107, 116. David A. Alhadeff, "Credit Controls and Financial Intermediaries," *American Economic Review, 50* (Sept. 1960), 655, however, holds the view that legal reserve requirements are not crucial for the control of a banking system.

Keynes, *Treatise, 2,* 70–1, argues that the only sound reason for having banks hold greater reserves than they require is to make them in this way contribute to the expenses incurred by the central bank in maintaining the currency. Ronald A. Shearer, "Significance of New Reserve Regulations: A Comment," University of Illinois, *Current Economic Comment, 22* (Aug. 1960), 49–50, holds that requiring banks to keep more cash than they otherwise would has the same effect as a differential tax on banks, and that the monetary authorities, as a quasi-taxing authority, should be made to demonstrate that the tax is justified by the results it produces. Cf. Frank E. Norton and Neil H. Jacoby, *Bank Deposits and Legal Reserve Requirements* (Los Angeles, University of California, 1959), p. 3.

John G. Gurley and Edward S. Shaw, *Money in a Theory of Finance*, pp. 262–4, 271, argue that a minimum-reserve requirement is unnecessary for monetary control. In their analysis monetary control requires only that the central bank regulate the supply of bank reserves and fix the price of these reserves in the form of a "reserve-balance rate." Presumably, if a central bank does not pay interest on reserve balances, it has fixed the reserve-balance rate (at zero) and so exercises control by regulating the supply of reserves.

137. Such specification of reserves for control purposes does not require that the total reserve burden imposed on the banking system vary with the deposits of the system. A fixed amount, varied only at the discretion of the authorities, is all that is needed to exercise control through movements in requirements. The allocation of any given fixed reserve burden among the members of the system could vary with the distribution of deposits among the members. Hence, the proponents for 100 per cent reserves must show that a specified reserve is necessary, and that a 100 per cent reserve is better than any other percentage.

ing of liquid assets into cash are also necessary to make a rise in legal requirements effective in getting the excess cash desired.

Given these conditions, any amount of excess cash can be generated by varying the reserve requirements imposed on the banking system.[138] This approach is most appropriate when control over the supply of cash is inadequate or impossible, for no close control over available cash is necessary to produce a given excess when legal requirements can be freely altered. For this reason the technique of variable reserve requirements is particularly apt for a non-banking financial system, for the available cash of such a system cannot be closely regulated.[139] The technique is also useful for banking systems operating in countries with thin or inadequate money markets. The supply of bank cash cannot then be regulated precisely by open-market operations, but undesirable fluctuations in supply can be countered by appropriate changes in reserve requirements.[140]

138. Gurley and Shaw, *Money in a Theory of Finance*, p. 269, appear to suggest that the bank demand for cash reserves could be manipulated by the central bank paying a varying rate of interest on reserve balances. No reserve ratio then need be specified, a rise in the rate on reserve balances being used to get the banks to hold more reserves.

139. That is, the cash base of a non-bank financial system cannot be controlled as can the cash base of a banking system, for non-banks by their own acts add to the cash base of their system as banks can not. Donald Shelby, "Some Implications of the Growth of Financial Intermediaries," *Journal of Finance, 13* (Dec. 1958), 539, implies that regulating the reserve ratios of non-banks would not contribute to monetary control, because such regulation would have little effect on the liabilities of the non-banks. Alhadeff, "Credit Controls and Financial Intermediaries," pp. 658–60, also argues against variable reserve ratios for non-banks for the same reason and for the reason that the effect of such variations on the earning assets of non-banks is less than it is on those of banks. It nevertheless follows that the excess cash of non-banks can be manipulated by means of variable reserve ratios and thus the volume of their earning assets regulated, which in turn affects the interest rates they charge and pay in accordance with the needs of monetary control. Warren L. Smith, "Financial Intermediaries and Monetary Controls," *Quarterly Journal of Economics, 73* (Nov. 1959), 545–6, appears to believe that simply imposing legal-reserve requirements on non-banks would be sufficient to control them.

140. Cf. Fousek, *Foreign Central Banking*, p. 55. The use of variable reserve ratios as the only means of manipulating the excess cash of the banking system in New Zealand is described in detail in Great Britain, Chancellor of the Exchequer,

Acting on the terms and conditions under which cash is made available to the banking system is another way of manipulating excess cash. The effectiveness of this technique depends on the system demand for earning assets or profit borrowing being elastic. An elastic system demand for earning assets means that banks stand ready to trade in earning assets even though they are in equilibrium; this means they operate a trading account in marketable securities and are prepared to buy or sell, within limits, whenever this is profitable, regardless of cash-position considerations. An elastic demand for profit borrowing means that changes in the lending rates of the central bank cause banks to vary the amount of their borrowing. In addition, the central bank may ration its loans so that variations in the degree of rationing, at existing rates, offer another way of causing the amount borrowed to vary.

Under these conditions excess cash can be injected into a banking system that is in equilibrium by the central bank changing its trading terms, and its terms and conditions for lending.[141] Thus, the central bank may induce the banks to give up cash to reduce profit borrowing either by calling for repayment or by raising rates to make the existing debt level an unprofitable one. This makes excess cash in the system negative so that the system must now contract.[142] The same effect may be achieved by the central bank inducing the system to acquire earning assets from it by offering securities at attractive prices. If banks accept, it is because they believe they can regain their equilibrium by liquidating lower-yielding assets. For the system, however, negative excess cash is created by trading with the central bank and attempts to eliminate it cause the system to contract. Similarly, posi-

---

Committee on the Working of the Monetary System, *Principal Memoranda of Evidence*, *1*, pp. 273, 275–6 (memorandum of evidence submitted by the Governor of the Reserve Bank of New Zealand).

141. Apparently open-market operations in West Germany are carried out largely by the central bank altering the rates at which it will buy and sell money-market paper. Cf. Deutsche Bundesbank, *Report*, 1960, p. 38. Turner, *Member-Bank Borrowing*, pp. 159–60, discusses the possibility of regulating the cash base of the banking system by appropriate variations in bank-rate.

142. If cash is not given up immediately to repay debt, it will be set aside for debt repayment and the system will then act as if it did not have sufficient cash.

tive excess cash can be injected into a banking system through the central bank offering banks cheaper loans or high prices for some of their earning assets. Acceptance of such offers generates positive excess cash and results in a banking expansion.

When a banking system is already out of equilibrium, its excess cash may be eliminated or modified by an appropriate change in the conditions or rates for profit borrowing. Thus, a variation in lending rates may induce banks to eliminate a positive excess by reducing profit borrowing, or a negative excess by increasing profit borrowing, when, without a change in rates, the excess would not have been so eliminated. Changes in the degree of rationing can also be used to achieve the same effect. Variations in the trading terms of the central bank are, however, unnecessary here for manipulating excess cash because the system will be trading in assets anyway in an attempt to regain its equilibrium. The central bank need be only a buyer or seller, as required, at existing prices in order to have an effect on excess cash.

In general, control of a banking system, or of any financial system, reduces, in the absence of liquidity complications, to a manipulation in some way of the amount of excess cash in the system, for no system willingly holds a positive excess or suffers a negative excess. Instead, given appropriate restraints and conditions, it attempts a substitution between earning assets and cash, with the sign of the excess governing the direction of the substitution, and the amount governing the strength of the effect. Therefore, by generating an excess or by modifying an excess generated by the system itself, the monetary authorities can get the banking system to move either up or down and at any desired rate. The authorities may do this by altering directly the supply of cash to the system, by varying the cash requirements imposed on the system, or by changing the terms and conditions under which they will deal with the system in supplying it with cash.[143]

143. This formulation perhaps takes account of the objection raised by Karl R. Bopp, "Central Banking Objectives, Guides, and Measures," *Journal of Finance*, 9 (Mar. 1954), 19–21, that the classical formulation of monetary control emphasizes too much the regulation of the volume of reserve balances. He points out that monetary control in Germany prior to World War I did not depend on regulating reserve balances but on influencing the liquidity of the banking system. His

Thus, all techniques for exercising general control over a banking system, or any financial system, reduce to a manipulation of excess cash, so that all monetary control may be said to take the form of shaping excess cash.[144]

Liquidity Ratios and Control

Difficulties in manipulating excess cash arise when a banking system holds money-market assets that are, for the system, a substitute for cash, in that variations in system holdings of the assets are accompanied by offsetting variations in bank cash. Such cash substitutes can exist only when some restraint is imposed on the operations of the central bank, perhaps by the financing needs of the government, or by the desire of the authorities to limit fluctuations in money-market interest rates. It is because of this restraint that, when the banking system acquires or disposes of cash-substitute assets, the cash of the system is decreased or increased by a like amount. Thus, cash-substitute assets are unlike other earning assets whose acquisition or disposal by the banking system alters bank deposits instead of bank cash. If the central bank could hold bank cash constant when the

---

formulation of monetary control in terms of operating on liquidity can, I think, be interpreted or explained in terms of manipulating the excess cash of the banking system.

144. This is a variation on a formulation by Robert V. Roosa, "Monetary and Credit Policy," *Economics and the Policy Maker*, Brookings Lectures, 1958–59 (Washington, D.C., The Brookings Institution, 1959), p. 107, who states that "under almost any circumstances . . . the general aims of the central bank can be expressed for purposes of current policy in terms of the direction and extent of the change that ought to be permitted at the margin, in the prevailing degree of pressure on bank reserves." For "bank reserves" in the foregoing statement I would substitute "excess cash."

A related point is whether monetary control, defined as regulation of the size of the banking system, is the primary concern of monetary policy. It clearly is when the immediate aim of policy is control of the money supply, of the amount of liquid financial assets held by the public, or of the amount of financing provided by banks. All these are a function of the size of the banking system. Even more remote aims, however, such as influencing interest rates, prices of financial assets, or expenditures and incomes, can be sought through regulating the size of the banking system, for monetary policy can pursue even these goals in this way.

banking system altered its holdings of money-market assets, there would be no cash-substitute assets.

The English banking system appears to provide the prime example of a banking system that holds cash substitutes, and the experience of that system indicates the nature of the difficulties that such cash substitutes can create for the manipulation of excess cash. Indeed, experience there suggests that for a banking system holding cash substitutes the basis for monetary control is not excess cash but liquidity requirements. A closer examination of the English banking system reveals, however, that this is not so.

The English clearing banks are committed to holding 8 per cent of their deposits in cash and at least 30 per cent of their deposits in the combined form of cash, money-market loans (at call and short notice), and bills, mainly treasury bills. Maintaining the 8 per cent cash ratio is said to be a purely technical problem for the English banks,[145] apparently because call loans and treasury bills can be exchanged for cash as required (and presumably the acquisition of these assets causes the banking system to lose cash).[146] Consequently, it is argued that control of the English banking system depends not on the 8 per cent cash ratio but on the 30 per cent "liquidity ratio."[147]

If the liquidity ratio of the English banks is exactly 30 per cent, the banks will not be able to expand even if they hold cash in excess of the 8 per cent requirement. Any attempt to expand will increase the need for liquid assets, but under English conditions additional money-

145. Great Britain, Chancellor of the Exchequer, Committee on the Working of the Monetary System, *Report*, p. 52. Also cf. W. Manning Dacey, "Treasury Bills and the Money Supply," *Lloyds Bank Review*, Jan. 1960, pp. 3–4.

146. R. S. Sayers, *Modern Banking*, 5th ed. (Oxford, At the Clarendon Press, 1960), p. 198, states that the English banks can always turn bills or call money into cash, or vice versa. This is also the interpretation of Warren L. Smith and Raymond F. Mikesell, "The Effectiveness of Monetary Policy: Recent British Experience," *Journal of Political Economy*, *65* (Feb. 1957), p. 25.

147. This forms the subject of a debate as to whether the liquidity ratio or the cash ratio is the crucial ratio in controlling bank credit. The issues in this debate are briefly summarized by M. Gaskin, "Monetary Policy and the Scottish Banks," *Scottish Journal of Political Economy*, *5* (Oct. 1958), 203–4.

market assets can be acquired only by giving up cash.[148] Hence, all the English banks can do in this situation is convert their excess cash into money-market assets which reduces the cash ratio to 8 per cent and leaves the liquidity ratio at 30 per cent. Similarly, the English banking system does not contract when its cash ratio falls below 8 per cent if its liquidity ratio is at 30 per cent. The system can dispose of money-market assets to raise its cash ratio to 8 per cent, but in so doing it obtains cash in the ratio of one for one for the money-market assets disposed of. Since cash forms part of the liquidity ratio, raising the cash ratio to 8 per cent in this way leaves the liquidity ratio at 30 per cent. Only if the liquidity ratio falls below 30 per cent will the banking system be compelled to contract, for the liquidity ratio can be built up to the required level only by disposing of earning assets not used in computing the liquidity ratio. The disposal of these other assets ordinarily does not raise cash, but lowers deposits so that the total assets of the banking system shrink. Even if the system has cash in excess of its needs here, it must contract because the additional liquid assets required can be acquired only for cash and there is not sufficient cash in the system to raise the liquidity ratio to 30 per cent.[149]

148. Roosa, "The Radcliffe Report," p. 6, in assessing the view that it is the liquidity ratio which limits the expansion of the English banking system, points out that the restraint exists only if the supply of eligible liquid assets is held exclusively by the authorities and the banks. He implies that this necessary condition does not exist in England and that, therefore, excess cash reserves would enable the banks to expand even though the liquidity ratio was at its minimum. Nevertheless, authorities on English banking, cited in the following note, appear to support the contention that English banks as a group can acquire additional liquidity assets only at the cost of reducing bank cash.

149. The illustrations used to show how variations in bank cash that leave the liquidity ratio unchanged at 30 per cent fail to affect the size of the banking system under English conditions suggest that the environment of the liquidity ratio in England is as described here. These illustrations are given by W. Manning Dacey, "The Floating Debt Problem," *Lloyds Bank Review*, Apr. 1956, pp. 27–30; idem, *Money under Review* (London, Hutchinson & Co., 1960), pp. 69–72; Kenen, *British Monetary Policy and the Balance of Payments*, pp. 50–3. Also cf. Great Britain, Chancellor of the Exchequer, Committee on the Working of the Monetary System, *Principal Memoranda of Evidence*, *1*, 9–10, which presents the views of the Bank of England on the control of bank credit in the United Kingdom.

The view that liquidity requirements or the liquidity ratio is crucial for monetary control in England is further strengthened by the difficulty encountered in altering the cash base of the English banking system. This difficulty arises because the money-market in London is financed primarily by the clearing banks and the Bank of England. Therefore open-market sales to the money market, designed to reduce bank cash, require additional financing of the money market by either the banking system or the central bank. If the money market finances the purchases of securities from the Bank of England with call money from the clearing banks, the banks lose cash to the Bank of England but at the same time gain money-market assets of a like amount. The total of liquid assets held by the banks is unchanged by the transactions so that both the liquidity ratio and the cash ratio can be preserved. If the Bank of England finances the money-market purchases, it defeats its effort to reduce bank cash. Liquidation of the money-market debt to the Bank of England is then brought about by the money market holding fewer treasury bills and the Bank of England more, so that bank cash is still not reduced.[150]

One way of making open-market operations effective is to develop a demand for treasury bills or other short-term government securities from sources outside the money market.[151] For this the authorities must permit interest rates on such securities to rise sufficiently to attract a substantial outside demand, which they may not be willing

150. This is the chain of events analyzed by Dacey, "The Floating Debt Problem," pp. 27–30; idem, *Money under Review*, pp. 69–71; Kenen, *British Monetary Policy and the Balance of Payments*, pp. 50–3.

151. Thomas Wilson, "The Rate of Interest and Monetary Policy," *Oxford Economic Papers*, 9 (Oct. 1957), 242–3, suggests this approach for making open-market sales effective in the United Kingdom. He argues that permitting the treasury-bill rate to fall would develop a demand for bills outside the banking system and money market. The same suggestion and analysis is put forward by A. N. McLeod, "Security-Reserve Requirements in the United States and the United Kingdom: A Comment," *Journal of Finance*, 14 (Dec. 1959), 538. The possibility is examined by Kenen, *British Monetary Policy and the Balance of Payments*, pp. 54–5, who concludes that it might require "a considerable increase in the interest cost of bill finance" to develop an outside market for U.K. bills, and that the Bank of England is not likely to be willing to accept such a high cost.

to do.[152] If, however, securities can be sold to the general public by the central bank, bank cash is reduced without the money-market assets of the banks being increased at the same time. Bank cash will also be reduced relative to bank holdings of money-market assets if the government sells long-term securities to the general public and pays the proceeds into an account with the central bank. The same result would be achieved by running a cash surplus on government transactions and letting government balances with the central bank accumulate. As long as the government funds are not paid out again, except to retire treasury bills, the liquid assets of the banking system remain reduced.

Even where there is no difficulty in reducing bank cash, liquidity requirements seem to provide the basis for control. Without such requirements, or with holdings of cash-substitute assets in excess of requirements, a reduction in bank cash can be offset or nullified by converting excess liquid assets into cash. Not until holdings of the cash-substitute assets are eliminated or reduced below minimum requirements will a loss of cash begin to affect the banking system. The function performed by liquidity requirements here, and in general in the English banking system, reveals however that monetary control still works through the manipulation of excess cash.

A banking system that holds cash-substitute assets in excess of minimum requirements after allowances for the cash position is similar to a banking system without cash-substitute assets, but whose supply of cash cannot be closely regulated by the central bank. In the latter type of banking system monetary control can be imposed by manipulation of the bank demand for cash, as discussed in the pre-

152. The Committee on the Working of the Monetary System, *Report*, p. 128, argue that the desire of the authorities "to secure reasonable stability of the Treasury Bill rate" is responsible for treasury bills in the hands of the English banks being almost the equivalent of cash. Mr. Dacey takes exception to this conclusion, arguing that a rise in bill rate would not reduce the supply of treasury bills, which for him provides the basis for effective control of bank credit. Cf. his "Treasury Bills and the Money Supply," pp. 3–5, and *Money under Review*, p. 63. He appears to overlook, however, the effect of higher rates on getting treasury bills into the hands of the public, a move which would enable the authorities to sell bills in a way that would reduce bank cash and the total liquidity assets of the banks at the same time.

vious section. The same means could be utilized in controlling a banking system holding cash-substitute assets. Legal requirements for cash could be raised to offset the conversion into cash of cash-substitute assets by the banking system, or to create a demand for cash in excess of what can be satisfied from the conversion of cash substitutes. Reductions in legal cash requirements foster expansion in either type of banking system.

An alternative to varying the cash requirements of a banking system holding cash-substitute assets is varying the liquidity requirements of the system and leaving the cash requirements fixed. Instead of restraining or contracting the system by compelling it to hold more cash, the central bank could compel the banking system either to hold the cash-substitutes that it would otherwise convert into cash, or to raise more cash in order to acquire cash substitutes to meet the higher requirements. Similarly, liquidity requirements, in lieu of cash requirements, can be reduced to help banks cover a cash deficit or to encourage a banking expansion.[153] In the latter situation a reduction in liquidity requirements, with cash requirements fixed, is less forceful than a reduction in cash demands. Unless the banks were being restrained from acquiring other earning assets by the previous liquidity requirement, the banks will simply continue to carry the cash-substitute assets made excessive by the reduction in requirements until opportunities for more profitable investments arise. But banks will not carry extra cash that earns no return and so a reduction in cash demands that makes excess cash greater than zero will at least cause the banks to acquire money-market assets. If money-market assets fall in price as a result of bank purchases, the lower prices might prompt the banks to seek or accept other earning assets that now offer a better yield.

Nevertheless, varying the requirements of the banking system for cash-substitute assets serves as an alternative to varying the cash demands of the system. Either can be used alone or in combination.[154]

153. Control over the activities of non-bank financial firms could also be exercised by imposing on them variable liquidity requirements as well as variable cash requirements.

154. Kenen, *British Monetary Policy and the Balance of Payments*, pp. 229–32, examines the arguments for a variable liquidity ratio as an instrument for monetary

In all cases, however, control over the banking system is a result of what the variation in requirements does to excess cash. Or, to put it the other way round, it is the manipulation of excess cash achieved through variations in requirements that makes for monetary control. Thus, making and keeping the excess cash of the system greater than zero still causes the banking system to expand. If the banking system is deficient in cash-substitute assets to at least the amount of the excess cash created, the excess cash will leave the system again as the banks build up their holdings of cash substitutes. The central bank has then failed to keep the supply of bank cash from contracting and so has failed to maintain excess cash above zero. The central bank has been frustrated in its attempt to provide the amount of excess cash that it wanted to. In such a situation an appropriate fall in liquidity requirements, whether brought about by a fall in cash requirements or in the requirements for cash substitutes, will enable the central bank to achieve any particular level of bank cash and excess cash.

Similarly, the banking system can be made to contract only if the central bank can make and keep excess cash negative. The central bank cannot do this if the banking system holds excess cash substitutes sufficient to at least cover its cash deficit. The banking system can then eliminate the negative excess cash without contracting. Again, the central bank has been unable to keep the supply of bank cash and the amount of excess cash at the level it wanted. Raising liquidity requirements by compelling the banks to hold more cash-substitute assets or more cash prevents the banking system from building up its cash to eliminate the negative excess, and so enables the central bank to maintain the level of bank cash required for control.

Thus, variations in liquidity requirements represent another technique for exercising general monetary control over a banking system which holds cash-substitute assets. The possibility for this also suggests that varying the supply of cash-substitute assets would represent yet another technique of monetary control. Again, English experience

---

control in the United Kingdom and decides in favour of variations that leave the cash ratio unchanged.

with monetary control appears to support this suggestion, and, indeed, that experience has even led some observers to conclude that altering the supply of cash substitutes is really the only way that effective control can be exercised over the English banking system.

In English banking the liquidity ratio will fall if bank cash falls relative to the money-market assets in the system, or if money-market assets in the system fall relative to bank cash. So if the supply of money-market assets to the banking system can be altered directly another way exists for imposing monetary control. The only money-market assets held by the banks subject to the direct control of the monetary authorities are treasury bills; and since the government can vary the supply of these, it follows that a key variable in controlling the English banking system could be the supply of treasury bills.[155]

This would, in fact, be the situation if the supply of treasury bills could be varied independently of the supply of bank cash. But there seems no way that the treasury bills held by the banking system can be varied by the authorities without the supply of cash being affected first. Thus, if the government decides to reduce the supply of treasury bills in the interest of monetary control, it will first either sell long-term government securities to the general public or run a cash surplus. In either case bank cash is reduced relative to bank holdings of money-market assets because proceeds of the security sales or of the cash surplus are added to government balances with the Bank of England. There is no need to do more in order to restrict the banking system, for the liquidity ratio of the banking system has been reduced. If treasury bills are now retired, bank cash will be restored although money-market assets of the banks will fall. The composition of the liquid assets held by the banking system are rearranged as a result of the treasury-bill retirements, but the liquidity ratio of the banking system is not thereby reduced. The reduction in the liquidity ratio occurred when the government first accumulated the cash with which

155. The Committee on the Working of the Monetary System, *Report*, p. 216, conclude that "the supply of Treasury Bills and not the supply of cash has come to be the effective regulating base of the domestic banking system." This view is championed by Dacey, *Money under Review*, pp. 62–3.

to reduce treasury bills so that reducing the supply of treasury bills here is not crucial to the control of the banking system.[156]

An expansion in the supply of treasury bills followed by a rise in the liquidity ratio of the banking system may appear to be directly responsible for encouraging any expansion in the banking system that occurs. The liquidity ratio of the banking system, however, can be affected here only if the increase in treasury bills forces the Bank of England to expand bank cash. The increase in treasury bills is then initially financed by the Bank of England so that when the proceeds are spent by the government an increase in bank cash occurs. If the central bank is unable to prevent or offset this increase in bank cash, which adds to the total liquid assets of the banks, control or restriction of the issue of treasury bills will, in effect, bestow control over bank cash. In this sense, it may be said that control of the treasury-bill issue gives control over the banking system. But even here it is actually control over the supply of bank cash as such that is the aim, and not control over the supply of money-market assets working independently of any effect on bank cash.

In general, all variations in the supply of cash-substitute assets to the banking system are preceded by a corresponding change in bank cash. The change in bank holding of cash substitutes is a result of banks reacting to their cash position. Such changes are not basic to the exercise of monetary control. Variations in the supply of cash-substitute assets to the banking system merely reflect changes in the supply of bank cash so that varying the supply of such cash substitutes does not constitute an independent means of exercising monetary control.

Thus, the presence of cash-substitute assets in a banking system, such as the English banking system, opens the way for one more technique of monetary control—that of a liquidity requirement. A

156. Dacey, "Treasury Bills and the Money Supply," pp. 7–8, admits that "a reduction in total liquid assets which in the first instance took the form of a reduction in cash holdings" would effectively bring about a contraction of the banking system, but he apparently does not see any way in which this can be brought about without reducing the money-market assets of the banks, especially treasury bills. I argue that, if only in a technical sense, the money-market assets cannot be reduced unless bank cash is reduced first. Sayers, *Modern Banking*, pp. 198–9, in considering the ways in which the liquid assets of the banks can be reduced, also points out that initially any reduction shows up in a fall in bank cash.

variable liquidity requirement in this situation can serve as an alternative or as a supplement to variable cash requirements in manipulating the excess cash of the banking system for purposes of monetary control. Despite the presence of cash-substitute assets, the basis for control is still excess cash. Liquidity requirements and variations in them just help the central bank to bring about the right degree of excess cash.

When liquidity conditions are the opposite from those for the English banking system, liquidity requirements in themselves make no direct contribution to general monetary control, for the liquid assets which satisfy the requirements are not then really cash-substitute assets for the banking system. Sales or purchases of the liquidity assets by the banking system do not need to be reflected in bank cash because the central bank is able to hold bank cash constant, if it wants to, in the face of such sales or purchases. The central bank can manipulate excess cash without having to rely on liquidity requirements so that transactions in the liquidity assets by the banking system do not differ in their effects on the system from transactions in any other type of earning assets. In such circumstances liquidity requirements serve to influence the composition but not the total of earning assets held by the banking system. But regardless of the function performed by liquidity requirements or ratios, monetary control still works by manipulating the excess cash of the banking system.

Averaging and Excess Cash

Another problem in dealing with excess cash arises when cash positions in a banking system are computed by averaging cash supplies and demands over a specified period of time,[157] known as the

157. When averaging is not used, the measurement of excess cash at any moment of time is simply a matter of comparing that day's cash supplies with cash requirements for that day. This is the basis on which the free reserves of the U.S. banking system are implicitly calculated. Daily cash supplies, averaged for a week and adjusted for borrowing from the Federal Reserve, are compared with legal requirements, which in effect amounts to a comparison of spot supply and spot demand. The possibility of carrying forward excess cash from one day to the next is not allowed for. In addition, no allowance is made for possible working needs in excess of the legal requirements.

reserve period. Such averaging seems to be prevalent among the banking systems of the world,[158] so that its effects on excess cash deserve more than passing mention. Furthermore, these effects are important for they bear on the identification, calculation, and effectiveness of excess cash.

The problem of identifying excess cash under averaging is one of finding the category of excess cash that tells whether or not the banking system is in equilibrium. Under averaging, the excess cash relevant for equilibrium is not the excess cash at the moment but the average of excess cash at all moments within a given reserve period. When this average is zero for a given period, it means that the banking system held all the earning assets it could have during the period, and that it held neither too much nor too little cash. Over the period as a whole the banking system was in a state of equilibrium. If average excess cash for a reserve period is negative, the system has not had all the cash it needed; if the average is positive, the system has not held all the earning assets that it could have. Hence, the equilibrium condition for a banking system in a given reserve period is that average excess cash be zero.

Thus, whether or not the system was in equilibrium for any reserve period that has expired can be determined by calculating the average excess cash in the system for that period. This average is simply the average of the individual or spot excesses at various moments of time within the period. In practice, the spot excesses are calculated at specified points of time, such as the opening or close of business each day,[159] by taking the available cash on hand at that moment and

158. "Various methods are used for administering reserve requirements. In most countries the arrangements are similar to those of the United States, and the reserve balances and deposit liabilities for each day are averaged over periods that range from one week to one month." Fousek, *Foreign Central Banking*, p. 49. The same statement appears in "Commercial Bank Reserve Requirements Abroad," Federal Reserve Bank of New York, *Monthly Review of Credit and Business Conditions*, Oct. 1955, p. 132. The presumption is that if the law permits averaging banks will compute their cash positions according to the averaging rules.

159. Regulations will determine whether calendar days or just business days are used. In the U.S. it is the former. Cf. Board of Governors of the Federal Reserve System, *Regulation D: Reserves of Member Banks*, s. 204.3 (a), the text of which corresponds to the (U.S.) Code of Federal Regulations, Title 12, Chapter II, Part

deducting the cash demand of the moment. The cash demand of the moment for a reserve period that has expired is, of course, the average demand for that period.

Whether the system is in equilibrium at any particular moment of time within a given reserve period can be determined by computing the indicated average excess for the period as things stand at the given moment. That is, given the spot excess as of the moment, the average excess to date in the reserve period, and the number of spot reserve observations remaining to be taken in the reserve period, the average excess cash for the period can be calculated on the assumption of no further change other than that caused by the mere passage of time. This calculation indicates what the average excess will be in the absence of autonomous changes in available cash and of expansion or contraction by the system. If the indicated average is zero, the system is in equilibrium as of that moment. There is then no reason for altering earning assets relative to available cash, for to do so is to change available cash and cash demands and so to prevent the average excess for the period from being zero. The system then will not have held enough cash, or too much cash, over the period. If the indicated average is not zero, the system is not in equilibrium. If greater than zero, the system can expand for it is holding too much cash; and if negative, it should contract for it is not holding enough cash.

In short, the indicated average excess at any given moment within a reserve period indicates whether or not the system is in equilibrium for that period, but it does not indicate the extent of the deviation from equilibrium. This deviation may be measured by the amount of excess cash that has to be eliminated at that moment in order to make the indicated average excess cash zero for the reserve period.[160] The

---

204, cited as 12 CFR 204. In Canada, juridical days are used. Cf. *Statutes of Canada*, 1953–54, 2-3 Elizabeth II, c. 48, s. 71 (2).

160. When the "excess" to be eliminated is positive, it is diminished by the amount outstanding, at the moment, of reserves borrowed from the central bank on the basis of need; when the "excess" is negative, the amount to be eliminated to restore equilibrium is increased by the amount of such need borrowing outstanding. That is, need borrowing is taken into account here by deducting it, algebraically, from the indicated average excess cash for the reserve period, which is calculated without any deduction for need borrowing.

elimination of this amount would then place the system in equilibrium.

Hence, under averaging, the excess cash in a banking system at any moment of time may be defined as the amount that shows the extent of the deviation from equilibrium in the foregoing sense. This may be styled the equilibrium concept of excess cash and its measurement begins with the indicated average excess for the reserve period. The indicated average excess is the sum of two products. One is the product of the average excess for the portion of the reserve period that has already expired and of the number of observations used in computing the average. This product gives the total amount of spot excess cash accumulated during the period to date. The other product gives the accumulation that will take place over the remainder of the period in the absence of any basic changes in the existing cash situation. It may be the product of the latest spot excess and the number of reserve observations remaining to be taken in the reserve period. If, however, the existing spot excess will change with the passage of time because cash demands vary with average deposits instead of spot deposits, the average of the expected future spot excesses must be used in computing the future accumulation. The sum of the products divided by the number of observations contained in both products gives the indicated average excess for the reserve period. The excess whose removal would put the system in equilibrium is then obtained by taking the aggregate used in computing the indicated average and dividing it by the number of observations remaining to be taken in the reserve period.

For example, a banking system has an average excess cash of 20 for 5 days and a spot excess at the end of the fifth day of 10 with 5 days left in the reserve period. The indicated average excess cash for the whole reserve period as at the end of the fifth day is

$$\frac{20 \times 5 + 10 \times 5}{10} = 15.$$

Excess cash as at the end of the fifth day is therefore

$$\frac{20 \times 5 + 10 \times 5}{5} = 30,$$

assuming that the existing spot excess of 10 is unaffected by the mere passage of time. If excess cash of 30 were removed from this banking system at the end of the fifth day,[161] the system would incur spot deficits of 20 for each of the 5 remaining days in the reserve period or a total deficit for these days of 100, although excess cash on any of these days, as calculated above, would be zero. This would exactly offset the surplus of 100 built up during the first five days of the period. Hence, by the end of the reserve period average excess cash for the whole period would be zero.

An alternative and more useful mode of expressing the method for calculating excess cash in the equilibrium sense runs in terms of converting the total excess accumulated over the expired portion of the reserve period into the equivalent amount of spot excess. The amount of the excess is then the algebraic sum of the conversion result and the last spot excess. Thus, in the foregoing example, the accumulated excess for five days was 100 (20 × 5). Dividing this by the number of days (5) remaining in the period and adding to the last spot excess (10) gives the amount of the excess (30), the elimination of which at that moment would put the banking system in equilibrium.

The identification and calculation of excess cash from the point of view of system equilibrium does not reveal anything about the effectiveness of this excess cash, although averaging opens up three possibilities: banks may not use the equilibrium concept of excess cash; they may delay their reaction to any given excess; and they may differ among themselves either in method of calculation or speed of reaction, thus introducing a distribution effect. These possibilities raise doubts about the usefulness of the equilibrium concept of excess cash.

The view banks take of their excess cash depends on how they pursue the objective of zero average excess cash for each reserve period. In pursuing this objective banks need not compute excess cash from the equilibrium view: other measures of excess cash will

161. It is excess cash of 30 and not available cash of 30 that must be taken from the system. If the elimination is affected by withdrawing available cash, the amount withdrawn will have to exceed 30, when cash demands fall with the withdrawal of cash, in order to achieve a net change of 30 in the spot excess.

serve as well. Thus, banks may treat as their excess cash the accumulated excess to date plus the latest spot excess. They are then treating their accumulated excess as an amount to be invested, or disinvested, for one day, which means that, in effect, they are converting their accumulated excess into the equivalent amount of spot by dividing by one day. Such a view of excess cash is not unlikely in banking systems where possibilities exist for investing and disinvesting funds for one day.

When such possibilities for one-day investment do not exist, or other reasons prevail, banks, if time permits, treat their accumulated excess as an amount to be worked off over a longer period than one day. They may, however, still prefer a shorter period than the number of days left in the reserve period. Working off an accumulated excess before a period ends would in the view of the banks enable them to adjust spot positions so as to end the reserve period with a zero spot excess as well as with zero average excess cash. This means that the divisor used to convert an accumulated excess into the equivalent amount of spot may vary between one and any number up to and including the number of days left in the reserve period. The number of days actually used is likely to be influenced by the cost and the possibility of making short-term cash adjustments, by the amount involved, and by the general cash policy.

The amount of excess cash at any moment of time as calculated by banks will vary with the divisor they use for converting their accumulated excess into the equivalent amount of spot excess. As many different measures of excess cash are possible as there are divisors. The smaller the divisor, given the accumulated excess, the larger the operational amount of excess cash and the more it departs from the equilibrium amount. Similarly, the larger the divisor the smaller the excess yielded by the operational calculation and the closer it approaches the equilibrium amount. Thus, excess cash as seen by the banks is never smaller than the equilibrium amount, but it may be larger.

Banks, no matter how they compute their excess cash, may not react immediately to their excess, for averaging enables them to delay their response. When excesses are not large banks may wait to see whether the passage of time brings elimination. In particular,

banks may be insensitive to excesses accumulated in the early part of
a reserve period, and indeed may welcome such accumulation. As
long as any accumulated excess remains within manageable proportions, banks may passively accept the accumulation, prefering to
wait till later in the reserve period before reacting to eliminate excess
cash.[162] Such behaviour means that banks do not necessarily react
immediately to any calculation of excess cash that they make.

When banks differ in their policies of calculating and of reacting
to excess cash, it means that a given excess in the equilibrium sense
then varies in its immediate effect on the banking system according
to its distribution among the members of the system. This is the only
true distribution effect that bears on the effectiveness of excess cash.
Another distribution effect may arise in the course of trying to generate a given excess but it bears on the size of the excess and not on
its effectiveness. This effect occurs when some banks permit their
cash requirements to vary with marginal changes in available cash:
an increase in cash made available to the system which favours such
banks results in a smaller amount of excess cash than would otherwise
appear.[163]

In short, excess cash in the equilibrium sense may not correspond
to the concept of excess cash used by banks, it may not be responded

162. It might even be the policy to wait till the last day before reacting. It might
also be the policy, however, near the end of a reserve period to ignore accumulations
if the spot excess is low or zero. Banks then prefer to hold cash rather than incur
a large spot deficit at the end of a period in order to use up prior accumulations.
In effect, this policy raises cash demands so that excess cash disappears.

163. The effectiveness of a given level of free reserves in the U.S. banking
system is said to depend, at least in part, on its distribution. Cf. Karl R. Bopp,
"The Rediscovery of Monetary Policy—Some Problems of Application," Federal
Reserve Bank of Philadelphia, *Business Review*, Aug. 1955, p. 10; "Guides to
Monetary Policy," ibid., Aug. 1959, p. 3; "The Significance and Limitations of
Free Reserves," Federal Reserve Bank of New York, *Monthly Review*, Nov. 1958,
p. 163. It is not clear, however, whether the distribution effect arises as a result of
the reasons mentioned in the text or as a result of a variation in demand among
banks for cash to hold in excess of legal requirements. The free-reserve concept in
ignoring such demand does not really measure excess cash. Therefore, the distribution of a given level of free reserves affects the amount of excess cash associated
with that level of free reserves, which would explain variations in the effectiveness
of a given amount of free reserves.

to immediately, and it may be affected by its distribution. Despite these defects, however, the equilibrium concept of excess cash still defines a variable that can be manipulated to control a banking system, for the sign and the amount of the variable can be regulated so as to allow for the defects.

Thus, if the immediate objective of policy is to bias the banking system to expand or to contract or to attain a new size, any equilibrium excess with the appropriate sign will be adequate. Since all other possible calculations of excess cash will be of the same sign initially, and cannot for long, if ever, be of contrary sign, differences between the operational and equilibrium calculations do not interfere with the policy objective. Furthermore, the shorter the reserve period, or the closer the end of the period, the sooner a given excess will make itself felt. The mere passage of time will itself cause any excess to be felt so that a delay in responding to a given excess will not interfere with the ultimate attainment of the policy objective. Nor will distribution effects affect the sign of the excess or its ultimate effect. Hence, establishing an equilibrium excess of a given sign and maintaining it for a sufficient length of time will eventually result in the desired movement or in the size of banking system wanted.

If rate of movement is important, an equilibrium excess of the appropriate size and sign will help bring about the desired rate. The larger the equilibrium excess the larger any other excess that may be calculated, and so the greater the response when it comes. And the larger the amount to be eliminated the less willing banks will be to postpone taking action. A larger excess will also counteract any sluggishness caused by distribution effects. Speed of movement will be very much a function of the size of the equilibrium excess.

Hence, averaging need not interfere with the central bank using excess cash for controlling the banking system. Averaging does complicate the measuring of excess cash but it may not add to the difficulty of control.[164] If a reserve ratio were specified for the banking system but averaging was not permitted, banks would have to work to a spot concept of excess cash. Such an arrangement might work

164. Under averaging, however, it is considerably more difficult to trace the expansion process of banking systems. Because the traditional analysis of the subject does not consider the matter, the problem is examined in the Appendix.

satisfactorily, but only if banks were able to switch with ease between cash and liquid assets, as they can in the United Kingdom. This raises problems for open-market operations of the nature examined under the previous head of this section. Yet without such provisions for rapid adjustments between cash and liquid assets, bank demand for cash might vary over a considerable range making it difficult to assess the effective amount of excess cash in the banking system. Coping with the effects of averaging may then present the lesser difficulty.

CONCLUSIONS

Central banking differs from other types of banking not because of any of the special attributes usually possessed by central banks but because of the discretionary power exercised by them in the national interest. Any banking institution that disregards its own profits in order to influence monetary events in the economy for some high purpose fulfils the essential function of a central bank. The means for effecting that function are open-market operations and bank-rate policies.

The special feature of open-market operations is that they do not alter the total wealth of the private sector of the economy, only the composition of that wealth through an exchange of idle balances and securities between the banking system and the non-bank sector. This is the major effect of open-market operations. Their effect on bank loans outstanding is weak because banking systems now usually have excess lending capacity, and because cash reserves are not usually reduced when a contraction or stabilization of loans is called for, and are expanded when the demand for loans is falling. For these reasons the main impact of open-market operations falls on the security holdings of the private sector, by involving the banking system in an exchange of securities and idle balances with the public.

Thus, an important dimension of open-market operations is their effect on security yields, and in general any stabilizing benefits that open-market operations have for the economy rest mainly with their destabilizing effects on security yields.

A policy of initiating open-market operations has the greatest effect on interest rates because the initiation will usually occur when the demand curve for idle balances, derived from the community preference for idle balances and securities, is stable. In contrast, an accommodating policy of open-market operations is carried out at a time when the demand curve is shifting so that movements in security yields tend to be moderated.

Apart from open-market operations, cash reserves may be altered in a number of ways, all of which alter the quantity of money in the private sector of the economy. These cash-reserve changes, like those produced from open-market operations, all affect security yields. The extent of their impact on yields may vary among themselves, and from that of open-market operations, but the difference is not sufficient to make it useful to distinguish different types of increases in the money supply. A meaningful distinction is that between increases in the money supply which represent increases in wealth, and increases in money which merely represent changes in the composition of existing wealth.

Bank-rate seems also to operate through costs although it too has a cash-reserve effect. Bank-rate policy is independent of open-market operations, and vice versa, even though they are closely linked. They can reinforce or conflict with each other, but this is a choice that is within the power of the monetary authorities. Bank-rate can only be effective if banks are restricted from borrowing from the central bank when the rate is not high enough to discourage borrowing. A rate that is just above that on the lowest yielding disposable asset held by the banks is an effective rate when the amount of such assets held by the banks is in excess of their needs. It is then more profitable for the banks to liquidate these assets than to borrow when they need cash. Banks do not need to borrow, but then bank-rate is serving no useful purpose: it may even serve the harmful purpose of encouraging the holding of excess liquid reserves.

Unfortunately, bank-rate policy today is based on considerations that lead to the foregoing results. The policy was inherited from pre-1914 banking conditions in England, under which bank-rate served the purpose of preserving the gold reserves of the Bank of England. As such it was a poor tool of monetary policy, and the change in the banking environment has not improved the tool. Today, bank-rate, at least in Canada and the United States, serves a purely technical function, devoid of all the richer connotations for monetary policy with which it is often invested. Bank-rate is now merely set at the level necessary to restrict as much as possible all borrowing from the central bank to that which is strictly necessary.

In these circumstances the only question that setting bank-rate raises is whether it should be set by discretion or by formula. The argument in favour of varying bank-rate automatically according to some formula is that this will eliminate interpreting all changes in bank-rate as changes in policy. This, so the argument goes, avoids wrong interpretation and perverse effects. The case for discretionary changes in bank-rate hinges on just the opposite reasoning: that such changes may provide a signal of intent of central-bank policy. Such a signal is essential if the central bank is trying to manipulate the size of the banking system in a flexible manner; if the timing and nature of the response by banks to pressure from the central bank is likely to be influenced favourably by knowledge of which way the central bank wishes the banking system to move; and if the central bank cannot always bring exactly the right degree of restraint to bear on the banking system. The advantages of both methods of setting bank-rate would be obtained by making non-policy changes in bank-rate according to formula, and policy changes by departing from the formula or by changing the formula.

Central-bank control of the banking system depends on the ability to manipulate the amount of excess cash in the system. Excess cash is the difference between the amount of cash held by banks and the amount that they desire to hold; it can be affected by altering the supply of cash to the banks or by working on their demand for cash. By creating a suitable differential between cash supplies and cash needs, the monetary authorities can cause the banking system to expand or contract. The existence of liquidity ratios does not change the principle of control, but it may enable the authorities to impose control simply by varying the liquidity ratio without altering excess cash. This possibility exists when liquidity assets are, to all intents and purposes, the equivalent of cash in the hands of the banks. Under such conditions variations in the supply of cash to the system must cause the liquidity ratio to vary also in order for the changes in cash to impose effective control on the system.

The possibilities for averaging cash requirements over a reserve period make it more difficult to identify and compute the exact amount of excess cash in the banking system at any given moment of time. Averaging also limits the effectiveness of a given amount of excess cash in promoting a movement in the system. Once recognized, however, these difficulties can be allowed for in manipulating excess cash for control purposes. Indeed, no matter how complex the regulations imposed upon a banking system, the basic principle of central-bank control remains the simple one of manipulating excess cash. If this were more clearly seen, less time and energy would be spent trying to devise new or more complex control regulations, and many existing regulations would be seen to be unnecessary.

Conclusions

From the analysis of the economic consequences of banking operations and transactions undertaken in this study several interesting conclusions may be drawn, not least of which is the general one that careful attention to modes of expression, details, and mechanics is particularly enlightening and rewarding in dealing with problems and controversies in the economics of banking.

This is perhaps most readily seen in the comparison of the lending activities of banks with those of other financial institutions. Although the mechanics of bank lending differ from the mechanics of lending by other financial institutions, the consequences of lending are the same when the cash reserves of the banks and the cash balances of the other lenders remain constant. Both must sell any securities they hold if they wish to expand their loans, and it makes no difference which type of lender is selling securities: the consequences are the same in both cases.

Another important conclusion is that credit rationing, properly defined, is not a conspicuous feature of modern banking. Rationing proper exists when lending capacity is insufficient to meet all credit-worthy demand for loans at existing rates. Most banks now usually have some excess lending capacity and so can adjust to pressures from borrowers or the monetary authorities by altering their holdings of open-market assets instead of the degree of rationing.

This does not mean that all excess demand for bank loans is eliminated. Loan requests are still refused or only partly met, but only unprofitable business is rejected. Credit risk and uncertainty about repayment are the main reasons for such rejections—not insufficient lending capacity.

The concept of the expansion path seems a useful one to apply to

459

banks in order to explain how bank loans and holdings of securities might vary for alterations in banking resources. Except when there is credit rationing, it appears that expansion paths in banking favour expansion and contraction in security holdings rather than in loans. Without credit rationing, however, any event that alters the size of the banking firm causes it to adjust its holdings of securities. A departure from this response may occur when the reaction on bank profits is adverse. But the adverse effect on banking profits may produce a change in lending conditions imposed by the banks, rather than in the nature of the expansion path.

It is through banking profits, and not necessarily through inter-related markets, that the link is forged between security prices and lending rates. Thus, when security yields are falling, banks are usually being forced out of loans into lower-yielding securities; bank profits are adversely affected, and the reaction of the banks is apt to express itself in lower lending rates. Thus, security yields and lending rates move down more or less together. A similar chain of events takes place when security yields are rising and banks are moving out of securities into loans: lending rates tend to follow security yields upwards.

A finding perhaps contrary to current thinking is that competition by a banking system for deposits may have long-run benefits for the system, even though in the short-run it raises costs without expanding deposits. The longer-run benefits might follow if bank competition restricts the growth of non-bank lenders sufficiently to cause the monetary authorities to permit the banking system to grow at a faster rate in order to meet the financing and credit needs of the economy. The faster rate of growth thus gained may more than offset the extra cost of competition for deposits.

Another major conclusion of this study is that branch banking did not arise to link areas of surplus funds with those deficient in funds. Branch banking developed and flourished because it had a cost or operating advantage. And the contribution that branch banking makes to the mobility of funds within an economy lies in the greater ease with which it can accommodate an interregional flow of funds produced by the interregional transactions of the banking public. The more extensive the branch-banking system, the less likely are transfers of cash reserves to be induced by interregional payments; thus, the less the possibility that a secondary banking repercussion will be imposed on the primary movement of deposits.

Above all, the contribution of branch banking to the mobility of funds cannot be explained in any very useful manner as a transfer of excess deposits from where they accumulate to where they can be used—either by head office or by branches deficient in deposits. Excess deposits merely reflect the movement of deposits by the public, not the activities of the banks, except when cash reserves are increasing: then the banking system expands deposits, and if these rise relative to loans, excess deposits must be created somewhere. Excess deposits arising in this way are certainly not detrimental to the areas in which they arise, and they are not necessarily at the expense of development in other areas. Therefore, it is meaningless to debate the merits of branch banking using the concepts of excess deposits and excess loans. These concepts are useful for bank accounting, but they make poor tools for the economic analysis of branch banking.

International transactions, like interregional ones, may produce a redistribution of deposits, but in this case between residents and non-residents. Such a redistribution occurs when cash payments on international account do not balance. The resulting deposit movements provide temporary accommodation for the balance of payments; more lasting accommodation is provided by international lending and investing on longer term. These longer-term transactions may tap foreign savings and may be as disturbing to internal stability as shorter-term movements in deposits. In particular, when the balance of payments for a debtor country discloses foreign borrowing in excess of a current-account deficit, foreign borrowing or direct investment is decidedly expansionary. Even when net foreign borrowing is less than the current-account deficit, it may still be expansionary, depending on how much domestic expenditures have been stimulated by the foreign borrowing or investment. Finally, if foreign borrowing and the current-account deficit balance, it does not necessarily follow that foreign borrowing has not been expansionary: it probably has been.

The financial transactions of a central government not only may produce income effects in the private sector of the economy but also may alter both the cash reserves of the banking system and the money supply of the private sector. In particular, government surpluses and deficits produce shifts in deposits between the government and private sectors. These shifts alter the money supply and also, when the un-balance in government transactions is on income account, total wealth in the private sector.

Because they stabilize government deposits, debt operations help to nullify the cash-reserve and deposit effects of government financial operations. The impact of these debt operations on the banking sys-tem is not likely to be momentous, especially when cash reserves are held constant: the impact on the private sector is much greater.

Deficit financing—financing a deficit by selling securities—is clearly expansionary when the deficit is an autonomous one; it is less expansionary when the deficit is merely induced by income changes. But in both cases the overall effect is less expansionary than it would be if securities did not have to be sold to finance the deficit.

Debt retirement—using a surplus to retire debt—is usually de-flationary, although not so deflationary as merely accumulating the surplus in the form of idle balances.

The examination of central-bank transactions suggests that open-market operations do not have strong direct effects. Their impact depends on price effects for they work through an exchange between securities and deposits. In the absence of credit rationing, bank loans are unlikely to be directly disturbed by open-market operations, ex-cept as a result of what happens to security prices. Hence, the main consequence of open-market operations is an alteration in the security holdings of the banking system and private sector. Any further conse-quences for the economy depend on how the behaviour of those two groups is influenced by the changes in security prices produced by open-market operations.

The practice of maintaining bank-rate just above the yield on the most liquid assets held by banks either induces banks to hold such assets to excess or penalizes those banks which do not and which, as a result, have to borrow from the central bank in an emergency. Such a bank-rate functions as a penalty rate.

Bank-rate may also be used as a signal of central-bank intentions. Such a signal is almost essential to the efficiency of monetary control except when the central bank can always apply the right degree of restraint, at the right time, to the banking system to get the behaviour desired. A bank-rate used as a signal indicates the direction in which the central bank would like the banking system to move. In a general sense, such a signal of intent makes sense when attempts are being made to influence the behaviour of a system of lenders in a particular direction and the methods available for doing so are not working perfectly.

Central-bank control of the banking system may be implemented by manipulating the amount of excess cash in the banking system, where excess cash is defined as the difference between the cash actually in the system and the amount that the system desires and requires at the given level of earning assets. No banking system will hold more cash than it needs and so it will react to an excess cash greater than zero by trying to expand. If excess cash is less than zero, the system will be forced to contract. Hence, by shaping the amount of excess cash in the banking system, the central bank can influence the direction in which the system will move as well as the speed of movement.

Excess cash can be manipulated by altering either the amount of cash supplied to the banking system or the requirements of the system for cash. From this point of view, it does not matter in which way a given amount of excess cash is generated. Even the existence of liquidity ratios does not necessarily eliminate excess cash as the target variable for control, although, to be effective, changes in excess cash may have to result in corresponding changes in the liquidity ratio.

Such are the more important conclusions that emerge from this analysis of banking operations and transactions. No doubt these could, with profit, be examined in still finer detail than they have been here. The present study is by no means exhaustive. Yet it justifies itself if it does no more than illustrate how economic theory may be applied to the understanding of the routine matters of banking.

Appendix: THE EXPANSION OF BANKING SYSTEMS

The expansion of banking systems bears examination in the light of the analysis in Chapter Seven dealing with the effects of averaging on the computation of excess cash. The traditional treatment of the subject takes no account of the effects of averaging on the expansion process, as a review of the standard formulations reveals. The usual presentations can be easily modified to take into account numerous complications, but not those associated with the averaging of cash requirements. These points are developed in what follows.

The basis for the traditional treatment of the subject is the attempt by a banking system to eliminate a given amount of "excess" cash, greater than zero—that is, cash held exceeds cash required—by trying to substitute earning assets for the excess cash. When excess cash appears in the banking system, banks react by attempting to substitute earning assets for the excess, which results in some excess cash being eliminated from the system but not all. Therefore, banks attempt again to substitute earning assets for excess cash. Once more some excess cash is eliminated and some remains in the system. Further substitutions are necessary, and after each substitution the amount of excess cash left in the system is less than before but still greater than zero. After an infinitely large number of substitutions the excess is finally eliminated and the earning assets and deposits of the banking system have reached a new higher level. It follows, therefore, that changes either in bank deposits or in earning assets may be used to trace the expansion path of the banking system.

This general account of a banking expansion covers the various descriptions usually encountered. Implicit is the condition that no excess cash is ever used to repay borrowings from the central bank or to acquire earning assets from the central bank or its customers. Under these conditions the standard formulations vary slightly in their presentations of the way in which excess cash is eliminated from the banking system.

Two slightly different views of the expansion process may be distinguished in the literature. In one the expansion is considered to proceed from bank to bank. Individual banks or groups of banks are identified and each bank or group of banks is considered to hold the excess cash of the moment, then to expand, and so to lose cash to the next bank or group of banks. Thus, excess cash spreads from bank to bank, in diminishing amounts as it gets distributed, each bank expanding as it gets the excess, losing cash to the next bank in the process, and eliminating its own excess at the same time.[1] The other view does not attempt to identify the banks that have the excess cash and gives no thought to the distribution of a given excess among the banks. Banks that have an excess expand, and any excess remaining after their initial reaction may accrue to the same banks that have just expanded as well as to banks that have not. Another round of expansion follows and again the distribution of the remaining excess is immaterial to the description. The expansion process is seen simply as a series of expansions by whatever banks happen to have excess

1. Thomas Joplin, *The Cause and Cure of Our Commercial Embarrassments* (London, 1841), pp. 33–4, as quoted by Lloyd W. Mints, *A History of Banking Theory in Great Britain and the United States*, p. 105, uses this approach to explain how a banking system expands, showing how excess cash acquired by one bank in being loaned out provides a second bank with excess cash with which it in turn expands, and so forth. The same sort of approach is adopted for purposes of exposition by the United States, Board of Governors of the Federal Reserve System, *The Federal Reserve System: Purposes and Functions*, 3rd ed. (Washington, the Board, 1954), pp. 22–4, and Paul A. Samuelson, *Economics: An Introductory Analysis*, 4th ed. (New York, McGraw-Hill Book Company, Inc., 1958), pp. 302–4. More involved presentations of a banking expansion expressed in terms of banks expanding in turn, one after the other, are those of Chester Arthur Phillips, *Bank Credit: A Study of the Principles and Factors Underlying Advances made by Banks to Borrowers*, pp. 60–2; J. H. Rogers, "The Absorption of Bank Credit," *Econometrica*, *1* (Jan. 1933), 66–7; and Karl Brunner, "A Schema for the Supply Theory of Money," *International Economic Review*, *2* (Jan. 1961), 89.

cash at the various points of time over which the expansion takes place.[2]

On either view the loss of excess cash that results from the acquisition of a given amount of earning assets may be restricted to a reserve leakage, or it may include a currency leakage as well. In the simplest presentations excess cash is eliminated solely through the effects of a banking expansion on deposits. The rise in deposits caused by an expansion raises the demand of the system for cash which consequently works to reduce excess cash—the reserve leakage. In the more sophisticated versions there is also an outright loss of cash because the public withdraw cash from the banking system to add to currency holdings as bank deposits expand. This currency leakage combines with the reserve leakage to reduce excess cash.[3]

Another variation in detail of presentation concerns the rate at which banks attempt to substitute earning assets for excess cash. The simpler assumption is to set the rate at one for one. This assumes that banks make no allowance for the effect of their asset acquisitions on their own deposits. The more complicated assumption is to set the rate at more than one for one, which means that banks count on their asset acquisitions to cause some expansion in their own deposits. They can therefore make a larger substitution of earning assets for a given excess.

All the foregoing variations in the standard presentations of the

2. This is similar to the approach used in explaining the process of income generation in multiplier analysis. It is applied to banking by Rutledge Vining, "A Process Analysis of Bank Credit Expansion," *Quarterly Journal of Economics*, 54 (Aug. 1940), 600–4; Procter Thomson, "Variations on a Theme by Phillips," *American Economic Review*, 46 (Dec. 1956), 965; and Leif Johansen, "The Role of the Banking System in a Macro-economic Model," *International Economic Papers*, No. 8 (1958), p. 94.

3. Only the reserve leakage is taken into account in the simple expositions of a banking expansion, such as those by Joplin, *Cause and Cure*, pp. 33–4; Board of Governors, *The Federal Reserve System*, pp. 22–4; and Samuelson, *Economics*, pp. 302–4. Even in the fuller analysis of Phillips, *Bank Credit*, pp. 60–2, and of Rogers, "The Absorption of Bank Credit," pp. 66–7, the only leakage recognized is the reserve leakage. Both a reserve and currency leakage are allowed for by Johansen, "The Role of the Banking System in a Macro-economic Model," p. 94; Thomson, "Variations on a Theme by Phillips," p. 965; and Brunner, "A Schema for the Supply Theory of Money," p. 89.

expansion process derive from a common pattern. First, changes in earning assets are used to measure the expansion of the banking system, for it is these changes, reflecting attempts to substitute earning assets for excess cash, that are responsible for the elimination of excess cash. Second, a rate of substitution between earning assets and excess cash of one for one is adopted. And third, two leakages are recognized: the reserve leakage and the currency leakage.

For these conditions the expansion of a banking system can be expressed in the form of the geometric progression

$$E + (1 - c)(1 - r)E + (1 - c)^2(1 - r)^2E + \ldots$$

The E term represents the initial excess cash, the parameter "r" stands for the marginal propensity of the banking system to hold cash against deposits (the reserve ratio), and the parameter "c" for the marginal propensity of the public to hold money in the form of currency (the currency ratio).

The first term in the series gives the amount of earning assets acquired as a result of an attempt to substitute earning assets of amount E for excess cash of amount E. Although earning assets increase by E, excess cash does not decrease by E. The cash loss is only cE, c being less than 1, which means that deposit liabilities rise by $(1 - c)E$ and that cash requirements rise by $r(1 - c)E$, r also being less than 1. Therefore, the original excess of E is reduced by $cE + r(1 - c)E$, leaving an excess of $(1 - c)(1 - r)E$, the second term in the series, with which a like amount of earning assets is acquired. The acquisition of earning assets of this amount leaves excess cash of $(1 - c)^2(1 - r)^2E$, the third term of the series, which serves to increase earning assets by the same amount. Further terms in the series can be interpreted in the same way. Thus, the geometric progression represents a series of diminishing incremental increases in earning assets; it also, in this case, represents a diminishing amount of excess cash.

Each term in the foregoing series may also be interpreted as the expansion of a specific bank or group of banks. Each term then reflects the excess cash gained from the previous expansion of some other bank or banks; it also represents the earning assets acquired by the receiving bank. This is a special situation, however, and, in general, there is no need to identify each term with particular banks. The same series may be used to represent the situation in which individual banks contribute to several or all of the terms in the series. The excess cash remaining after a given attempt to substitute earning assets for a previous excess may accrue to the same banks as were involved in the substitution without the terms of the series thereby being affected. In either interpretation, however, it is necessary to assume that all banks behave in the same way.[4]

The concept of excess cash implicit in the standard formulation of a banking expansion is a spot concept, for any one excess is simply the previous excess reduced by the drain of cash to circulation and the rise in the cash demands of the banks which follow an attempt to substitute earning assets for the previous excess. Such a calculation gives the latest spot excess only, and contains no provisions for carrying forward previous excesses. Furthermore, if the reserve ratio remains constant over the course of the expansion, it means that banks arrive at this excess cash by figuring their cash requirements as a constant percentage of each day's deposits. In other words, banks never permit their cash-demand ratio to vary from day to day, another possible indication that there is no averaging of excess cash.[5]

4. Differences among banks in their cash needs and in their substitution rates can be allowed for, however, in the description of a banking expansion by means of a matrix multiplier analysis, as has been ably shown by Karl Brunner, "The Micro-Structure of the Monetary System and the Derivation of an Aggregative Money Supply Function" (Los Angeles, By the author, 1959), pp. 7–14. (Mimeographed.) A summary of this analysis was presented at a session of the 72nd annual meeting of the American Economic Association, Washington, D.C., Dec. 29, 1959.

5. Banks can operate in this way only when money markets are sufficiently perfect that temporary excess cash need not be held idle or future needs anticipated by holding additional cash in reserves. Some of the large English banks operate by computing their daily cash needs as a fixed percentage, in this case 8, of their day's deposits, computing the deviation from the day's cash, and acting that day to eliminate the difference. The very sketchy discussion of this point in Great Britain, Chancellor of the Exchequer, Committee on the Working of the Monetary System, *Report*, Cmd. 827 (London, Her Majesty's Stationery Office, 1959), pp. 52, 119, suggests that all the English clearing banks do not always operate like this. It is the view of R. S. Sayers, *Modern Banking*, 5th ed. (Oxford, At the Clarendon Press, 1960), pp. 36n3, 193, that the 8 per cent cash ratio is held only on a weekly basis, the aim being to have 8 per cent at midweek, but to permit some variation from this within the week.

The reserve ratio need not be held constant, however, from term to term in the expansion series. It may be permitted to vary, thus reflecting imperfect money markets, without affecting the basic pattern of the process of eliminating excess cash from a banking system. The amount of excess cash remaining after each attempted substitution of earning assets for cash is affected by the value assumed by the reserve ratio, but the general relation of the remaining excess to the previous is not thereby altered in any basic fashion.[6]

Likewise, a rate of substitution greater than one for one can also be allowed for without disturbing the basic pattern of the elimination process. A rate of substitution greater than one for one means that banks allow for the effect of their asset acquisitions on their own deposits. That is, they consider the elimination of a given excess to require a purchase of earning assets of some amount greater than the excess to be eliminated. Such an attitude or banking policy affects the amount of assets acquired as a result of a given excess but it does not have any drastic effect on the process of eliminating excess cash. Each term in the expansion series is simply larger as a result of containing a coefficient greater than one representing the substitution rate assumed.[7]

6. The process of expansion still forms a converging geometric progression so long as any coefficient in which the reserve ratio appears for purposes of expressing the cash loss of a substitution is less than one. Even variations in the currency ratio and substitution rate from term to term in the expansion process do not interfere with the series converging as a geometric series so long as each coefficient formed by these variables is always less than one. The formal analysis of this convergency condition is given by Brunner, "The Micro-Structure of the Monetary System . . .," pp. 11–12 and Appendix II.

7. Both Rogers, "The Absorption of Bank Credit," p. 66, and Thomson, "Variations on a Theme by Phillips," p. 968, show that introducing a coefficient to represent a rate of substitution greater than one does not interfere with summing the expansion series as a converging geometric series.

Brunner, "A Schema for the Supply Theory of Money," pp. 88–9, seems to think that a rate of substitution (which he calls the expansion coefficient of individual banks) greater than one can be introduced satisfactorily into the elementary formulations of a banking expansion only if the expansion is expressed in terms of each bank expanding alone and in turn. His reason is that grouping the reaction of all banks together on a consolidated basis eliminates interactions among the banks and produces an expansion coefficient that has no clear meaning

The existence of a liquidity ratio similar to that which prevails in English banking also calls for a minor modification to the standard formulation of the expansion process. Under English conditions, as noted in Chapter Seven, the acquisition of liquidity assets apparently causes a loss of cash of a like amount, which the acquisition of other earning assets does not. Therefore, to get the usual expansion series under these conditions, it is necessary to assume that banks do not use excess cash to raise their liquidity ratios above the minimum required. Further, the expansion in deposits that then follows under this assumption absorbs excess cash at a rate determined by the liquidity ratio and not by the cash ratio. Thus, under English conditions an expansion in deposits absorbs directly an amount of cash equal to 8 per cent of that expansion, and another 22 per cent indirectly through the acquisition of liquidity assets required to maintain the liquidity ratio at 30 per cent of deposits. This means that under these conditions the parameter used for computing the reserve leakage of the expansion process must take the value of the liquidity ratio, 30 per cent, and not the value of the cash ratio, 8 per cent.[8]

Excess cash may not be a spot concept as it is in the standard formulations, and indeed will not be if banks resort to averaging in making up their cash positions. This is one complication, however, that cannot be easily handled by slightly modifying the standard

for the individual bank. The action of individual banks may be combined, however, without consolidating any accounts, so that nothing is lost in grouping banks together. A common or average expansion coefficient can be applied as readily to all banks so combined as to any one bank. That is, if each bank decides that a certain proportion of its excess cash can be converted into earning assets, a behaviour characteristic is available that can be averaged for the banking system, or that can be assumed identical for all banks, and then applied to the total amount of excess cash in the banking system. In other words, there seems to be no need to assume that a banking expansion proceeds by each bank expanding in turn, in order to introduce a rate of substitution between earning assets and excess cash of more than one, which the individual bank applies to its excess cash.

8. W. Manning Dacey, *Money under Review* (London, Hutchinson & Co., 1960), pp. 56–9, shows how under English conditions, in the absence of a currency drain, a given injection of bank cash expands deposits by 3.33 times the injection, the reciprocal of the liquidity ratio, and not by 12.5 times, the reciprocal of the cash ratio.

formulation, for computing excess cash from averages greatly affects the process of eliminating an excess. At least, when averaging has to be allowed for, problems arise that are foreign to the standard formulations of a banking expansion. For one thing, the use of averaging requires deciding what is excess cash. For another, averaging complicates the determination of the excess cash remaining after a given substitution attempt. Finally, a problem of lags is introduced by averaging.

Under averaging the question of what is excess cash may be answered in a number of ways, and a decision has to be reached on which calculation of excess cash to use. There is no problem of choice when banks compute their excess cash in the equilibrium sense: that is, as the amount of excess which if eliminated would make average excess cash zero for the whole reserve period. The equilibrium concept is then the obvious concept to use in analyzing the elimination of excess cash from the banking system. This concept, however, is not a simple one to work with for it takes into account the number of days left in a reserve period, which introduces a variable into the calculation of excess cash that falls continuously from a maximum at the start of a period to a minimum at the end, and which jumps from its minimum at the end of one period to its maximum at the start of the next. Hence, when the equilibrium concept is used, time is a variable in the calculation of excess cash, which complicates the computation of the excess for any given moment.[9]

When banks compute their excess cash on some other basis than the equilibrium one, a decision has to be made whether to use the operational or the equilibrium concept in analyzing the elimination of excess cash from the banking system. The needs or objectives of the analysis decide the issue in favour of the operating concept. The concern of the analysis is with tracing the step-by-step acquisition of

9. Time is a complicating factor here even when the expansion of the banking system proceeds on a bank-by-bank basis. The excess cash gained by any bank in its turn in the process has to be adjusted for the date of receipt, expressed in terms of the time left in the reserve period, unless the excess can be eliminated on the same day as it is received. If elimination on the day of receipt is impossible, as it usually will be because of bank float, the bank will have a carry-over of excess cash to the next day and this accumulation must be taken into account in computing the excess to be eliminated. Time then enters into the calculation.

earning assets through a series of attempted substitutions for excess cash, and these substitutions are governed by the operational concept of excess cash, which in this case differs from the equilibrium concept.

An operational computation of excess cash that deviates from the equilibrium calculation will be easier to work with when the passage of time does not enter into its calculation. This will be the case when banks use a constant divisor, such as one day, to convert their accumulated excess into the equivalent amount of spot. Another complication may arise, however, because any difference between the operational and equilibrium view of excess cash means that the operational excess will be larger than the equilibrium excess. This raises the possibility that banks in reacting to the larger operational excess may over-expand. Some terms of the expansion series will then be negative indicating the sale of assets to eliminate the negative excess cash caused by over-expansion.[10]

Regardless of the concept of excess cash used under averaging, a problem arises in calculating the amount of excess cash that remains in the system after an attempted substitution of earning assets for excess cash. The problem arises because averaging may affect the calculation of the reserve leakage of a given substitution as well as the actual procedure for working out the remaining excess.

Under averaging the reserve leakage may be based on average deposits and not on the latest deposit total, as it is in the standard formulations of a banking expansion. When it is, allowance must be made for the effect of an attempted substitution, not on spot deposits, but on average deposits.[11] It is then more difficult to determine the

10. The expansion series then alternates. This possibility can be handled satisfactorily only by combining the reaction of all banks together at each moment of time. A bank-by-bank description of the expansion process would not be possible because as the receiving bank is expanding the losing bank might be contracting to correct for its over-expansion. The reaction of both banks would have to be combined to determine the net effect on the banking system.

11. Under U.S. reserve regulations cash requirements are based on average deposits. Cf. United States, Board of Governors of the Federal Reserve System, Regulation D, "Reserves of Member Banks," s. 204.3 (a). At the beginning of a new reserve period reserve requirements will jump when spot deposits at the end of the old period differ from the average for the period, for the last spot deposit always forms the reserve base at the start of a new period. Furthermore, allowance

rise in the cash demands of a banking system following an attempt to substitute earning assets for a given amount of excess cash. There is no difficulty when cash requirements do not vary at all with deposits of the current reserve period, as they will not when requirements are based on deposits of a previous period: cash requirements vary then only with a change of periods.[12]

The steps in calculating, under averaging, the excess remaining after an attempted substitution may perhaps be explained best by postulating conditions that correspond most closely to those of the basic formulation: namely, that banks use the equilibrium calculation of excess cash, that they respond immediately to any excess, that the attempted rate of substitution is one for one, and that the initial excess cash appears in the banking system at the start of a new reserve period. Under these conditions the banking system has a spot

---

might have to be made here for the delay that bank float and security-market conventions governing deliveries impose between the act of acquiring earning assets and the final effect on cash and deposits. For example, purchase orders executed today for securities may not require payment until one or two days later. Payment might then be in clearing-house funds which introduces another delay before cash is lost or deposits, proper, are raised. If a bank so desired, it could take account of these delays, under averaging, in planning its substitutions of earning assets for excess cash.

12. This is the situation under Canadian reserve regulations: legal requirements are fixed within any given reserve period and can vary only with the change of periods. Deposits of the previous period form the reserve base for the current period. Cf. Canada, Laws, Statutes, *Statutes of Canada*, 1953–54, 2-3 Elizabeth II, c. 48, s. 71.

Reserve requirements in West Germany appear to contain a combination of the Canadian and U.S. averaging provisions. Up to the 15th of the month, the reserve period being the calendar month, required reserves vary with average daily deposits computed from the 16th of the previous month to the 15th of the current one. After the 15th, required reserves are fixed for the remainder of the month because the reserve base for the month is equal to average deposits in the period from the 16th of one month to the 15th of the next. With the beginning of a new month and reserve period, requirements may be changed and will again become subject to daily variation during the first half of the month. This is my interpretation of Articles 7, 8, and 9 of "The Deutsche Bundesbank's Order on Minimum Reserves of April 16, 1959," as amended to April 20, 1961, which is reproduced in Deutsche Bundesbank, *Report*, 1960, pp. 62–5.

excess, greater than zero, at the end of the first day of the new reserve period. This also means that the amount of excess accumulated during the reserve period up to this point of time is the same as the spot excess. Thus, the amount of excess cash in the banking system at the end of the first day is this accumulated excess (which corresponds to the spot excess) divided by the number of days remaining in the reserve period and added to the spot excess.[13]

The attempt to substitute earning assets for this initial excess cash results in a cash leakage made up of a loss of cash to circulation and a rise in the cash demands of the banking system. This is a leakage from the previous spot excess and it results in a new spot excess lower than the first. That is, the effect of the leakage on excess cash is accounted for entirely by its effect on the spot excess. To calculate the total excess remaining in the system, the new spot excess must be added to the previous accumulation of excess cash to bring the accumulation up to date. This new accumulation is then divided by the number of days now remaining in the reserve period. The results of this division added to the new spot excess gives the amount of excess cash remaining in the banking system after the initial substitution attempt. The amount remaining after any other substitution attempt is calculated in the same way.

From the way in which the remaining excess cash has to be worked out under averaging, it can be seen that a possibility exists for excess cash to move temporarily in a contrary fashion to that expected in a banking expansion. Thus, for sufficiently small reserve and currency leakages, the rising accumulation of excess cash which occurs during a reserve period, combined with a falling divisor for converting the accumulation into the equivalent amount of spot, may more than outweigh the decline in the spot excess. If this occurs, excess cash actually increases within a given reserve period while the banking system is expanding. With the passing of one reserve period to the

13. Under a bank-by-bank expansion the excess cash remaining after each bank took its turn in expanding would always be calculated in this way. That is, the receiving bank would gain a spot excess, and having had no prior accumulation of excess, would divide this excess by the number of days remaining in the reserve period and add the result to the spot excess.

next, however, excess cash will drop as the accumulated excess of a period expires with that period.

A further complication in the computation of excess cash, ruled out of the foregoing discussion, is the possibility of delayed or lagged responses. This is a very real possibility under averaging for banks then need not respond immediately to any given excess. Within a reserve period banks have a choice of responding immediately or at any date prior to the expiration of the reserve period. The effect of a delay in responding may also be worked out by using the equilibrium calculation of excess cash.

A lag in responding to excess cash affects the size of the excess in two ways. First, unless the spot excess is zero, the accumulation of excess cash will change with the passage of time because of the influence of the spot excess on the accumulation. The longer a spot excess of a given size continues to exist, the greater the change it produces in the accumulated excess and so the greater the change in excess cash. Any delay in responding to excess cash permits a given spot excess to have this effect on excess cash. The second way that excess cash is affected by a lagged response is through the passage of time which reduces the divisor used to convert the accumulated excess into the equivalent amount of spot excess. Again, any delay in responding to a given excess will cause that excess to grow.

Consequently, a lagged response means that for each response excess cash will differ from what it would have been had the response been made as soon as the excess was recognized. Each term in the expansion series, showing the accumulation of earning assets over the course of the expansion, may be larger than it otherwise would be, but the interval of time between the terms will also be longer. Furthermore, the extent of this effect may vary from term to term for the length of the lag may be a function of the size of the excess as well as of the point of time within the reserve period. Any lag in responding then varies over the course of an expansion.

Thus, the effects of averaging on the process of eliminating excess cash from a banking system are extensive and involved. They cannot be easily allowed for by means of slight modifications to the basic formulation of a banking expansion. Therefore, for a banking system that is working to keep average excess cash zero, rather than spot excess cash, the standard formulations for the expansion of a banking system are far from satisfactory. They fail to reveal the actual steps by which excess cash is eliminated from a system making use of provisions for averaging cash requirements.

Selected Bibliography

(A selection from works cited of Canadian sources and of other material on banking or on subjects especially dealt with here.)

I. Books and Pamphlets

ALHADEFF, David A. *Monopoly and Competition in Banking*. Publications of the Bureau of Business and Economic Research, University of California. Berkeley, California, University of California Press, 1954.

AMERICAN BANKERS ASSOCIATION. Economic Policy Commission. *Member Bank Reserve Requirements*. New York, the Association, 1957.

ANGELL, James W. *The Behaviour of Money: Exploratory Studies*. New York, McGraw-Hill Book Company, Inc., 1936.

ASCHHEIM, Joseph. *Techniques of Monetary Control*. Baltimore, The Johns Hopkins Press, 1961.

AUBURN, H. W. (ed.). *Comparative Banking*. London, Waterlow and Sons Limited, 1960.

BAGEHOT, Walter. *Lombard Street: A Description of the Money Market*. New York, Charles Scribner's Sons, 1902.

BLOOMFIELD, Arthur I. *Monetary Policy under the International Gold Standard: 1880–1914*. New York, Federal Reserve Bank of New York, 1959.

BRECHER, Irving. *Monetary and Fiscal Thought and Policy in Canada, 1919–1939*. Canadian Studies in Economics, No. 8. Toronto, University of Toronto Press, 1957.

BRECKENRIDGE, Roeliff Morton. *The Canadian Banking System, 1817–1890*. Publications of the American Economic Association, Vol. X, Nos. 1, 2 and 3. New York, Macmillan and Company, Limited, 1895.

BROWALDH, E. and Thunholm, L. E. *Changes in Bank Balance Sheets, 1938–1952*. Paris, Institut International d'Etudes Bancaires, 1954.

BURGESS, W. Randolph. *The Reserve Banks and the Money Market*. New York, Harper and Brothers, 1927.

CHAPMAN, John M. *Concentration of Banking: The Changing Structure and Control of Banking in the United States*. New York, Columbia University Press, 1934.

——, and Westerfield, Ray B. *Branch Banking: Its Historical and Theoretical Position in America and Abroad*. New York, Harper and Brothers, 1942.

CLAPHAM, Sir John. *The Bank of England: A History*. 2 vols. Cambridge, At the University Press, 1944.

CONANT, Charles A. *A History of Modern Banks of Issue: With an Account of the Economic Crises of the Present Century*. [Second edition]. New York, The Knickerbocker Press, [1896].

COPELAND, Morris A. *A Study of Moneyflows in the United States*. Publications of the National Bureau of Economic Research, Inc., Number 34. New York, National Bureau of Economic Research, Inc., 1952.

——. *Trends in Government Financing*. A Study by the National Bureau of Economic Research. Princeton, Princeton University Press, 1960.

CURRIE, Lauchlin. *The Supply and Control of Money in the United States*. Harvard Economic Studies, 47. Cambridge, Massachusetts, Harvard University Press, 1934.

DACEY, W. Manning. *Money under Review*. London, Hutchinson and Co., 1960.

DAVENPORT, Herbert Joseph. *The Economics of Enterprise*. New York, The Macmillan Co., Limited, 1918.

DAY, A. C. L. *Outline of Monetary Economics*. Oxford, At the Clarendon Press, 1957.

DAY, John Percival. *Considerations on the Demand for a Central Bank in Canada*. Toronto, The Macmillan Company of Canada, Limited, 1933.

ECKARDT, H. M. P. *Manual of Canadian Banking*. Fourth edition. Toronto, Monetary Times, [1913].

———. *A Rational Banking System: A Comprehensive Study of the Advantages of the Branch Bank System.* New York, Harper and Brothers, 1911.

EINZIG, Paul. *Foreign Balances.* London, Macmillan and Co., Limited, 1938.

———. *The Theory of Forward Exchange.* London, Macmillan and Co., Limited, 1937.

FINNEY, Katherine. *Interbank Deposits: The Purpose and Effects of Domestic Balances, 1934–54.* New York, Columbia University Press, 1958.

FOSTER, Major B., et al. *Money and Banking.* Fourth edition. New York, Prentice-Hall, Inc., 1953.

FOUSEK, Peter G. *Foreign Central Banking: The Instruments of Monetary Policy.* New York, Federal Reserve Bank of New York, November, 1957.

FRIEDMAN, Milton. *A Program for Monetary Stability.* The Millar Lectures, No. 3. New York, Fordham University Press, 1959.

GILBART, James W. *The Principles and Practice of Banking.* New edition, ed. anon. London, Bell and Daldy, 1871.

GREGORY, T. E. (comp.). *Select Statutes, Documents and Reports Relating to British Banking, 1832–1928.* 2 vols. London, Oxford University Press, 1929.

GURLEY, John G. and Shaw, Edward S. *Money in a Theory of Finance.* Washington, D.C., The Brookings Institution, 1960.

HACKETT, W. T. G. *A Background of Banking Theory.* Toronto, The Canadian Bankers' Association, 1945.

HART, Albert G. *Money, Debt and Economic Activity.* New York, Prentice-Hall, Inc., 1948.

HAWTREY, R. G. *The Art of Central Banking.* London, Longmans, Green and Co., 1932.

———. *A Century of Bank Rate.* London, Longmans, Green and Co., 1938.

———. *Currency and Credit.* Fourth edition. London, Longmans, Green and Co., 1950.

———. *Trade and Credit.* London, Longmans, Green and Co., 1928.

Historical Outline of Canadian Banking Legislation and Some Features of the Present Working of the Canadian Banking System. Presentations by

J. A. McLeod, President, The Canadian Bankers' Association, before the Royal Commission on Banking and Currency, at Ottawa, 1933. [n.p., n.n., n.d.].

HOLLADAY, James. *The Canadian Banking System*. Boston, Bankers Publishing Company, 1938.

HOLMES, Alan R. *The New York Foreign Exchange Market*. New York, Federal Reserve Bank of New York, 1959.

HOOD, William C. *Financing of Economic Activity in Canada*. A Study for the Royal Commission on Canada's Economic Prospects. [Ottawa, Queen's Printer], 1957.

JAMES, F. Cyril. *A Colloquy on Branch Banking: Contemporary Questions and Answers*. New York, American Economists Council for the Study of Branch Banking, 1939.

———. *The Economics of Money, Credit and Banking*. Third edition. New York, The Ronald Press Company, 1940.

JAMIESON, A. B. *Chartered Banking in Canada*. Revised edition. Toronto, The Ryerson Press, 1957.

JOHNSON, Joseph French. *The Canadian Banking System*. National Monetary Commission. Washington, Government Printing Office, 1910.

KATZ, Samuel I. *Two Approaches to the Exchange-Rate Problem: The United Kingdom and Canada*. Essays in International Finance, No. 26. Princeton, International Finance Section, Department of Economics and Sociology, Princeton University, 1956.

KENEN, Peter B. *British Monetary Policy and the Balance of Payments, 1951–1957*. Harvard Economic Studies, *116*. Cambridge, Massachusetts, Harvard University Press, 1960.

KEYNES, John Maynard. *The General Theory of Employment, Interest and Money*. London, Macmillan and Co., Limited, 1936.

———. *Monetary Reform*. New York, Harcourt, Brace and Company, 1924.

———. *A Treatise on Money*. 2 vols. New York, Harcourt, Brace and Company, 1930.

KING, W. T. C. *History of the London Discount Market*. London, George Routledge and Sons, Ltd., 1936.

KISCH, Sir Cecil H. and Elkin, W. A. *Central Banks: A Study of the Constitutions of Banks of Issue, with an Analysis of Representative*

Charters. Fourth edition. London, Macmillan and Co., Limited, 1932.

KOCK, M. H. de. *Central Banking*. Third edition. London, Staples Press Limited, 1954.

LEAF, Walter. *Banking*. Home University Library of Modern Knowledge, *124*. London, Williams and Norgate, Ltd., [1926].

LINDBECK, Assar. *The "New" Theory of Credit Control in the United States: An Interpretation and Elaboration*. Stockholm Economic Studies, Pamphlet Series I. Stockholm, Almqvist and Wiksell, 1959.

MACLEOD, Henry Dunning. *The Theory and Practice of Banking*. 2 vols. Fifth edition. London, Longmans, Green and Co., 1892.

MARSH, Donald Bailey. *World Trade and Investment: The Economics of Interdependence*. New York, Harcourt, Brace and Company, 1951.

MILLER, Harry E. *Banking Theories in the United States before 1860*. Harvard Economic Studies, *30*. Cambridge, Massachusetts, Harvard University Press, 1927.

MINTS, Lloyd W. *A History of Banking Theory in Great Britain and the United States*. Chicago, University of Chicago Press, 1945.

NEUFELD, E. P. *Bank of Canada Operations, 1935–54*. Canadian Studies in Economics, No. 5. Toronto, University of Toronto Press, 1955.

NEW YORK CLEARING HOUSE ASSOCIATION. *The Federal Reserve Re-Examined*. New York, The Association, 1953.

PATINKIN, Don. *Money, Interest, and Prices: An Integration of Monetary and Value Theory*. Evanston, Illinois, Row, Peterson and Company, 1956.

PATTERSON, E. L. Stewart. *Canadian Banking*. Revised edition. Toronto, The Ryerson Press, 1941.

PHILLIPS, Chester Arthur. *Bank Credit: A Study of the Principles and Factors Underlying Advances Made by Banks to Borrowers*. New York, The Macmillan Company, 1921.

PIGOU, A. C. *Industrial Fluctuations*. London, Macmillan and Co., Limited, 1927.

PLUMPTRE, A. F. W. *Central Banking in the British Dominions*. Toronto, The University of Toronto Press, 1940.

PRITCHARD, Leland J. *Money and Banking*. Boston, Houghton Mifflin Company, 1958.

RAE, George. *The Country Banker: His Clients, Cares, and Work from an Experience of Forty Years.* Revised by Ernest Sykes. Seventh edition. London, John Murray, 1930.

Relations Between the Central Banks and Commercial Banks. Lectures delivered at the Tenth International Banking Summer School, Garmisch-Partenkirchen, Germany, September, 1957. Frankfort on Main, Fritz Knapp Verlag, for Bundesverband des privaten Bankgewerbes e.V., 1957.

RIEFLER, Winfield W. *Money Rates and Money Markets in the United States.* New York, Harper and Brothers, 1930.

RIST, Charles. *History of Monetary and Credit Theory: From John Law to the Present Day.* Trans. Jane Degras. New York, Macmillan and Company, 1940.

ROBERTSON, D. H. *Banking Policy and the Price Level: An Essay in the Theory of the Trade Cycle.* New York, Augustus M. Kelley, 1949.

————. *Money.* Cambridge Economic Handbook.—II. Fourth edition. London, Nisbet and Co., Ltd., 1948.

ROBINSON, Roland I. *The Management of Bank Funds.* New York, McGraw-Hill Book Company, Inc., 1951.

ROOSA, Robert V. *Federal Reserve Operations in the Money and Government Securities Markets.* New York, Federal Reserve Bank of New York, 1956.

ROSS, Victor. *A History of The Canadian Bank of Commerce: With an Account of the Other Banks Which Now Form Part of Its Organization.* Vol. II. Toronto, Oxford University Press, 1922.

SAYERS, R. S. *Central Banking After Bagehot.* Oxford, At the Clarendon Press, 1957.

————. *Modern Banking.* Third edition. Oxford, At the Clarendon Press, 1951.

SCHUMPETER, Joseph A. *Business Cycles: A Theoretical, Historical, and Statistical Analysis of the Capitalist Process.* 2 vols. New York, McGraw-Hill Book Company, Inc., 1939.

SEN, S. N. *Central Banking in Undeveloped Money Markets.* Calcutta, Bookland Limited, 1952.

SHEPHERD, Sidney A. *Foreign Exchange in Canada: An Outline.* Toronto, University of Toronto Press, 1953.

SMITH, Warren L. *Debt Management in the United States.* Joint Economic

Committee: Study of Employment, Growth, and Price Levels: Study Paper No. 19. Washington, Government Printing Office, 1960.

SOUTHWORTH, Shirley Donald. *Branch Banking in the United States*. New York, McGraw-Hill Book Company, Inc., 1928.

THOMAS, Rollin G. *Our Modern Banking and Monetary System*. New York, Prentice-Hall, Inc., 1946.

The Treasury and the Money Market, New York, Federal Reserve Bank of New York, 1954.

TURNER, Robert C. *Member-Bank Borrowing*. Columbus, Ohio, The Ohio State University, 1938.

VINER, Jacob. *Canada's Balance of International Indebtedness, 1900–1913: An Inductive Study in the Theory of International Trade*. Harvard Economic Studies, *26*. Cambridge, Massachusetts, Harvard University Press, 1924.

WALKER, B. E. *A History of Banking in Canada*. Toronto, [n.n.], 1899.

WESTERFIELD, Ray B. *Money, Credit and Banking*. New York, The Ronald Press Company, 1938.

WILLIS, H. Parker. *The Theory and Practice of Central Banking*. New York, Harper and Brothers Publishers, 1936.

WILLIS, J. Brooke. *The Functions of the Commercial Banking System*. New York, King's Crown Press, 1943.

WILLIS, Parker B. *The Federal Funds Market: Its Origin and Development*. Boston, The Federal Reserve Bank of Boston, 1957.

WOOD, Elmer. *English Theories of Central Banking Control, 1819–1858: With Some Account of Contemporary Procedure*. Harvard Economic Studies, *64*. Cambridge, Massachusetts, Harvard University Press, 1939.

II. *Articles and Parts of Books*

ALFORD, R. F. G. and Paish, F. W. "Debate on Monetary Control—Basic Principles and Modern Mechanics," *The Banker* (London), August 1956, pp. 476–87.

ALHADEFF, D. A. "Credit Controls and Financial Intermediaries," *American Economic Review*, *50* (Sept. 1960), 655–71.

———, and Alhadeff, C. P. "A Note on Bank Earnings and Savings Deposit Rate Policy," *Journal of Finance*, *14* (Sept. 1959), 403–10.

R

ARNDT, H. W. "Overseas Borrowing—The New Model," *Economic Record, 33* (Aug. 1957), 247–61.

BECKHART, Benjamin Haggott. "The Banking System of Canada," *Foreign Banking Systems.* H. Parker Willis and B. H. Beckhart, editors. New York, Henry Holt and Company, 1929. Pp. 289–492.

BOPP, Karl R. "Central Banking Objectives, Guides, and Measures," *Journal of Finance, 9* (Mar. 1954), 12–22.

———. "A Flexible Monetary Policy," Federal Reserve Bank of Philadelphia, *Business Review,* March 1958, pp. 3–7.

———. "The Rediscovery of Monetary Policy—Some Problems of Application," ibid., August 1955, pp. 3–12.

BRECHLING, Frank P. R. "A Contribution to the Liquidity Preference Theory of Interest," Banca Nazionale del Lavoro (Rome), *Quarterly Review,* December 1957, pp. 416–50.

———. "A Note on Bond-Holding and the Liquidity Preference Theory of Interest," *Review of Economic Studies, 24* (June 1957), 190–7.

BRUNNER, Karl. "A Schema for the Supply Theory of Money," *International Economic Review, 2* (Jan. 1961), 78–109.

CANNAN, Edwin. "The Meaning of Bank Deposits," *Economica, 1* (Jan. 1921), 28–36.

CARSON, Deane. "Bank Earnings and the Competition for Savings: A Reply," *Journal of Political Economy, 69* (June 1961), 286–7.

———. "Bank Earnings and the Competition for Savings Deposits," ibid., *67* (Dec. 1959), 580–8.

CHANDLER, L. V. "Monopolistic Elements in Commercial Banking," *Journal of Political Economy, 46* (Feb. 1938), 1–22.

CLARK, W. C. "Financial Administration of the Government of Canada," *Canadian Journal of Economics and Political Science, 4* (Aug. 1938), 391–419.

CRICK, W. F. "The Genesis of Bank Deposits," *Readings in Monetary Theory.* Blakiston Series of Republished Articles on Economics, 5. New York, The Blakiston Company, 1951. Pp. 41–53. Reprinted from *Economica, 7* (1927), 191–202.

CULBERTSON, J. M. "Intermediaries and Monetary Theory: A Criticism of the Gurley-Shaw Theory," *American Economic Review, 48* (Mar. 1958), 119–31.

CURTIS, C. A. "Banking," *Encyclopedia Canadiana*. Ottawa, The Canadiana Company Limited, 1957. *1*, 292–303.

———. "Credit Control in Canada," *Papers and Proceedings of the Annual Meeting of the Canadian Political Science Association, 2* (May 1930), 101–22.

———. "History of Canadian Banking," *Readings in Money and Banking*. Elizabeth M. Rosengren, editor. Toronto, University of Toronto Press, 1947. Pp. 14–34. Reprinted with revisions from the *Encyclopedia of Canada*. Toronto, University Associates of Canada, Limited, 1935.

DACEY, W. Manning. "The Floating Debt Problem," *Lloyds Bank Review*, April 1956, pp. 24–38.

———. "Treasury Bills and the Money Supply," ibid., January 1960, pp. 1–16.

DEWALD, William G. "Bank Earnings and the Competition for Savings," *Journal of Political Economy, 69* (June 1961), 279–82.

"Dollar Deposits in London," *The Economist* (London), July 11, 1959, pp. 109–10.

DUE, John F. "Government Expenditures and Their Significance for the Economy," *Fiscal Policies and the American Economy*. Kenyon E. Poole, editor. New York, Prentice-Hall, Inc., 1951. Pp. 201–51.

EASTMAN, Harry C. "Aspects of Speculation in the Canadian Market for Foreign Exchange," *Canadian Journal of Economics and Political Science, 24* (Aug. 1958), 355–72.

EINZIG, Paul. "Dollar Deposits in London," *The Banker* (London), January 1960, pp. 23–7.

———. "Some Recent Changes in Forward Exchange Practices," *Economic Journal, 70* (Sept. 1960), 485–95.

ELLIOTT, Courtland. "Bank Cash," *Canadian Journal of Economics and Political Science, 4* (Aug. 1938), 432–59.

ELLIS, H. S. "The Rediscovery of Money," *Money, Trade, and Economic Growth: In Honor of John Henry Williams*. New York, The Macmillan Company, 1951. Pp. 253–69.

FRIEDMAN, Milton. "A Monetary and Fiscal Framework for Economic Stability," *Essays in Positive Economics*. Chicago: The University of Chicago Press, 1953. Pp. 133–56. Reprinted from *American Economic Review, 38* (June 1948), 245–64.

GIBSON, J. D. "The Trend of Bank Loans and Investments in Canada," *Readings in Money and Banking*. Elizabeth M. Rosengren, editor. Toronto, University of Toronto Press, 1947. Pp. 52–65. Reprinted from *Canadian Investment and Foreign Exchange Problems*. J. F. Parkinson, editor. Toronto, University of Toronto Press, 1940.

GOODE, Richard, and Gurley, John G. "Open-Market Operations *versus* Reserve Requirement Variation: Comment," *Economic Journal, 70* (Sept. 1960), 616–18.

"Guides to Monetary Policy," Federal Reserve Bank of Philadelphia, *Business Review*, August 1959, pp. 2–10.

GURLEY, J. G. and Shaw, E. S. "Financial Aspects of Economic Development," *American Economic Review, 45* (Sept. 1955), 515–38.

——. "Financial Intermediaries and the Saving-Investment Process," *Journal of Finance, 11* (May 1956), 257–76.

——. "The Growth of Debt and Money in the United States, 1800–1950: A Suggested Interpretation," *Review of Economics and Statistics, 38* (Aug. 1957), 250–62.

——. "Reply," *American Economic Review, 48* (Mar. 1958), 132–8. A reply to J. M. Culbertson, "Intermediaries and Monetary Theory: A Criticism of the Gurley-Shaw Theory," ibid., pp. 119–31.

HAGGER, A. "Movements in Tasmania's 'International Reserves'," *Economic Record, 36* (Apr. 1960), 242–9.

HALD, Earl C. "Monetary Aspects of Changes in Treasury Balances," *Southern Economic Journal, 22* (Apr. 1956), 448–56.

HARTLAND, Penelope. "Interregional Payments Compared with International Payments," *Quarterly Journal of Economics, 63* (Aug. 1949), 392–407.

HELLWEG, Douglas. "Comments on Task Force Report," *Record of the Federal Reserve System Conference on the Interregional Flow of Funds*. Washington, Federal Reserve System, 1955. III–(6)–1–4.

HOLMES, Alan R. and Klopstock, Fred H. "The Market for Dollar Deposits in Europe," Federal Reserve Bank of New York, *Monthly Review*, November 1960, pp. 197–202.

"Influence of Credit and Monetary Measures on Economic Stability," *Federal Reserve Bulletin*, March 1953, pp. 219–34.

JOHNSON, Harry G. "The Revival of Monetary Policy in Britain," *Three Banks Review*, No. 30, June 1956, pp. 3–20.

KAREKEN, John H. "Lenders' Preferences, Credit Rationing, and the Effectiveness of Monetary Policy," *Review of Economics and Statistics*, *39* (Aug. 1957), 292–302.

——. "Monetary Policy and the Public Debt: An Appraisal of Post-war Developments in the USA," *Kyklos*, *10* (1957), 401–31.

——. "On the Relative Merits of Reserve-Ratio Changes and Open-Market Operations," *Journal of Finance*, *16* (Mar. 1961), 65–72.

——. "Post-Accord Monetary Developments in the United States," Banca Nazionale del Lavoro (Rome), *Quarterly Review*, September 1957, pp. 322–51.

KATZ, Samuel I. "The Canadian Dollar: A Fluctuating Currency," *Review of Economics and Statistics*, *35* (Aug. 1953), 236–43.

LAND, Brian. "How Canada's Money Market Keeps Idle Cash at Work," *Canadian Business* (Montreal), February 1958, pp. 26–31, 100–2, 104–6, 108.

MACINTOSH, R. M. "Broadening the Money Market," *Canadian Banker*, *61* (Autumn 1954), 63–73.

McLEOD, A. N. "Security Reserve Requirements in the United States and the United Kingdom: A Comment," *Journal of Finance*, *14* (Dec. 1959), 531–42.

MARSH, Donald B. "Canada," *Banking Systems*. Benjamin H. Beckhart, editor. New York, Columbia University Press, 1954. Pp. 119–82.

METZLER, Lloyd A. "Wealth, Saving, and the Rate of Interest," *Journal of Political Economy*, *59* (Apr. 1951), 93–116.

MILLER, Erwin. "Monetary Policy in a Changing World," *Quarterly Journal of Economics*, *70* (Feb. 1956), 23–43.

MINSKY, Hyman P. "Central Banking and Money Market Changes," ibid., *71* (May 1957), 171–87.

MORTON, Walter A. "A Zero Deposit Rate," *American Economic Review*, *30* (Sept. 1940), 536–53.

MURPHY, Henry C. "Debt Management," *Fiscal Policies and the American Economy*. Kenyon E. Poole, editor. New York, Prentice-Hall, Inc., 1951. Pp. 158–200.

MUSGRAVE, R. A. "Credit Controls, Interest Rates, and Management of Public Debt," *Income, Employment and Public Policy: Essays in Honor of Alvin H. Hansen.* New York, W. W. Norton and Company, 1948. Pp. 221–54.

———. "Debt Management and Inflation," *Review of Economics and Statistics, 31* (Feb. 1949), 25–30.

———. "Money, Liquidity and the Valuation of Assets," *Money, Trade and Economic Growth: In Honor of John Henry Williams.* New York, The Macmillan Company, 1951. Pp. 216–42.

NEUFELD, E. P. "The Bank of Canada's Approach to Central Banking," *Canadian Journal of Economics and Political Science, 24* (Aug. 1958), 332–44.

PAISH, F. W. "Banking Policy and the Balance of International Payments," *Readings in the Theory of International Trade.* Blakiston Series of Republished Articles on Economics, *4.* Philadelphia, The Blakiston Company, 1949. Pp. 35–55. Reprinted from *Economica, 3* (Nov. 1936), 404–22.

PEACH, W. N. "Treasury Investment Funds and Open-Market Operations," *Journal of Finance, 6* (Mar. 1951), 46–53.

PENTLAND, H. C. "The Role of Capital in Canadian Economic Development before 1875," *Canadian Journal of Economics and Political Science, 16* (Nov. 1950), 457–74.

PFISTER, Richard L. "State and Regional Payments Mechanisms: Comment," *Quarterly Journal of Economics, 74* (Nov. 1960), 641–8.

PLUMPTRE, A. F. W. "The Role of Interest Rates and Bank Credit in the Economies of the British Dominions," *Economic Journal, 49* (June 1939), 222–36.

POINDEXTER, J. Carl. "Some Misconceptions of Banking and Interest Theory," *Southern Economic Journal, 13* (Oct. 1946), 132–45.

PORTER, Richard C. "Open-Market Operations *versus* Reserve Requirement Variation: Comment," *Economic Journal, 70* (Sept. 1960), 618–20.

PRITCHARD, Leland J. "A Note on the Relationships of Bank Capital to the Lending Ability of the Commercial Banks," *American Economic Review, 43* (June 1953), 362–6.

RADFORD, R. A. "Canada's Capital Inflows, 1946–53," International Monetary Fund, *Staff Papers, 4* (Feb. 1955), 217–57.

"Reserve Adjustments of City Banks," Federal Reserve Bank of Kansas City, *Monthly Review*, February 1958, pp. 3–8.

RITTER, Lawrence S. "Functional Finance and the Banking System," *American Journal of Economics and Sociology*, *15* (July 1956), 395–404.

———. "A Note on the Retirement of Public Debt During Inflation," *Journal of Finance*, *6* (Mar. 1951), 66–70.

ROBERTSON, Sir Dennis H. "More Notes on the Rate of Interest," *Economic Commentaries*. London, Staples Press Limited, 1956. Pp. 59–70. Reprinted from *Review of Economics Studies*, No. 55, 1953–54.

———. "A Squeak from Aunt Sally," *The Banker* (London), December 1959, pp. 718–22.

ROELSE, Harold V. "The Money Market," *Money Market Essays*. New York, Federal Reserve Bank of New York, March 1952. Pp. 1–7.

ROLPH, Earl R. "Principles of Debt Management," *American Economic Review*, *47* (June 1957), 302–20.

ROOSA, Robert V. "Monetary and Credit Policy," *Economics and the Policy Maker*. Brookings Lectures, 1958–1959. Washington, D.C., The Brookings Institution, 1959. Pp. 89–116.

———. "The Radcliffe Report," *Lloyds Bank Review*, October 1959, pp. 1–13.

ROSA, [now Roosa], R. V. "Interest Rates and the Central Bank," *Money, Trade, and Economic Growth: In Honor of John Henry Williams*. New York, The Macmillan Company, 1951. Pp. 270–95.

RUDD, A. "Changes in Lombard Street," *The Bankers' Magazine* (London), April 1957, pp. 316–19.

SAMUELSON, Paul A. "The Effect of Interest Rate Increases on the Banking System," *American Economic Review*, *35* (Mar. 1945), 16–27.

———. "Recent American Monetary Controversy," *Three Banks Review*, No. 29 (Mar. 1956), pp. 3–21.

SAYERS, R. S. "The Bank in the Gold Market, 1890–1914," *Papers in English Monetary History*. T. S. Ashton and R. S. Sayers, editors. Oxford, At the Clarendon Press, 1953. Pp. 132–50. Reprinted from *Bank of England Operations, 1890–1914*. London, P. S. King and Son Ltd., 1936. Chapter IV.

————. "Central Banking in the Light of Recent British and American Experience," *Quarterly Journal of Economics*, *63* (May 1949), 198–211.

————. "The New York Money Market Through London Eyes," *Three Banks Review*, No. 28, December 1955, pp. 21–37.

SCITOVSKY, Tibor. "The Theory of the Balance of Payments and the Problem of a Common European Currency," *Kyklos*, *10* (1957), 18–42.

SHACKLE, G. L. S. "The Deflative or Inflative Tendency of Government Receipts and Disbursements," *Oxford Economic Papers*, No. 8 (Nov. 1947), pp. 46–64.

SHORTT, Adam. "The Early History of Canadian Banking: IV. The First Banks in Lower Canada," *Journal of The Canadian Bankers' Association*, *4* (July 1897), 341–60.

————. "The History of Canadian Currency, Banking and Exchange: The Crisis of 1857–58," ibid., *11* (Apr. 1904), 199–218.

"The Significance and Limitations of Free Reserves," Federal Reserve Bank of New York, *Monthly Review*, November 1958, pp. 162–7.

SIMMONS, Edward C. "A Note on the Revival of Federal Reserve Discount Policy," *Journal of Finance*, *11* (Dec. 1956), 413–21.

SMITH, Warren L. "Areas of Regional Research," *Record of the Federal Reserve System Conference on the Interregional Flow of Funds*. Washington, Federal Reserve System, 1955. III–(7)–1–22.

————. "The Discount Rate as a Credit-Control Weapon," *Journal of Political Economy*, *66* (Apr. 1958), 171–7.

————. "Financial Intermediaries and Monetary Controls," *Quarterly Journal of Economics*, *73* (Nov. 1959), 533–53.

————. "On the Effectiveness of Monetary Policy," *American Economic Review*, *46* (Sept. 1956), 588–606.

"Some Observations on Excess Reserves of Member Banks," Federal Reserve Bank of St. Louis, *Monthly Review*, October 1960, pp. 6–8.

TETHER, Gordon C. "Dollars—Hard, Soft, and Euro," *The Banker* (London), June 1961, pp. 395–404.

THANOS, C. A. "The Definition of a Central Bank and Its Practical Implications," *Economia Internazionale*, *11* (Feb. 1958), 110–17.

TOBIN, James. "Asset Holdings and Spending Decisions," *American Economic Review*, *42* (Papers and Proceedings, May 1952), 109–23.

——. "Monetary Policy and the Management of the Public Debt: The Patman Inquiry," *Review of Economics and Statistics*, *35* (May 1953), 118–27.

"Towards a More Stable Money Supply," Federal Reserve Bank of Cleveland, *Monthly Business Review*, September 1954, pp. 3–9.

"The Treasury's Deposit Balances and the Banking System," Federal Reserve Bank of New York, *Monthly Review of Credit and Business Conditions*, April 1958, pp. 51–6.

TRUED, M. N. "Interest Arbitrage, Exchange Rates, and Dollar Reserves," *Journal of Political Economy*, *65* (Oct. 1957), 403–11.

TURK, Sidney. "Foreign Exchange Market in Canada," *Canadian Chartered Accountant*, *63* (Aug. 1953), 58–68.

TURVEY, Ralph. "Consistency and Consolidation in the Theory of Interest," *Economica*, *21* (Nov. 1954), 300–7.

——. "Some Notes on Multiplier Theory," *American Economic Review*, *43* (June 1953), 275–95.

WALLICH, H. C. "The Changing Significance of the Interest Rate," ibid., *36* (Dec. 1946), 761–87.

——. "Recent Monetary Policies in the United States," ibid., *43* (Papers and Proceedings, May 1953), 27–41.

——. "Some Current Features of Bank Liquidity in the United States," Banca Nazionale del Lavoro (Rome), *Quarterly Review*, July–September 1951, pp. 109–18.

WHITE, William H. "Measuring the Inflationary Significance of a Government Budget," International Monetary Fund, *Staff Papers*, *1* (Apr. 1951), 355–78.

WHITTLESEY, C. R. "Memorandum on the Stability of Demand Deposits," *American Economic Review*, *39* (Dec. 1949), 1192–203.

——. "Monetary Policy and Economic Change," *Review of Economics and Statistics*, *39* (Feb. 1957), 31–9.

WILSON, J. S. G. "The Canadian Money Market Experiment," Banca Nazionale del Lavoro (Rome), *Quarterly Review*, March 1958, pp. 19–55.

III. Official Documents

CANADA. Parliament. House. Standing Committee on Banking and Commerce. *Proceedings: Decennial Revision of the Bank Act.* 1st Session, 22nd Parliament, 1954.

CANADA. Royal Commission on Banking and Currency in Canada. *Report.* Ottawa, King's Printer, 1933.

THE CANADIAN BANKERS' ASSOCIATION (comp.). *Bank Act Revision Proceedings: Extracts from and Synopses of Debates in the House of Commons and Proceedings and Discussions of and Evidence Received by the Select Standing Committee on Banking and Commerce . . . in the Years 1913, 1924 and 1928.* [Montreal], The Canadian Bankers' Association, 1933.

GREAT BRITAIN. Chancellor of the Exchequer. Committee on the Working of the Monetary System. *Principal Memoranda of Evidence.* 3 vols. London, Her Majesty's Stationery Office, 1960.

———. *Report.* Cmd. 827. London, Her Majesty's Stationery Office, 1959.

GREAT BRITAIN. Committee on Finance and Industry. *Report.* Cmd. 3897. London, His Majesty's Stationery Office, 1931.

UNITED STATES. Congress. Joint Committee on the Economic Report. *Monetary Policy and the Management of the Public Debt: Hearings before the Subcommittee on General Credit Control and Debt Management.* 82nd Congress, 2nd Session, 1952.

———. *Monetary Policy and the Management of the Public Debt: Report of the Subcommittee on General Credit Control and Debt Management.* 82nd Congress, 2nd Session, 1952.

———. *Monetary Policy and the Management of the Public Debt: Their Role in Achieving Price Stability and High-level Employment—Replies to Questions and Other Material for the Use of the Subcommittee on General Credit Control and Debt Management.* 2 Pts. 82nd Congress, 2nd Session, 1952.

Cited herein as U.S. Congress, *Monetary Policy . . . Public Debt: Compendium.*

UNITED STATES. Federal Reserve Board. *Annual Report,* 1923.

UNITED STATES. National Monetary Commission. *Interviews on the*

Banking and Currency Systems of Canada. Washington, Government Printing Office, 1910.

IV. Unpublished Materials

BRUNNER, Karl. "The Micro-Structure of the Monetary System and the Derivation of an Aggregative Money Supply Function." Los Angeles, by the author, 1959. (Mimeographed.)

MOORE, John Basil. "The Effects of Counter-Cyclical Monetary Policy on the Canadian Chartered Banks, 1935–1957." Unpublished Ph.D. dissertation, The Johns Hopkins University, 1958.

SUBJECT INDEX

Accommodating open-market operations, defined, 384–5
Active balances, defined, 44
Availability of credit, defined, 56 n. 3
Availability doctrine, 54–9

Balance of international payments. *See* International payments
Balanced-budget theorem, 304 n. 14
Balances:
  active and inactive, 44–5
  idle, 370–1
    and bonds, 366–70
    See also Bonds
Bank:
  borrowing from central bank, 408–11
  capital, 162–3
  capital expenditures by, 162
  cash, 51
    borrowed from central bank, 430–1
    composition of, 431
    effect of banking expansion on, 432 n. 133
    and monetary control, 432–3
    See also Cash
  credit:
    inherent instability of, 29–31
    stability of, 35–6
    and trade credit, 66 n. 26
  expenses, 155–6
  investments, 26–8. *See also* Securities
  as lender, 14–15
  loans:

    applications for, 74
    capacity for, 62–4
    control over, 22–3
    and investments, 28
    nature of, 20–2
    and open-market operations, 380–1
    rejection of, 75
    See also Lending; Lending rates; Loans
  profits, 150–7
  revenues, 156
  See also Banking; Banks
Bank Act:
  on lending rates, 84 n. 66
  on reserve requirements, 473 n. 12
Bank of Canada:
  and bank-rate, 424 n. 125
  borrowing from, 421 nn. 116–17
  clearing arrangements with, 355 n. 27
  and currency drain, 317 n. 32
  deposits with, 141 n. 2
  foreign exchange transactions, 220 n. 6
  on loan expansion, 52 n. 92
  open-market operations, 365 n. 47, 385–6, 391 n. 81
  profits of, 357 n. 28
  and security yields, 49 n. 88
Bank of England:
  and bank-rate, 411 ff.
  credit rationing by, 76
  as lender of last resort, 415–18

INDEX TO PERSONAL NAMES

*1000 copies of
this book have been printed
from Baskerville type
by Latimer, Trend & Co., Ltd.,
Plymouth.
The dust jacket was
designed by
Peter Matthews.*